READINGS IN PSYCHOLOGY

The Search for Alternatives

READINGS IN PSYCHOLOGY

The Search for Alternatives

Third Edition

James A. Dyal
William C. Corning
Dale M. Willows

University of Waterloo

McGRAW-HILL BOOK COMPANY

New York   St. Louis   San Francisco   Auckland
Düsseldorf   Johannesburg   Kuala Lumpur   London   Mexico   Montreal
New Delhi   Panama   Paris   São Paulo   Singapore
Sydney   Tokyo   Toronto

READINGS IN PSYCHOLOGY:
THE SEARCH FOR ALTERNATIVES

Library of Congress Cataloging in Publication Data

Dyal, James Albert, date   comp.
  Readings in psychology.

  Includes bibliographies.
    1. Psychology—Addresses, essays, lectures.
2. Human behavior—Addresses, essays, lectures.
I. Corning, William C., joint comp. II. Willows,
Dale M., joint comp. III. Title. [DNLM: 1. Behavior—
Collected works. 2. Psychology— Collected works.
BF21 D994r]
BF149.D96 1975   150'.8   74-20759
ISBN 0-07-018537-9

1 2 3 4 5 6 7 8 9 0 DODO 7 9 8 7 6 5

This book was set in Times Roman by Creative Book Services, division of McGregor &
Werner, Inc. The editors were Richard R. Wright and Phyllis T. Dulan; the designer was
Joseph Gillians; the production supervisor was Thomas J. LoPinto.
R. R. Donnelley & Sons Company was printer and binder.

ACKNOWLEDGMENTS

Judith M. Bardwick and Elizabeth Douvan, excerpted from "What are big boys/girls made of?" by Judith M. Bardwick and Elizabeth Douvan in *Woman in a sexist society: Studies in power and powerlessness,* edited by V. Gornick and B. R. Moran, 1971, p. 147. Published by Basic Books.

Jerome S. Bruner, excerpted from *On knowing: Essays for the left hand,* 1964, pp. 108, 123–124. Published by Harvard University Press.

Jerome S. Bruner, excerpted from *The relevance of education,* 1971, pp. xi, 100. Published by Norton.

J. S. Clark, excerpted from "Starvation in the affluent society" by J. S. Clark in *Deprivation in America,* edited by V. B. Ficker and H. S. Graves, 1971, pp. 16–18. Published by Glencoe Press.

Robert Coles, excerpted from *Still hungry in America,* 1969, p. 8. Published by The World Publishing Co.

William C. Corning, excerpted from "So's yer ole man" by William C. Corning. From personal communication written to James Dyal, 1973.

Simone de Beauvoir, excerpted from *The coming of age,* 1972, p. 283. Published by Putnam.

Jose M. R. Delgado, excerpted from "Psychocivilized direction of behavior" by Jose M. R. Delgado. Appeared in *The Humanist,* March/April, 1972, p. 15.

James Dyal, excerpted from *Readings in psychology: Understanding human behavior,* 1962, p. 485. Published by McGraw-Hill.

James Dyal, excerpted from "Images in the lonely crowd," by James Dyal. Appeared in *Vital Speeches,* 1965, **31,** pp. 729–735.

Ellis D. Evans, excerpted from *Contemporary influences in early childhood education,* 1971, p. 281. Published by Holt, Rinehart and Winston.

Minna Field, excerpted from *The aged, the family, and the community,* 1972, pp. 114–115. Published by Columbia University Press.

W. Gaylin, excerpted from "What's normal?" Appeared in *New York Times Magazine,* April 1, 1973, pp. 14–15.

V. E. Headings, excerpted from "Optimizing the performance of human genes" by V. E. Headings. Appeared in *The Humanist,* September/October, 1972, **32,** p. 9.

Charles W. Hobart, extracted from "Commitment, value conflict, and the future of the American family" by Charles W. Hobart. Appeared in *Marriage and Family Living,* 1963, **25,** p. 407.

Arthur Jensen, excerpted from "Genetics and education: A second look" by Arthur Jensen. Appeared in *New Scientist,* October, 1972, p. 98.

Sigmund Koch, excerpted from "Reflections on the state of psychology" by Sigmund Koch. Appeared in *Social Research,* 1971, **38,** pp. 672–696.

vi ACKNOWLEDGMENTS

Sigmund Koch, excerpted from "The image of man implicit in encounter group theory" by Sigmund Koch. Appeared in *The Journal of Humanistic Psychology*, 1971, **11** (2), pp. 109–128.

Herbert Kohl, excerpted from "The open classroom" by Herbert Kohl. Appeared in *The New York Review of Books*, 1972, p. 28.

Joshua Lederberg, excerpted from "Racial alienation and intelligence" by Joshua Lederberg. Appeared in *Harvard Educational Review*, 1969, **39**, p. 614.

Melvin J. Lerner, excerpted from "On the injustice of believing in justice" by Melvin J. Lerner. From personal communication written to James Dyal, 1973.

Frank A. Logan, excerpted from "Experimental psychology of animal learning and behavior," by F. A. Logan. Appeared in *American Psychologist*, 1972, **27**, pp. 1061–1062.

Abraham H. Maslow, excerpted from *The psychology of science*, 1969, pp. 16–17. Published by Henry Regnery Co.

Keith Melville, excerpted from *Communes in the counter culture*, 1972, pp. 99–100. Published by William Morrow & Co.

Keith Melville, excerpted from "Fresh possibilities and untested alternatives" by Keith Melville in *Communes in the Counter Culture*, edited by Keith Melville, 1972. Published by William Morrow.

George A. Miller, excerpted from "Psychology as a means of promoting human welfare" by George A. Miller. Appeared in *American Psychologist*, **24** (12), 1969, p. 1069.

Ashley Montagu, excerpted from "Animals and man: Divergent behavior." Appeared as a letter in *Science*, 1968, p. 963.

R. L. Marrone, excerpted from "Scarcity/survival—abundance/actualization" by R. L. Marrone. From personal communication written to James Dyal, 1973.

Herbert Otto, excerpted from "Has monogamy failed?" by H. Otto. Appeared in *Saturday Review*, April 25, 1970, pp. 23–25, 62.

Neil Postman and Charles Weingartner, excerpted from *Teaching as subversive activity*, 1969, pp. 2–3. Published by Delta Books.

Everett Reimer, excerpted from *School is dead: Alternatives in education*, 1971. Published by Doubleday.

Carl Rogers, excerpted from "Freedom from isolation" by Carl Rogers. Appeared in *The Humanist*, 1969, **29**, p. 1.

Charles E. Silberman, excerpted from *Crisis in the classroom*, 1970, pp. 23, 114. Published by Random House.

R. L. Sinsheimer, excerpted from "Genetic engineering: The modification of man" by R. L. Sinsheimer. Appeared in *Impact of Science on Society*, 1970, **20**, p. 291.

B. F. Skinner, excerpted from *Beyond freedom and dignity*, 1971, p. 57. Published by Alfred Knopf.

B. F. Skinner, excerpted from "Some issues concerning the control of human behavior" by B. F. Skinner. Appeared in *Science*, **124**, 1956, pp. 1064–1065.

Time, excerpted from "Crackup in mental care" by *Time*, Dec. 17, 1973, p. 61.

Alfred North Whitehead, excerpted from *Science and the Modern World*, 1953, p. 35. Published by Macmillan.

Daniel Yankelovich, excerpted from "The new naturalism" by Daniel Yankelovich. Appeared in *Saturday Review*, Apr. 1, 1972, p. 33.

To Amy, Cass, Clay, Jack, Jessie, Keith, Kurt, Mark, Seth, and Shanti
who will continue the search for alternatives

Contents

Special Acknowledgments   xvii

CHAPTER 1 THE PSYCHOLOGY CONNECTION   1
            Provocations   1
Selection 1 Who Are You and What Are You Doing Here?
            (Don't Read This Book!)   2
            James A. Dyal, William C. Corning, and Dale M. Willows
   Comment These "New" Students   3
            Charles E. Silberman
   Comment Schooling—Man's Inhumanity to Man   6
            John Amos Comenius
   Comment The Fear of Knowing: Fear of Personal and Social Truth   8
            Abraham H. Maslow
   Comment To Read Is Less Commendable . . .   10
            B. F. Skinner

Selection 2 Psychology as a Science: Relevant Criticisms and Criticisms of Relevance   13
            Jonathan L. Freedman
   Comment Reflections on the Discipline of Psychology   13
            Sigmund Koch

Selection 3 The Possibility of a Science of Human Behavior   20
            B. F. Skinner
   Comment Understanding and Prediction Are Better Goals   23
            George A. Miller
   Comment Learning Freedom and Dignity   24
            Frank A. Logan

Selection 4 The Place of the Person in the New World of the Behavioral Sciences   25
            Carl R. Rogers
   Comment I Cannot Quite Agree   31
            B. F. Skinner

Selection 5 Psychology: The Necessary and Relevant Science   32
            James A. Dyal, William C. Corning, and Dale M. Willows

            USEFUL RESOURCES   36

CHAPTER 2 EDUCATIONAL ISSUES   38
            Provocations   38
Selection 6 Educational Issues for the Seventies   39
            James A. Dyal
   Comment What Is Worth Knowing?   41
            Jerome S. Bruner

Comment   Education and the Lower Class—The Social Psychology of Failure   41
Jerome S. Bruner

Comment   Toward Educational Diversity   52
Arthur Jensen

Comment   The Genetic Hypothesis—Irrelevance and Relevance   54
Joshua Lederberg

Comment   Conservation and Change   56
Alfred North Whitehead

Comment   Questions for the Open Classroom   58
Ellis D. Evans

Comment   The Revolutionary Role of Education   62
Everett Reimer

Selection 7   Beyond Crap Detection: The Inquiry Medium Is the Message   65
Neil Postman and Charles Weingartner

Comment   "Crap Detecting"   65
Neil Postman and Charles Weingartner

Comment   On Learning to Learn   67
Charles E. Silberman

Selection 8   What Education Is: Excellence and Relevance   70
Jerome S. Bruner

Comment   An Educational Theory Is a Political Theory   74
Jerome S. Bruner

Selection 9   Education and Equality   75
Charles E. Silberman

Comment   Teachers' Expectations—A Self-fulfilling Prophecy   76
Herbert Kohl

Selection 10   Tough and Tender Learning   81
David Nyberg and Donald H. De Lay

Comment   The Virtues of Encouraging Discovery   83
Jerome S. Bruner

Comment   Suspended Expectations   85
Herbert Kohl

Selection 11   The Early Years and the Preschool Strategy   86
Burton L. White

USEFUL RESOURCES   91

CHAPTER 3   **AND MAN CREATED MAN**   94
Provocations   94

Selection 12   And Man Created Man: What Kind of Man Shall We Build?   95
William C. Corning

Comment   Genetic Control Is an Old Idea   96
V. E. Headings

Selection 13   Man into Superman: The Promise and Peril of the New Genetics   97
Time

Comment	Maxims for Genetic Manipulation *Robert Sinsheimer*	100
Comment	Who Is to Decide? *José Delgado*	108
Selection 14	Psychosurgery: Legitimate Therapy or Laundered Lobotomy *C. Holden*	109
Selection 15	Brain Power: The Case for Bio-Feedback Training *Barnard Law Collier*	113
Selection 16	Behavior Control and Social Responsibility *Leonard Krasner*	120
	USEFUL RESOURCES	125

CHAPTER 4 ON WOMANKIND   126
	Provocations	126
Selection 17	On Womanhood *Dale M. Willows*	127
Selection 18	Male & Female: Differences between Them *Time*	130
Selection 19	Sexual Stereotypes Start Early *Florence Howe*	135
Comment	What Are Big Boys/Girls Made Of? *Judith M. Bardwick and Elizabeth Douvan*	135
Selection 20	He and She: The Sex Hormones and Behavior *Maggie Scarf*	142
Selection 21	Feminine Intellect and the Demands of Society *Eleanor E. Maccoby*	149
Selection 22	Man's Role in Women's Liberation *Mary Louise Briscoe and Elsie Adams*	152
	USEFUL RESOURCES	155

**CHAPTER 5 ON BEING POOR, OLD, OR "BLACK" IN A RICH,
YOUNG, AND "WHITE" CULTURE**   161
	Provocations	161
Selection 23	On Being Poor, Old, or "Black" in a Rich, Young, and "White" Culture. *James A. Dyal*	162
Comment	What Is There to Say? *Robert Coles*	162
Comment	Mental Health of the Elderly *Minna Field*	164
Comment	On the Injustice of Believing in Justice *Melvin J. Lerner*	165

Selection 24   The Many Faces of the Poor   166
Elton B. McNeil

Selection 25   You're Asking Me What Deprivation Is?   171
Victor B. Ficker and Herbert S. Graves
Comment   The Poverty Syndrome   171
Thelma McCormack
Comment   On Starvation in America   174
Raymond Wheeler, M.D., Robert Coles, M.D., Report to Senate Subcommittee on Poverty by a Distinguished Panel of Medical Experts

Selection 26   Old Age: End Product of a Faulty System   175
Simone de Beauvoir
Comment   Personalizing Death Transforms Life   176
James A. Dyal
Comment   The Discovery of Old Age   178
Simone de Beauvoir

Selection 27   Age-Ism: Another Form of Bigotry   179
Robert N. Butler

Selection 28   The Pathology of the Ghetto   182
Kenneth B. Clark

Selection 29   In Juvenile Court   189
Susan K. Strahm

USEFUL RESOURCES   191

CHAPTER 6   **ON AGGRESSION**   193
Provocations   193
Selection 30   Violence Depends on Your Point of View   194
William C. Corning
Comment   On "Good" and "Bad" Aggression   194
Jerome Skolnick

Selection 31   On War and Peace in Animals and Man   196
N. Tinbergen
Comment   Animals and Man: Divergent Behavior   200
Ashley Montagu

Selection 32   The *Human* Nature of Human Nature   205
Leon Eisenberg

Selection 33   The Problem with Porky Pig   206
William C. Corning

Selection 34   Television and Growing Up: The Impact of Televised Violence   210
Surgeon General's Scientific Advisory Committee

Selection 35   If Hitler Asked You to Electrocute a Stranger, Would You? Probably   218
Philip Meyer

Selection 36   Home from the War: The Psychology of Survival   227
Robert Jay Lifton

USEFUL RESOURCES   244

CHAPTER 7   ON MADNESS   246
Provocations   246
Selection 37   Introduction to Madness: Or What's in a Name?   247
William C. Corning
Comment   Psychiatric labels: semantic blackjacks   248
Thomas Szasz
Comment   "Psychiatrosis"   249
R. D. Laing
Comment   "Blaming the Victim"   249
William Ryan
Comment   A Homosexual for President?   250
W. Gaylin

Selection 38   The Schizophrenic Experience   251
R. D. Laing

Selection 39   Laing's Models of Madness   261
Miriam Siegler, Humphry Osmond, and Harriet Mann

Selection 40   On Being Sane in Insane Places   272
D. L. Rosenhan

Selection 41   On Being Insane in Insane Places   278
Ailon Shiloh
Comment   Crackup in Mental Care   279
Time

USEFUL RESOURCES   292

CHAPTER 8   THE SEARCH FOR ALTERNATIVE LIFE STYLES   293
Provocations   293
Selection 42   The Search for Alternative Life Styles   294
James A. Dyal
Comment   Scarcity/Survival—Abundance/Actualization   294
Robert L. Marrone
Comment   Suburbia—The Symbolic Centerpiece of the American Dream   295
Keith Melville
Comment   Value Conflict and the Suburban Family   296
Charles W. Hobart
Comment   The Middle Class Revolt—Old and New   297
Keith Melville
Comment   The New Naturalism   298
Daniel Yankelovich
Comment   Freedom from Isolation   300
Carl Rogers
Comment   The Image of Man Implicit in Encounter Group Therapy   302
Sigmund Koch
Comment   Has Monogamy Failed?   307
Herbert A. Otto
Comment   Fresh Possibilities and Untested Alternatives   313
Keith Melville

Selection 43   On Hanging Loose and Loving: The Dilemma of Present Youth   314
Henry Miller

Selection 44   We Are Leaving, You Don't Need Us   320
                 David Bailey
Comment   And the Inorganic Makes the Organic *DEAD*   322
                 James A. Dyal

Selection 45   Teen-Age Sex: Letting the Pendulum Swing   323
                 Time

Selection 46   Communes: The Alternative Life-Style   330
                 Herbert A. Otto

                 USEFUL RESOURCES   337

CHAPTER 9   THE SEARCH FOR ALTERNATIVE REALITIES   339
             Provocations   339
Selection 47   The Search for Alternative Realities   340
                 James A. Dyal
Comment   Product versus Process   340
                 James A. Dyal

Selection 48   The Search for Alternative Realities   345
                 Keith Melville

Selection 49   Altered States of Consciousness   350
                 Andrew Weil

Selection 50   Conclusions and Recommendations of the Commission of Inquiry into the
                 Non-Medical Use of Drugs: Majority Report on Cannabis   355
                 Gerald Le Dain, Heinz Lehmann, and J. Peter Stein

Selection 51   On Meditation   364
                 Edward W. Maupin

Selection 52   Transcendental Meditation and the Science of Creative Intelligence 368
                 Paul H. Levine

Selection 53   A Psychology of the Future   375
                 Abraham H. Maslow

                 USEFUL RESOURCES   376

Special Acknowledgments

As with most book projects, many people are responsible for the creation of a book in addition to those who are the authors. In this case, of course, we are particularly indebted to the authors of the various articles for their creative understanding and to the publishers for their permission to reproduce the material.

Also there is always someone ... "without whose efforts we would never ..."; on this project that person is Doris Leland. Doris's dedication to this project has been extraordinary—far beyond that which could be attributed to the meager extrinsic reward. We thank you, Doris. Diane Cox has also made an important contribution to this book in some of the same ways as Doris. We are also indebted to Chris Levesque, who suffered in good spirit through the typing of innumerable drafts of our commentaries. Gayle Stevens and Pam Butcher also provided helpful secretarial support.

Since this book has been extensively classroom-tested, we are indebted to the several hundred students enrolled in courses in Introductory Psychology for their critically helpful comments. We also wish to express our appreciation to several advanced students who have served as discussion leaders for seminars based on "Search for Alternatives." These student colleagues are: Alison Atkins, Beverly Behar, Shari Bender, Sue Berry, Marsha Faubert, Sue Ogurzsoff, David Peltz, and David Robertson. Shari Bender also was of great help in proofreading.

We are also particularly grateful to Sue Prosser for the use of her drawing for the book cover. Sue was a student in a seminar taught by James Dyal and had prepared the drawing as a part of her "model of man."

James A. Dyal

READINGS IN PSYCHOLOGY
The Search for Alternatives

CHAPTER 1

THE PSYCHOLOGY CONNECTION

PROVOCATIONS

On our planet, and possibly on others, the astonishing outcome is that the collection of atoms making up living organisms have now become sophisticated enough to ask why they exist. In us, the privileged animals, nature becomes self-conscious.

Nigel Calder

The heart of the psychological revolution will be a new and scientifically based conception of man as an individual and as a social nature. When I say that the psychological revolution is already upon us, what I mean is that we have already begun to change man's self conception. If we want to further that revolution, not only must we strengthen its scientific base, but we must also try to communicate it to our students and to the public.

George A. Miller

Psychology is peculiarly prey to parochialism. Left to their own devices, psychologists tend to construct models of a man who is neither a victim of history, a target of economic forces, nor even a working member of a society.

Jerome S. Bruner

Psychological facts and impressions have to be explained, not by oversimplifying them to conform with what we know about the brain, but by enlarging our knowledge of the brain to accommodate them. As a distinguished Canadian psychologist, Donald Hebb, would put it, this is not degrading mind to matter. Instead, it is upgrading the properties of matter to account for mind.

Nigel Calder

WHAT DO YOU THINK?

---

1 WHO ARE YOU AND WHAT ARE YOU DOING HERE? (DON'T READ THIS BOOK!)

JAMES A. DYAL, WILLIAM C. CORNING, and DALE M. WILLOWS

MOTIVES FOR ATTENDING UNIVERSITY

We often begin our courses in Introductory Psychology by asking some of the students to say something about themselves and why they are in the university.

● Why don't you stop reading for a moment and think about who you are and why you are here? . . . Go ahead, stop for a moment and *let yourself think, don't just read.* Before you read the next section, write some of your reasons in the space below.

While we do not know *your* thoughts on this problem, some of the common answers which students have given are:

(a) "I am here because I want to become certified to (enter a particular occupation) and I can't get in without a degree." *(b)* "I came to college because, as long as I can remember, my parents have planned for my education and it was just expected that I would come." *(c)* "I came to this university because all my friends were coming here." *(d)* "There are a lot of different things that I am into—weaving, potting, free preschools, people, and psychology—like this just seemed to be a place that I could put them all together." *(e)* "Let's face it, I'm here to make as good marks as I

●

can so I can get a good job and live a good, normal, successful life." *(f)* "I guess I'm here because I usually enjoy learning things and talking about things—ideas—I just really like playing around with ideas." *(g)* "I don't know why I'm here, there just doesn't seem to be anything else to do right now; there sure are places I'd hell-of-a-lot rather be than here, but then again, what difference does it make, it's the same crummy world wherever you go." *(h)* "Well, I think it's a really cool place: lots of groovy chicks, lots of action." *(i)* "I believe that the only way we are going to change this corrupt society is to bring it down and—like—the university is one of the prime pillars that holds up this dehumanizing structure—like—I'm here to tear it down so we can build a new world which is responsive to real human needs and values." *(j)* "I'm still trying to work that out, I don't know what I want my life to be like—I need some time to figure out what I'm doing here—in the world as well as in the university—I'm glad for some time to work on me." *(k)* "Buzz off, Jack. It's none of your business" (usually implicit rather than overt).

Several important features of the youth in our Western society of the 1970s are revealed by these open and direct answers: (1) Your choices are often heavily determined by what other people expect of you, especially "significant others" such as parents and peers *(b, c)*. (2) One of the major devices used by our society to control social mobility is "certification" by educational institutions; many of you are here to be stamped "Grade A Prime" so that you can bring a higher price in the marketplace *(a, e)*. (3) Many of you have learned society's lessons quite well and are anxious to take your rightful place in a comfortable middle-class life which provides few alternatives to being "successful" *(e)*. (4) Yet, in spite of the lure of this promised land, many of you are dissatisfied with yourselves; you find yourselves being apathetic and alienated from other people who may be viewed only as objects to manipulate, impress or defy *(g, h, i, k)*. (5) Yet again, despite the overwhelming odds against it, some of you have survived and are seeking to make your own way through the educational wasteland and you sometimes find it

exciting and fulfilling *(d, f)*. (6) Many of you are beginning (or continuing) to ask existential questions about the meaning of your existence *(j,* and may be even *g* and *i)*.

You do not have to have much sophistication in psychology to suspect that these different students are going to be having quite different experiences in college. Your own experiences will probably confirm the notion that the motives which you have for doing something strongly influence the style with which you do it. It should also be apparent that what you learn, how well you learn it, and how long you retain it will depend in part on why you want to learn it in the first place. New learning will also depend on the learnings which you bring with you to each new classroom setting, not the least of which are complex and often conflicting attitudes, emotions, and conceptualizations about "teachers," "parents," "the school," "what they make me do," . . . etc. In other words, your style of coping with "authority figures" may greatly influence your performance in a learning situation.

COMMENT: THESE "NEW" STUDENTS

What these "new" students understand, far better than their parents, is that the choice of a career involves far more than a choice of how to earn a livelihood. They understand, viscerally if not intellectually, that the question, "What shall I do?" really means "What shall I do with myself?" or rather, "What shall I make of myself?" And that means asking "Who am I?" "What do I want to be?" "What values do I want to serve?" "To whom, and to what, do I want to be responsible?" As Drucker rightly observes, "These are existential questions, for all that they are couched in secular form and appear as choices between a job in government, in business, or in college teaching." That the students' answers are not always relevant is less important than the fact that they are forcing us to confront the most fundamental questions of value and purpose.

CHARLES E. SILBERMAN

"SOME OF MY BEST FRIENDS ARE STUDENTS . . . "

Psychologists are concerned about all aspects of behavior and are committed to try to bring the light of reason and careful observation to bear on the search for greater understanding of human behavior and experience. Considerable research has been devoted to clarifying the complex problem of how motivations, personality characteristics, attitudes, and abilities of the teacher and the student interact sometimes to facilitate and sometimes to inhibit learning in the university. Some of the most extensive research in this area has been reported by Mann and his colleagues.[1] Perhaps you will recognize aspects of yourself or your friends in the following gallery of mini-portraits. They are composite drawings based on Mann's research and upon our own experiences with students over many years of teaching.

The Independent As an independent student you tend to think of yourself as superior to other students in your class, expecially if you are male and an active participant in class discussion. Your feeling of classroom superiority is often accurate since you tend to make valuable contributions to class discussion. Because you feel self-confident, you are able to bring your richer past experience together with your critical abilities to focus on the material under discussion. As a result of your success in this type of classroom you tend to prefer discussion/seminar type classes to lecture courses. When others in the class may be "losing their head" in anxiety, dependency, or anger, you tend to persist in the intellectual task-oriented work of the course.

The Compliant Student If you are a compliant student, you tend to hold conventional attitudes with regard to teaching and learning; you

are more likely to be female than male; you are generally contented with your role as a student; you probably had good relations with your parents, have seldom felt a strong need to rebel, and are generally trusting of authority. You tend to rely on the *extrinsic* motivation induced by rewards and punishments to stimulate you to pursue your course work (e.g., approval, praise, criticism from parents, peers, or professors). Although the course work may be interesting to you, you probably would do little or no work without these extrinsic motivators. You are the typical "good student" in the conventional classroom.

The Anxious-Dependent Student You are very concerned about what authorities think of you and are quite dependent upon them for feedback about your performance. You tend to doubt your intellectual competence and tend to have generally low self-esteem. As a consequence of these two characteristics you tend to be uncomfortable in classes that have a lot of *student* participation and discussion because this format tends to provide less information from the professor and you are afraid you will not know what facts the professor thinks are important in order to pass the tests. For similar reasons you tend to avoid involvement in course material which does not seem likely to "pay off" on the tests.

The Authority Rebel Strong reaction against persons in authority (or their products, such as books) is the central defining trait of this classroom personality. Like the independent student, the Rebel tends to see himself as superior to the other students in the class; again with some justification, since he is actually more creative and has the potential of being more involved and productive. However, because he is quite rebellious and resentful of authority, his classroom performance is quite erratic. If the instructor is authoritarian, then the Rebel is likely to do little or nothing in the course; on the other hand, the Rebel may become deeply involved in the course and produce exciting and challenging ideas.

The Attention Seeker You want to be liked by all, especially those in authority. As a result you

[1]R. D. Mann, S. M. Arnold, J. Binder, S. Cytrynbrum, B. N. Newman, B. Ringwald, J. Ringwald, & R. Rosenwein. *The college classroom: Conflict, change, and learning.* New York: Wiley, 1970; and B. E. Ringwald, R. D. Mann, R. Rosenwein, and W. J. McKeachie. Conflict and style in the college classroom—an intimate study. *Psychology Today,* 1971, 4, 45–47.

are very concerned about the impression you are making, especially when you feel that you are being judged (and you feel that you are being judged most of the time). Your orientation to the instructor and to your classmates is social rather than intellectual. Nonetheless, you try to make good grades because they are symbols of approval by authorities and provide needed reassurance that you are liked.

The Silent Student   If you are a Silent Student, you may never say anything in the classroom unless specifically called upon by the Instructor. While the dynamics of such nonparticipatory behavior are often complex, they quite often involve a feeling of helplessness and vulnerability in relation to the teacher, who is seen as either too threatening or too manipulative to interact with. Many such silent students are girls who describe themselves as being ''good little girls'' who did not make trouble for their parents. It has been suggested that the Silent Student sometimes tends to equate verbal interaction in the classroom with aggressive competition. She may feel failure in this competition and also may have learned to inhibit responses which are hostile and aggressive. This syndrome could also be produced by boredom or utter confusion about the content of the course.

• Some of you may be feeling hostile toward us at this point for appearing to ''pigeonhole'' you and put you into little ''personality boxes.'' If so—good! You have your ''crap detector'' working (read Ernest Hemingway's comments on page 65, and the kind of ''crap'' which you have detected is that of oversimplication and overgeneralization. Yet there is some truth in what has been said and it is important that you develop your truth-detecting ability as well.

Even if you were not disturbed by the foregoing thumbnail sketches, we hope that you did realize that they were more like caricatures than accurate portraits, for indeed that is so. Nonetheless, like all caricatures, they emphasize the dominant features of the style in which the individual presents himself to others. Yet several cautions are in order. First, as with all such personality typologies, most people do not actually fit comfortably into one or the other of these molds. Furthermore, the face which we present to others is very much dependent upon the situation itself. This means that a person who acts like a compliant student in one class may be somewhat more rebellious in another class, or somewhat more independent. Furthermore, it would be expected that through growth and further learning these styles of reactions may change over time. For example, the Rebel may begin to resolve his identity crisis and find that he can cope more constructively even in authoritarian structures. He may thus evolve into the more independent student.

We cannot conclude this section without some further comments on ''teacher'' and ''school.'' Like students, professors are also complex and heterogeneous; and much of your behavior in the classroom *is* elicited by the professor's teaching style and course organization. For example, there are some professors (all too often in required courses) who adopt a dictatorial manner and, within a lecture or so, have created a whole classroom of compliant and silent students. We certainly do not intend to lay the failures of classroom learning entirely at your feet. Indeed, if we have the courage to look behind these caricatures, we may come to a better understanding of how the ''brain bending'' of the conventional classroom may have contributed to making you the kind of learner you are today. It is unfortunately true that many of you have not had experiences in school which would serve to free your desire to learn. On the contrary, many of you have learned to dislike the whole process of schooling and see college as a matter of ''putting in time.'' Even those of us who have devoted our lives to ''education'' must admit that the atrocities which have been perpetrated in the name of ''learning'' are all too reminiscent of the techniques used by the inquisition to save the souls of sinners. Together they constitute a weird and compelling documentation of man's inhumanity to man.

COMMENT: SCHOOLING—MAN'S INHUMANITY TO MAN

Teachers almost invariably take their pupils as they find them; they burn them, beat them, card them, comb them, drill them into certain forms, and expect them to become a finished and polished product; and if the result does not come up to their expectations (and I ask you how could it?) they are indignant, angry, and furious. And yet we are surprised that some men shrink and recoil from such a system. Far more is it a matter for surprise that any one can endure it at all.

JOHN AMOS COMENIUS The Great Didactic, 1632

What does the traditional classroom teach? Most often it is structured to teach compliance, conformity, and apathy, or competition and motivation to get a good grade. These qualities are, of course, not listed in the course objectives of any teacher—but look beyond the teacher—look at the structure of the learning environment. Young students rapidly learn what the academic environment has to teach them. Look at what the students actually spend their time doing. What is expected of them? Most of the time they are trained to be quiet and listen to the teacher. This may be entertaining and interesting to students for a few weeks . . . but twelve to seventeen years? It turns out, however, that students have an option of whether or not to "turn off" the teacher. Typically, the middle-class student does not totally turn off, he just switches to a more interesting channel (e.g., fantasies, day-dreaming, the behavior of other students, how-to-get-teacher, etc.). However, as each of these alternatives come to be punished, it is either inhibited or greatly exaggerated. We have in this situation the beginning of the Compliant Student on the one hand or the Authority Rebel on the other.[2]

[2]Our society tends to permit males to be more aggressively rebellious than females. Also, it may be that females are inher-

A person who has been systematically robbed of the ability to respond with enthusiasm and awe, a person who perceives the learning process as one of incorporating the "food for thought" dished out by the teacher, who must take these morsels, digest them, and then excrete them back onto the exam paper—such a person is legitimately described as a starving victim of emotional/intellectual poverty.[3] He is certainly among the disadvantaged of our world. It is not surprising that he is apathetic and alienated from the whole process. It is not a part of him, he is not involved in it; he is only a passive observer of what is happening to him and he does not want to get involved. He has been successfully trained for his role of "nonparticipant" in the Submissive Society.

Let us quickly admit that many of the statements in this section have been deliberately provocative. They have been designed to get you to react to this book—preferably positively, but we will be satisfied with a negative reaction if it will help to get you involved in your psychology course. On the other hand, we believe that our comments were more than just provocative; that in some important sense they are "true." Nonetheless, at this point we find the words of Sigmund Koch to be particularly apt: "If I cannot persuade the reader, I will settle for making him uneasy."[4]

THE SEARCH FOR ALTERNATIVES: AN OVERVIEW

In an unprecedented fashion mankind is today seeking to expand its freedom and searching for alternatives to assure its survival. In the service of these goals we are increasingly willing to challenge even the most sacred precepts from the past.

ently more sensitive to punishment and the threat of punishment and thus tend to be more docile and conforming. You may find out more about these sex differences in the selcleions in Chapter 4.

[3]See R. W. Leeper and P. Madison, "Emotional richness and emotional poverty." In J. A. Dyal (Ed.), *Readings in psychology: Understanding human behavior* (2nd ed.) New York: McGraw-Hill, 1967.

[4]Sigmund Koch.

As members of the youth generation you have examined your inheritance from the established culture and have found it wanting along many dimensions. As psychologists we are immersed in these currents of change both as participants and as observer/interpreters. Thus, throughout this book we will emphasize the analysis of some of the crucial problem dimensions of our society and try to provide some perspective on alternative approaches toward solutions.

One of the major recurring themes of concern both to mankind in general and psychologists in particular is that of personal freedom versus control by others. In Chapter 1, we find that the differing approaches to psychology represented by behaviorism and humanism provide alternative perspectives on some of the crucial questions which are a part of this issue: What does personal freedom mean? Are we controlled? How? By whom? To what ends? Can the social sciences help to increase personal freedom and quality of life? Are the social sciences value free? Can they be? Should they be? Why is it important for you to know something about psychology?

As we noted in previous sections, what you learn in this course is heavily determined by your attitudes and motivations, which, in turn, have been molded by your experience in a school system. Some of these experiences have served to make you unfree rather than serving as a liberating force. Some of the ways in which your ability to function in college is conditioned by your previous

---

• Pick one of the above questions and comment below.

experiences in "the system" are discussed in Chapter 2. The most severe restrictions of freedom and opportunity are found among the lower socioeconomic classes, and these cultural disabilities are reflected in and exaggerated by the present system of "schooling." Low socioeconomic status and social mobility are linked with problems of the relative positions and abilities of the races. The chapter concludes with commentaries regarding some meaningful alternative approaches to "freeing-up" the educational system (preschool, reschool, free-school and deschool).

Of course the school system is not the only arena in which the struggle for freedom continues. In Chapter 3 we examine some of the many technologies which are now being developed by biological and behavioral sciences. These technologies, if used "properly," possess the potential for great benefits for mankind. On the other hand, they also raise the specter of extensive genetic and psychosocial control of man beyond the year 2000. As a prospective citizen of the twenty-first century, you must consider the possibility that man may tend to overcontrol himself. During your lifetime, man will make himself over in his own image—but *which* image, and who shall decide?

Contemporary concern regarding liberation of the human spirit has focused on the "female of the species" as a downtrodden and underprivileged group. This is our subject in Chapter 4. Somewhat less than half of you who will be reading this book are members of this beleaguered "minority." Are there real biological differences between the species besides the anatomical differences? Can these differences be related to the differences in "female psychology"? How are girl and boy babies raised differently? What consequences might these differences make in the female's self-concept, role definition, and behavior? What do you think may be some of the consequences of a blurring of sex role distinctions? Chapter 4 is definitely not "for women only." We hope that all of you, regardless of sex, will come to a better understanding of sex differences in behavior and a greater appreciation of the factors which mold you into

your sex roles. We hope that your new understanding will help you to become less sexist in your own life.

In Chapter 5 we consider the fact that our society is not only a "sexist" society; it is also a "racist" society. The period in which most of you were born and raised has been one in which the primary domestic issue in the United States, and to a lesser extent throughout the world, has been racism. The way in which socioeconomic institutions and personal perceptions are structured to perpetuate racial discrimination has been documented again and again by the media, by expert psychocultural analysts, and by agencies of government. Yet, in spite of the fact that the entire lifetime of most college students has been spent in a culture which has documented its own racist flaws, only 37 percent of American college students in 1971 considered the United States to be a racist nation.[5] Our psychological defenses against knowing the truth about ourselves seem most difficult to breach!

COMMENT: THE FEAR OF KNOWING; FEAR OF PERSONAL AND SOCIAL TRUTH
More than any other scientists we psychologists have to contend with the astonishing fact of resistance to the truth. More than any other kind of knowledge we fear knowledge of ourselves, knowledge that might transform our self-esteem and our self-image. A cat finds it easy to be a cat, as nearly as we can tell. It isn't afraid to be a cat. But being a full human being is difficult, frightening, and problematical. While human beings love knowledge and seek it—they are curious—they also fear it. The closer to the personal it is, the more they fear it. So human knowledge is apt to be a kind of dialectic between this love and this fear. Thus knowledge includes the defenses against itself, the repressions, the sugar-coatings, the inattentions, the forgettings. Therefore any methodology for

[5]Daniel Yankelovich. *The changing values on campus.* New York: Washington Square Press, 1972.

WHO ARE YOU AND WHAT ARE YOU DOING HERE?

getting at this truth must include some form of what psychoanalysts call "analysis of the resistance," a way of dissolving fear of the truth about oneself, thus permitting one to perceive himself head on, naked—a scary thing to do.

A. H. MASLOW

Western culture is also guilty of the most flagrant discrimination against those who are elderly; ours is an age and culture of "ageism." The elderly constitute an exploited minority to which we will all someday belong (if we are lucky). Our passing from the culturally valued status of producer-consumer to the non-status of "expendable-end-product" will be eased by "adequate retirement income" and a "generous old-age policy." Yet we will be waiting to die in a culture which no longer regards us as significant.

• We realize that it is almost impossible for you to really believe and know in your gut that you will someday be old, even though we all know it with our head. Do you think that Maslow's comments about fear of knowing are relevant here also?

The poor are always with us! But of course the problems of poverty are not equally distributed; they vary with age and race. We hope Chapter 5 will help you to understand both intellectually and emotionally the problems of being poor, old, and black in a rich, young, and white culture.

It would appear that more and more college students are coming to accept the possibility that ours is a "sick society." The proportion who either agreed or were not sure has risen from 46 percent in 1968 to 62 percent in 1971. From one-half (53 percent) to three-quarters (75 percent) of college students regarded the following social problems as significant signs that our society was not working properly: the Vietnam war (76 percent), pollution (71 percent), racial prejudice (62 percent), poverty

(60 percent), drug addiction (54 percent), and rising crime (53 percent).[6] In Chapters 6 (Violence) and 7 (Madness) we are concerned with manifestations of the fact that our society is not working properly for a significant segment of our people. Violence seems to be endemic in our society; violence against our fellow man, against ourselves, and against other forms of life on this planet. Some of us are legitimately concerned, in part, because many of us seem so unconcerned! But what can be done? Here is an obvious case in which our lack of understanding of the roots of man's behavior retards our efforts toward solution of social problems. Is man inherently violent—spawned eons ago from a killer ape? Or is it our aggressive societal structures and frustrating interpersonal relations which are primarily to blame? How much of our violence is *learned*, learned from parents, peers, and the public media? Is the decade of the 1970s to be a decade of peace internationally and interracially? Or are we simply licking our wounds and waiting for another chance to strike out? Would you do violence?

If society is "sick," then maybe those who are mad are really the sane ones. It now seems clear that the majority of people who are insane are *not* suffering from a malfunctioning nervous system. They are suffering the consequences of maladaptive learning; they have not been able to "adjust" themselves to cope with the moral conflicts which are inherent in our society. Over the past three decades more and more professional psychologists and psychiatrists have begun to question the appropriateness of the "sickness" model of mental illness, which treats the troubled person "as if" he were suffering from something analogous to a physical disorder. The alternative view is based on a social-learning model which emphasizes interpersonal conflict as the major source of personality disturbance and also points to the prevention of such disorders by reforming the community. Unfortunately, at the present time a substantial portion of our total expenditures on "mental health" are devoted to maintaining the "custodial ethic"

[6] D. Yankelovich, ibid., pp. 61–65, 233.

which says in effect " . . . if you are too deviate, we will put you away." The fact that some asylums are being used as places "to put away" societal rebels in Russia raises the even more frightening question of how extensively the rights of the insane are being violated in our own society. Some of the issues relating madness to societal values are examined in Chapter 7.

Chapter 8 is devoted to alternative life styles, with particular attention being focused on the attitudes and values of the youth generation. As people who have grown up during the 1960s and 1970s, you have witnessed, and perhaps participated in, the rise of a new consciousness—a consciousness which is especially sensitive to social injustice and which despairs because interpersonal trust and a feeling of community with one's fellows so seldom exists. "Your time" has been a time in which young people, more than ever before, define themselves as a unique class in our society and in many ways stand against the values which are held by the preceding generations. You are a generation which has refused to see the emperor resplendently clothed when in fact he is naked. Yet how long can we continue to gaze directly at the truth, especially when it is not flattering to our neurotically idealized conception of ourselves? Are we seeing the beginning of a new conservatism among youth—a tendency to be more concerned with the practical problems of everyday living and "getting ahead in the world" than with "spiritual" or social values? Your own views and reactions will help to determine whether or not the values of the counterculture will continue to provide alternatives to the established views.

The counterculture has moved the whole culture toward views of the world other than the traditional Western perspective which emphasizes the pragmatic, scientific, and technological. Your generation has been the first in the history of modern industrialized societies to seek alternative realities through psychedelic drugs, mysticism, and Eastern religions. This general cultural revolution has also influenced the perspectives of psychology. During the nineteenth century psychology regarded itself as that science which was devoted to the study of consciousness. But during the twentieth century psychology has been dominated by a behavioristic conception which excluded conscious experience as appropriate subject matter. More recently, paralleling the rise of the drug culture, psychologists have become increasingly interested in conscious experiences and their alteration by a variety of psychological treatments and physical agents. In Chapter 9 we will examine some of the psychological and sociocultural aspects of the search for alternative realities.

We cannot conclude this overview of the book without posing some overarching questions —questions with which we hope you can become involved: How will schools of the future differ from those which you have experienced? Will the biological/behavioral sciences be used to expand man's freedom or limit his alternatives? Will we be successful in challenging and reducing the "sexism," "racism" and "ageism" that exists in the structure of our society and in the minds and hearts of our citizens? What can be done about our increasingly violent culture? Can positive regard for the political structure of a democratic society be restored? Will the counterculture provide real alternatives to the Establishment? Is encounter grouping "the most important social invention of the twentieth century" or a phoney-baloney fad? Will the sexual revolution in North America continue on the swing toward sexual freedom or react toward a new puritanism? Will communes become an increasingly selected way of living? Will the values of the counterculture be coopted and prostituted by the media and the Establishment? What realities can I (should I) experience and believe in? Will the forces of good and right triumph over the *dark sinister forces of affluence and superscience*? Tune in next decade for the next thrilling episode in the continuing true-life adventure

---

COMMENT: TO READ IS LESS COMMENDABLE . . .

In Plato's *Phaedrus,* Thamus, the Egyptian king, protests that those who learn from books have only the show of wisdom, not wisdom itself. Merely reading what someone has written is less commendable than saying the same thing for arcane reasons. A person who reads a book appears to be omniscient, yet, according to Thamus, he "knows nothing." And when a text is used to aid memory, Thamus contended that memory would fall into disuse. To read is less commendable than to recite what one has learned.

B. F. SKINNER

DON'T READ THIS BOOK!
WRITE ON IT

"Don't read this book?" Right! That's what we mean—but it *does* need some elaboration. More precisely we mean "Don't *just* read this book."

It is unfortunately true for many of you that your years of schooling have taught you to "just read" and "memorize the facts." These will not be easy habits to overcome, but one of the purposes of this book is to *help* you to do just that. We hope that it will provide experiences which will encourage you to break the spell of automatic, passive reading and will challenge you to begin *thinking* about what you are reading. Thinking about what you are reading is much more difficult, much more work. Perhaps that is why we so seldom do it.

We have tried to structure this book to help you to become more involved in your psychology course. One of the ways in which we have tried to make the book more interesting and challenging to you is by breaking up the continuity of the articles by inserting "on-the-spot" questions, comments, and opportunities for you to react. For example,

---

● Heresy! We are distracting you from your reading!

Yes, indeed, we are trying to distract you from "just reading" in the hope that you will give some *thought* to what you are reading—and that you will get involved with what the author has written so

that you are actively questioning and commenting to yourself. We believe question asking to be important because it is demonstrably effective in increasing students' sense of personal power, (i.e., competence and confidence). We thus strongly agree with Postman and Weingartner when they say, "Once you have learned how to ask questions—relevant and appropriate and substantial questions—you have learned how to learn and no one can keep you from learning whatever you want or need to know." (Selection 7, p. 65.) And because we also agree with their view that " . . . asking questions is behavior. If you don't do it, you don't learn it," we have tried to help you to learn to ask questions.[7] We have done that in several ways. First, we have introduced our own questions and comments in the "on the spot" sections. As you have already seen, each of these is designated with a black spot (●). Second, we have provided space for you to write some comments or questions of your own. We have indicated these by a blank space in which you can write your questions and comments. Your comments may range from a superficial but honest "bullshit," to more probing questions which could serve to initiate further search (e.g., library, laboratory, or "learning-in-life" research) on your part. Some of you will be able to use these sections as opportunities to learn to be "active seekers" rather than "passive recipient knowers." They are yours to be used as you see fit. Third, we encourage you to write in this book whenever you have a thought about the material. We cannot anticipate where this will occur for you so use the margins, but—*don't (just) read this book, write in it!* Fourth, we have tried to begin each chapter with provocative statements that focus on some of the central issues in the chapter. Again, we have left room for you to react. Fifth, immediately following the "Provocations" we have written more

---

[7]Those of you who are interested in constructive ways to challenge the system will find numerous practical tactics described in two books: Harold Taylor. *How to change colleges.* New York: Holt, Rinehart and Winston, 1971; and Neil Postman and Charles Weingartner. *The soft revolution: Student handbook for turning schools around.* New York: Delacorte, 1971.

lengthy but equally provocative editorial introductions to the basic issues to be considered in some of the articles. In some instances we have become so involved in formulating these sections that they have grown to be article length statements in their own right (Selection 1, 6, and 42). In other cases these editorial introductions may be relatively brief (but, we hope, still provocative). In any case, *be sure to read them,* because they set the stage, provide the context, and add new ideas for your consideration as you read the other selections in the chapter. And sixth (and finally), we hope that the articles which we have selected for this book are ones which will provide you with an enjoyable reading/thinking/feeling experience *and* provide a basis for intellectual/emotional travel beyond where you are now.

In conclusion, we recognize that no matter what we have done to help you get involved in this book, in the course, and in your university experience, in the last analysis the key to the whole effort is *you*. Although we hope there are many times when you will be able to get a little help from your friends (including your professor), it is *you* who must eventually assume responsibility for your education and your own life. No one else can *give* you an education. That is your right, freedom, obligation, and responsibility. Now let's go on with it.

Remember, "Once you have learned how to ask questions—relevant and appropriate and substantial questions—you have learned how to learn and no one can keep you from learning whatever you want or need to know . . . asking questions is behavior. If you don't do it, you don't learn it."

The space below is left for you to begin to practice asking questions. What questions or comments do you have about what we have said in this article? Write them below.

- Once you have learned how to ask questions - relevant and appropriate and substantail questions - you have learned how to learn.

2   PSYCHOLOGY AS A SCIENCE: RELEVANT CRITICISMS AND CRITICISMS OF RELEVANCE*

JONATHAN L. FREEDMAN

Almost everyone who thinks about the matter at all seems dissatisfied with the social sciences. In a sense, of course, this is as it should be. Satisfaction with progress in a field generally reflects smugness or arrogance by practitioners and ignorance or naiveté by outsiders. Most good scientists have doubts about their own field. Physicists suffered from dissatisfaction and self-doubt even during the marvelously productive years between 1930 and 1960, as do biologists now during a period of spectacular growth in their field. Nevertheless, dissatisfactions with the social sciences seem to be more widespread and deeper than those that have affected most other sciences. This dissatisfaction is so profound that there is talk of abandoning the field entirely or no longer treating it as a science, which comes to much the same thing. I share many of these doubts. My colleagues will confirm that I am generally considered overly critical of the social sciences, and it is thus somewhat anomalous for me to be writing mainly in their defense. Yet I feel that the social sciences are exceedingly important and, with all their faults, perhaps our only hope.

COMMENT: REFLECTIONS ON THE DISCIPLINE OF PSYCHOLOGY

In psychology, for almost a hundred years, we have been vigorously erecting a discipline on a pattern unique in the history of scholarship. The hallmarks of our scholarly style have been: "advance by asseveration," "progress by proclamation," "proof by pronunciamento," "truth by trivialization," "experiment by exculpation,"

*Abridged from J. L. Freedman, Psychology as a science. *Social Research*, 1971, 38, 710–731. Reprinted by permission of the author and publisher.

"rigor by role-playing." If this be discipline, it is a discipline of deceit. The few areas in which genuine insights or hard discoveries have been possible under these circumstances are seen as pockets of sedition—or, better, just not seen. A discipline of this character must rely upon an obsessive orthodoxy which exacts a terrible price from the self-determining or spontaneous of any age, and especially from the young. . . . A generation of students is upon us who will not succumb to an orthodoxy merely because it is there. . . . In a word, the customer (i.e., student) is no longer buying the dear, musty, turgid scientist rhetoric. For good or for ill—and probably for both—world sensibility has been going through a sea change and recent generations of students have been at the forefront of those making the waves. To my cynical mind, the last two sentences taken together *imply* the inevitable demise of orthodox social science.

SIGMUND KOCH

It is interesting that the increasing dissatisfaction with the social sciences coincides with increasing interest and activity in these fields. During the 1960s, college students gradually and then more rapidly lost interest in the physical sciences and turned instead to the biological and social sciences. In the last few years the turn to the social sciences has been pronounced. . . .

It is not surprising that dissatisfaction with and interest in the social sciences have increased at the same time. As people have found that technology and the traditional physical and biological sciences do not have the answers to mankind's burning questions, and as they then turn to the social sciences only to find that the latter do not now have the answers either, it is natural that there should be dissatisfaction. This is felt by people active in the field as well as those who simply read about it. These dissatisfactions give rise to several types of criticisms, and it is important to distinguish among them.

First, there are people, most or whom are in the arts of humanities, who say that the kinds of problems with which the social sciences deal should not be studied through scientific methods. Such broad and sweeping indictments are based largely on ethical or moral grounds. Second, there are some, mostly scientists in other fields, who say that the scientific approach is fine in principle, but that the techniques actually used by people in the field are too primitive and sloppy to prove effective. Third, there are many, either social scientists themselves or others deeply involved with social problems, who accept the scientific approach and believe that current methods could be productive, but feel that the field has degenerated into a search for trivia and fails to deal with important or interesting questions. I will try to cope with each of these criticisms in turn.

1. Science should not probe into human feelings, thought or behavior. The argument goes that the scientific method is acceptable when you want to determine the effect of gravity on a falling body or discover whether penicillin cures pneumonia, but it should not be used to find out how children learn to read, or how to reduce prejudice, the effects of overcrowding or why human beings fight wars. I consider this criticism either frivolous or absurd and find it hard to take seriously. But I understand that many people, some of whom I respect in their own fields, do take it seriously and so it must be dealt with.

The basis for this attack is that it is irreligious or inhumane to study human beings scientifically. I cannot answer the religious objection—that is a matter of faith. But the humanist position is subject to argument. I remember reading an essay by Joseph Wood Krutch in which he objected to social scientists trying to study happiness. He was appalled by the idea and, in addition to suggesting that it

was impossible (a quite separate argument), expressed the view that studying happiness scientifically would change its special human quality. Presumably Mr. Krutch would have felt the same about human pain, although perhaps preserving its special quality would have been less important to him. The point is that studying any aspect of human thought, feeling or behavior is held to be repugnant because it makes the object of study "less human."

To return to Mr. Krutch's criticism: Assuming that appropriate and ethically acceptable methods can be found, I do not see why studying happiness scientifically is any more demeaning or dehumanizing than studying the effects of penicillin on pneumonia or ascertaining how many chromosomes human beings have. Nor do I see why it is more dehumanizing than fiction or biography. Humanists do not object to intimate biographies such as Boswell's *Life of Johnson* nor to James Joyce's attempt to picture mental life in Molly's soliloquy in *Ulysses*. A social scientist who studies human problems is often doing very much what the novelist or biographer does—except that the scientist tries to do it systematically. Surely no one would object to an author making an occasional note in his journal about his daily activities, how his friends behave, how a child looked at him as he passed a playground, or how a waitress complained that she did not like standing on her feet all day. Yet critics complain about a social scientist who takes the same kinds of notes and then publishes them as a study of social mores and structure in a large city in Connecticut. In both cases we are observing human behavior—the major difference is that the social scientist does it more systematically, sometimes in a controlled environment.

The humanists' distrust and dislike of the scientific approach to the social sciences seems to be based on two somewhat different complaints. They feel that human life has a special, indescribable quality that is threatened by scientific exploration. Even if happiness could be quantified, it should not be, because, once put into numbers, it is no longer special. Descriptions of life in prose or poetry do not threaten because they are themselves human forms of expression and thus necessarily preserve the humanness of what is being described. On the other hand, numbers and science are cold and machine-like, and therefore do not have that human quality.

The second cause of the humanists' distrust is their feeling that the descriptions of human life given by social scientists are oversimplified. One study or even a hundred studies of happiness cannot possibly reflect the richness and complexity of the experience, and thus scientific articles on happiness are empty and misleading. They suggest a simplistic shallow view of man. The humanist sees the social scientist as threatening the human quality of man by measuring and quantifying and in the end providing no more than an oversimplified version of reality.

There is obviously considerable truth in both criticisms. Most descriptions of human life by social scientists tend to be dry and mechanistic. Saying that 36.4 percent of women between the ages of 19 and 35 have an orgasm at least one a week (made up figures) may communicate interesting information about female sexual behavior, but not the excitement and richness of the experience. And descriptions of human behavior currently being provided by the social scientists are certainly oversimplified. This is true even in the case of relatively simple behaviors such as rote learning, and becomes more evident as the phenomenon increases in complexity. For example, social psychology has a considerable amount to say about why people like each other. It can predict with some accuracy whether individuals are likely to become friends, on the basis of various factors such as how much mutual contact they have, their similarities and the quality of their interactions. But, as students always complain when they study this problem, these factors do not explain why two particular individuals like each other, or why two people fall in love when two other quite similar people do not Thus, when social psychologists say that familiarity, similarity and reinforcement history are major factors determining liking, it

sounds terribly simplistic because everyone knows that these factors do not explain liking in detail or begin to include the richness and depth of the feelings involved.

I agree. Social science does tend to make human beings sound less human and more mechanical, and to present a far too simple view of man. Yet I do not think these are legitimate criticisms. It all depends on what you expect from a science. In the long run, of course, we all agree that the goal of the investigation should be a thorough, full understanding of man that reflects the richness of the human experience. That is in the long run —probably the very very long run. The essential point is that all science progresses by concentrating on relatively simple phenomena and trying to discover something about them. In fact, it tends to operate by deliberately simplifying the situation, by excluding or ignoring most of the rich detail in order to focus on one or two factors at a time. You cannot study the growth process in trees by observing the whole forest; you must focus on particular trees. Admittedly, you then cannot see the beauty of the forest for concentrating on the trees. But at the moment you are not interested in the forest as a whole; you are studying a more limited problem.

Social science functions in the same way. It focuses on limited problems and on limited aspects of them in the hope of accumulating small bits of information about human beings. One can complain about the tediousness of the process and be disappointed by the individual accomplishments, but not about the process itself. This is how it is in all sciences and how it must be in the social sciences as well.

Thus, although I sympathize with the feelings of the humanists regarding the mechanistic, shallow view of man that is sometimes given by the social sciences, I do not accept this as a basic criticism of the field. Surely we do want to know about human behavior and it is apparent that speculations and novels do not tell us all we want to know. Accordingly, if appropriate methods are used to preserve human dignity and privacy, humanistic indictment of the social sciences is simply untenable. Man has always been fascinated by himself, and he will use all of the tools available to him in pursuit of that interest. One of the most powerful tools is the scientific method.

2. The problem with the social sciences is that their techniques are not good enough, or, "How can you expect to discover anything if you measure in inches rather than in millimeters?" If social scientists used better methods, more powerful statistics, more elaborate and precise equipment, and paid more attention to scaling and measurement they would make progress; but their present methods are simply inadequate.

Admittedly, there is considerable truth to this criticism. In fact, I recently wrote an article criticizing a technique that was becoming quite popular among some psychologists. This was the use of role-playing instead of actual research. The investigator asks someone how he would behave or how he thinks someone else would behave *if* he were in a given situation. Instead of placing someone in the situation and observing his behavior, the "experimenter" relies on this kind of self-report or guess. Obviously this is not science, yet research using this method is being done and has been reported in the journals. Thus, I recognize the existence of poor techniques in the social sciences and agree that they cause considerable damage and confusion. However, I do not accept this as a blanket description of all of the social sciences. As with the previous criticism, even if it were true, it would not be a reason to abandon the attempt at scientific exploration; and I do not think it is true.

Let us be clear that at least in some social sciences there is considerable sophistication in both methodological techniques and statistical procedures. I think it fair to say that the social sciences (for better or worse) use the most powerful, complicated, and high-powered statistics of all of the scientific fields. Most of the major advances in statistical inference have received their impetus from agricultural, biomedical and social science research, largely because these kinds of fields involve problems and types of data that require very sophisticated statistical analyses. Other sciences obtain results that are so obvious and striking that

statistics are hardly needed, or they accumulate so many observations that they can rely simply on estimates of margin of error. The social sciences rarely obtain such powerful effects and almost never have enough observations to preclude the necessity of inferential statistics. This is hardly a strength; on the contrary, the necessity of using such complicated statistics can be seen as one of the unfortunate aspects of the social sciences. But there can be no question that the statistical techniques used by social scientists are the best available and that criticism on these grounds is totally unjustified.

In sum, I do not believe that the available techniques, methods, and procedures are inadequate for studying most problems in the social sciences. Naturally we are constantly finding new and better methods. Research done in the 1960s was considerably more sophisticated and in some respects more productive than similar research done 10 or 20 years earlier. Generally, problems investigated by the social scientists are difficult to get a handle on, partly because they involve variables that cannot be measured directly. Yet I believe that the current methods, if appropriately and intelligently applied, are adequate for investigating these problems.

3. The final criticism of the social sciences is that they have not really discovered anything about human behavior, that there has been no accumulation of knowledge, and that they are making no progress in solving the problems with which they should be concerned. This is by far the most serious criticism and one that weighs heavily on the minds of a great many people in the field. The social sciences that once promised so much seem to have yielded very little. Knowledge from the social sciences should enable us to understand ourselves more fully, to solve many of the world's problems, and to expand and enrich our lives. That is the dream, presumably the goal of the social sciences—obviously a largely unfulfilled dream.

But dreams are rarely fulfilled by the generation that first dreamed them. The question is not whether the social sciences have totally explained human behavior and solved all of the ills of mankind, but rather whether the social sciences have made any reasonable progress along this path, whether they have discovered anything we did not know before. I think the answer is that the amount of knowledge accumulated by the social sciences is substantial, but disappointing. When backed into a corner, many social scientists point out that it is a very young field and not much can be expected of it so soon. Certainly it is young, certainly the number of people involved in active research has been small until recently, certainly relatively little money has been invested in the social sciences, and certainly a science has the right to stumble around for a while before making real progress. But it is also true that a great part of the resources, both human and financial, have been wasted through poor techniques and concentration on trivia.

Dissatisfaction with progress in the field is exacerbated by those practitioners who pretend that they know a great deal more than they actually do. Social scientists seem especially prone to pomposity and arrogance. Since the general public supposes, at times, that social scientists have all the answers, it is tempting for a social scientist to pretend that he does. Unfortunately this happens all too often; the public is misled and more legitimate scientists dismayed. We hear economists telling us with absolute certainty that they know exactly how to solve the nation's inflation without causing too much unemployment (despite the fact that other economists suggest almost opposite procedures). Then, when the plans do not work, they blandly say (as Professor McCracken, head of the President's Council of Economic Advisors recently did) that the plan really was correct but perhaps should have been carried out a little differently. Sociologists and social psychologists tell us exactly how to reduce racial prejudice or how to elect a peace candidate when, in most cases, there is little hard data on which to base their conclusions and in fact their techniques are demonstrably ineffective. A great man in the field of learning tells us that he knows exactly how to raise children in order to produce an utopian society—a statement based largely on research with pigeons and

rats. Ethologists make virtually unlimited pronouncements about human nature when they know more about other animals than they do about human beings. Educational psychologists offer endless courses in how to teach, yet they do not know much about it themselves and their students do not necessarily become better teachers. And so on. Since most competent and respected social scientists will not make such pronouncements because they understand that their knowledge is limited, most of the public posturing is left to the less scrupulous, but more famous people in the field. I suppose this is inevitable, but the sad result is that the trusting public is deceived and then disillusioned.

This is a pretty dismal picture to be painted by someone actively involved in the field. Despite these negative feelings, however, I am ready to defend the social sciences even in respect to criticisms of their productivity. The crucial point here is that, even though they have produced less than they might have, the social sciences have made appreciable progress and there is good reason to believe they will continue to do so.

Finally, I would like to discuss the whole issue of relevance, importance and trivia. Every science, indeed every field of human endeavor, must deal with the question of whether its work is worth doing. Space ships, atomic reactors, literary criticism, nuclear accelerators, napalm, new plastics, art, astronomical observatories, the structure of DNA and even heart and kidney transplants are scrutinized in terms of their value to society and mankind. This kind of scrutiny is particularly prevalent in the social sciences, which are expected to deal with crucial social problems and are therefore criticized when they do not. Why study how to teach a rat to run a maze when you can study how to teach a child to read? Why study the relationship between the physical and psychological property of sound when you could be studying how to bring a schizophrenic's world closer to reality? Why investigate how people play some silly game in the laboratory when you could be studying how to end war and aggression? And why publish all those papers on the intricacies of attitude change and so little specifically on how to reduce racial prejudice?

One answer to these kinds of questions, an answer that still appeals to many and is difficult to reject, is that the sciences seek knowledge and that this is a justification in its own right. The scientist studies whatever he thinks is interesting. He does not ask whether this is the best problem to study, whether it is the most important or the most practical, whether it is the one society most needs to have answered. He does not make value judgments in terms of practical application or broad social significance. When he uncovers a piece of knowledge he does not wonder whether it will be useful or to what use it will be put. That is not his job. He tries to find truth and when he does he has been successful.

- Do you believe that "pure science" is, or can be, value-free? Why, or why not?

A second answer is that scientists should and do worry about the practical application of their discoveries and the social worth of what they are doing; at the same time, they may be able to make greater contributions through basic rather than applied research. Social scientists who would like to solve the problems of racial prejudice, war and ignorance may feel that the best way to do this is not through a direct frontal attack. Basic research, it is argued, will be more likely to produce the knowledge necessary to solve these problems than applied research directly related to them. For example, rather than study how to reduce the prejudice of Southern whites toward blacks, the social scientist studies attitude change in general and trusts that eventually the knowledge he obtains will be applicable to the reduction of all prejudices.

- Let us distract you a moment! Why "Southern whites" in this sentence? If you are an observant student you will see that this is an ex-

ample of how our language fosters miscommunication and perpetuates overgeneralization and stereotype. While it is true that the problem of prejudice against blacks had its seeds in the Southern regions of the United States, it is by no means confined to that area. Indeed, many Southern whites are leaders in the fight against discrimination. We know that, you know that, and Professor Freedman knows that; and indeed he would probably be among the first to emphasize that point. Yet all too often our unconscious stereotypes lead us to the unintended practice of this form of "reverse prejudice." Think about it!

Now, back to the basic-research argument.

There are several grounds for this basic-research argument. The first is that basic research is designed to discover general principles, while applied research is too specific to generalize to other situations. Even if the applied research produced results, it would not add much to our understanding of the issue. In contrast, successful basic research might uncover laws that would help us understand the issue in general and could be applied to many situations.

The second reason given in favor of basic research is that we do not really know enough as yet to do good applied work. Only when you know something can you apply it and, because the discipline is so new, too little knowledge has been accumulated in most areas to enable social scientists to do productive applied research.

Both the pure-science and basic-research positions are held by many social scientists; I think both arguments are reasonable and defensible. There are, however, many who feel that more applied research should be done and that basic research could be directed more closely to current problems. They feel that applied research often does produce results while, even in the long run, much basic research will prove useless. . . .

My own feeling is that the field desperately needs a combination of basic and applied research and that the balance has been too much on the side of the former. I would like to see the best researchers doing both kinds of work. That is, the typical social scientist should do some basic research trying to discover underlying principles and general laws and also some applied research using his experience and knowledge to solve specific problems in the real world.

. . . we have to some extent slighted applied research, at least in psychology, and, more particularly, we have failed to work back and forth between actual situations and laboratory experiments. We often talk about doing this, but it is rarely carried out in practice.

Even if we accept the pure science or basic research arguments, however, it is possible to criticize many who adhere to them. There is a tendency in psychology and probably in other fields to concentrate on smaller and smaller problems. While it is possible to disregard the practical importance of a problem, the scientist should take into account how important it is in the context of his own field. A problem without obvious relevance to society might still be extremely important within psychology, because it is central to a theoretical position or has major implications for a whole field of investigation. All too often scientists focus on a particular issue even though it has few implications and would be considered trivial or unimportant by other scientists in the field.

The social sciences differ from most of the other sciences in that the layman can usually understand enough about a problem in the field to feel that he can evaluate its importance; and often he decides that it is not an important problem. When someone in chemistry or physics describes his area of interest to a layman, most of us listen with awe but little understanding. We hardly feel competent to decide whether he is working on an important problem in the field. In contrast, everyone is to some extent an expert in the social sciences. Thus when someone says that he is working on the effects of partial reinforcement on speed of extinction (even when he describes exactly what that means in non-jargon terms), some laymen will decide that it is an uninteresting problem without fully understanding its implications. The point is that the social sciences tend to be criticized more freely because they are more accessible to those not in them. While there may be just as much emphasis on trivia in the physical as in the social sciences, it is more obvious in the latter and therefore gives rise to more dissatisfaction. But the fact remains that there is a great deal of work on trivia, very little on the crucial problems facing society. Very little work in the social sciences is particularly interesting or important, either inside or outside the field. To that extent, dissatisfactions are justified. Not everyone has to work on relevant social problems, but the work should concentrate as much as possible on problems that are important either to the field itself or to the general human condition. To the extent that this is not done now the field should be criticized, and it is of course the major source of dissatisfaction for those of us in the field. Nevertheless this is no reason to abandon scientific inquiry in the social sciences. I think that the social sciences have produced considerable knowledge, and are likely to produce more in the future. History has, I think, amply demonstrated that the insights and brilliance of the most gifted men are not enough to reveal all the truths of human thought and behavior. Only a systematic, scientific inquiry (combined with human insight) has any chance of producing such revelations and that is why we must continue this attempt.

Criticisms of the social sciences:

① Many humanists dislike + distrust the scientific approach

- They feel human life has a special indescribable quality which is threatened by scientific exploitation.

② Techniques aren't good enough. That is present methods in V.H.B are inadequate

③ No knowledge of human behavior has really been accumulated that no progress has been made in solving the numerous problems with which psychologists are concerned.

3 THE POSSIBILITY OF A SCIENCE OF HUMAN BEHAVIOR*

B. F. SKINNER

Man's power appears to have increased out of all proportion to his wisdom. He has never been in a better position to build a healthy, happy, and productive world; yet things have perhaps never seemed so black. Two exhausting world wars in a single half century have given no assurance of a lasting peace. Dreams of progress toward a higher civilization have been shattered by the spectacle of the murder of millions of innocent people. The worst may be still to come. Scientists may not set off a chain reaction to blow the world into eternity, but some of the more plausible prospects are scarcely less disconcerting.

In the face of this apparently unnecessary condition men of good will find themselves helpless or afraid to act. Some are the prey of a profound pessimism. Others strike out blindly in counteraggression, much of which is directed toward science itself. Torn from its position of prestige, science is decried as a dangerous toy in the hands of children who do not understand it. The conspicuous feature of any period is likely to be blamed for its troubles, and in the twentieth century science must play the scapegoat. But the attack is not entirely without justification. Science has developed unevenly. By seizing upon the easier problems first, it has extended our control of inanimate nature without preparing for the serious social problems which follow. The technologies based upon science are disturbing. Isolated groups of relatively stable people are brought into contact with each other and lose their equilibrium. Industries spring up for which the life of a community may be unprepared, while others vanish leaving millions unfit for productive work. The application of science prevents famines and plagues, and lowers death rates—only

to populate the earth beyond the reach of established systems of cultural or governmental control. Science has made war more terrible and more destructive. Much of this has not been done deliberately, but it has been done. And since scientists are necessarily men of some intelligence, they might have been expected to be alert to these consequences.

It is not surprising to encounter the proposal that science should be abandoned, at least for the time being. This solution appeals especially to those who are fitted by temperament to other ways of life. Some relief might be obtained if we could divert mankind into a revival of the arts or religion or even of that petty quarreling which we now look back upon as a life of peace. Such a program resembles the decision of the citizens of Samuel Butler's *Erewhon,* where the instruments and products of science were put into museums—as vestiges of a stage in the evolution of human culture which did not survive. But not everyone is willing to defend a position of stubborn "not knowing." There is no virtue in ignorance for its own sake. Unfortunately we cannot stand still: to bring scientific research to an end now would mean a return to famine and pestilence and the exhausting labors of a slave culture.

SCIENCE AS A CORRECTIVE

Another solution is more appealing to the modern mind. It may not be science which is wrong but only its application. The methods of science have been enormously successful wherever they have been tried. Let us then apply them to human affairs. We need not retreat in those sectors where science has already advanced. It is necessary only to bring our understanding of human nature up to the same point. Indeed, this may well be our only hope. If we can observe human behavior carefully from an objective point of view and come to understand it for what it is, we may be able to adopt a more sensible course of action. The need for establishing some such balance is now widely felt, and those who are able to control the direction of science are acting accordingly. It is understood that there is no point in furthering a science of nature unless it includes a sizable science of human nature, because only in that case will the results be wisely used. It is possible that science has come to the rescue and that order will eventually be achieved in the field of human affairs.

This possibility is offensive to many people. It is opposed to a tradition of long standing which regards man as a free agent, whose behavior is the product, not of specifiable antecedent conditions, but of spontaneous inner changes of course. Prevailing philosophies of human nature recognize an internal "will" which has the power of interfering with causal relationships and which makes the prediction and control of behavior impossible. To suggest that we abandon this view is to threaten many cherished beliefs—to undermine what appears to be a stimulating and productive conception of human nature. The alternative point of view insists upon recognizing coercive forces in human conduct which we may prefer to disregard. It challenges our aspirations, either worldly or otherworldly. Regardless of how much we stand to gain from supposing that human behavior is the proper subject matter of a science, no one who is a product of Western civilization can do so without a struggle. We simply do not want such a science.

SOME OBJECTIONS TO A SCIENCE OF BEHAVIOR

When a science of behavior reaches the point of dealing with lawful relationships, it meets the resistance of those who give their allegiance to prescientific or extrascientific conceptions. The resistance does not always take the form of an overt rejection of science. It may be transmuted into claims of limitations, often expressed in highly scientific terms.

It has sometimes been pointed out, for example, that physical science has been unable to maintain its philosophy of determinism, particularly at the subatomic level. The Principle of Indeterminacy states that there are circumstances under which the physicist cannot put himself in possession of all relevant information: if he chooses to observe one event, he must relinquish the possibility of observing another. In our present state of knowledge, certain events therefore appear to be unpredictable. It does not follow that these events are free or capricious. Since human behavior is enormously complex and the human organism is of limited dimensions, many acts may involve processes to which the Principle of Indeterminacy applies. It does not follow that human behavior is free, but only that it may be beyond the range of a predictive or controlling science. Most students of behavior, however, would be willing to settle for the degree of prediction and control achieved by the physical sciences in spite of this limitation. A final answer to the problem of lawfulness is to be sought, not in the limits of any hypothetical mechanism within the organism, but in our ability to demonstrate lawfulness in the behavior of the organism as a whole.

● If you assume, along with Skinner, that all behavior is completely determined, can the concept of personal freedom continue to have any useful meaning? We believe that it can. Discuss it in your class and with your professor—see if you can figure out why.

If you are interested in this problem, you would probably enjoy Skinner's latest book on the topic, *Beyond Freedom and Dignity*.

The extraordinary complexity of behavior is sometimes held to be an added source of difficulty. Even though behavior may be lawful, it may be too complex to be dealt with in terms of law. Sir Oliver Lodge once asserted that "though an astronomer can calculate the orbit of a planet or comet or even a meteor, although a physicist can deal with the structure of atoms, and a chemist with their possible combinations, neither a biologist nor any scientific man can calculate the orbit of a common fly." This is a statement about the limitations of scientists or about their aspirations, not about the suitability of a subject matter. Even so, it is wrong. It may be said with some assurance that if no one has calculated the orbit of a fly, it is only because no one has been sufficiently interested in doing so. The tropistic movements of many insects are now fairly well understood, but the instrumentation needed to record the flight of a fly and to give an account of all the conditions affecting it would cost more than the importance of the subject justifies. There is, therefore, no reason to conclude, as the author does, that "an incalculable element of self-determination thus makes its appearance quite low down the animal scale." Self-determination does not follow from complexity. Difficulty in calculating the orbit of the fly does not prove capriciousness, though it may make it impossible to prove anything else. The problems imposed by the complexity of a subject matter must be dealt with as they arise. Apparently hopeless cases often become manageable in time. It is only recently that any sort of lawful account of the weather has been possible. We often succeed in reducing complexity to a reasonable degree by simplifying conditions in the laboratory; but where this is impossible, a statistical analysis may be used to achieve an inferior, but in many ways acceptable, prediction. Certainly no one is prepared to say now what a science of behavior can or cannot accomplish eventually. Advance estimates of the limits of science have generally proved inaccurate. The issue is in the long run pragmatic: we cannot tell until we have tried.

A final objection deals with the practical application of a scientific analysis. Even if we assume that behavior is lawful and that the methods of science will reveal the rules which govern it, we may be unable to make any technological use of these rules unless certain conditions can be brought under control. In the laboratory many conditions are simplified and irrelevant conditions often eliminated. But of what value are laboratory studies if we must predict and control behavior where a comparable simplification is impossible? It is true that we can gain control over behavior only insofar as we can control the factors responsible for it. What a scientific study does is to enable us to make optimal use of the control we possess. The laboratory simplification reveals the relevance of factors which we might otherwise overlook.

We cannot avoid the problems raised by a science of behavior by simply denying that the necessary conditions can be controlled. In actual fact there is a considerable degree of control over many relevant conditions. In penal institutions and military organizations the control is extensive. We control the environment of the human organism in the nursery and in institutions which care for those to whom the conditions of the nursery remain necessary in later life. Fairly extensive control of conditions relevant to human behavior is maintained in industry in the form of wages and conditions of work, in schools in the form of grades and conditions of work, in commerce by anyone in possession of goods or money, by governmental agencies through the police and military, in the psychological clinic through the consent of the controlee, and so on. A degree of effective control, not so easily identified, rests in the hands of entertainers, writers, advertisers, and propagandists. These controls, which are often all too evident in their practical application, are more than sufficient to permit us to extend the results of a laboratory science to the interpretation of human behavior in daily affairs—for either theoretical or practical purposes. Since a science of behavior will continue to increase the effective use of this control, it is now more important than ever to understand the processes involved and to prepare ourselves for the problems which will certainly arise.

● The processes involved from Skinner's point of view are those based on operant conditioning using rewards to elicit and maintain the desired behavior. You should look up "token economies" in your text to see how these principles are applied in institutional settings.

COMMENT: UNDERSTANDING AND PREDICTION ARE BETTER GOALS

Personally, I believe there is a better way to advertise psychology and to relate it to social problems. Reinforcement is only one of many important ideas that we have to offer. Instead of repeating constantly that reinforcement leads to control, I would prefer to emphasize that reinforcement can lead to satisfaction and competence. And I would prefer to speak of understanding and prediction as our major scientific goals.

. . . therefore, I want to try to make the case that understanding and prediction are better goals for psychology than is control—better both for psychology and for the promotion of human welfare—because they lead us to think, not in terms of coercion by a powerful elite, but in terms of the diagnosis of problems and the development of programs that can enrich the lives of every citizen.

GEORGE A. MILLER

THE FATE OF THE INDIVIDUAL

Western thought has emphasized the importance and dignity of the individual. Democratic philosophies of government, based upon the "rights of man," have asserted that all individuals are equal under the law, and that the welfare of the individual is the goal of government. In similar philosophies of religion, piety and salvation have been left to the individual himself rather than to a religious agency. Democratic literature and art have emphasized the individual rather than the type, and have often been concerned with increasing man's knowledge and understanding of himself. Many schools of psychotherapy have accepted the philosophy that man is the master of his own fate. In education, social planning, and many other fields, the welfare and dignity of the individual have received first consideration.

The use of such concepts as individual freedom, initiative, and responsibility has, therefore, been well reinforced. When we turn to what science has to offer, however, we do not find very comforting support for the traditional Western point of view. The hypothesis that man is not free is essential to the application of scientific method to the study of human behavior. The free inner man who is held responsible for the behavior of the external biological organism is only a prescientific substitute for the kinds of causes which are discovered in the course of a scientific analysis. All these alternative causes lie *outside* the individual. The biological substratum itself is determined by prior events in a genetic process. Other important events are found in the nonsocial environment and in the culture of the individual in the broadest possible sense. These are the things which make the individual behave as he does. For them he is not responsible, and for them it is useless to praise or blame him. It does not matter that the individual may take it upon himself to control the variables of which his own behavior is a function or, in a broader sense, to engage in the design of his own culture. He does this only because he is the product of a culture which generates self-control or cultural design as a mode of behavior. The environment determines the individual even when he alters the environment.

The conception of the individual which emerges from a scientific analysis is distasteful to most of those who have been strongly affected by democratic philosophies. As we saw in Chapter I, it has always been the unfortunate task of science to dispossess cherished beliefs regarding the place of man in the universe. It is easy to understand why men so frequently flatter themselves—why they characterize the world in ways which reinforce them by providing escape from the consequences of criticism or other forms of punishment. But although flattery temporarily strengthens behavior, it is questionable whether it has any ultimate survival value. If science does not confirm the assumptions of freedom, initiative, and responsibility in the behavior of the individual, these assumptions will not ultimately be effective either as motivating devices or as goals in the design of culture. We may not give them up easily and we may, in fact, find it difficult to control ourselves or others until alternative principles have been developed. But the change will probably be made. It does not follow that newer concepts will necessarily be less acceptable. We may console ourselves with the reflection that science is, after all, a cumulative progress in knowledge which is due to man alone, and that the highest human dignity may be to accept the facts of human behavior regardless of their momentary implications.

COMMENT: LEARNING FREEDOM AND DIGNITY

The message that needs to be accepted is this: Man is not free in any absolute sense, but he can *learn* to be motivated to control his own behavior and can *learn* effective habits of self-control. Man is not born dignified, but he can *learn* to be moti-

vated to behave accordingly. Man does not inherently feel a personal or social conscience, but he can *learn* the rules that history has shown to be best for individual and cultural survival.

The point is that many of the ills of our society can be traced to the false doctrine that man is by nature "good" and has a natural free will to express this goodness. This is not to say that man is by nature "bad." It is to say that one's sense of personal freedom is in no way lost by the knowledge that this was learned in interaction with an appropriate environment. Dignity is no less dignified by the fact that the concept itself was learned and the requisite behaviors learned. Conscience is no less personal and meaningful from the fact that our understanding of what is "right" and what is "wrong" reflects learning to behave on the basis of society's collective drive for survival.

The goal is not to get the experimental psychology of learning out of the basement into an ivory tower. It should be in the home, in the street, in the school; it also should be in the individual. We must conquer the traditional belief in what Skinner calls "autonomous man," but not by threatening to deprive him of meaning and purpose. This view makes learning even more important. It is more than learning reading, writing, and arithmetic. It is more even than learning a trade or profession. Surely principles of learning can be used to improve on those, but now is none too soon to promote the role of learning human values.

FRANK A. LOGAN

Man is not free in any absolute sense, but he can learn to be motivated to control his own behavior and can learn effective habits of self control.

4 THE PLACE OF THE PERSON IN THE NEW WORLD OF THE BEHAVIORAL SCIENCES*

CARL R. ROGERS

The science of psychology, in spite of its immaturities and its brashness, has advanced mightily in recent decades. From a concern with observation and measurement it has increasingly moved toward becoming an "if then" science. By this I mean it has become more concerned with the discernment and discovery of lawful relationships such that *if* certain conditions exist, *then* certain behaviors will predictably follow. It is rapidly increasing the number of areas or situations in which it may be said that if certain describable, measurable conditions are present or are established, then predictable, definable behaviors are learned or produced.

Now in one sense every educated person is aware of this. But it seems to me that few are aware of the breadth, depth, and extent of these advances in psychology and the behavioral sciences. And still fewer seem to be aware of the profound social, political, ethical, and philosophical problems posed by these advances. I would like to focus on some of the implications of these advances.

I should like to try to present, as well as I can, a simplified picture of the cultural pattern which emerges if we endeavor to shape human life in terms of the behavioral sciences. This is one of two possible directions I wish to consider.

There is first of all the recognition, almost the assumption, that scientific knowledge is the power to manipulate. Dr. B. F. Skinner of Harvard says: "We must accept the fact that some kind of control of human affairs is inevitable. We cannot use good sense in human affairs unless someone engages in the design and construction of environmental conditions which affect the behavior of men."[1]

Let us look at some of the elements which are involved in the concept of the control of human behavior as mediated by the behavioral sciences. What would be the steps in the process by which a society might organize itself so as to formulate human life in terms of the science of man?

First would come the selection of goals. In a recent paper [Freedom and the control of men] Dr. Skinner suggests that one possible goal to be assigned to the behavior technology is this: "Let man be happy, informed, skillful, well-behaved, and productive." In his book, *Walden Two*, where he can use the guise of fiction to express his views, he becomes more expansive. His hero says, "Well, what do you say to the design of personalities? Would that interest you? The control of temperament? Give me the specifications, and I'll give you the man! What do you say to the control of motivation, building the interests which will make men most productive and most successful? Does that seem to you fantastic? Yet some of the techniques are available, and more can be worked out experimentally. Think of the possibilities . . . Let us control the lives of our children and see what we can make of them."[2]

What Skinner is essentially saying here is that the current knowledge in the behavioral sciences, plus that which the future will bring, will enable us

*Abridged from C. R. Rogers, The place of the person in the new world of the behavioral sciences. *Personnel and Guidance Journal*, 34, 442–451. Copyright © by American Personnel and Guidance Association. Reprinted by permission of the author and the publisher.

[1]B. F. Skinner, "Freedom and the Control of Men," *American Scholar*, 25, 47–65, 1955–1956. Reprinted with permission of the author and copyright holder.
[2]B. F. Skinner, *Walden Two*, The Macmillan Company, New York, 1948.

to specify, to a degree which today would seem incredible, the kind of behavioral and personality results which we wish to achieve.

The second element in this process would be one which is familiar to every scientist who has worked in the field of applied science. Given the purpose, the goal, we proceed by the method of science—by controlled experimentation—to discover the means to these ends. The method of science is self-correcting in thus arriving at increasingly effective ways of achieving the purpose we have selected.

The third element in the control of human behavior through the behavioral sciences involves the question of power. As the conditions or methods are discovered by which to achieve our goal, some person or group obtains the power to establish those conditions or use those methods. There has been too little recognition of the problem involved in this. To hope that the power which is being made available by the behavioral sciences will be exercised by the scientists, or by a benevolent group, seems to me a hope little supported by either recent or distant history.

The fourth step in this process whereby a society might formulate its life in terms of the behavioral sciences is the exposure of individuals to the methods and conditions mentioned. As individuals are exposed to the prescribed conditions this leads, with a high degree of probability, to the behavior which has been desired. Men then become productive, if that has been the goal, or submissive, or whatever it has been decided to make them.

To give something of the flavor of this aspect of the process as seen by one of its advocates, let me again quote the hero of *Walden Two*. "Now that we *know* how positive reinforcement works, and why negative doesn't" he says, commenting on the method he is advocating, "we can be more deliberate and hence more successful, in our cultural design. We can achieve a sort of control under which the controlled, though they are following a code much more scrupulously than was ever the case under the old system, nevertheless *feel free*. They are doing what they want to do, not

what they are forced to do. That's the source of the tremendous power of positive reinforcement—there's no restraint and no revolt. By a careful cultural design, we control not the final behavior, but the *inclination* to behave—the motives, the desires, the wishes. The curious thing is that in that case *the question of freedom never arises*.''[3]

THE PICTURE AND ITS IMPLICATIONS

Let me see if I can sum up very briefly the picture of the impact of the behavioral sciences upon the individual and upon society, as this impact is explicitly seen by Dr. Skinner and implied in the attitudes and work of many, perhaps most, behavioral scientists. Behavioral science is clearly moving forward; the increasing power for control which it gives will be held by some one or some group; such an individual or group will surely choose the purposes or goals to be achieved; and most of us will then be increasingly controlled by means so subtle we will not even be aware of them as controls. Thus whether a council of wise psychologists (if this is not a contradiction in terms) or a Stalin or a Big Brother has the power, and whether the goal is happiness, or productivity, or resolution of the Oedipus complex, or submission, or love of Big Brother, we will inevitably find ourselves moving toward the chosen goal, and probably thinking that we ourselves desire it. Thus if this line of reasoning is correct, it appears that some form of completely controlled society—a Walden Two or a 1984—is coming. The fact that it would surely arrive piecemeal rather than all at once, does not greatly change the fundamental issues. Man and his behavior would become a planned product of a scientific society.

You may well ask, "But what about individual freedom? What about the democratic concepts of the rights of the individual?" Here too Dr. Skinner

---

[3]B. F. Skinner, *Walden Two*. The Macmillan Company, New York, 1948, p. 218. Quotation reprinted with permission of the author and publisher.

THE PLACE OF THE PERSON IN THE NEW WORLD OF THE BEHAVIORAL SCIENCES

is quite specific. He says quite bluntly, "The hypothesis that man is not free is essential to the application of scientific method to the study of human behavior. The free inner man who is held responsible for his behavior . . . is only a prescientific substitute for the kinds of causes which are discovered in the course of scientific analysis. All these alternative causes lie *outside* the individual."[4]

I have endeavored, up to this point, to give an objective picture of some of the developments in the behavioral sciences and an objective picture of the kind of society which might emerge out of those developments. I do however have strong personal reactions to the kind of world I have been describing, a world which Skinner explicitly (and many another scientist implicitly) expects and hopes for in the future. To me this kind of world would destroy the human person as I have come to know him in the deepest moments of psychotherapy. In such moments I am in relationship with a person who is spontaneous, who is responsibly free, that is, aware of his freedom to choose whom he will be and aware also of the consequences of his choice. To believe, as Skinner holds, that all this is an illusion and that spontaneity, freedom, responsibility, and choice have no real existence would be impossible for me.

I feel that to the limit of my ability I have played my part in advancing the behavioral sciences, but if the result of my efforts and those of others is that man becomes a robot, created and controlled by a science of his own making, then I am very unhappy indeed. If the good life of the future consists in so conditioning individuals through the control of their environment and through the control of the rewards they receive, that they will be inexorably productive, well behaved, happy or whatever, then I want none of it. To me this is a pseudo-form of the good life which includes everything save that which makes it good.

And so I ask myself, is there any flaw in the logic of this development? Is there any alternative view as to what the behavioral sciences might mean to the individual and to society? It seems to me that I perceive such a flaw and that I can conceive of an alternative view. These I would like to set before you.

ENDS AND VALUES IN RELATION TO SCIENCE

It seems to me that the view I have presented rests upon a faulty perception of goals and values in their relationship to science. The significance of the *purpose* of a scientific undertaking is, I believe, grossly underestimated. I would like to state a two-pronged thesis which in my estimation deserves consideration. Then I will elaborate the meaning of these two points.

1 In any scientific endeavor—whether "pure" or applied science—there is a prior personal subjective choice of the purpose or value which that scientific work is perceived as serving.

2 This subjective value choice which brings the scientific endeavor into being must always lie outside of that endeavor and can never become a part of the science involved in that endeavor.

Let me illustrate the first point from Dr. Skinner's writings. When he suggests that the task for the behavioral sciences is to make man "productive," "well-behaved," etc., it is obvious that he is making a choice. He might have chosen to make men submissive, dependent, and gregarious, for example. Yet by his own statement in another context man's "capacity to choose," his freedom to select his course and to initiate action—these powers do not exist in the scientific picture of man. Here is, I believe, the deepseated contradiction or paradox. Let me spell it out as clearly as I can.

Science, to be sure, rests on the assumption that behavior is caused—that a specified event is fol-

[4]B. F. Skinner, *Science and Human Behavior*, The Macmillan Company, New York, 1953, p. 447. Quotation reprinted with permission of the author and publisher.

lowed by a consequent event. Hence all is determined, nothing is free, choice is impossible. But we must recall that science itself and each specific scientific endeavor, each change of course in a scientific research, each interpretation of the meaning of a scientific finding, and each decision as to how the finding shall be applied rests upon a personal, subjective choice. Thus science in general exists in the same paradoxical situation as does Dr. Skinner. A personal, subjective choice made by man sets in motion the operations of science, which in time proclaims that there can be no such thing as a personal, subjective choice. I shall make some comments about this continuing paradox at a later point.

I stressed the fact that each of these choices, initiating or furthering the scientific venture, is a value choice. The scientist investigates this rather than that, because he feels the first investigation has more value for him. He chooses one method for his study rather than another because he values it more highly. He interprets his findings in one way rather than another because he believes the first way is closer to the truth, or more valid—in other words that it is closer to a criterion which he values. Now these value choices are never a part of the scientific venture itself. The value choices connected with a particular scientific enterprise always and necessarily lie outside of that enterprise.

I wish to make it clear that I am not saying that values cannot be included as a subject of science. It is not true that science deals only with certain classes of "facts" and that these classes do not include values. It is a bit more complex than that, as a simple illustration or two may make clear.

If I value knowledge of the "three R's" as a goal of education, the methods of science can give me increasingly accurate information as to how this goal may be achieved. If I value problem-solving ability as a goal of education, the scientific method can give me the same kind of help.

Now if I wish to determine whether problem-solving ability is "better" than knowledge of the three R's, then scientific method can also study those two values, but *only*—and this is very important—only in terms of some other value which I have subjectively chosen. I may value college success. Then I can determine whether problem-solving ability or knowledge of the three R's is more closely associated with that criterion. I may value personal integration or vocational success or responsible citizenship. I can determine whether problem-solving ability or knowledge of the three R's is "better" for achieving any one of these values. But the value or purpose which gives meaning to a particular scientific endeavor must always lie outside of that endeavor.

My point then is that any scientific endeavor, pure or applied, is carried on in the pursuit of a purpose or value which is subjectively chosen by persons. It is important that this choice be made explicit, since the particular value which is being sought can never be tested or evaluated, confirmed or denied, by the scientific endeavor to which it gives birth and meaning. The initial purpose or value always and necessarily lies outside the scope of the scientific effort which it sets in motion.

● While this may be true of any given scientific program, does this necessarily mean that investigation of values and purposes is outside of the realm of science?

Perhaps, however, the thought is that a continuing scientific endeavor will evolve its own goals; the initial findings will alter the directions, and subsequent findings will alter them still further and that the science somehow develops its own purpose. This seems to be a view implicitly held by many scientists. It is surely a reasonable description, but it overlooks one element in this continuing development, which is that subjective, personal choice enters in at every point at which the direction changes. The findings of a science, the results of an experiment, do not and never can tell us what next scientific purpose to pursue. Even in the purest of science, the scientist must decide what the findings mean and must subjectively choose what next step will be most profitable in the pursuit of his purpose. And if we are speaking of the application of scientific knowledge, then it is distressingly clear that the increasing scientific knowledge of the structure of the atom carries with it no necessary choice as to the purpose to which this knowledge will be put. This is a subjective personal choice which must be made by many individuals.

Thus I return to the proposition with which I began this section of my remarks—and which I now repeat in different words. Science has its meaning as the objective pursuit of a purpose which has been subjectively chosen by a person or persons. This purpose or value can never be investigated by the particular scientific experiment or investigation to which it has given birth and meaning. Consequently, any discussion of the control of human beings by the behavioral sciences must first and most deeply concern itself with the subjectively chosen purposes which such an application of science is intended to implement.

- Does Rogers' phrase "subjectively chosen" necessarily imply that the *choosing process itself* and the final decision are "free" and not in themselves determined?

AN ALTERNATIVE SET OF VALUES

If the line of reasoning I have been presenting is valid, then it opens new doors to us. If we frankly face the fact that science takes off from a subjectively chosen set of values, then we are free to select the values we wish to pursue. We are not limited to such stultifying goals as producing a controlled state of happiness, productivity, and the like. I would like to suggest a radically different alternative.

Suppose we start with a set of ends, values, purposes, quite different from the type of goals we have been considering. Suppose we do this quite openly, setting them forth as a possible value choice to be accepted or rejected. Suppose we select a set of values which focuses on fluid elements of process, rather than static attributes. We might then value:

Man as a process of becoming; as a process of achieving worth and dignity through the development of his potentialities;

The individual human being as a self-actualizing process, moving on to more challenging and enriching experiences;

The process by which the individual creatively adapts to an ever new and changing world;

The process by which knowledge transcends itself, as for example the theory of relativity transcended Newtonian physics itself to be transcended in some future day by a new perception.

If we select values such as these, we turn to our science and technology of behavior with a very different set of questions. We will want to know such things as these.

Can science aid us in the discovery of new modes of richly rewarding living? More meaningful and satisfying modes of interpersonal relationships?

Can science inform us as to how the human race can become a more intelligent participant in its own evolution—its physical, psychological and social evolution?

Can science inform us as to ways of releasing the creative capacity of individuals, which seem so necessary if we are to survive in this fantastically expanding atomic age? Dr. Oppenheimer has pointed out that knowledge, which used to double in millennia or centuries, now doubles in a generation or a decade. It appears that we will need to discover the utmost in release of creativity if we are to be able to adapt effectively.

In short, can science discover the methods by which man can most readily become a continually developing and self-transcending process, in his behavior, his thinking, his knowledge? Can science predict and release an essentially "unpredictable" freedom?

It is one of the virtues of science as a method that it is as able to advance and implement goals and purpose of this sort as it is to serve static values such as states of being well-informed, happy, obedient. Indeed we have some evidence of this.

A POSSIBLE CONCEPT OF THE CONTROL OF HUMAN BEHAVIOR

It is quite clear that the point of view I am expressing is in sharp contrast to the usual conception of the relationship of the behavioral sciences to the control of human behavior, previously mentioned. In order to make this contrast even more blunt, I will state this possibility in a form parallel to the steps which I described before.

1 It is possible for us to choose to value man as a self-actualizing process of becoming; to value creativity, and the process by which knowledge becomes self-transcending.

2 We can proceed, by the methods of science, to discover the conditions which necessarily precede these processes, and through continuing experimentation, to discover better means of achieving these purposes.

3 It is possible for individuals or groups to set these conditions, with a minimum of power or control. According to present knowledge, the only authority necessary is the authority to establish certain qualities of interpersonal relationship.

4 Exposed to these conditions, present knowledge suggests that individuals become more self-responsible, make progress in self-actualization, become more flexible, more unique and varied, more creatively adaptive.

5 Thus such an initial choice would inaugurate the beginnings of a social system or subsystem in which values, knowledge, adaptive skills, and even the concept of science would be continually changing and self-transcending. The emphasis would be upon man as a process of becoming.

I believe it is clear that such a view as I have been describing does not lead to any definable Utopia. It would be impossible to predict its final outcome. It involves a step by step development, based upon a continuing subjective choice of purposes, which are implemented by the behavioral sciences. It is in the direction of the "open society," as that term has been defined by Popper, where individuals carry responsibility for personal decisions. It is at the opposite pole from his concept of the closed society, of which *Walden Two* would be an example.

I trust it is also evident that the whole emphasis is upon process, not upon end states of being. I am suggesting that it is by choosing to value certain qualitative elements of the process of becoming, that we can find a pathway toward the open society.

THE CHOICE

It is my hope that I have helped to clarify the range of choice which will lie before us and our children in regard to the behavioral sciences. We can choose to use our growing knowledge to enslave people in ways never dreamed of before, depersonalizing them, controlling them by means so carefully selected that they will perhaps never be aware of their loss of personhood. We can choose to utilize our scientific knowledge to make men necessarily happy, well-behaved, and productive, as Dr. Skinner suggests. We can, if we wish, choose to make men submissive, conforming, docile. Or at the other end of the spectrum of choice we can choose to use the behavioral sciences in ways which will free, not control; which will bring about constructive variability, not conformity; which will develop creativity, not contentment; which will facilitate each person in his self-directed process of becoming; which will aid individuals, groups, and even the concept of science to become self-transcending in freshly adaptive ways of meeting life and its problems.

If we choose to utilize our scientific knowledge to free men, then it will demand that we live openly and frankly with the great paradox of the behavioral sciences. We will recognize that behavior, when examined scientifically, is surely best understood as determined by prior causation. This is the great fact of science. But responsible personal choice, which is the most essential element in being a person, which is the core experience in psychotherapy, which exists prior to any scientific endeavor, is an equally prominent fact in our lives. That these two important elements of our experience appear to be in contradiction has perhaps the same significance as the contradiction between the wave theory and the corpuscular theory of light, both of which can be shown to be true, even though incompatible. We cannot profitably deny the freedom which exists in our subjective life, any more than we can deny the determinism which is evident in the objective description of that life. We will have to live with that paradox.

COMMENT: I CANNOT QUITE AGREE

I cannot quite agree that the practice of science requires a prior decision about goals or a prior choice of values. The metallurgist can study the properties of steel and the engineer can design a bridge without raising the question of whether a bridge is to be built. But such questions are certainly frequently raised and tentatively answered. Rogers wants to call the answers "subjective choices of values." To me such an expression suggests that we have had to abandon more rigorous scientific practices in order to talk about our own behavior. In the experimental analysis of other organisms I would use other terms, and I shall try to do so here. Any list of values is a list of reinforcers—conditioned or otherwise. We are so constituted that under certain circumstances food, water, sexual contact, and so on, will make any behavior which produces them more likely to

occur again. Other things may acquire this power. We do not need to say that an organism chooses to eat rather than to starve. If you answer that it is a very different thing when a man chooses to starve, I am only too happy to agree. If it were not so, we should have cleared up the question of choice long ago. An organism can be reinforced by—can be made to "choose"—almost any given state of affairs.

The values I have occasionally recommended (and Rogers has not led me to recant) are transitional. Other things being equal, I am betting on the group whose practices make for healthy, happy, secure, productive, and creative people. And I insist that the values recommended by Rogers are transitional, too, for I can ask him the same kind of question. Man as a process of becoming—*what*? Self-actualization—for what? Inner control is no more a goal than external.

What Rogers seems to me to be proposing, both here and elsewhere, is this: Let us use our increasing power of control to create individuals who will not need and perhaps will no longer respond to control. Let us solve the problem of our power by renouncing it. At first blush this seems as implausible as a benevolent despot. Yet power has occasionally been foresworn. A nation has burned its Reichstag, rich men have given away their wealth, beautiful women have become ugly hermits in the desert, and psychotherapists have become nondirective. When this happens, I look to other possible reinforcements for a plausible explanation. A people relinquish democratic power when a tyrant promises them the earth. Rich men give away wealth to escape the accusing finger of their fellowmen. A woman destroys her beauty in the hope of salvation. And a psychotherapist relinquishes control because he can thus help his client more effectively.

The solution that Rogers is suggesting is thus understandable. But is he correctly interpreting the result? What evidence is there that a client ever becomes truly *self*-directing? What evidence is there that he ever makes a truly *inner* choice of ideal or goal? Even though the therapist does not do the choosing, even though he encourages "self-actualization"—he is not out of control as long as he holds himself ready to step in when occasion demands—when, for example, the client chooses the goal of becoming a more accomplished liar or murdering his boss. But supposing the therapist does withdraw completely or is no longer necessary—what about all the other forces acting upon the client? Is the self-chosen goal independent of his early ethical and religious training? of the folk-wisdom of his group? of the opinions and attitudes of others who are important to him? Surely not. The therapeutic situation is only a small part of the world of the client. From the therapist's point of view it may appear to be possible to relinquish control. But the control passes, not to a "self," but to forces in other parts of the client's world. The solution of the therapist's problem of power cannot be *our* solution, for we must consider *all* the forces acting upon the individual.

If we are worthy of our democratic heritage we shall, of course, be ready to resist any tyrannical use of science for immediate or selfish purposes. But if we value the achievements and goals of democracy we must not refuse to apply science to the design and construction of cultural patterns, even though we may then find ourselves in some sense in the position of controllers. Fear of control, generalized beyond any warrant, has led to a misinterpretation of valid practices and the blind rejection of intelligent planning for a better way of life. In terms which I trust Rogers will approve, in conquering this fear we shall become more mature and better organized and shall, thus, more fully actualize ourselves as human beings.

B. F. SKINNER

---

5 PSYCHOLOGY: THE NECESSARY AND RELEVANT SCIENCE
JAMES A. DYAL, WILLIAM C. CORNING, AND DALE M. WILLOWS

PSYCHOLOGY AS A SURVIVAL SCIENCE

Despite the criticisms which have been leveled at psychology as a science both by those who know it best and by those who reveal their profound ignorance in their naïve criticisms, one thing seems sure: The further development of this human science is a necessary condition for man's survival. Without such a science we are finished. In order to show you that this is no overstatement let us sample a few of the current survival questions with which society is now grappling.

How can we reduce and control environmental pollution? What effects do various types of pollution have on our stress reactions? Can we learn how to reduce the violent interactions among humans on both a personal level and an international level? Can we learn how to create environments for our children so that they can become competent and confident persons? Should we use our scientific knowledge to improve the basic nature of man through genetic engineering? Can we educate our emotions as well as our intellects? Should we? How? How can we help people to get more enjoyment from their lives? What economic/political system will be best for Western man in the twenty-first century? By what criteria? Would it be a good thing to establish a guaranteed annual income? Why? Why not? Is it a good idea to get rid of sex roles? How can we convince people to regulate the size of their families in order to achieve zero population growth? Should we? How can we solve the myriad problems of the ghetto? Is the nuclear family no longer a useful social structure? How can we best solve personal and social problems associated with drug abuse? With the high crime rate?

How can we move to genuine psycho-social equality for women? For minorities? For the aged?

ad traumatum

It should be readily apparent to you that a satisfactory solution to all of these questions *requires* more and better information about basic human psychological functions: how we think, feel, hope, fear, problem-solve, love, imagine, learn, remember, dream, achieve, attract others, repel others, react to stress, etc., etc.

Yet it can still be asked, is it really desirable to understand man better? Some would point out the many ways in which new knowledge has been used to make man's position in the world more precarious. After all, knowledge is power—and power corrupts. Each technological advance seems to have only created more devastating problems so that now we are entering a period of crisis—the crisis of survival. Failure to solve the problems created by science and technology carries with it the possible extinction of man as a species on this planet. Yet we are obviously not ready to accept our own demise without a struggle. Knowledge has been and can be used for the long-term welfare of man. Even the most dedicated anarchistic critic of our culture must agree that we have traveled far since the dawn of civilization in rescuing man from the capriciousness of such natural enemies as famine and disease. Perhaps we have even made it more possible for more men to live in more comfort with a greater chance for freedom and happiness than ever before.

We could thus affirm that it is not only desirable to have a better understanding of human behavior and experience, but that it is one of man's most insistent psychological imperatives—*man is that creature who must strive to understand himself*. But there are many paths to understanding and each has its special methodology and power —philosophy, theology, literature, biology, sociology, anthropology—all contribute useful and legitimate perspectives. As psychologists our domain of interest spans the broad range from molecular psychobiology to existential psychotherapy. And as psychologists we are committed to applying the method of science to advance our understanding of man. We opt for the scientific approach because it has been shown to be a powerful technique of discovery. Although errors of fact and interpretation are sometimes made, the scientific approach tends to be self-correcting in the long run.

As a consequence of its self-correcting characteristics and its ability to provide reliable facts, the scientific approach offers the advantage of advancing our understanding because its facts and theories tend to be cumulative: They build on what has been discovered previously. While it must be admitted that depressingly little of our current psychological knowledge has been cumulative, we *have* done some building on previous facts and theories. For example, on the basis of experiments conducted around 1900 E. L. Thorndike formulated the law of effect which specified the critical importance of rewards and punishments in determining what is learned. During the succeeding 75 years psychologists have conducted thousands of experiments and formulated powerful theories to establish the boundaries and the subtleties of this principle. Today, extensive applications of the principle are found in classrooms and mental institutions in the form of behavior modification programs. The demonstrable power of the principle continues to be expanded and, at the same time, its limitations are beginning to be established. The limitations point us in the direction of trying to understand how control and modification of behavior can be achieved through internal cognitive processes as well as external rewards and punishments.

The question of whether or not it is *possible* to build a science which analyzes human behavior and experience is no longer at issue. The answer to that is clear: *It is being done*. And yet this answer is reminiscent of the person who asked a friend, "Do you believe in baptism by total immersion?" only to receive the response, "Believe in it? Why I've seen it done!" Similarly, while we may have seen a science of human behavior "appearing before our very eyes," it is still an open question as to whether or not we believe in it. As Skinner says, "Regardless of how much we may stand to gain from supposing that human behavior is the proper subject matter of science, no one who is a product of Western culture can do so without a struggle. We simply do not want such a science."[1]

● Be sure that you understand the reasoning behind and the implication of this strong assertion by Skinner. If you cannot get the feel for this from the selection, you might want to examine Skinner's more recent book, *Beyond Freedom and Dignity*.

The failure of layman to appreciate the usefulness of a scientific approach to human behavior is nowhere more evident than in a class of students taking their first psychology course. As professors we are often struck by the fact that the typical student either behaves as though one opinion were as good as another in matters of human behavior or, if there is a priority, it is obviously his common sense judgment based on his limited experience which is most commanding. Indeed, it often does not seem to occur to the student that *research* on human behavior can provide a sounder, more reliable basis for his own personal "world building" than can the simple-minded strategy of assertion and counterassertion. "Common sense" explanations are often useful, but they attain greater power and generalizability after surviving close scientific scrutiny. It is informed opinion, based upon a disciplined use of intellect, *along with* a sensitivity to one's own experiences, which can best provide a thinking/feeling framework in which our (and your) understanding of human behavior can continue to grow. We thus opt for a relevant and disciplined science of human behavior which accepts the challenge of real life problems *as well as* the problems of the traditional laboratory. We believe that it is possible to create a psychology that is

[1]B.F. Skinner. *Science and human behavior*. New York: MacMillan, 1953. p. 7.

relevant to the personal lives of individuals and to the problems of human survival without sacrificing our devotion to sound and valid scientific principles. After all, the essence of science is *disciplined inquiry*, not a particular method. It is now imperative that psychology accept its role as a "survival science" and a "growth science," which engages man at all levels of his functioning.

A NEW ECLECTICISM

It is unfortunately the case that until relatively recently psychology has not provided an intellectual climate which encouraged the growth of a wide variety of perspectives. During the first half of the twentieth century North American psychology was dominated by two approaches to understanding human behavior. One was psychoanalysis, which emphasized how much of *man's behavior is controlled by unconscious processes* over which he had little control. The basic sources of data to support this view came from extended psychoanalytic interviews with people who were emotionally troubled. The other approach was that of behaviorism which emphasized that *man's behavior is controlled by the external situations* to which his reactions had been conditioned. Much of the behavioristic thesis was based on models of man derived from research on lower animals, especially pigeons and white rats. The generalizability of these models is now being subjected to a healthy, skeptical criticism. It is finally becoming apparent to psychologists that "man is not a rat" and that the model of man which one holds does make a difference. Even so, we do not suggest that animal research is not valuable in helping us to understand certain basic mechanisms—it is, and it should be pursued. However, we do suggest that the overemphasis on any particular approach, especially one which involves problems which are obviously far removed from real human problems, can no longer be permitted to preempt our approach to understanding man.

Both behaviorism and psychoanalysis tended to

regard man as a rather pitiable creature, determined by inner and outer forces over which he had little or no control. However, during the past twenty years another approach has challenged these deterministic models. This "third force" is called humanistic psychology. It provides a basically optimistic perspective and emphasizes man's striving toward personal growth and integration. It asserts the basic freedom of the individual to "choose" his life even in the face of obvious constraints on his freedom. Pure "freedom" is of course a fiction which would imply a total randomness of behavior; thus the humanistic approach chooses to emphasize those ways in which man is "free within constraints." Abraham Maslow was a leader in opposing the behaviorist conception of man as no different *in principle* from any other physical object. He questioned the philosophy of science which stands behind behaviorism. Central to this philosophy was the belief that psychology should approach its subject matter in the same way that physics has advanced, namely by analyzing complex events into "smaller," less complex units, and then seeking to derive laws or principles which govern the interactions of these subunits to yield the more complex event. Maslow also questioned the appropriateness of limiting our understanding of man to that which could be based on externally exhibited behavior. He contended that conscious experiences should be again included as part of the subject matter of psychology. Although he was often misinterpreted by his critics as being antiscientific Maslow contended:

> It is very difficult, I have found, to communicate to others my simultaneous respect for and impatience with these two comprehensive psychologies. So many people insist on being either pro-Freudian or anti-Freudian, pro-scientific psychology or anti-scientific-psychology, etc. In my opinion all such loyalty-positions are silly. Our job is to integrate these various truths into the whole truth, which should be our only loyalty. . . .
>
> It is quite clear to me that scientific methods (broadly conceived) are our only ultimate ways of being sure that we do have the truth. But here also it is too easy to misunderstand and to fall into a pro-science or anti-science dichotomy. I have already

written on this subject . . . I intend to continue with this enterprise, of enlarging the methods and the jurisdiction of science so as to make it more capable of taking up the tasks of the new, personal, experiential psychologies.

> Science, as it is customarily conceived by the orthodox, is quite inadequate to these tasks. But I am certain that it need not limit itself to these orthodox ways. It need not abdicate from the problems of love, creativeness, value, beauty, imagination, ethics and joy, leaving these altogether to "non-scientists," to poets, prophets, priests, dramatists, artists, or diplomats. All of these people may have wonderful insights, ask the questions that need to be asked, put forth challenging hypotheses, and may even be correct and true much of the time. But however sure they may be, they can never make mankind sure. They can convince only those who already agree with them, and a few more. Science is the only way we have of shoving truth down the reluctant throat. Only science can overcome characterological differences in seeing and believing. Only science can progress. I wish to be understood as trying to enlarge science, not destroy it. It is not necessary to choose between experiencing and abstracting. Our task is to integrate them.[2]

We believe that the humanistic approach can serve as a necessary redirection away from a behaviorism which was tending to increasingly trivialize and molecularize the subject matter of psychology. We thus applaud the fresh new breeze which takes us on a new course which may be more in contact with problems of real human significance. Unfortunately, at times it has seemed that the humanistic psychology movement has been captured by "lunatic fringe" elements (e.g., nude marathon therapies) which tended to be not only antiscientific but also anti-intellectual. Thus, in addition to the "distortions at the fringe," the humanistic perspective has often suffered from preoccupation with rhetoric and a lack of a rigorous methodology with which to pursue its objectives. The backlash against several hundred years of Western civilization's overemphasis on rationality seemed to center in some of the perversions of

[2]A. H. Maslow. *Toward a psychology of being.* (2nd ed.) Princeton: Van Nostrand, 1968. pp. vii–viii.

humanistic psychology. Yet the pendulum has begun to swing back to the recognition that, as Maslow emphasized, our task is to integrate experiential and cognitive/abstracting approaches to man, a task which requires the fine honeying of our sharpest intellectual and emotional tools. We thus caution against the view that a humanistic emphasis is necessarily an antiscientific emphasis.

It is possible that we are on the threshold of a scientific humanism which will provide the base for our necessarily eclectic psychology. Note that since "eclectic" means selecting and using the best elements of all systems, this broadened conception requires recognition of the fact that science involves value judgments both with regard to the problems which are worth engaging our efforts and the procedures of disciplined inquiry which shall be useful. Such a psychology is not a comfortable one for those who would prefer a more traditional approach based on the model of science provided by physics. Indeed, it is painfully true that the acceptance of an eclectic approach means that psychology typically fails to be a coherent, integrated discipline; on the contrary, it is rather often a discipline which seems to be going off in all directions at the same time. Despite the discomfort engendered by such a perverse polymorphic science we have no alternative but to accept the challenge of an eclectic and relevant science of human behavior. Such a rigorously involved science can represent the center of man's search for understanding himself in relation to the universe—past, present, and future. We invite you to participate in the ongoing creation of this necessary science.

USEFUL RESOURCES

ALEXANDER, T. Psychologists are rediscovering the minds. *Fortune*, November, 1970. Discusses many facets of the new cognitive psychologies which hold that ". . . the stimulus-response model is simplistic when it comes to actually describing why people do what they do. It suggests that psychologists have been arrogant, or perhaps naïve, in dismissing the innate wellsprings of behavior.

COREN, S. Is relevance relevant in research? *American Psychologist*, 1970, 25, 649–650.

DOHERTY, M., and Shernburg, K. *What is*

psychology: An introduction to how psychologists work. Glenview, Ill.: Scott, Foresman, 1970.

GARNER, W. R. The acquisition and application of knowledge: A symbiotic relation. *American Psychologist*, 1972, 27, 941–949.

HITT, W. P. Two models of man. *American Psychologist*, 1969, 24, 651–658. This paper contrasts the behavioristic and the humanistic (phenomenological) views of man by elaborating the following dimensions:

1 Man can be described meaningfully in terms of his behavior; or man can be described meaningfully in terms of his consciousness.
2 Man is predictable; or man in unpredictable.
3 Man is an information transmitter; or man is an information generator.
4 Man lives in an objective world; or man lives in a subjective world.
5 Man is a rational being; or man is an arational being.
6 One man is like other men; or each man is unique.
7 Man can be described meaningfully in absolute terms; or man can be described meaningfully in relative terms.
8 Human characteristics can be investigated independently of one another; or man must be studied as a whole.
9 Man is a reality; or man is a potentiality.
10 Man is knowable in scientific terms; or man is more than we can ever know about him.

KALISH, R. A. *Making the most of college: A guide to effective study*. (2nd ed.) Belmont: Brooks/Cole, 1969. Contains valuable discussion and "workbook" material to help the beginning college/university student become more responsible to himself and more *effective* in using his time. *A really valuable aid* ask your book store to stock it for you.

KARLINS, M., and ANDREWS, L. M. *Psychology: What's in it for us?* New York: Random House, 1973. An excellent little paperback dealing with some of the same topics and issues raised throughout this book. For example, biofeedback, electrical stimulation of the brain, expanding human awareness, and the political implications of behavior control.

MASLOW, A. H. *Toward a psychology of being*. Princeton, N.J.: Van Nostrand, 1962. A book in which Maslow spells out in detail his psychology of self-actualization. Including such basic concepts as the heirarchy of motives, peak-experiences, maturity, human values, and self-actualization.

MASLOW, A. H. *The psychology of science.* Chicago: Henry Regnery Co., 1966. Argues that the concept of science must be broadened to include methods whereby we achieve personal (subjective) knowledge.

MILLER, G. A. Psychology as a means of promoting human welfare. *American Psychologist,* 1969, 24, 1063–1075. The basic take-home message of this article is that psychologists should work toward helping the layman become more enlighted concerning some of the basic concepts of the psychological revolution which is now in progress. We should "give psychology away to the unwashed."

PSYCHOSOURCES: *A psychology resource catalog. PsychoSources* defines itself as an access device for the field of psychology. Something of a psychological yellow pages with over-sized pages and soft cover, it catalogs films, books, etc., on childhood, ethology, identity, education, women, aging, oppression, becoming a revolutionary, sleep and dreaming, simulations and games, with listings of hotlines, schools of humanistic psychology, growth centers, cutouts to illustrate perceptual phenomena, tests you can take and score and much much more.

PSYCHOLOGY TODAY BOOK CLUB

SKINNER, B. F. *Walden two.* New York: Macmillan Co., 1948. A utopian novel which shows how principles of behavioral engineering could be applied to create a community of happy, confident and competent people.

SKINNER, B. F. *Beyond freedom and dignity.* New York: Alfred A. Knopf, 1971. Shows how the belief in an "autonomous inner man" (mind/self) was at one time advantageous in initiating and maintaining countercontrol against tyrannical societal institutions but that it now is a disabling myth which interferes with man's control of his own destiny through control over his environment.

SKINNER, B. F. *Science and human behavior.* New York: MacMillan, 1953. Devoted to the proposition that we can best develop our understanding of ourselves and others by the rigorous application of the principles and methods of science and technology to the analysis of human behavior.

STEINER, I. D. The evils of research: or what my mother didn't tell me about the sins of academia. *American Psychologist,* 1972, 27, 766–768.

It has come to my attention that many professors of psychology are requiring their students to take examinations without obtaining the student's prior consent and that such professors often withhold information concerning the questions that will be asked on their examination. Students allege that participation in examinations is frequently a traumatic experience, that it sometimes has lasting effects on their self-perceptions and job opportunities, and that it occasionally causes a student to alter his entire life plan. Moreover, students contend that examinations frequently serve no learning function whatever and that they are administered merely for the purpose of evaluating the student, deciding whether he shall be permitted to continue in college, or whether he is entitled to a diploma or admittance to graduate school. On checking with my colleagues, I discovered that these nefarious practices are indeed very common.

Steiner then goes on to suggest that in order to protect students from such outrageous abuses we need a code of ethics. He proposes that we adapt the current code on ethical principles in human research to deal with examination ethics. This leads to a set of "tongue in cheek" principles which are summarized in the following principle.

No examination may be given unless all parties agree that no evaluative purpose will be served and that no one but the student will ever see the examination paper. Whenever there is reason to doubt that these procedures will be followed, the professor must clear his examination with an ethics board consisting of two football coaches, one custodian, and Abbie Hoffman.

This is a fun article—perhaps you should look it up and make it assigned reading for your professor.

CHAPTER 2
EDUCATIONAL ISSUES

PROVOCATIONS

Surely, I said, knowledge is the food of the soul; and we must take care, my friend, that the Sophist does not deceive us when he praises what he sells, like the dealers wholesale or retail who sell the food of the body; for they praise indiscriminately all their goods, without knowing what are really beneficial or hurtful: neither do their customers know, with the exception of any trainer or physician who may happen to buy of them. In like manner those who carry about the wares of knowledge, and make the round of the cities, and sell or retail them to any customer who is in want of them, praise them all alike; though I should not wonder, O my friend, if many of them were really ignorant of their effect upon the soul; and their customers equally ignorant, unless he who buys of them happens to be a physician of the soul. If, therefore, you have understanding of what is good and evil you may safely buy knowledge of Protagoras or any one; but if not, then, O my friend, pause, and do not hazard your dearest interests at a game of chance. For there is far greater peril in buying knowledge than in buying meat and drink. . . .

Plato, Protagoras

"The most deadly of all possible sins," Erik Erikson suggests, "is the mutilation of a child's spirit." It is not possible to spend any prolonged period visiting public school classrooms without being appalled by the mutilation visible everywhere–mutilation of spontaneity, of joy in learning, of pleasure in creating, of sense of self. The public schools are the kind of institution one cannot really dislike until one gets to know them well. Because adults take the schools so much for granted, they fail to appreciate what grim, joyless places most schools are, how oppressive and petty are the rules by which they are governed, how intellectually sterile and esthetically barren the atmosphere, what an an appalling lack of civility obtains on the part of teachers and principals, what contempt they unconsciously display for children as children.

Charles E. Silberman

The game is called "Let's Pretend," and if its name were chiseled into the front of every school building in America, we would at least have an honest announcement of what takes place there. The game is based on a series of pretenses which include: Let's pretend that you are not what you are and that this sort of work makes a difference to your lives; let's pretend that what bores you is important, and that the more you are bored, the more important it is; let's pretend that there are certain things everyone must know, and that both the questions and answers about them have been fixed for all time; let's pretend that your intellectual competence can be judged on the basis of how well you can play Let's Pretend.

Neil Postman and Charles Weingartner

WHAT DO YOU THINK?

6 EDUCATIONAL ISSUES FOR THE SEVENTIES

JAMES A. DYAL

EXCELLENCE AND RELEVANCE

"What is a good education?" "What is worth knowing?" "How can we best facilitate the teaching/learning process?" These and similar questions have preoccupied curriculum builders throughout the history of education. Some of their answers have been so widely affirmed as to constitute the literal meaning of the word education.

● It might be "educational" for you to know the dictionary definition of "education"; why not look it up? Then think about what values are implied.

It should be apparent that there is no universally appropriate answer to the question "What is worth knowing?" Your own answers to that question depend on the demands of society and on your life style—your goals, needs, and aspirations. If your goal is "acquiring knowledge," then what is worth knowing is "facts" and a framework (usually provided by the teacher) within which these facts can be related. On the other hand, suppose your goal is to develop your reasoning ability and critical judgment, then what is relevant and worth knowing is quite different from what is implied by "acquiring knowledge." Or suppose your educational goal is to acquire and develop the skills of an engineer—or an accountant—or an electrician—or a nurse. What is relevant then? The point is that both the *content* and the *process* of teaching/learning vary rather dramatically with the goal which is being pursued. The learning process may appropriately range from rote memorization of facts to learning how to ask questions and to be critical of one's own productions (called crap detection by Hemingway—see Selection 10), to learning specific skills and techniques. It is thus not surprising that the most heated controversies among professional educators focus on the question of proper goals for the educational process. Should students be taught to "possess knowledge," or "be critical consumers," or to do specific jobs, or to be "cultured persons," to be "whole, fully functioning persons," or to do all and be all these things? And who should decide?

During the past decade a new force has entered the debate. Students have become aware that the educational goals which they hold for themselves are often in conflict with the goals held for them by the faculty. For example, knowledge acquisition (based on the "mind-as-a-container-to-be-filled" model of learning) has long been the dominant model in teaching practice. The goal was to create a student who would eagerly acquire facts and cognitive skills; the faculty watchword was "high standards of excellence." More recently the faculty demand for "excellence" has been drowned out by the increasingly strident student demand for "relevance" has meant "social relevance" and "personal relevance." In this context "relevance." Those students and faculty who demand more social relevance emphasize the continuing

complex interpenetration between schools and society. Thy recognize that the educational goals which they can pursue depend upon the models of a "good person" which are accepted and proclaimed by society at large.

● Do you understand this assertion? Think about it.

They oppose the conventional value systems which teach peer competition, eager acquisition of facts, and passivity/docility toward educational responsibility; they offer an alternative set of values which are more humanistic, which emphasize the development of the whole person, not just his intellectual/cognitive abilities, and which develop a sensitivity to the social ills of our time.

For example, in his book *Education and Ecstasy*, George B. Leonard (31) emphasizes a three-component definition of education:

1 *"To Learn is to change. Education is a process that changes the learner."*

2 *"Learning involves interaction between the learner and the environment; and its effectiveness relates to the frequency, variety and intensity of that interaction."*

The implication of these two propositions is that the emphasis shifts from the teacher's presentation of a limited set of information to the *response* of the student to a learning environment. This point of view is also emphasized by Postman and Weingartner's dictum (p. 65), "It is not what you say to people that counts; it is what you have them do." That is, what is important is the *interaction* between critical characteristics of a learning environment and the responses the learner is able to make to the environment. As Leonard says:

The environment may be a book, a game, a programmed device, a choir, a brainwave feedback mechanism, a silent room, an interactive group of students, even a teacher—but in every case, the educator will turn his attention from mere *presentation* of the environment (a classroom lecture, for example) to the *response* of the learner. He will study and experiment with the learning process, the series of responses, at every step along the way, better to utilize the increasing capacities of environment and learner as each changes.

3 *"Education, at best, is ecstatic."*

While Leonard may be overstating the case by the use of the term "ecstatic," it is clear that the best kind of learning generates a feeling of satisfaction and delight which is far beyond the extrinsic rewards which come from "pleasing the teacher"—it is pleasing to the learner. Leonard rhapsodizes that:

> The new educator will seek out the possibility of delight in every form of learning . . . He will find that even education now considered nothing more than present drudgery for future payoff . . . can become joyful when a skillfully designed learning environment . . . makes the learning quick and easy. Indeed, the skillful pursuit of ecstasy will make the pursuit of excellence, not for the few, but for the many, what it never has been—successful. And yet, make no mistake about it, excellence, as we speak of it today, will be only a by-product of a greater unity, a deeper delight.

It is not just the members of the educational "radical chic" who propose that the "educational ecstasy experience" is a valid index of the value of what is learned. Jerome Bruner, an authority on cognitive development and pedagogy, also accepts "delight" as a legitimate and important criterion for deciding what is worth learning. However, he adds a second criterion: the degree to which the new knowledge permits the learner to "travel," to grow intellectually beyond where he is, the degree to which it empowers the learner with new confidence, competence, and desire to learn. He declares that relevance, in either the social or the personal sense, "depends upon what you know that permits you to move toward goals you care

about." Are excellence and relevance incompatible? Bruner does not think so, neither does Leonard, and neither do we.

COMMENT: WHAT IS WORTH KNOWING?

We may well ask of any item of information that is taught or that we lead a child to discover for himself whether it is worth knowing. I can think of only two good criteria and one middling one for deciding such an issue: whether the knowledge gives a sense of delight and whether it bestows the gift of intellectual travel beyond the information given, in the sense of containing within it the basis of generalization. The middling criterion is whether the knowledge is useful. It turns out, on the whole, as Charles Sanders Peirce commented, that useful knowledge looks after itself. So I would urge that we as schoolmen let it do so and concentrate on the first two criteria. Delight and travel, then.

JEROME S. BRUNER

● As you read the articles in this section, attend to the problem of reconciling excellence and relevance. See if you can formulate some points which would support (or refute) the view that they are not incompatible.

COMMENT: EDUCATION AND THE LOWER CLASS—THE SOCIAL PSYCHOLOGY OF FAILURE

My work on early education and social class, for example, had convinced me that the educational system was in effect our way of maintaining a class system—a group at the bottom. It crippled the capacity of children in the lowest socioeconomic quarter of the population to participate at full power in society and did so early and effectively . . . (This) charge has been made by Royal Commissions and advisers to Presidents as well as by the anti-Establishment New Left that educational and socializing practice, before the school years as after, reflects and reinforces the inequities of a class system. This it does by limiting access to knowledge of the poor while facilitating it for those better off. The charge is even more serious: that our practice of education, both in and out of school, assures uneven distribution not only of knowledge but also of competence to profit from knowledge. It does so by limiting and starving the capabilities of the children of the poor by leading them into failure until they are convinced that it is not worth their while to think about school-like things.

JEROME BRUNER

EDUCATION AND SOCIAL CLASS: SUCCESS AND FAILURE

Education and the Lower Class

Why are you in college? As we noted in Selection 1, most of you are here because your parents, your friends, and you just naturally expected that you would go to college. It is just the "normal" thing to do; it is what everyone does. *But* this is true *if and only if* you were fortunate enough to be born into the white, middle, or upper class. If, on the other hand, you were born into the lower class and you are now reading these words, not only are you very exceptional but also something of a miracle has happened. Your being here is especially miraculous if you are black, chicano, Puerto Rican, etc. and were raised in a large urban ghetto, or if you are Indian and were raised on a reservation. Not only did you have to be quite bright intellectually, but you had to be willing to "learn the white man's ways" in order to escape the ghetto. Thus for a highly selected few of you, and against almost insurmountable odds, the educational system has provided a way out even though the personal cost may have been high. Yet because we have always been able to point to a few people who "made it," we have continued to believe in the myth that through schooling a democratic society based on ability can be maintained. Unfortunately this humanistic, liberal assumption may turn out to be more utopian dream than realistic strategy for social change. In fact there is now convincing evidence that rather than helping the poor and disadvantaged to move into the mainstream of socioeconomic life in America, the schools most often serve to perpetuate class differences or, at the very best, are ineffective in reducing them.

Indeed, it is all too often the case that rather than serving to alleviate the learning disabilities which are engendered by lower-class and minority-group backgrounds the schools actually exacerbate the problem. It works something like this: "The schools"—i.e., the school boards, the administrators, the teachers, the textbooks, etc.—typically reflect middle-class experience and values. The disadvantaged students often deviate from the behavior expected by this reference group in terms of language facility, social behavior, emotional control, or values and goals. The standardizing/socializing forces of the school are immediately brought to bear on the child to shape him up to expectations. He is required to "conform or fail." The almost inevitable failure is typically attributed to the individual's inadequacies rather than to the school's failure to create an environment in which he could be "led out" (educated), an environment which could capitalize on his strengths rather than exploit and condemn his weaknesses. Not only is the deviant child confronted with the "conform or fail" dilemma, but his teachers probably are supportive and understanding of his failure—after all, he is not expected to succeed in school. This puts him into a vicious double bind in which he is called upon both to "conform (to middle-class values) *or* fail" and to "conform (to our low expectations of you) *and* fail." What does the "disadvantaged" child learn in school? He learns that learning is not for him and becomes another victim of the self-fulfilling prophecy (see Selection 10, *Education and Equality* by Charles E. Silberman).

Education and the Middle Class

It is clear that the psychological/sociological/ economic consequences of schooling can be devastating for the "disadvantaged" child. But it is well to note that even if you come from an "advantaged" home you may not escape unscarred by the educational process. In many instances the psychological consequences of "success" in the school may have been equally disabling for you as a middle-class child. Most of the important forces in your world (e.g., parents, peers, and public places) converge to reinforce the school requirement for docility and submission. You were subtly coerced to "conform and succeed." Indeed, it *is* important that some aspects of the "going-along-to-get-along" message be accepted as a part of the basic socialization process whereby we learn to define ourselves in interdependence with others. The problem is not that we are socialized, but that we become oversocialized. Pacified and domesticated, we have learned the lesson too well, and as a result we have great difficulty in increasing our autonomy from the evaluations of others. Our cultural conditioning makes it difficult to achieve an "internal locus of evaluation" based on our own real feelings and experiences rather than on attitudes and opinions taken over from others (who are "significant," "knowledgeable," "powerful," or "sanctified"). As students you become increasingly hooked on blue-ribbon motivation; you become more deeply enmeshed in your "student nigger" role; you become the Compliant Student, the Silent Student, the Attention-Getter. By the time the schooling process is completed, you have been transformed into the typical product of Western society, the "other-directed man."

An alternative is to react with anger and rebellion (either overt or covert). This mode of reaction seems to be more easily available to the males of our society since it is more consistent with social role demands. However, neither rebellion and rejection of "authority" nor unthinking submission to authority provides a secure base for establishing constructive relations with other persons. Self-

actualization depends upon being able to work out problems of dependence/independence toward a solution of *creative interdependence*. Through its reward systems which emphasize submission to adult authority and competition with peers, the school often serves as a powerful obstacle to achieving creative interdependence for the "successful" middle-class student.

EDUCATION, RACE, AND IQ

Any society which limits access to the social, economic, and educational prerequisites for the "good life" on the basis of race and social class may legitimately be viewed as "racist." In our racist society the lower socioeconomic class is occupied by a disproportionate number of Negroes. As we have noted above, one consequence of this fact is that the educational experiences of black children are less adequately matched to their abilities and interests and are generally more frustrating than for middle-class whites. The black children tend to become dropouts and thus perpetuate the vicious circle of poverty–poor education–poverty. (Other disabling aspects of being poor and black are discussed in Chapter 5). While the disproportionate representation of blacks in the lower class is readily regarded as a product of such environmental vicious circles, the question is often raised as to whether or not there are real differences in abilities between blacks and whites which may account for the inferior achievements of the blacks. Indeed, there is a considerable amount of research which indicates that American Negroes, on the average, score substantially lower on IQ tests than the average score for American whites. If this is a true reflection of differences in ability, it would seem to have important implications for educational practice. At the very least it raises the practically important question of how much of this IQ difference can be eliminated by compensatory training programs. But this question, in turn, plunges us into the more general issue of how much of the individual differences in IQ are due to heredity and how much to environment. This troublesome question has generated heated debate and substantial research for several decades. Recently a controversial paper was published on these issues by A. R. Jensen (25). After reviewing a vast array of literature, Jensen concludes that: (1) the extensive programs of compensatory education which were supported by the United States government during the 1960s have failed to have a substantial and permanent effect on the IQ or scholastic achievement of the children, (2) one of the reasons they have failed is that the observed difference of 15 IQ points between Negroes and whites is *in part* due to genetic differences which in the individual are not susceptible to change. The paper touched a socially explosive issue; emotions flared and charges of racism and bigotry soon began to obscure the scientific and educational issues. One of the problems is that a clear understanding of the issue hinges on complex technical knowledge that is not possible to teach to an intelligent layman via the medium of the popular press (or even in an introductory psychology course). Besides being rather technical at many points, the problem is often compounded by the fact that even the experts disagree on the meaning of certain aspects of the data.

Despairing of the possibility of providing you with the technical knowledge necessary for you to evaluate the arguments yourself, we considered the possibility of ignoring the question altogether. The problem with that approach is that this is such an explosive issue that you are likely to form opinions on the basis of popular press reports. If nothing else, your introductory psychology course should help you to read such reports more critically. Moreover, because the "race and IQ controversy" seems to raise many important social and educational issues, to ignore it would be intellectually irresponsible. The issue has been raised, and we must deal with it. However, the recent history of the controversy has generated such a voluminous literature of argument and counterargument that no single paper is adequate to deal with the major issues. Thus we have chosen to present the controversy in the form of several problem areas

which contain specific questions which are at issue. If there are clearcut answers to some of these questions, we will state them, but more often than not the answers will be controversial. In this case we will present the major alternative views and, where appropriate, indicate our own conclusion regarding the question.

Problem Area 1 The Effectiveness of Large-Scale Compensatory Education Programs
Question 1. How effective were the large-scale compensatory education programs such as Project Head Start, in overcoming the intellectual/educational deficit of lower socioeconomic level children?

> *Jensen's 1969 Answer:* "Compensatory education has been tried and it apparently has failed. . . . The chief goal of compensatory education—to remedy the educational lag of disadvantaged children and thereby narrow the achievement gap between 'minority' and 'majority' pupils—has been utterly unrealized in any of the programs which have been evaluated thus far (25)."
> *Rebuttal:* The programs were evaluated too early to give them a fair test.
> *Counterrebuttal (Jensen, 1972):* "Has any new research appeared since the original publication of the HER (Harvard Educational Review) article in 1969 that would require extensive revision of any of the main points? None has come to my attention, although I have been closely in touch with research in this field (27)."

Question 2. Why were these large-scale compensatory education programs ineffective?
The answer to this question is debatable:

> *Answer 1:* "All too often the Head Start programs have merely supplied poor children with an opportunity to play in traditional nursery schools that were designed chiefly to exercise large muscles and to enable middle-class children to escape from their overly strict and solicitous mothers. Such opportunities are unlikely to be very effective in overcoming the deficient skills and motives to be found in the children of the poor. . . . Our traditional belief that class

differences in ability are the inevitable consequence of heredity left Americans with little
inclination to provide nursery schools for children of the poor. Thus, the schools got adapted
to what were conceived to be the needs of the
middle-class children. When the decision to
mount Project Head Start was made, only these
programs were widely available for deployment
on a large scale. It should be no surprise, then if
the success of Project Head Start in improving
the future academic success of children of the
poor is highly limited.

"In consequence of this unfortunate history,
we have no ready-made technology of compensatory early childhood education designed to
foster in children of the poor those abilities and
motives underlying competence in the dominant
society which circumstances prevented their
acquiring (18)."

Answer 2: The programs started too *late* in the
child's development. You can find support for
this point of view in Burton White's article
(Selection 11).

Answer 3: The programs started too *early* in the
child's development (39).

Answer 4: The programs failed because they
were not comprehensive enough. There are two
aspects of this argument. The first points to the
fact that the large-scale programs failed to train
the mothers as models and as sources for continuing reinforcement for the new habits which
were learned in the Head Start school.

Smaller-scale programs which trained the
mothers as well as the children were much more
successful (51, 53). Second, since following
the Head Start preschool programs, the children
were typically returned to conventional
"ghetto" classrooms, it is not surprising that
the gains in intellectual performance and
academic achievement were short-lived. While
Project Follow Through has been implemented
in localities to attempt to carry the compensatory education beyond the preschool level, it is
too early to evaluate its success (11).

Answer 5: Compensatory education failed because the intellectual deficits are due primarily
to hereditary differences in ability rather than to
depressed environments. (This argument will
be elaborated below.)

*Question 3. Are there any small-scale research
programs in compensatory education which show
that intellectual/educational deficits can be overcome by some methods?*

Answer: Yes. For the specific details see References 2, 11, 33, 51, 52, and 53.

Conclusions.

Yours? Before reading our conclusion, why
not try to formulate your own conclusion regarding compensatory education programs and
write it in the space provided. If your conclusion is different from ours, you might want to
discuss it with your instructor or discussion
group.

Ours. Large-scale compensatory education programs have failed to provide substantial and persistent improvements in intellectual/educational performance for disadvantaged children. However, this failure seems to reflect the inadequacies of the training programs and does not mean that substantial gains in educational performance and measured IQ cannot be attained with other methods; indeed, there is now evidence that other approaches are successful.

Problem Area 2   Racial Differences in Intellectual Abilities
Question 1. Is it true that there are measurable differences between North American blacks and North American whites in overall intellectual abilities?
Answer: Yes, as measured by performance on standard intelligence tests, the size of difference varies from 10 to 20 IQ points and can generally be regarded as about 15 IQ points on average.
Question 2. Does this difference reflect a real difference in intellectual abilities or is it the result of characteristics of the test which bias the results against blacks?

● Before proceeding to try to understand this section you probably would be wise to take a short ten- to fifteen-minute detour. Skim through the section in your basic text which describes intelligence tests so that you get the basic idea of what these tests are all about. Then come back to this question.

The answer to this question is controversial.
Answer 1: The differences are due primarily to the cultural bias of the tests as evidenced by the fact that some of the content of such tests as the Stanford-Binet and the Wechsler Intelligence Scale for Children (WISC) reflects the experiences in white middle-class society. Not only is the *content* biased in the direction of favoring

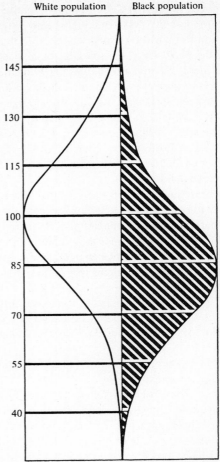

White population   Black population

Distribution of IQ scores. On most intelligence tests, black scores average about 15 points lower than white scores.

white middle-class experience but the standardization group (the group which sets the norms against which all others are judged) was white Americans whose socioeconomic status was slightly higher than the average. The standardization group contained no Negroes. A consequence of this "white only" standardization samples is that these tests are only tests of white abilities. The tests are constructed on the basis of what white Americans can do at particular ages. Therefore, in as much as they are considered tests of intelligence, they do not and can not measure the intelligence of black Americans. To do this, new tests, standardized on blacks only, would have to be constructed. We can still compare black and white children on the existing IQ tests. However in doing this, we are not comparing black and white intelligence, but instead how blacks do on tests of white intelligence.

"It is probably impossible to standardize a test perfectly and without bias. This would not matter if it were explicitly recognized that a test is only applicable to populations resembling the standardization sample in all relevant respects. This limitation on the applicability of tests is not sufficiently appreciated, especially by those who attempt to make generalizations about interracial differences in intelligence on the basis of tests constructed by and standardized on one race only (42)."

Answer 2: First, the above argument assumes that black intelligence and white intelligence are not only different in level but also different in kind, at least as measured by these "white-intelligence" tests. This would appear to be correct. Blacks seem to do relatively better on rote memory and association type subtests. On these subtests there are no differences between blacks and whites. It is on the tests of abstract reasoning that the whites tend to score higher than the blacks.

Second, we must distinguish between cul-turally *loaded* items and culturally *biased* items. "The fact that a test is culture *loaded* does not necessarily mean it is culture-biased (28)." For example, the WISC contains subtests which are culturally loaded; that is, they require experiences which are easily obtained by white middle-class children but which are less accessible to black lower-class children. There are also subtests on the WISC which are more like standard culture-fair tests which test "reasoning power rather than specific bits of knowledge (28)."

"Surprisingly, blacks tend to perform relatively better on the more culture-loaded or verbal kinds of tests than on the culture-fair type. For example, on the widely used Wechsler Intelligence Scale, comprised of 11 different subtests, blacks do better on the culture-loaded subtests of vocabulary, general information, and verbal comprehension than on the nonverbal performance test such as the block designs. Just the opposite is true for such minorities as Orientals, Mexican-Americans, Indians, and Puerto Ricans. It can hardly be claimed that culture-fair tests have a built-in bias in favor of white, Anglo, middle-class Americans when Arctic Eskimos taking the same tests perform on a par with white, middle-class norms (28)."

Conclusions.

Yours?

Ours. The basic IQ tests (WISC and Stanford-Binet) *are* loaded in favor of white-middle class experience; but it is unclear at this point how much of this loading acts to depress the test performance of blacks. Nonetheless, it is our judgment that "culture-bias" probably accounts for a meaningful but relatively small part of the obtained black-white IQ difference.

Question 3. Are there other aspects of the typical IQ test situations which could depress black performance?

Answer 1: The performance of Negroes on IQ tests is not comparable to that of whites because being evaluated is more stressful for blacks. Blacks have been conditioned to expect to fail, while whites have greater expectations for success. Experiments by Irwin Katz and his colleagues strongly suggest that IQ testing is more stressful for blacks than for whites, *especially if the blacks are tested by a white examiner and they expect that their performance will be evaluated in relation to whites* (50). (This is of course a typical test situation for many blacks.) "It would seem, therefore, that there is at least a double handicap to your intellectual performance when you are black: 1. the white environment, particularly in America, is threatening and stressful, evoking reactions that are a drain on your performance; 2. your expectancy of success is low (realistically, usually) and this only makes matters worse. In testing disadvantaged groups, much less attention has been paid to these handicaps than to those arising from differences in upbringing or, in the case of immigrants, from language problems. . . . There is enough evidence to enable one to say this: till now, psychologists, whatever their views on the origins of I.Q. have recognized only two kinds of environmental influence—those relating to child rearing and those relating to cultural differences. It is time a third was added —differences in motivation due to chronically poor race relations. If the results of the experiments are to be believed . . . this could be one of the strongest draws of all on ability (50)."

Answer 2: Jensen contends that most of the studies which have attempted to test the hypothesis that a white examiner might inhibit the performance of the child have not obtained support for it. He says "In my own study in which 9,000 black and white children took a number of standard mental and scholastic tests given by black and white examiners, there was no systematic difference in scores according to the race of examiners (28)."

Conclusions.

Yours?

•

Ours. It seems likely that the effects of discrimination and low expectations may operate to interfere with performance of the blacks by decreasing motivation and increasing stress. At this point it is not known how much of the IQ differences should be attributed to this motivational/stress factor, although when combined with other environmental factors noted below, the total effect could be substantial.

Question 4. Are the observed differences due primarily to genetic differences or to differences in environmental factors?

Answer 1: (The genetic hypothesis) Jensen's approach to this question was to first show what proportion of the individual differences in IQ *within* the population of United States whites was due to differences in genotypes. He says, "Much of my paper (The Harvard Educational Review paper) was a review of the methods and evidence that led me to the conclusion that individual differences in intelligence—that is, IQ—are predominantly attributable to genetic differences, with environmental factors contributing a minor portion of the variance among individuals (27)." Now the precise proportion of genetic variance which is obtained varies from study to study and depends in part on the genetic model which is assumed. Jensen's early papers suggested that the appropriate figure was about 80 percent, but geneticists have convinced him that the figure is too high. He now suggests that for the North American white population the more accurate figure is about 66 percent; that is, genetic factors are about twice as important as environmental factors. Jensen says that he knows of no "reason to believe that the heritability of IQ for blacks, when adequately estimated should differ appreciably from that for whites. Of course the absence of reliable data makes this a speculative assumption. (28)"

Jensen acknowledges that knowing the heritability of a trait *within* a given population does not tell us anything regarding how much of the difference *between* two populations is genetic, and yet he goes on to say, "The fact of

substantial heritability of IQ within the populations does increase the *a priori* probability that the population difference is partly attributable to genetic factors. Biologists generally agree that, almost without exception throughout nature, any genetically conditioned characteristic that varies among individuals within a subspecies (i.e., race) also varies genetically between different subspecies. Thus, the substantial heritability of IQ within the Caucasian and probably black populations makes it likely (but does not prove) that the black population's lower average IQ is caused at least in part by a genetic difference(28)."

In the same article Jensen contends that he has tried to emphasize the uncertainty of our knowledge regarding the causes of racial differences in IQ. He maintains that he does not claim that there is definitive genetic evidence to support the hypothesis of genotypic differences in intelligence between human races. Rather, he has argued that the evidence which is available does not support the environmentalist hypothesis.

Rebuttal: Research by Sandra Scarr-Salapatek (43) suggests quite strongly that the degree of heritability of IQ should not be regarded as fixed for a white or a black population but depends on the characteristic being measured (verbal aptitude or nonverbal aptitude) and whether the children lived in an advantaged or disadvantaged environment. "The major finding . . . is that advantaged and disadvantaged children differ primarily in what proportion of variance of aptitude scores can be attributed to environmental sources . . . the percentage of the total variance attributable to genetic sources was always higher in the advantaged groups of both races." The implication is that the amount of variance in measured aptitude which is due to genotype differences may be substantially reduced for disadvantaged children so that suppressive environmental factors have more weight for disadvantaged children but genetic factors have more weight for advantaged children. Thus it does not make much sense to talk about a general heritability value such as 66 percent. Indeed, some authorities contend that the most reasonable overall value is around 50 percent (34), whereas, other critics contend that there is no reason to believe that IQ scores have any heritability at all (29, 30).

Jensen's argument that "substantial heritability of IQ within the populations does increase the *a priori* probability that the population difference is partly attributable to genetic factors" is simply not true according to highly regarded experts in genetics (32).

Answer 2: (The environmentalist hypothesis): The environmentalists emphasize several factors which could account for the poorer performance of blacks on the IQ tests. Two of these we have already noted: (1) the IQ tests are culturally biased in favor of middle-class whites;

(2) blacks are more stressed and less motivated by intelligence tests than whites.

Several other environmental factors are commonly implicated as depressing the performance of blacks both in school and on IQ tests. These include: (1) discrimination and prejudice result in social isolation which limits the opportunity and desire of blacks to develop the language facility and abstracting ability which are required for success in white society; (2) many more blacks than whites are subjected to poverty-level living conditions which result in nutritional deprivation which may impair intellectual functioning; (3) blacks are victims of a self-fulfilling prophecy of low expectations —low motivation—low performance—low expectations etc. (see Selection 10).

Conclusions.

Yours?

Ours. We conclude that neither the genetic nor the environmentalist hypothesis has been able to encompass all the evidence in a convincing manner. The uncomfortable fact is that, at the present time, *we do not know whether the observed intellectual differences between North American blacks and whites are due in large part or in small part to genetic differences between the races.* We thus tend to agree with Bodmer, a geneticist at Oxford University, who concludes that "currently available data are inadequate to resolve this question in either direction and we cannot see how the question could be satisfactorily answered using available techniques (4)."

On the other hand, we *do* know that there are substantial differences between blacks and whites in environmental factors which we *suspect* might influence intellectual functioning and school performance (e.g., nutrition, type of care and attention provided by the parents, self-fulfilling prophecies, etc.). It would seem to be obvious that we should proceed to attempt to improve intellectual/educational performance by modifying the environments in which the children are raised. We would agree with J. McV. Hunt, an expert on child development, who says:

"Although one cannot with certainty rule out the possibility of racial differences in potential for competence, the whole issue is of very little import so long as the great majority of black, Puerto Rican, and Indian children grow up in poverty with extremely limited opportunities to acquire the language and number abilities and the motivation that underlie full participation in our society (18)."

Problem Area 3   Intellectual Freedom and Implications of the Research

Question 1. Should research on this problem be discontinued?

Answer 1: Intellectual/scientific freedom must be preserved. The "race-IQ controversy" has proven to be the most explosive psychological issue of this decade. It has resulted in extensive personal abuse being showered upon the pro-

tagonists (Jensen, Herrnstein, and Eysenck) by professional radicals (for example, Students for a Democratic Society), professional organizations (Society for the Psychological Study of Social Issues), and peers and colleagues (for example, Morton Deutsch claimed to have found "53 major errors or misinterpretations, . . . all of them antiblack (39)." Indeed, the abuse reached such spectacular proportions that fifty prominent professors in psychology and related fields, including four Nobel Laureates, signed a declaration affirming Jensen's right to study the effect of genetic variables on human behavior. They cited instances of previous abuse of unpopular views (e.g., Galileo and Darwin) and stated that: "Today, a similar suppression, censure, punishment and defamation are being applied against scientists who emphasize the role of heredity in human behavior . . . it is virtually heresy to express a hereditarian view . . . (39)." And D. O. Hebb, Chancellor of McGill University and former president of the American Psychological Association and of the Canadian Psychological Association, denounced such abuse as "dogmatic and emotional." He goes on to argue that "if Jensen's argument is socially dangerous, it must be more dangerous in the long run to suppress it (39)." Jensen argues that: "Colleagues have brought up a variety of more intellectual reasons for denying a genetic basis for behavioral differences. One of the commonest reasons is that such knowledge, if it is established and generally accepted by the scientific and intellectual community, might be used by some persons for evil purposes, to promote racial prejudice, discrimination, and segregation and to justify or rationalize the political suppression and economic exploitation of racial minorities and the nation's working class in general. As I point out in my paper on ethical issues in genetic research, these consequences do not logically follow from the recognition of genetic behavioral differences. Nearly all scientifically important knowledge can be used for food or ill (27)."

• While these consequences may not *logically* follow from the recognition of genetic behavioral differences, our knowledge of social psychology, prejudice, and discrimination would lead us to expect that such consequences *would* follow at least in some local situations and *could* be used by some people to strengthen a discriminatory belief structure. As a consequence that dilemma is deepened! If we feel quite certain that *some* people will use new knowledge in an "evil" way, should we suppress this new knowledge? What do *you* think? Discuss it with your friends.

Answer 2: "Suggestion" without "proof" is socially irresponsible. One Nobel Laureate asserts that Jensen's "hypothesis" is as socially irresponsible as yelling "Fire" in a crowded theater when no fire exists. The point is that the negative personal and social consequences resulting from publicizing the genetic hypothesis are too devastating to justify public discussion until there is definite proof which is accepted by the general scientific community.

Question 2. What are the educational implications?

Answer 1: Jensen contends that even if it were clearly established that the measured differences in IQ performance reflected a heavy contribution of genetic factors, the "only morally tenable position in human relations would remain unchanged: that all persons should be treated according to their own individual characteristics and not in terms of their group identity. Let me stress that none of the research I have discussed here allows one to conclude anything about the intelligence of any individual black or white person (28)."

• Were you surprised that Jensen holds this view? Do you believe he actually holds it? Why? Why not? If you believe that he does hold it, but you were surprised, what do you think that means about your understanding of Jensen's views? . . . of your emotional reactions to his views?

On a more specific level Jensen believes that one educational implication which follows from his genetic hypothesis is that we should increase the diversity of our school programs so that they can encompass a wide variety of educational goals and instructional means toward those goals. As he indicates in the following comment, the aim of such a pluralistic system would be to increase the opportunity of all children to actualize their potential to become socially useful and self-fulfilling adults.

COMMENT: TOWARD EDUCATIONAL DIVERSITY

We have invested so much for so long in trying to equalize scholastic performance that we have given little or no thought to finding ways of diversifying schools to make them rewarding to everyone while not attempting to equalize everyone's performance in a common curriculum. Recommendations have almost always taken the form of asking what next we might try to make children who in the present school system do not flourish academically become more like those who do. The emphasis has been more on changing philosophy of equalization, however laudable its ideals, cannot work if it is based on false premises and no amount of propaganda can make it appear to work. Its failures will be forced upon everyone.

Educational pluralism of some sort, encompassing a variety of very different educational curricula and goals will, I think, be the inevitable outcome of the growing realization that the schools are not going to eliminate human differences. Rather than making over a large segment of the school population so they will not be doomed to failure in a largely antiquated elitist-oriented educational system, which originally evolved to serve only a relatively small segment of society, the educational system will have to be revamped in order to benefit everyone who is required by the society to attend schools. It seems incredible that a system can still survive which virtually guarantees frustration and failure for a large proportion of the children it should intend to serve. From all the indications, public education in such a form will not much longer survive.

But we should not fail to recognize that to

propose radical diversity in accord with individual differences in abilities and interests, as contrasted with uniformity of educational treatment, puts society between Scylla and Charybdis in terms of insuring for all individuals equality of opportunity for the diversity of educational paths. The surest way to maximize the benefits of schooling to all individuals and at the same time to make the most of a society's human resources is to ensure equality of educational opportunity for all its members.

Monolithic educational goals and uniformity of approaches guarantee unnecessary frustration and defeat for many. On the other hand, educational pluralism runs the risk that social, economic, ethnic background or geographic origin, rather than each child's own characteristics, might determine the educational paths available to him. The individual variety of educational paths and goals are to be found everywhere, in every social stratum, ethnic group, and neighborhood. Academic aptitudes and special talents should be cultivated wherever they are found, and wise society will take all possible measures to ensure this to the great possible extent. At the same time, those who are poor in the traditional academic aptitudes cannot be left by the wayside. Suitable means and goals must be found for making their years of schooling rewarding to them, if not in the usual academic sense, then in ways that can better their chances for socially useful and self-fulfilling roles as adults.

ARTHUR JENSEN

Answer 2: Geneticist Walter Bodmer concludes his analysis of the controversy by posing the question "What use can be made of knowledge concerning genetic components to race-I.Q. differences?" His answer is that "No one surely should argue against the need for a better scientific understanding of the basis of intellectual ability and the benefits to society that might accrue from such an understanding. But why concentrate this effort on the genetic basis for the race-I.Q. difference? Apart from the intrinsic, almost insurmountable difficulties in answering this question at the present time, it is not in any way clear what practical use could be made of the answer. Perhaps the only practical argument is that, since the question that the difference is genetic has been raised, an attempt should be made to answer it. Otherwise those who now believe that the difference is genetic will be left to continue their campaigns for an adjustment of our educational and economic systems to take account of 'innate' racial differences.

"A demonstration that the difference is not primarily genetic could counter such campaigns. On the other hand, an answer in the opposite direction should not, in a genuinely democratic society free of race prejudice, make any difference (4)."

Conclusions (regarding intellectual freedom).
Yours?

Ours. We agree, in principle, with the statement issued by the Council of the Society for the Psychological Study of Social Issues to the effect that: "The Council of the Society for the Psychological Study of Social Issues reaffirms its long-held position of support for open inquiry on all aspects of human behavior. We are concerned with establishing high standards of scientific inquiry and of scientific responsibility. Included in these standards must be careful interpretation of research findings, with rigorous attention to alternative explanations. In no area of science are these principles more important than in the study of human behavior, where a variety of social factors may have large and far-reaching effects. When research has bearing on social issues and public policy, the scientist must examine the competing explanations for his findings and must exercise the greatest care in his interpretation. Only in this way can he minimize the possibility that others will overgeneralize or misunderstand the social implications of his work."

However we contend that, like all sociopolitical principles, the principle of freedom of inquiry is not absolute. It is bounded and constrained at those points where it infringes on the welfare of others. We have ample precedent to suggest the importance of deciding "not to know" or "taking care" regarding the means and consequences of our "truth seeking." For example, most civilized men believe that mankind should impose limits on itself in the manner in which it goes about researching thermonuclear reactions. Thus, by mutual agreement we have chosen to ban unlimited atmospheric tests of thermonuclear devices. Within the psychosciences considerable concern is now being expressed regarding the use of "psychosurgery" (see Selection 14). Psychosurgery is a "brain operation" which has as its primary purpose the alternation of thoughts, emotions, and social behavior of humans. The potential for misuse of this technique for the control of political dissent is apparent and frightening. The Society for Neuroscience

and other interested professional groups are now considering calling for a moratorium on psychosurgery until the appropriate neurological and societal safeguards can be established (36).

As we consider the societal/personal implications of further research on racial differences in IQ, we confront an issue of similar magnitude to those involved in control of thermonuclear reactions and psychosurgery. In order to sharpen the focus let us suppose that it were established beyond a reasonable scientific doubt that 65 percent of the black-white IQ difference was due to differences in genotypes. (This would mean that approximately 10 IQ points difference in *mean* performance is due to genotypes.) What would be the likely consequence of this knowledge?

As we have seen, even Jensen admits that no direct *educational* implications *should* follow from establishing the genetic hypothesis. He holds that the only morally defensible view is that each person should be judged and educated on the basis of his own individual abilities and not on the basis of group membership. Bodmer also holds this view, so does Scarr-Salapatek, and so do we. Thus, it would appear as noted below by Joshua Lederberg (a leading geneticist) that "the genetic hypothesis is almost irrelevant to Jensen's most cogent point."

COMMENT: THE GENETIC HYPOTHESIS—IRRELEVANCE AND RELEVANCE

The genetic hypothesis is almost irrelevant to Jensen's most cogent point. Our educational systems often neglect a child's strongest capabilities and hold him back, while focusing on his weaknesses. He reports very encouraging results in teaching deprived children how to read by rote learning, leaving more complicated abstractions to a later stage of their schooling. If the 6-year-old has a deficit in abstract thinking, it is relatively unimportant for educational policy whether this is the fault of his genes or a cultural maladaptation. In many situations, a genetic defect might be easier to repair: certainly we are better equipped to deal with diabetes or deafness than with overt racial hostility.

The social crime would be to characterize a child by his color rather than by his individually tested capabilities, and Jensen may be doing a great service by insisting on this kind of differentiation.

The genetic hypothesis does matter if it discourages educators and scientists from probing more deeply into the crucial early years of child development. The period from one to three years of age is, in fact, almost a blank page of scientific development. This is no accident: children of that age are hidden in the bosom of their families; in many states it is even legally forbidden to establish "schools" for them, on the theory that maternal deprivation would be fatal to their proper development. The most crucial level in compensatory education may be an effort to reach and teach the mothers of these young children. Teach what? We have no scientific guidelines yet, and there are pitifully few programs along these lines.

JOSHUA LEDERBERG

What about "*positive*" *societal* consequences which might be gained from this knowledge? Some positive eugenics advocates would contend that we should implement a program of guided reproduction which would overcome "dysgenic" trends in the gene pool. The purpose would be to selectively breed for a particular genotype. We regard this proposal as unacceptable on scientific, moral, and political grounds.

In sum, we find no reason to believe that any *positive* societal or educational consequences would be likely to occur from establishing the genetic hypothesis of racial-IQ differences.

What of possible *negative* *societal* consequences? Given what we know of about the social psychology of prejudice, discrimination, and intergroup conflict it would not be prudent to believe that what Jensen and Bodmer think we *should* do will in fact happen. On the contrary, confirmation of the genetic hypothesis is likely to strengthen the views and programs of racial bigots and outright segregationists. Furthermore, it would lead to decreased support for environmental interventions designed to reduce inequality of opportunity. According to Deutsch, such fears are well founded since

> Jensen's article, through its use by attorneys in some desegregation cases and by some legislators with respect to appropriations bills (and from its overinterpretation in the public media), has had a negative effect on social progress: less money for education cannot lead to better education; casting and court desegregation decisions canot lead to greater equality (8, p. 552).

And what of *negative educational* consequences? They are likely to be of two sorts. First, it would seem to virtually guarantee (even more frequently than now—see Selection 9) that racial stereotypes rather than individual abilities would influence the kind of educational experience which is received by a disadvantaged black child. Even more than today the power of stereotyping and self-fulfilling prophecy would become an educational reality. Second, as noted by Lederberg and by Deutsch, economic support for research on environmental intervention would be curtailed and schools in "disadvantaged" neighborhoods would be likely to suffer from economic malnutrition.

If we are seriously interested in individualizing the educational process in the present racist culture of North America, it seems reasonable to believe that establishing the validity of the genetic hypothesis would be counterproductive for achieving that goal. Rather than reinforcing involuntary incarceration in the "black racial box" we need to develop a society in which there are many avenues to success. Then differences can be "valued variations on the human theme regardless of their environmental or genetic origins (43)"; then differences in performance, interest, and personality can be seen as just that *differences rather than deficits* (10).

In the light of the foregoing it does not seem unreasonable to advocate that (1) *behavioral scientists should agree to establish a moratorium on all research which has as its primary aim the estab-*

lishment of a genetic base for racial differences in intelligence and personality; (2) the governments of the United States and Canada should provide a large-scale massive infusion of research and development funds directed toward establishing techniques of compensatory education which are powerful enough to eliminate or substantially reduce intellectual/educational deficits due to environmental disadvantages; (3) the effect of such programs should be evaluated longitudinally and continuously for a long enough period to establish the ways in which they have been successful and the ways in which they have failed (about three decades would probably be required); (4) if this all-out effort to establish the environmental hypothesis should meet with little success and if there exists at that time adequate behavior genetic techniques to permit a valid test of the genetic hypothesis, and if the cultural consciousness has developed to a level in which "differences are not deficits," then we can in good conscience reopen the race-IQ controversy. Until then let us conscientiously try to relate to people as individuals rather than members of a category and get on with the job of creating a better environment for all citizens.

● What do you think about the above recommendations? Do you understand the basis for recommendation (1)? Do you think it is justified? Do you agree with recommendation (2)? What can you do about it? Write your congressman or M.P.? What else?

SOME ALTERNATIVE APPROACHES

In the previous sections we have reminded you of the many real and serious shortcomings of the traditional school systems which continue to dominate education throughout North America, indeed throughout the world. Many of you have your own horror stories to add to the long documentation of classroom atrocities. Immersion in the problems of the present system is an important step toward change; many defenses operate to keep us from becoming aware of the full enormity of our plight. Such awareness is necessary if we are to mobilize and direct the tremendous energies which are required to change a major societal institution in a truly significant way. Yet, beyond our analysis of the problem we need a dream which carries at least glimpses of a more ideal system. We have characterized the belief that the schools could/should serve to equalize opportunity as a utopian dream which is contrary to reality. Yet it may be that the crisis in the schools is so serious that to dream in any less idealistic terms is to doom the educational enterprise to sterility and to condemn mankind to extinction. Be that as it may, it is abundantly clear that the school must play a dual role as conservator and communicator of culture as well as an agency of change. It cannot do this without a simultaneous reformation of the priorities and values of society at large and a dramatic restructuring (destructuring?) of the schools within that transformed society.

COMMENT: CONSERVATION AND CHANGE

There are two principles inherent in the very nature of things, the spirit of change, and the spirit of conservation. There can be nothing real without both. . . . Mere conservation without change cannot conserve, mere change without conservation is a passage from nothing to nothing.

ALFRED NORTH WHITEHEAD

Continued immersion in the failures of the school eventually leads us to cry, "Enough! Enough of this dismal litany. What can be done?" Is there any hope that the educational enterprise can move beyond its current encapsulation? Some people think so; indeed, some would assert that we have available at the present time many models which embody not only promise for the future, but real accomplishments in the present (43).

The alternatives may be viewed as occuring in four primary strategy clusters which we call the *preschool* strategy, the *reschool* strategy, the *free-school* strategy and the *deschool* strategy.

The Preschool Strategy: The Spirit of Preformation

In 1965 the Harvard Pre-School Project was begun under the direction of Dr. Burton White. The rationale for the project as stated by White was based on the fact that:

> Accumulating evidence suggested that while most educators were concerning themselves with the educational process of children age six and older, much of a child's crucial development was over by then. By six, so it seemed, it might already be too late to prevent stunted development and to insure full growth. Thus the Pre-School Project was designed as a cornerstone for the whole research and development effort with older children. The object was to find out as much as possible about the preschool-age child and, in particular, to study the attributes and development of the successful or educable child. The phrase we used then was that we were concerned with the development of educability.
>
> Our mandate was maddeningly simple to express: to learn how to structure the experiences of the first six years of life so that a child might be optimally prepared for formal education. Though the problem was easily stated, the solution was not likely to be achieved with ease (52).

During the first years of the program White and his collaborators identified many specific ways in which children who were judged to be highly confident and competent six-year-olds (A group) differed from other children (C group) who never seemed to be able to cope. However, it became clear that whatever produced these differences in competence occurred well before the age of six. Indeed, it seemed to happen before the age of three. Thus the basic principle of the preschool strategy is simple: The early years are critical for setting cognitive and social competence, therefore it is important to intervene early—even beginning at birth. In Selection 11 White provides insight into the child's world in the early years and suggests some educational implications of this new understanding of the preschool child.

In addition to the research findings, strong impetus has come to this preschool strategy from the practical experience gained in hundreds of day-care centers throughout North America. Unfortunately, in the United States, governmental support for day-care centers has been drastically cut back. Hopefully the support for research programs in this area will not suffer a similar fate.

● Is there anything that you can do to help restore these important efforts? Are there local day-care programs to which you could contribute?

The Reschool Strategy: The Spirit of Reformation

The reschool strategy encompasses a wide variety of efforts which aim to improve the present system through changes in techniques, tactics, and technologies. It is a strategy of reformation rather than revolution; it creates change through restructuring rather than destructuring. One example of this approach is the nongraded school, which attempts to organize the curriculum in a "vertical" rather than "horizontal" manner. That is, each course of study (e.g. mathematics) is organized into sequential units so that each student may proceed at his own pace. A school which was properly restructured according to this tactic would have no grade levels (horizontal structure). Several meaningful educational/psychoemotional benefits are said to accrue from this approach. For example, the child's rate of progression is more closely paced to his own cognitive/emotive development than to some theoretical average pace. As a consequence it helps to eliminate the emotional and intellectual trauma which often results from non-promotion in the conventional graded curriculum (14).

While the nongraded approach opens up the structure of the school, it does not necessarily change many aspects of the teaching/learning process itself. Other restructuring approaches focus more on the characteristics of the learning environment and the teaching methods. One approach which has generated considerable interest among education reformers is called by several names: the informal classroom, the open classroom, and in England where it originated, the Leicestershire method.

It is clear that not all children (or parents or teachers) would find the goals and procedures advocated by a free-school (see below) to be compatible with their educational needs or convictions. For those who feel that there is no psychological/educational justification for advocating a permissive, unstructured, free-play approach to classroom learning, the open classroom alternative is becoming increasingly available. It shares the free-school's emphasis on freedom with a collateral emphasis on providing a rich learning environment and a teacher who is sensitive to the cognitive/emotive growth of the whole child. Several features of the informal classroom method are notable: (1) the *"integrated"* day—the day is not divided up into specific class lessons to be accomplished at specified times. Rather, there are various activity areas (e.g., science and math, visual arts, language arts, and general purpose). The child is free to spend time in the various learning centers as he chooses. The child's productivity is believed to be heavily dependent on the teacher's skill in setting up the learning centers; (2) *vertical groupings,* children are grouped into "families" who stay together for two to three years and consist of children ranging in age from five to eight; (3) *inductive thinking* (as opposed to specific fact learning) is emphasized; (4) *children are trustworthy and responsible for their own learning.* Coercive measures designed to force children's learning are avoided. So are artificial incentives. Preferred are motivational strategies which capitalize on children's exploratory responses and natural curiosity (11); (5) *training for the future is deemphasized.*

Instead, the prevalent teaching value is placed upon making the most of the child's current learning situation. In other words, the enrichment of children's lives in infant school takes precedence over concern about what they will be able to do at the end of one, two or three years. This is several degrees away from most American approaches, which generally gauge program effectiveness in terms of the long range results (11).

COMMENT: QUESTIONS FOR THE OPEN CLASSROOM

In addition to the need for empirical research, several important questions about infant school practice need clear answers. For example, when each child determines by individual choice how he will use his time, is there a danger of excessive random activity (Yeomans, 1969)? In other words, who is accountable if a given child does not achieve the praiseworthy, if ambiguous, aims of informal education? If there are certain curriculum "universals" (content areas) that all children need to share, can these be left to personal choice? Is there, as Barth (1969) suggests, a danger that infant school practices will be "haphazard, disordered, and misunderstood" unless they are guided by a clear theoretical framework? To what extent does the emphasis upon intuitive teaching and evaluation conflict with educators' attempts to build a science of teaching? To what extent is informal education, with its potential strengths and weaknesses, consistent with a society's national goals? Why, as it is often claimed, does the educational "establishment" in England and the United States seemingly resist change in the direction of broad-scale open education? How does one best prepare teachers and children for a successful open education experience? Are infant school children developing greater independence and responsibility, as is generally claimed? Is the near-idyllic existence of new infant and junior school children too far divorced from the realities of life for it to be the best sort of learning experience?

ELLIS D. EVANS

Again we find ourselves asking, "Can we reconcile excellence with ecstasy? Competence with creativity? Caring with detachment? Being-as-a-child with being-as-an-adult?" We believe, with Washburne and Silberman, in the practical possibility of a dual focus in which "Every child has the right to be prepared adequately for later effective living as an adult." It is our opinion that "later effective living as an adult" is most likely to be attained in a learning environment which is responsive to the child's needs, especially his need to get love and give it, his need to know and be known, his needs to work and to play.

Other approaches to restructuring the teaching/learning process make extensive use of children as teachers (13), programmed instruction (46), computer assisted instruction (1). These latter methods involve the student as an active participant in the learning process rather than a passive recipient of information which is "presented" by the teacher. The restructuring of the classroom based on the inquiry method would of course be another example of this strategy for change (cf. Postman and Weingartner, Selection 7).

The Free-School Strategy

The idea is that freedom is a supreme good, that people, including young people, have a right to freedom and that people who are free, will in general be more open, more humane, more intelligent than people who are directed, manipulated, ordered about . . ."

The Santa Barbara Community School

The prototype of contemporary free-schools was established in England in the 1920s by A. S. Neill. It was founded as a protest against the coercion and authoritarian structures of the traditional school and it was based on the belief that happy, contented, and socially responsible people could be raised better in an atmosphere of love and freedom. The publication in 1960 of *Summerhill: A Radical Approach to Child Rearing* (37) provided a powerful stimulus to similar efforts throughout North America. There is now a vigorous, diverse,

and rapidly growing free-school movement in America. As with any such movement based on freedom, the particular forms vary widely and each school tends to reflect the views and personalities of its founders, teachers, and, of course, the students themselves. Yet all free-schools are predicated on the principle that learning is something that the child does best for himself and the function of the school is to provide the freedom whereby the inherent capacity of the child to be a "good chooser" can be expressed. Two points of clarification are in order and should be strongly emphasized. First, *freedom is not license*. The whole point of learning to be free is that we recognize our search for autonomy does not give us the right to infringe on the other person's freedom. As Neill says: "I define license as interfering with another's freedom. For example, in my school a child is free to go to lessons or stay away from lessons because that is his own affair, but he is not free to play a trumpet when others want to study or sleep."

Second, *freedom is not anarchy*. There are many rules which govern the behavior of the students at Summerhill; indeed, probably more rules than in a traditional school. But the difference is that the rules are made by the students themselves and reflect their needs, interests, and concerns. Freedom is never freedom from structure and constraint. It is rather the ability to generate and modify one's own structures with their attendant constraints. Learning to be free is learning to live with nonfreedom in a creative, meaningful way. That a free-school *can* provide the climate in which a person can begin to learn to be responsibly free is suggested by the report of the British government inspectors regarding the Summerhill pupils:

They are full of life and zest, there is no sign of boredom or apathy. The children hold an attitude of deep affection for the school. They are friendly, easy and natural. They have a lack of shyness and self-consciousness. They are very easy, pleasant people to get on with. The system encourages initiative, responsibility and integrity (6, p. 84).

Neill says that Summerhill should be regarded as a way of life, not as a school, and it would appear that the prototypical free-school does achieve its goal of freeing the child to be more creative, spontaneous, and zestful in his living. Yet, many advocates of change in the present system would contend that the *academic* results must be taken into account. They would question the intellectual competence of the graduates of the free-schools, and again, the report of the British government inspectors tends to support their case: "On the whole the results of this system are unimpressive—the children work with a willing interest that is most refreshing but their achievements are meagre."

Consistent with this point is that many "graduates" of Summerhill indicate that they needed a one-or two-year-long "reentry" period in order to catch up in their academic work.

The problem of reconciling individual choice with structure is a difficult one; but one thing is clear—the solution will take many forms; there is no one best way. And another thing, too—the "best way" for a given child varies from day to day. A free-school teacher must be willing to help a child learn to come to terms with structure and intellectual competence and at the same time preserve and foster his striving toward creative interdependence—a monumental task.

The philosophy behind the *informal* classroom contends that a good school "is a community in which children learn to live first and foremost as children and not as future adults (43)." The philosophy behind Summerhill as a prototypical free-school emphasizes that play is the serious work of all children. Yet it would seem that "merely to let children live free, natural, childlike lives may be to fail to give them the training they need to meet the problems of later life (44, p. 116)." And in a similar vein Bertrand Russell observed shortly before his death:

> I think freedom is not a panacea. . . . Both in education and in other matters I think that freedom must have very definite limitations, where you come to things that are definitely harmful to other people, or things that prevent you yourself from being useful, such as the lack of knowledge (41).

• What is your opinion about how you can best reconcile freedom and limits within a school context? Talk with your friends about what principles you would form *your* school on; seek arguments against your views as well as those which agree.

The Deschool Strategy

The most radical of the alternatives which have been proposed to the traditional education system is simply to do away with schools altogether. The three most vocal spokesmen for this point of view have been Ivan Illich, Everett Reimer, and Paul Goodman. While these revolutionaries differ somewhat among themselves as to the details of a new system, they tend to agree on their diagnosis of the malignancy known as school. We may formulate some principles on which they would tend to agree:

1 The present school systems actually tend to arrest and stunt intellectual and emotional growth for the majority of students; perhaps only 10 to 15 percent of the students are able to thrive on this activity without being harmed.

Do these percentages really mean anything? How could they possibly be established? Is your crap detector working?

---

2 Most of the schooling process does not prepare the student for competence in the real world; it is largely carried on for its own sake.

3 The compulsory nature of schooling contributes to its ineffectiveness as either a skill-training procedure or as a vehicle for liberal education; the compulsion also plays a major role in stunting the intellectual and emotional growth of the participants, student and teacher alike.

4 The whole educational system in the Western world is geared to produce avid consumers of the products of a technological society.

5 The education monopoly controls the attitudes and behavior of the students by inculcating the values of consumerism and unlimited technological progress such as *(a)* "bigger is better than smaller," *(b)* "more is better than less," *(c)* a "good man" is one who is successful in the marketplace of exchange of goods and services for profit, *(d)* the more goods one can consume, the more "successful," i.e. more valued, he is, *(e)* education consists in accumulating knowledge packages which can be traded for more and better knowledge packages or access to specific "ways of life," *(f)* the products which will be produced are those which fit the needs of the most successful consumers (middle and upper class), *(g)* as a consequence,

> Once basic needs have been translated by a society into demands for scientifically produced commodities, poverty is defined by standards which the technocrats can change at will. Poverty then refers to those who have fallen behind as an advertised ideal of consumption in some important respect. In Mexico the poor are those who lack three years of schooling and New York City they are those who lack twelve (21).

Do you think the energy crisis and the ecological crises have had any real impact in reorienting our society toward a "conserving ethic" as opposed to a consuming ethic?" See Selection 47 for more on the consumer culture.

---

6 Our schools isolate and alienate our young from those who are older; from their feelings;

from the real work of most people; from intimate knowledge of tools and "things," from each other via eager acquisition and competition; and from the natural world by usurping most of their time and energies during a critical one or two decades (six to sixteen or twenty-six) of their lives

Again we say, "Enough of the dismal litany. What can be done?" For the "deschoolers" meaningful solutions cannot be comprised of halfway measures aimed at restructuring the schools. It must involve deschooling society.

Illich proposes that the total schooling system be dismantled and that the vast funds which are now expended on the educational establishment be used to create learning networks into which each person can freely enter. The networks are based on his view

> . . . that no more than four . . . distinct "channels" or learning exchanges could contain all the resources needed for real learning. The child grows up in a world of things, surrounded by people who serve as models for skills and values. He finds peers who challenge him to argue, to compete, to cooperate, and understand; and if the child is lucky, he is exposed to confrontation or criticism by an experienced elder who really cares. Things, models, peers and elders are four resources each of which requires a different type of arrangement to ensure that everybody has ample access to it (21).

Illich's educational revolution focuses its goals and means around this analysis of things, models, peers, and elders as the critical learning resources. He describes his goal as

> 1. To liberate access to things by abolishing the control which persons and institutions now exercise over their educational values. 2. To liberate the sharing of skills by guaranteeing freedom to teach or exercise them on request. 3. To liberate the critical and creative resources of people by returning to individual persons the ability to call and hold meetings—an ability now increasingly monopolized by institutions which claim to speak for the people. 4. To liberate the individual from the obligation to shape his expectations to the services offered by any established

profession—by providing him with the opportunity to draw on the experience of his peers and to entrust himself to the teacher, guide, adviser, or healer of his choice. Inevitably the deschooling of society will blur the distinctions between economics, education, and politics on which the stability of the present world order and the stability of nations now rest (21).

These goals are to be reached by establishing four learning networks which provide:

1 *Reference services to educational objects*—through laboratories, libraries, museums, factories, airports, farms, etc., etc., greater access is provided to real learning environments containing the "tools of the trade."

2 *Skill exchanges*—a kind of "yellow pages" of persons who possess skills and who are willing to serve as "skill models."

3 *Peer-matching*—this is a communication network which would use mass media and computers to help people who are interested in learning the same thing get together for interchange on that topic.

4 *Reference services to educators-at-large*—the professional and freelance educator would describe his services and the conditions under which he renders them. There would be no certification to "guide" the quality of instruction. Rather, a prospective student would contact former students for their evaluation of the educator's services.

Critics of Illich's deschooling strategy contend that the system would be exceptionally difficult to implement and that there are better, "less chancy" reforms which can achieve the goals (17). It does seem clear that such a system would result in a complete restructuring of society and would also need to be preceded by widespread changes in society. Can anything actually be done? In a chapter entitled "What Each of Us Can Do," Everett Reimer suggests a revolutionary triad as follows: "Lowering consumption, sharing, and conserving are three actions which most of us can take, and

yet, jointly, they constitute a powerful revolutionary program (38)."

COMMENT: THE REVOLUTIONARY ROLE OF EDUCATION

Effective alternatives to schools cannot occur without other widespread changes in society. But there is no point in waiting for other changes to bring about a change in education. Unless educational alternatives are planned and pursued, there is no assurance they will occur, no matter what else happens. If they do not, the other changes are likely to be superficial and short-lived. Educational change, on the other hand, will bring other fundamental social changes in its wake.

True education is a basic social force. Present social structures could not survive an educated population even if only a substantial minority were educated. Something more than schooling is obviously in question here. People are schooled to accept a society. They are educated to create or recreate one.

Education has the meaning here that deep students of education and of human nature have always given it. None has defined it better than Paulo Freire, the Brazilian educator, who describes it as becoming critically aware of one's reality in a manner that leads to effective action upon it. An educated man understands his world well enough to deal with it effectively. Such men, if they existed in sufficient numbers, would not leave the absurdities of the present world unchanged.

EVERETT REIMER

REFERENCES

1. ATIKINSON, R. C., & WILSON, H. A. (Eds.), Computer assisted instruction. *New York:* Academic Press, *1969.*

2. BEREITER, C., & ENGLEMANN, S. *Teaching disadvantaged children in the pre-school*. Englewood Cliffs, N.J.: Prentice-Hall, 1966.

3. BREMER, J., & VON MOSCHZISKER, M. *The school without walls:* Philadelphia's parkway program. New York: Holt, Rinehart and Winston, 1971.

4. BODMER, W. F. Race and IQ: The genetic background. In K. Richardson, D. Spears, & M. Richards (Eds.), *Race and intelligence*. Baltimore: Penguin Books, 1972.

5. BURTON, A. *The horn and the beanstalk*. Toronto: Holt, Rinehart and Winston, 1972.

6. Central Advisory Council for Education (England), *Children and their primary schools*, London, Her Majesty's Stationery Office, 1967.

7. COLEMAN, JAMES S., *et al. Equality of educational opportunity*. Washington, D.C.: U.S. Government Printing Office, 1966.

8. DEUTSCH, M. Happenings on the way back to the forum. *Harvard Educational Review*, 1969, **39**, 523–557.

9. DEUTSCH, M., KATZ, I., & JENSEN, A. (Eds.), *Social class, race and psychological development*. Holt, Rinehart and Winston, 1968.

10. DOBZHANSKY, T. Differences are not deficits. *Psychology Today*, December 1973, 97–101.

11. EVANS, E. D. *Contemporary influences in early childhood education*. New York: Holt, Rinehart and Winston, 1971.

12. FEATHERSTONE, J. *Schools where children learn*. New York: Avon Books, 1971.

13. GARTNER, A., KOHLER, M. C., & RIESSMAN, F. *Children teach children: Learning by teaching*. New York: Macmillan, 1969.

14. GOODLAD, J. J., & Anderson, R. H. *The nongraded elementary school*. New York, Harcourt, Brace and World, 1963.

15. HEBB, D. Quoted in Berkeley Rice, The high cost of thinking the unthinkable. *Psychology Today*, December 1973, 89–93.

16. HODGSON, GODFREY. Do schools make a difference? *The Atlantic Monthly*, March 1973, 35–46.

17. HOOK, S. Illich's de-schooled utopia. *Encounter*, January 1972, 53–57.

18. HUNT, J. McV. Black genes—white environment. *Trans-Action*, June 1969, pp. 12–22.

19. HUNT, J. McV. Has compensatory education failed? Has it been attempted? *Harvard Educational Review*, 1969, **39**, 278 300.

20. HUNT, J. McV. Early childhood education and social class. *The Canadian Psychologist*, 1972, **73**, 305–328.

21. ILLICH, I. *Deschooling society*. New York: Harper and Row, 1970.

22. JACKSON, P. W. *et al.* Perspectives on inequality: A reassessment of the effects of family and schooling in America. *Harvard Educational Review*, 1973, **43**, 37–166.

23. JENCKS, CHRISTOPHER. A reappraisal of the most controversial document of our time. *New York Times Magazine*, August 10, 1969.

24. JENCKS, C. *et al. Inequality: A reassessment of the effect of family and schooling in America*. New York: Basic Books, 1972.

25. JENSEN, ARTHUR. How much can we boost IQ and scholastic achievement? *Harvard Educational Review.* 1969, **39**, 1–124.

26. JENSEN, ARTHUR. Race and the genetics of intelligence: A reply to Lewontin. *Bulletin of the Atomic Scientists*, May 1970, 17 23.

27. JENSEN, ARTHUR. Genetics and education: A second look. *New Scientist* October 12, 1972, 96–98.

28. JENSEN, ARTHUR. The differences are real. *Psychology Today*, 1973, **7**(7), 79–86.

29. KAMIN, L. J. *Heredity, intelligence, politics, and psychology*. Unpublished paper presented at the 1973 meetings of the Eastern Psychological Association.

30. KAMIN, L. J. *The science and politics of I.Q.*, Potomac, Md.: Erlbaum Associates, **In** press.

31. LEONARD, G. B. *Education and ecstasy*. New York: Dell Publishing Co., 1968.

32. LEWONTIN, R. C. Race and intelligence.

Bulletin of the Atomic Scientist. March 1970. Pp. 2–4.

33. MCCARTHY, J. Changing parent attitudes and improving language and intellectual abilities of culturally disadvantaged four-year-old children through parental involvement. *Contemporary Education,* 1969, **40,** 166–168.

34. MCCLEARN, G. E., & DEFRIES, J. C. *Introduction to behavioral genetics.* San Francisco; Freeman, 1973.

35. MARSHALL, L. H. Psychosurgery's tortuous path. *Neurosciences Newsletter.* 1973, **4**(4), 3.

36. MORRISON, T., & BURTON, A. *Options: Reforms and alternatives for Canadian education.* Toronto: Holt, Rinehart and Winston of Canada Ltd., 1973.

37. NEILL, A. S. *Summerhill: A radical approach to child rearing.* New York: Hart, 1960.

38. REIMER, E. *School is dead: Alternatives in education.* Garden City: Doubleday, 1971.

39. RICE, B. The high cost of thinking the unthinkable. *Psychology Today.* December 1973, 89–93.

40. ROHWER, W. D. Jr. Prime time for education. Early childhood or adolescence? *Harvard Educational Review,* 1971, **41,** 316–341.

41. RUSSELL, B. As quoted in Postman, N., & Weingartner, C. *The soft revolution.* New York: Delacorte Press, 1971.

42. RYAN, Joanna. IQ—the illusion of objectivity. In K. Richardson, D. Spears, & M. Richards (Eds.), *Race and intelligence.* Baltimore, Penguin, 1972, 35–55.

43. SCARR-SALAPATEK, SANDRA. Race, social class and IQ, *Science,* 1971, **174,** 1285–1294.

44. SILBERMAN, CHARLES E. *Crisis in the classroom,* New York: Random House, 1970.

45. SILBERMAN, CHARLES E. *The open classroom reader,* New York: Random House, 1973.

46. STOLUROW, L. M. Programmed instruction. In R. L. Ebel (Ed.), *Encyclopedia of educational research.* New York: Macmillan, 1969.

47. TORRANCE, E. P. An alternative to compensatory education. *Educational Horizons,* 1972, **50,** 176–182.

48. TORRANCE, E. P. Influence of alternative approaches to pre-primary educational stimulation and question asking skills. *The Journal of Educational Research,* 1972, **65,** 204–206.

49. WASHBURNE, C. As quoted in Silberman, C. E. *Crisis in the classroom.* New York: Random House, 1970.

50. WATSON, P. Can racial discrimination affect IQ? In K. RICHARDSON, D. SPEARS, & M. RICHARDS (Eds.), *Race and intelligence,* Baltimore: Pelican, 1972.

51. WEIKART, D., & LAMBIE, D. Z. Preschool intervention through a home teaching program. In Jerome Hellmuth (Ed.), *Disadvantaged child.* Vol. **II.** New York: Brunner/Mazel, 1968. Pp. 435–500.

52. WHITE, B. L. An analysis of excellent early education practices: Preliminary report. *Interchange,* 1971, **2**(2), 71–88.

53. WILLMON, B. Parent participation as a factor in the effectiveness of Head Start programs. *Journal of Educational Research,* 1969, **62,** 406–410.

7 BEYOND CRAP DETECTION: THE INQUIRY MEDIUM IS THE MESSAGE*

NEIL POSTMAN and CHARLES WEINGARTNER

COMMENT: "CRAP DETECTING"

Try this: In the early 1960s, an interviewer was trying to get Ernest Hemingway to identify the characteristics required for a person to be a "great writer." As the interviewer offered a list of various possibilities, Hemingway disparaged each in sequence. Finally, frustrated, the interviewer asked, "Isn't there any one essential ingredient that you can identify?" Hemingway replied. "Yes, there is. In order to be a great writer a person must have a built-in, shock-proof crap detector."

It seems to us that, in this response, Hemingway identified an essential survival strategy and the essential function of the schools in today's world. One way of looking at the history of the human group is that it has been a continuing struggle against the veneration of "crap." Our intellectual history is a chronicle of the anguish and suffering of men who tried to help their contemporaries see that some part of their fondest beliefs were misconceptions, faulty assumptions, superstitions, and even outright lies. The mileposts along the road of our intellectual development signal those points at which some person developed a new perspective, a new meaning, or a new metaphor. We have in mind a new education that would set out to cultivate just such people—experts at "crap detecting."

NEIL POSTMAN AND CHARLES WEINGARTNER

*Abridged from Neil Postman and Charles Weingartner, *Teaching as a subversive activity*. Copyright © 1969 by Neil Postman and Charles Weingartner. Reprinted by permission of the publisher, Delacorte Press.

"The medium is the message" implies that the invention of a dichotomy between content and method is both naïve and dangerous. *It implies that the critical content of any learning experience is the method or process through which the learning occurs.* Almost any sensible parent knows this, as does any effective top sergeant. It is not what you say to people that counts; it is what you have them *do*.

● This a critically important point! Let us repeat it. *"It is not what you say to people that counts; it is what you have them do."* A whole theory of pedagogy is implied by this sentence. Yet in how many of your classes is this taken seriously? Could you make constructive suggestions as to how this principle could be better implemented in your courses—including this one!

If most teachers have not yet grasped this idea, it is not for lack of evidence. It may, however, be due to their failure to look in the direction where the evidence can be seen. In order to understand what kinds of behaviors classrooms promote, one must become accustomed to observing what, in fact, students actually *do* in them. What students do in the classroom is what they learn (as Dewey would say), and what they learn to do is the classroom's message (as McLuhan would say). Now, what is it that students *do* in the classroom? Well, mostly, they sit and listen to the teacher. Mostly, they are required to believe in authorities, or at least pretend to such belief when they take tests. Mostly, they are required to *remember*. They are almost never required to make observations, formulate definitions, or perform any intellectual operations that go beyond repeating what someone else says is true. They are rarely encouraged to ask substantive questions, although they are permitted to ask about administrative and technical details. (How long should the paper be? It is practically unheard of for students to play any role in determining what problems are worth studying or what procedures of inquiry ought to be used. Examine the types of questions teachers ask in classrooms, and you will find that most of them are what might technically be called "convergent questions," but which might more simply be called "Guess what I'm thinking" questions.

It is safe to say that just about the *only* learning that occurs in classrooms is that which is communicated by the structure of the classroom itself. What are these learnings? What are these messages? Here are a few among many, none of which you will ever find officially listed among the aims of teachers:

Passive acceptance is a more desirable response to ideas than active criticism.

Discovering knowledge is beyond the power of students and is, in any case, none of their business.

Recall is the highest form of intellectual achievement, and the collection of unrelated "facts" is the goal of education.

The voice of authority is to be trusted and valued more than independent judgment.

One's own ideas and those of one's classmates are inconsequential.

Feelings are irrelevant in education.

There is always a single, unambiguous Right Answer to a question.

English is not History and History is not Science and Science is not Art and Art is not Music, and Art and Music are minor subjects and English, History and Science major sub-

jects, and a subject is something you "take" and, when you have taken it, you have "had" it, and if you have "had" it, you are immune and need not take it again. (The Vaccination Theory of Education?)

What all of us have learned (and how difficult it is to unlearn it!) is that it is not important that our utterances satisfy the demands of the question (or of reality), but that they satisfy the demands of the classroom environment. Teacher asks. Student answers. Have you ever heard of a student who replied to a question, "Does *anyone* know the answer to that question?" or "I don't understand what I would have to do in order to find an answer," or "I have been asked that question before and, frankly, I've never understood what it meant?" Such behavior would invariably result in some form of penalty and is, of course, scrupulously avoided, except by "wise guys." Thus, students learn not to value it. They get the message. And yet few teachers consciously articulate such a message. It is not part of the "content" of their instruction. No teacher ever said: "Don't value uncertainty and tentativeness. Don't question questions. Above all, don't think." The message is communicated quietly, insidiously, relentlessly, and effectively through the structure of the classroom: through the role of the teacher, the role of the student, the rules of their verbal game, the rights that are assigned, the arrangements made for communication, the "doings" that are praised or censured. In other words, the medium is the message.

Now, if you reflect on the fact that most classroom environments are managed so that such questions as these will not be asked, you can become very depressed. Consider, for example, where "knowledge" comes from. It isn't just *there* in a book, waiting for someone to come along and "learn" it. Knowledge is produced in response to questions. And new knowledge results from the asking of new questions; quite often new questions about old questions. Here is the point: *Once you have learned how to ask questions –relevant and appropriate and substantial questions–you have learned how to learn and no*

● Something to think about?

---

one can keep you from learning whatever you want or need to know.

● It seems so obvious that Postman and Weingartner are right here—after all they even put it in italics—but let us carry it a bit further. Ask yourself the question, "Why is it important to learn to ask questions?" What are some of your answers? There are many "answers" (at least tentative ones) to be found in your library. Do you know how to use it? Do you know how to use various "search aids" such as *Psychological Abstracts?* Ask your professor to teach you! Do you see how this is related to "learning-by-doing" rather than "learning-by-saying?"

COMMENT: ON LEARNING TO LEARN

Of what does the capacity to educate oneself consist? It means that a person has both the desire

and the capacity to learn for himself, to dig out what he needs to know, as well as the capacity to judge what is worth learning. It means, too, that one can think for himself, so that he is dependent on neither the opinions nor the facts of others, and that he uses that capacity to think about his own education, which means to think about his own nature and his place in the universe—about the meaning of life and of knowledge and of the relations between them.

CHARLES E. SILBERMAN

In sum..., the process that characterizes school environments: what students are restricted to (solely and even vengefully) is the process of memorizing (partially and temporarily) somebody else's answers to somebody else's questions. It is staggering to consider the implications of this fact. The most important intellectual ability man has yet developed—the art and science of asking questions—is not taught in school! Moreover, it is *not* "taught" in the most devastating way possible: by arranging the environment so that significant question asking is not valued. It is doubtful if you can think of many schools that include question asking, or methods of inquiry, as part of their curriculum. But even if you knew a hundred that did, there would be little cause for celebration unless the classrooms were arranged so that students could *do* question asking; not talk about it, read about it, be told about it. Asking questions is behavior. If you don't do it, you don't learn it. It really is as simple as that.

• Asking questions is not as hard as you might think—let yourself go and give it a try.

• Question your psychology prof. Ask him why . . . Write the questions below.

• Ask yourself questions about what is happening to you in your life now outside of the university as well as questions about what you are experiencing this year in the university.

8 WHAT EDUCATION IS: EXCELLENCE AND RELEVANCE*

JEROME S. BRUNER

What Education Is Education seeks to develop the power and sensibility of mind. On the one hand, the educational process transmits to the individual some part of the accumulation of knowledge, style, and values that constitutes the culture of a people. In doing so, it shapes the impulses, the consciousness, and the way of life of the individual. But education must also seek to develop the processes of intelligence so that the individual is capable of going beyond the cultural ways of his social world, able to innovate in however modest a way so that he can create an interior culture of his own. For whatever the art, the science, the literature, the history, and the geography of a culture, each man must be his own artist, his own scientist, his own historian, his own navigator. No person is master of the whole culture; indeed, this is almost a defining characteristic of that form of social memory that we speak of as culture. Each man lives a fragment of it. To be whole, he must create his own version of the world, using that part of his cultural heritage he was made his own through education.

For me the yeast of education is the idea of excellence, and that comprises as many forms as there are individuals to develop a personal image of excellence. The school must have as one of its principal functions the nurturing of images of excellence.

A detached conception of idealized excellence is not enough. A doctrine of excellence, to be effective, must be translatable into the individual lives of those who come in contact with it.

I believe, then, that the school must also contain men and women who, in their own way, seek

*Abridged by permission of the publishers from Jerome Bruner, *On knowing: Essays for the left hand* (pp. 115, 119–124), Cambridge, Mass.: Belknap Press of Harvard University Press, copyright 1962, by the President and Fellows of Harvard College.

and embody excellence. This does not mean that we shall have to staff our schools with men and women of great genius but that the teacher must embody in his own approach to learning a pursuit of excellence.

The Subject Matter of Education The issue of subject matter in education can be resolved only by reference to one's view of the nature of knowledge. Knowledge is a model we construct to give meaning and structure to regularities in experience. The organizing ideas of any body of knowledge are inventions for rendering experience economical and connected. We invent concepts such as force in physics, the bond in chemistry, motives in psychology, style in literature as means to the end of comprehension.

The history of culture is the history of the development of great organizing ideas, ideas that inevitably stem from deeper values and points of view about man and nature. The power of great organizing concepts is in large part that they permit us to understand and sometimes to predict or change the world in which we live. But their power lies also in the fact that ideas provide instruments for experience.

Indeed, we know now, after a quarter of a century of research on perception, that experience is not to be had directly and neatly, but filtered through the programmed readiness of our senses. The program is constructed with our expectations and these are derived from our models or ideas about what exists and what follows what.

From this, two convictions follow. The first is that the structure of knowledge—its connectedness and the derivations that make one idea follow from another—is the proper emphasis in education. For it is structure, the great conceptual inventions that bring order to the congeries of disconnected observations, that gives meaning to what we may learn and makes possible the opening up of new realms of experience. The second conviction is that the unity of knowledge is to be found within knowledge itself, if the knowledge is worth mastering.

To attempt a justification of subject matter, as Dewey did, in terms of its relation to the child's social activities is to misunderstand what knowledge is and how it may be mastered. The significance of the concept of commutativity in mathematics does not derive from the social insight that two houses with fourteen people in each is not the same as fourteen houses with two people in each. Rather, it inheres in the power of the idea to create a way of thinking about number that is lithe and beautiful and immensely generative.

● From the section of your basic psychology text which discusses the information processing ability, you can learn about "the magic number 7 plus or minus 2." If it is not in your text, ask your professor what it means. Can you make a connection between that concept and Bruner's emphasis on the importance of making *connections* and developing *cognitive structures?* Write what you think the connection is below.

●

● How could you train yourself to have the "mind set" which helps you to continually look for connections?

This is one consideration of cognitive economy, that is paramount. One cannot "cover" any subject in full, not even in a lifetime, if coverage means visiting all the facts and events and morsels. Subject matter presented so as to emphasize its structure will perforce be of that generative kind that permits reconstruction of the details or, at very least, prepares a place into which the details, when encountered, can be put.

Finally, it is as true today as it was when Dewey wrote that one cannot foresee the world in which the child we educate will live. Informed powers of mind and a sense of potency in action are the only instruments we can give the child that

will be invariable across the transformations of time and circumstance. The succession of studies that we give the child in the ideal school need be fixed in only one way: whatever is introduced, let it be pursued continuously enough to give the student a sense of the power of mind that comes from a deepening of understanding. It is this, rather than any form of extensive coverage, that matters most.

The Nature of Method The process and the goal of education are one and the same thing. The goal of education is disciplined understanding; that is the process as well.

Insofar as possible, a method of instruction

should have the objective of leading the child to discover for himself. Telling children and then testing them on what they have been told inevitably has the effect of producing bench-bound learners whose motivation for learning is likely to be extrinsic to the task—pleasing the teacher, getting into college, artificially maintaining self-esteem. The virtues of encouraging discovery are of two kinds. In the first place, the child will make what he learns his own, will fit his discovery into the interior world of culture that he creates for himself. Equally important, discovery and the sense of confidence it provides is the proper reward for learning. It is a reward that, moreover, strengthens the very process that is at the heart of education —disciplined inquiry.

The Problem of Relevance This brings us directly to the problem of relevance, that thumb-worn symbol in the modern debate about the relation of education to man and society. The word had two senses. The first is that what is taught should have some bearing on the grievous problems facing the world, the solutions of which may affect our survival as a species. This is social relevance. Then there is personal relevance. What is taught should be self-rewarding by some existential criterion of being "real," or "exciting," or "meaningful." The two kinds of relevance are not necessarily the same, alas.

I am with those who criticize the university for having too often ignored the great issues of life in our time. But I do not believe that the cure in the classroom is to be endlessly concerned with the immediacy of such issues—sacrificing social relevance to personal excitement. Relevance, in either of its senses, depends upon what you know that permits you to move toward goals you care about. It is this kind of "means-ends" knowledge that brings into a single focus the two kinds of relevance, personal and social. It is then that we bring knowledge and conviction together, and it is this

requirement that faces us in the revolution in education through which we are going.

I have suggested that the human, species-typical way in which we increase our powers comes through converting external bodies of knowledge embodied in the culture into generative rules for thinking about the world and about ourselves. It is by this means that we are finally able to have convictions that have some consequences for the broader good. Yet I am convinced, as are so many others, that the way in which our ordinary educational activities are carried out will not equip men with effective convictions. I would like to propose, in the light of what I have said about skill and intentionality, and to honor what I believe about the two faces of relevance, that there be a very basic change in pedagogical practice along the following lines.

First, education must no longer strike an exclusive posture of neutrality and objectivity. Knowledge, we know now as never before, is power. This does not mean that there are not canons of truth or that the idea of proof is not a precious one. Rather, let knowledge as it appears in our schooling be put into the context of action and commitment. The lawyer's brief, a parliamentary strategy, or a town planner's subtle balancings are as humanly important a way of knowing as a physicist's theorem. Gathering together the data for the indictment of a society that tolerates, in the United States, the ninth rank in infant mortality when it ranks first in gross national product—this is not an exercise in radical invective but in the mobilizing of knowledge in the interest of conviction that change is imperative. Let the skills of problem solving be given a chance to develop on problems that have an inherent passion—whether racism, crimes in the street, pollution, war and aggression, or marriage and the family.

Second, education must concentrate more on the unknown and the speculative, using the known and established as a basis for extrapolation. This will create two problems immediately. One is that the shift in emphasis will shake the traditional role of the teacher as the one who knows, contrasting with the student who does not. The other is that, in

*The remaining portion of this selection is abridged and reprinted from *The relevance of education* by Jerome S. Bruner. Edited by Anita Gil. By permission of W. W. Norton & Company, Inc. Copyright © 1971 by Jerome S. Bruner.

any body of men who use their minds at all, one usually gets a sharp division between what Joseph Agassis (1969) calls "knowers" and "seekers." Knowers are valuers of firm declarative statements about the state of things. Seekers regard such statements as invitations to speculation and doubt. The two groups often deplore each other. Just as surely as authority will not easily be given up by teachers, so too will knowers resist the threatening speculations of seekers. Revolution does have difficulties!

With respect to encouraging speculative extrapolation, I would particularly want to concentrate on "subjects" or "disciplines" that have a plainly visible growing edge, particularly the life sciences and the human sciences: human and behavioral biology, politics, economics, sociology, and psychology, organized around problems which have no clearly known solutions. The reward for working one's way through the known is to find a new question on the other side, formulated in a new way. Let it be plain that inquiry of this kind can be made not just through "the social sciences" but equally via the arts, literature, and philosophy, as well as by the syntactical sciences of logic and mathematical analysis.

Third, share the process of education with the learner. There are few things so exciting as sensing where one is trying to go, what one is trying to get hold of, and then making progress toward it. The reward of mastering something is the mastery, not the assurance that some day you will make more money or have more prestige. There must be a system of counseling that assures better than now that the learner knows what he is up to and that he has some hand in choosing the goal. This may be raising the spectre problem of totally individualized instruction. But learning *is* individual, no matter how many pupils there are per teacher. I am only urging that in the organization of curricula, units, and lessons, there be option provided as to how a student sets his goal for learning.

Fourth and finally, I would like to propose that as a transition we divide the curriculum into a Monday-Wednesday-Friday section that continues during the transition to work with what has been best in our school curricula up to this point, and a Tuesday-Thursday curriculum that is as experimental as we care to make it—seminars, political analyses, the development of position papers on school problems, "problem-finding" in the local community, you name it. Let it be as controversial as needs be. We are lacking diversity in experiment and can afford controversy in order to get it. Tuesday and Thursday need be no respecter of conventional teaching qualification. Indeed, it might provide the proper occasion for bringing outsiders into the school and "hooking" them with its challenge. I would also want to bring to the school—other than the conventional media of learning—film, political debate, and the carrying out of plans of action, all to be subject to scrutiny, discussion and criticism.

I am no innocent to matters of schooling and the conduct of instructional enterprises. What I am proposing involves a vast change in our thinking about schools, about growth, about the assumption of responsibility in the technological world as we know it. I have wanted to highlight the role of intention and goal directedness in learning and the acquisition of knowledge, and the conversion of skill into the management of one's own enterprises. The objective is to produce skill in our citizens, skill in the achieving of goals of personal significance, and of assuring a society in which personal significance can still be possible.

COMMENT: AN EDUCATIONAL THEORY IS A POLITICAL THEORY

A theory of instruction is a political theory in the proper sense that it derives from consensus concerning the distribution of power within the society—who shall be educated and to fulfill what roles? In the very same sense, pedagogical theory must surely derive from a conception of economics, for where there is division of labor within the society and an exchange of goods and services for wealth and prestige, then *how* people are educated and in what number and with what constraints on the use of resources are all relevant issues. The psychologist or educator who formulates pedagogical theory without regard to the political, economic, and social setting of the educational process courts triviality and merits being ignored in the community and in the classroom.

JEROME S. BRUNER

9 EDUCATION AND EQUALITY*

CHARLES E. SILBERMAN

What is it in the schools that leads to failure? Professor Robert K. Merton of Columbia University, one of the most distinguished American sociologists, suggested the answer in his theory of the "self-fulfilling prophecy."[1] Stated as simply as possible, the theory holds that in many, if not most, situations, people tend to do what is expected of them—so much so, in fact, that even a false expectation may evoke the behavior that makes it seem true. As Merton formulated the theory in his essay, "men respond not only to the objective features of a situation, but also, and at times primarily, to the meaning this situation has for them. And once they have assigned some meaning to the situation," their subsequent behavior, and the behavior of others, are both determined by it. Whether the meaning they ascribe to the situation is initially true or false is beside the point; the definition evokes the behavior that makes it come true. "The specious validity of the self-fulfilling prophecy," as Merton put it, "perpetuates a reign of error."[2]

Thus, a teacher's *expectation* can and does quite literally affect a student's *performance*. The teacher who assumes that her students cannot learn is likely to discover that she has a class of children who are indeed unable to learn; yet another teacher, working with the same class but without the same expectation, may discover that she has a class of interested learners. The same obtains with respect to behavior: the teacher who assumes that her students will be disruptive is likely to have a disruptive class on her hands. "You see, really and truly, apart from the things anyone can pick up [the dressing and the proper way of speaking, and so on]," Eliza Doolittle explains in Shaw's *Pygmalion*, "the difference between a lady and a flower girl is not how she behaves, but how she's treated. I shall always be a flower girl to Professor Higgins, because he always treats me as a flower girl, and always will; but I know I can be a lady to you, because you always treat me as a lady, and always will."

In most slum schools, the children are treated as flower girls. One cannot spend any substantial amount of time visiting schools in ghetto slum areas, in fact, be they black, Puerto Rican, Mexican American, or Indian American, without being struck by the modesty of the expectations teachers, supervisors, principals, and superintendents have for the students in their care.

[1] Robert K. Merton, "The Self-Fulfilling Prophecy," *The Antioch Review*, Summer 1948 (reprinted in Merton, *Social Theory and Social Structure*, New York: Free Press, revised and enlarged edition, 1957).

[2] For a review of the voluminous literature documenting the phenomenon, cf. Robert Rosenthal and Lenore Jacobson, *Pygmalion in the Classroom*, New York: Holt, Rinehart, and Winston, 1968, Chapters 1 to 4. The rest of the volume is a report of an experiment designed to show that raising teachers' expectations about some children's intellectual capacity results in higher achievement by these children. The hypothesis is reasonable and probably correct; unfortunately, the data presented are defective and contradictory, and so do not, by themselves, support the conclusion. Cf. the review by Robert L.

Thorndike in the *Teachers College Record*, Vol. 70, No. 8, May 1969.

*Abridged from C. E. Silberman, *Crisis in the classroom*, New York: Random House, 1970. Reprinted by permission of the publisher.

COMMENT: TEACHERS' EXPECTATIONS —A SELF-FULFILLING PROPHECY

Teachers know the type of class they are expected to be teaching.[a] Before the teacher has even met his students his expectations of bright, mediocre, or dull individuals are set.

Even in schools which have abandoned tracking, the teacher is given a set of record cards by his supervisor which document the child's school life as perceived by his previous teachers. These cards usually contain achievement and I.Q. scores, personality evaluations, descriptions of conferences with the students' parents, judgments about his behavior in class and "study habits." Difficult pupils are identified as well as good (i.e., conforming and performing) ones. The record cards are probably designed not only as analyses of their pupils' careers at school, but as warnings to teachers on what to expect.

When the teacher meets his class on the first day of the school year, he is armed with all of this "professional" knowledge. Anticipating a dull class, for example, a teacher may have spent several weeks preparing simple exercises to keep his students busy. On the other hand, faced with the prospect of teaching a bright class, he may have found a new and challenging textbook or devised some ingenious scientific experiments.

If the record cards indicate that several pupils are particularly troublesome or, what is more threatening, "disturbed," the teacher will single them out as soon as they enter the room and treat them differently from the other pupils. He may do the same with bright students or ones rumored to be wise, funny, lazy, violent, scheming, deceitful. . . . The students will sense this and act in the manner expected of them. Thus the teacher traps both himself and his pupils into repeating patterns that have been set for years.

Expectations influence behavior in subtle ways:

a successful though nervous and unhappy student may try to relax. His teacher says, "What's the matter? You're not yourself this week." This may produce feelings of guilt in the student, who then drives himself to succeed in spite of feeling that the price he is paying for academic achievement may be excessive.

A "difficult" student tries to make a new start and is quiet and obedient. His teacher responds to this behavior by saying, "You're off to a good start this year," and so informs the student that a bad start was expected of him. The student becomes angry and defiant.

A supposedly dull student gives a correct answer in class and is praised excessively. He is embarrassed and becomes withdrawn.

Even in kindergarten a teacher will have expectations. Some children are "disadvantaged," others have language problems. The teacher anticipates that they may not do well. Others come from intellectual or privileged homes and if they don't perform well something must be wrong.

Teachers' expectations have a tendency to become self-fulfilling.[b] "Bad" classes tend to act badly, and "gifted" classes tend to respond to the special consideration that they expect to be given to them if they perform in a "superior" way.

HERBERT KOHL

Prejudice is not the only problem; expectations can be lowered by empathy as well as by distaste. Indeed, one has the uneasy feeling that many of the books, courses, and conferences designed to sensitize teachers and administrators to the problems of the "disadvantaged" have backfired. By learning why black (or Puerto Rican, Mexican American, or Indian American) youngsters fail through no fault of their own, teachers learn to understand and to sympathize with failure—and thereby to expect it. James C. Conant's widely hailed volume,

[a]In some Union contracts there are even provisions for rotation of teachers from top to bottom, through the middle to the top again.

[b]For a study of self-fulfilling prophecies, see *Pygmalion in the Classroom: Teacher Expectation and the Pupil's Intellectual Ability*, by Robert Rosenthal and Lenore Jacobson, Holt, Rinehart & Winston, 1968.

Slums and Suburbs, which called attention to the "social dynamite" contained in the failures of ghetto education, provides a nice case in point, for the book amounted to a plea to educators to lower their sights. "One lesson to be drawn from visiting and contrasting a well-to-do suburb and a slum is all important for understanding American public education," Dr. Conant announced on the first page. *"The lesson is that to a considerable degree what a school should do and can do is determined by the status and ambitions of the families being served."* [Emphasis his]

When schoolmen do try to adjust the school to fit the students' needs, therefore—for example, by creating separate curricula for the "disadvantaged"—all too often they compound rather than relieve the problem. Thus many schools have tried to follow Conant's recommendation that "in a heavily urbanized and industrialized free society the educational experiences of youth should fit their subsequent employment." But as James Coleman points out, the recommendation "takes as *given* what should be problematic—that a given boy is going into a given post-secondary occupational or educational path. It is one thing to take as given that approximately 70 percent of an entering high school freshman class will not attend college; but to assign a *particular child* to a curriculum designed for that 70 percent closes off for that child the opportunity to attend college."[c] [Emphasis his]

The problem begins well before high school; it starts, in fact, in the first grade. The anthropologist Eleanor Burke Leacock has described with exquisite detail how different are the expectations regarding both academic achievement and behavior among teachers in middle-class and lower-class schools, and how, in all kinds of subtle ways, these expectations serve to teach lower-class children *not* to learn.[d] In the study she directed, teams of observers studied classrooms and interviewed

teachers and students in schools representing four socioeconomic categories: low-income black, low-income white, middle-income black, and middle-income white. They discovered, as Professor Leacock writes, that "even with the best will in the world and the application of considerable skill" in their teaching, teachers "unwittingly help perpetuate a system of inequalities" by transmitting to the children "in myriad ways the message: 'This is your station in society; act, perform, talk, *learn* according to it and no more.' " [Emphasis hers]

These expectations are transmitted to the children in all sorts of ways. Like almost everyone who studies ghetto schools, Leacock and her observers were struck by the liveliness and eager interest children in the lower grades displayed, and by the passivity and apathy that is evident later on; in the schools they studied, the children's interest and eagerness had disappeared by the fifth grade.

The reason was not hard to find: the teachers in the low-income black school did remarkably little to evoke the children's interest. A careful count of the frequency and nature of teacher-student interchanges, for example, showed that teachers in the low-income classrooms discussed the curriculum with their students less than half as often as did the teachers in the middle-income rooms. There is considerable truth, in short, to Kenneth Clark's insistence that black children do not learn because they are not taught.[e]

Low-income students are discouraged from learning in another way. The teachers in the low-income black school not only taught less, they also evaluated their students' work less than half as frequently as the teachers in the middle-class rooms. More important, perhaps, their evaluations were almost always negative; in the low-income black classes, teachers made negative comments about their students three times as often as they made positive ones. In the middle-class rooms, by contrast, teachers offered positive evaluations more often than negative ones. The result, as

[c]James S. Coleman, "The Concept of Equality of Educational Opportunity," in Harvard Educational Review, *Equal Educational Opportunity.*
[d]Eleanor Burke Leacock, *Teaching and Learning in City Schools,* New York: Basic Books, 1969.
[e]Kenneth B. Clark, *Dark Ghetto,* New York: Harper & Row, 1965.

Leacock writes, is that by the fifth grade, "the low expectations for their achievement, combined with the lack of challenge in the classroom, had taken their toll. The children fidgeted listlessly, looked distractedly and aimlessly here and there, and waited until something captured their attention." The classroom observers, Professor Leacock writes, "were struck by the fact that standards in the low-income Negro classrooms were low for both achievement and behavior." This was not what they had expected to find, for "they had assumed that the middle-income schools would stress achievement and that the lower-income schools would emphasize behavior. Yet it was in the middle-income schools, both Negro and white," the researchers discovered, "that the strictest demands were made" on behavior, as well as on achievement, with students expected to adhere to high standards for everything from "self-control" and "being nice" to posture and such inane teacher idiosyncrasies as "Are our thumbs in the right place?" In the low-income schools, the demands were fewer and more modest, with the emphasis, as noted earlier, on "learning to take orders," and the expectation was that disorder would prevail. As often as not, it did.

It is a gross oversimplification, therefore, to attribute the failures of the slum school to lower-class students' inability to understand or unwillingness to accept middle-class values. What teachers and administrators communicate to lower-class students, Leacock suggests, in what is perhaps her most useful insight, is not middle-class *values* but middle-class *attitudes* toward lower-class people and their role in society. The school, she writes, conveys *"a middle-class image of how working-class children are and how they should be*—an image which emphasizes obedience, respect, and conscientiousness . . . rather than ability, responsibility, and initiative, and which expects . . . unruliness with regard to behavior and apathy with regard to curriculum." [Emphasis hers] By conveying this image to their students, "teachers perpetuate the very behavior they decry." And the behavior, in turn, confirms the teachers' initial expectations, thereby perpetuating

the reign of error for still another generation of students.

The teachers whom Leacock & Company interviewed and observed, it is important to realize, "were all experienced, hardworking, and capable people who were trying to do their best for the children in their classrooms within the limits of their training and situations." So far as the observers could tell, the teachers were free from racial prejudice (as free, that is to say, as anyone growing up in the United States can be). Some of the teachers were themselves black; those who taught in low-income black schools expected as little from their students as did their white colleagues. Their prejudices, in short, were prejudices of class.

Where racial and ethnic prejudice exists, however, the vicious circle of low expectations = low achievement = low expectations becomes even more vicious. And such prejudice does exist; there is little reason to expect teachers to be any freer from prejudice than the rest of us. In all too many schools, therefore, minority-group children are exposed to a steady flow of insult and humiliation that blocks their learning in a number of ways. Experiencing prejudice reinforces the sense of inferiority, even of worthlessness, which the culture and society outside the school instills. It destroys the incentive to learn, persuading students that there is no use trying, since the cards are stacked against them anyway. And it evokes a burning anger and hostility against the school that makes students want to leave as soon as they can, and that diverts their energies from learning into a search for ways of striking back.

Teachers and administrators convey their prejudice in a variety of ways, some subtle, some not so subtle, all damaging.

ITEM A sixth-grade class in a racially mixed school. A black girl calls out the answer to a question the teacher had asked of the entire class. "Don't you call out," the teacher responds. "You sit where I put you and be quiet." A few minutes later, when a blond-haired, blue-eyed girl calls out an answer to another question, the teacher responds, "Very good, Annette; that's good thinking."

ITEM A fifth-grade class in a racially-mixed school. A black youngster has his hand raised to ask a question; before the teacher can respond, the principal, who is visiting, tells the child, "Put your dirty hand down and stop bothering the teacher with questions."

Sometimes—more frequently than those outside the schools realize, and more frequently than those inside the schools are willing to admit—prejudice manifests itself in harsh and even brutal ways.

ITEM An assistant principal, monitoring the main corridor in a large urban high school, sees a black student, one leg in a cast, hobbling along on crutches. He waits until the student has reached his destination, and then orders him to return to the other end of the two-block-long corridor and retrace his steps. The student had been walking on the left side of the corridor, and an obscure and never-before enforced school regulation requires students to walk on the right side.

Black children are not the only ones who are harmed in these ways. In California and the Southwest, prejudice against Mexican Americans is almost as great; teachers, administrators, school boards, and even state legislatures and boards of education convey their contempt for these youngsters and their parents by forbidding the use of Spanish anywhere in the schools. Until it was repealed in the late 1960s, Section 288 of the Texas State Penal Code made it illegal for a teacher, principal, or school superintendent to teach or conduct school business in any language but English; Texas tradition makes it illegal for students to use Spanish.[f]

ITEM In a South Texas school, children are forced to kneel in the playground and beg forgiveness if they are caught talking to each other in Spanish; some teachers require students using the forbidden language to kneel before the entire class.

ITEM In a Tuscon, Arizona, elementary school classroom, children who answer a question in Spanish are required to come up to the teacher's desk and drop pennies in a bowl—one penny for every Spanish word. "It works!" the teacher boasts. "They come from poor families, you know."

The reasons for failure are clear enough. But is success possible? Are there any grounds, other than blind faith, for believing that the schools *can* educate children from lower-class and minority-group homes, that they *can* reduce the disparities in academic achievement attributable to poverty and ethnicity?

● If you take seriously the waste of human potential which results from debilitating environments of lower-class minority groups, and if you regard education as an important force for social change, then you must require yourself to do some serious thinking about how the present educational structures serve to maintain the self-fulfilling prophecy! What can you do in your situation in terms of practical action? Write down some things you could do and some information you would need to be an effective "change agent."

[f]Stan Steiner, "La Raza: The Mexican-Americans," *The Center Forum*, Vol. 4, No. 1, September 1969. The following items are also taken from that article.

• Think about your own behavior and that of your peers and professors to see if you can detect instances of the self-fulfilling prophecy. Describe in the space provided below one such "item."

• Think of some ways that you may have profited or suffered by your teacher's "self-fulfilling" image of you and your potential. List them below and discuss them with friends in your class.

10 TOUGH AND TENDER LEARNING*

DAVID NYBERG and DONALD H. DE LAY

In the fourteenth century, before books became an available public commodity, scholars stood before large crowds of students reading from manuscript scrolls. The students were expected to memorize what they heard. In the twentieth century we have available not only all the books that we could possibly read in a lifetime, but an incredibly rich resource of other media and travel opportunities as well; yet our teachers still stand in front of large crowds of students and read from scrolls (albeit somewhat more up to date). The students are still expected to memorize what they hear. In six hundred years there have been a few relatively brief flurries of concern about how people learn, but the basic and ancient model of lecture-memorize-test is still, incredibly enough, accepted as *the* way.

Classrooms are so far out of step with what is going on in the world outside (a discrepancy with which every student and teacher is familiar) that they have virtually become halls for an habitual conformity game. A child learns from his elders to play the school game in order to dissipate fear —fear of parent and teacher reprisal, of peer ridicule, of some sort of abstract failure to keep within the horizontal blue lines and the vertical red line margins, and, most sad of all, fear of making a mistake (which is to say, in many cases, being inventive). The fear comes largely from the same reprehensible adult behavior that provoked Alfred Adler to define education as "the process of transferring the notes of the teacher to the notebook of the pupil without passing through the head of either." He was joined in his outrage by Albert Einstein, who quipped that "Education is *what's left* when you have forgotten everything you learned in school."

*Abridged from D. Nyberg, *Tough and tender learning*, Palo Alto: National Press Books, 1971. Reprinted from *Tough and tender learning* by D. Nyberg by permission of National Press Books.

It would be frighteningly easy to go on deriding the traditions of institutionalized education in this country, but the more important task is formulating a sound basis for improving learning opportunities. We cannot improve education without changing it, and we are reluctant to begin because changing always involves a risk. However, in light of the state of education now, a refusal to risk change seems a gross irresponsibility, for it means perpetuating a severe and general failure. Six hundred years is enough time for caution.

Our essential concern is for human beings. The assumption underlying the presentation of this theory is that schools abound with good people who really want to do a better job of helping students, who really care about their work, and who are willing to spend the vast amount of energy necessary for breaking through into improvement. If this were not true, we would have no reason for hope at all.

BASES FOR LEARNING

Hundreds of statements have been made about what the purpose of school is; to us, the best one is simply *to help students want to learn*. What we mean by learning is a change in personal behavior of which the person is aware. It may seem redundant if not naive to say this, yet many schools operate as if learning were a function of information accumulation alone. Learning, in our opinion, is a product of two functions: acquiring information and, more important, discovering and developing *personal meaning*. It is the combination of information plus its personal meaning to the learner that creates a behavioral change.

Learning = Information + *Personal Meaning* → Behavioral Change

Too often formal learning is artificially terminated by tests at the informational level. The behavioral change resulting from preparation for such tests comes in the form of finger movements on a test paper. Any first year algebra student can tell you how fast this imprint of "learning" fades and how significant it remains to him.

If we are serious about improving schools, we must look carefully at what we believe about learning, for we cannot make a solid case for change on any other basis. For the most part, learning is a unique, lonesome, personal process, even in a crowded classroom. The number of variances that exist in one human being, let alone among a group of people, is fantastic. These variances in multiple combinations account for differences in the ways people learn. It follows that if we want to be as effective as we can in facilitating learning, we cannot afford to ignore individual differences. To "individualize instruction" is a valid and desirable goal. What is astonishing, however, is the frequency of its verbalization contrasted with the paucity of its practice. We seem to find comfort in talking about better things, good things, even though we haven't the courage to do them.

● Right on! In our own attempts to reform the university teaching/learning process we are often almost totally stymied by colleagues or administrators who pay lip service to "individual differences" in theory but refuse to acknowledge them in their own practice. Indeed, they often block attempted reforms by insisting on "standards" and standardizations based on the assumption that students *should* desire the same goals and have the same interests and values that he (or *she)* has.

Just as we tend to fear the unknown, change of any sort, we also tend to avoid personal matters in education. Yet learning is a personal matter. We must push ourselves to find ways of dealing with the ambiguous and of overcoming our fear of approaching people on a personal, individual level—the level at which we find personal meaning.

One obstacle to change is the traditional ethos or context of assumptions in which learning takes place. Currently most schools are fashioned after military or penal models which are basically control-oriented. The prime assumption is that persons within the confines of the institution need control because they are untrustworthy. This attitude is surely not conducive to inventive, risky, highly personalized behavior, which is to say, learning. For personal learning to take place in a school, the institution must be operated in such a way as to encourage teachers and students to act on the belief that learning and independence are more important than control. If this action is not permitted by the administration, any attempts to improve learning will be crushed into insignificance. Personal meaning cannot flourish in a tightly controlled, mistrustful context which does not allow for ambiguity and surprise.

Student Choice   This basis for learning is easily abused. There is nothing more restrictive for a learner than to be given alternatives of only token dimensions (for example, between A and a), or to be given no choice at all. It is important that a teacher provide as broad an array of alternatives as practicable at every juncture of learning for every student. This requires a lot of work. It is important, however, so that the learner feels correctly that he has the *right* to select what he *wants* to learn. One of the teacher's jobs is to inform the student of what probable consequences he will face once he begins acting on his choice. In this way the student takes responsibility (or at least shares it with the teacher) for what he does, for what he wants to do. This is a much different form of behavior than following rules and assignments against one's wishes. Alternatives are important, but student selection is vital for allowing learning to become a personal process.

Active Involvement   It is not what we put into a student through his auditory canals but what he displays through various behaviors that makes the difference in learning. To require a student to sit passively absorbing (or ignoring) teacher-talk is to encourage all forms of passive, nonproductive, sedentary behavior. Learning is essentially an active process, a *behavior* change. The behavior change may take many different forms, but insofar as the change is a consequence of learning (as we use the term), the new behavior will tend to indicate that an integration is taking place between a personal sense of meaning and action. It will be apparent that a connection is forming between character and conduct, belief and behavior, integrity and individuality. In other words, the learner will show that he knows what he is doing and that he feels responsible for his behavior. Sitting quietly and listening dutifully is passive and therefore a deterrent to learning as we have defined it. Personal meaning cannot evolve when a person is not involved in what is going on around him. It is difficult to be involved when not allowed to be active; without involvement choice is irrelevant. The only thing you can get out of a sponge is what you allow it to soak up, and you generally have to squeeze pretty hard to get back what you already had. The sponge, by the way, is left empty again.

One of the fundamental skills that we want students to have is verbal dexterity—the ability to handle thoughts in terms of words. We want them to learn how to talk. Why then are teacher talking and student quietude the core elements of teaching? Why do we expect a student to learn how to talk when we are forever telling him to be quiet? Most teacher talk is lecturing that has a negative effect on learning. It prevents active involvement on the part of the learner.

● You probably find yourself agreeing with these assertions, but be careful to avoid the "rhetoric trap" and the "overgeneralization trap." Your own experience will also tell you that you *have* learned and incorporated ideas which were first presented in lectures. While "the lecture" may well have the disadvantage

of reducing active involvement, it *may* have other advantages. Can you think of any? Perhaps the real problem is not the lecture *method* but the lecture *system* in which almost all of a student's "educational" experience is based on the lecture method. Lectures do seem to be effective devices for doing certain things—(What? you ask incredulously.) Look it up, find out the facts for yourself.

Inquiry The power for learning resides in keeping questions open. A rhetoric of conclusions presented in rapid-fire style does not provoke inquiring behavior in students. Instead it deadens curiosity. We should encourage curiosity in learners by raising questions, not by repeating conclusions, for it is in the search for answers (or further questions) by the learner that learning takes place. Learning is an *inquiring process*. We cannot present all pertinent knowledge or information to students—there is too much of it and it changes too rapidly. But we can help equip students with the necessary tools for inquiry so they may learn to deal with change per se and so they may search out their own meanings in terms of their own interests.

COMMENT: THE VIRTUES OF ENCOURAGING DISCOVERY

Insofar as possible, a method of instruction should have the objective of leading the child to discover for himself. Telling children and then testing them on what they have been told inevitably has the effect of producing bench-bound learners whose motivation for learning is likely to be extrinsic to the task—pleasing the teacher, getting into college, artificially maintaining self-esteem. The virtues of encouraging discovery are of two kinds. In the first place, the child will make what he learns his own, will fit his discovery into the interior world of culture that he creates for himself. Equally important, discovery and the sense of confidence it provides is the proper reward for learning. It is a reward that, moreover, strengthens the very process that is at the heart of education —disciplined inquiry.

JEROME S. BRUNER

● Also remember Postman's and Weingartner's views on inquiry. Why not review their basic points now? First see how many you can recall, then skim the article (pp. 65-69) and then review them again.

Intrinsic Reward Perhaps the most talked about issue in learning today is reinforcement or reward. Educators are inundated with a mass of commercially prepared material that is based on the notion that information properly defined, segmented, and sequenced (programmed) can be "learned" more efficiently. The principal idea behind this kind of programmed material is *immediate* reinforcement, that is, the learner is reinforced after each frame or segment of the program. This reinforcement or reward can be anything from a "correct" to a smile to a jellybean, and the process seems to be equally effective with pigeons or people (although pigeons do prefer corn). When properly used, this reinforcement schedule is a powerful adjunct to learning. Most often, however, it is directed at informational levels and seldom does it have any relation to meaning of a personal sort. It seems to us that this issue could stand a reevaluation; teachers have better things to do than act as reinforcement agents with their pockets full of jellybeans or with their faces set to smile.

The main trouble with this type of reward system is that the learner perceives it as extrinsic to himself, in the same way that he perceives the most common reward system used in education, namely, grades. Extrinsically perceived rewards tend to separate and barricade the learner from the subject and from the person directing the process

and issuing the rewards. This may explain, in part, the need for *control* of students in most schools. It is ironic that the most common rewards given by educators drive students away from learning.

Sometime ago one of the authors (Don De Lay) devised a plan (CRAM: Comprehensive Random Achievement Monitor) to monitor student progress on a continuous basis through the duration of a course (De Lay and Nyberg, 1970). The idea was to give a rather short test in several different forms which represented a sample of the entire subject of the course several times during the semester. The questions were randomly selected from a master list of course objectives. By sampling responses to the material by different students at random intervals, he was able to monitor the progress of each student and the entire class. The tests were never announced ahead of time, and the questions sometimes were new and sometimes were repeated because of the way they were selected. The initial student response to this infringement of the rules of the game was silent and vocal disapproval, and in some cases real anger. For several weeks hostility was evident but gradually subsiding. The tests were always returned and never graded; the only marks were small checks on items the student seemed confused about. As the course progressed students began to realize that they were not being evaluated. Instead, the test procedure let them know how they were progressing, where they were weak, and what they already knew, and it gave them some idea of what they might like to pursue next. *Students began to request the test rather than object to it.* Their perceptions of the same test given under the same conditions were reversed from "an extrinsic evaluation" to "an intrinsic feedback"—or knowledge leading toward the learner's own goals. We think Carl Rogers was right in saying that "evaluation destroys communication"; when evaluation was eliminated, communication improved between the teacher and the students and among the students themselves. We are certain that personal communication is intimately related to learning.

When a student feels he is being *assisted* by knowing his own progress toward his own goals, he soon assumes an attitude of wanting to know and enjoying the process of inquiry. Feedback can lead to the joy of learning for its own sake, which in turn leads to the teacher's ultimate goal: to become unnecessary. Learning is a lifelong process. To become a "learning person," a student must consciously pursue learning and be comfortable in an indeterminate, ever-changing, exciting world.

In our efforts to be efficient with student feedback, we run the danger of losing the important human element of *concern*. We have never met a human being who did not respond to what he perceived as authentic, spontaneous concern about his progress or well-being from another person. This authentic human warmth of real concern transposes feedback from something that is merely important to something that is really powerful. It is vital that teachers lower their "stranger level" with students and risk really knowing students as persons. Concern is the heart of the process of human feedback, the force that raises learning to a personalized level. The ultimate loss in teaching is to insulate oneself from students by abstracting them into objects, for every student knows that he really exists right in the "here and now," and that his is a very personal, concrete existence.

COMMENT: SUSPENDED EXPECTATIONS

A teacher in an open classroom needs to cultivate a state of *suspended expectations*. It is not easy. It is easy to believe that a dull class is dull, or a bright class is bright. The words "emotionally disturbed" conjure up frightening images. And it is sometimes a relief to discover that there are good pupils in the class that is waiting for you. Not reading the record cards or ignoring the standing of the class is an act of self-denial; it involves casting aside a crutch when one still believes one can't walk without it. Yet if one wants to develop an open classroom within the context of a school which is essentially totalitarian, such acts of will are necessary.

What does it mean to suspend expectations when one is told that the class one will be teaching is slow, or bright, or ordinary? At the least it means not preparing to teach in any special way or deciding beforehand on the complexity of the materials to be used during a school year. It means that planning does not consist of finding the class's achievement level according to the record cards and tailoring the material to those levels, but rather preparing diverse materials and subjects and discovering from the students as the year unfolds what is relevant to them and what isn't.

Particularly it means not reading I.Q. scores or achievement scores, not discovering who may be a source of trouble and who a solace or even a joy. It means giving your pupils a fresh chance to develop in new ways in your classroom, freed from the roles they may have adopted during their previous school careers. It means allowing children to become who they care to become, and freeing the teacher from the standards by which new pupils had been measured in the past.

There are no simple ways to give up deeply rooted expectations. There are some suggestions, however:

> talk to students outside class
>
> watch them play and watch them live with other young people
>
> play with them—joking games and serious games
>
> talk to them about yourself, what you care about
>
> listen

In these situations the kids may surprise you and reveal rather than conceal, as is usual in the classroom, their feelings, playfulness, and intelligence.

HERBERT KOHL

Respect A great deal of evidence supports the notion that the way a teacher feels about his students and the way each student feels about himself are of critical importance for learning. When a teacher expects a student's achievement level to be high, the student's achievement level tends to be high. When a student is convinced that he *can* learn and that another (the teacher) also is convinced that he can learn, he in fact does learn. Conversely, when neither teacher nor student is confident that a task can be done well, the task probably will not be done well (Rosenthal and Jacobson, 1968).

It is extremely important that teachers believe in each student and that this belief be open enough to be perceived by the student. The expectations of the teacher and of the student tend to be fulfilled. In brief, positive self-respect is a requisite for learning.

All Together Student choice, active involvement, inquiry, intrinsic reward, and respect have been considered one by one as bases for learning. The learning process exists, however, as a complete experience with all its parts in motion, flowing as part of the living person. We have tried to establish the rudiments of a learning theory that acknowledges the flow and individuality of learning. Our theory points to the absence of any cure-alls for education, either in technical systems or structures of thought, including our own. If the freedom and concern that are essential to learning can come alive only in the context of a particular group of people, with all their limitations, then much of our theory may be wrong for that group. Freedom extends to the choice of theories, and we can only hope that each teacher would commit himself to some position in learning he believes in and then do something about it. As he shifts from an intellectual commitment to a behavioral commitment as well, *experiencing* the consequences of his ideas with other persons, then the refinement process of experimental learning can begin.

School presently is a game for most students. If the incentives for playing the game were removed and the potentials for freedom and concern were provided, then students would have good reason to give of themselves, to risk the unknown in learning, and to enjoy the whole process. We believe that the vast majority of adults in public education are willing to risk themselves to make this happen.

11 THE EARLY YEARS AND THE PRESCHOOL STRATEGY*

BURTON L. WHITE

THE EMERGENCE OF DIVERGENCE

Under the variety of early rearing conditions prevalent in modern American homes, divergence with respect to the development of educability and overall competence first becomes manifest sometime during the second year of life, and becomes quite substantial, in many cases, by three years of

*Abridged from Burton L. White, An analysis of excellent early educational practices: Preliminary report. *Interchange*, 1971, 2(2), 71–88. Reprinted by permission of the author and the publisher.

age. We therefore resolved to focus our effort on the process of the development of competence during the second and third years of life. Nothing that we have learned since has changed our confidence in that judgment. In fact, what we have learned has suggested a reasonable explanation.

Two major factors that underlie the effectiveness of early child-rearing practices have suggested themselves in our recent work: the development of locomotor ability (walking) and the emergence of language. For the better part of the first year, the infant's ability to move about is very limited. For the first eight months he usually cannot even crawl. Even when he begins to crawl and then walk about while holding on to a support (cruise) he is considerably less mobile than the 14- to 18-month-old who can usually walk and climb both furniture and stairs. This increased mobility, combined with the curiosity typical of a child this age, produces a very real stress on the caretaker (usually the mother). After all, though he can move about, he is still clumsy and unsure of his large muscle skills; and though he is curious, he is inexperienced, so that razor blades and electric outlets are perceived simply as additional objects to explore. His clumsiness and lack of practiced judgment mean that he is prone to personal injury and also likely to damage breakable household items. None of these factors confront the infant's mother until the end of his first year of life and they become most pressing during the second and third years.

Families adopt a variety of methods of dealing with the toddler. Some "childproof" the home, others follow the child everywhere, others restrict the child's range of mobility, and some use various combinations of these techniques. *It appears from our work that part of the answer to why some children develop better than others during this age period lies in the manner of response of the mother to the emergence of locomotor mobility in her child.*

The second major factor is language. In a manner virtually parallel to locomotor ability, language ability is essentially nil during the first eight or nine months of life, then moves ahead dramatically (especially *receptive* language) during the second and third years of life. What families provide in the way of elaborate or simple, clever or dull, voluminous or sparse language during the first eight months of life is far less likely to influence development than what they do in regard to language in the second and third years of a child's life.

Add to these two factors the impression that few mothers (as yet) have clear ideas about the particular psychological needs of very young infants in cribs and the result is at least a reasonable explanation of why developmental divergence often does not become clear until the second year of life.

The Relevance of Child-Rearing Practices

We want to identify differences in the history of experience of A and C children in order to be able to generate hypotheses about excellent child-rearing practices. Again, I am obliged to counsel the reader about the *tentative* nature of what follows. Much of what I suggest is based on other data we have been collecting and also on the general informal information we have gained because of the many visits we have made to the homes of the families in the study.

The Child at One Year of Age Most one-year-olds appear to resemble each other in a few interesting and fundamental ways. First of all, *perhaps the hallmark of this age is curiosity.* The one-year-old seems genuinely interested in exploring his world throughout the major portion of his day. Aside from meal times, and the need to relieve various occasional physical discomforts, his consuming interest is in exploration. But not all situations are optimal for nurturing that curiosity nor are the rules governing exploratory behavior equivalent across homes. Nonetheless, the one-year-old is primed for expending enormous amounts of energy exploring and learning about his world.

Second, the one-year-old is an incomplete master of his body. The development of gross motor skills such as walking, climbing, and running, along with special variations such as sliding down ramps, and pushing and hauling large objects, will occupy much of his time during the second year of life. In addition, fine motor skills having to do with the use of his hands seem to be at the heart of many of the activities of the second year.

Third, and of especial importance, is that the one-year-old seems to be in the middle of two social developmental processes wherein he is learning gradually about his potential as an *agent,* as an "I" or "me," and about his power over and dependence upon his mother. During the second year, unlike any other time in his life, he seems to develop along these directions in a manner that may produce a vigorous, secure, loving, and healthy social animal or he may take other paths. He may become a modest form of social tyrant by two, whose major orientation during his waking hours is clinging to and dominating his mother, or he may learn that his mother is rather unpredictable, someone to fear while at other times someone who will protect him.

There are many more ideas of possible consequence that could be expressed about the one-year-old but I would rather move at this point to a discussion of the role of the mother in the development of the child of this age.

Mothering, a Vastly Underrated Occupation

I begin with the bold statement that the mother's direct and indirect actions with regard to her one- to three-year-old child are, in my opinion, the most powerful formative factors in the development of a preschool child. Further, I would guess that if a mother does a fine job in the preschool years, subsequent educators such as teachers will find their chances for effectiveness maximized. Finally, I would expect that much of the basic quality of the entire life of an individual is determined by the mother's actions during these two years. Obviously, I could be very wrong about these declarative statements. I make them as very strong hunches that I have become committed to, as a kind of net result of all our inquiries into early development.

Let me quickly add that I believe most women are capable of doing a fine job with their one- to three-year-old children. Our study has convinced us that a mother need not necessarily have even a high school diploma, let alone a college education. Nor does she need to have very substantial economic assets. In addition, it is clear that a good job can be accomplished without a father in the home. In all of these statements I see considerable hope for future generations.

Best Guesses about Most Effective Child-Rearing Practices

Our most effective mothers do not devote the bulk of their day to rearing their young children; most of them are far too busy to do so; many of them, in fact, have part-time jobs. *What they seem to do,* often without knowing exactly why, *is to perform excellently the functions of designer and consultant.* By that I mean they design a physical world, mainly in the home, that is beautifully suited to nurturing the burgeoning curiosity of the one- to three-year-old. It is full of small manipulable, visually detailed objects, some of which were originally designed for young children (toys), others normally used for other purposes (plastic refrigerator containers, bottle caps, baby food jars and covers, shoes, magazines, television and radio knobs, etc.). It contains things to climb such as chairs, benches, sofas, stairs, etc. It includes a rich variety of interesting things to look at such as television, people, and the aforementioned types of physical objects.

In addition to being largely responsible for the type of environment the child has, this mother sets up guides for her child's behavior that seem to play a very important role in these processes. She is generally *permissive and indulgent.* The child is encouraged in the vast majority of his explorations. When the child confronts an interesting or difficult situation, he often turns to his mother for help. Though usually working at some chore, she is generally within earshot. He then goes to her and usually, but *not always,* is *responded to* by his mother with help or shared enthusiasm plus, occasionally, an interesting, naturally related idea. These 10- to 30-second interchanges are usually oriented around the child's interest of the moment rather than toward some need or interest of the mother. At times, under these circumstances, the child will not receive immediate attention. These effective mothers do not always drop what they are doing to attend to his request, but rather if the time is obviously inconvenient, they say so, thereby probably giving the child a realistic small taste of things to come.

These mothers very rarely spend five, 10, or 20 minutes teaching their one- or two-year-olds, but they get an enormous amount of teaching in "on the fly," and usually at the *child's* instigation. Though they do volunteer comments opportunistically, they mostly act in response to overtures by the child.

These effective mothers talk a great deal to their infants and, very often, at a level the child can handle. Furthermore, they seem to be people with high levels of energy. The work of a young mother, without household help, is, in spite of modern appliances, very time- and energy-consuming. Yet, we have families subsisting at a welfare level of income, with as many as eight closely spaced children, who are doing every bit as good a job in child-rearing during the early years as the most advantaged homes.

To the extent that our study is correct about the formative effects of the experiences of the second and third year of life, the performance of mothers during that age period is extremely important and government will have to show more concern for this problem. It seems to me that it is quite possible to learn how some families manage to get their children off to a good start and just as possible that such knowledge could be delivered to society, particularly to those families currently rearing young children. Why, for example, shouldn't our public schools be preparing children for their roles as parents? They clearly do very little of such work now. Adding this requirement to the elementary and secondary school core curricula would be quite consistent with a "preparation for life" orientation toward the goals of education.

Our study also may have implications for the education of three- to six-year-olds as well. Why not consider our description of the competent six-year-old as a possible guide for defining the goals of early education? Preschool education for non-disadvantaged children might move toward more specific goal definitions than those that prevail, with greater potential for designing really effective preschool curricula.

PRESCHOOL: HAS IT WORKED? *

What have we learned about preschool education in the past decade? In the early 1960s, the

*Abridged from Burton L. White, Preschool: Has it worked? *Compact*, July/August 1973, 6–7. Reprinted by permission of the author and the publisher.

federal government became seriously concerned with the education of children less than six years of age.

Children whose earliest school performances were below average often fell further behind the longer they went to school, it was found. Indeed, this pattern was very common, especially in lower-income population areas. Project Head Start was conceived to deal with this national problem.

Since then, Head Start has attempted preventive or remedial education in thousands of settings for many children, at a cost of many hundreds of millions of dollars. A variety of educational programs have been tried with many different kinds of children, 3 to 6 years of age.

After nearly a decade of such activity, at least one central fact is clear: Given our current resources, a poorly developing 3-, 4-, or 5-year-old is not often converted to an average or above-average elementary school student. As far as academic effects are concerned, Head Start has clearly not worked for most of the target population.

I do not mean to say that Head Start has had no important benefits. Certainly, there have been substantial health benefits. Certainly, more families have a heightened awareness of educational issues in early childhood. There may even be benefits for the social development of Head Start children that we have not yet measured. But, as for the central goal of heading off educational underachievement, the results have been disappointing.

Early signs of the inadequate benefits of Head Start prompted the federal government to begin two new programs. The first, Project Follow Through, rested on the assumption that continuation of special educational assistance was needed to maintain preschool gains. Enrichment programs in the elementary years were tried. As far as I can tell, such programs have shown even fewer positive results than Head Start.

The second program rested on the assumption that Head Start began too late—that children had to be reached before they became three years old. Called the Parent-Child Center Project, it was designed to provide preventive education during the first three years of life. Unfortunately, shortly after its inception, the country experienced an economic recession and funds for government programs in education were cut back severely. As a result, we have accumulated little or no evidence to date on the effectiveness of parent-child centers.

The events of the past decade have led me to three rather momentous conclusions:

If a 3-year-old is six months or more behind in academically relevant areas, such as language and problem-solving skills, he is not likely to ever be successful in his future educational career. There are exceptions to this generalization, but the results of Head Start, Follow Through and other remedial programs clearly support this statement for large numbers of American children.

We have apparently overemphasized the role of the schools in the total education of children.

We have apparently underemphasized the role of the family as the child's first educational delivery system. We do not prepare prospective parents to help children acquire the foundation for formal education.

At least four fundamental areas can be identified as part of the foundation normally achieved in some fashion in the years before a child enters the first grade.

1 Language development. From about the age of 6 to 8 months on to about 36 months, most children acquire the ability to understand most of the language they will use in ordinary conversation throughout their lives. No educator denies the central role of language in a child's educational career.

2 Social attachment, social style and basic self-perceptions. Much recent research has described how babies form their first vital social relationship (usually to their mother), how they adopt their first social style and how they form their early impressions of themselves during the first three years of life. Much of that research also has indicated strongly the underlying importance of those social developments for a child's future educational success.

3 The development of curiosity and intrinsic interest in learning. Nothing alive is more curious or more interested in exploration and learning than the typical 8-month-old baby. It is difficult to destroy or even badly suppress that urge during the first months of an infant's life. Sadly, the compelling urge to learn found in nearly every baby, rich or poor, is not invulnerable beyond the first year of life. By age two or three, many babies are much less curious, much less interested in learning for its own sake. Often the causes of such educational setbacks are clearly discernible in the child-rearing practices in the home.

4 Learning to learn skills. Jean Piaget, the Swiss student of the origins of children's intelligence, has stimulated much recent intensive research on that topic. Suffice to say that most children look fine in this area up to the middle of the second year of life, but that many begin to fall behind at that point.

Not everyone in early education would endorse this description of developmental process in the early years; many professionals would. I believe the evidence for the special importance of development in the first three years is very convincing. What, then, are the ramifications for public policy?

I have noted that by three years of age identifiable educational deficits have already developed in many children. This conclusion is now beyond dispute. Moreover, such deficits often do not appear until the middle of the second year of life. Each month that passes subsequently finds more future underachievers. If we are to sponsor preventive education, it has to be from the first year of life on. Since most infants receive their early education in their homes—and quite informally as a consequence of child-rearing practices of the family—we will have to provide support for the family or somehow arrange for infants to go to school.

Our research of the last eight years at the Harvard pre-school project has focused on how a minority of families from many backgrounds regularly do an outstanding job of rearing their children during the first years of life. We have become convinced that the job is best done in the home by the family.

We have also concluded that most families have the potential to do the job. We have observed first-rate development in low-income homes in situations where there are many closely spaced children, where the mother holds a part-time job and where the marriage is shaky or nonexistent. Such successes notwithstanding, most families need help and our educational system isn't providing it.

Isn't it time we took a good look at why we wait to start educating children at age five or six when children start to learn at birth?

USEFUL RESOURCES

ACKERMAN, N. *et al. Summerhill: For and against.* New York: Hart Publishing, 1970. A. S. Neill's ideas about education and child raising have generated an enormous amount of controversy. This collection combines a spectrum of views and reactions ranging from, "I would as soon enroll a child of mine in a brothel as in Summerhill" (Max Rafferty, California State Superintendent of Public Instruction), (Maybe this attitude is partly the reason so many free schools have been founded in California.— Ed.), to "Summerhill . . . is a holy place" (John M. Culkin, Jesuit priest). It is an excellent book for revealing basic issues and attitudes regarding freedom and learning.

AXELROD, J., FREEDMAN, M. B., HATCH, W. R., KATZ, J., & SANFORD, N. *Search for revelance.* San Francisco, Jossey-Bass, 1969.

BURTON, ANTHONY *The horn and the beanstalk.* Toronto: Holt, Rinehart and Winston, 1972. Among the critics of contemporary educational institutions, Burton is unique in directing his book to "Mr. and Mrs. America, be they in Canada or the United States." It is only the silent majority that can change the world without catastrophe.

COX, D. W. *The city as a schoolhouse: The story of the parkway program.* Valley Forge: Judson Press, 1972. Describes the development and implications of the Parkway Program in Philadelphia; the original school without walls program which utilizes the institutions of the city as its prime resources in the teaching/learning process.

DEUTSCH, M. Some psychological aspects of learning in the disadvantaged. *Teachers College Record,* 1969, **67,** 260–265.

DEUTSCH, M., KATZ, I., & JENSEN, A. (Eds.), *Social class, race and psychological development.* New York: Holt, Rinehart and Winston, 1968.

EVANS, E. D. *Contemporary influences in early childhood education.* New York: Holt, Rinehart and Winston, 1971. Describes a variety of "early education" (age three to six) programs emphasizing educational and psychological features. Discusses the Montessori method, Project Head Start, behavior analysis and the British infant school program. A good source for term paper material.

FADER, D. *The naked children.* New York: Macmillan, 1971. "This is the story of one school year in the life of Cleo, Wentworth, Snapper, Rubbergut, and Uncle Wiggly. Thirteen and fourteen years old in the 1965–1966 academic year, eighth and ninth grade students in Washington's Garnet-Patterson Junior High School, organized and led by Cleo, the only girl—they were my companions, my friends, and my colleagues. They were also the single most powerful force I have ever known for good change in bad education."

GARTNER, A., KOHLER, M. C., & RIESMANN, F. *Children teach children: Learning by teaching.* New York: Harper and Row, 1971.

GERBER, W. Human intelligence. *Editorial Research Reports,* 1969, **2,** 617–632. Contains nice summaries of the major issues and good references. A most helpful article if you are writing a paper on intelligence.

GLAZER, N. Y., & CREEDON, C. F. *Children and poverty: Some sociological and psychological perspectives.* Chicago: Rand McNally, 1968.

GOODLAD, J. I., & ANDERSON, R. H. *The nongraded elementary school.* (Rev. ed.) New York: Harcourt, Brace and World, 1963.

GROSS, B., & GROSS, R. *Radical school reform*. New York: Simon and Schuster, 1970. An excellent anthology of the views of the major leaders of the movement. Reviewed by Michael B. Katz in *Saturday Review*, June 20, 1970, 88–89.

HASKETT, G. J. Research and early education: relations among classroom, laboratory and society. *American Psychologist*, 1973, **28**, 248–256.

HERRNSTEIN, R. J. *I.Q. in the meritocracy*. New York: Little, Brown and Co., 1973. A lucid and comprehensive presentation of the thesis that progress toward equalization of opportunity results in an "hereditary meritocracy." Herrnstein discusses: the reliability of IQ testing, the nature of intelligence, the relation between IQ, school grades, and social status, and the interplay of heredity and environment. The essence of the argument is formulated in the "I.Q. and Social Status Syllogism" as follows:

If differences in mental abilities are inherited, and If success requires those abilities, and If earnings and prestige depend upon success, Then social standing (which reflects earnings and prestige) will be based to some extent on inherited differences among people.

HOLT, J. *How children fail*. New York: Pitman, 1969.

HOLT, J. I oppose testing, marking and grading. *Today's Education*. March 1971, 28–31. Indicates some of the pedagogical and psychological problems associated with grading and suggests short-run "subversive" strategies that may be used by teachers and students to overcome the problems.

ILLICH, I. *Deschooling society*. New York: Harper and Row, 1970. "Schooling has become a sacred cow which all must worship, serve, and submit to, yet from which little true nourishment is derived. . . . We must provide for . . . legal protection from the obligatory, graded curriculum; laws forbidding discrimination on the basis of prior schooling; the forma-tion of skill centers where useful skills can be learned, taught by those best equipped to teach them; peer matching by which the learned may share their knowledge with those seeking instruction."

JENCKS, C. *et al. Inequality: A reassessment of the effect of family and schooling in America*. New York: Basic Books, 1972.

JENSEN, A. R. *Genetics and education*. London: Methuen, 1972. A book of reprints on genetics, race, and intelligence. For a review of this book see "Race, intelligence and I. Q." by David Cohen in *New Scientist*, October, 1972, p. 168.

JENSEN, A. R. Race and the genetics of intelligence: A reply to Lewontin. *Bulletin of the Atomic Scientists*. May 1970, 17–23.

JENSEN, A. R. The Differences are real. *Psychology Today*. December 1973, 80–86. "Let me stress that none of the research I have discussed here allows one to conclude anything about the intelligence of any individual black or white person."

JEROME, J. *Culture out of anarchy: The reconstruction of American higher education*. New York: Herder and Herder, 1970. Discusses the history, success, and failures of several "free university" experiments.

KOZOL, J. *Death at an early age*. Boston: Houghton Mifflin, 1967.

LEWONTIN, RICHARD C. Race and intelligence. *Bulletin of the Atomic Scientist*. March 1970, 2–8. Written by a well-known geneticist, this article is one of the more easily understandable critical evaluations of Jensen's thesis that differences between races in IQ are due primarily to hereditary differences. See above for the complete references for Jensen's reply to Lewontin. Both articles reveal substantive issues, personal bias, and rhetorical polemics.

McNEIL, E. B. *Being human: The psychological experience*. San Francisco: Canfield Press, 1973. Chapter 4 is devoted to a good review of educational issues paralleling our presentation in this book from "current critics" to "education tomorrow." An excellent overview.

NEILL, A. S. *Summerhill: A radical approach to*

child rearing. New York: Hart, 1960. The classic in free-school literature.

NYBERG, D. *Tough and tender learning*. Palo Alto: National Press Books, 1971. A most readable book in which Nyberg helps you understand the importance of "minding your feelings," "feeling your mindings," and the theory and practice of respecting persons in theory (Chapter 9, a flea for your ear, or why most plans for humanizing education probably won't work) and in practice (Chapter 13 on the possibilities of being a respectable teacher without having to push people around).

POSTMAN, N., & WEINGARTNER, C. *The soft revolution: A student handbook for turning schools around*. New York: Delacorte Press, 1971. "This book was written mainly for students, somewhere between the ages of fifteen and twenty-five. But not for all of them. We are not talking to those who have been able to accommodate themselves, without discomfort, to the schooling process. Neither are we talking to those whose discomfort is so acute that they are prepared to burn buildings down."

REPO, S. (Ed.), *This book is about schools*. New York: Pantheon Books, 1970.

REUDER, G. F., MOON, C. E., & TREFFINGER, D. J. Directory of organizations and periodicals on alternative education. *Journal of Creative Behavior*, 1973, **7**, 54–66.

RICHARDSON, K., SPEARS, D., & RICHARDS, M. *Race and intelligence*. Baltimore: Penguin, 1972. One of the best paperback books dealing with the race-IQ controversy at a level which, with effort, is understandable to the layman. Presents psychological, genetic and sociological perspectives.

RYAN, T. J. *Poverty and the child: A Canadian study*. Toronto: McGraw-Hill Ryerson, 1972.

SARASON, S. B. *The culture of the school and the problem of change*. Boston: Allyn and Bacon Inc. "The more things change the more they remain the same—that is a recurring statement in this book, which in part is devoted to trying to understand why this is so."

Saturday review of education. 450 Pacific Avenue, San Francisco, Calif. 94133.

SILBERMAN, C. E. *Crisis in the classroom*. New York: Random House, 1970. A classic critique of contemporary educational practice in North America. A most valuable source book.

SILBERMAN, C. E. *The open classroom reader*. New York: Random House, 1973. "This companion volume to Silberman's bestselling *Crisis in the Classroom* has been designed for teachers, students, administrators, parents, school board members—anyone who is dissatisfied with the status quo in the elementary school and who wants to explore the alternative approaches that go under the rubric of informal education, open education, and the open/classroom. The most complete reader available on the open classroom."

Psychology Today Book Club

This magazine is about schools. 56 Esplanade St. East, Suite 408, Toronto 215, Ontario.

WEBER, L. *The English infant school and informal education*. Englewood Cliffs, N.J.: Prentice-Hall, 1971. An excellent review of the history, practice, and psychological foundations of the informal classroom by an educator who has been very instrumental in the movement in North America.

CHAPTER 3

AND MAN CREATED MAN

PROVOCATIONS

Some scientists, however, frankly believe that laymen are ill equipped to discuss issues with them, let alone share control of what they do. The matters they contend are quite technical and should be decided by the technical men who understand them.

Time Magazine

Man not only creates his own environment, but in so doing eventually presides over the programming and realization of his own evolution—however inadvertent and stumbling he may be about it.

Jerome S. Bruner

Freedom is a manufactured myth to which I subscribe in order to explore my limitations.

Shari Bender

The hypothesis that man is not free is essential to the application of scientific method to the study of human behavior. The free inner man who is held responsible for his behavior is only a prescientific substitute for the kinds of causes which are discovered in the course of scientific analysis.

B. F. Skinner

"Mr. Castle," said Frazier very earnestly, "let me ask you a question. I warn you, it will be the most terrifying question of your life. What would you do if you found yourself in possession of an effective science of behavior? Suppose you suddenly found it possible to control the behavior of men as you wished. What would you do?"

B. F. Skinner

Freedom is what you do with what's been done to you.

Jean-Paul Sartre

WHAT DO YOU THINK?

12 AND MAN CREATED MAN: WHAT KIND OF MAN SHALL WE BUILD?

WILLIAM C. CORNING

We are caught in something of a paradox these days. . . . Our western heritage is an egalitarian ideology that teaches us we are born equal and free with the same opportunities. We reject predeterministic notions and constantly assert that we indeed possess a "free will" and are independent of biological, behavioral, and social controls. We do accede to the weather, taxes, and dying. It is our technology that underscores the paradox. While we desire and worship our freedom on the one hand, at the same time we are fascinated by the idea of the manipulation and control of man and willingly support a science and technology that is developing with incredible speed techniques for engineering our structure and behavior. The escapades of Baron Frankenstein with his tragic human conglomerate born of electricity and graveyard parts has always fascinated us. Today, science is bringing this early fantasy into the realm of reality.

This section is concerned with some interesting and in some cases frightening possibilities. Science is close to providing the means of determining man's structure and physiology, of controlling both his offspring's future characteristics as well as his present patterns. What is peculiar is that the public appears unaffected by these possibilities in spite of their publication via television and the newspapers, and their dramatization in motion pictures. In *The Manchurian Candidate,* a returning Korean War veteran (Laurence Harvey) is unaware that he has been conditioned to kill while a prisoner of war; in *The President's Analyst,* James Coburn fights a plot by the telephone company to gain control over minds by the mass implantation of miniature computers; behavioral control and the issue of freedom at any price versus control was starkly presented in the novel (and film) *A Clockwork Orange,* where a hoodlum of futuristic London is transformed via conditioning techniques into an "acceptable" member of society who is repelled by violence and lust. Perhaps these dramatizations are too unreal. What is being discovered in laboratories around the world, however, should be sufficient to mobilize the public. The headline below is typical:

RESEARCHERS COMPLETE ANALYSIS OF
MAKE-UP OF GENE

For various reasons, the implications of this sort of headline are not making an impact on the public. It is the scientist who is most concerned about the implications of these discoveries and who is most insistent that the public begin discussions and debate over future technological advances. As Gaylin puts it, it is ". . . analogous to Dr. Frankenstein chastising the Swiss citizenry for failing to storm his laboratories."

What are the possibilities of controlling those aspects of man's biology that are most relevant to psychology? What will our guidelines be when it becomes possible to control or seriously influence the genetic potential which will eventually be expressed in IQ scores? Should we "delete" potential human beings who have a strong probability of being different? Historically, it has been the "different" people who have led mankind to new insights, higher levels of understanding, to a richer life. "Different" people have also wrought destruction and retarded advances of civilization. Should we gamble on a full spectrum of human beings or attempt to genetically weed out what we now consider "deviants" in an attempt to create our image of perfect man? In the old days, the weeding out was after the fact—the bizarre idea or behavior was handled by the guillotine or prison. It may be possible in the near future to prevent the deviant person, a distinctly greater danger. At least Galileo's views were known before official suppression occurred; soon we may be able to prevent a Galileo or to jump in and alter his brain processes when the first signs of antiestablishmentarian behavior appear.

The following selections provide an overview of the "state of the art" with respect to control technology; they hint at futuristic possibilities, but possibilities that at this point in time have high probabilities of payoff in terms of behavioral control. The possibilities are: genetic engineering, organism assembly, artificial brains, experiential influences on brain structure, biochemical methods of brain control, the uses of hypnosis to alleviate pain, etc., and the electrical control of brain activity. At one time or another, these possibilities were in the realm of science fiction and we could go to the movies and be titillated by *Donovan's Brain* (a brain removed from the skull and kept alive in a bowl), Frankenstein stories, other-world beasts descending upon earth and electronically controlling our brain's thoughts—these science fiction fantasies now merge with real life possibilities so that political and scientific leaders are beginning to ask, "Who is to play God?" Is the issue as simple as that of choosing between ". . . something mechanical that appears organic (Hyman, 1963)" such as the conditioned hoodlum of *A Clockwork Orange,* or the "free" animal capable of intense rage, bestiality, and abundant love? Can our attempts to remake man ever exceed the system within which we do the deciding, or is our society so limiting that our molded man will simply be a caricature of the best and the worst of us? Consider the diversity of cultures, ethical systems, physical traits, and psychological phenomena, and then try to decide what kind of man we are to build: he will most likely be someone like yourself.

COMMENT: GENETIC CONTROL IS AN OLD IDEA

A brief survey of relatively recent history reveals that the interest in manipulating man's genetic composition preceded the era of molecular biology. The eugenics movement of Europe and North America during the 19th and early 20th centuries revealed a distinct pattern of the privileged making and implementing decisions about the social value of the less privileged. The techniques for designing genetic change were intended to operate at the level of changing the gene frequencies. Accordingly, individuals of the presumed socially unfit class were to be restrained from reproducing, while those of the fit class were to be encouraged to reproduce. On an expanded scale, the Nazi eugenics program instituted a classification of individuals according to social value, followed by radical negative selection on the one hand and positive selection on the other. The history of slave-breeding practices in the Americas is notably absent from most discussions of designed genetic change. Firsthand accounts record that some North American slaveholders selectively mated persons who possessed physical characteristics judged to be economically valuable. Likewise, in more recent years, a rubber company operating in Brazil developed a practice of systematically killing the free Indian population and establishing stud farms where selected Indian girls were to breed slave labor.

In all the instances cited, the objectives of the designed genetic changes were to protect society, to establish political superiority, or to amass economic wealth. In no instance was the objective the well-being of the individuals at stake. We can ill afford to submerge into the subconscious such painful experiences, since they provide a key insight into those old-fashioned human characteristics of greed and pride that extort their dividends from the other fellow.

V. E. HEADINGS

---

13 MAN INTO SUPERMAN
The Promise and Peril of the New Genetics*

THE BODY: FROM BABY HATCHERIES TO "XEROXING" HUMAN BEINGS

Man today is heir to a host of inherited imperfections, ranging from diabetes to degenerative nerve disease. Each individual, geneticists have determined, carries between five and ten potentially harmful genes in his cells, and these flawed segments of DNA can be passed down to his progeny along with the messages that determine whether a child will have red hair or blue eyes.

Nature itself takes care of the worst genetic mistakes. One out of every 130 conceptions ends before the mother even realizes she is pregnant because the defective zygote, or fertilized egg, never attaches itself to the wall of the uterus. Fully 25% of all conceptions fail to reach an age at which they can survive outside the womb, and of these, at least a third have identifiable chromosomal abnormalities. Still, as many as five out of every 100 babies born have some genetic defect, and Nobel-Prizewinning Geneticist Joshua Lederberg believes the proportion would be even higher were it not for nature's own process of quality control.

The most obvious deformities result from chromosomal abnormalities. Down's syndrome, or mongolism, which occurs once in every 600 births, is caused when one set of chromosomes occurs as a triplet rather than a pair. Hydrocephalus, or water on the brain, and polydactyly, the presence of extra fingers or toes, also result from faulty genes.

But the majority of genetic stigmas have somewhat more subtle symptoms and occur when

*Abridged from "Man into superman: The promise and peril of the new genetics," *Time*, Apr. 19, 1971, pp. 35–50. Reprinted by permission from *Time*, The Weekly Newsmagazine; Copyright Time Inc.

defective genes fail to order the production of essential enzymes that trigger the body's biochemical reactions. Phenylketonuria (PKU) is caused by the absence of the enzyme necessary for the metabolism of the amino acid phenylalanine; as a result, toxins accumulate in the body and eventually cause convulsions and brain damage. Cystic fibrosis, which causes abnormal secretion by certain glands and respiratory-tract blockage that can lead to death by pneumonia, is the most common inborn error of metabolism; it is believed to be caused by a deficiency in a single gene.

Most people are unaware that they are carrying defective genes until they have a deformed, diseased or mentally retarded child. While medical science has not yet developed the techniques for repairing the bad genes, it can increasingly determine that they are present. Genetic counselors can thus advise prospective parents on the possibilities that their offspring will be born with genetic diseases. Properly informed, a couple that runs a high risk of producing a defective child may well decide to forgo having children.

If both parents carry genes for diabetes, for example, the chances are one in four that their children will inherit an increased risk for developing the disease. If either parent actually suffers from diabetes, the odds are even worse. Members of one large South Dakota family afflicted with a rare degenerative nerve disease have been advised, for example, that the odds are 50-50 that any children they have will suffer loss of balance and coordination and die, probably of pneumonia, by age 45 (*Time*, Jan. 25).

Genetic counseling once relied more heavily on mathematics than medicine to predict the chance of hereditary handicaps. But it is now possible for doctors to identify and catalogue chromosomes. If there are certain chromosomal abnormalities, the prospective parents are informed that they will almost definitely produce deformed offspring. While this knowledge may take some of the mystery and romance out of procreation, it also eliminates much of the uncertainty. As one geneticist puts it, "There is nothing very romantic about a mongoloid child or a deformed body."

● Toulouse Lautrec was born with a deformed body. . . .
Ray Charles is blind. . . .
Arlo Guthrie may have inherited Hodgkin's disease. . . .
Prevent them? Breed only the perfect?

An even more important technique enables physicians to examine the cells of the unborn only months after conception and to determine with accuracy whether or not the infant will inherit his parents' defective genes. The procedure is known as amniocentesis, from the Greek *amnion* (membrane) and *kentesis* (pricking); it is performed by inserting a long needle through the mother's abdomen and drawing off a small sample of the amniotic fluid, the amber liquid in which the fetus floats. Physicians then separate the fetal skin cells from the fluid and place the cells in a nutrient bath where they continue to divide and grow. By examining the cells microscopically and analyzing them chemically, the doctors can identify nearly 70 different genetic disorders, most of them serious.

Amniocentesis, performed between the 13th and 18th weeks of pregnancy, is not without some risk to both mother and baby. But in cases where family history leads them to suspect genetic defects, physicians feel that the benefits more than justify the danger; for the tests, which have been carried out on more than 10,000 women in the U.S. alone in the past 40 years, have proved extremely accurate. Using amniocentesis, Dr. Henry Nadler, a Northwestern University pediatrician, diagnosed mongolism in ten of 155 high-risk pregnancies tested. Subsequent examination of the fetuses showed that his diagnosis was correct in all cases.

At present, the woman who learns through amniocentesis that she is carrying a seriously deformed fetus has only two choices: abortion or the heartbreak of delivering a hopelessly defective infant. But the mother whose unborn baby is found to have one of several hereditary enzyme deficiencies has a more acceptable alternative, for medicine has developed techniques for treating many such illnesses. An amniotic test for fetal lung maturity, for example, has helped warn doctors when a child may be born with hyaline membrane disease, which blocks proper breathing. In those cases, birth can be delayed by sedation until tests show the baby ready to breathe on its own. Tests that permit prompt postnatal detection of PKU give doctors an opportunity to place babies so affected on special diets that prevent the accumulation of the deadly toxins and allow them to live relatively normal lives.

Some treatments are even possible before birth. Physicians routinely perform intrauterine transfusions on fetuses suffering from Rh disease, a genetic condition that results from the incompatibility of maternal and fetal blood.

Artificial insemination, once the exclusive province of livestock breeders, also offers escape from some genetic mishaps. An estimated 25,000 women whose husbands are either sterile or carry genetic flaws have been artificially inseminated in the U.S. each year, many of them with sperm provided by anonymous donors whose pedigrees have been carefully checked for hereditary defects. Some 10,000 children are born annually of such conceptions.

Doctors also see possibilities in artificial inovulation, a procedure in which an egg cell is taken directly from the ovaries, fertilized in a test tube and then reimplanted in the uterus. By carefully scrutinizing the developing embryo in the test tube, doctors could spot serious genetic deficiencies and decide not to reimplant it, thus avoiding an abortion later on. If the embryo is normal, it could even be reimplanted in the womb of a donor mother and carried to term there, enabling the woman either unable or unwilling to go through pregnancy to have children that were genetically her own.

Even test-tube babies, once the stuff of science fiction, are now not only possible, but probable. Dr. Landrum Shettles of Columbia University and Dr. Daniele Petrucci of Bologna, Italy, have shown that considerable growth is possible in test tubes. Shettles has kept fertilized ova growing for six days, the point at which they would normally attach themselves to the lining of the uterus. Petrucci kept a fertilized egg alive and growing for nearly two months.

Indeed, only development of an "artificial womb" capable of supporting life stands in the way of routine ectogenesis, or gestation outside the uterus, and now even this problem may yield to solution. Scientists at the National Heart Institute have developed a chamber containing a synthetic amniotic fluid and an oxygenator for fetal blood, and have managed to keep lamb fetuses alive in it for periods exceeding two days. Once their device is perfected, the baby hatchery of Aldous Huxley's *Brave New World* will be a reality and life without birth a problem rather than a prophecy.

Man may eventually be able to abandon sexual reproduction entirely. That startling and perhaps unwelcome possibility has been demonstrated by Dr. J. B. Gurdon of Britain's Oxford University. Taking an unfertilized egg cell from an African clawed frog, Gurdon destroyed its nucleus by ultraviolet radiation, replacing it with the nucleus of an intestinal cell from a tadpole of the same species. The egg, discovering that it had a full set of chromosomes, instead of the half set found in unfertilized eggs, responded by beginning to divide as if it had been normally fertilized. The result was a tadpole that was the genetic twin of the tadpole that provided the nucleus. Gurdon's experiment was also proof of what geneticists have long known: that all of the genetic information necessary to produce an organism is coded into the nucleus of every cell in that organism.

Man, say the scientists, could one day clone (from the Greek word for throng), or asexually reproduce himself, in the same way, creating thousands of virtually identical twins from a test tube full of cells carried through gestation by donor mothers or hatched in an artificial womb. Thus, the future could offer such phenomena as a police force cloned from the cells of J. Edgar Hoover, an invincible basketball team cloned from Lew Alcindor, or perhaps the colonization of the moon by astronauts cloned from a genetically sound specimen chosen by NASA officials. Using the same technique, a woman could even have a child cloned from one of her own cells. The child would inherit all its mother's characteristics including, of course, her sex.

Dramatic as cloning may be, it is overshadowed in significance by a technique that may well be practiced before the end of this century: genetic surgery, or correction of man's inherited imperfections at the level of the genes themselves. When molecular biologists learn to map the location of specific genes in human DNA strands, determine the genetic code of each and then create synthetic genes in the test tube, they will have the ability to perform genetic surgery.

Some molecular biologists envisage using laser beams to slice through DNA molecules at desired points, burning out faulty genes. These would then be replaced by segments of DNA tailored in the test tube to emulate a properly functioning gene and introduced into the body as artificial—and beneficial—viruses.

● How would we know a "gifted" and unique individual before the fact? Suppose we noticed a "deviant" genetic structure in developing human brain cells. Would we be more likely to "correct" the deviant structure to make the brain "normal" or would we let it develop to see what it is like?

Prophylaxis is important, but man's molecular manipulations need hardly be confined to the prevention and cure of disease. His understanding of the mechanisms of life opens the door to genetic engineering and control of the very process of evolution. DNA can now be created in the laboratory. Soon, man will be able to create man—and even superman.

Researchers have found that they can increase the life span of laboratory animals by underfeeding them and thus delaying maturation. This phenomenon, they believe, occurs because a smaller intake of food results in the formation of fewer cross linkages—connecting rods that link together and partly immobilize the long protein and nucleic acid molecules essential to life. If scientists can retard cross linking in man, they may well slow his aging process. Scientists also hope that they can some day do away with disease, genetically breeding out hereditary defects while breeding in new immunities to bacterial and other externally caused ailments. Finally, they look forward—in the distant future and with techniques far beyond any now conceived—to altering the very nature of their species with novel sets of laboratory-created genetic instructions.

Current predictions about the appearance of re-engineered man seem singularly uninspired. Some scientists argue that man's head should be made larger to accommodate an increased number of brain cells. They do not, however, explain what man would do with this additional gray matter; there is good reason to believe that man does not use all that he presently possesses. A few others note that the efficiency of man's hands could be increased by an extra thumb and his peripheral vision enhanced by protruding eyes—improvements that seem unnecessary in the light of man's expanding technology.

Some favor less obvious alterations. They have suggested that man be given the genes to produce a two-compartment stomach (a cow has four) that could digest cellulose; that mutation could be advantageous if man fails to increase his food supplies fast enough to feed the planet's growing population, but superfluous if he does. They also want man programmed to regenerate other organs, such as he now does with the liver, so that he can repair his damaged or diseased heart or lungs if necessary.

Others call for even more specialized humans to perform functions that in reality will probably be done better by machines. British Geneticist J.B.S.

Haldane called for certain regressive mutations to enable man to survive in space, including legless astronauts who would take up less room in a space capsule and require less food and oxygen (larger and more powerful spacecraft would seem to be an easier and less monstrous solution). Haldane also suggested apelike men to explore the moon. "A gibbon," he said only half-jokingly, "is better preadapted than a man for life in a low gravitational field."

Eventually, scientists fantasize, man will escape entirely from his inefficient, puny body, replacing most of his physical being with durable hardware. The futuristic cyborg, or combination man and machine, will consist of a stationary, computerlike human brain, served by machines to fill its limited physical needs and act upon its commands.

Such evolutionary developments could well herald the birth of a new, more efficient, and perhaps even superior species. But would it be man?

COMMENT: MAXIMS FOR GENETIC MANIPULATION

I would offer five maxims for the future genetic technology; they are couched in borrowed terms:

Do not eliminate all of chance and novelty—for that is the way to extinction.

Do not create defined sub-types—for that is the way of the ant.

Do not chill all passion—for that is the way of the drone.

Do not diminish the heart—for that is the way of the robot.

Do not erase the ego—for that is the way of the slave.

Paul Tillich wrote: 'Man becomes truly human only at the moment of decision.' We should aim always to enlarge his opportunities and capacities for decision.

R. SINSHEIMER

THE MIND: FROM MEMORY PILLS TO ELECTRONIC PLEASURES BEYOND SEX

In all of his 35,000-year history, Homo sapiens has found it harder to fathom the depths of his mind than to unlock the secrets of his body. But the discoveries of molecular biology may well show the way to a new comprehension; they may make it possible, through genetic engineering, surgery, drug therapy and electrical stimulation, to mold not only the body but also the mind.

Man cannot wait for natural selection to change him, some scientists warn, because the process is much too slow. Yale Physiologist José Delgado likens the human animal to the dinosaur: insufficiently intelligent to adapt to his changing environment. Caltech Biophysicist Robert Sinsheimer calls men "victims of emotional anachronisms, of internal drives essential to survival in a primitive past, but undesirable in a civilized state." Thus, by his own efforts, man must sharpen his intellect and curb his aboriginal urges, especially his aggressiveness.

To most laymen, the idea of remaking man's mind is unthinkable; "You can't change human nature," they insist. But many scientists are convinced that the mind can be altered because it is really matter. Explains Physicist Gerald Feinberg: "What sets us apart from inanimate matter is not that we are made of different stuff, or that different physical principles determine our workings. It is rather the greater complexity of our construction and the self-awareness that this makes possible."

That self-awareness resides in the brain, the organ about which scientists have the most to learn. To Physiologist Charles Sherrington, the brain's 10 billion nerve cells were like "an enchanted loom" with "millions of flashing shuttles." For some functions, M.I.T. Professor Hans-Lukas Teuber explains, brain cells are preprogrammed with "enormous specificity of configuration, chemistry and connection." Some are sensitive only to vertical lines, others only to horizontal or oblique ones. "Each of these little creatures does his thing," Teuber says.

In the hope of deciphering this staggering variety, hundreds of scientists, including molecular biologists, in the U.S. and abroad, are now turning to brain research. One day in the distant future, their discoveries may help man to improve his already remarkable brain—for despite its dazzling versatility and subtlety, it is not without limitation. "Computers slashing from circuit to circuit in microseconds can cope with the input and response time of dozens of human brains simultaneously," Biophysicist Sinsheimer laments. Besides, the brain can call up only a limited amount of stored information at a time to focus it on a particular problem. And while it can grasp as many as 50 bits of visual information at once, it cannot file away more than 10 of them per second for later reference.

To most scientists, this reference system, or memory, is one of the most important tools of man's intelligence. Long before the development of molecular biology, Marcel Proust pondered the mystery of memory in *Remembrance of Things Past*. About a man's own past, he wrote that "it is a labor in vain to attempt to recapture it: all the efforts of our intellect must prove futile. The past is hidden somewhere beyond the reach of the intellect." In *Swann's Way*, it was a tea-soaked *petite madeleine* that touched off the hero's long-forgotten childhood memories. In the scientific world, the stimulus is sometimes a surgeon's probe. Montreal Surgeon Wilder Penfield, for example, while performing operations under local anesthesia, by chance found brain sites that when stimulated electrically led one patient to hear an old tune, another to recall an exciting childhood experience in vivid detail, and still another to relive the experience of bearing her baby. Penfield's findings led some scientists to believe that the brain has indelibly recorded every sensation it has ever received and to ask how the recording was made and preserved.

Initially, some brain researchers believed that memories were stored in electrical impulses. But scientists could not comprehend how a cranial electrical system, however complex its interconnections, could accommodate the estimated million billion pieces of information that a single brain collects in a lifetime.

Their doubts increased when they found that a trained animal generally remembered its skills despite attempt to disrupt its cerebral electrical activity by intense cold, drugs, shock or other stress; only short-term memory—of recently learned skills—was impaired. There was an obvious conclusion: while short-term memory may be partly electrical, long-term memory must be carried in something less ephemeral than an electric current.

That something, theorists believed, was chemical. Scientists had long known that chemical as well as electrical activity goes on in brain neurons: these cells carry on metabolism and protein synthesis like other body cells. Researchers soon learned that the leap of message-carrying nerve impulses across the gap between one cell and another takes place only with the help of chemical transmitter substances. One of these, acetylcholine, was promptly identified, and investigators began to look for other brain chemicals, specifically for varieties that might contain memories.

Their reasoning was that just as DNA carries genetic "memories," so other molecules might encode and carry information plucked from transient electrical impulses. Some early researchers proposed the idea of a separate brain molecule for each memory. The hypothesis of Swedish Neurobiologist Holger Hydén of the University of Göteborg was a bit more sophisticated; he thought that RNA was the key to memory formation and was encouraged in his belief by the results of his experiments with rats. When he taught them special tasks, he discovered that the RNA had not only increased in quantity but was different in quality from ordinary RNA. In short, what Hydén did was to lay the groundwork for a molecular theory of memory.

As Hydén's rat experiments demonstrated, RNA itself does not store memories; instead, it may play an intermediary role, stimulating the brain to produce proteins that are perhaps the actual repositories of memory. In one experiment inspired by that theory, University of Michigan Biochemist Bernard Agranoff taught goldfish to swim over a barrier, then injected them with puromycin, an antibiotic that prevents protein synthesis. When the injection was given hours after learning, it had no effect, suggesting that memory proteins had already formed. Injected just before or just after training, the drug prevented learning.

Other experiments based on the RNA-protein theory may demonstrate actual chemical memory transfer. Among the most publicized are those of University of Michigan Psychologist James McConnell and Neurochemist Georges Ungar of the Baylor College of Medicine. McConnell works with planaria, or flatworms, conditioning them by electrical shock to contract when a light is flashed. He then grinds them up and feeds them to untrained worms. Once they have cannibalized their brothers, the worms learn to contract twice as fast as their predecessors. What may happen, McConnell theorizes, is that the first batch of worms form new RNA, which synthesizes new proteins containing the message that light is a signal to contract. Having consumed these memory proteins, the second group of planaria presumably do not need to manufacture so much of their own; they have swallowed memory, as it were.

Ungar's experiments are similar. Using shock, he conditions rats to shun the darkness they normally prefer, then makes a broth of their brains. This he injects into the abdominal cavities of mice, which seem to react with a parallel unnatural aversion to the dark. Moreover, the more broth Ungar injects, the faster the mice seem to learn this fear. His theory: the memory message (that darkness should be avoided) is encoded by the rats' DNA-RNA mechanism into an amino-acid chain called a peptide, a small protein that Ungar managed to isolate and then synthesize. His name for it: scotophobin, from the Greek words for "darkness" and "fear."

The experiments done by both men are hard to repeat, and investigators are still trying to decide whether the few apparent replications are sound. There is controversy, too, over the meaning of results: critics say it is hard to interpret the behavior of worms and other lower creatures objectively. Some say that Ungar may have discovered not a memory molecule but a molecule that blocked a normal response (to seek darkness) instead of teaching a new reaction (to seek light). Most investigators doubt that a single memory molecule will be found, but they believe that molecular biology will eventually reveal the secret of memory. If so, the blue-sky possibilities are limitless. It might be possible to develop "knowledge pills" that would impart instant skill in French, tennis, music or math. McConnell jokingly proposes another idea: "Why should we waste all the knowledge a distinguished professor has accumulated simply because he's reached retirement age?" His solution: the students eat the professor.

Many less frivolous proposals for improving memory and other aspects of mental life are emerging from molecular biology and genetics. It is known that genes do not cause behavior. But they influence it and set limits to physical structure, temperament, intelligence and special abilities.

Psychiatrist Alexander Thomas of New York University finds that babies show a characteristic style (easy, difficult or slow-to-warm-up) from their earliest days. When he admits that this temperament may develop in the months after birth, he does not rule out the possibility that it is inborn. Other life scientists warn that "when we strive for equality of opportunity, we must not deceive ourselves about equality of capacity." For example, it is believed that genetic influence is especially great in such areas as mathematics, music and maybe acrobatics. Unless genetic potential is tapped by the environment, it will not develop: kittens prevented from walking will not learn normal form and depth perception. Says Geneticist Joshua Lederberg: "There is no gene that can ensure the ideal development of a child's brain without reference to tender care and inspired teaching."

This interaction between environment and heredity is one of the factors that make it so difficult to change human characteristics. Another is that nearly all behavioral traits are polygenic —dependent on several genes. But even so complex a trait as intelligence may eventually come under the control of molecular biologists. Some scientists fantasize that super-geniuses will some day be produced by increasing brain size, through either genetic manipulation or through transplantation of brain cells to newborn infants or to the fetus in the womb. (Such cells might be synthesized in the laboratory or developed by taking bits of easily accessible tissue from a contemporary Newton or Mozart and inducing them to turn into brain neurons.)

Another prospect is to alter genes so that babies will be born with rote knowledge—language skills, multiplication tables—just as birds apparently emerge from the egg with genetic programs that enable them to navigate. Some researchers hope to develop shared consciousness among several minds, thus polling intellectual resources.

Most observers continue to feel that reining in man's aggressiveness is as important as spurring his intelligence. Harvard Neurosurgeon Vernon Mark advocates a non-genetic approach. "There are basic brain mechanisms that will stop violent behavior, and we are born with them," Mark asserts. To tap those mechanisms, scientists would like to develop an anti-aggression pill (estrogens, or female hormones, have already been used experimentally to inhibit aggressive behavior). Until they do, Mark and two Harvard colleagues —Psychiatrist Frank Ervin and Surgeon William Sweet—are fighting aggression by using surgery to destroy the damaged brain cells that sometimes cause violence in people with specific brain disease. Typical of their patients is a gifted epileptic engineer named Thomas, who used to erupt in rages so frenzied that he would hurl his children or his wife across the room. First, Mark and Ervin sent electric current into different parts of Thomas' brain; when the current sparked his rage, the doctors knew they had found the offending cells. Surgeons Mark and Sweet then destroyed them, and in the four years since, Thomas has had no violent episodes.

Physiologist Delgado has developed even more dramatic methods of aggression control in animals. In one famous experiment, he implanted electrodes in the brain of a bull bred for fierceness. Then, with only a small radio transmitter as protection, he entered the ring with the bull and stopped the angry animal in mid-charge by sending signals into what he believes was its violence-inhibiting center. Similarly, Neuroanatomist Carmine Clemente of U.C.L.A. has shocked cats into dropping rats they were about to kill. But neither man sees any early prospects for remote control of human aggression.

Other mental problems may well succumb to molecular biology. Many therapists resist the idea that emotional problems have biochemical equivalents; yet Freud himself believed that they do and that they would one day be identified. Researchers are already convinced that schizophrenia has some genetic basis, although, as Psychologist David Rosenthal explains, it is not the disease that is inherited but a tendency to it. As a match must be struck before it will burn, so must the tendency be triggered by something in the environment. No one is yet sure whether the trigger is cultural or familial, electrical or chemical, but some investigators back the chemical theory on the ground that certain drugs enable schizophrenics to live outside institutions, at least for short periods. To date, drugs for schizophrenia have been administered on a trial-and-error basis; as molecular biologists learn more, it will become possible to use specific drugs to achieve specific ends.

Further research may provide a bonus of new genetic, chemical and electronic ways to enhance sexual pleasure. Physicist John Taylor, in fact, professes to fear that sex will become so much fun that people will want to give up practically all nonsexual activities. Author Gordon Rattray Taylor predicts that it may become possible to "buy desire," or switch it on or off at will; the playboy might opt for continuous excitement and the astronaut for freedom from sexual urges during space flight.

Unlikely as it may seem, there are researchers who claim to have discovered something better than sex. At McGill University in Canada, Psychologist James Olds used electrodes to locate specific "pleasure centers" in the brains of rats, and then allowed the animals, electrodes still in place, to stimulate themselves by pressing a lever. Given a choice, the rats preferred this new pleasure to food, water and sex. Some pressed the lever as many as 8,000 times an hour for more than a day, stopping only when they fainted from fatigue.

Such experiments lead Herman Kahn of the Hudson Institute to predict that by the year 2000, people will be able to wear chest consoles with ten levers wired to the brain's pleasure centers. Fantasies Kahn: "Any two consenting adults might play their consoles together. Just imagine all the possible combinations: 'Have you ever tried ten and five together?' couples would ask. Or, 'How about one and one?' But I don't think you should play your own console; that would be depraved."

Author Taylor, on the other hand, sees nothing wrong with solitary pleasure. Some day, he writes, a man may be able to put on a "stimulating cap" instead of a TV set, and savor a program of visual, auditory and other sensations. He and other futurists envision "experience centers" or "drug cafés" that would replace bars and coffeehouses. There, perhaps with the help of "dream machines," one might order a menu of "enhanced vision, sensory hallucinations and self-awareness." One might also be able to experience the mental states of a great man, or even of an animal. Molecular Biologist Leon Kass of the National Academy of Sciences projects a world in which man pursues only artificially induced sensation, a world in which the arts have died, books are no longer read, and human beings do not bother even to think or to govern themselves.

Some life scientists see even greater perils in man's new knowledge. "I would hate to see manipulation of genes for behavioral ends," warns Stanford Geneticist Seymour Kessler, "because as man's environment changes, and as man changes his environment, it is important to maintain flexibility." Professor Gerald McClearn of the Institute for Behavioral Genetics at the University of Colorado agrees, explaining that a gene that is considered "bad" now might become necessary for survival in the event of drastic environmental change. "It is foolhardy to eliminate genetic variability," he says. "That is our evolutionary bankroll, and we dare not squander it. Species that ran out of variability ran out of life."

Such worries are probably premature. To some experts, the more radical forms of behavior control, especially genetic modification, belong to the realm of science fiction. Yet others believe that biological predictions are always too conservative, and that man will soon proceed, and succeed, with his experiments. If he does, he must prepare himself for a social and moral revolution that would affect some of his most cherished institutions, including religion, marriage and the family. With such possibilities in mind, Nobelist George Beadle has warned that "man knows enough but is not yet wise enough to make man."

THE SPIRIT: WHO WILL MAKE THE CHOICES OF LIFE AND DEATH?

The quantum leap in man's abilities to reshape himself evokes a sense of uneasiness, a memory of Eden. Eat of the forbidden fruit, God warns, and "you shall surely die." Eat, promises the serpent, and "you shall be like God."

That temptation—to be "like God"—is at the root of the ethical dilemmas posed by molecular biology. In one sense, the new findings have continued the work of Newton, Darwin, and Freud, reducing men to even tinier cogs in a mechanistic universe. At the same time, it was man himself who deciphered the code of life and who can now, in Teilhard de Chardin's phrase, "seize the tiller of the world." If he is only a bundle of DNA-directed cells, more sophisticated but hardly dissimilar from those of animals and plants, he can at least use that knowledge to improve, even to re-create himself. But should he?

In his persuasive 1969 book *Come, Let Us Play God,* the late biophysicist Leroy Augenstein argued that man takes the role of God by default or design and has always done so. Ecologically, he changes the very face of the earth: first with plows, then with dams, insecticides and pollution, he has seriously upset the balance of nature. His humane instincts and scientific curiosity team up to preserve life so well that the world faces a population crisis. Moreover, by extending the lives of those with defective genes, science increases the chance that damaging genes will be passed down to ever-larger portions of succeeding generations. Germany's pre-eminent Protestant ethicist, Helmut Thielicke, notes that men must recognize how

"the act of compassion to one generation can be an act of oppression to the next." Thielicke argues that men must be willing to make hard choices. If society intervenes to keep alive the hereditarily ill (as he believes it should), then it must also be willing to intervene again, perhaps even sterilizing some with hereditary diseases.

This is only one kind of ethical problem raised by the new genetics, and it is already close at hand. Other problems are still in the far future but how the dilemmas of population control are handled will set important patterns for later issues.

Population pressures increase the likelihood of widespread government drives, or even coercion, to limit births. Couples who are warned by genetic counseling that they risk producing deformed offspring would face far greater pressure than they do now to avoid having children; those with defective genes could become, in effect, second-class citizens, a caste of genetic lepers.

One current example illustrates the problem. Amniocentesis can now quite accurately predict whether a fetus is mongoloid; women carrying such abnormal fetuses are now encouraged, where it is legal, to have abortions. Already a number of medical planners are pointing up the cost-effectiveness of abortion in those cases. Unless the birth rate of mongoloid children is reduced, their care by 1975 may well cost some $1.75 billion nationally.

Methodist Paul Ramsey, Professor of Religion at Princeton and one of the top Protestant ethicists in the U.S., protests the aborting of such abnormal fetuses as an unjustified taking of human life. But he does not think moral men can avoid the problems of population and genetic crises. Indeed, he urgently recommends that society develop an "ethics of genetic duty." The right to have children can become an obligation not to have them, Ramsey asserts; it is shocking to him that parents will refuse genetic counseling and take the "grave risk of having defective children rather than remain childless." Dead set as he is against abortion in all but the most serious cases, Ramsey would prefer to see one parent undergo voluntary sterilization, "Genetic imprudence," he says, "is gravely immoral."

To Ramsey and others, genetic surgery —repairing, replacing or suppressing a "sick" gene—could be profoundly moral. Depending on the defect, genetic surgery before or after birth could prevent abnormality, and also insure that it was not passed on. Moral Theologian Bernard Häring of Rome's Accademia Alfonsiana applauds basic remedial intervention as "corrective foresight."

But Häring is one among many, both scientists and ethicists, who find it considerably harder to justify "positive" genetic engineering, restructuring the genes to make the "perfect" man. The prospect suggests apocalyptic possibilities: M.I.T. Biologist Salvador Luria approaches it "with tremendous fear of its potential dangers." Biologist Joshua Lederberg of Stanford University disowns such Utopian aims as a proper goal for serious biology, and even doubts that techniques sophisticated enough to achieve them could be perfected in the near future. But the possibility nonetheless tantalizes: Who would decide what qualities to preserve, and by what standards? Even remedial genetic engineering could pose a distressing problem if it achieved the ability to remove "undesirable" behavior tendencies. Asks Thielicke: "Would one try to eradicate Faust's restlessness, Hamlet's indecision, King Lear's conscience, Romeo and Juliet's conflicts?"

Human cloning, the asexual reproduction of genetic carbon copies, raises similar questions. Who shall be cloned, and why? Great scientists? Composers? Statesmen? When Geneticist Hermann J. Muller first broached the idea of sperm banks in *Out of the Night* (1935), he suggested Lenin as a sperm donor. In later editions, Lenin was conspicuously absent, replaced on Muller's list by Leonardo da Vinci, Descartes, Pasteur, Lincoln and Einstein. Society could well be as fickle—or worse—about cloning. It might create a caste of subservient workers, as in *1984,* or a breed of super-warriors out of a "genetics race" between the U.S. and the U.S.S.R. An even more hideous nightmare would be the "clonal farm," where anyone could keep a deep frozen identical twin on hand for organ transplants.

Such fanciful fears tend to obscure deeper ethical and practical objections to cloning. The process could be used, for example, to allow a woman to produce a child without passing on her own or her mate's defective gene. A cell nucleus from the genetically sound parent could be substituted for the nucleus in her egg. But even that quite reasonable application could introduce a novel set of complications. Would the cloned child develop a sibling rivalry with its biological parent? Would he face a severe identity crisis, being someone else's "duplicate"? Beyond such considerations, a number of scientists and ethicists would list cloning among those things that men should never do, even if they can. Says Embryologist Robert T. Francoeur, author of *Utopian Motherhood:* "Xeroxing of people? It shouldn't be done in the labs, even once, with humans."

To many critics cloning is only one of several biological developments that threaten what Paul Ramsey calls "a basic form of humanity": the family. Ramsey thinks that artificial insemination by a donor, which is already fairly common, has opened the door to further invasions of family integrity. In his recent book *Fabricated Man,* he mentions other possible developments: artificial inovulation (the "prenatal" adoption of someone else's fertilized egg), "women hiring mercenaries to bear their children," and "babies produced in hatcheries." Beyond finding some of the possibilities repellent, Ramsey argues that they violate "covenant-fidelity," a bond of spiritual and physical faithfulness, between wife and husband or parent and child.

Francoeur, on the other hand, feels that the new embryology can lead to a fresh flexibility in the family structure. He favors host mothers (Ramsey's "mercenaries") because some women want children but cannot carry them to term. In an opposite way, artificial inovulation could be the means for a sterile mother to bear a child, even if not from her own egg. But he draws the line at artifical wombs, which, he says, "would produce nothing but psychological monsters." Others emphasize that the family itself must survive to fill important psychological needs. Molecular Biologist Leon Kass, who left the research labs to become executive secretary of the National Academy of Science's Committee on the Life Sciences and Social Policy, puts it effectively: "The family is rapidly becoming the only institution in an increasingly impersonal world where each person is loved not for what he does or makes, but simply because he is. Can our humanity survive its destruction?"

Beyond population control, beyond "Xeroxing" and patterning people, beyond the survival of the family lies the ultimate ethical question: the sanctity of life itself. The move toward new knowledge requires experimentation. The new generation of experiments, however, involves human life, and many moralists suggest that many of those experiments are intrinsically evil because they toy with life. They point, for example, to the experiments by Italian Biologist Daniele Petrucci, who in 1961 announced that he had kept a fertilized egg alive for 29 days *in vitro* (in the glass) before letting it die because it was monstrously deformed. Another Petrucci embryo lived for 59 days before it died because of a laboratory mistake. The Vatican, which sternly forbids all experimentation with fertilized eggs, demanded that Petrucci cease his investigations. He agreed to comply.

In a recent experiment conducted by Landrum Shettles at Columbia University, a 100-cell human embryo growing in a petri dish was unceremoniously pipetted in a salt solution onto a glass slide. For those who believe that human life begins with fertilization, Shettles' simple laboratory procedure was an act of unjustifiable killing, even though such experiments might help perfect a morally justified technique like genetic surgery. Even in the case of laboratory mistakes that might produce monsters, argues Bernard Häring, only those that are clearly inhuman should be destroyed. A number of scientists, on the other hand, subscribe to an alternate ethical view that an embryo is not human until later in its development—perhaps as early as two months or as late as six months.

Most scientists, naturally, fight what they see as arbitrary limits on their right to experiment. But not all. Testifying before the House subcommittee on science in January, Molecular Biologist James Watson took time off from his cancer investigations to express concern about developments in embryo research, predicting that many biologists would soon join Britain's R.G. Edwards in experimenting with human eggs. Watson suggested that one course of action could be to prohibit all research on human cell fusion and embryos. Failing that, he proposed international agreements limiting such research before it becomes widespread and irresponsible, and before "the cat is totally out of the bag."

Watson is not alone in his worries. Last summer Biologist James Shapiro, one of three young scientists who successfully isolated a bacterial gene, gave up his promising career to take up social work because he feared government misuse of genetic achievements. An Episcopal priest, Canon Michael Hamilton of Washington (D.C.) Cathedral, called Shapiro's action a "loss of nerve." Yet the looming issues are enough to test the nerve of any thoughtful man. Central is the question: Who will decide? Who will make the choices not only of life and death, but what kind of life?

To consider such issues, Roman Catholic Lay Theologian Daniel Callahan and a number of like-minded ethicists and scientists have set up the Institute of Society, Ethics and the Life Sciences. Among the 70 members are Geneticist Theodosius Dobzhansky, Psychiatrist Willard Gaylin, Theologian John C. Bennett, and U.S. Senator Walter F. Mondale of Minnesota, who three years ago introduced a bill to establish an interdisciplinary committee to examine new scientific problems. It did not pass, but Mondale is trying again this year. "There may still be time," he says, "to establish some ground rules."

The long-term goal of the institute, says Callahan, is "legitimizing the problems," making the study of ethical issues a respectable part of the scientific curriculum. Too many scientists, says Gaylin, "see this as something mushy, something for Sunday morning, beyond the realm of science." To change that situation, the institute is trying to educate legislators on the importance of ethical considerations, and is encouraging universities to offer a solid background in ethical studies for "every scientific professional." At the Texas Medical Center in Houston, a similar interdisciplinary effort has been started by the Institute of Religion and Human Development and the Baylor College of Medicine. The Sunday School Board of the Southern Baptist Convention has developed a thorough adult-education course on biomedical issues as one of its electives for this spring.

Cancer Researcher Van Rensselaer Potter of the University of Wisconsin has suggested in a new book, *Bioethics,* that the U.S. create a fourth branch of Government, a Council for the Future, to consider scientific developments and recommend appropriate legislation.

Indeed, some form of super-agency may be the only solution to the formidable legal problems sure to arise. Already, laws relating to artificial insemination by a donor are in confusion; developments such as donor mothers and cloning will raise even more complicated questions. If a mother had herself cloned without her husband's permission, for only one example, would he be legally responsible for the child?

Some scientists, however, frankly believe that laymen are ill equipped to discuss issues with them, let alone share control of what they do. The matters, they contend, are technical and should be decided by the technical men who understand them. Even if government does enter the field, points out Daniel Callahan, much of the success of any ethical policy will depend on a responsible professional code. "If you depend solely on laws, sanctions and enforcements," says Callahan, "the game is over." Molecular Biologist Francis Crick is confident that basic morals and common sense will prevail. Some of the wilder genetic proposals will never be adopted, he claims, because "people will simply not stand for them."

Some ethicists and scientists argue that the worries, the plans and the proposals are premature, that ethics has always been an *ad hoc* thing, dealing with the world as it is, not as it might be in the future. Given the enormousness of the new problems and the speed of change, that attitude may be a luxury.

Beyond the sanctity of human life, the single criterion that ethicists most often mention as an absolute, or nearly one, is human freedom. Scientific advances, as they see it, can either promote freedom or inhibit it, but the distinctions are not always obvious or easy. The danger is that a democratic society might therefore fail to act at all, and by default pass the problems—and the solutions—to a small, uncontrolled elite, leading perhaps ultimately to a totalitarian government. The late author C. S. Lewis warned more than a quarter century ago that "man's power over Nature is really the power of some men over other men, with Nature as their instrument."

COMMENT: WHO IS TO DECIDE?

Our understanding of intracerebral mechanisms is growing at an impressive rate. Our power to influence the physical and functional properties of the brain is also increasing rapidly, and very soon we may be able to enhance or diminish specific behavioral qualities. Who, then, is going to decide the mental shape of future man, and what will be the bases for his decisions? Should we encourage individuality or conformism, rebellion or submissiveness, emotion or intellect? What are the risks of misusing this as yet incalculable power? What ethical principles should be established?

Rejecting the myth that each individual is born with a mental homunculus, and accepting the fact that we are merely a product of genes plus sensory inputs provided by the surroundings, we approach a conclusion similar to that formulated so lucidly by Skinner: Cultures must be designed with a human purpose. Just as we have developed city planning, we should propose mental planning as a new and important discipline to formulate theories and practical means for directing the evolution of future man. We should not consider ourselves the end product of evolution; rather, we should try to imagine that thousands of years from now the inhabitants of the earth could differ more from present man than we differ from gorillas and chimpanzees.

The key factor for our future development is human intelligence, which could play a decisive role in evolution.

In confronting the question "Who is to decide the qualities of future men?" we should remember that when a machine or an ideology has enough appeal and applicability, it will spread and it will be used. Our present task is to investigate the biological and mental capabilities of man and to evaluate the choices for future development. Then these choices should be made available to society and to the individual.

JOSÉ DELGADO

14 PSYCHOSURGERY: LEGITIMATE THERAPY OR LAUNDERED LOBOTOMY?*

C. HOLDEN

The controversy over what some call the "new wave" of psychosurgery has been gaining momentum over the past year. It has rushed into a realm where data are scanty and unreliable, and where there are few legal, medical, or ethical guideposts. Neither the government nor the medical profession has established standards for the selection and treatment of psychosurgery patients, and some people think the way is clear for a new lobotomy boom like that which occurred in the 1940's and early 1950's.

One measure of the visibility of the problem is that Senator Edward Kennedy (D—Mass.) recently devoted a morning to hearings on the subject in connection with a bill he plans to introduce on medical experimentation with human beings.

If any single individual is responsible for getting the issue out in the open, it is Peter Breggin, a Washington psychiatrist who writes "brave new world" novels about psychosurgery. Breggin opposes any and all psychosurgery on the grounds that the operations have a general blunting effect on emotions and thought processes and that there is no theoretical or empirical justification for any of them.

This argument presupposes general agreement on a precise definition of "psychosurgery," but no such agreement exists. Grossly speaking it can be defined as the destruction or removal of brain tissue for the purpose of altering certain behavior. There are many kinds of procedures—what has aroused most concern is the fact that some surgeons are doing brain surgery on subjects prone to habitual violence. Critics think this is only a step away from using psychosurgery or the threat of it as a tool for social control.

The antipsychosurgery factions see little difference between current procedures and the old prefrontal lobotomies, of which about 50,000 were performed for disorders ranging across the spectrum of mental illness and brain disease. Lobotomies reduced the populations of mental hospitals. They also left an indeterminate number of semi-vegetables in their wake.

It was not the medical profession that called a halt to these operations. Rather, it was the development of a new family of tranquilizing drugs called phenothiazines. But as it became evident that there are some people whose condition intensive drug therapy can't alleviate, psychosurgery began a tentative comeback, this time in a far more

*From C. Holden, Psychosurgery: Legitimate therapy or laundered lobotomy? *Science*, Mar. 16, 1973, **179**, 1109–1112. Copyright 1973 by the American Association for the Advancement of Science.

refined form. The lobotomy has been abandoned in favor of interventions in various parts of the limbic system—the portion of the brain that rules the higher functions of emotion, self-awareness, and creativity. Stereotaxic surgical procedures, which enable electrodes to be inserted and directed to any part of the brain, have made operations highly selective. The trouble is, there is still no conclusive evidence correlating specific brain structures with specific behavior.

At present, probably no more than 500 psychosurgery operations per year are being performed in this country, by perhaps a dozen neurosurgeons. Nonetheless, the new ways scientists are finding to tamper with the nature of life itself, combined with the social awareness born of the political upheavals of the 1960's, have produced a considerably higher level of sensitivity than that which governed brain surgery two decades ago.

The controversy centers upon brain operations to control violent behavior allegedly associated with epilepsy, and criticism has been focused on a trio of doctors associated with Harvard University: William Sweet, chief of neurosurgery at Massachusetts General Hospital; Vernon Mark, neurosurgery chief at Boston City Hospital; and Frank Ervin, a psychiatrist and neurologist who is now on the faculty of the University of California at Los Angeles and associated with the newly formed Center for the Prevention of Violence there.

In 1967, these three wrote the *Journal of the American Medical Association* a letter that has now become a staple exhibit among the opponents of psychosurgery. The letter suggested that, while environmental and social factors undoubtedly played a role in the urban riots that were then raging through the country's metropolitan centers, another factor was being ignored: namely, the possible role played by brain disease—"focal lesions" that spur "senseless" assaultive and destructive behavior. There is a need, said the letter, for research and clinical studies to "pinpoint, diagnose, and treat those people with low violence thresholds before they contribute to further tragedies."

Around the same time, the group set up a Neuro Research Foundation at Boston City Hospital to carry out the appropriate studies and identify possible subjects for brain surgery. In 1970, through various mysterious maneuvers that no one seems to be able to explain, they persuaded Congress to direct the National Institute of Mental Health (NIMH) to award them a $500,000 grant to carry on their work. Louis Wienkowski, director of NIMH extramural research, says NIMH was not prepared to support such activity and tried to fulfill congressional intent by using the money for animal studies. But the funds eventually found their way to the Sweet group in the form of a closely monitored contract, with the stipulation that no brain operations on human beings be performed. While Sweet's work was regarded with apprehension by the medical community, the law enforcement community has shown more enthusiasm: at about the same time, the foundation obtained a grant of $108,000 from the Law Enforcement Assistance Administration of the Justice Department to test procedures for screening habitually violent male penitentiary inmates for brain damage.

Congressional interest, too, remained alive last year. The Senate Labor-Health, Education, and Welfare appropriations subcommittee, headed by Warren Magnuson (D—Wash.), was so impressed with Sweet's testimony on the need to investigate the relationship between violence and brain disease that they stuck a $1 million line item in the budget of the National Institute for Neurological Diseases and Stroke (NINDS) to be applied to research in this area. The appropriation was killed when President Nixon vetoed the Labor-HEW bill last September, and its resurrection is unlikely.

Murray Goldstein of NINDS says Congress did not earmark the funds for Sweet's work in particular and that the money would not have been used to support experimental surgery on human beings in any case. Nonetheless, the issue of the $1 million has mobilized protests from a number of government scientists and mental health professionals. Calling themselves the NIMH-NINDS Ad Hoc Committee on Psychosurgery, they have circulated petitions opposing the appropriation. "Since psychosurgery can severely impair a person's intellectual and emotional capacities, the prospects for repression and social control are disturbing,'' says the petition.

POLARIZATION

As this wording indicates, the public controversy has picked up the whole range of procedures that fit into the category of psychosurgery and placed them firmly in the political realm —with those at the extreme ends of the debate, such as Breggin and a University of Mississippi neurosurgeon named O. J. Andy, doing most of the talking.

Staging a Breggin-Andy confrontation seems to be the currently popular way of trying to cast light on the psychosurgery question. (Most recently, these two were key witnesses at the Kennedy hearings). Breggin, who has been labeled a ''fanatic'' by at least one respectable neuroscientist, flatly opposes any intervention in the brain for the purpose of altering behavior. Psychosurgery is an ''abortion of the brain'' and is being used to repress and vegetabilize the helpless: the poor, the women, the black, the imprisoned, and the institutionalized. Andy has allowed himself to be made something of a scapegoat by critics of psychosurgery. He operates on institutionalized individuals whom, he says, ''everyone else has found hopeless.'' Many are wards of the state; most are children. His motives have not been impugned, but his methods of diagnosis, patient selection, and follow-up—''casual to the point of irresponsibility,'' as psychiatrist Willard Gaylin of the Hastings Institute has called them—as well as his limited sensitivity to the ethical issues involved, make him a handy target.

Another highly vocal commentator is David Eaton, an influential Washington, D.C., minister who states flatly that, if somebody doesn't do something, psychosurgery will be used to repress blacks, if it isn't already. A recent article in *Ebony* carried the same message and was entitled, ''New threat to blacks: Brain surgery to control behavior.''

It is not difficult to understand the concern among blacks and other relatively powerless groups about a procedure that is hedged by virtually no legal safeguards. For example, Santa Monica neurosurgeon M. Hunter Brown is quoted as saying he did 20 operations on people who came to him as a result of an article in the *National Enquirer,* a human interest tabloid in which Brown tells how, with thermal probes, he can turn ''vicious killers'' into ''happy peaceful citizens.''

The issue has become highly confused, partly because discussions of psychosurgery fail to differentiate among various procedures and the purposes for which they are used. The cingulumotomy is probably the most prevalent kind of operation, according to Paul Fedio of NINDS. This is not performed for violence-associated disorders and is probably psychosurgery in its purest form because it is done for behavioral disorders in persons with no apparent brain pathology. H. T. Ballantine of Massachusetts General Hospital is probably the most prolific cingulotomist, and he does it for alleviation of pain as well as for various ''neuropsychiatric illnesses'' such as depression, anxiety states, and obsessional neuroses that have not proved amenable to other kinds of treatment.

Then there is the thalamotomy, which was used in the past to curb the psychomotor effects of Parkinson's disease, and has since been replaced by the drug L-dopa. Thalamotomies are still in the running, though, with O. J. Andy using this procedure for persons suffering from ''hyperresponsive syndrome,'' a vaguely defined disorder marked by violence and total unmanageability. Andy says all his patients suffer from ''structural pathology'' of the brain.

Finally (for the purpose of this article), there is the amygdalotomy. Fedio says this procedure was originally developed to curb epilepsy. Sweet and his colleagues are extending this procedure to people with diagnosable brain damage—who suffer outbursts of uncontrollable violence, but who do not necessarily have epilepsy. One problem is that the connection between violence and epilepsy is extremely murky. Furthermore, says Fedio, there is no concrete evidence that an individual's violent behavior is associated with the specific damage that has been located in his brain.

Many neuroscientists who believe some forms of psychosurgery are beneficial have heavy reservations about intervention to alleviate violence.

But since no one seems to know what to do about it, it looks as though some decisions are about to be made willy-nilly by the courts. One such case, apparently the first of its kind, is scheduled to be decided soon by a court in Detroit. It all began with a proposal by two doctors associated with the Lafayette Clinic, the psychiatric teaching hospital of Wayne State University. The doctors, Jacques S. Gottlieb and Ernst A. Rodin, put together 3 years ago a "Proposal for the Study of the Treatment of Uncontrollable Aggression at Lafayette Clinic." The Michigan legislature subsequently appropriated $228,400 for the research project, which was designed to compare the use of amygdalotomy and drug therapy on two comparable groups of patients. The subjects were all to be nonpsychotic, brain damaged males (because females have "more diffuse brain diseases") over 25, with I.Q.'s over 80, hospitalized for at least 5 years, who had been subjected unsuccessfully to all other known forms of treatment, who remembered their violent acts and felt remorse about them, and who were capable of understanding and deciding whether they wanted to undergo the treatment.

The first subject chosen was a 36-year-old man, known as a criminal sexual psychopath, who had been in Ionia State Hospital for 18 years since he murdered and raped a nurse (in that order). The subject and his parents have both signed the consent form, and he is said to be very eager to have the operation, although he was fully informed of possible undesirable side-effects, including death. With the concurrence of two committees, one to review candidate selection, the other to guard the patient's interests, the operation was scheduled for 15 January.

Then Gabe Kaimowitz, a Michigan Legal Services lawyer and member of the Medical Committee for Human Rights, found out about it, and the matter blew up in the press. Kaimowitz asked for court review of the matter, claiming that the patient is being detained under a now-obsolete law, that the circumstances (the subject wants the operation so he can get out) make informed consent impossible, and that the use of public funds for the project is inappropriate.

One likely outcome of the case—to be decided by a three-judge panel of the Wayne County Circuit Court—could be a ruling that this type of surgery should not be performed on involuntarily institutionalized patients. It has focused a good deal of public attention on the matter and has drawn the attention of public interest groups, including Washington's Center for Law and Social Policy. "The case will establish an important precedent for efforts to impose social control on the uses of psychosurgery," says Charles Halpern of the center.

"Psychosurgery," says Ayub K. Ommaya of NINDS, "is a failure of medicine." Far more research needs to be done before guidelines for its appropriate use can be formulated. On the other hand, he points out, there are rare instances —intractable pain or *anorexia nervosa* (self-induced starvation), for example—where a brain operation appears to be the only answer.

There now appears to be a gradually coagulating body of "responsible opinion." One possible move, proposed at the symposium on behavior control at the last AAAS meeting, would be for the government to establish regulations that would surround the use of an experimental surgical procedure with the same kind of safeguards the Food and Drug Administration applies to new pharmaceutical procedures. Protocols might be set up to govern the selection of patients—requiring the approval of various review committees, assuring that all alternatives have been exhausted, and defining "informed consent." The last is particularly difficult, for, as Gaylin says, "The damaged organ is the organ of consent."

Operations on institutionalized individuals might be banned, as might surgery for controlling violence, because of the political implications and the rudimentary state of knowledge about the connection between violence and brain disease.

So far, professional organizations such as the American Medical Association have had little to say. Exceptions are the American Orthopsychiatric Association, which is filing an *amicus curiae* brief in the Detroit case, and the Society for Neuroscience, which has made psychosurgery its theme for the year.

The federal health establishment is taking an increasingly visible interest in the questions surrounding psychosurgery. Bertram Brown, director of NIMH, made the strongest public declaration by a high government official to date when he said at the Kennedy hearings that he believes there is not enough known about the brain to supply clear justification for such operations. Meanwhile, NIMH and NINDS have set up an "inter-institute work group" to define problems surrounding psychosur-

gery and make recommendations, due next June, on future priorities in brain research.

A lot of defining needs to be done. Broadly speaking, "psychosurgery" could include electroshock therapy, prolonged drug therapy, and the insertion of electrodes for diagnostic purposes, since all of these can make permanent alterations in brain tissue.

Some people think the psychosurgery issue is getting more attention than it deserves. It is really at the extreme end of a massive spectrum of increasingly sophisticated ways people are learning to manipulate each other. But as such, it may spur people to find ways of assessing how new behavioral technologies encroach on individual freedom and to decide on the extent to which they are desirable.

15 BRAIN POWER:
The Case for Bio-Feedback Training*

BARNARD LAW COLLIER

Inside a darkened chamber in the laboratory of Dr. Lester Fehmi sits Ralph Press, a nineteen-year-old mathematics student at the State University of New York in Stony Brook, Long Island. Relaxed in an armchair with his eyes closed, Ralph is undergoing his eleventh session of bio-feedback training to help him learn to control his brain waves.

Four silver electrodes are pasted to Ralph's scalp, their orange lead wires plugged into an electroencephalograph that is tracing his brain-wave activity on thick ribbons of EEG paper in the next room. The silence in the soundproofed chamber is broken only by the long and short

*From B. L. Collier, Brain power: The case for bio-feedback training. *Saturday Review*, Apr. 10, 1971, pp. 10–13, 58. Reprinted by permission of the author and the publisher.

beepings of a rather high-pitched tone: the key to Ralph's bio-feedback training.

Dr. Fehmi, a professor of psychology at Stony Brook, has told Ralph that he can learn to increase his brain's output of an eight-to-fourteen-cycle-per-second brain sine wave called alpha. Alpha waves are one of four known brain waves. They are generated, billions of them, by the tiny electrical pulses that surge through the brain as it does its complex chores. High production of alpha waves is often associated with the objective state of peak mental and physical performance, a relaxed yet extremely sensitive alertness.

Dr. Fehmi and George Sintchak, the Stony Brook psychology department's chief electronic engineer, have rigged the EEG machine and a computer so that each time Ralph's brain generates a burst of alpha activity the occurrence is recorded, timed, and almost instantly made known to Ralph by means of the beeping tone. The tone is Ralph's bio-feedback. It is an audible signal that lets Ralph be consciously aware of a visceral function, in this case the production of his alpha brain waves, which his mind ordinarily blocks out, ignores, or is unable to perceive without external assistance. When Ralph's brain generates only snippets of alpha radiation, the tone comes in staccato little blips. As he produces more and more alpha, the tone stays on longer and longer. Ralph, of course, wants to succeed by producing as much alpha as he can.

For nearly an hour, Ralph shows minute-by-minute improvement in his ability to keep the tone on. A computer read-out verifies that he is maintaining the tone for a cumulative average of twenty-eight seconds out of each minute. "He's one of our super-subjects," Dr. Fehmi remarks. "He's not the best, but he's getting pretty good."

Ralph's alpha waves are of high amplitude, very rhythmic and regular. This is what they look like as they are traced by the jiggling pens of the EEG machine:

"OK, Ralph," Dr. Fehmi says quietly over the intercom, "I want you to turn the tone off and keep it off."

The tone that Ralph has learned to sustain for upwards of three seconds now goes beep, beep, *blip;* within seconds, it has died away except for tiny random beeps. This what it looks like on the EEG tracing as Ralph begins to stop his alpha waves:

"Now turn the tone back on," Dr. Fehmi says.

A pause of a second or so and the tone beeps back to life and stays on for seconds at a time. Then on, off, on, off. The tests continue until it is clear that Ralph is in personal command of his brain's alpha-wave activity as evidenced by the EEG machine's record.

A steady flow of new scientific findings indicates that, with the aid of the teaching technique called bio-feedback training, man can learn to control willfully his body and his state of consciousness to a degree that traditionally has been dismissed in Western cultures as mere trickery or condemned as somehow wicked or blasphemous.

Projects in hospitals and research laboratories around the world are convincingly demonstrating that it may be possible to learn personal mastery over the functions of our visceral organs—the heart, liver, kidneys, intestines, glands, and blood vessels—in the same specific way that we learn to manipulate our fingers to play Chopin or our legs to kick a field goal. There is also highly intriguing research going on in laboratories like Dr. Fehmi's to demonstrate that with bio-feedback training we can learn self-control over the electrical activity of our brain. These studies indicate that man may possess the ability to will himself into whatever state of consciousness seems most appropriate to his environment, to accomplishing a task at hand, or to some special pursuit.

The implications of bio-feedback training are proving terribly easy to overstate, given the limited amount of solid experimental evidence that presently exists. People seem peculiarly ready nowadays to lunge at the adventurous prospect of employing new methods and modern technology to explore and conquer one's own brain and body instead of, say, the moon or Southeast Asia. The propensity for exaggeration about progress in this area frightens prudent scientists. Already they are encountering the con artists, the charlatans, and the quacks who are taking people's money by glibly mouthing the jargon associated with bio-feedback research and similar studies of the mind's control over internal organs. This caveat is offered early because it is difficult to keep one's imagination reined in unless one is warned that much of the data accumulated so far are limited to experiments with rats, monkeys, rabbits, or other lab animals. And the remarkable results with animals may not travel well from the laboratory to humans. Nevertheless, research teams are reporting an ever increasing number of cases in which human subjects have unquestionably gained conscious control over visceral organs once thought beyond the mastery of the mind.

In Baltimore, for example, Dr. Bernard T. Engel, a psychologist, and Dr. Eugene Bleecker, a cardiovascular specialist, have conducted bio-feedback training sessions with eight patients suffering from premature ventricular contractions, a dangerous irregularity of the heartbeat involving the heart's main pumping chamber. With significant success, these patients have learned to speed, slow, and narrowly regulate their heart by force of mental discipline alone.

At the Gerontology Research Center of the National Institute of Child Health and Human Development, Dr. Engel and Dr. Bleecker use a visual form of bio-feedback training to help patients control their heart. In a typical experiment, the patient lies quietly on a hospital bed in a small, windowless laboratory near Dr. Engel's office. The electrodes of an electrocardiograph are attached to his chest and pulse points, and the EKG machine is hooked up with a specially programmed computer. On the bed table in front of the patient sits a small metal box fitted with a red, a yellow, and a green light in the same pattern as a regular traffic signal. The display is hooked into the computer, which almost instantly analyzes the EKG readings and provides bio-feedback information to the patient by means of the flashing colored lights.

The first phase of the training is speeding the heart rate. The patient may be told that when the yellow light goes on he will know that his heart is beating faster; the green light flashing on means it is slowing down. A small meter next to the light box indicates to the patient what percentage of time he is succeeding in keeping the yellow light lit. The goal for the heart patient, of course, is to gain control over the lights and his heartbeat in the same way Ralph Press controlled the beeping tone and his alpha-wave production: by sheer mental effort, and without any muscular exertion—which amounts to cheating.

After a patient learns to speed his heart, he is then taught to slow it down with the red light and later to keep it beating within narrow normal limits, with the three lights acting as too fast, too slow, and normal signals. Some of Dr. Engel's patients have achieved a 20 percent speeding or slowing of their hearts—about sixteen beats a minute from an eighty-beat-per-minute base. This self-willed rate change in one direction or the other tends to even out the irregular beats. Why? Researchers are not quite sure, but it works.

But what happens when the patient goes home, away from Dr. Engel's bio-feedback light box? The final stage of the five-phase training program is the stepped withdrawal of the bio-feedback light signals. The patient, after extensive training, finds he can deliberately alter his heartbeats in the desired direction without artificial feedback. One of Dr. Engel's patients could still remember how to control his rate after two years. That Dr. Engel's patients retain what they have learned without the aid of an electronic device to provide feedback is what excites many researchers who feel that we may be capable of discovering unknown mechanisms, or "feedback loops," within ourselves that will allow us, after some basic training, to monitor our viscera and their functions at will throughout life.

In Boston and New York City, scientists are trying to see how people with hypertension can effectively lower their abnormally high blood pressure by thinking it down. Under the direction of Dr. Neal E. Miller, a professor of physiological psychology at Rockefeller University in New York and a pioneer in the brain sciences, experiments are now proceeding to discover if human subjects can learn to control the contractions of their intestinal tract. Laboratory rats have learned to control these contractions with notable success. If humans can do as well, it could mean relief from much suffering for people with spastic colons and similar gastrointestinal ailments usually associated with stress and psychosomatic illness.

Dr. Miller was in the forefront of what seemed, just a decade or so ago, a vain and somewhat foolhardy challenge to the bedrock idea that the viscera and the autonomic nervous system that controls them operate entirely independently of an animal's deliberate control. Dr. Miller has traced back to Plato the dogma that the organs controlled by the autonomic nervous system function at a kind of cave-mannish level, learning only in classical Pavlovian fashion to react to such stimuli as sour lemons and growling bears. On the other hand, the somatic, or cerebrospinal, nervous system, which transmits nerve signals from the brain to the spinal cord and directly to the skeletal muscles, can learn by the sophisticated trial-and-error instrumental process. Perhaps the Greeks considered it an act of hubris to believe that they, not the gods, exercised command of their heart, brain, and guts. Dr. Engel, who also has studied the accumulated prejudices against the viscera, can recite a chain of erroneous proofs put forth until only a few years ago by scientists who, with a kind of religious fervor, had shunned anatomical facts and new information in order to steadfastly support Plato.

At the root of the research reports on bio-feedback training is what Dr. Miller describes as "an almost complete change in our way of thinking about viscera and their ability to learn. We are now able to regard the activities of our internal organs as behavior in the same sense that the movements of our hands and fingers are behavior. This is the basic stem of it all, but just where this rather radical new orientation will lead, we can't be sure yet."

Some indications that we can possibly control our viscera have been around for centuries without anyone's grasping their import. Dr. Miller points out that actors and actresses can control their tear glands, which are visceral organs, to make themselves cry on cue. It is possible that some classical conditioning is involved: The actor recalls something sad and the sadness makes him cry. But many actors and actresses say they can cry without any recalling, that all they have to do is think "cry" and the tears flow.

Magicians and mystics and meditators have often gained mental control over visceral organs to a significant degree. Harry Houdini is said to have been able to swallow and regurgitate a key that would unlock him from some otherwise unopenable box. If he did this, it would mean he had gained mastery over the muscles of his esophagus and stomach, part of the viscera.

A few yogis, it would seem, can control their metabolism to some extent. But whether or not they "cheat" by using skeletal muscles instead of only their mind to perform their tricks is unknown. Scientists have found that some yogis who can "stop" their hearts so that no pulse or sound of beating can be detected are actually performing what is called the Valsalva maneuver. By taking a deep breath, closing their windpipe, and breathing hard to increase the pressure inside their chest and around their heart, they collapse the veins to the heart and clamp off the return of blood. This arrests heart sounds and the pulse, but an EKG shows that the heart is still beating and usually quite fast. "We must reexamine a lot of phenomena we may have dismissed as fakery before," Dr. Miller says.

The belief in a "superior" somatic nervous system and an "inferior" autonomic nervous system was so strong that, according to Dr. Miller, "for more than a dozen years I had extreme difficulty getting students or even paid assistants to conduct experiments on the control of internal organs." But Dr. Miller persisted, and his research has led many other scientists to abandon the old dogma. He has shown that the internal organs in animals and to a significant extent in man, as well, are capable of learning by trial and error—and with a startling degree of specificity and discrimination. In one experiment, which Dr. Miller particularly enjoys mentioning, he and his research colleague, Dr. Leo V. DiCara, tuned their instrumental conditioning process down so fine that a rat learned to blush one ear and blanch the other. In almost all of his animal experiments, Dr. Miller paralyzes the rats and other lab animals with curare, a powerful drug used by South American Indians to tip their poison darts. The curare interferes with all the nerve impulses that keep the skeletal muscles working—including respiration. The paralyzing of the skeletal muscles ensures that the animals do not "cheat" by somehow using their skeletal muscles to affect their visceral responses. (It is thus far a frustration for Dr. Miller and others that non-curarized animals are slower to learn viscerally than the curarized ones.)

The difference between the way the body learns by classical conditioning and by instrumental conditioning is crucial to understanding how bio-feedback training works. Classical conditioning, or learning, always demands a stimulus that elicits an innate response. For example, the first time you ever saw a lemon, nothing much happened with your saliva glands, which are visceral organs. But after you first tasted its sour juice, your saliva glands automatically secreted lots of saliva to dilute and wash away the puckering citric acid. You cannot control the response of your saliva glands to the lemon juice, and after you have tasted several lemons your mouth will start watering at the very sight of one. You have been classically conditioned to salivate at the sight of lemons. The same thing works for other such stimuli: a mad dog, for example. The sight of one will boost your heart rate, increase your adrenaline flow, and generally activate other innate fear responses.

The process of instrumental learning is much less limited since it requires no specific stimulus to provoke a response. If you want to sink a twelve-foot golf putt, for instance, there is nothing anyone can offer you, not a lemon or $5,000, that will get your body to hole the ball out with Pavlovian sureness. But by the process of trial and error, or instrumental conditioning, you can learn to coordinate your muscles and other responses. You stroke the ball toward the hole and it glides by. You try again and again. Each time you get closer. You are not aware of precisely what you are doing to improve; you cannot say which muscles are contracting or relaxing and in what order. But you get closer nonetheless, and each near success is a reward that is likely to keep you trying. At last you are in control of your muscles, your responses, and the golf ball. It plunks into the hole. This trial-and-error process is called instrumental learning.

Now imagine that you are trying to make the same putt blindfolded. Very difficult, if not impossible. Why? Because something essential is missing from the learning process: feedback. In this case, the feedback is the sight of the ball getting closer to the cup. Of course, you could learn to make the putt blindfolded if you substituted for the feedback of your visual perception the voice (feedback) of your caddy. He might, at the simplest level say "yes" when your direction was right and say nothing or "no" when it wasn't. He might offer more guidance: "A little more to the right" or "A little to the left and harder." You would still be badly handicapped by the impreci-

sion of your caddy's secondhand information, but eventually you would sink one and then perhaps quite a few.

Our mind is in some ways like the blindfolded golfer where the viscera are concerned. Scientists are trying to find new ways to remove the blindfold, which is enormously difficult indeed, or to substitute the guidance of the caddy-type feedback for sensory information about visceral organs that the mind for some reason dismisses or never perceives. Dr. Fehmi's beeping tone and the mini-volt currents of pleasurable brain stimulation that lab rats get are simple reward bio-feedback signals; Dr. Engel's colored lights represent more guidance. All are examples of bio-feedback used to instrumentally condition internal organs by letting the mind know, within predetermined limits, what those organs are up to.

One path of bio-feedback research has branched slightly away from the strictly therapeutic approach and is investigating the ability of human beings to exert purposeful control over their visceral functions, especially their brain functions, with the goal of making the essentially healthy person better able to cope with his world. At the United States Navy Medical Neuropsychiatric Research Unit in San Diego, California, Dr. Ardie Lubin and Dr. David Hord, both psychologists, are studying the relationship between the output of alpha waves and sleep. What they want to determine is whether or not a person deprived of sleep can be returned to a state of effectiveness and acceptable decision-making capacity by willing himself into an alpha state for a certain length of time. Some preliminary tests have shown that alpha states may be recuperative.

At the Langley Porter Neuropsychiatric Institute, part of the University of California Medical Center in San Francisco, a research group headed by Dr. Joe Kamiya is exploring the possibility that brain-wave control may have important effects on health, creativity, and such mental functions as perception and memory. Dr. Kamiya is regarded by most psychologists as the pioneer in the field of brain-wave control. Dr. Kamiya and his research team have found that subjects who do best at mastering their alpha-wave output are those who have had some training in meditation, as in Zen. At Stony Brook, Dr. Fehmi has noted that musicians, athletes, and artists are especially adept at control over their brain waves. Conversely, he has found that subjects who come into his chamber and slouch in their armchair in the spaced-out way associated with drug trips produce precious little alpha.

It is frustrating to researchers that the subjects who are most proficient in gaining brain-wave control are often strangely tongue-tied when it comes to telling just how they do it. Some say they relax and wipe everything from their mind. Others concentrate on some infinite point like a mystical third eye in the middle of their forehead. Some are unable to verbalize the experience at all.

"The best way I can describe the feeling of alpha," says Dr. Fehmi, "is a relaxed but alert and sensitive 'into-it-ness.'" Dr. Edgar E. Coons, a physiological psychologist at New York University and a musician, has been trained to produce alpha waves in Dr. Fehmi's lab; he says the alpha state "makes me feel as if I'm floating about half an inch above my seat." A talented young musician named David Rosenboom, who recently presented a bio-feedback brain-wave concert at Automation House in New York (brain-wave activity was fed into a computer and an ARP synthesizer; the result was a weird but not unpleasing effect), is the reigning champion brain-wave producer for Dr. Fehmi. When his alpha is really going strong in all parts of his brain, Rosenboom says he is plugged in to a "great energy source." Another musician named LaMonte Young, who keeps a forty-cycle "home" tone going in his Manhattan studio at all times, explained that he had no trouble generating alpha the first time he ever tried it, because his mind "is tuned to frequencies and intervals."

At the University of Colorado Medical School, Dr. Hans Stoyva has had notable success in teaching his patients how to relax specific muscles that tense up and cause certain kinds of tension headaches. The easing of pain has been swift and dramatic.

Dr. Martin Orme, director of experimental psychiatry at the University of Pennsylvania Medical School in Philadelphia, is studying the alpha-wave phenomenon with an eye toward finding out what exactly an alpha state does to or for an individual and how it might be beneficial to him. "It's not enough to know you can contemplate your navel," Dr. Orme says. "You then have to ask, 'What happens?'" Experiments conducted with subjects who have been trained to produce a reliably high alpha-wave output show, according to Dr. Orme, that critical thinking tends to interfere with alpha waves, but that alpha-wave production does not mean blunted intellectual capacity. What alpha production seems to do best for the alpha producer is relax him, insulate him from stressful critical thought, and rehabilitate his autonomic nervous system to some degree.

"What this may mean," Dr. Orme says, "is that alpha might be used to bring down the level of a person's anxiety to a point where he can function at his best. We all need a certain amount of anxiety to function. It is well accepted that we function best as anxiety rises to a certain point on a bell-shaped curve, and past that point we do increasingly worse as anxiety increases. If alpha can be used to knock down anxiety to the point on the curve where we work most effectively, it can be a most important development." However, Dr. Orme is quick to point out that "this is three levels or more from where we are now, but it is something to consider."

Another prospect for visceral learning is its use as a possible alternative to drugs. If, for example, a high alpha output can cause deep relaxation, or a specific focusing of bio-feedback training can loosen up a taut muscle, this could well substitute for the billions of tranquilizers consumed to achieve essentially the same effect. The advantage over drugs might be considerable. For instance, while a tranquilizer acts in a general way on the whole body or an entire bodily system (perhaps with unwanted side effects), bio-feedback training might be specific enough to do the job required and let the rest of the body function undisturbed.

"There is also," says Dr. Orme, "the general

question of personal control and how we might be able to bring our emotions under control. We want to know, of course, to what extent an individual can gain control with precision and reliability over the things he fears. A good part of fear is the fear of fear. If you know you are going to be hurt, you will hurt more with exactly·the same degree of hurting stimulus. If we can break into some of the feedback loops that are part of the fear cycle, we may be able to control unpleasant and unproductive anxiety.''

To Dr. Orme, the goal is clear. ''We may be able to become actual masters of our destiny. As a psychiatrist, my purpose is to enable man to decide his own fate instead of his juices deciding for him.''

At Rockefeller University, Dr. DiCara, a burly ex-football player, is attempting to unravel some of the whys and hows of visceral learning. In one recent experiment, he and Dr. Eric Stone found that rats trained to increase their heart rate had significantly more of a powerful group of chemicals called catecholamines in their brains and hearts than rats who learned to *lower* their heart rates. In humans, catecholamines are associated with hypertension and coronary artery disease. The possibility of learning to slow the heart rate to achieve beneficial effects on hypertension and heart ailments is intriguing; however, a major obstacle still to be overcome is the inability at present to measure catecholamines in the human brain.

An equally intriguing possibility has been raised by an experiment conducted by Dr. DiCara and Dr. Jay M. Weiss. Rats that had learned to slow their heart rates subsequently showed excellent ability to learn to move back and forth in a shuttle box to avoid an electric shock. Rats trained to speed their hearts learned very poorly and exhibited signs of extreme fearfulness by leaping into the air, squealing, and turning toward their tails with each pulse of shock instead of getting away from it. In contrast, the slow heart-rate rats took each shock in stride, with only ''mild jerks,'' and slowly walked out of the electrified side of the box.

''It is crystal-clear,'' says Dr. Miller, with whom Dr. DiCara has worked as co-experimenter on many projects, ''that heart rate training affects rats' learning. What is further indicated is that the training also affects their emotionality. We cannot jump from the laboratory to the clinic, but we may indeed find that in human subjects trained to lower their heart rates there could be an increased capacity to adapt to stressful situations and a corresponding decrease in emotionality.''

The field of bio-feedback training and visceral learning is still only crudely charted. New research teams are forming to explore further; the mechanical and electronic spin-offs of the space age are providing the new tools and infinitely more sensitive measuring devices that are required for progress. But most of all there seems to be a new attitude.

''We have brought four to five thousand years of cultural myths into the laboratory to be investigated,'' says Dr. Miller, who, in just a few years, has seen the pendulum of interest swing from ''great resistance to great readiness.'' Although he is understandably reluctant to speculate on what the future holds, he is nonetheless confident that the new knowledge about our internal organs will stimulate much more research into the astonishing ability of human beings to learn.

16 BEHAVIOR CONTROL AND SOCIAL RESPONSIBILITY*

LEONARD KRASNER

In recent years, research in psychotherapy has increasingly focused on investigations which could be interpreted as being part of a broad psychology of behavior control. The essential element of behavior control studies is the influence, persuasion, and manipulation of human behavior. Two broad categories of controlling techniques have been utilized. The first can be termed the "social reinforcement" process, namely, those techniques which utilize the behavior of the examiner and structure of the interview situation as a means of influencing behavior. These include studies of psychotherapy, hypnosis, operant conditioning, attitude influence, placebos, and brainwashing. A second category of influence techniques involves the use of physical devices or drugs, such as tranquillizers, brain stimulation, sensory deprivation, or teaching machines. Both categories of investigation have in common the development of techniques for enhancing the effectiveness of the control or manipulation of individual behavior. Many investigators in this field have been influenced by Skinnerian behaviorism with its emphasis on environmental control and shaping of behavior. Although there is as yet no direct evidence on this point, it is hypothesized that the social reinforcement type of influence is more effective than physical devices because the subject is less likely to be aware of them and thus is more likely to respond to them.

It is in the field of psychotherapy that the issues of the *moral and ethical implications* of behavior control first arose as a relevant problem. Psychotherapy involves the direct application of the finding of behavior control. A professionally

trained individual uses a variety of techniques to change, modify, or direct the behavior of another person. It differs from brainwashing in the implied assent given by the patient to this manipulation. This view of the therapist as a manipulator of behavior is one that arouses considerable opposition from many therapists who deny that they are actively involved in controlling behavior. This is perhaps best expressed by Rogers, both in his debate with Skinner (Rogers & Skinner, 1956) and in his article on "Persons or Science" (1955). In this latter paper, he goes into the dangers of control and deplores the tendency toward social control implicit in the results of the kinds of studies discussed in this paper. His attitude is that therapy is a process which is "intensely personal, highly subjective in its inwardness, and dependent entirely on the relationship of two individuals, each of whom is an experiencing media." Rogers contends that:

> Therapists recognize—usually intuitively—that any advance in therapy, any fresh knowledge of it, any significant new hypothesis in regard to it, must come from the experience of the therapists and clients, and can never come from science.

He feels that there is a danger in science which may lead toward manipulation of people, and cites as examples of this the attempts to apply laws of learning to control people through advertisements and propaganda. Skinner's *Walden Two* is cited as a psychologist's picture of paradise:

> A paradise of manipulation in which the extent to which one can be a person is greatly reduced unless one can be a member of the ruling council.

This point of view can be best summarized as Rogers does, as follows:

> What I will do with the knowledge gained through scientific method—whether I will use it to under-

*From Leonard Krasner, Behavior control and social responsibility. *American Psychologist,* 1962, **17,** 199–204. Copyright 1962 by the American Psychological Association and reproduced by permission.

stand, enhance, enrich, or use it to control, manipulate, and destroy—is a matter of subjective choices depending upon the values which have personal meaning for me.

Yet in another paper (Rogers & Skinner, 1956) even Rogers is willing to concede that:

> In client-centered therapy, we are deeply engaged in the prediction and influencing of behavior, or even the control of behavior. As therapists, we institute certain attitudinal conditions, and the client has relatively little voice in the establishment of these conditions. We predict that if these conditions are instituted, certain behavioral consequences will ensue in the client.

The "anti-control" view is also well presented in a series of papers by Jourard. He contends that manipulation will have harmful effects both on the patient and on the therapist. Jourard (1959) contends that:

> "Behavioristic" approaches to counseling and psychotherapy, while rightly acknowledging a man's susceptibility to manipulation by another, ignore the possibly deleterious impact of such manipulation on the whole man and, moreover, on the would-be manipulator himself—whereas the essential factor in the psychotherapeutic situation is a loving, honest and spontaneous relationship between the therapist and the patient.

In contrast, a "behavioristic" viewpoint might argue that apparent spontaneity on the therapist's part may very well be the most effective means of manipulating behavior. The therapist is an individual programmed by his training into a fairly effective behavior control machine. Most likely the machine is most effective when it least appears like a machine.

Despite the views of Rogers and of other therapists, the evidence seems quite strong that psychotherapy as a social reinforcement process is part of a broader psychology of behavior control in which the therapist is actively influencing the behavior, attitudinal and value system of the patient. Further, recent research has begun to put the therapist back into the therapy situation insofar as studying his personality and other personal attributes, including his value system. Marmor points

out that psychoanalysis, as well as other types of psychotherapy, involves the communication of the therapist's implicit values and behavioral characteristics. Marmor's conviction is that:

> Whether or not the analyst is *consciously* "tempted to act as a teacher, model, and ideal" to his patients, he *inevitably* does so to a greater or lesser extent; and this is a central aspect of the psychoanalytic process.

One of the reasons for denial on the part of therapists that they control behavior, or that they even desire to do so, is that such control would raise many moral, ethical, and legal problems, which the therapist is not prepared to handle. Thus, therapists are put in the paradoxical position of saying to the patient, "we will change your behavior, but we do not really want to change your behavior." Generally, science fiction is more willing to come to grips with some of the basic issues involved than is the professional therapist.

Yet, we cannot avoid facing the issue of values. In fact, psychology is in the process of having a strong revival of interest in values. Recognition of the need for concern with the *ethics* or *moral values* of the therapist is implicit in an increasing number of articles. For example, May (1953) points out that the progress of psychoanalysis in the last decade can be judged by the increasing recognition that it is an illusion for the analyst to suppose that he can avoid value judgments. He feels that this recognition is explicit in the writings of Fromm and Horney and implicit in the works of Fromm-Reichman, Kubie, Alexander, and French. May cites a statement of J. McV. Hunt, who says ". . . I have reluctantly come to the conclusion that the scientist cannot avoid the value assumptions merely by deciding to do so." Hunt concludes, and May agrees, that values do belong to the subject material of science and must be taken into account in devising measuring instruments of behavioral or situational change. The study of Rosenthal on changes in "moral values" following psychotherapy is an illustration. Patients who are rated as "improved" changed significantly in their performance on a value test in the direction of values held by their therapists in sex, aggression, and authority, whereas unimproved patients tended to become less like their therapists in these values.

Lowe points out some of the ethical dilemmas involved insofar as the therapist is concerned, with possible conflicts over four sets of values. After reviewing value systems in four different categories, called naturalism, culturism, humanism, theism, Lowe concludes that "there is no single professional standard to which the psychologist's values can conform." The dilemma for the psychologist, as he sees it, is that if *one* set of values is to become absolute, psychology would cease to be a science and would become a social movement. However, he feels that psychologists cannot, on the other hand, do research without intending it to serve a particular value orientation. His suggestion is that value orientations be dealt with as objectively as possible, and that each area in psychology become more fully aware of the implications of its efforts. Further, since value orientations are in such conflict that at this point they are unresolvable, each therapist must understand his own values and those of others.

There have been infrequent attempts to measure attitudes of therapists, but most of these have been in terms of attitudes to therapy rather than attitudes to the broader implications of their social role. There have certainly been investigations of personality variables of the therapist, or psychologist, or psychiatrist, but these have been generally oriented towards traditional personality variables rather than value attitudes. Shaffer, for example, found in his analysis of objective versus intuitive psychologists, that the differences are not in terms of personality but in terms of attitudes toward role. Skinner (Rogers & Skinner, 1956), who was among the first to call attention to the ethical problems inherent in a psychology of behavior control, has pointed out that an important reinforcement for the therapist himself is his success in manipulating human behavior.

While the issue of behavior control first arose in regard to psychotherapy, it is now far broader and covers other areas such as operant conditioning, teaching machines, hypnosis, sensory deprivation, subliminal stimulation, and similar studies.

There is considerable public interest, concern, and misunderstanding about the range and power of psychological findings.

How does a "psychology of behavior control" differ from the science of psychology? The differences are subtle, but important. A science of psychology seeks to determine the lawful relationships in behavior. The orientation of a "psychology of behavior control" is that these lawful relationships are to be used to deliberately influence, control, or change behavior. This implies a manipulator or controller, and with it an ethical and value system of the controller. As we learn more about human behavior it is increasingly obvious that it is controllable by various techniques. Does this mean that we, as psychologists, researchers, or even therapists, *at this point* could modify somebody's behavior in any way we wanted? The answer is no, primarily because research into the techniques of control thus far is at the elementary stage. Science moves at a very rapid pace, however, and now is the time to concern ourselves with this problem before basic knowledge about the techniques overwhelms us.

The obvious analogy is with the atomic physicists, who have been very concerned about the application of their scientific findings. Of course, many of the comments from the physical scientists have come *since* the dropping of the first atom bomb. The concern of the psychologist must come before the techniques of behavior control are fully developed. *Public* concern is more readily discernible at this point as shown by popular articles and the cries of indignation some years back when subliminal stimulation was a going fad.

Carl Rogers has recently been quoted as saying that:

> To hope that the power which is being made available by the behavioral sciences will be exercised by the scientists, or by a benevolent group, seems to me to be a hope little supported by either recent or distant history. It seems far more likely that behavioral scientists, holding their present attitudes, will be in the position of the German rocket scientists specializing in guided missiles. . . . If behavioral scientists are concerned solely with advancing their science, it

seems most probable that they will serve the purpose of whatever group has the power (Brecher & Brecher, 1961).

This rather pessimistic quotation is from a popular article in a recent issue of *Harper's* magazine. The authors cite this and other research, particularly the work of Olds on brain stimulation, as evidence for deep concern about the role of the behavioral scientist. In what is perhaps an overdramatization of the situation, yet one which may legitimately express lay concern, they conclude that:

New methods of controlling behavior now emerging from the laboratory may soon add an awe-inspiring power to enslave us all with our own engineered consent.

Oppenheimer (1956), in comparing the responsibility of the physicist with that of the psychologist, makes the cogent point that:

The psychologist can hardly do anything without realizing that for him the acquisition of knowledge opens up the most terrifying prospects of controlling what people do and how they think and how they behave and how they feel.

We can approach the problem of social responsibility by asking three basic questions:

1 Is human behavior controllable? Overwhelming experimental evidence in fields of motivation, conditioning, and personality development indicates that this is true.

2 If so, is it desirable or wise for psychologists to continue research in these fields? Psychologists have no choice but to continue their research. The findings can be used just as meaningfully to help man as to hinder him. Further, methods of counter control can be developed. The danger is *not* in the research findings but in their potential misuse.

3 What safeguards can be incorporated into this type of research? The answer to this is the crux of the psychologist's dilemma. First, a code of ethics such as that of the APA is a good first step, but certainly not enough. An ethical code merely says that the psychologist will not deliberately misuse his findings. It does not go into the more basic question of the psychologist or behavior controller's value system. If we see him as one who is in a position to change or modify others' behavior, this implies a value decision as to what is "good behavior," what is "mental health," and what is desirable adjustment. To deny control is to do a disservice and, in effect, to hide one's head in the sand like the proverbial ostrich. The fact that the behavior controllers are professional individuals is no guarantee that behavior control will not be misused. We have only to turn to the role of German physicians in medical atrocities as evidence of misuse by a supposedly professional group.

Berg goes into one aspect of the ethical and value problem in discussing principles that should guide the use of human subjects in psychological research. His concern with the problem is an outgrowth of the "barbarous medical experiments" performed on human subjects by Nazi physicians in the name of science. These German physicians were not mere tools, but were leaders in their profession. Berg suggests that future researchers using human subjects adhere to the principles of "consent," "confidence," and "standard procedure." He cites the basic principles governing permissible government experiments laid down at the Nuremberg trials. These are relevant for future discussion of the kinds of behavior permissible, or not permissible, to behavior controllers.

Basically, they are similar to the principles that Roe (1959) pointed out, namely, that *awareness* is a major ingredient in defense against manipulation. Roe makes pertinent comments in stressing the need for man to be aware of himself and the world around him:

Awareness of our own needs and attitudes is our most effective instrument for maintaining our own integrity and control over our own reactions.

A somewhat similar view is expressed by Cattell, who also calls for research into ethical values and feels that moral laws can be derived from psychological and physiological investigation of living matter. He does not accept the viewpoint, which he attributes to a majority of psychologists and most laymen, that ethical values lie outside the realm of science. Creegan also concerns himself with the need for scientific investigation of ethical problems. In comparing the responsibility of the psychologist with that of the atomic physicist he points out that:

> Psychology does not produce nuclear warheads, nor does it produce the apocalyptic birds which may take them to a selected target, but psychology is concerned with human decisions. . . . The greatest power in the world is the power of rational decision. Atomic physics deals with the release of great forces, but answers to ethical questions may be the decisive ones for the future of humanity.

Creegan further goes into questions of whether force and hidden persuasion ought to be used for a good cause. Once we have committed ourselves on economic, social, and religious problems, how should we go about implementing our ideas? How does the psychologist define "the good life"? Does the psychologist constitute an ethical elite? Creegan points out that at present it is the physicist who communicates with the public about moral problems, rather than the psychologist. Muller also feels that values are a legitimate source of scientific investigation. He disagrees with those who say that man's values are determined by a higher authority outside of himself or those who say that values are a private matter. But Muller is a biologist, not a psychologist.

The attacks on psychological investigators of behavior control are often quite unfair. For example, Krutch is highly critical of the implications of Skinner's *Walden Two* because of a fear that social control will pass into the hands of experimentalists who are not concerned with moral issues. Yet it is often these experimenters who are most concerned with value problems and who are in a position to approach on an objective basis the whole question of moral and value issues.

We would suggest two major steps be taken at this point. The first is to develop techniques of approaching experimentally the basic problem of

social and ethical issues involved in behavior control. One initial approach would be to investigate the attitudes and fantasies of experimenters and therapists toward their own role as behavior controllers in studies in which the effectiveness of their influence can be readily tested. As an example, in our laboratory we are presently devising ways of measuring attitudes toward mental health, "the good life," and applications of science. Fantasy behavior will be elicited in response to special stimuli and reports of role perception and role reaction will be obtained from therapists and from experimenters in psychotherapy, verbal conditioning, and other behavior controlling experiments. The attitude measures will be associated with behavioral ratings of these "controllers" and subject responsivity to them. These studies are undertaken within a framework of investigating the variables that go into resisting influence situations.

A second major step in dealing with this problem is communication between the general public and the research investigators. In this field, particularly, researchers must keep in contact with each other. Any kind of research which is kept secret, such as work in sensory deprivation, is to be deplored. Furthermore, it is the psychologist-researcher who should undertake the task of contact with the public rather than leaving it to sensationalists and popularizers.

In summary, behavior control represents a relatively new, important, and very useful development in psychological research. It also may be horribly misused unless the psychologist is constantly alert to what is taking place in society and unless he is active in investigating and controlling the social uses of behavior control.

REFERENCES

BRECHER, RUTH, & BRECHER, E. The happiest creatures on earth? *Harper's*, 1961, **222**, 85–90.

JOURARD, S. I-thou relationship versus manipulation in counseling and psychotherapy. *Journal of Individual Psychology*, 1959, **15**, 174–179.

MARMOR, J. Psychoanalytic therapy as an educational process: Common denominators in the therapeutic approaches of different psychoanalytic "schools." Paper presented to the Academy of Psychoanalysis, Chicago, May 1961.

MAY, R. Historical and philosophical presuppositions for understanding therapy. In O. H. Mowrer (Ed.), *Psychotherapy theory and research*. New York: Ronald Press, 1953.

OPPENHEIMER, J. R. Analogy in science. *American Psychologist*, 1956, **11**, 127–135.

ROGERS, C. R. Persons or science: A philosophical question. *American Psychologist*, 1955, **10**, 267–278.

ROGERS, C. R., & SKINNER, B. F. Some issues concerning the control of human behavior: A symposium. *Science*, 1956, **124**, 1057–1066.

USEFUL RESOURCES

CRICHTON, M. *The terminal man*. New York: Bantam Books, 1973. A human bomb is created when 40 electrodes are implanted.

DELGADO, J. M. *Physical control of the mind*. New York: Harper & Row, 1969.

FERGUSON, M. *The brain revolution: The frontiers of mind research*, 1973.
"*The Brain Revolution* is more than an account of biological and medical breakthroughs; it documents an international social and cultural transformation." "The topics covered range from brain chemistry to sleep and dream research, from genetics and evolution to drug therapy and hypnosis, from creativity and learning to meditation and mental illness, from parapsychology to the control of pain. And there is a common thread running through the dozens of subjects discussed: we have grossly underestimated the potential of the normal brain." Psychology Today Book Club.

FISHLOCK, D. *Man modified*. London: Paladin, 1971. Discusses machine interactions with man.

HEATH, R. G. (Ed.) *The role of pleasure in behavior*. New York: Hoeber, 1964. A collection that includes articles on controlling brain states with drugs and electrical stimulation.

KESEY, K. *One flew over the cuckoo's nest*. New York: Viking Press, 1962. A dramatic account of one man's revolution in a mental hospital.

LONDON, P. *Behavior control*. New York: Harper and Row, 1969. A well-written review by a psychologist covering drugs, psychosurgery, electrical stimulation of the brain, conditioning, etc.

MARK, V., & ERVIN, F. *Violence and the brain*. New York: Harper and Row, 1970. Controlling aggression—with brain surgery.

MULLER, H. J. *The children of Frankenstein*. Bloomington: Indiana University Press, 1970. What are the implications of our advanced technology for man's future?

RAMSEY, P. *Fabricated man: The ethics of genetic control*. New Haven: Yale University Press, 1970.

SHAFFER, H. B. Human engineering. *Editorial Research Reports*, May 19, 1971, No. 19, 369–386. A concise compilation of current technological possibilities.

WOLPE, J. *The practice of behavior therapy*. New York: Pergamon Press, 1969.

CHAPTER 4
ON WOMANKIND

PROVOCATIONS

*Culture makes clothes
but God gives gonads.*

> *Harry Harlow*

*Nobody objects to a woman being a good writer
or sculptor or geneticist if, at the same time, she
manages to be a good wife, a good mother,
good-looking, good-tempered, well-groomed and
unaggressive.*

> *Marya Mannes*

*The core of the problem for women today is not
sexual but a problem of identity–a stunting or
evasion of growth that is perpetuated by the
feminine mystique. As the Victorian culture did
not permit women to accept or gratify their basic
sexual needs, our culture does not permit women
to accept or gratify their basic needs to grow and
fulfill their potentialities as human beings.*

> *Betty Friedan*

*To be a woman is something so strange, so
confused, so complicated . . . so contradictory,
that only a woman could put up with it.*

> *Soren Kierkegaard*

*A woman, if she have the misfortune to know
anything, should conceal it as well as she can.*

> *Jane Austen*

*Wives, submit yourselves unto your own hus-
bands, as unto the Lord.
    For the husband is the head of the wife, even
as Christ is the head of the church: and he is the
saviour of the body.
    Therefore as the church is subject unto Christ,
so let the wives be subject to their own husbands
in everything.*

> *St. Paul: Ephesians, 6*

Anatomy is destiny.

> *Sigmund Freud*

WHAT DO YOU THINK?

---

17 ON WOMANHOOD

DALE M. WILLOWS

One of the most conspicuous features of all cultures of the world is the inequality of the sexes. It is claimed, by those who would justify this form of oppression that men are dominant in society because males are *naturally* superior to females in certain physical and mental abilities. The current Women's Liberation movement has challenged this claim of women's inferiority. They characterize it as a disabling myth whose primary function is to perpetuate the preferential status accorded to men.

● Since people generally support beliefs which are complimentary to themselves it is not surprising that many women are becoming increasingly vocal in asserting their right to equality with men; nor is it surprising that many men are resistant to changing the traditional dominance/submission relationship. Similarly, it is perhaps understandable that many women "over thirty" tend to accept the status quo. However, it is surprising (and regrettable) to find that many *young* women, including college women, accept the view that men are naturally superior to women. Sexual stereotyping does indeed begin early! (See Selection 19 by Florence Howe.)

What are the "facts"? Are there real innate differences between males and females which are significantly related to socially valued behavior? There are, of course, the obvious differences in primary and secondary sex characteristics, and those of Freudian persuasion have made much of the structural differences in the genitalia. In feats of symbolizing approaching verbal magic they have used these structural differences to conceptualize the male as being one who "penetrates,"

who "probes," who "stands out," whereas the female "incorporates," "receives," "engulfs," and passively "takes in." Freudian theory has thus tended to perpetuate a view of woman which assigns her to a lower status because of her physical/emotional dependence on man. The roles and status which were assigned to females by a male-dominated society strongly influence women's own conception of themselves. Not surprisingly these male definitions of "a good woman" have often prevented the full development of the potential of women. They have extended to all facets of womanhood even to the specification of which emotions and feelings would be positively or negatively valued by the male. Perhaps the ultimate of such male mind-bending was achieved by Freud's insistence that the "good" female orgasm was a vaginal orgasm—one which required the penetration of the male penis. Clitoral orgasm (which could be more easily achieved through other stimulation including automanipulation) was held to be inferior, less complete, less mature, or infantile.

Within the past decade much new information has been gained about the physiology of the female orgasm, primarily through the research efforts of Masters and Johnson.[1] After measuring many physiological reactions which occur during orgasm, both during intercourse and masturbation, Masters and Johnson have concluded:

That the dichotomy of vaginal and clitoral orgasms is entirely false. Anatomically, all orgasms are centered in the clitoris, whether they result from direct manual pressure applied to the clitoris, indirect pressure resulting from the thrusting of penis during intercourse or generalized sexual stimulation of other erogenous zones like the breasts.

The implication of this fact is not that females

[1]W. H. Masters and V. E. Johnson. *Human sexual response.* Boston: Little Brown and Co., 1966.

are now "liberated" to imitate masculine sexuality but that "if the Masters and Johnson material is allowed to filter into the public consciousness, hopefully to replace the enshrined Freudian myths, then woman at long last will be allowed to take the first step toward her emancipation, to define and enjoy the forms of her own sexuality."[2]

Much of the controversy regarding observed differences in behavioral style between the sexes focuses on the question of whether the differences are biologically based or primarily the result of social conditioning. If the behavioral differences are biologically based, they are likely to be more resistant to change through social interventions. Thus, if it could be shown that females are passive, dependent, sensitive, irrational, intuitive, and gentle (and all those other "feminine" characteristics) as a result of immutable biological factors, attempts to open up more career opportunities to women in areas which clearly demand aggression, independence, rationality (and all those other "masculine" qualities) would be exercises in futility. Women would not be able to develop the necessary characteristics to do the jobs. If, on the other hand, it is a complex of sociocultural factors which have prevented women from pursuing various "masculine" activities, there is hope for reform and elimination of sexist attitudes and bias. The necessary reform could be achieved both through legislation and education.

We should note that the problem of determining the degree to which a certain behavioral trait (e.g. "warm receptiveness") has a biological base is greatly complicated by the fact that almost from birth girls are treated differently than boys by their parents. Of course this differential experience can serve as the basis for different personality characteristics. The real complication arises from the fact that the tendency of parents to react to girl babies differently than boy babies may be based on differential biologically determined capacities and tendencies of the two sexes. For example, girl infants

. . . are talked to more than boy infants at very early ages, a fact which might explain differential language acquisition, for it is known that girls show precocious development *vis a vis* boys. We also know that girl infants respond more to auditory signals than do boys; thus girls may be spoken to more because they are more responsive to this stimulation. This would suggest that there are basic biological differences accounting for differential experience.[3]

A word of caution is in order regarding scientific objectivity and the selection and interpretation of "facts." Unfortunately, as in most debates in which the participants have a vested interest in the outcome, the arguments in the controversies have not always been entirely objective. In fact, in the process of selecting the articles for this chapter, your editor was struck by the fact that *she* could usually tell the sex of the writer by the biases which were communicated in the article. Individuals who are acknowledged experts in fields such as biology, anthropology, sociology, and psychology have all too often allowed sociopolitical considerations to color their interpretation of facts when it comes to questions about equality of the sexes. Lack of objective reporting of data is evident everywhere in the literature on this controversial subject. In some cases "statistics" have even been reported in such a biased way as to make them appear to support an argument which they in fact refute. For example, the critics of the Women's Liberation movement (including at least one quite prestigious male physician/politician) frequently argue that women are biologically unsuited to serve in positions of power and responsibility because they are emotionally unstable as a result of their monthly "raging hormonal storms." The statistics on which this claim is based show that "Women have a higher incidence of car accidents and suicides during their 'periods.'" However, it is rarely added that the percentage of women who have accidents or commit suicide is still much lower than the comparable percentage for men.

---

[2]Susan Lydon. The Politics of Orgasm in M. H. Garskof (Ed.), *Roles women play: Readings toward women's liberation.* Belmont, Cal.: Brooks/Cole, 1971.

[3]Michael Lewis. Parents and children: Sex-role development. *School Review.* February 1972, pp. 229–240.

From the fact that women have fewer car accidents and commit fewer suicides a feminist might argue that women are *better* equipped than men to function in positions which require emotional stability.

● Note that this "feminist" perspective on the "facts" is also subject to the critisism of being a biased interpretation. A more reasonable view is that before we can use the "facts" of car accidents or suicides to support one argument or another we must first show that there are significant differences among the sexes in the number of accidents or suicides *for those persons who occupy high-stress jobs which require emotional stability*. Valid and reliable information on this issue does not seem to be available.

The point which is relevant for you the student is this: Examine the facts and interpretations provided by the author closely to see if the facts actually support the interpretations, also be on guard that your own biases do not color *your* attempts to *find out* the truth.

We have already seen that the road to success in our society is through the school system and that this system like all other major institutions is dominated by male values and attitudes. It fosters eager acquisition and aggressive competitiveness. The female student is thus placed in a double bind, if she is successful in the competitive/aggressive behavior demanded by the school, she is viewed by her male peers with disdain as a "castrator." "It seems there is nothing more distasteful than 'an uppity' woman who opts to beat a man, especially at 'his own game'—be it law, medicine, physics or rational thought."[4] On the other hand if she chooses not to compete in the man's world, she risks failing to develop her real abilities and potential. Furthermore, and somewhat ironically, if she chooses to compete in the intellectual striving and succeeds, she also runs the risk of depreciation by women. Furthermore, the double bind into which the bright woman is placed often generates a good deal of anxiety, self-doubt, and concern about her normality or femininity. This conflict between maintaining her feminine image and developing her ability is resolved by most women by "relinquishing that ability and abdicating from competition in the outside world."[5] Other compromise solutions involve attempting to override the social pressures by being successful at both. Such women are then able to have the best of both worlds, especially if they have a husband who supports and takes pride in their achievements outside the home. However, these women are in the minority, and Horner's research, discussed in Selection 21, shows that in competitive situations with males, females seem to be characterized by a desire to avoid competitive success, by what Horner calls—"the will to fail."

● Think about discussion groups that you have been in. Who typically does the most talking, males or females? Many of you females who are reading this book will have had extensive experience with conflict. How many of you can remember trying to make sure your boyfriend does not think you are as smart as he is? Would you share some of these experiences with your discussion group? What are some solutions to this conflict which are available to you?

---

[4]Riesman, D. Two generations. *Daedalus*, 1964, **93**, 711–735.

[5]Horner, M. Fail: Bright woman. *Psychology Today*, November, 1969.

18 MALE & FEMALE: DIFFERENCES BETWEEN THEM*

"The Book of Genesis had it wrong. In the beginning God created Eve," says Johns Hopkins Medical Psychologist John Money. What he means is that the basic tendency of the human fetus is to develop as a female. If the genes order the gonads to become testicles and put out the male hormone androgen, the embryo will turn into a boy; otherwise it becomes a girl. "You have to add something to get a male," Money notes. "Nature's first intention is to create a female."

Nature may prefer women, but virtually every culture has been partial to men. That contradiction raises an increasingly pertinent question (as well as the hackles of militant feminists): Are women immutably different from men? Women's Liberationists believe that any differences—other than anatomical—are a result of conditioning by society. The opposing view is that all of the differences are fixed in the genes. To scientists, however, the nature-nurture controversy is oversimplified. To them, what human beings are results from a complex interaction between both forces. Says Oxford Biologist Christopher Ounsted: "It is a false dichotomy to say that this difference is acquired and that one genetic. To try and differentiate is like asking a penny whether it is really a heads penny or a tails penny." As Berkeley Psychologist Frank Beach suggests, "Predispositions may be genetic; complex behavior patterns are probably not."

The idea that genetic predispositions exist is based on three kinds of evidence. First, there are the "cultural universals" cited by Margaret Mead. Almost everywhere, the mother is the principal caretaker of the child, and male dominance and aggression are the rule. Some anthropologists believe there has been an occasional female-

dominated society; other insist that none have existed.

Sex Typing Then there is the fact that among most ground-dwelling primates, males are dominant and have as a major function the protection of females and offspring. Some research suggests that this is true even when the young are raised apart from adults, which seems to mean that they do not learn their roles from their society.

Finally, behavioral sex differences show up long before any baby could possibly perceive subtle differences between his parents or know which parent he is expected to imitate. "A useful strategy," says Harvard Psychologist Jerome Kagan, "is to assume that the earlier a particular difference appears, the more likely it is to be influenced by biological factors."

Physical differences appear even before birth. The heart of the female fetus often beats faster, and girls develop more rapidly. "Physiologically," says Sociologist Barbette Blackington, "women are better-made animals." Males do have more strength and endurance—though that hardly matters in a technological society.

Recent research hints that there may even be sex differences in the brain. According to some experimenters, the presence of the male hormone testosterone in the fetus may "masculinize" the brain, organizing the fetal nerve centers in characteristic ways. This possible "sex typing" of the central nervous system before birth may make men and women respond differently to incoming stimuli, Sociologist John Gagnon believes.

In fact, newborn girls do show different responses in some situations. They react more strongly to the removal of a blanket and more quickly to touch and pain. Moreover, experiments demonstrate that twelve-week-old girls gaze longer at photographs of faces than at geometric figures. Boys show no preference then, though eventually

*Abridged from Male & female: Differences between them. *Time*, March 20, 1972, 56–59. Reprinted by permission from *Time*, The Weekly Newsmagazine; Copyright Time Inc.

they pay more attention to figures. Kagan acknowledges the effect of environment, but he has found that it exerts a greater influence on girls than on boys. The female infants who experienced the most "face-to-face interaction" with their mothers were more attentive to faces than girls whose mothers did not exchange looks with them so much. Among boys, there was no consistent relationship.

Internal Organs   As some psychologists see it, this very early female attention to the human face suggests that women may have a greater and even partly innate sensitivity to other human beings. Perhaps this explains why girls seem to get more satisfaction from relationships with people.

Even after infancy, the sexes show differential interests that do not seem to grow solely out of experience. Psychoanalyst Erik Erikson has found that boys and girls aged ten to twelve use space differently when asked to construct a scene with toys. Girls often build a low wall, sometimes with an elaborate doorway, surrounding a quiet interior scene. Boys are likely to construct towers, facades with cannons, and lively exterior scenes. Erikson acknowledges that cultural influences are at work, but he is convinced that they do not fully explain the nature of children's play. The differences, he says, "seem to parallel the morphology [shape and form] of genital differentiation itself: in the male, an external organ, erectible and intrusive; internal organs in the female, with vestibular access, leading to statically expectant ova."

In aptitude as well as in interest, sex differences become apparent early in life. Though girls are generally less adept than boys at mathematical and spatial reasoning, they learn to count sooner and to talk earlier and better. Some scientists think this female verbal superiority may be caused by sex-linked differences in the brain. Others believe it may exist because, as observation proves, mothers talk to infant girls more than to baby boys. But does the mother's talking cause the child to do likewise, or could it be the other way round? Psychologist Michael Lewis suggests the possibility that girls are talked to more because, for biological reasons, they respond more than boys to words and thus stimulate their mothers to keep talking.

Evidence that parental behavior does affect speech comes from tests made by Kagan among poor Guatemalan children. There, boys are more highly valued than girls, are talked to more and become more verbal. In the U.S., Psychiatrist David Levy has found that boys who are atypically good with words and inept with figures have been overprotected by their mothers. Psychologist Elizabeth Bing has observed that girls who excel at math and spatial problems have often been left to work alone by their mothers, while highly verbal girls have mothers who offer frequent suggestions, praise and criticism.

While girls outdo boys verbally, they often lag behind in solving analytical problems, those that require attention to detail. Girls seem to think "globally," responding to situations as a whole instead of abstracting single elements. In the "rod and frame test," for instance, a subject sits in a dark room before a luminous rod inside a slightly tilted frame, and is asked to move the rod to an upright position. Boys can separate the rod visually from the frame and make it stand straight; girls, misled by the tipped frame, usually adjust the rod not to the true vertical but to a position parallel with the sides of the frame.

In another experiment, children are asked to group related pictures. Boys again pay attention to details, perhaps putting together pictures that show people with an arm raised; girls make functional groupings of, for example, a doctor, a nurse and a wheelchair.

In all such differences, environmental influence is suggested by the fact that children who think analytically most often prove to have mothers who have encouraged initiative and exploration, while youngsters who think globally have generally been tied to their mother's apron strings. In Western society, of course, it is usually boys who are urged toward adventure. Herein, perhaps—there is no proof—lies an explanation for the apparent male capacity to think analytically.

In IQ tests, males and females score pretty much alike. Since this is true, why do women seem less creative? Many social scientists are convinced that the reasons are cultural. Women, they say, learn early in life that female accomplishment brings few rewards. In some cases, women cannot be creative because they are discriminated against. In other instances, a woman's creativity may well be blunted by fear of nonconformity, failure or even success itself (see following story). Unlike men, Kagan says, women are trained to have strong anxiety about being wrong.

To many psychoanalysts, however, the explanation lies in the fact that women possess the greatest creative power of all: bringing new life into being; thus they need not compensate by producing works of art. Men, it is theorized, are driven to make up for what seems to them a deficiency. That they feel keenly, though unconsciously, their inability to bear children is shown in dreams reported on the analyst's couch, in the behavior of small boys who play with dolls and walk around with their stomachs thrust forward in imitation of their pregnant mothers and in primitive rites and ancient myths. According to these myths, presumably conceived by males, Adam delivered Eve from his rib cage, Zeus gave birth to Athena out of his head, and when Semele was burned to death, Zeus seized Dionysus from her womb and sewed him up in his thigh until the infant had developed.

There are personality differences between the sexes too. Although no trait is confined to one sex—there are women who exceed the male average even in supposedly masculine characteristics—some distinctions turn up remarkably early. At New York University, for example, researchers have found that a female infant stops sucking a bottle and looks up when someone comes into the room; a male pays no attention to the visitor.

Another Kagan experiment shows that girls of twelve months who become frightened in a strange room drift toward their mothers, while boys look for something interesting to do. At four months, twice as many girls as boys cry when frightened in a strange laboratory. What is more, Kagan says, similar differences can be seen in monkeys and baboons, which "forces us to consider the possibility that some of the psychological differences between men and women may not be the product of experience alone but of subtle biological differences."

Female Passivity Many researchers have found greater dependence and docility in very young girls, greater autonomy and activity in boys. When a barrier is set up to separate youngsters from their mothers, boys try to knock it down; girls cry helplessly. There is little doubt that maternal encouragement—or discouragement—of such behavior plays a major role in determining adult personality. For example, a mother often stimulates male autonomy by throwing a toy far away from her young son, thus tacitly suggesting to him that he leave her to get it.

Animal studies suggest that there may be a biological factor in maternal behavior; mothers of rhesus monkeys punish their male babies earlier and more often than their female offspring; they also touch their female babies more often and act more protective toward them.

As for the controversial question of female "passivity," Psychoanalyst Helene Deutsch believes that the concept has been misunderstood. "There is no contradiction between being feminine and working. The ego can be active in both men and women," she says. It is only in love and in sex that passivity is particularly appropriate for women. As she sees it, passivity is no more than a kind of openness and warmth; it does not mean "inactivity, emptiness or immobility."

Another controversy rages over the effect of hormones. Militant women, who discount hormonal influence, disagree violently with scientific researchers, who almost unanimously agree that hormones help determine how people feel and act.

● Although some militant women may prefer to discount the facts of hormonal influence on behavior, this is really not the main point which is made by those concerned with equality for women. The point is that even though hormones do affect behavior, the more important question is—what evidence is there that these effects make women inferior in their work situation?

So far, there have been few studies of male hormones, but scientists think they may eventually discover hormonal cycles in men that produce cyclic changes in mood and behavior. As for females, studies have indicated that 49% of female medical and surgical hospital admissions, most psychiatric hospital admissions and 62% of violent crimes among women prisoners occur on premenstrual and menstrual days. At Worcester State Hospital in Massachusetts, Psychologists Donald and Inge Broverman have found that estrogen sharpens sensory perception. They believe that this heightened sensitivity may lead more women than men to shy away from situations of stress.

Fierce Bulls   One trait thought to be affected by hormones is aggressiveness. In all cultures, investigators report, male infants tend to play more aggressively than females. While scientists think a genetic factor may be involved, they also observe that society fosters the difference by permitting male aggression and encouraging female adaptability. Some suggest that females may be as aggressive as men—but with words instead of deeds.

The definitive research on hormones and aggression is still to be done. However, it has been established that the female hormone estrogen inhibits aggression in both animal and human males. It has also been proved that the male hormone androgen influences aggression in animals. For example, castration produces tractable steers rather than fierce bulls.

The influence of androgen begins even before birth. Administered to pregnant primates, the hormone makes newborn females play more aggressively than ordinary females. Moreover, such masculinized animals are unusually aggressive as long as they live, even if they are never again exposed to androgen.

According to some experts, this long-lasting effect of hormones administered or secreted before birth may help explain why boys are more aggressive than girls even during their early years when both sexes appear to produce equal amounts of male and female hormones. Other observers have suggested that the spurt in male-hormone production at puberty could be one of the causes of delinquency in adolescent boys, but there is no proof that this is so.

Will there some day be a "unisex" society with no differences between men and women, except anatomical ones? It seems unlikely. Anatomy, parturition and gender, observes Psychologist Joseph Adelson, cannot be wished away "in a spasm of the distended will, as though the will, in pursuit of total human possibility, can amplify itself to overcome the given." Or, as Psychoanalyst Therese Benedek sees it, "biology precedes personality."

"Nature has been the oppressor," observes Michael Lewis. Women's role as caretaker "was the evolutionary result of their biological role in birth and feeding." The baby bottle has freed women from some of the tasks of that role, but, says University of Michigan Psychologist Judith Bardwick, "the major responsibility for child rearing is the woman's, even in the Soviet Union, the Israeli kibbutz, Scandinavia and mainland China." Furthermore, though mothering skills are mostly learned, it is a fact that if animals are raised in isolation and then put in a room with the young of the species, it is the females who go to the infants and take care of them.

"Perhaps the known biological differences can be totally overcome, and society can approach a state in which a person's sex is of no consequence for any significant activity except childbearing," admits Jerome Kagan. "But we must ask if such a society will be satisfying to its members." As he sees it, "complementarity" is what makes relationships stable and pleasurable.

Psychoanalyst Martin Symonds agrees. "The basic reason why unisex must fail is that in the sexual act itself, the man has to be assertive, if tenderly, and the woman has to be receptive. What gives trouble is when men see assertiveness as aggression and women see receptiveness as submission." Unisex, he sums up, would be "a disaster," because children need roles to identify with and rebel against. "You can't identify with a blur. A unisex world would be a frictionless environment in which nobody would be able to grow up."

The crucial point is that a difference is not a deficiency. As Biologist Ounsted puts it, "We are all human beings and in this sense equal. We are not, however, the same." In the opinion of John Money, "You can play fair only if you recognize and respect authentic differences."

Though scientists disagree about the precise nature and causes of these differences, there is no argument about two points: society plays a tremendous part in shaping the differences, and most women are capable of doing whatever they want. Only in the top ranges of ability, says Kagan, are innate differences significant; for typical men and women, "the biological differences are totally irrelevant." Psychiatrist Donald Lunde agrees. "There is no evidence," he asserts, "that men are any more or less qualified by biological sex differences alone to perform the tasks generally reserved for them in today's societies."

● This same point was made in another context earlier in this book. Do you remember where?

Situation Report

If statistics mean anything, American women are having a harder time today than they were a few years ago. For one thing, female suicide is on the rise. While it has long been true that more men than women kill themselves, the ratio has changed. This is true across the country, but the change is particularly marked in certain large cities. In Los Angeles in 1960, for example, 35% of the people who committed suicide were women. Last year the figure had risen to 45%. Another change: while women have always failed more often in suicide attempts than men, the difference is no longer as great—women are becoming more adept at killing themselves.

The higher suicide rate is only one evidence that women are experiencing more conflict. A recent University of Wisconsin study suggests that women psychiatric patients today complain of more anxiety, depression, alienation and inability to cope with stress than did their counterparts of ten years ago. The researchers found no such trend among men. Relatively unchanged over the past few years is the fact that more women than men are in therapy for minor emotional troubles, and, according to some psychiatrists, more male than female patients are "seriously impaired." A major reason for these differences may well be society's willingness to let women complain of feeling anxious while frowning on men who do likewise. As a result, men may keep their symptoms to themselves until they break down completely.

In drug addiction, there appears to be a tiny decrease among women: in 1969, 16% of the nation's addicts were women, compared with 15% last year. Now, as in the past, there are estimated to be five times more men than women alcoholics.

Women still begin drinking heavily later than men—in their early 30s instead of 20s. But once started, women drinkers deteriorate faster into alcoholism.

Another difference is the increase in the out-of-wedlock birth rate among girls from 15 to 19; from 8.3 per 1,000 unmarried teen-agers in 1940 to 19.8 in 1971. Surprisingly, Indiana University Sociologist Phillips Cutright believes that increased sexual activity at this age level is a "relatively minor factor"; a more important cause is improved health. There is also a striking rise in the number of unmarried mothers who keep their babies. No nationwide records are kept, but one Boston social agency reports an increase among whites from 10% a decade ago to 45% in 1970.

19 SEXUAL STEREOTYPES START EARLY*

FLORENCE HOWE

COMMENT: WHAT ARE BIG BOYS/GIRLS MADE OF?

"What are big boys made of? What are big boys made of?"

Independence, aggression, competitiveness, leadership, task orientation, outward orientation, assertiveness, innovation, self-discipline, stoicism, activity, objectivity, analytic-mindedness, courage, unsentimentality, rationality, confidence, and emotional control.

"What are big girls made of? What are big girls made of?"

Dependence, passivity, fragility, low pain tolerance, nonaggression, noncompetitiveness, inner orientation, interpersonal orientation, empathy, sensitivity, nurturance, subjectivity, intuitiveness, yieldingness, receptivity, inability to risk, emotional liability, supportiveness.

These adjectives describe the idealized, simplified stereotypes of normal masculinity and feminity. They also describe real characteristics of boys and girls, men and women. While individual men and women may more resemble the stereotype of the opposite sex, group differences between the sexes bear out these stereotypic portraits. How does American society socialize its members so that most men and women come close to the society's ideal norms?

JUDITH M. BARDWICK and ELIZABETH DOUVAN

"I remember quite clearly a day in sixth grade," a college freshman told me a year ago, "when the class was discussing an article from a weekly supplementary reader. The story was about a chef, and someone in the class ventured the opinion that cooking was women's work, that a man was a 'sissy' to work in the kitchen. The teacher's response surprised us all. She informed us calmly that men make the best cooks, just as they make the best dress designers, singers, and laundry workers. 'Yes   she said, 'anything a woman can do a man can do better.' There were no male students present; my teacher was a woman.''

How much blame should be placed on public education? A substantial portion, although it is true that schools reflect the society they serve. Indeed, schools function to reinforce the sexual stereotypes that children have been taught by their parents, friends, and the mass culture we live in. It is also perfectly understandable that sexual stereotypes demeaning to women are also perpetuated by women—mothers in the first place, and teachers in the second—as well as by men—fathers, the few male teachers in elementary schools, high school teachers, and many male administrators and educators at the top of the school's hierarchy.

Sexual stereotypes are assumed differences, social conventions or norms, learned behavior, attitudes, and expectations. Most stereotypes are well-known to all of us, for they are simple—not to say simple-minded. Men are smart, women are dumb but beautiful, etc. A recent annotated catalogue of children's books (distributed by the National Council of Teachers of English to thousands of teachers and used for ordering books with federal funds) lists titles under the headings ''Especially for Girls'' and ''Especially for Boys.'' Verbs and adjectives are remarkably predictable through the listings. Boys ''decipher and discover,'' ''earn and train,'' or ''foil'' someone; girls ''struggle,'' ''overcome difficulties,'' ''feel lost,'' ''help solve,'' or ''help [someone] out.'' One boy's story has ''strange power,'' another moves ''from truancy to triumph.'' A girl, on the other hand, ''learns to face the real world'' or makes a ''difficult adjustment.'' Late or early, in catalogues or on shelves, the boys of children's books are active and capable, the girls passive and in trouble. All studies of children's literature—and there have been many besides my own—support this conclusion.

Ask yourself whether you would be surprised to find the following social contexts in a fifth-grade arithmetic textbook:

1 girls playing marbles; boys sewing;

2 girls earning money, building things, and going places; boys buying ribbons for a sewing project;

3 girls working at physical activities; boys babysitting and, you guessed it, sewing.

Of course you would be surprised—so would I. What I have done here is to reverse the sexes as found in a fifth-grade arithmetic text. I was not surprised, since several years ago an intrepid freshman offered to report on third-grade arithmetic texts for me and found similar types of sexual roles prescribed: Boys were generally making things or earning money; girls were cooking or spending money on such things as sewing equipment.

The verification of sexual stereotypes is a special area of interest to psychologists and sociologists. An important series of studies was done in 1968 by Inge K. Broverman and others at Worcester State Hospital in Massachusetts. These scientists established a ''sex-stereotype questionnaire'' consisting of ''122 bipolar items'' —characteristics socially known or socially tested as male or female. Studies by these scientists and others established what common sense will verify: that those traits ''stereotypically masculine . . . are more often perceived as socially desirable'' than those known to be feminine. Here are some ''male-valued items'' as listed on the questionnaire:

very aggressive

very independent

not at all emotional

very logical

very direct

very adventurous

very self-confident

very ambitious

These and other characteristics describe the stereotypic male. To describe the female, you need only reverse those traits and add "female-valued" ones, some of which follow:

very talkative

very tactful

very gentle

very aware of feelings of others

very religious

very quiet

very strong need for security

and the one I am particularly fond of citing to men who control my field—"enjoys art and literature very much."

The Worcester scientists used their 122 items to test the assumptions of clinical psychologists about mental health. Three matched groups of male and female clinical psychologists were given three identical lists of the 122 items unlabeled and printed in random order. Each group was given a different set of instructions: One was told to choose those traits that characterize the healthy adult male; another to choose those of the healthy adult female; the third, to choose those of the healthy adult—a person. The result: The clinically healthy male and the clinically healthy adult were identical—and totally divergent from the clinically healthy female. The authors of the study concluded that "a double standard of health exists for men and women." That is, the general standard of health applies only to men. Women are perceived as "less healthy" by those standards called "adult." At the same time, however, if a woman deviates from the sexual stereotypes prescribed for her—if she grows more "active" or "aggressive," for example—she doesn't grow healthier; she may, in fact, if her psychiatrist is a Freudian, be perceived as "sicker." Either way, therefore, women lose or fail, and so it is not surprising to find psychologist Phyllis Chesler reporting that proportionately many more women than men are declared "sick" by psychologists and psychiatrists.

The idea of a "double standard" for men and women is a familiar one and helps to clarify how severely sexual stereotypes constrict the personal and social development of women. Studies by child psychologists reveal that while boys of all ages clearly identify with male figures and activities, girls are less likely to make the same sort of identification with female stereotypes. With whom do girls and women identify? My guess is that there is a good deal of confusion in their heads and hearts in this respect, and that what develops is a pattern that might be compared to schizophrenia: The schoolgirl knows that, for her, life is one thing, learning another. This is like the Worcester study's "double standard"—the schoolgirl cannot find herself in history texts or as she would like to see herself in literature; yet she knows she is not a male. Many women may ultimately discount the question of female identity as unimportant, claiming other descriptions preferable—as a parent, for example, or a black person, or a college professor.

Children learn sexual stereotypes at an early age, and, by the time they get to fifth grade, it may be terribly difficult, perhaps hardly possible by traditional means, to change their attitudes about sex roles—whether they are male or female. For more than a decade, Paul Torrance, a psychologist particularly interested in creativity, has been conducting interesting and useful experiments with young children. Using a Products Improvement Test, for example, Torrance asked first-grade boys and girls to "make toys more fun to play with." Many six-year-old boys refused to try the nurse's kit, "protesting," Torrance reports, "'I'm a boy! I don't play with things like that.'" Several creative boys turned the nurse's kit into a doctor's kit and were then "quite free to think of improvements." By the third grade, however, "boys excelled girls even on the nurse's kit, probably because," Torrance explains, "girls have been conditioned by this time to accept toys as they are and not to manipulate or change them."

Later experiments with third, fourth, and fifth-graders using science toys further verify what Torrance calls "the inhibiting effects of sex-role conditioning." "Girls were quite reluctant," he reports, "to work with these science toys and frequently protested: 'I'm a girl; I'm not supposed to know anything about things like that!' " Boys, even in these early grades, were about twice as good as girls at explaining ideas about toys. In 1959, Torrance reported his findings to parents and teachers in one school and asked for their cooperation in attempting to change the attitudes of the girls. In 1960, when he retested them, using similar science toys, the girls participated willingly and even with apparent enjoyment. And they performed as well as the boys. But in one significant respect nothing had changed: The boys' contributions were more highly valued—both by other boys and by girls—than the girls' contributions, regardless of the fact that, in terms of sex, boys and girls had scored equally. "Apparently," Torrance writes, "the school climate has helped to make it more acceptable for girls to play around with science things, but boys' ideas about science things are still supposed to be better than those of girls."

Torrance's experiments tell us both how useful and how limited education may be for women in a culture in which assumptions about their inferiority run deep in their own consciousness as well as in the consciousness of men. While it is encouraging to note that a year's effort had changed behavior patterns significantly, it is also clear that attitudes of nine-, ten-, and eleven-year-olds are not so easily modifiable, at least not through the means Torrance used.

Torrance's experiments also make clear that, whatever most of us have hitherto assumed, boys and girls are *not* treated alike in elementary school. If we consider those non-curricular aspects of the school environment that the late anthropologist Jules Henry labeled the "noise" of schools, chief among them is the general attitude of teachers, whatever their sex, that girls are likely to "love" reading and to "hate" mathematics and science. As we know from the Rosenthal study of teacher expectations, *Pygmalion in the Classroom,* such expectations significantly determine student behavior and attitudes. Girls are not expected to think logically or to understand scientific principles;

they accept that estimate internally and give up on mathematics and science relatively early. And what encouragement awaits the interested few in high school? For example, in six high school science texts published since 1966 and used in the Baltimore city public schools—all of the books rich in illustrations—I found photographs of one female lab assistant, one woman doctor, one woman scientist, and Rachel Carson. It is no wonder that the percentage of women doctors and engineers in the United States has remained constant at 6 percent and 1 percent respectively for the past fifty years.

● Here is another area of discriminatory behavior which seems to be related in part at least to the self-fulfilling prophecy. Make connections to Chapter 2 and to Chapter 7.

Though there is no evidence that their early physical needs are different from or less than boys', girls are offered fewer activities even in kindergarten. They may sit and watch while boys, at the request of the female teacher, change the seating arrangement in the room. Of course, it's not simply a matter of physical exercise or ability: Boys are learning how to behave as males, and girls are learning to be "ladies" who enjoy being "waited on." If there are student-organized activities to be arranged, boys are typically in charge, with girls assisting, perhaps in the stereotyped role of secretary. Boys are allowed and expected to be noisy and aggressive, even on occasion to express anger; girls must learn "to control themselves" and behave like "young ladies." On the other hand, boys are expected not to cry, though there are perfectly good reasons why children of both sexes ought to be allowed that avenue of expression. Surprisingly early, boys and girls are separated for physical education and hygiene, and all the reports now being published indicate preferential treatment for boys and nearly total neglect of girls.

In junior high schools, sexual stereotyping becomes, if anything, more overt. Curricular sex-typing continues and is extended to such "shop" subjects as cooking and sewing, on the one hand, and metal- and woodworking, printing, ceramics, on the other. In vocational high schools, the stereotyping becomes outright channeling, and here the legal battles have begun for equality of opportunity. Recently, the testimony of junior high and high school girls in New York has become available in a pamphlet prepared by the New York City chapter of NOW [National Order of Women]. Here are a few items:

Well, within my physics class last year, our teacher asked if there was anybody interested in being a lab assistant, in the physics lab, and when I raised my hand, he told all the girls to put their hands down because he was only interested in working with boys.

There is an Honor Guard . . . students who, instead of participating in gym for the term, are monitors in the hall, and I asked my gym teacher if I could be on the Honor Guard Squad. She said it was only open to boys. I then went to the head of the Honor Guard . . . who said that he thought girls were much too nasty to be Honor Guards. He thought they would be too mean in working on the job, and I left it at that.

We asked for basketball. They said there wasn't enough equipment. The boys prefer to have it first. Then we will have what is left over. We haven't really gotten anywhere.

Finally, I quote more extensively from one case:

MOTHER: I asked Miss Jonas if my daughter could take metalworking or mechanics, and she said there is no freedom of choice. That is what she said.

THE COURT : That is it?

ANSWER: I also asked her whose decision this was, that there was no freedom of choice. And she told me it was the decision of the board of education. I didn't ask her anything else because she clearly showed me that it was against the school policy for girls to be in the class. She said it was a board of education decision.

QUESTION: Did she use that phrase, "no freedom of choice"?

ANSWER: Exactly that phrase—no freedom of choice. That is what made me so angry that I wanted to start this whole thing.

* * *

THE COURT: Now, after this lawsuit was filed, they then permitted you to take the course; is that correct?

DAUGHTER: No, we had to fight about it for quite a while.

QUESTION: But eventually they did let you in the second semester?

ANSWER: They only let me in there.

Q: You are the only girl?

A: Yes.

Q: How did you do in the course?

A: I got the medal for it from all the boys there.

Q: Will you show the court?

A: Yes (indicating).

Q: And what does the medal say?

A: Medal 1970 Van Wyck.

Q: And why did they give you that medal?

A: Because I was the best one out of all the boys.

THE COURT: I do not want any giggling or noises in the courtroom. Just do the best you can to control yourself or else I will have to ask you to leave the courtroom. This is no picnic, you know. These are serious lawsuits.

Such "serious lawsuits" will, no doubt, continue, but they are not the only routes to change. There are others to be initiated by school systems themselves.

One route lies through the analysis of texts and attitudes. So long as those responsible for the education of children believe in the stereotypes as givens, rather than as hypothetical constructs that a patriarchal society has established as desired norms—so long as the belief continues, so will the condition. These beliefs are transmitted in the forms we call literature and history, either on the printed page or in other media.

Elementary school readers are meant for both sexes. Primers used in the first grades offer children a view of a "typical" American family: a mother who does not work, a father who does, two children—a brother who is always older than a sister—and two pets—a dog and sometimes a cat—whose sexes and ages mirror those of the brother and sister. In these books, boys build or paint things; they also pull girls in wagons and push merry-go-rounds. Girls carry purses when they go shopping; they help mother cook or pretend that they are cooking; and they play with their dolls. When they are not making messes, they are cleaning up their rooms or other people's messes. Plots in which girls are involved usually depend on their inability to do something—to manage their own roller skates or to ride a pony. Or in another typical role, a girl named Sue admires a parachute jumper: "What a jump!" said Sue. "What a jump for a man to make!" When her brother puts on a show for the rest of the neighborhood, Sue, whose name appears as the title of the chapter, is part of his admiring audience.

The absence of adventurous heroines may shock the innocent; the absence of even a few stories about women doctors, lawyers, or professors thwarts reality; but the consistent presence of one female stereotype is the most troublesome matter:

> Primrose was playing house. Just as she finished pouring tea for her dolls she began to think. She thought and thought and she thought some more: "Whom shall I marry? Whomever shall I marry?
>
> "I think I shall marry a mailman. Then I could go over to everybody's house and give them their mail.
>
> "Or I might marry a policeman. I could help him take the children across the street."

Primrose thinks her way through ten more categories of employment and concludes, "But now that I think it over, maybe I'll just marry somebody I love." Love is the opiate designated to help Primrose forget to think about what she would like to do or be. With love as reinforcer, she can imagine herself helping some man in his work. In another children's book, Johnny says, "I think I will be a dentist when I grow up," and later, to Betsy, he offers generously, "You can be a dentist's nurse." And, of course, Betsy accepts gratefully, since girls are not expected to have work identity other than as servants or helpers. In short, the books that schoolgirls read prepare them early for the goal of marriage, hardly ever for work, and never for independence.

If a child's reader can be pardoned for stereotyping because it is "only" fiction, a social studies text has no excuse for denying reality to its readers. After all, social studies texts ought to describe "what is," if not "what should be." And yet, such texts for the youngest grades are no different from readers. They focus on families and hence on sex roles and work. Sisters are still younger than brothers; brothers remain the doers, questioners, and knowers who explain things to their poor, timid sisters. In a study of five widely used texts, Jamie Kelem Frisof finds that energetic boys think about "working on a train or in a broom factory" or about being President. They grow up to be doctors or factory workers or (in five texts combined) to do some hundred different jobs, as opposed to thirty for women.

Consider for a moment the real work world of women. Most women (at least for some portion of their lives) work, and if we include "token" women—the occasional engineer, for instance—they probably do as many different kinds of work as men. Even without improving the status of working women, the reality is distinctly different from the content of school texts and literature written for children. Schools usually at least reflect the society they serve; but the treatment of working women is one clear instance in which the reflection is distorted by a patriarchal attitude about who *should* work and the maleness of work. For example, there are women doctors—there have been women doctors in this country, in fact, for a hundred years or so. And yet, until [very recently], there were no children's books about women doctors.

In a novel experiment conducted recently by an undergraduate at Towson State College in Maryland, fourth-grade students answered "yes" or "no" to a series of twenty questions, eight of which asked, in various ways, whether "girls were smarter than boys" or whether "daddies were smarter than mommies." The results indicated that boys and girls were agreed that 1) boys were not smarter than girls, nor girls smarter than boys; but 2) that daddies were indeed smarter than mommies! One possible explanation of this finding depends on the knowledge that daddies, in school texts and on television (as well as in real life), work, and that people who work know things. Mommies, on the other hand, in books and on television, rarely stir out of the house except to go to the store—and how can someone like that know anything? Of course, *we* know that half of all mothers in the United States work at some kind of job, but children whose mommies do work can only assume—on the basis of evidence offered in school books and on television—that their mommies must be "different," perhaps even not quite "real" mommies.

School systems can and should begin to encourage new curricular developments, especially in literature and social studies, and at the elementary as well as the high school level. Such changes, of course, must include the education and re-education of teachers, and I know of no better way to re-educate them than to ask for analyses of the texts they use, as well as of their assumptions and attitudes. The images we pick up, consciously or unconsciously, from literature and history significantly control our sense of identity, and our identity—our sense of ourselves as powerful or powerless, for example—controls our behavior. As teachers read new materials and organize and teach new courses, they will change their views. That is the story of most of the women I know who, like me, have become involved in women's studies. The images we have in our heads about ourselves come out of literature and history; before we can change those images, we must see them clearly enough to exorcise them and, in the process, to raise others from the past we are learning to see.

That is why black educators have grown insistent upon their students' learning black history —slave history, in fact. That is also why some religious groups, Jews for example, emphasize their history as a people, even though part of that history is also slave history. For slave history has two virtues: Not only does it offer a picture of servitude against which one can measure the present; it offers also a vision of struggle and courage. When I asked a group of young women at the University of Pittsburgh last year whether they

were depressed by the early nineteenth-century women's history they were studying, their replies were instructive: "Certainly not," one woman said, "we're angry that we had to wait until now—after so many years of U.S. history in high school—to learn the truth about some things." And another added, "But it makes you feel good to read about those tremendous women way back then. They felt some of the same things we do now."

Will public education begin to change the images of women in texts and the lives of women students in schools? There will probably be some movement in this direction, at least in response to the pressures from students, parents, and individual teachers. I expect that parents, for example, will continue to win legal battles for their daughters' equal rights and opportunities. I expect that individual teachers will alter their courses and texts and grow more sensitive to stereotypic expectations and behavior in the classroom. But so far there are no signs of larger, more inclusive reforms: no remedial program for counselors, no major effort to destereotype vocational programs or kindergarten classrooms, no centers for curricular reform. Frankly, I don't expect this to happen without a struggle. I don't expect that public school systems will take the initiative here. There is too much at stake in a society as patriarchal as this one. And schools, after all, tend to follow society, not lead it.

● It would be a most interesting and instructive project to keep a notebook on the number and type of occasions in which you encounter sexual stereotypes which result in "sexism" (i.e., the discrimination against a person on the basis of sex). Try the project for just 1 twelve-hour period.

---

20 HE AND SHE: THE SEX HORMONES AND BEHAVIOR*

MAGGIE SCARF

Freud always maintained that human psychology had, as one of its components, some unknown biological "bedrock." He thought that we all, male and female alike, were captives of our physiology; that inborn propensities and tendencies exerted a profound effect upon behavior—and that these inner propensities were different in the two sexes. (Hence his now-infamous remark: "Anatomy is Destiny.") This belief is, however, not popular in the present, more "environmentalist" intellectual climate. The common assumption nowadays appears to be that where male behavior and female behavior are different they are so because of acculturation: that the display of their "masculinity" or "femininity" is by and large the result of social training.

Recent research on the sex hormones suggests that it is Freud's ideas which may be the more valid approximation of the reality. Endocrine studies have now established the critical role played by the sex hormones during prenatal life: These hormones are not only crucial to differentiation of the (male or female) sexual organs; but they "program" the brain, during fetal development, for the later display of either masculine or feminine behavior.

The word *hormone,* in the Greek, means "to arouse"—and this is what hormones do. They are chemical substances, secreted first in one place (usually, but not always, a gland or organ), then released into the bloodstream to move through the body and exert their ultimate effects elsewhere —on other "target" organs. The hormones and hormone-producing glands are part of an interrelated chemical system, as intricately balanced as the body's "electrical" system (brain, spinal cord, nerves, sense organs). Hormones must be present in order for the initiation—or in some cases, inhibition—of a multitude of complex chemical processes. They are involved, for example, in the vital maintenance of correct blood sugar in the body; of the over-all rate of metabolism; in the regulation of water retention, of growth, of body responses to stress; and in the mediation of reproductive behavior.

The major sex hormones are secreted either in the testes in males (testosterone) or in the ovaries of females (progesterone and the estrogens, the important ones being 17 *beta*-estradiol and estrone). The adrenals, small yellowish organs lying just above each kidney, also secrete some sex hormones, including small amounts of testosterone and larger amounts of the weaker male hormone androstenedione (AD)—as well as a variety of other important hormones, including cortisol, cortisone and the "fight-or-flight" epinephrine (adrenalin).

Both sexes produce hormones of the opposite sex. In fact, men produce as much of the potent 17 *beta*-estradiol as adult women early in their menstrual cycle (when estrogen levels are at a low ebb). Men also have as much, or more, 17 *beta*-estradiol and estrone in their bloodstreams as do most postmenopausal women.

It is not the lack of estrogens which make a male a male, but the far higher levels of testosterone, antagonizing and nullifying the biological effects of the female hormones.

Puberty is a time when the sex hormones are said to be "awakening." The pituitary or "master gland" (an organ just under the brain, not much larger than a small pea) now begins sending increasing amounts of hormones called gonadotropins into the bloodstream. These are chemical messengers which, in the case of the male, stimulate sperm production and the secretion of testosterone by the cells of the testes. In the female the same gonadotropins (chemically identical to those of the male) are released by the pituitary; but in females they appear in sequence, rather than simultaneously. The first of these hormones stimulates the growth of the egg and its nest cells within the ovary, with an accompanying rise in estrogen secretion. The second gonadotropin, appearing slightly later in the cycle, subserves the production of progesterone, the female hormone which prepares the uterine lining to receive the fertilized egg. The sex hormones bring about, in their turn, the onset of secondary sexual characteristics —breast development in girls, growth of facial hair in boys, etc.—as well as the behavioral changes seen in adolescence.

Puberty, however, it now appears, does not constitute an "awakening" so much as it does a *reawakening*. Research during the past several decades has demonstrated that the sex hormones are, in fact, present during prenatal development. The concentrations in which they appear in utero are crucial not only to sexual differentiation (to produce a male or a female) but, it now appears, to differentiation of central nervous system tissues which will mediate masculine or feminine behavior during adult life.

The primitive gonad, it should be mentioned here, is sexually bipotential: it contains everything necessary for the fetus to develop either as male or female. There is a "rind," capable of becoming an ovary; a "core" which can develop as a testis; and two sets of internal duct systems, male and female. (One of them will become vestigial during sexual differentiation.) The "genital tubercle" grows into either a clitoris or a penis; the tissue above the urogenital groove either fuses, in the male, to become a scrotum or remains separate as the lips of the vagina.

What makes the embryonic gonad move toward differentiation as male or female? Surely it is

genetic sex which sets a "direction"—and, it used to be assumed, determined everything that followed. But a series of brilliant experiments begun in the late forties by the French physiologist Alfred Jost gave definitive proof that it was in fact the prenatal hormones which played the decisive role in sexual differentiation of the developing fetus.

Jost, using surgical methods so delicate that they have been difficult for other investigators to imitate, castrated a male rabbit in utero. The infant male, when it was born, had completely *female* external genitalia: It appeared that in the absence of the testes (and therefore, testosterone) a genetic XY male fetus had developed in a female direction.

What would happen, then, to an ovariectomized female fetus? Jost removed the ovaries of a developing female rabbit fetus: At birth she had normal female internal ducts and external genitalia. It seemed that the ovaries—and therefore, prenatal estrogens—were not vital to the female in order to ensure her normal differentiation. Indeed, given that no interference (such as the presence of testosterone) occurred, the fetus would always develop along female lines. Jost's work suggested that Nature had some fundamental bias in favor of producing females. Femaleness thus could not be—as Freud had suggested—some state of incompleted maleness; it appeared to be the basic form of life. Maleness was itself the correction: to achieve it, something had to be added on—male hormones.

(One psychoendocrinologist tells a story of how he explained to a very religious friend that the Adam and Eve story in Genesis was unlikely—that all biological evidence now available suggested that if one sex arose from the side of the other, it would have had to have been Adam who came from Eve. "Isn't God wonderful?" retorted his friend. "When He created the sexes, He even did it the hard way!")

Later work of Jost's, and a variety of other studies, have now demonstrated that testosterone must not only be present in utero in order for normal male differentiation to occur; it must be present during a sensitive "critical period." A male rabbit fetus, castrated by the 19th day after conception, will develop a completely female internal duct system and female genitalia. If castrated on day 24, however, when the crucial phase is over, its development will be completely male.

Similarly, a male rat castrated in utero (this can now be done using chemical methods) will differentiate in a female direction—with a vaginal pouch, unfused scrotal tissues and a miniaturized penis which is indistinguishable from a clitoris. If castration is delayed until the critical period has passed, however—in this species, several days before birth—the rat will be irreversibly male.

In females, the presence of testosterone during the sensitive phase is as dramatic as its absence in males: A female rat receiving injections of male hormone during the critical period will become virilized, develop male-appearing genitalia, grow at an increased (male-type) rate, lose her reproductive cycle and become sterile. The same hormone doses, given 10 days after birth, will achieve none of these effects.

Hormones—the right concentrations at the right times—are decisive to normal sexual differentiation. In the middle fifties, the group of researchers working with the great pioneer in hormones and behavior, Dr. William C. Young (who died in 1965), began to wonder: Was it possible that fetal hormones also had some determining effect upon the type of sexual behavior that would be shown much later on, at puberty? What actually caused males to show masculine sexual responses during mating, and females to display feminine responses? It had always been assumed that the reason, in each case, was genetic. A genetic male simply looked like a male and was expected to behave like one.

But if prenatal hormones could feminize his

Behavioral Principle: "Testosterone Rules"

Numerous animal studies have confirmed that there is a curious link between the male hormone, testosterone, and levels of ongoing aggression. In the mouse, for example, fighting among males commences with the onset of puberty, when hormone levels are rising abruptly. Female mice fight only rarely, as is the case for males which have been castrated. When male mouse castrates are given testosterone injections, however, they display normal male adult fighting behavior within a matter of hours.

Does high testosterone level in the male bear a direct, one-to-one relationship to high levels of displayed aggression? In a study published last year, Dr. Robert Rose of the Boston University School of Medicine used new hormone assay techniques to take precise readings of male hormone levels in the bloodstreams of 34 male rhesus monkeys. At the same time, Rose, working with colleagues Irwin Bernstein and John Holaday, measured the frequency with which each monkey became involved in aggressive interactions with other members of the colony; and also assessed the dominance rank of each rhesus within the entire group.

Rose and his co-workers found that there was a high correlation between the levels of the animals' testosterone and the position which each held within the dominance hierarchy. The higher a monkey's male hormone concentration was, the higher his position in the "pecking order" tended to be. Those monkeys who were the more dominant were those who were more aggressive. And testosterone levels related, with almost startling simplicity, to levels of displayed aggression: The five animals showing the greatest degree of threat and confrontation behavior were the five with the highest hormonal level. If a clear-cut principle can be said to have emerged from the Rose study it was that, at least among male rhesus monkeys, Testosterone Rules.

Dr. Rose, 35, who trained as both a physician and a psychiatrist, is chief of the Department of Psychosomatic Medicine at Boston University Medical School. He is currently, he notes, trying to investigate some of the questions raised by last year's male rhesus study. For example, was the superior status of the more dominant monkeys predicated on the fact that their male hormone levels were high in the first place? Or had testosterone levels risen as a *result* of dominance? Or both: Had raised hormonal levels meant more aggressiveness, which in turn lent itself to higher dominance position, which in turn had the effect of raising testosterone level—a question of the rich getting richer?

Rose and his colleagues, in order to test these possibilities, took several of the male monkeys and placed them, individually, into new colonies consisting only of females (13 or more). The lone male, in each instance, assumed the highest dominance position immediately. He had frequent copulations and, says Rose, had "what appeared to be a fairly blissful existence. After several weeks in these paradisiacal circumstances, we tested each male for levels of testosterone circulating in his bloodstream. We found that, across the board, the levels had risen —something like a fourfold increase."

It seemed that male hormone levels were not set and fixed within the body; they could be "turned up" as a consequence of environmental stimuli. The next question was, would the reverse also hold true? The researchers took each of their experimental monkeys and introduced them into new and far different groups—colonies of strange males in which the dominance hierarchy was already well established. In this situation, each lone "new boy" in the colony was set upon by the other males, outnumbered and subjected to total defeat. After a mere half-hour of such treatment, the monkeys were rescued from their respective fields of disgrace, and testosterone measurements were taken once more. In all cases, hormone levels had fallen sharply.

"Defeat was associated with behavioral withdrawal. The monkeys all did, after their experience with the strange males, show every sign of real depression," said Rose. "And that withdrawal involved a concomitant drop in sexual levels." Rose is now interested in finding out what happens to a male rhesus's level of displayed aggressiveness, and to his position within the social hierarchy, when testosterone levels are manipulated upward or downward by adding or removing fixed amounts of male hormone.

—M. S.

---

genitalia, and masculinize those of the female, could they also affect the two, complementary sets of behavior and the type of sexual responses each would show?

In a now-classic experiment, Young and his colleagues demonstrated that a female guinea pig which had been virilized during prenatal life (through testosterone shots to the mother) would, when given male hormones at puberty, respond with startling amounts of male behavior. In subsequent work, Dr. Arnold A. Gerall showed that such females would not only mount other females and display pelvic thrusting, but (granted that genital development had been sufficiently anomalous) even intromission and ejaculation. In contrast, even when given high doses of estrogens, the capacity for showing normal female behavior —such as the "lordotic" response, typical in female rats and guinea pigs, in which the back is deeply arched and the genitals raised and presented to the male—was dramatically diminished. It was as if, during the period of prenatal life, some inner behavioral dial had been set at "male."

Experimental studies of the past 10 years have now established that, at least in lower animals, there are sensitive neural tissues which (like the primitive gonad) are bisexual in potential. These tissues, located in the hypothalamic region at the base of the brain, differentiate during fetal development to produce an unequivocally "male" or "female" brain; that is, they become imprinted during prenatal life to mediate either masculine or feminine mating behavior at puberty. Again, the key to what happens is testosterone. If it is present, the "female" pattern will be suppressed and the "male" tissues will become organized for the steady release of gonadotropins at puberty, and for male sexual responses during reproductive behavior. If, on the other hand, testosterone is absent in uterine life, the sensitive brain areas will differentiate as "female." They will become programed for the cyclical release of pituitary hormones at puberty, and for female sexual responses during mating.

Might homosexuality in the male be tied to a less-than-adequate supply of testosterone during the critical period when brain tissues are differentiating and becoming "programed" for the display of later sexual behavior? A number of researchers, intrigued by a vast animal literature on the subject, have recently begun looking for a possible correlation between homosexual behavior and the actions of fetal hormones.

In a [recent] British report, it was found that a group of homosexual males had lower levels of testosterone in their urine than did a comparison group of heterosexual males; and that a group of lesbian women had higher testosterone in urinary samples than did a control group of female heterosexuals.

[Recently] in an investigation carried out at the Masters and Johnson research institute in St. Louis, the blood plasma testosterone values and sperm counts of 30 young homosexual college students were carefully analyzed. It was found that among the 15 men in the group who were totally, or almost totally, homosexual, testosterone readings were much lower than they were among the other half of the men, who had definite heterosexual proclivities also. Sperm scores were also astonishingly lower among exclusively homosexual males. There appeared, interestingly enough, to be no great difference either in hormone levels or sperm counts when the bisexual males were compared with a "control" group of heterosexuals. According to the director of this research project, Dr. Robert C. Kolodny, the important question to be studied now is whether diminished testosterone supply is somehow a *result* of homosexual behavior—or whether it reflects an endocrine makeup that is simply different from that of heterosexuals in the first place.

One cannot of course generalize from rats to humans. (And the psychoendocrinological journals are as full of cautions about this temptation as the old temperance tracts once were about the dangers of drink.) Nevertheless, as one researcher remarked privately: "We do, in fact, work with the implicit assumption that what is found to be true in one species will hold true up and down the phylogenetic scale. It's usually an exception when one discovers a physiological mechanism in one species and then finds it absent—or totally reversed—in others. After all, aren't we making the same sorts of assumptions when we test out our drugs on rats?"

The presumption is, then, that the higher animals including monkeys, apes and human beings are, like the rat and the guinea pig, *not* psychosexually neutral at birth: That they are, even before the onset of learning and social experience, "programed" or predisposed by early hormonal influences to acquire specific, either masculine or feminine, patterns of behavior. In a study carried out in the late nineteen-sixties by Dr. Robert W. Goy, it was demonstrated that female rhesus monkeys, exposed to male sex hormones during prenatal development, would later behave in more malelike, than femalelike, fashion. Dr. Goy, working at the Oregon Regional Primate Research Center, injected a group of expectant monkey mothers with periodic doses of testosterone. The result was, not surprisingly, a generation of female offspring whose genitalia were male in appearance. These female ''pseudohermaphrodites'' were separated from their mothers at birth, and henceforth socialized only with their agemates.

Goy carefully studied the behavior of the virilized females as they grew into childhood. It had already been well established, through the famous monkey studies of Dr. Harry Harlow and others, that the play behavior of juvenile male monkeys was measurably different from that of the young females (and that these differences were not ''taught'' by the parent monkeys, because they manifested themselves even when the juveniles had no contact whatsoever with the older generation). The young males, for example, showed much more social threat behavior; they initiated play more often than did the young females; and they engaged in rough-and-tumble and pursuit play to a far greater degree. The males also withdrew less from threats and approaches made by others; and they engaged in more sexual play, including the frequent mounting which was in effect a ''game'' in which the future sexual role was being rehearsed.

The impressive thing about Goy's experimentally masculinized females was that they too behaved in all of these ways. They displayed the elevated levels of energy and activity commonly seen in young male monkeys: In fact their play behavior was much more similar to that of the male than to anything normally encountered in the behavior of the juvenile female.

In a 1967 study carried out at the Psychohormonal Research Unit of Johns Hopkins Medical School, the same unusually high levels of energy and activity were found in a group of 10 young girls who had been accidentally masculinized in utero. This research investigation was carried out by Dr. Anke Ehrhardt, working in collaboration with the Psychohormonal Unit's well-known director, Dr. John Money. The 10 young females taking part had all been virilized as a result of what was essentially a medical mishap: Their mothers were given progestin, a synthetic hormone, during pregnancy (in order to prevent unwanted abortion). It was not known at this time—during the 1950's—that certain progestins have a masculinizing effect on the developing female fetus. Nine of the 10 girls had been born with malelike genitalia, including an enlarged clitoris and a fused, empty scrotum. They received surgical correction early in life, and development proceeded normally from that point onward; psychosexual development, carefully evaluated by Dr. Ehrhardt in extensive tests and interviews, was certainly within the normal female range also. But it did seem to point toward some interesting questions about what the influence of those masculinizing fetal hormones had been.

Of the 10 girls, ranging in age from almost 4 to almost 15, nine were out-and-out tomboys. They preferred trucks, guns and other boys' toys to dolls. They loved being outdoors, climbing trees, playing football and baseball. They preferred being with boys to being with other girls; they wore boys' clothing styles and were more or less indifferent—some were actively opposed—to skirts and more feminine modes of dress. All displayed a high frequency of self-assertion and self-reliance, some of them to such an extent that their mothers were concerned about their behavior. ''My daughter acts like a boy,'' complained one woman. ''It might be because of the hormones. She is the opposite from me. I was the dainty type.'' Another family was having problems because their fetally virilized daughter was far better in sports than was her older brother.

Says Dr. Ehrhardt, who is now an assistant research professor of pediatrics and psychiatry at the New York State University at Buffalo: ''The girls were consistently less interested in doll-playing than were a 'control' group of 10 girls, who were matched with them in every possible way—age, race, socioeconomic level, I.Q., etc. Also, the 'control' girls did a great deal of bridefantasying, and involved themselves frequently in those sorts of games which are actually childhood rehearsals of the future maternal and wifely roles. In contrast, the fetally masculinized girls tended to fantasize about future careers.''

In studies which she and Dr. Money have done on girls suffering from adrenogenital syndrome, notes Dr. Ehrhardt, the same tomboyish element and high-energy level regularly appear. Adrenogenital syndrome is a genetically transmitted condition which causes masculinization of the female fetus during prenatal development. The condition is due, briefly, to an error in metabolism which causes the adrenals to become overactive and produce too many hormones, including too many male hormones. It is now possible to stabilize this dysfunction with cortisone, so that overproduction of male hormones in the adrenogenital girl can be stopped postnatally, and her genitals can be surgically feminized. Still, psychosexual development of these girls, similarly to the progestin-induced masculinized girls, is toward the more "malelike" end of the normal female spectrum—high degrees of activity expressed in more masculine kinds of behavior.

In assessing which behaviors were to be called "masculine" and which were to be called "feminine," Drs. Ehrhardt and Money relied on criteria such as energy expenditure (much higher in boys), toy and sports preferences, career ambitions, maternalism (girls are usually fascinated by infants and infant care; boys are usually not) and several other items, including body image, clothing choice, etc. In statistical analyses of responses of large groups of boys and girls, sex-related "male" and "female" clusters about these items do reliably emerge.

"Nevertheless, isn't it possible," I asked Dr. Ehrhardt, who is a fair-haired, pretty German-born woman in her early 30's, "that these 'sex differences' are merely artifacts of our culture? Most psychiatrists and psychologists (and of course, most Women's Liberationists) believe that they result primarily from social experience. That is, a small female child is taught very early, or learns by imitation, those 'feminine' ways in which she is expected to behave—and responds by doing it.''

"I would agree," she answered, "that the most powerful factors in the shaping of gender identity are probably experiential and social. In other words the primary thing is whether a person is called and thought of (and calls himself or herself) male or female. This is of course fundamental to identity. But within the broad spectrums of behavior which we call either masculine or feminine, there are certainly very wide variations. You can have, on the one hand, a woman who is totally domestic and maternal; and on the other, a person who is uninterested in children and wants only a career. My speculation would be that there is a fetal hormonal history, in both these cases, disposing the individual in one direction or the other. In other words, what I'm suggesting is that there may very well be normal female hormone correlates to the variations of normal female behavior.

"The main message of most of this work, both with animals and with humans," she added, "is that hormones before birth may have an organizing effect upon behavior that will appear only much later—that social environment is the mold in which basic tendencies, already present, will be shaped and formed. The idea is that testosterone, by its presence or absence, sets some kind of behavioral potential; and that postnatal experiences are actually acting upon a physiologically biased substrate.''

● This last paragraph is important. It suggests that physiological differences between males and females do not *control* (strictly determine) behavior but that they bias the individual in certain directions, and that the biases may be enhanced or played down by cultural factors. Anatomy is *not* destiny; it is a biased die. Our view is that no biological difference can be cited which would justify the past and present oppression of woman. What is *your* conclusion on this issue?

---

21 FEMININE INTELLECT AND THE DEMANDS OF SOCIETY*

ELEANOR E. MACCOBY

It is universally known that the intellectual achievements of women, over the course of history, rank considerably lower, in quality and quantity, than those of men.

One explanation offered for this difference is that up until very recently women have had far less access to the opportunities of education than have men. Yet even today, some forty years after the opportunities for higher education have been opened to large numbers of women, the differences persist. In the field of letters, where women are presumed to have special aptitudes, more men than women are productive, creative writers. And in the field of science the imbalance is even greater: the Madame Curies are notable by their rarity and our colleges and universities turn out but few women who become intellectually excited by a scientific research problem or who organize varied data into a new hypothesis or theory.

What are the reasons for the relatively low level of feminine intellectual achievement?

It is reasonable to believe—and has been offered as an explanation—that woman's social sex-role is more incompatible with the life of an intellectual than is a man's. It is difficult to continue in the single-minded pursuit of a set of ideas while being a competent wife and mother—more difficult than for a man to do so while a competent husband and father. Yet it is necessary to ask whether these matters of conflicting interests and responsibilities constitute the entire explanation for women's lack of signal accomplishment in the intellectual sphere. I am inclined to think they do not.

If we examine woman's intellectual performance through a large range of her life cycle, we find other reasons for suspecting that it is not just the conflicting demands upon her time created by marriage and children that interfere with her achievement. Rather, it appears that some of the constraints upon her intellectual achievement make themselves felt long before marriage and continue to be present during those long years from thrity-five to sixty-five when the most demanding phase of child-rearing is over—the period when many men are at the peak of their productive careers.

It seems possible that these constraints may be some relevant early-formed personality traits, or even some early-established basic qualities of mind, that characterize women and that bear upon intellectual performance. Likewise, the possibility exists that innate hereditary qualities, mental and behavioural, affect woman's intellectual productivity. It is these factors that I would like to explore in this article.

SOCIAL MOULDING OF FEMININE INTELLECT

Studies of girls have repeatedly shown that they develop early a greater interest in other people, and in what other people think of them, than do boys; they tend to be more influenced by the opinions of others, and they are more conforming to what they perceive to be the social demands of the situations they are in. It is probably these conformist tendencies that help them to excel at spelling and punctuation—the kinds of performance for which there is only one socially prescribed right answer. But for higher-level intellectual productivity, it is independence of mind that is required—the ability to turn one's back on others at least for a time,

*Abridged from Eleanor M. Maccoby, Feminine intellect and the demands of science. *Impact of Science on Society*, quarterly published by Unesco, XX(1), 1970, 13–20. © Unesco.

while working alone on a problem—and it is just this which girls, from an early age, appear to find so difficult to do.

But of course, this is not true for all girls. So it is interesting to consider now what happens to a little girl who at preschool age does have the qualities that could make her into an analytic thinker. She is full of curiosity, likes to explore things, is dominant and independent, probably likes to play with boys and wear blue jeans, and isn't especially interested in dolls. Assuming that her parents have been tolerant of her temperament, what takes place when she enters school?

One of the first blows is that the boys won't play with her any more; they form their own exclusive play groups, and she must fall back upon the company of girls. In many ways she is made to discover that she is not behaving as girls are expected to behave, and the disapproval she encounters generates a certain amount of anxiety.

This may sound like pure speculation, but there is some evidence that this is the course that development does take in girls who start out as tomboys. Sears traced the development of aggression, and anxiety about aggression, to be between the ages of 5 and 12.[a] The boys who were most anxious about aggression at age 12 were the ones whose parents had forbidden fighting when they were younger; at the age of 5 they had already become fairly unaggressive children. The girls who showed most anxiety about aggression at age 12, however, were the ones who had been fairly aggressive at kindergarten age. What is important for our present discussion is this: that the ones who showed the most of this kind of anxiety in middle childhood were the ones who had been trained in ways inappropriate to their sex in pre-school years.

In most American homes, the mothers assume a larger role in the discipline and caretaking of daughters, and the fathers in that of sons. However, the girls with high aggression anxiety levels in middle childhood had received an unusually high amount of both discipline and caretaking from their fathers. Furthermore, they had been encouraged to fight back when attacked by other children in the neighbourhood—an encouragement which is more often reserved for boys in the American culture. We see, then, that these girls were being to some degree masculinized in early childhood, and we can only assume that it was at least partly the social disapproval they encountered over their unfeminine behavior that produced the anxiety they later manifested.

Social disapproval can have even more direct effects on the expression of feminine intellectuality, by affecting the will to try.

While the evidence is not clear as to whether boys or girls have a higher correlation between ability (as measured by IQ tests) and achievement, there are some indications that boys lead in this. One 1960 study of seventh-grade children, for example, found the correlation between ability and achievement to be higher for boys. Then, Coleman, in 1961, reported that among secondary-school students who were named as 'best scholar' the boys had higher IQ scores than the girls, despite the fact that the girls in the general population studied had higher average IQ scores.[b] He suggests that girls of this age are caught up in a 'double bind.' They wish to conform to their parents' and teachers' expectations of good academic performance, but fear that high academic achievement will make them unpopular with boys. As a result of these dual pressures, Coleman suggests, the brightest girls do creditably in school but less than their best. On the other hand, the brightest boys feel free to excel in scholarship and do so in fact.

Matina Horner has recently come to similar conclusions, based upon studies with intelligent college-aged men and women.[c] The subjects in her studies are asked to tell a story based on a 'clue'. For the women, one clue is: 'After first-term finals, Anne finds herself at the top of her medical school class.' A similar clue, but this time about John being at the top of his medical school class, is

[a]R. R. Sears, 'Relation of Early Socialization Experiences to Aggression in Middle Childhood,' *Journal of Abnormal and Social Psychology*, No. 63, p. 466–92, 1961.

[b]J. S. Coleman, *The Adolescent Society*, Glencoe, Ill., The Free Press, 1961.
[c]Matina A. Horner, 'Fail: Bright Women,' *Psychology Today*, November, 1969, p. 36.

given to men. Men show few signs of conflict over success in the stories they write to this clue. Women, however, quite often manifest what Horner calls a 'motive to avoid success'. They say such things as that Anne is hated, that she is an unattractive bookworm, or that she lowers her performance on the next exam so that her boy friend can do better.

Horner also finds that in working on standard achievement tests, women do best working alone, and much worse when competing against men. Men, however, do better when competing against either sex than they do alone.

Many girls, in other words, are prevented from trying to do their best, particularly in competitive situations, by the belief that they will be seen as unfeminine.

A study following up a group of gifted children to determine what becomes of them in adulthood disclosed that, for girls, there was no relationship between IQ as measured during the school years and the level of subsequent achievement in their adult occupations; for boys there was good correlation.

There is also evidence that girls who are under-achievers in secondary school usually begin to be so at about the onset of puberty. This is a further indication that the achievement drop-off among girls as they reach maturity is linked to the adult female sex role—to finding a mate and marrying.

Let me link up these findings with our present concerns with woman's intellect. Suppose a girl does succeed in maintaining, throughout her childhood years, the qualities of dominance, independence and active striving that appear to be requisites for good analytic thinking. In so doing, she is defying the conventions concerning what is appropriate behavior for her sex. She may do this successfully in many ways, but I suggest that it is a rare intellectual woman who will not have paid a price for it: a price in anxiety. And this anxiety can do more than affect a woman's emotional life and personality; it can also have repercussions on her intellectual activity.

We are beginning to know a good deal about the effects of anxiety on thinking. It is especially damaging to creative thinking, for it narrows the range of efforts to find solutions to difficulties, interferes with breaking set, and prevents scanning of the whole range of elements open to perception. When anxiety facilitates performance, as it sometimes does, it facilitates already well-learned tasks, but it is antagonistic to breaking new ground.

INTELLECTUALITY AT THE PRICE OF FEMININITY?

From the standpoint of those who want women to become intellectuals, the above is something of a horror story. It would appear that even when a woman is suitably endowed intellectually and develops the right temperament and habits of thought to make use of her endowment, she must be stout of heart to resist society's pressures and remain a whole and happy person while pursuing her intellectual bent.

For parents and educators who are charged with the responsibility of raising and training girls, the requisites for intellectual development in girls appear to pose something of a dilemma. Shall mothers encourage whatever tomboy tendencies they find in their young daughters? Shall teachers attempt to free girls from the emotional involvement with others that helps to make them so tractable in the class-room?

I do not mean to imply that the concerted efforts of parents and teachers together would necessarily serve to make girls just like boys intellectually. I think it is quite possible that there are genetic factors that differentiate the two sexes and bear upon their intellectual performance, other than those having to do with what we have thought of as innate 'intelligence'. For example, there is good reason to believe that boys are innately more aggressive than girls—aggressive in the broader sense, not just as it implies fighting, but as it implies dominance and initiative as well. If this quality is indeed one which underlies the later growth of analytic thinking, then boys have an advantage which most girls, being endowed with more passive qualities, will find difficult to overcome.

Yet it appears likely that the way children are dealt with by the adults responsible for their care, and the social roles girls know they are preparing themselves for, also have a major bearing on whether girls will develop the characteristics that will be conducive to the growth of higher-level intellectual skills.

In so far as child training does have an influence, parents and educators have some difficult value judgements to make. What kinds of women do they want to produce? Do we want to encourage intellectuality in women if it must be done at the expense of femininity?

We appear here to be caught in another double-bind. Yet need it be so? May not there be some other alternative? Could not our current definitions of the feminine woman and girl undergo some revisions without any damage to the essential functions of woman? Does a woman really need to be passive and dependent in order to be sexually attractive to men, or in order to be a good mother? Could we not accept and encourage the active, dominant, independent qualities of the intellectual girl without labelling her as masculine, while encouraging in her whatever aspects of femininity *are* compatible with an analytic quality of mind?

I recognize that I am raising some controversial and intricate issues here, for the social and economic role of woman is by very necessity a dependent one during her child-bearing years. But these years have become a much smaller segment of her life span than they once were. I ask whether our whole definition of femininity should be such as to prepare a woman only for this short segment of her life.

22   MAN'S ROLE IN WOMEN'S LIBERATION*

MARY LOUISE BRISCOE and ELSIE ADAMS

The following essay is reformist, not revolutionary, in nature. It represents what strikes us as a reasonable and moderate appeal to men to reevaluate and then to change their attitudes toward women. It also reflects what we conceive to be the present attitude of most women in the Women's Liberation movement: optimistic, hopeful. Current history of other political movements has taught some depressing lessons about "working within the system for peaceful change"; nevertheless, at this time the Women's Liberation movement is non-violent and non-separatist. What women will be saying five years hence depends on their progress toward equality in the immediate future.

*Abridged from M. L. Briscoe and E. Adams, Man's role in women's liberation. *Up against the wall, mother,* . . . Beverly Hills, Calif.: Glencoe Press, 1971, pp. 375–383. Reprinted by permission of the publisher.

At present, very few men do anything to actively liberate women. There are those who have sacrificed traditional roles by helping to cook and clean a bit, but most of their basic attitudes about women are shrouded by historical myths. If, for example, they "instinctively" protect their women from physical or emotional threat, or if, indeed, they talk about "their women" with all the pride of ownership that derives from the cave or slave market, then they are really enacting the patterns of ancient culture in which the distinction between the sexes was dependent on physical differences only, i.e., bearing the club or the child.

It is no secret that no one is really free. The question is, how can more people obtain greater freedom? And if men must dominate women, or imagine that they must, in order to feel freer themselves, are they really free at all? The answer seems obvious. But although most people today are confronted by many problems of social sickness, the need for Women's Liberation within this society has been relegated to the bottom of the pile. The responses from men vary: "What are they so excited about? They have an easy life while we have to support them." "They're sick. They talk about freedom but what they really want is to castrate and dominate men (i.e., they want to be like us)." "All they really need is a good screw to settle them down." "If they keep it up they will destroy important sexual differences and therefore sexual attraction." "Women's Liberation is not a political issue—why don't the women spend their time on real problems?"

The fact of the matter is that women have spent their time on real problems, and their participation in political activity is the very thing that has made them cognizant of their lack of freedom. By this time most literate people know that women throughout the U.S. are getting organized to protest the denial of their basic freedoms. It has happened rapidly, spontaneously, and to such an extent that it looks like a master plan has prompted a movement. However the organizing factor is not a master plan but the idea of a master who excels and dominates his mistress. The peace movement began as a small campus voice—male or female—and was soon joined by various groups of women working actively for peace on local and national levels. The cry against war seemed "natural" to women, but young men who protested the war in those days were called cowards and thought to be unmanly. Now, after ten years, the cry for peace is heard in state as well as federal government, and the women who supported the cause, who helped convince men that it was a cause, have had some time to examine their own positions. They are joined by many young women on and off the campuses who have had their own freedom denied by their friends who claim to live for the greater freedom of all people.

The motivation of women to change their roles, or to develop roles that are more human and less subordinate, is clear enough. But they cannot change unless society also changes, and that means that men must work toward the liberation of women as well as men in all racial groups. Fewer people are startled these days when they hear talk about the need for equal rights of blacks, red, yellows and whites. They see that skin color does not necessarily suggest qualitative differences among races. The terms male and female should operate in a similar way: to describe the characteristics which distinguish people of different sexes who have equal rights to be human. Current studies in psychology, sociology and anthropology indicate that no one is really certain just how the sexes are different; we have until now assumed differences that are based only on inherited value judgments, not fact. Because men have been instrumental in developing and maintaining the value judgments which determine the traditional role of women, they are morally obligated to help change that role if they sincerely desire social change.

The first thing men must do is to discover and examine their own chauvinism, then try to free themselves from the need to suppress another group. This is probably the most difficult stage in the process of male liberation from male supremacist attitudes, since no one wants to admit that he is an oppressor. The process of discovery and liberation should be continual, because as in all forms of prejudice, the underlying attitudes are difficult to find and get rid of. The initial discovery is not enough. Traditional patterns of behavior are sometimes subtle and elusive to those who are pleased by them. When men feel alienated from a society they fear or distrust, they are pleased by the comforting presence they hope or imagine to have in their women. The ties of the nuclear family may seem to form a safe harbor from the ghastly business of a computerized world for many. But few men can honestly say they have this kind of comfort in any form but fantasy. They fear change in the role of women because they are afraid to lose what they probably don't even have. Psychic isolation is frightening to women as well as men, and if men realize they cannot tolerate it, they ought to realize that women's cry for greater freedom is not an attempt to destroy humane bonding among individuals but to create a more satisfactory bonding for both sexes. The defensive reaction most men have when they hear of Women's Liberation probably comes from their fear of losing their position as king of an imaginary mountain. They must examine their kingdom to see how it creates problems for both sexes. Women do not usually want to do men in, they simply want to improve their own position, which will also improve their relationship with men and other women. Women become hateful to men when their rights and recognition are continually evaded or deliberately ignored.

Once men begin to see their chauvinism they should talk seriously to other men and women about the problem and its damaging effects on both sexes. It is imperative that men take the problem seriously. There have been as many bad jokes about women as about minstrel shows, and neither are funny. Often men ask why women don't have a sense of humor about Women's Liberation—but they would not dare ask a Black or an Indian a comparable question. The answer is clear—there is nothing funny about being oppressed, and the male need for laughter usually reveals either unconscious fear of castration or blind refusal to see that the problem exists. The effect on women is the same eventually—they get more frustrated because they are not being taken seriously, and soon become more resentful, more bitter, and more militant.

Castration jokes are among the most frequent. A man who feels threatened by castration ought to read Freud again. It will become obvious, as it has to contemporary psychology, that Freud's theory of penis envy may describe his own sexual problems, but it hasn't much to do with those of little girls. In fact, the more recent studies of castration indicate that it is a ritual among men, not women. Examples of actual castration by women are rare, and usually represent women who have been mentally and physically exploited by men to such extremes that they were left with no alternative to suicide but violence against their oppressor. The fear of castration is nonetheless very real among many men who feel that women, by asking for equal human rights, want to un-man them.

Another common joke is that a liberated woman simply means free sex. The idea that

freedom of spirit could be interpreted as a means to cheaper sex is hideous to women working for their liberation. One male student interviewed in *Woodstock* explained with a grin that he was going to the rockfest because there would be a lot of girls around with freer ideas about sex. Many so-called radical men profess sympathetic understanding of Women's Liberation, then expect sex as a reward for their benevolence. Many simply use Women's Liberation as a front for sexual exploitation; they pass out the latest Women's Liberation literature, and admit that they are chauvinists but can't help it. Some men have, however, taken serious steps to put aside the veil of humor and investigate its cause.

In addition to increasing self-awareness, men can take many practical steps to prevent their automatic and traditional oppression of women. In political action groups, for instance, men can learn to type and run mimeo machines and volunteer to use these skills instead of depending on women to work for them. There is often no good reason why men are chairmen and women the secretaries at movement meetings: men can volunteer to take notes. Men can learn to understand and actively support the demands of Women's Liberation groups, like the need for day-care centers, abortion reform, and equal employment rights. They can offer to help with, but not to run, the organization of women's action groups. In all social activities, men should learn to respond to women as human beings rather than merely physical objects. Hardly anyone is interested in destroying the basis of physical attraction, but to emphasize only physical qualities in women de-humanizes them and enforces a barrier between the sexes. Men should consider what women say instead of merely how they look, and not conclude automatically that what they say will be insignificant because spoken by women.

Men can learn to actively participate in home life. Since one of the real sicknesses in our society is momism, men should take more time and interest in the actual work of child rearing to give the child the benefit of a humane, sympathetic male model instead of the usually absent patriarch. They would undoubtedly learn to appreciate the responsibility of caring for children, and greatly contribute to the needed change in children's attitudes toward both parents. At the same time they could avoid the alienation from the family circle common to so many fathers which has enforced the silent matriarchy in our culture. Since more women are working outside the home than ever before, the need for parents to share the labor in the home is great. Yet most men expect working wives to fulfill the traditional housewife and mother roles while working at another job full or part time. Men can volunteer to share in the jobs that must be done regularly, like cleaning, the laundry, grocery shopping, cooking and washing dishes. When both parents are working outside the home, contributing significantly to the economic and social well being of the family, there is no viable reason for men to expect women to do all of this work themselves. Even if only the man works outside the home, his parental responsibilities are the same as the woman's, and his obligation to at least help with the housework remains.

There is also a need for men to encourage women in their pursuit of freedom. This costs men a great deal, since from their point of view they will lose a power over another segment of humanity that they have enjoyed for over 5000 years. Nevertheless, for the improvement of both sex roles, men should encourage women to evaluate their own image. Many women are afraid to demand their own freedom because they have been taught to believe in the moral value of their submission. Men should encourage women to respect themselves as individuals, to develop their talents and interests in significant ways, to develop and act on their own opinions, and to reject their traditional role as submissive women whose primary purpose in life is to fulfill and support the desires of men. Men should encourage women to become active in things that matter, and avoid the usual rationalizations that women are less capable, too temperamental, unreliable, and unavailable when needed. These phrases describe men as well as women, and men must have the courage to face this fact.

And what should women do? Plenty, but this essay is about man's responsibility. Thousands of women are actively working to liberate themselves and their sisters in order to bring about a better society. The purpose of this essay is to state what should be obvious: that no one is free as long as someone is oppressed; that those who oppress must recognize it and act responsibly to free those they oppress; that the oppressed cannot peacefully gain their freedom without responsible action by their oppressors. Peacefully. That is the key. Men have nothing to fear from Women's Liberation if they truly believe in freedom. On the contrary, they have everything to gain, because freedom provides greater happiness for everyone.

● The male dominated government of Sweden has broken through the problem by *actually* making women equal socioeconomically. Women there have found that when "equal pay for equal work" actually exists most of the other problems of inequality tend to dissipate. The males in the society seem to be very pleased with the increased freedom and equality. North American men and women need to continue to pressure their legislators to make good on promises and actually enforce laws which are now on the books.

USEFUL RESOURCES

ADAMS, E., & BRISCOE, M. L. *Up against the wall, mother.* Beverly Hills, Calif.: Glencoe Press, 1971.
"The title of our book is intentionally ambiguous. On the most obvious level, it echoes the threat that has become a part of militant black rhetoric. The threat was first expressed in Leroi Jones' poem *Black People,* and it constitutes the denouement of a Black Panther Party film: 'Up against the wall, motherfucker. This is a stick-up. We've come for what's ours.' It is the oppressed talking to the oppressor—black to white, or, in our book, woman to man. Deliberately drawing on the analogy between white

oppression of black and male oppression of female, our title is a warning to those who have kept woman down: She is ready to take what has been stolen from her—that is, control of her own life.

"On another level, the title serves not as a command but as a description of woman's place: she has been pushed up against the wall by a culture that defines her as inferior and prescribes roles (especially the wife-mother role) for her, thus giving her little or no choice about what she can do with her life. As the selections in 'The "Better Half" make abundantly clear, marriage and motherhood often result in frustration, even desperation, for the woman. Mother is literally driven up against the wall. Our goal is to liberate woman so that she can be free to choose her own life style.

"Rebellion—the focus of the present Women's Liberation movement—is the theme of this book; rebellion against the traditional definitions of woman; against male assumptions about her function in society; against her systematic exploitation as a sex object, wife, mother, and worker; against the gigantic brainwashing that serves in place of her education and which begins so early that, by the time she is five years old, she understands and accepts the fact that certain jobs are closed to her ('I want to be a nurse. I like to take care of people.' 'Why not be a doctor?' 'Men are doctors. Women are nurses.') and that housework and mothering are her destiny ('I play with my dolls. I wash them, dress them, cook for them, serve them meals, take care of them when they are sick. Johnny builds houses and drives trucks and goes fishing.')."

ALTBACH, EDITH H. *From feminism to liberation.* Cambridge, Mass.: Schenkman Publishing Co., Inc., 1971.
This books aims at a thoughtful analysis of the Women's Liberation Movement. "It is too early to say anything conclusive on the directions the Women's Liberation Movement will take. We can, however, see its strength and potential for human liberation and there is reason to believe that the movement has a good chance of drawing a mass base and avoiding the errors of past women's movements. . . . Not since the beginning of the century has the institution of the family been exposed to such a total and critical reappraisal. . . . Women's Liberation has been concerned with the process whereby a woman begins to assert her rights with her family and her man."

Several of the articles present depthful historical, sociological, and political analyses of the status and role of women in Western society.

BARDWICK, J. M. (Ed.) *Readings on the psychology of women.* New York: Harper & Row, 1972.
"Feminine rage and accusations—and occasionally the backlash of traditionalists—dominate the media. Book stores suddenly have new collections of Women's Liberation books and Sex Role has hit the best seller list. This is a different book: it is an academic's collection of theory and research papers from the professional literature of psychology, sociology, anthropology, endocrinology, obstetrics, and psychosomatics. This collection is primarily intended to generate discussion in class and research in the professions."

In the long run, an understanding of why women behave differently from men will come from careful research on all aspects of the question. Most of the literature stimulated by the Women's Liberation movement, however, has been more political than psychological. It has focused on the questions rather than on the answers. *Readings in the Psychology of Women* is an exceptional book both because it is oriented toward *answering* some of the questions raised by the Women's Liberation movement, and because it is research oriented.

For the student who is interested in finding out what is really "known" (as opposed to "believed," "asserted," or "speculated") about why women behave differently from men, this book is probably the most thorough, informative, and thoughtful source available. It provides an excellent starting point and reference source for writing papers on the psychology of women.

A *must* book for any serious student of female psychology.

CHESLER, P. *Women and madness.* Garden City, N. Y.: Doubleday, 1972.

A well-documented treatise which supports the view that the constraints which our society imposes on women not only makes it difficult for them to achieve full personhood but also literally drives them crazy—only to be treated by male psychiatrists who seek to help them adjust to the female role. The book elaborates on the following analysis: (1) that for a number of reasons, women "go crazy" more often and more easily than men do; that their craziness is mainly self-destructive; and that they are punished for their self-destructive behavior, either by the brutal and impersonal custodial care given them in mental asylums, or by the relationships they have with most (but not all) clinicians, who implicitly encourage them to blame themselves or to take responsibility for their unhappiness in order to be "cured."; (2) that both psychotherapy and marriage, the two major socially approved institutions for white, middle-class women, function similarly, i.e., as vehicles for personal "salvation" through the presence of an understanding and benevolent (male) authority. In female culture, not being married, or being unhappily married, is experienced as an "illness" which psychotherapy can, hopefully, cure.

Embattled human male, The *Impact of Science and Society,* 1971, **21** (1).

The entire issue is devoted to analysis of the changing role of the *male* in a changing society.

EPSTEIN, C. F. *The other half: Roads to women's equality.* Englewood Cliffs, N. J.: Prentice-Hall, 1971.

"The issues of the 'women's problem' are the basic issues of power and privilege, domination and subordination, dependence and autonomy. We hope that this book, by bringing together analyses of current issues, sociological studies of women's position in society, and historical perspectives on the present movement, can shed light on some far-reaching and fundamental forces in our time—forces that have deep historical roots and that have been exerted in all societies.

"As the pressure toward attainment of freedom is great, so is the resistance against granting freedom. All of us are participants in today's struggles. There is no way to escape these conflicts and polemics because the problem is part of our lives and we are obliged to understand it, and to search for its solution as wisely as possible. It is our lives that are at stake."

GARSKOF, M. H. *Roles women play: Readings towards women's liberation,* Belmont, Calif.: Brooks/Cole, 1971.

"No one, no matter how radical, denies the existence of physical differences between males and females. Their genitals are obviously different. In addition, women tend to have larger breasts, to be smaller and less muscular, to have less body hair, and to have smaller lungs than men do. There are also differences in the sex hormones secreted by each. Women today do not question the existence of these biological differences, but rather they question the psychological and sociological implications of these differences."

This book is devoted to exploring the dual questions, "Do psychological differences between the sexes really exist? And, if they do exist, what causes them?"

GORNICK, V. & MORAN, B. K. *Woman in sexist society: Studies in power and powerlessness,* New York: Basic Books, 1971.

"Woman's condition, here and now, is the result of a slowly formed, deeply entrenched, extraordinarily pervasive cultural (and therefore political) decision that—even in a generation when man has landed on the moon—woman shall remain a person defined not by the struggling development of her brain or her will or her spirit, but rather by her childbearing properties and her status as companion to men who make, and do, and rule the earth. Though she is a cherished object in her society, she shall remain as an object rather than becoming a subject; though she is exposed to education, wealth, and independence, apparently exactly as though she were an autonomous being and the equal of men, every genuine influence in her life is actually teaching her that she may educate herself only in order to be a more fit companion to her husband. She may use wealth but not make it; she may learn about independence only so that she can instill it in her male children, urge it forward in her husband, or admire its presence or despise its absence in her father. Her sense of these characteristics of adult life is sharp and distinct, once removed: it never really occurs to her that these necessities are there for her, as well as for those to whom she is attached. Everything in her existence, from early childhood on, is bent on convincing her that the reality of her being lies in bearing children and creating an atmosphere of support and nurturance for those who aggress upon the world and the intent of asserting the self, grasping power, taking responsibility—in other words, those who are living life as it has always been defined by human principle. Woman shall never be allowed to forget that her ego is passive and her will to independence lies fallow; that the urgent desire for self-assertion that spurs the development of intellect, genius, and complex capacities is, in her, a weak and flickering mechanism; that, in reality, woman is a differently made creature, one whose proportions are more childlike, if you will, less given to maturity than are the proportions of men.

This is the substance of sexism. This is the creation of thousands of years of thought and reinforced patterns of behavior so deeply imprinted, so utterly subscribed to by the great body of Western conviction, that they are taken for "natural" or "instinctive." Sexism has made of women a race of children, a class of human beings utterly deprived of self-hood, of autonomy, of confidence—worst of all, it has made the false come true. Women have so long shared acquiescently in society's patriarchal definition of them as being composed of warmth, passivity, nurturance, inert egos, and developed intuition, that they have become the very thing itself and can no more see themselves in that mirror of life that declares independence, aggression, intellectual abstraction, and primary responsibility to be the silhouette of human development than can men. As a result, women have long suffered from an image of the self that paralyzes the will and short circuits the brain, that makes them deny the evidence of their senses and internalize self-doubt to a fearful degree. They have been raised to be the bearers of children by other bearers of children. They have been treated primarily as bearers of children by everyone they have ever known; parents, teachers, friends, lovers, busdrivers, landlords, employers, policemen, culture heroes. . . . Should they reveal strong wishes that their lives form themselves around an altogether other definition, they are branded unnatural.

Sexism, like any other cultural characteristic, lives through institutions—those that blindly perpetuate it and those that depend upon it for their very life. Altogether, the essays in this book form a detailed examination of these institutions—these attitudes, these responses, these ignorant convictions about woman's nature, and these religiously blind observations about her need—that, petrified by custom, have determined woman's unchanging position throughout the patriarchal centuries.

And the greatest of these is marriage.

In marriage, as in the economy, woman's position is essentially subservient and supportive. Within the home and without, she performs the services of the society without sharing in its decisions or in the freedoms it grants other adults. Women perform the day-to-day tasks of maintaining humanity—preparing food, keeping up the home, caring for children, and giving emotional support. These functions to a large degree determine the social definition of femininity. "Feminine" women are supportive, nurturative, kind, gentle, selfless, and giving and—in the bargain—pliant and stupid enough never to resent their subservient position. In short, they have variously all the virtues of an ideal servant or an ideal companion. The qualities one might well wish for oneself—intelligence, bravery, ingenuity, creativity, or mastery—are neither necessary nor desirable.

The book consists of a collection of essays of generally high quality and diversity, most of which rely on extensive research to support their all too convincing documentation that ours is a highly sexist society. The essays are grouped into four general topic areas: (1) "Beauty, love and marriage: the myth and the reality"; (2) "Woman is made, not born"; (3) "Woman at work"; and (4) "social issues and feminism: education, homosexuality, race and radicalism."

HOWARD, JANE. *A Different Woman*. New York: E. P. Dutton, 1973.

Describes the process of coming of age in America for the female and makes womanhood the psychological equivalent of manhood.

A Different Woman is an autobiographical mirror that reflects the experience of an entire generation. Americans who reached adulthood in the fifties, sixties, and seventies will see in Jane Howard's account of her life, her family, her loves, and her lovers, the outlines of what they lived and are living.

Jane Howard set out to write about the women's movement and women in modern America. She ended up writing about herself, but in plumbing the depths of her own consciousness she uncovered the truth that existence is a shared reality that makes each different woman not so different after all, and that life is measured by joy and passion as much as desperation.

HUBER, J. *Changing women in a changing society*, Chicago: University of Chicago Press, 1973.

This work also appeared as Volume 78, Number 4 (Jan., 1973) of the *American Journal of Sociology*. It consists of a collection of essays which emphasize the sociological and social-psychological factors in occupational discrimination.

JANEWAY, ELIZABETH. *Man's world. Woman's place: A study of social mythology.* New York: William Morrow, 1971.

A psychological, sociological, historical, and literary analysis of such cultural myths as "woman's place is in the home," and "penis envy." She shows how the "myth of female weakness" and its dialectical oppositive "the myth of female power" stem from the fact that all mankind, male and female alike, first came to understand femaleness through an all powerful mother who at the same time is paradoxically protected by a man.

A subtle, provocative and scholarly work, rich in its clarifying capacity.

KORDA, M. *Male chauvinism: How it works.* New York: Random House, 1973.

"The last stronghold of male dominance in our society, which this book explores, is the business world. It operates to the advantage of men because it was created by men and because they see themselves as deserving of special privileges. Although the bulk of the book concerns itself with case histories of the ways in which men abuse women in work conditions, Korda does, in one succinct chapter, lay waste to all of the philosophic flim-flam that men use to legitimize their despotism . . . may I suggest that Michael Korda has written the single most important book you'll find available this year. Lawrence Dietz, Los Angeles Times Book Review." Psychology Today Book Club.

MEDNICK, M. S., & TANGRI, S. S. (Eds.). New perspectives on women, *The Journal of Social Issues,* **28,** No. 2, 1972.

This issue reflects the growing awareness of "shibboleths and lacunae (Laws, 1969)" in the study of women, and includes some of the recent attempts to correct these. The issue focuses on methodological and theoretical criticism, analysis of female stereotypes and roles, and achievement and motivation in women. The feminist movement which is responsible for these new perspectives on women also raises fundamental questions regarding present institutions like the family, and provides fresh views on such vital issues as peace, racism, population, and environment.

MILLETT, KATE. *Sexual politics,* Garden City, N. Y.: Doubleday, 1970.

The first two chapters attempt to provide an awareness of the way in which power and dominance are reflected in sexual activity itself and to present a systematic overview of patriarchy as a political institution. Chapters 3 and 4 are mainly historical and the remainder of the book is devoted to a literary criticism of the politics of sexual relations as revealed in the writings of D. H. Lawrence, Henry Miller, Norman Mailer, and Jean Genet. It is a scholarly analysis.

MONEY, J., & EHRHARDT, A. A. *Man & woman, boy & girl.* Baltimore: The Johns Hopkins Press, 1972.
"At a time when public interest in the character of human sexuality is increasingly widespread, this book provides accurate, comprehensive and authoritative information on just what distinguishes males from females . . . it is the most important volume in the social sciences to appear since the Kinsey reports." James Lincoln Colier, *The New York Times Book Review.*

Role of women, The *Dialogue,* **3** (4), 1970.
A special section is devoted to biological and cultural analysis of the role of women. Also includes articles entitled "The literature of feminism" and "Art and the female form."

SCHAEFFER, D. L. (Ed.) *Sex differences in personality: Readings,* Belmont, Calif.: Wadsworth, 1971.

The book is divided into three sections. The first section, Perception of the Self and Others, deals with the way people of both sexes feel about themselves and others in terms of other unconscious attitudes, expectations and prejudices. The second section, Intrapersonal and Interpersonal Behavior, discusses some of the behavioral manifestations on sex differences that research has discovered. . . . The final section, Sex-Related Behavior, deals with sex differences in the psychological expression of sexuality. It examines the effects of sex role and of some differences in physiological sexual functions (within normal limits) on sex-related behaviors.

The selections are primarily relevant to either Freudian or social learning theories of development.

Sexism in family studies. *Journal of Marriage and the Family,* 1971, **33,** (3).
The entire issue is devoted to provocative papers dealing with sexism in society and in the family.

Women in the age of science and technology. *Impact of Science on Society,* 1970, **20** (1).
The entire issue is devoted to examining feminine intellect and the demands of science and technology. It also includes a controversial paper by Lionel Tiger, "The possible biological origins of sexual discrimination."

CHAPTER 5

ON BEING POOR, OLD, OR "BLACK" IN A RICH, YOUNG, AND "WHITE" CULTURE

PROVOCATIONS

The poor you have always with you.

                Jesus Christ

Why?

                James Dyal

If I were God, what would I do to improve the lot of the Negroes? If I were God, I'd make everybody white.

                Anonymous

When they are old, the exploited classes are condemned, if not to utter destitution, then at least to extreme poverty, to uncomfortable, inconvenient dwellings, and to loneliness, all of which results in feelings of failure and a generalized anxiety.

            Simone de Beauvoir

*Will you still need me,
Will you still feed me
When I'm sixty-four.
You'll be older, too . . .*

             The Beatles

It is now generally understood that chronic and remediable social injustices corrode and damage the human personality, thereby robbing it of its actual hamanity. No matter how desperately one seeks to deny it, this simple fact persists and intrudes itself. It is the fuel of protests and revolts.

             Kenneth B. Clark

The average Mexican-American lives ten years less than the average Anglo. There is no biological reason why this should be so. The only reason is because the Mexican-American is starving and does not have enough medical care.

      Senator Ralph Yarborough, D–Texas

The American Indians are by any measure save cultural heritage the country's most disadvantaged minority.

             McGeorge Bundy

WHAT DO YOU THINK?

---

23 ON BEING POOR, OLD, OR "BLACK" IN A RICH, YOUNG, AND "WHITE" CULTURE

JAMES A. DYAL

"It is difficult for most of us to recognize the poor because most of the time they are invisible. When, for example, was the last time you were in close contact with a truly poverty stricken person?"[1]

● Think about it!

The poor constitute an invisible minority to middle-class citizens, in part because they simply live in places that we normally have little occasion to go. But of course other causes of their invisibility are more profound than their merely being "out of the way." There are characteristic failures of our society which constitute the politics of power, the economics of scarcity, the anthropology of the outcast, and the psychology of chronic but quiet despair. The poor are invisible to us because to really become aware of them is all too often too devastating and guilt-provoking. Again we prefer not to know. In the classic manner of Scarlett O'Hara we defend against reality by telling ourselves, "I'll not think about that today; *I'll think about that tomorrow.*"

After immersing myself in the all too voluminous documentation of the mind-sapping, marrow-sucking world of expendable humans I found myself at a loss for words to help you to become involved. Any words which I could put down on

paper seemed all too impotent, all too feeble. I found that my sense of the inadequacy of words to carry the communication load was shared by Robert Coles, a Harvard psychiatrist who has written most extensively and sensitively on the plight of the poor.[2]

COMMENT: WHAT IS THERE TO SAY?

What is there to say? I sometimes wonder what indeed there is to say about the tenant farmers I know, or the children of the ghetto I am now getting to know. Sometimes, when I sit down to write up the life—the life history and often enough the case history—of one or another man or woman I've been talking with, the task seems hopeless. There is so much to communicate, and yet several of the snapshots my wife and I have taken seem to more than do it: everything, just about everything I would want to say seems there, in those Kodachromes, waiting for eyes that have any awareness and sympathy. And from a sharecropper's wife in Alabama I once heard my doubts more than confirmed:

> People don't know what they don't see, I guess. There's no other way of explaining it, not that I can see. Out of sight, out of mind. You can't go telling them anything. No sir, I don't believe you can. They're used to shutting their eyes

[1]Elton B. MacNeil. *Being human: The psychological experience.* San Francisco: Canfield Press, 1973.

[2]See his trilogy, *Children of crisis,* for which he won the Pulitzer Prize and the Mental Health Association Research Achievement Award. They are: *Children of crisis: A study of courage and fear; Migrants, sharecroppers and mountaineers;* and *The south goes north,* published in Boston by Little, Brown, 1967–1971.

on you, but if you get them to stop and take a look around, then if they're the least bit partial to begin with, well they'll possibly come over to your side.

ROBERT COLES

● Note this, the poor understand that they most often simply are not seen by other people. They are non-persons. They are invisible. Think about how it must be to exist and not be recognized as a person.

I do not believe that I can best help you experience the everyday trauma and tragedy of millions of North Americans only by marshalling before you vast arrays of statistics. Like Coles, I have chosen to let the people speak for themselves directly or through the poignant portrayals made by other observers. Through these testimonials of our inhumanity to our fellow men perhaps we will all come to a better understanding and deeper feeling for what it means to be poor, in a rich culture.

Ageism: You'll Be Older Too

Ageism is, of course, discrimination and deprivation of status which is directed toward those who are of a different age than that of the dominant cultural group. Thus it may be seen that ageism is directed toward both those who are "too young" and those who are "too old." As persons who are just now emerging into "full adulthood," instances of discrimination against you on the basis of your age (as opposed to lack of competence) are probably still all too easy to recall.

● Why don't you try that now? Think of limitations of your freedom which were based strictly on an arbitrary ruling about age—(make sure that your example is not based on lack of competence). What sorts of restrictions do these tend to be? Why do they exist?

While recognizing that ageism includes discrimination against the young, our primary concern in the present section is that which is directed against the old. How old is old? Of course aging is a continuing process, but old age in our culture is primarily defined by economic, production-oriented considerations, rather than physical, psychological, or social considerations. If you are retired and thus no longer contributing to the economy, you are considered to be old. (Note also that the discrimination against "youth" ceases when that person begins a full-time job.)

The absolute number of older people (sixty-five plus) in the United States today (1975) is about 21 million, and the proportion of the population which is sixty-five and over has been steadily increasing since 1900. This has been due to the lower mortality rates as a result of medical advances which have substantially reduced infant mortality and better medical care throughout the life span. The average life span in North America in 1900 was about fifty, whereas the average life expectancy in 1975 is somewhat above seventy-two. If the present trend toward zero population growth in the United States continues, the *proportion* of older people in the total population will continue to increase at least until the year 2000. Furthermore, the trend in retirement age is for earlier and earlier retirement. These factors suggest that the "wave of the future" is toward greater numbers of older people, and a likelihood that older people will have greater impact on the society than has been the case in the "youth"-oriented culture of the first three-fourths of the twentieth century.

As psychologists we have tended to devote much of our energies to trying to understand the aging/maturing process during the childhood and adolescent phases of life. But more recently there has been an increased concern with the psychology of the full life span. We have begun to learn that some of the memory loss and mental health problems which are often regarded as an inevitable consequence of aging are more likely to be caused by sociocultural factors than by any inexorable physiological process.

COMMENT: MENTAL HEALTH OF THE ELDERLY

Advanced age often brings with it a deterioration of mental health. Unfortunately, the neglect of ailments among the elderly has been even more pronounced where mental ill-health was concerned. As a result, we find that there has been less understanding of mental disorders among the elderly and less ability—or even inclination—to study its causes or to institute treatment procedures than was the situation in the case of physical ill-health. Here too, it was assumed that mental illness was part of the process of aging and that therefore it predetermined an unfavorable prognosis and consequently underlined the uselessness of attempts at treatment. The elderly mentally disturbed patients frequently found their way to mental hospitals, where they remained indefinitely, forgotten and untreated, with a consequent further deterioration in the majority of cases. There is evidence that within recent years, concomitant with a general increase of interest in mental health, the attitude toward mental illness among the aged has shown a significant change. The medical profession is now recognizing that deterioration of mental health and behavior disorders are not always—and in fact need not be—part of the aging process. It is now accepted by many physicians that a variety of factors may be responsible for the symptoms of disorder manifested by the elderly. Such symptoms as withdrawal, forgetfulness, and temporary confusion may be due to intolerable social situations. One might cite suc precipitating factors as bereavement, loneliness, economic in-

security or insecurity in any other area, despair, loss of self-esteem, loss of social status and prestige, loss of hope—all of these, so frequently seen among the elderly, may create feelings of worthlessness, frustration and loss of a significant role and purpose in life. Serious physical illnesses too may give rise to a variety of mental symptoms which disappear if and when the physical condition is treated successfully. It is important to keep in mind also that the neurotic tendencies and unhealthy personality patterns which the elderly person may manifest can be a carry-over from his earlier years and may become aggravated as the individual is faced with the numerous deprivations so often imposed by aging. As a result of this better understanding of the causes which frequently underlie disturbed behavior, physicans no longer regard its manifestations as irreversible or untreatable. Custodial care in mental institutions is now not only seen to be inadequate and failing to meet the needs of the elderly, but is recognized as being wasteful both economically and in terms of human happiness. It is believed that many of the elderly could be removed from the unfavorable institutional environment and treated successfully in the community.

MINNA FIELD

Of course the emotional, medical, and social problems of an old person are compounded when that person is also a member of an oppressed minority group. Racism, ageism, and sexism combine to make death a welcome relief for many human beings in our young, "white," affluent culture. Whether or not our society is really willing to make it·desirable to live longer is questioned by some authorities. For example, at a recent conference, "Extension of Human Life Span," held at the Center for the Study of Democratic Institutions at Santa Barbara, California, it was asserted that

There is little evidence that society can make available the money, personnel, energy, and skills required to meet their aged persons' needs. . . . For maximum social benefit and minimum social harm, it might be wise to postpone extension of the human life-span until balancing social changes are achieved. . . . If we decrease the length of senescence by advances in aging control, we may prolong tedium, drudgery, years of depression and anxiety.[3]

Racism: On Being "Black" of Whatever Stripe

Much has been made of the problems which confront members of nondominant racial groups in countries which are racist in their practice, if not in their principles. Indeed, we have heard so much of the problems, issues, and controversies that we may well be so satiated that our sensitivities have turned off to the whole issue. And yet, although some progress has been made, the fact remains that racism is still rampant in our "free" society. For example, busing in order to achieve racial balance in the schools is still a major issue in many parts of the United States. It would not be an issue if there were in fact equal economic opportunity and non-discrimination in housing.

Ask any black, chicano, Indian, or French Canadian that you meet if racism is still a part of his personal everyday experience. The destruction and warping of personality which is inherent in such racial discrimination has been well documented by social scientists. Remember what Kenneth Clark, an outstanding black psychologist, has said:

It is now generally understood that chronic and remediable social injustices corrode and damage the human personality, thereby robbing it of its actual humanity. No matter how desperately one seeks to decry it, this simple fact persists and intrudes itself. It is the fuel of protests and revolts.[4]

If we understand this, why has the problem not been solved? Why do we stand by and let such injustice continue?

[3]A. A. Goldfarb, Harmful psychological effects of increased life expectancy. *Geriatric Focus*, 1970, **9**, 5–6.
[4]Kenneth Clark, *Dark ghetto: Dilemmas of social power*. New York: Harper & Row, 1965.

COMMENT: ON THE INJUSTICE OF BELIEVING IN JUSTICE

It is a common observation that the *victims* of social injustice are often condemned by those who are instrumental in causing or perpetuating the injustice. It is easy to understand that the harm-doer would try to avoid feelings of guilt by asserting that the victims deserve their fate. What is more perplexing is that "innocent bystanders" observing the injustice also tend to devalue the victim. It is as though merely witnessing an injustice creates a demand to set things right by defending the victim or alleviating his suffering. However, actions to help the victims can obviously be costly in terms of one's own resources and security. On the other hand, failure to meet these demands is also costly. It carries with it the guilt of one's own complicity in the fate of the victim and the implicit threat that one does not live in a just world; that one lives in a jungle where sheer power rules. This conflict represents for you and I, the innocent bystanders, a real and present danger to our personal sense of well-being. What shall we do to resolve the dilemma?

Research in the laboratory has confirmed what shrewd observers have suspected happens in society. The results throw light on why we let gross social injustices continue to exist. It turns out that there is available an easy resolution of the conflict. The observer can merely persuade himself that no real injustice exists—*the victims deserve their fate either because of their own active failures because they are inherently inferior.* What should be remembered in thinking about this is that the motivation underlying those acts of "oppression by omission" can be traced to the desire to believe that "I am a just person in a just world—a world where people deserve their fate." By some tragic irony it is the desire for a just world which serves to perpetuate social injustice.

How could we turn ourselves around so that this decent human need for justice could be used to foster constructive social change? The research which has been done thus far indicates that there is at least one critical ingredient. It is simply whether or not the ''innocent bystander'' has the resources to eliminate the injustice without at the same time making himself a victim. The fact that the ''justice motive'' can elicit two diametrically opposed consequences—cruel condemnation of victims or acts of help and protection—carries with it an important implication. We should be wary of persuading someone that injustice exists in his world either as a result of his own hand or that of another, without at the same time giving him the useable power to make it right.

MELVIN J. LERNER

The selections which we have included on racism dramatically illustrate the personal pathology which results from racism directed toward blacks, and chicanos. Perhaps they will help you to a better intellectual/emotional understanding of what it is like to be ''black'' in a ''white'' racist culture.

24   THE MANY FACES OF THE POOR*

ELTON B. McNEIL

It is difficult for most of us to recognize the poor because most of the time they are invisible. When, for example, was the last time you were in close contact with a truly poverty stricken person? They are invisible mainly because they live in rural areas, they are members of minority groups, and usually they are old.

THE AGED POOR

The invisibility of the aged poor is due to the fact that they are physically and financially unable to move about much in our society. They may sit out their remaining days in rented rooms or in decaying houses in neighborhoods that have long ago changed from the character they had in the old days. More so than any of the ethnic minority groups, white people who are impoverished and old and who live in the inner city are cut off from

*From Elton B. McNeil, *Being human: The psychological experience*, pp. 117–123. Copyright © 1973 by Elton B. McNeil. Reprinted by permission of Harper & Row, Publishers, Inc.

the familial supports necessary to sustain their waning powers. They are surrounded by people but suffer isolation, invisibility, and grinding poverty.

The modern problem of the poverty-stricken old people can be traced to the emergence of the modern, industrialized state. The state provides the circumstances for survival for its citizens over 65 years of age, but it fails to furnish gainful employment for them. The improved practices of medicine, public health, and public sanitation have let us live longer, but this has become a mixed blessing to the industrial state.

Between the ages of 65 and 75, a significant population shift occurs as women begin to outnumber men. These are usually husbandless women trapped by a low, fixed income and incapable of meaningful employment. For these women and for the aged men, the longer one lives the worse one's plight becomes, since old people are ignored and no longer needed in the industrial state. In 1890, 70 percent of the aged were gainfully employed, but this figure fell to less than 33 percent in 1960 and has declined steadily since that time. Today fewer than 20 percent of the aged continue to earn money. The problem of the aged poor has already become a critical social issue and will become an increasingly severe problem in the years ahead.

THE RURAL POOR

In the richest nation in history nearly 14 million rural Americans are poor, and a high proportion of them could be described as destitute. It surprises most Americans to learn that there is proportionately more poverty in rural America than in our cities. In metropolitan areas, one person in eight is poor and in the suburbs the ratio is one in 15. In rural areas, one of every four persons is poor. Only one in four of these rural families actually lives on a farm; most live in small towns and villages.

Rural low-income areas have steadily lost population through the migration of rural farm people. From 1790 to the present, the nation's population has shifted from being about 95 percent to 30 percent rural. As recently as 65 years ago, 33 percent of the entire population was living on farms, but this figure has dropped to only 6 percent. This mass exodus from rural areas means that those left behind are often worse off than before. The many old people and children are too heavy a burden for the few working-age members of the family to support, and the chances of escaping from poverty or avoiding deeper poverty are greatly diminished as the young take flight to the cities. The problems of the rural poor are compounded in a variety of additional ways. Large families are traditional in rural areas, and the result is that meager resources have to be stretched past the breaking point to feed, clothe, and educate the children. The rural household may include several generations of the family, since families take pride in caring for the old folks at home.

Since more than 19 million persons in rural American have not completed high school and more than three million have fewer than five years of schooling, even migration does not promise much increase in income. But years of schooling is an inadequate index to the skill or ability of the rural poor, since rural schools pay low salaries, do not attract the better teachers, and do not always deliver quality in education. It is evident that, in whatever direction the poor may turn, they confront only another obstacle to the escape from poverty.

The continuing problem of Appalachia is one illustration. This region of original American frontier covers 182,000 square miles extending from southern Pennsylvania to nothern Alabama and is rich in natural resources. Yet, Appalachia is now raising its third welfare generation. It has counties in which as many as one-third of the inhabitants are unemployed—some of whom have not worked for decades. In Appalachia, the average adult has a sixth-grade education and three-fourths of the children are drop-outs before they complete the twelfth grade. The additional burdens of human pathology (tuberculosis, silicosis, infant mortality, and so on) are so high that they do not fit into our concept of the Western world at all. As each new generation is born it has only poverty to look forward to—the young grow, marry, go on welfare, have children and keep the cycle of poverty going.

The plight of children caught in the poverty trap is particularly tragic. Migrant children, for example, are in the deepest trouble of all. Each year 150,000 of them move across our land harvesting crops carrying with them poverty, disease, and ignorance of formal education. They are unwelcome in the communities where they serve as cheap labor, and, constantly on the move, they are not eligible for public assistance to relieve their misery. The longer they remain migrant workers, the greater will be their cultural and educational deprivation and the more certain it will be that they will never escape from poverty. It has become fashionable to speak of "pockets of poverty." The truth is that there are concentrations rather than "pockets" of poverty. Poverty refuses to stay isolated; it can be found anywhere in America.

● And anywhere in Canada or Mexico. Look—open your eyes and hearts to it.

Spanish Americans are only slightly better off than blacks → have the least education.

SPANISH-AMERICAN POVERTY

A little recognized concentration of poverty can be found among the Spanish-Americans of the Southwest. The ancient romantic history of this region of our land set the stage for a serious social problem. "Colonization of what is now the Southwest was started more than three centuries ago when this entire area, along with Mexico, was part of Spain's vast overseas empire. Santa Fe was an important urban settlement in 1609. By 1790 the white population of the Southwest was practically all Spanish and included an estimated 23,000 persons."

From these modest beginnings have sprung more than three and one-half million modern Spanish-Americans—and they have a problem. They rank as low or lower in education than any other ethnic group in America, with the singular exception of the American Indian woman. They are unemployed twice as frequently as are their counterpart Anglos and only slightly better employed than blacks in America. Thus, Spanish-Americans are just barely better off financially than are blacks. Further, if the Spanish-American has any advantage at all, it is to be found in his more cohesive family life, 75 percent of Spanish-American households have both husband and wife present.

Recent reports by the Census Bureau show evidence that persons of Spanish origin are gaining in income more rapidly than are blacks, but they still lag far behind whites. Spanish-Americans still have less education than others. An average of five or fewer years of education for 20 percent of the Spanish group may be compared with 14 percent among blacks, and 4 percent among whites. The contrast among whites, the 23 million black Americans and the more than nine million persons of Spanish origin (five million from Mexico, one and one-half million from Puerto Rico, and 700,000 from Cuba) includes a number of other dimensions. For one, the median age for Mexican-Americans, blacks, and persons of Spanish origin is substantially younger than that for the white population. Blacks are more likely than Spanish to work as laborers or service employees; and more black women work than do Spanish or white women.

These details indicate that the dominant white Americans are selectively and differentially prejudiced and discriminatory. The advances Spanish-Americans have achieved to date are a likely prophecy of things to come in the years ahead, but their impatience is as great as any minority group condemned to poverty.

HELP FOR THE POOR

The measures we have been taking to help the poor reflect the beliefs and attitudes we hold about poverty sticken people. Historically, with a very few exceptions, the more affluent members of our society have believed that the poor deserved their fate as a consequence of shiftlessness, lack of virtue, and the absence of character.

● Stop! Turn to page 165 and make the connection to M. J. Lerner's Comment, "The Injustice of Believing in Justice."

"Probably the most enduring attitude toward the problem of poverty was that the poor should not be made too comfortable in it. There was serious concern that any real kindness or generosity shown the poor would merely encourage poverty and that the poor would come to enjoy it. Thus, aid was to be grudgingly, even meanly, given."

In the nineteenth century, the public poorhouse was fashioned to remove from public vision a variety of social discards—the blind, the lame, the old, the feeble, and the orphaned. Housed all in one building and maintained at a bare minimum level of subsistence, poorhouses became pesthouses that soon evoked outraged cries for reform. The private charitable organizations of that time helped selectively—by choosing who among the

Welfare → an urban phenomenon — *took place in countries where political turmoil greatest.*   → *1960's — welfare explosion.*

THE MANY FACES OF THE POOR **169**

poor were truly deserving of assistance and deciding how much aid could be given without encouraging them to remain poverty ridden.

Today the view of poor people has become less moralistic as the list of reasons for poverty has expanded. Race, age, geographic area, technological obsolescence, sickness, separation, and many other factors contribute to poverty. Today poverty is inextricably bound up with welfare programs such as Aid to Families with Dependent Children (AFDC). But our society is foundering in its attempt to deal with the recent explosion of relief rolls. As one report revealed: "Between 1950 and 1960, only 110,000 families were added to the rolls, yielding a rise of 17 percent. In the 1960s, however, the rolls exploded, rising by more than 225 percent. At the beginning of the decade, 745,000 families were receiving aid; by 1970, some 2,500,000 families were on the rolls."

The rapid expansion of relief rolls in the 1960s occurred during the years of the greatest civil disorder in our history; the turmoil of the civil rights struggle, the outbreak of rioting in the cities, and the mass protests mounted by relief recipients compounded an already difficult situation. The welfare rise coincided with the enactment of Federal programs designed to restore calm to the ghettos. Among other benefits, these programs hired thousands of poor people, social workers, and lawyers who worked actively to get relief for more families. The result was a quick doubling of the welfare rolls. By early 1969, 800,000 families had been added to the relief burden—an increase over 1960 of 107 percent. Moreover, the welfare explosion, while generally an urban phenomenon, had its greatest impact in that handful of large metropolitan counties where political turmoil had been the greatest.

The relief rolls surged upward at an even faster rate beginning in 1969. By the end of 1970, only two years later, another 900,000 families were receiving aid. Then, in November 1971, welfare statistics revealed that 14.6 million persons received a total of $1.5 billion in cash and services; 10.5 million recipients were those in the Aid to Families with Dependent Children program. This

incredible expansion of request for financial aid has jeopardized the liberal concept of social care for the poor. In the past when mass unemployment produced social turmoil, programs of public relief were instituted to absorb and control the unemployed. Once the social disorders were smoothed out, however, the welfare system quickly contracted to service only the aged, crippled, or disabled who were unable to contribute to the labor market. The theory has been that mass unemployment weakens social and psychological constraints on the poor and undermines the established network of social control. Thus, government aid is forthcoming only so long as disorder seems probable.

To rationalize the increase in public welfare, a system of make-work for the dependent poor has always appeared to soothe the public's moral concern about supporting the indigent. During the depression of the 1930s, the immediate humanitarian response of the federal government was to appropriate billions of dollars for direct relief payments. It shortly became apparent, however, that no one was happy with direct relief since it seemed no more than a temporary expedient to keep body and soul together—if not one's dignity. Direct relief did little to renew personal pride or restore the dignity of a previous way of life. An ancient remedy was then reinvented—abolish direct relief and put the unemployed to work on subsidized projects that might dignify subsistence aid. If the past is predictive of the future, it is likely we will repeat history by shrinking relief rolls and services as soon as full employment exists.

Michael Harrington in his book *The Other America* argued that we have a new kind of poverty—a poverty of automation, a poverty of the minority poor, and a poverty that is almost hereditary, invariably transmitted from generation to generation. Harrington had a solution. He suggested instituting a G.I. bill in the war against poverty whereby we would pay people to go to school—paying for their tuition and their books and giving them a reasonable living allowance if they had a family. Convinced that the G.I. bill was one

— direct relief → no good →

of the most successful social experiments this society has ever undertaken, Harrington asks why it requires a shooting war for us to be so smart. If our society really believes that the most productive thing young persons can do is go to school, then we ought to put up the money to make it possible for *every* youngster to take advantage of such opportunity. Over time, that person would be able to strike a blow against the seemingly unbreakable cycle of poverty.

The poverty issue may better be described as one of inequality, since the poor in our country are often rich by the standards of other cultures. Still, the very poor are clearly extremely unequal when compared to others in America. But this shift in terms redefines the problem and can lead us to study different issues and search for different kinds of solutions. Should we focus, for example, on "changing opportunity" or "changing conditions"? Much of the anti-poverty effort in the 1960s was designed to increase educational opportunity for the young in order to promote individual social mobility. It was a bitter theory since it encouraged a higher rate of movement out of the ranks of poverty, even if those left behind were as badly off as before.

We lack an adequate social psychological theory to specify the interdependence between our socioeconomic system and the individual's way of life. As a consequence, social scientists have invested most of their energy in studying the children of poverty since there was some degree of agreement that the forces exerted on early socialization are particularly critical for adult behavior. Following this line of thought, scientists assumed that the earlier they could remedy or influence the effects of poverty, the greater the impact they would have. In time, given the lack of public readiness to put money where the sentiments were, this hope was abandoned. One writer has stated: "The discovery of a relationship between background (i.e., poverty) and behavior is no longer very satisfactory as an end in itself. Much more worthwhile is an understanding of the specific variables and detailed means by which environmental conditions produce the psychological dispositions, which in turn are responsible for a particular behavior."

To measure exactly the effects of poverty, we must devise a means of subtracting out the influences of a host of related variables. To date, researchers have made only sweeping generalizations about poverty based on unsystematic and uncontrolled experiments. There seems to be no way to make poverty "popular" in the scientific world.

● How might a "humanistic psychologist" and a "behavioristic psychologist" differ in the way that they would approach the study of the causes, the effects, and the remedies of the poverty problem?

G.I. bill → pay poverty
(Harrington)   stricken to go
                     to school.

25 YOU'RE ASKING ME WHAT DEPRIVATION IS?*

VICTOR B. FICKER AND HERBERT S. GRAVES

COMMENT: THE POVERTY SYNDROME

The poverty syndrome is produced not by economic deprivation but by a pattern of social relations symbolized and maintained by income differences. Being poor means being powerless, being treated as inferior in a variety of contexts throughout one's life . . . The Old Left called these people the "lumpenproletariat" to suggest that they were not just poorer than most but outcasts too. The probability is high that their children will be outcasts too. Everything conspires against them. With few exceptions their fate is sealed before they ever walk across the threshold of schools that would have failed them in any event.

THELMA McCORMACK

While deprivation is not a respecter of race, religion, or national origin, it does befall the lower social and economic groups of our society. It is often said that anyone with the desire to do so can climb out of his environment and forever be rid of the deprivations of poverty and want. See if you agree with that thought after you read the case study that follows.

This case study is not fiction—it is the *true* story of a woman of twenty-eight or twenty-nine years of age who looks more nearly fifty. The story is in the subject's own words—slightly cleaned up to eliminate the profanity and some of her bitter resentment toward a society which does not in-

clude her. It is her report to a case worker in a field office of the Office of Economic Opportunity.

Read her story with compassion. It is one of desperation and utter hopelessness; it covers all categories of deprivation. This woman seems trapped in the bottom of a deep well with sides too steep to climb, with no handholes or ropes to grasp. If you feel no compassion for her, then think of her children, for she sees no way out for them either.

The authors have never read an account that better describes the many types of deprivation experienced by our disadvantaged citizens. Here in one package is what the present means for one family and what little hope exists for its future. The woman is white; the locale is Tennessee. She could just as easily have been Black, Mexican-American, or Puerto Rican—families such as hers exist in each of our fifty states. As a matter of fact, families such as this exist in all of our communities. We can find them if we only will look; we can help if only we take the trouble to understand and decide to help. Can we do less?

A CASE STUDY IN DEPRIVATION *

Here I am, dirty, smelly, with no proper underwear beneath this rotting dress. I don't know about you, but the stench of my teeth makes me half sick. They're decaying, but they'll never be fixed. That takes money.

Listen to me without pity, now, for I don't need your pity; it won't help me at all, and it won't help my hungry children. Listen to me with understand-

*From the files of the Office of Economic Opportunity.

ing, if you can. Try to put yourself in my dirty, worn out, ill-fitting shoes—if you can stand the thought, much less the reality.

What is poverty? Poverty is getting up every morning from a dirty and illness-stained mattress —a hard, lumpy mattress. Sheets? There are no sheets. They have long since been used for diapers, for there are no real diapers here, either.

That smell? That other smell? You know what it is—plus sour milk and spoiled food. Sometimes it's mixed with the stench of onions cooked too often. Onions are cheap.

We're like dogs in that we live in a world of smells and we've learned to identify most of them without searching them out. There is the smell of young children who can't make it down that long path at night. There is the smell of the filthy mattress. There is the smell of food gone sour because the refrigerator doesn't work. I don't re-member when the refrigerator did work. I only know it takes money to get it fixed. And there is the smell of garbage. I could bury it, but where do you get a shovel without money?

Poverty is being tired—dog tired all the time. I can't remember when I wasn't tired. When my last baby came, they told me at the hospital that I had chronic anemia caused by a poor diet, a bad case of worms, and the need for a corrective operation.

When they told me about my condition, I listened politely. The poor are always polite, you know. We can't afford to offend those who might decide to be big and give us something. The poor always listen, for there really isn't much we can say. If we were to say anything, it might prejudice somebody with a little money. What good would it do to say there is no money for iron pills, better food, or necessary medicine?

The idea of an operation is frightening even if you have the money required. If I had dared, I would have laughed. Who would have taken care of my children while I was in the hospital for a prolonged period?

The last time I left my children with their grandmother was when I had a job. I came home to find the baby covered with fly specks and wearing a diaper that had not been changed since I left. When the dried diaper was removed, bits of my

baby's flesh were on it. My middle child was playing with a sharp piece of glass, and my oldest was playing alone at the edge of an unprotected lake. On my job I made $22 a week. A nursery school charges $20 a week for three children. So I had to quit my job.

Poverty is dirt. You may say, in your clean clothes and coming from your clean house, "Any-body can be clean." Let me explain housekeeping with no money. For breakfast, I give my children grits with no margarine, or cornbread made with-out eggs or oleo. For one thing, that kind of food doesn't use up many dishes. What dishes there are, I wash in cold water. No soap. Even the cheapest soap has to be saved for washing the old sheets I use for the baby's diapers.

Look at these cracked red hands. Once I saved up for two months to buy a jar of Vaseline for my hands and for the baby's diaper rash. When I had the money and went to buy the Vaseline, the price had gone up two cents, and I didn't have another two cents. Every day I have to decide whether I can bear to put these cracked, sore hands into that cold water and strong soap. Why don't I use hot water? It takes money to get something with which you can heat it. Hot water is a luxury. We don't have luxuries.

You would be surprised if I told you my age. I look twenty years older than I am; my back has been bent over tubs so long I can't stand up straight any more. I can't remember when I did anything but wash, but we're still dirty. I just can't seem to keep up with all the washing. Every night I wash every stitch my school-age child had on and just hope the clothes will be dry enough to wear when morning comes.

Poverty is staying up all night when it is cold to guard the one fire we have; one spark striking the newspaper we have on our walls would mean my sleeping children would die in the flames. In the summer, poverty is watching gnats and flies de-vour my baby's tears when he cries, which is most of the time. I've never been in an air-conditioned house. I've just heard folk talk about them. Our screens are torn, but we pay so little rent that I know it's foolish to even talk about getting them fixed. Poverty means insects in your food, in your nose, in your eyes, and crawling over you while you sleep. Poverty is children with runny noses, even in the summer. Paper handkerchiefs take money, and you need all your rags for other things. Antihistamines are for the rich.

Poverty is asking for help. Have you ever had to swallow what pride you had left and ask for help, knowing your children will suffer more if you don't get it? Think about asking for a loan from a relative, if that's the only way you can really understand asking for help.

I'll tell you how asking for help feels: You find out where the office is, the one from which paupers are supposed to get help. When you find it, you circle that block four or five times trying to get up nerve enough to go in and beg. Finally, the thought of your children's need and suffering pushes you through the door. Everybody is very busy and official. After an eternity, a woman comes out to you and you tell her you need help, and you force yourself to look at her.

She isn't the one you need to see. The first one never is. She sends you to see someone else and, after spilling your poverty and shame all over the desk, you find out this isn't the right office. Then you repeat the whole procedure. It doesn't get any easier.

You ask for help in two or three places, until you're sick of the whole procedure, but you're always told to wait. You are told why you have to wait but you don't really hear, because the dark cloud of shame and despair deafens you with its roar of recrimination.

Poverty is remembering—remembering quitting school in junior high school because the nice children from nice homes were so cruel about your clothes and your smell. (There have always been smells—you think you should have been a bloodhound.) I remember when I quit and the attendance teacher came to see my mother. She told him I was pregnant. I wasn't, but my mother knew they wouldn't make me go back to school if she told them that. She thought I could get a job and bring home some money. I had jobs off and on, but never long enough to earn money.

I remember mostly being married. I was so young. I'm still young, but you can't tell it. In another town, for a little while we had most of the things you have; a little house with lights, hot water and everything. Then my husband lost his job. For a little while there was some unemployment insurance, but soon all our nice things were repossessed and we moved back here—I was pregnant at the time. This house didn't look so bad when we first moved in. Every week it got worse, though. Nothing was ever fixed. Soon we didn't have any money at all.

My husband got a few odd jobs, but everything went for food—just as it does now. I'll never know how we lived through three years and three babies, but we did. After that last baby, I just plain destroyed my marriage. Would you want to bring another baby into this filth? I didn't, and birth-control measures take money. I knew the day my husband left that he wasn't coming back, but neither of us said anything. What was there to say? I hope he has been able to climb out of this mess somewhere. He never could hope to do it here, with us to drag him down.

It was after he left that I first asked for help. I finally got it: $78 a month for the four of us. That's all we'll ever get. That's why there is no soap, no medicine, no needles, no hot water, no aspirin, no hand cream, no shampoo—none of those things ever. And forever. I pay $20 a month rent. The rest goes for food: grits, cornmeal, rice, beans and milk.

Poverty is looking into a future colored only the blackest black. There is no hope. Your children wouldn't play with my children; you wouldn't allow it. My boys will someday turn to boys who steal to get what they need. I can already see them behind prison bars, but it doesn't bother me as it would you. They'll be better off behind prison bars than they would be behind the bars of my poverty and despair. They'll find the freedom of alcohol and drugs—the only freedom they'll ever know.

My daughter? She'll have a life just like mine, unless she's pretty enough to become a prostitute. I'd be smart to wish her dead already.

You say there are schools? Sure there are, but my children have no paper, no pencils, no crayons, no clothes, no anything worthwhile or useful. All they have is worms, pinkeye, infections of all sorts all the time. They aren't hungry, but they are undernourished. There are surplus commodity programs some places, I hear, but not here. Our county said it would cost too much. There is a school lunch program, but I have two children who are already too damaged for that to do them any good.

Yes, I know there are health clinics. They are in the towns, and I live eight miles from any town. I can walk that far, but my little children can't, and I can't carry them.

I have a neighbor who will take me to town when he goes, but he expects to be paid one way or another. No thanks; at least the hungry children I have are legitimate. You may know my neighbor. He is the large fellow who spends his time at the gas station, the barber shop, and the corner complaining loudly about the government spending money on the immoral mothers of illegitimate children.

Poverty is an acid that eats into pride until pride is burned out. It is a chisel that chips at honor until honor is pulverized. You might do something if you were in my situation—for a week or a month. Would you do it year after year, getting nowhere?

Even I can dream. I dream of a time when there is money—money for the right kind of food, for medicine, for vitamins, for a toothbrush, for hand cream, for a hammer and nails, for screens, for a shovel, for paint, for sheets, for needles, and thread and . . . but I know it's a dream, just like you know it's a dream when you see yourself as President.

Most, though, I dream of such things as not having wounded pride when I'm forced to ask for help. I dream for the peace of sincerely not caring any more. I dream of a time when the offices I visit for help are as nice as other government offices, when there are enough workers to get to you quickly, when those workers don't quit in defeat and despair just as poor folk quit hoping. I dream of the time when I have to tell my story just once each visit, to just one person. I'm tired of proving my poverty over and over and over.

I did not come from another place, and I did not come from another time. I'm here, now, and there are others like me all around you.

● If you were able to read this article without implicit tears of sorrow and anger—and maybe a little guilt—then you now know something about yourself! You are part of the problem rather than part of the solution.

COMMENTS: ON STARVATION IN AMERICA

Only one of the [Mississippi Delta] families I visited ever had milk at all and this was reserved for "the sickliest" one. One mother summed up the question of diet in a single, poignant sentence: "These children go to bed hungry and get up hungry and don't ever know nothing else in between." Thin arms, sunken eyes, lethargic behavior, and swollen bellies were everywhere to be seen.

RAYMOND WHEELER, M.D.

There are thousands and thousands of children in the Delta we didn't see, out of sight, out of reach, out of mind, out of access to white doctors and Negro doctors. There must be between 50,000 and 100,000 children suffering from malnutrition in the Delta. . . . I fear that we have among us now in this country hundreds of thousands of people who have literally grown up to be and learned to be tired, fearful, anxious, and suspicious. . . . The children need food, the kind of food that will enable their bones to grow, their blood to function as it should, their vital organs to remain healthy, and their minds to stay alert. It is inconceivable to us that children at this stage of American history, and in the context of American wealth, continue to live like this in Mississippi, in Alabama, in Kentucky, in West Virginia, in the Southwest, and, indeed, carry this condition of life to all of our Northern cities.

ROBERT COLES, M.D.

We do not want to quibble over words, but "malnutrition" is not quite what we found, the boys and girls we saw were hungry—weak, in pain, sick, their lives are being shortened; they are, in fact, visibly and predictably losing their health, their energy, and their spirits. They are suffering from hunger and disease and directly or indirectly they are dying from them—which is exactly what "starvation" means.

Report to Senate Subcommittee on Poverty by a Distinguished Panel of Medical Experts

It is old age rather than ~~life~~ death that should be contrasted to life.

26 OLD AGE: END PRODUCT OF A FAULTY SYSTEM*

SIMONE DE BEAUVOIR

Old age is not a necessary end to human life. It does not even represent what Sartre has called the "necessity of our contingency," as the body does. A great many creatures—the mayflies, for example—die after having reproduced their kind, without going through any phase of degeneration. However, it is an empirical and universal truth that after a certain number of years the human organism undergoes a decline. The process is inescapable. At the end of a certain time it results in a reduction in the individual's activities. Often it also brings a diminution in his mental faculties and an alteration in his attitude toward the world.

A particular value has sometimes been given to old age for social or political reasons. But the vast majority of mankind looks upon the coming of old age with sorrow or rebellion. It fills men with more aversion than does death itself.

And indeed it is old age, rather than death, that is to be contrasted with life. Old age is life's parody, whereas death transforms life into a destiny.

Not all old people give up the struggle. Far from it—many are remarkable for their stubborn perseverance. But in these cases they often become caricatures of themselves. Their will goes on, by its own impetus, with no reason or even against all reason. They began by forming their desire, their will, with a given end in view. Now they desire, because they have desired. Broadly speaking, among the old, habit, automatic reactions, and hardened, set ways take the place of invention.

Morality teaches a serene acceptance of those ills that science and technology are powerless to abolish—pain, disease, old age. It claims that the courageous endurance of that very condition that lessens us is a way of increasing our stature. If he lacks other projects, the elderly man may commit himself to this. But here we are playing with words. Projects have to do only with our activities. Undergoing age is not an activity. Growing, ripening, aging, dying—the passing of time is predestined, inevitable.

● "One's life has value so long as one attributes value to the lives of others by means of love, friendship, indignation, compassion. When this is so, then there are still valid reasons for activity or speech."

*Abridged from Simone de Beauvoir, Old age: End product of a faulty system. Copyright 1972 by Saturday Review Co. First appeared in *Saturday Review*, April 8, 1972, 39–42. Used with permission.

Old age ⇒ not necessary to end life.

COMMENT: PERSONALIZING DEATH TRANSFORMS LIFE

Man is alienated from himself to the degree that he refuses to choose to recognize his own limitations, his primary limitation being his own contingency—the realization that there is nothing necessary about one's existence—that man may cease to exist at anytime. However, the real force of man's predicament becomes existentially meaningful to a person when that person avoids thinking of death in general terms and refers it to himself —that is, the important thing is not the abstraction that all men are mortal, but the fact that I am mortal—that I will die—that there is a specific moment in the future when I will cease to exist.

Thus, as Kierkegaard has put it, the individual "achieves full recognition of himself through being saddled with a tragic sense of life and death." But it is too often the case that this tragedy is too hard for a person to bear and he thus, time after time, chooses to forget or avoid his contingency. Because the average person is afraid to realize that he is *unique and alone*, he learns many ways to avoid confronting himself by the use of all the mechanisms of adjustment and defense which the psychologists have discovered.

JAMES A. DYAL

There is only one solution if old age is not to be an absurd parody of our former life, and that is to go on pursuing ends that give our existence a meaning—devotion to individuals, groups, or causes, to social, political, intellectual, or creative work. In spite of the moralists' opinion to the contrary, in old age we should still wish to have passions strong enough to prevent our turning in upon ourselves. One's life has value so long as one attributes value to the lives of others by means of love, friendship, indignation, compassion. When this is so, then there are still valid reasons for activity or speech. People are often advised to "prepare" for old age. But if this merely means

setting aside money, choosing the place for retirement, and laying on hobbies, we shall not be much the better for it when the day comes. It is far better not to think about it too much but to live a fairly committed, fairly justified life so that one may go on in the same path even when all illusions have vanished and one's zeal for life has died away.

But these possibilities are granted only to a handful of privileged people. It is in the last years of life that the gap between them and the vast majority of mankind becomes deepest and most obvious. When we set these two old ages side by side we can answer the essential questions of aging: What are the inescapable factors in the individual's decline? And to what degree is society responsible for them?

As we have seen, the age at which this decline begins has always depended upon the class to which a man belongs. Today a miner is finished, done for, at the age of fifty, whereas many of the privileged carry their eighty years lightly. The worker's decline begins earlier; its course is also far more rapid. His shattered body is the victim of disease and infirmity, whereas an elderly man who has had the good fortune of being able to look after his health may keep it more or less undamaged until his death.

When they are old, the exploited classes are condemned, if not to utter destitution, then at least to extreme poverty, to uncomfortable, inconvenient dwellings, and to loneliness, all of which results in a feeling of failure and a generalized anxiety. They sink into a torpid bewilderment that has physical repercussions. Even the mental diseases from which they suffer are to a great extent the products of the system. Even with health and clarity of mind, the retired man is nevertheless the victim of that terrible curse, boredom. Deprived of his hold upon the world, he is incapable of finding another, because his time apart from his work, his free time, was alienated, rendered sterile. With age his gloomy idleness leads to an apathy that endangers what physical and intellectual balance he still has.

The injury he has suffered during the course of his life is still more radical. The reason that the

solution of old age: go on pursuing ends that give our existance meaning.

retired man is rendered hopeless by the want of meaning in his present life is that the meaning of his existence has been stolen from him from the very beginning. A law, as merciless as Lassalle's "iron law" of wages, allows him no more than the right to reproduce his life. It refuses him the possibility of discovering any justification for it. When he escapes from the fetters of his trade or calling, all he sees around him is an arid waste. He has not been granted the possibility of committing himself to projects that might have peopled the world with goals, values, and reasons for existence.

● "When they are old, the exploited classes are condemned, if not to utter destitution, then at least to extreme poverty, to uncomfortable, inconvenient dwellings, and to loneliness, all of which results in a feeling of failure and a generalized anxiety."

That is the crime of our society. Its "old-age policy" is scandalous. But more scandalous still is the treatment that it inflicts upon the majority of men during their youth and their maturity. It prefabricates the maimed and wretched state that is theirs when they are old. It is the fault of society that the decline of old age begins too early, that it is rapid, physically painful, and, because men enter in upon it with empty hands, morally atrocious. Some exploited, alienated individuals inevitably become "throw-outs," "rejects," once their strength has failed them.

● "A man should not start his last years alone and empty-handed."

That is why all the remedies that have been put forward to lessen the distress of the aged are such a mockery; not one of them can possibly repair the systematic destruction that has been inflicted upon some men throughout their lives. Even if they are treated and taken care of, their health cannot be given back. Even if decent houses are built for them, they cannot be provided with the culture, the interests, and the responsibilities that would give their life a meaning. I do not say that it would be entirely pointless to improve their condition here and now, but doing so would provide no solution whatsoever to the real problem of old age. What should a society be so that in his last years a man might still be a man?

The answer is simple: He would always have to have been treated as a man. By the fate it allots to its members who can no longer work, society gives itself away; it has always looked upon them as so much material. Society confesses that as far as it is concerned profit is the only thing that counts and that its "humanism" is mere window dressing. In the nineteenth century the ruling classes explicitly equated the proletariat with barbarism. The struggles of the workers succeeded in making the proletariat part of mankind once more, but only insofar as it is productive. Society turns away from the aged worker as though he belonged to another species.

That is why the whole question of aging is buried in a conspiracy of silence. Old age exposes the failure of our entire civilization. It is the whole man that must be remade; it is the whole relationship between man and man that must be recast if we wish the old person's state to be acceptable. A man should not start his last years alone and empty-handed. If culture were not a mere inactive mass of information, acquired once and for all and then forgotten, if it were effectual and living, and if it meant that the individual had a grasp upon his environment that would fulfill and renew itself as the years go by, then he would be an active, useful citizen at every age. If he were not atomized from his childhood, shut away and isolated among other atoms, and if he shared in a collective life, as necessary and as much a matter of course as his own, then he would never experience banishment.

Nowhere and in no century have these conditions obtained. Although the socialist countries may have come a little closer to them than the capitalist, they still have a very long way to go.

We may dream that in the ideal society I have just spoken of old age as we know it would be virtually nonexistent. As it does happen in certain privileged cases, the individual, personally weakened by age but not obviously lessened by it, would one day be attacked by some disease from which he would not recover. He would die without having suffered any degradation. Old age would really comply with the definition that is given to it by certain bourgeois ideologists—a period of life different from youth and maturity but possessing its own balance and leaving a wide range of options open to the individual.

We are far from this state of affairs. Society cares about the individual only insofar as he is profitable. The young know this. Their anxiety as they enter upon social life matches the anguish of the old as they are excluded from it. Between these two ages, the problem is hidden by routine. The young man dreads this machine that is about to seize hold of him, and sometimes he tries to defend himself by throwing bricks; the old man, rejected by it, exhausted and naked, has nothing left but his eyes to weep with. Between youth and age there turns the machine, the crusher of men—of men who let themselves be crushed, because it never even occurs to them that they can escape it. Once we have understood what the state of the aged really is, we cannot satisfy ourselves with the calling for a more generous "old-age policy," higher pensions, decent housing, and organized leisure. It is the whole system that is at issue, and our demand cannot be otherwise than radical —change life itself.

COMMENT: THE DISCOVERY OF OLD AGE

Die early or grow old: there is no other alternative. And yet, as Goethe said, 'Age takes hold of us by surprise.' For himself each man is the sole, unique subject, and we are often astonished when the common fate becomes our own—when we are struck by sickness, a shattered relationship, or bereavement. I remember my own stupefaction when I was seriously ill for the first time in my life and I said to myself, 'This woman they are carrying on a stretcher is me.' Nevertheless, we accept fortuitous accidents readily enough, making them part of our history, because they affect us as unique beings: but old age is the general fate, and when it seizes upon our own personal life we are dumbfounded. 'Why, what has happened?' writes Aragon. 'It is life that has happened; and I am old.' The fact that the passage of universal time should have brought about a private, personal metamorphosis is something that takes us completely aback. When I was only forty I still could not believe it when I stood there in front of the looking-glass and said to myself, 'I am forty.' Children and adolescents are of some particular age. The mass of prohibitions and duties to which they are subjected and the behaviour of others towards them do not allow them to forget it. When we are grown up we hardly think about our age any more: we feel that the notion does not apply to us; for it is one which assumes that we look back towards the past and draw a line under the total, whereas in fact we are reaching out towards the future, gliding on imperceptibly from day to day, from year to year. Old age is particularly difficult to assume because we have always regarded it as something alien, a foreign species: 'Can I have become a different being while I still remain myself?'

SIMONE DE BEAUVOIR

27 AGE-ISM: ANOTHER FORM OF BIGOTRY*

ROBERT N. BUTLER

Malcolm X, the Kerner Commission Report, and a variety of other persons, events, and materials have made the concept of racism familiar. Social class discrimination also needs no introduction. However, we may soon have to consider very seriously a form of bigotry we now tend to overlook: age discrimination or age-ism, prejudice by one age group toward other age groups. If such bias exists, might it not be especially evident in America; a society that has traditionally valued pragmatism, action, power, and the vigor of youth over contemplation, reflection, experience, and the wisdom of age?

In the affluent community of Chevy Chase, recent events have revealed a complex interweaving of class, color, and age discrimination that may highlight the impact of these forces in our national life.

On January 30, 1969, the National Capital Housing Authority, the public housing agency of the District of Columbia, held hearings on its proposal to purchase Regency House, a high-rise apartment building in Chevy Chase, for the elderly poor. If finally approved, Regency House would be the first public housing project west of Rock Creek Park, the traditional boundary between black and white in Washington, D.C.

The middle-class and middle-aged white citizenry of Chevy Chase appeared at both the hearings and at the Chevy Chase Citizens' Association meeting at a local public school on February 17. They vigorously protested on a variety of grounds the National Capital Housing Authority proposal. Some of these aroused citizens demonstrated that they could practice the politics of

*Abridged from R. N. Butler, Age-ism: Another form of bigotry. *The Gerontologist*, Winter, 1969, **9** (4), Pt. 1, 243–246. Reprinted by permission of the author and the publisher.

protest and confrontation in a manner as impassioned as that of the young and alienated.

Chevy Chase residents were irritated and angered by a proposal to provide what they considered luxury housing (there is a swimming pool on the roof of Regency House) for older people who were not accustomed to "luxury."

Among statements heard at the meetings and quoted in the local newspapers were: "You would open the door for people who don't know how to live." "Slums are made by the people who live in them." "It (public housing) has to come sometime but not this time or in this place." "I am not against old folks, believe me." "Who wants all those old people around." Zoning, tax losses, costs, and property values were also mentioned, but it was clear that more than concern over the pocketbook was operating.

Class, color, and age have always been parts of the structure of American communities. Since the passage of the Public Housing Act of 1937, we have tended to increase the divisions within America by separating the poor and segregating the non-white. Today, despite Social Security, the elderly poor are common, and they are frequently black. There has also been a trend in recent years toward segregation of the middle-class elderly in "retirement communities" and "housing for the elderly."

Neighborhood reaction against the use of Regency House for the elderly poor carries implications beyond Chevy Chase. The classic or scapegoat explanation for prejudice turns upon the unconscious effort to justify one's own weaknesses by finding them in others—in other races, religions, or nationalities. Personal insecurity, once generalized, becomes the basis of prejudice and hostility.

Age-ism describes the subjective experience implied in the popular notion of the generation gap. Prejudice of the middle-aged against the old in this instance, and against the young in others, is a serious national problem. Age-ism reflects a deep seated uneasiness on the part of the young and middle-aged—a personal revulsion to and distaste for growing old, disease, disability; and fear of powerlessness, "uselessness," and death.

Cultural attitudes in our society reinforce these feelings. We have chosen mandatory retirement from the work force and thus removed the elderly from the mainstream of life. Age-ism is manifested in the taunting remarks about "old-fogeys," in the special vulnerability of the elderly to muggings and robberies, in age discrimination in employment independent of individual competence, and in the probable inequities in the allocation of research funds. Although persons 65 years of age and over account for 25% of all public mental hospital admissions, only 3% of the research budget of the National Institute of Mental Health is spent in relevant research. Less than 1% of the budget of the entire National Institutes of Health is devoted to the study of aging phenomena.

The issue goes deeper. It is the middle-aged after all, upon whom the "burdens imposed" by both ends of the life cycle, the young and the old, necessarily fall. From their purses come hard-won earnings to educate the young and to care for the elderly (in our time collectively, although inadequately, through Medicare and Social Security). Middle life has been labeled the period of "gravity" because of its manifold responsibilities. It is not surprising that some members of the middle group "cop out" of marriages, of jobs, even of society while others rigidly and tenaciously hold on to what they have struggled so hard to achieve. Many middle-aged people, of course, respond flexibly and creatively to both young and old.

Many different objections were raised to the National Capital Housing Authority proposal for housing the elderly poor in Chevy Chase. Color and class were surely most significant, yet racism alone cannot account for the "middle-aged riot"—for screeching, shouting, booing, and stomping of feet that occurred at the hearings and

the citizens' meeting. A local official noted that the same arguments against public housing had been heard from middle-class Negro families in the Northeast, a predominantly black section of Washington.

The proposed purchase of the nine-story 172-unit apartment building gave rise to an extraordinary amount of misinformation. In the first place, Regency House is not particularly luxurious. Second, contrary to the apparent fears that only elderly Negroes on welfare could occupy Regency House, NCHA housing is for low-income elderly and not just for welfare or black elderly. . . . Some opponents of the Regency House proposal expressed fear that families with children would eventually move in, although the apartment house contains only efficiencies and one-bedroom apartments. Others considered that "these people" were undeserving and should have been more provident. Yet the stereotype of the undeserving poor seems curiously outmoded. Many of "these people" were at the height of their earning power and productive years during the Depression when income and the possibility of saving were minimal. . . . Other opponents of the Regency House proposal misunderstood the financial basis of the plan. They feared that monies for the purchase of this building would come out of their own pockets through local taxes. . . . Still another point in the opposition was that "these people" would have a higher cost of living in Chevy Chase than elsewhere. Actually there has been some evidence that living costs are higher in Washington's ghetto areas. . . . There was talk among the middle-aged opponents of legal action against the decision. One stated ground was that public monies should not be used to enforce social policies.

H. G. Wells once said that history is a race between education and catastrophe. The NCHA might have mitigated the storm of controversy and, more important, facilitated the reception of the elderly poor into Chevy Chase through an educational campaign with the assistance of the press and various interested groups and individuals within and without the community. . . . There was a large measure of good will within the community that was not mobilized.

The experience of other housing for the elderly sponsored by NCHA could have been reported and potential residents themselves asked to participate in neighborhood meetings. Chevy Chase residents, imprisoned in such myths as "deterioration," could have been invited to visit other NCHA housing.

Such a program would have been political education in the very best sense. Perhaps the same number of Chevy Chase residents would have objected; but their protests would have been drowned out by a better informed, articulate majority. Moreover, both the youth and the middle-aged of the area would have learned something about themselves, including the implacable course of their own aging.

To explore the bigotry in age-ism is not to minimize the other more salient features of racial and class discrimination observed in Chevy Chase. But aging is the great sleeper in American life. By the year 2000, according to current population projections, there will be approximately 33 million retired people each with an average of 25 years of retirement time. Should there be major breakthroughs in finding deterrents to aging along with the present steady pace of medical progress, there would be still greater numbers of old and retired people. How are they (that is, we) to be supported: What are they (we) to do? The Beatles sing:

"Will you still need me,
Will you still feed me,
When I'm sixty-four.
You'll be older, too. . . ."

Chevy Chase residents, like Americans in general, are unaware of or unwilling to acknowledge the poverty of the elderly. George Santayana said that, but for the excellence of the typical single life in a society, no nation deserves to be remembered more than the sands of the sea. If it may be said that the quality of a culture can be measured by its regard for its least powerful members, for exam-

ple, its care for the elderly and its protection and education of its children, the readings for ours are disappointingly low.

Social Security and Medicare, which most Americans consider landmarks in social legislation, are little more than sops to the conscience. The average income of the person over 65 in America is $1,800 per year. Nearly 7 million of our 19 million elderly are below the poverty line. The average monthly Social Security check of a retired male worker in America today is $86.04. Since Medicare pays an average of only 35% of medical bills, it has thus far failed to provide adequate financial support for the health care of the elderly. Medicare, Social Security, and public housing are examples of tokenism. They are not fundamentally meeting human needs for health care, income, and housing.

Ironically, one could question the wisdom of concentrating old people in specific housing. Sweden, for example, has been giving up high-rise enclaves for its older citizens. Rather than a housing program for older citizens, it might be more desirable socially to provide rent supplements or, ultimately, appropriate income maintenance so that the elderly could live anywhere throughout the city. Of course, some older people do want to live together and coordinated services—medical, social, and recreational—can be placed in housing for the elderly. For those with increasing limitation, congregate living with available services is mandatory. Thus, it is probably wisest for a society to provide a range of alternatives. One of the greatest losses of old age is that of choice.

One thing is certain: further concentration of public housing in limited sections of any city —concentrating the poor or the rich or the black or the old or the young—only contributes to the divisiveness of our society.

I do not want my children to grow up in an isolated neighborhood, knowing neither the realities of old age nor the meaning of racial heterogeneity. Age, race and social class discrimination are clearly inimical to the developing human community and to the extent that our community of Chevy Chase is "closed," *it* is inherently disadvantaged.

Age-ism might parallel (it might be wishful thinking to say replace) racism as the great issue of the next 20 to 30 years and age bigotry is seen within minority groups themselves.

Seventeen percent of our electorate is over 65 already, but at present it is not voting as a group; consequently politicians are not zealously seeking the votes of older citizens. Yet this may well change; perhaps one day we will be hearing of Senior Power. We don't all grow white or black, but we all grow old.

28 THE PATHOLOGY OF THE GHETTO*

KENNETH B. CLARK

The dark ghetto is institutionalized pathology; it is chronic, self-perpetuating pathology; and it is the futile attempt by those with power to confine that pathology so as to prevent the spread of its contagion to the "larger community."

It would follow that one would find in the ghetto such symptoms of social disorganization and disease as high rates of juvenile delinquency, venereal disease among young people, narcotic addiction, illegitimacy, homicide, and suicide. All of these forms of social pathology do thrive in the ghettos, except suicide; only in suicide statistics does Harlem fall below the norms of New York City as a whole.

Not only is the pathology of the ghetto self-perpetuating, but one kind of pathology breeds another. The child born in the ghetto is more likely to come into a world of broken homes and illegitimacy; and this family and social instability is conducive to delinquency, drug addiction, and criminal violence. Neither instability nor crime can be controlled by police vigilance or by reliance on the alleged deterring forces of legal punishment, for the individual crimes are to be understood more as symptoms of the contagious sickness of the community itself than as the result of inherent criminal or deliberate viciousness.

EMOTIONAL ILLNESS

The emotional ill health of the dark ghetto is a continuum ranging from the anxious but "normal" individual to the criminally psychotic. The harmful effects of American racism on personality development and psychological balance are unmistakable. Still, it is one thing to show that prejudice damages individuals and another to show that the emotional illness of a particular individual has been caused by prejudice and its social consequences. The link between the phenomenon of the dark ghetto and individual destructiveness and withdrawal seems clear in many cases; in others the relationship is less sharply drawn.

The evidence concerning the nature and extent of individual psychoses and neuroses in the ghetto is far less available and not easy to interpret. There are comparatively few Negro or white psychiatrists in the ghettos; and psychotherapy has not had the vogue among Negroes that it has in white middle- and upper-class urban communities in large part because the middle class is the central group in the white community and it is not in the Negro community. Individual psychotherapy tends either to be restricted to those sufficiently and destructively ill enough to require the intervention of society —and here it is largely custodial in nature—or to those less seriously damaged who have the funds and the inclination to seek help for themselves. It would be, in fact, surprising to find many Negro

*Abridged from Chapters 4 and 5 in *Dark ghetto* by Kenneth Clark. Copyright © 1965 by Kenneth B. Clark. Reprinted by permission of Harper & Row, Publishers, Inc.

patients receiving extensive voluntary personal treatment, though the number doubtless will rise as Negroes move into more high-status jobs, thereby gaining both the money to pay the high cost of prolonged therapy and the psychological orientation to accept it.

One would expect, however, given the pathology of the dark ghetto, to find a high rate of admission of Negro patients to the state and city psychiatric wards. Harlem has the highest rate of admission to state mental hospitals of any area in New York City. The crude rate per 10,000 population is 38.5 for Harlem compared to a mean rate for the rest of the city of 13 per 10,000.

But admission to state hospitals is only one index of mental illness, and if statistics for patients in private hospitals and under home or office therapy were known, the ghetto's rate of treated illness would significantly decline in comparison with that of the white community. There are, of course, no statistics for untreated or undiagnosed illness.

In the absence of adequate and urgently needed research into the degree of actual prevalence of emotional illness in Negro urban communities, one can do little more than speculate. Is the pathology of the dark ghetto so pervasive that mental disturbance does not stand out as clearly as it does elsewhere? Is the city government less observant of deviant behavior in the ghetto because it is subconsciously less concerned to protect the community from threat? Is less illness reported—or even recognized *as* illness—by ghetto families and friends? Are persons who are emotionally disturbed already institutionalized for other pathologies—drug addiction, delinquency, homicide—and hence not diagnosed or treated as ill? Does the pattern of violence in the ghetto provide an outlet for emotional release that would in another culture be turned inward into phobias and depression? Do ghetto residents feel too alienated from the clinics and social agencies to seek help? Do the agencies tend to prefer as clients those who are "reachable" and hence indirectly weed out prospective Negro patients?

Or are the problems to be dealt with in the nation's dark ghettos so demanding of individual energies that there is not even the strength for emotional illness? Is mental illness—other than the starkly and destructively psychotic—itself a luxury of the middle and upper classes?

Whatever the facts about the incidence and the causes of emotional illness in the Negro ghetto, it is clear that facilities for treatment are inadequate. In Harlem, for example, there are four services for emotionally disturbed children, two of them public, and two private. According to data supplied by three of these agencies, they serve 560 young people under twenty-four.[a] But if one in ten of the general population is emotionally disturbed, as the National Association for Mental Health estimates, more than twelve times this number of young people alone in Harlem need help, not counting the adults.

HOMICIDE AND SUICIDE

The homicide rate for ghetto areas, like the delinquency rate, is startling. In Harlem it is nearly six times the rate for New York City. In one area of about fourteen square blocks in New York the rate is fifteen times that of the city as a whole.

The rate of suicide for the ghetto is, on the other hand, lower than the city average. For Harlem the rate is 8.2 per 100,000 population compared to the city rate of 9.7. Throughout the country Negroes, and communities with a high proportion of Negroes, ordinarily have lower suicide rates. The meaning of this consistent finding is still subject to dispute. One current view holds that low suicide rates mirror high social homogeneity. Another view holds that high suicide rates accompany the "middle-class rat race."

Like suicide rates elsewhere, therefore, the incidence in Harlem seems to be related to higher

[a]Data are available only for the two private agencies within the community and one additional agency located outside the community but drawing 90 percent of its caseload from the Harlem area.

status and its concomitant anxieties; and, where suicide does occur in the Harlem ghetto, it appears to occur with the intensity and frequency of homicide.

It is interesting to speculate upon the comparative difference between the rates of homicide and suicide for Harlem. Suicide may be conceived of as aggression turned inward. In this, Harlem, except for a few areas, is low. Homicide, on the other hand, is the ultimate aggression turned outward. In this, Harlem ranks high. Furthermore, the victims in homicide cases in the ghetto and elsewhere are for the most part friends and relatives, and not the feared and hated "Whitey." A tantalizing deduction about the social pathology of the community, therefore, is that it is primarily manifested in aggression directed toward intimates and fellow victims of the ghetto. This may mean that the victim of oppression is more prone to attack his fellow victim than to risk aggression against the feared oppressor.

Other factors which may be related to the high intra-ghetto homicide rate are the sheer social abrasiveness of population density, the general purposelessness and irrelevance of constricted lives, and the fact that aggressions of Negroes against whites are more likely to be punished severely than similar aggressions against other Negroes. In a disturbing sense, there remains the possibility that homicide in the ghetto is consistently high because it is not controlled, if not encouraged, as an aspect of the total network of the human exploitation of the ghetto. The unstated and sometimes stated acceptance of crime and violence as normal for a ghetto community is associated with a lowering of police vigilance and efficiency when the victims are also lower-status people. This is another example of the denial of a governmental service—the right of adequate protection—which is endured by the powerless ghetto.

● Does this lack of protection for minority groups characterize *your* city? Are the police *less* persistent in solving ghetto crimes? How about arranging a class meeting in which police

and local ghetto representatives could exchange views? Could you do it? You might learn a lot about interracial attitudes from such an encounter.

As for suicide, one would expect its incidence to increase rather than decline as the members of the ghetto are admitted into the mainstream of American society. There is no human society where total happiness can be reliably found, as the national suicide rate affirms, but the American Negro is determined to share the total American culture with all its tension and trouble.

DRUG ADDICTION

The statistics on addiction are unreliable. Probably the most important reason for their unreliability is that the use of narcotics is, under present American governmental policy, considered to be illegal and a criminal act. This policy demands that narcotic users blend with the more furtive, illicit, and criminal elements and style of the ghetto. The fact that those who use marijuana, a nonaddictive stimulant, are also required to see themselves as furtive criminals could in some part account for the presumed tendency of the majority of, if not all, drug addicts to start out by using marijuana. It is a reasonable hypothesis that the movement from the nonaddictive drugs or stimulants to the addictive is made more natural and likely because both are forced to belong to the same marginal, quasicriminal culture.

Harlem is the home of many addicts; but as a main center for the distribution of heroin, it attracts many transients, who, when the "panic" is on, cannot buy drugs at home. The social as well as the personal price of the drug industry is immense, for though addicts are victims of the system so, too, are nonaddicts: Many addicts resort to crime in their desperate need for money to feed the expensive habit. Most Harlem residents cannot afford or cannot obtain insurance against prevalent burglary of their apartments, but the addicts do not steal only in Harlem, moving into the white community as well.

Narcotic addiction is chiefly an economic and class problem in any ghetto. Addicts who have the funds do not have to steal to buy drugs. The affluent addict can be reasonably sure of the quality of his heroin; the poor addict has no choice and may find he has bought milk sugar or too strong a dose. The addict of the ghetto shares with others of his community the fact that they are all powerless to protect themselves from a complex and interrelated pattern of multiple exploitation.

For many ghetto young people, narcotics offer a life of glamour and escape, or the illusion of personal importance or even success. Various programs have been periodically announced to stamp out this notorious traffic, but so far Harlem has had no successful program for prevention or treatment. The possibility of an effective solution through the treatment of adolescent addicts seems remote.

Haryou workers interviewed many drug addicts and tape recorded their responses—the plaintive stories that follow, drawn from *Youth in the Ghetto,* need no embellishment.

All you have to do is to stop that white man from selling us the drug, like that. Then you won't have any drug addiction. We don't have any connection for getting drugs, we don't produce them or process them, we don't have anything to bring them into Harlem, or any place, with. So the real crime rate in drugs doesn't stem from us. You have to get to the hoard where it really comes from in the beginning. When you stop that, when you find that, you have your answer right there. You can't blame it on us. We couldn't find it, we couldn't touch it, if it wasn't for him.

Besides, most of us don't know anything about drugs, or anything else, until we meet one of these types of people, and they introduce us to it—telling us about a way to make a dollar. That way we are deteriorating our race, by listening to them and by participating. But we don't have jobs, what can we do? We all need a dollar. We have to eat—we have to raise our families.

The Man, he wants these things to exist in Harlem. Everything that exists in Harlem the government wants it to exist. If they didn't want it, they would stop it.

—Man, age about 30

I was just born black, poor and uneducated. And you only need three strikes all over the world to be out, and I have nothing to live for but this shot of dope.

I have nothing to shoot at. All I have to look forward to is a thrill and it's in a bag, and they run me up on the roof to get that. I don't have any place to turn, but I imagine you have. I'm poor and all I can look forward to is what I can get out of this bag. That's the only thrill in life for me, you know. I've never had anything, no opportunity, you know, to get any money, no nothing. All I can look forward to is what I can get out of this bag, and that's nothing really.

When I started I was fourteen years old, and that's twelve years ago. Drugs were much different then. For a dollar a cap poor people got rich. I started back where a man could shoot dope—hey cook that up for me, Eddie. Can you cook? Okay, hit me, man. I started back when I was fourteen years old in 1951, you understand, and I've been using dope ever since, except for the time I spent in the penitentiary. I figure if Whitey gives me half a chance, you know, when I came through school, I could have done something more than this, you know. I know it. But I didn't have the chance because, like I say, I had those three strikes against me.

I'm not really blaming him, you know, the younger ones, but all Whiteys are associated with their race, and I blame them all because there isn't anything else I can do, you know, but shoot dope.

Well, I don't think anything can be done to correct it. Me, because I'm too far gone on it, you know. But, I mean, for my brothers and sisters, you know, people that are coming up younger than I, you know, they can do something. Give them a better education and better job opportunities.

Because I've been in this so long, this is part of my life. I'm sick now, I'm supposed to be in a hospital. They tried to admit me into the hospital three days ago, but knowing that it will be detrimental for me to stay out here, I stayed anyway because I'd rather have this shot of dope than go into anyone's hospital.

Like I say, it's only natural. It's part of my life after twelve years. I never come out of jail and try to do something else but go to this cooker. So, like I say, this is all that's left to me. Look, I started when I was fourteen. I'm not going to say that I never tried to get a job. I tried to get a job, but what references can I give. When I go to State Employment Agency, and they ask where have you been working for the last—since 1952, and I tell them, well, I've been in jail—that's no reference. They won't give me a job. Or, if I get a job you tell them I've been in jail, they turn me loose anyway, you know.

There's nothing I can do, you know. What the hell else can I do? I can't get a legitimate job, but anything else I do they say is against the law. And as long as I stay in this, I'm going to stay in dope, because everyone that's doing something against the law is in dope.

Your environment, I read somewhere, is just a mirror of yourself, you know. So what can I do?

I mean, I have to get my thrills from life some-way. I can't lay back. I think I can enjoy working, and raising a family, like the next man, but this is all they left me. I can't work, so I must steal. And mostly the women who will accept me are thieves, or in the trade. And I mean, they're not thinking about raising a family. I mean, they think about what would be good for them, you know. The relief won't take them, so if I had a woman she would have to go out and turn tricks. I have to go out and steal to support my habit. So what can we do but shoot dope for enjoyment. They have left us nothing else.

Work, work, some kind of work program setup where a man can work and get ahead and support himself. Then he can go to some type of school at night, you know, to learn some type of trade, be-cause in jail you can't learn a trade. You know, they tell you that you can, but you can't. If you go there, it's just a house of brutality, you know, that's all I've ever found. A bunch of people—I don't know how the administration thinks, but I know the guards that are head over you—all the fellows are interested in are confining you there, working you, making sure you obey, not the administration's orders, but their orders, you know.

So you can't learn anything in jail, you know. All you can do there is learn to hate more. You can't learn a trade or anything. All you learn there is how to stay out of the police's way as much as possible, even if it means ducking work. You duck work—you stay away from the law, because you know the more that you stay around them, the more they see you, the more they want to whip you. I know that, because I started going to jail when I was a kid.

I don't think I could be rehabilitated, you know, not now, in this society. Maybe if I see something better offered. But I hope that in the future they offer kids, or my sister's kids, or someone's kids, a better opportunity than they offered me, because they didn't offer me anything. I either accepted a porter job for the rest of my life regardless of how much education I had, or went to jail. In fact, I think jails were built for black men. You understand? If you look at the population up there, the black man is more popular in jail than the white man. The black man makes parole less frequently than the white man; the black man gets more time than the white man; and the black man goes to the chair more often than the white man. Whitey gets all the breaks in this world.

—Drug addict, male, age 26

The fact that the kind of creative sensitivity reflected in these testimonies has been made alien to the larger society is one of the major tragedies of the ghetto and the society as a whole.

It is now generally understood that chronic and remediable social injustices corrode and damage the human personality, thereby robbing it of its effectiveness, of its creativity, if not its actual hu-manity. No matter how desperately one seeks to deny it, this simple fact persists and intrudes itself. It is the fuel of protests and revolts. Racial segrega-tion, like all other forms of cruelty and tyranny, debases all human beings—those who are its vic-tims, those who victimize, and in quite subtle ways those who are merely accessories.

This human debasement can only be com-prehended as a consequence of the society which spawns it. The victims of segregation do not ini-tially desire to be segregated, they do not "prefer to be with their own people," in spite of the fact that this belief is commonly stated by those who are not themselves segregated. A most cruel and psychologically oppressive aspect and conse-quence of enforced segregation is that its victims can be made to accommodate to their victimized status and under certain circumstances to state that it *is* their desire to be set apart, or to agree that subjugation is not really detrimental but beneficial. The fact remains that exclusion, rejection, and a stigmatized status are not desired and are not voluntary states. Segregation is neither sought nor imposed by healthy or potentially healthy human beings.

Human beings who are forced to live under ghetto conditions and whose daily experience tells them that almost nowhere in society are they respected and granted the ordinary dignity and courtesy accorded to others will, as a matter of course, begin to doubt their own worth. Since every human being depends upon his cumulative experiences with others for clues as to how he should view and value himself, children who are consistently rejected understandably begin to question and doubt whether they, their family, and their group really deserve no more respect from the larger society than they receive. These doubts become the seeds of a pernicious self- and group-hatred, the Negro's complex and debilitating prejudice against himself.

WHITE RATIONALIZATIONS

It is now rare even for the most ardent apologist for the *status quo* seriously to assert that the American pattern of segregation has beneficial consequences. Some do, however, continue to argue that the Negro's inferiority and inherent character defects demand that he be segregated. Others suggest that the chances of his developing those traits and characteristics which would make him more acceptable to the white community would be greater if he would function within his own community until he demonstrates that he is worthy of associating with others. Among the questions which remain unanswered by this type of argument are: Under what circumstances is the Negro ever adjudged worthy or deserving of association with others, and how can he be expected to develop these traits of "worthiness" under conditions which tend to perpetuate characteristics of unworthiness as described by the proponents of this position themselves? In the belief no doubt that this was a statement of compassion, one white opponent of New York's school integration plan said: "If I were God, what would I do to improve the lot of the Negro? If I were God, I'd make everybody white." To sensitive Negroes, this betrays the ultimate condescension—the belief that to *be* Negro means irrevocable rejection.

Even this point of view is not logically consistent, since the same individuals who reject Negroes as offensive have no difficulty, as we have noted above, in accepting Negroes in close and at times intimate association and relationship, for example, as servants or menials or mistresses, as long as the inferior position of the Negro and the dominant position of the white is clearly perceived and accepted by both.

The answers to these questions cannot be found in any single devil—but must be sought in the compliant or accessory role of many in society. However, more privileged individuals understandably may need to shield themselves from the inevitable conflict and pain which would result from their acceptance of the fact that they *are* accessories to profound injustice. The tendency to discuss disturbing social issues such as racial discrimination, segregation, and economic exploitation in detached, legal, political, socio-economic, or psychological terms as if these persistent problems did not involve the suffering of actual human beings is so contrary to empirical evidence that it must be interpreted as a protective device. After World War II, the bulk of the German people *could not know* what was going on in the death camps.

● What psychological defense mechanism(s) are illustrated here? Look up defense mechanisms in your dictionary and see if you can figure it out.

The people of Mississippi *had to believe* in 1964 that the disappearance and death of the three civil rights workers in that state was a diversionary strategy plotted by civil rights groups. Negroes generally expected that a grand jury in New York City *would have found* that it was justifiable homicide performed in the line of duty for a white policeman to kill a fifteen-year-old Negro boy who was "attacking him with a penknife." Insensitivity is a protective device. Among its more primitive examples are: The prevalent beliefs that the predicament of the masses of Negroes reflects their inherent racial inferiority; that the poor are to blame for the squalor and despair of the slums; that the victims of social injustice are somehow subhuman persons who cause and perpetuate their own difficulties; that the more responsible and superior people of the society not only have no obligation for the "irresponsibles" but must be vigilant to see that all of the power of government is used to protect them and their children from them; and that any contrary or compassionate interpretation of the plight of the poor or the rejected is merely the sentimental and naive expression of impractical do-gooders or "bleeding hearts."

● Stop. Turn back to page 165 and reread M. J. Lerner's comment on injustice. Do you see the connection?

More subtle and obscure forms of protection against facing the consequences of social injustice are to be found among those social scientists who cultivate that degree of academic detachment which blocks meaningful or insightful study of human affairs. The preoccupation with trivia—as if this were the ultimate scientific virtue and goal—leads to the irrelevance of much social science research. It is interesting to speculate on the significance of the fact that during the ten years after the U.S. Supreme Court school desegregation decision, an increasing number of social scientists have raised questions concerning the "scientific validity" of the psychological and sociological data cited by the Court as evidence of the damage which segregation inflicts upon personality. Not one of these critics had questioned these data and their interpretations prior to the Court's decision, although the studies on which they were based had been published and available for critical reactions for many years prior to their use in the historic decision.

The pervasive need to turn one's back on any clear evidence of man's inhumanity to man exemplified in the cool objective approach is probably most clearly seen, though in a more subtle form, in the detached "professionalism" of many social workers and in the selective isolation of many psychiatrists and clinical psychologists. Some members of these "helping fields," too, have often defended as objectivity what, to the client, feels more like insensitivity. Furthermore, in their preoccupation with the problem of the individual and their insistence upon reducing him to a manageable system of assumptions, the disturbing and dehumanizing social realities behind his personal agony may be avoided. With the professional perspective which constricts social vision to the impulses, strengths, and weaknesses of the individual "client" as if these can be isolated from the injustices and pathologies of his life, these professionals need not confront the difficult problems of the nature and origin of the social injustices nor run the risks of conflict with the many vested interests which tend to perpetuate the problems of the poor and the rejected. This posture is built into the nature of their training and reinforced by their complex role as agents of the more privileged classes and the admitted and irrevocable fact of their identification with the middle classes. The professionals themselves would point out, also, that the routinizing pressure of bureaucratic procedures, and a heavy case load of human suffering dull the edge of concern and that the most sensitive among them feel, within the structure, uncertain and helpless as to how to address themselves to the problem of social change. It is not surprising, altogether, that compassion is usually sooner or later subordinated to accommodation; yet it is hard for many to understand why they are irrelevant to the root problems of the poor.

Some theorists and practitioners maintain that it is not within their power or training to attempt to help workingclass and low-status people because the problems of these people are psychosocial and, since they cannot be "reached," are not amenable to the psychotherapeutic and casework techniques thought to be helpful in working with middle-class individuals. Some professionals tend to limit their role to that of models or interpreters of the middle-class norms of speech, behavior, dress, values, and ways of handling problems and feelings. In view of their status and psychological distance, the social worker's concern to "relate to" the "client" seems pathetic in its failure of elemental empathy. The stated or unstated goal of this type of "therapeutic" relationship must then become that of helping the client "adjust" to his life realities, i.e., to keep him from "acting out" his rebellion in antisocial or self-destructive ways and thereby to function more effectively *within* the continuing pathology of his society. These goals are consistent with the *status quo* convenience of the middle class. They are consistent with the benign artificiality of response from these professionals which repels the members of the working class, for whom the immediate and pressing realities of their daily lives alone seem relevant. That middle-class individuals are not equally repelled may be an indication of the extent to which pretenses and protective detachment have become norms of middle-class adjustment—particularly in a society of accepted injustice. This is not to say that individual therapy is not needed and cannot be effective. It is to say that such procedures are not effective where social pathology is at the root of the individual's maladjustment. It is a real question whether adjustment or indifference to the reality of injustice is not the real neurosis, and rebellion the evidence of health.

29 IN JUVENILE COURT

IN THE SUPERIOR COURT OF THE STATE OF CALIFORNIA
IN AND FOR THE COUNTY OF SANTA CLARA
Juvenile Division
Honorable Gerald S. Chargin, Judge
Courtroom No. 1

TRANSCRIPT OF PROCEEDINGS

San Jose, California   September 2, 1969

APPEARANCES:

For the Minor: FRED LUCERO, ESQ.,
                        Deputy Public Defender
For the Probation Department:WILLIAM TAPOGNA, ESQ.,
                        Court Probation Officer
Offical Court Reporter: SUSAN K. STRAHM, C.S.R.
September 2, 1969   10:25 a.m.

PROCEEDINGS

THE COURT : All right. This is the time regularly set for the hearing of this matter. Under the law, I wish to advise you of your legal rights. You are represented by the Public Defender's office. You have a right to call witnesses on your behalf, and you have the right to cross-examine any witnesses who testify against you. The minor has a right to remain silent. Anything that you say may be used against you.

Are you willing to proceed with the hearing at this time?

MR. LUCERO: Yes.

THE MINOR: Yes, sir.

THE COURT: All right. We will read the Petition to you, . . . Pay attention because you will be asked to admit or deny the allegations.

Please read the Petition.

. . . the Petitioner alleges the person whose name, address and age are shown in the above caption is under 21 years of age. This person comes within the provisions of Section 602 of the Juvenile Court Law of California, in that in the County of Santa Clara, State of California, during the month of December, A.D., 1968, a felony, to wit, a violation of California Penal Code Section 285, incest, was committed by the above-named minor as follows, to wit: The said minor did unlawfully accomplish an act of sexual intercourse with his sister.

Certified from the Justice Court for the Gilroy-Morgan Hill Judicial District on the 25th day of July, 1969.

THE COURT: All right. Will the minor and his parents please stand up and raise your right hand to testify in case you care to testify in this matter.

THE COURT: All right. Be seated.

Now, young man, you've heard this Petition read to you, . . . It, in effect, charges you that during the month of December of last year, 1968, a felony was committed by you, in that you did unlawfully accomplish an act of sexual intercourse with your sister.

Before you answer, consult your attorney. Do you admit or deny the allegations?

(Discussion off the record between the minor and his attorney.)

THE MINOR: Yes.

THE COURT: All right. In view of the admission by the minor, the Court determines that the allegations of the Petition are true, and the minor comes within the provisions of Section 602 of the Juvenile Court Law.

I have before me a report prepared by the probation officer and its recommendation, which I don't go along with. But I guess there ought to be some other way—just sending you to some relatives isn't the answer on this kind of charge.

Counsel, what do you have to say about this?

MR. LUCERO: Well, Your Honor, this is the first time that this youngster has been referred to the Probation Department for any violation. He seems to be doing well in school. He's not a behavior problem at the school. He has never given any difficulty at home.

I think that perhaps the recommendation of the Probation Department is in line with the needs of this youngster and that he's not violent. He's not taking things from people, destructive of property. Separation of the family—him from the other family members is probably the answer to this particular violation, although I don't think that the youngster, in view of what has transpired since then, is going to reengage in that type of activity.

THE COURT: There is some indication that you more or less didn't think that it was against the law or was improper. Haven't you had any moral training? Have you and your family gone to church?

THE MINOR: Yes, sir.

THE COURT: Don't you know that things like this are terribly wrong? This is one of the worst crimes that a person can commit. I just get so disgusted that I just figure what is the use? You are just an animal. You are lower than an animal. Even animals don't do that. You are pretty low.

I don't know why your parents haven't been able to teach you anything or train you. Mexican people, after 13 years of age, it's perfectly all right to go out and act like an animal. It's not even right to do that to a stranger, let alone a member of your own family. I don't have much hope for you. You will probably end up in State's Prison before you are 25, and that's where you belong, any how. There is nothing much you can do.

I think you haven't got any moral principles. You won't acquire anything. Your parents won't teach you what is right or wrong and won't watch out.

Apparently your sister is pregnant; is that right?

THE MINOR: . . . Yes.

THE COURT: . . . How old is she?

THE MINOR'S MOTHER: . . . Fifteen.

THE COURT: Well, probably she will have a half a dozen children and three or four marriages before she is 18.

The County will have to take care of you. You are no particular good to anybody. We ought to send you out of the country—send you back to Mexico. You belong in prison for the rest of your life for doing things of this kind. You ought to commit suicide. That's what I think of people of this kind. You are lower than animals and haven't the right to live in organized society—just miserable, lousy, rotten people.

There is nothing we can do with you. You expect the County to take care of you. Maybe Hitler was right. The animals in our society probably ought to be destroyed because they have no right to live among human beings. If you refuse to act like a human being, then, you don't belong among the society of human beings.

MR. LUCERO: Your Honor, I don't think I can sit here and listen to that sort of thing.

THE COURT: You are going to have to listen to it because I consider this a very vulgar, rotten human being.

MR. LUCERO: The Court is indicting the whole Mexican group.

THE COURT: When they are 10 or 12 years of age,

going out and having intercourse with anybody without any moral training—they don't even understand the Ten Commandments. That's all. Apparently, they don't want to.

So if you want to act like that, the County has a system of taking care of them. They don't care about that. They have no personal self-respect.

MR. LUCERO: The Court ought to look at this youngster and deal with this youngster's case.

THE COURT: All right. That's what I am going to do. The family should be able to control this boy and the young girl.

MR. LUCERO: What appalls me is that the Court is saying that Hitler was right in genocide.

THE COURT: What are we going to do with the mad dogs of our society? Either we have to kill them or send them to an institution or place them out of the hands of good people because that's the theory—one of the theories of punishment is if they get to the position that they want to act like mad dogs, then, we have to separate them from our society.

Well, I will go along with the recommendation. You will learn in time or else you will have to pay for the penalty with the law because the law grinds slowly but exceedingly well. If you are going to be a law violator—you have to make up your mind whether you are going to observe the law or not. If you can't observe the law, then, you have to be put away.

Said minor will be adjudged a ward of the Juvenile Court in and for the County of Santa Clara, that the welfare of the minor requires that his physical custody be taken from his parents, said minor be committed to the care, custody and control of the relative home placement, with approval of placement in the home of his grandmother. . . .

Now, when you get down there with your grandmother, you have to pay attention to her because she is going to act as your parent. Mind her. After school also stay home and keep out of trouble. Do better in school.

It might be a good idea to read the Ten Commandments to find out what life is all about and what duties the Supreme Being imposes on every one of us to act like ordinary human beings and not like a pig.

All right. That's all.

STATE OF CALIFORNIA   )
) ss.
COUNTY OF SANTA CLARA)

I, SUSAN K. STRAHM, do hereby certify that the

foregoing is a full, true and correct transcript of the proceedings had in the within-entitled action taken on the 2nd day of September, 1969; that it is a full, true and correct transcript of the evidence offered and received, instructions, acts and statements of the Court, also all objections and exceptions of counsel, and all matters to which the same relate; that I reported the same in stenotype, being the qualified and action Official Court Reporter of the Superior Court of the State of California, in and for the County of Santa Clara, appointed to said Court, and thereafter had the same transcribed into typewriting as herein appears.

Dated: This 29th day of September, 1969.

(signed) Susan K. Strahm
SUSAN K. STRAHM, C.S.R.

USEFUL RESOURCES

ADAMS, I. *The poverty wall.* Toronto: McClelland and Stewart, 1970.
Combines basic hard data about low-income Canadians with casebook stories about specific individuals.

AMERICAN SOCIOLOGICAL ASSOCIATION. *The incidence and effects of poverty in the U.S.* New York: Allyn and Bacon, 1970.
Treats key issues regarding poverty from a sociological perspective.

DURFEE, D. (Ed.) *Poverty in an affluent society.* Englewood Cliffs, N. J.: Prentice Hall, 1970.
A collection of articles examining poverty in the United States. It includes an excellent bibliography of novels, reports, and films.

KATZ, I., & GURIN, P. (Ed.) *Race and the social sciences.* New York: Basic Books.

JONES, R. L. *Black psychology.* New York: Harper & Row, 1972.

LEACOCK, E. (Ed.) The culture of poverty: A critique. New York: Simon and Schuster, 1970.

REID, T. E. *Canada's poor: Are they always to be with us?* Toronto: Holt, Rinehart and Winston of Canada, 1972.
". . . attempts to fill the gap with its exploration of the meaning of poverty—its causes, the problems faced by the poor, and possible solutions to this spectre that continues to haunt us."

The bibliography demonstrates "that though the books on poverty in Canada do not fill shelf after shelf in the library they nevertheless provide a lot of basic information on the subject. We can, if we want, find out about poverty as it exists in the Maritimes instead of the Appalachians, in Cabbagetown rather than Harlem, in Norway House, Manitoba instead of in Navajo villages in New Mexico."

RILEY, M. W., & A. FONER. *Aging and society*. New York: Russell Sage Foundation, 1968.

Aging and Society summarizes the results of recent social science research on middle-aged and older people and interprets this knowledge in terms of sociological theory and professional practice. Its three volumes are addressed to social scientists and teachers engaged in research and education on the aging process and to practitioners concerned with prevention and treatment of the problems associated with aging. Research findings on this topic, hitherto widely scattered, are summarized in Volume One; their implications for the practicing professions are set forth in Volume Two, and for sociological understanding in Volume Three. The aim is to stimulate both the application of existing knowledge and the development of new knowledge through further research.

A truly monumental effort toward integration and interpretation of the implications of what we know about aging in our society. A must for any serious student of aging. *It will provide much of the basic data which you need for your term papers in this area.*

SCHLESINGER, B. *Poverty in Canada and in the United States*. Toronto: University of Toronto Press, 1966.

Provides extensive reference material.

SHEFFE, NORMAN. *Issues for the seventies: Poverty*. Toronto: McGraw-Hill Co. of Canada, 1970.

A collection of articles examining poverty in Canada with some suggestions toward remedies, including a sympathetic discussion of the possibility of a guaranteed annual income.

VALENTINE, CHARLES A. *Culture and poverty: Critique and counterproposals*. Chicago: University of Chicago Press, 1968.

SENNETT, R., & COBB, J. *The hidden injuries of class*. New York: Random House, 1972.

"In this intrepid, ground-breaking book, Richard Sennett and Jonathan Cobb uncover and define a new form of class conflict in America—an internal conflict in the heart and mind of the blue-collar worker who measures his own value against those lives and occupations to which our society gives a special premium."

CHAPTER 6
ON AGGRESSION

PROVOCATIONS

If animals are inadequately or abnormally socialized, aggressive behavior becomes distorted and exaggerated. Animals that are correctly socialized in normal habitats, or in richly stimulating artificial ones, show moderate amounts of aggression, and only in certain circumstances. . . . Under normal conditions, aggression plays little part in other aspects of primate social life. The idea that the function of maleness is to be overbearingly aggressive, to fight constantly and to be dominant makes little evolutionary sense.

David Pilbeam

Can Education End Aggression?

Niko Tinbergen

The body count [in Vietnam] is the perfect symbol of America's descent into evil. . . . the amount of killing becomes the total measure of achievement.

Robert Jay Lifton

WHAT DO YOU THINK?

30 VIOLENCE DEPENDS ON YOUR POINT OF VIEW

WILLIAM C. CORNING

Of all exponential curves, that referring to progress in destructive power is the most spectacular and the best known.

Arthur Koestler

• Think about it

It seems that violence is increasing in North America. We see marked increases in crimes, riots, and senseless assaults and find these real-life happenings more and more intolerable. Curiously enough, we seem to be fascinated by it too, as evidenced by the popularity of ultra-violent films. We can attempt to escape the threat of real-life violence by moving to the suburbs or by renting apartments in security-tight buildings, but violence is still there—on television, in the movies, and in the newspapers. Our frustration over the apparent rise in violence forces us to adopt some conclusions about its causes and to effect programs and research efforts aimed at prevention.

COMMENT: ON "GOOD" AND "BAD" AGGRESSION

In a war, each side typically labels the other side as the aggressor and calls many of the latter's violent acts atrocities. The definition of the winner usually prevails. . . . Exuberant football crowds or fraternal conventions frequently produce considerable property damage yet are rarely condemned. The violence of the poor against each other is substantially ignored until it spills out into the communities of the more comfortable. . . . Generally, American society tends to applaud violence conducted in approved channels, while condemning as "violent" lesser actions which are not supportive of existing social and political arrangements.

JEROME SKOLNICK

How we view violence and aggression may, to some extent, depend upon our position in society. We could assume that the riots in ghettos and on campuses, the crime in the streets, and the activities of various "guerilla" groups are due to socioeconomic conditions and accordingly work for change in the environment, i.e., in the political structure, in social programs, in housing, in education, and so on. Such an assumption requires the eventual commitment of tremendous amounts of government funds, funds that are derived, of course, from taxes. Removal of the deprivation and frustration will remove the causes of violence, which as Rap Brown put it, ". . . is as American as cherry pie." The environmentalist position also points to models for violence which also must be dealt with. Such models are said to exist in the operations of the police, in comic books, in the behavior of parents, and in movies. On a larger scale, we support institutionalized (and legal) violence—war—and provide the child with flags, toy guns, John Wayne movies, and the possibility of heroism, glory, and medals of honor. Changing the institutions and the models and even our politics is difficult because it means giving up things we have come to like and depend upon: the lucrative defense contract job, the home in a white, middle-class suburb, the neighborhood school, the exclusive clubs—the "silent majority" scene.

A way out is to view aggression and violence in naturalistic terms, to assume it is an endogenous drive as inevitable as food-seeking and sex. From an economic point of view, this removes the necessity of instituting large-scale alterations in our society's structure. After all, what good would it do when underneath the surface there is a biological stink. Adoption of this point of view would require the more altruistic to develop ways in which those who have a propensity for violence may vent their drives—sports, for example. At the other extreme, we could adopt legal means to cleanse the population of these biologically maladaptive types either by institutionalizing them, "ghettoizing" them, and/or fostering a sort of economic genocide.

The latter view is gaining in popularity these days, perhaps as a rationalization for objecting to the rising costs of government and perhaps as a result of the frustration over the ineffectiveness of many social programs. A picture of man as a primeval beast wearing the thin veneer of civilization is supplemented by recent findings that suggest (but do not prove) that some manlike apes may have been killers, that a particular chromosomal aberration may predispose man to criminal acts, and by the entertaining writings of zoologists (Desmond Morris's *Naked Ape*), playwrights *(The Bad Seed)*, and novelists *(A Clockwork Orange)*. The man who appears to gather the most attention and who stimulates the most acrimony is Konrad Lorenz, whose books *(On Aggression* and *The Evolution and Modification of Behavior)* have had a large impact. Lorenz assumes that aggression is an innate drive and like other drives in his conceptualization, it strives for discharge. Since it is instinctive, its origins and characteristics can be studied in animals where we can readily see instincts in operation. Man is a product of evolution, and many of the conclusions which Lorenz arrives at are derived from animal analogies. Unlike many animals, however, man has not developed a system of checks and balances to control his aggressive impulses. This deficiency "accounts for" his carrying of an aggressive act to its ultimate conclusion—killing. This view of the innate depravity and moral ineptitude of man was also expressed by Robert Ardrey in *African Genesis*. Ardrey's argument is based on the findings that

one of the earliest manlike apes, Australopithecus, was a tool-user and may have used a certain bone to smash in the heads of other apes. Since an early ape may have been a killer, it is therefore safe to conclude that we have a killer instinct. These views are not new—Freud at one time had postulated a "death instinct" (Thanatos) which had the purpose of lessening stimulation and in its ultimate form it meant a return of life to the inorganic world. The self-destructive aspects of this instinct could be turned outward, an act that actually aided survival of a people since they were no longer *self* destructive. Thus, war was seen as a means for surviving.

All the above reflect a social Darwinistic influence where man's behavior is explained away by attributing events and catastrophes to nature. These are facile attributions and as consumers, academically, politically, and morally, we should develop a most cautious attitude about the messages:

> Militant enthusiasm, in one particular respect, is dangerously akin to the triumph ceremony of geese and to analogous instinctive behavior patterns of other animals.   Konrad Lorenz

> . . . when one contemplates the streak of insanity running through human history, it appears highly probable that *homo sapiens* is a biological freak, the result of some remarkable mistake in the evolutionary process.   Arthur Koestler

> The rise of the human neocortex is the only example of evolution providing a species with an organ which it does not know how to use.   Arthur Koestler

> I am alone in the African street, lost, afraid, and without allies. I understand nothing. Yet this is the street where I was born. I too once delighted in massacre, slavery, castration, and cannibalism, and my conscience told me that these things were right. . . . What prevents me today? Nothing prevents me, excepting only the wisdom of my civilization and the conditioning it has brought to my instincts in my life time.   Robert Ardrey

31 ON WAR AND PEACE IN ANIMALS AND MAN*

N. TINBERGEN

I am an ethologist, a zoologist studying animal behavior. What gives a student of animal behavior the temerity to speak about problems of human behavior? Of course the history of medicine provides the answer. We all know that medical research uses animals on a large scale. This makes sense because animals, particularly vertebrates, are, in spite of all differences, so similar to us; they are our blood relations, however distant.

But this use of zoological research for a better understanding of ourselves is, to most people, acceptable only when we have to do with those bodily functions that we look upon as parts of our physiological machinery—the functions, for instance, of our kidneys, our liver, our hormone-producing glands. The majority of people bridle as soon as it is even suggested that studies of animal behavior could be useful for an understanding, let alone for the control, of our own behavior. They do not want to have their own behavior subjected to scientific scrutiny; they certainly resent being compared with animals, and these rejecting attitudes are both deep-rooted and of complex origin.

But now we are witnessing a turn in this tide of human thought. On the one hand the resistances are weakening, and on the other, a positive awareness is growing of the potentialities of a biology of behavior. This has become quite clear from the great interest aroused by several recent books that are trying, by comparative studies of animals and man, to trace what we could call "the animal roots of human behavior." As examples I select Konrad Lorenz's book *On Aggression* and *The Naked Ape* by Desmond Morris. Both books were best sellers

*Abridged from N. Tinbergen, On war and peace in animals and man. *Science*, June 28, 1968, **160**, 1411–1418. Copyright 1968 by the American Association for the Advancement of Science.

from the start. We ethologists are naturally delighted by this sign of rapid growth of interest in our science (even though the growing pains are at times a little hard to endure). But at the same time we are apprehensive, or at least I am.

We are delighted because, from the enormous sales of these and other such books, it is evident that the mental block against self-scrutiny is weakening—that there are masses of people who, so to speak, want to be shaken up.

But I am apprehensive because these books, each admirable in its own way, are being misread. Very few readers give the authors the benefit of the doubt. Far too many either accept uncritically all that the authors say, or (equally uncritically) reject it all. I believe that this is because both Lorenz and Morris emphasize our knowledge rather than our ignorance (and, in addition, present as knowledge a set of statements which are after all no more than likely guesses). In themselves brilliant, these books could stiffen, at a new level, the attitude of certainty, while what we need is a sense of doubt and wonder, and an urge to investigate, to inquire.

POTENTIAL USEFULNESS OF ETHOLOGICAL STUDIES

Now, in a way, I am going to be just as assertive as Lorenz and Morris, but what I am going to stress is how much we do not know. I shall argue that we shall have to make a major research effort. I am of course fully aware of the fact that much research is already being devoted to problems of human, and even of animal, behavior. I know, for instance, that anthropologists, psychologists, psychiatrists, and others are approaching these problems from many angles. But I shall try to show that the research effort has so far made insufficient use of the potential of ethology.

I feel that I can cooperate best by discussing what it is in ethology that could be of use to the other behavioral sciences. What we ethologists do not want, what we consider definitely wrong, is uncritical application of our results to man. Instead, I myself at least feel that it is our method of approach, our rationale, that we can offer, and also a little simple common sense, and discipline.

The potential usefulness of ethology lies in the fact that, unlike other sciences of behavior, it applies the method or "approach" of biology to the phenomenon behavior. It has developed a set of concepts and terms that allow us to ask:

1 In what ways does this phenomenon (behavior) influence the survival, the success of the animal?

2 What makes behavior happen at any given moment? How does its "machinery" work?

3 How does the behavior machinery develop as the individual grows up?

4 How have the behavior systems of each species evolved until they became what they are now?

The first question, that of survival value, has to do with the effects of behavior; the other three are, each on a different time scale, concerned with its causes.

These four questions are, as many of my fellow biologists will recognize, the major questions that biology has been pursuing for a long time. What ethology is doing could be simply described by saying that, just as biology investigates the functioning of the organs responsible for digestion, respiration, circulation, and so forth, so ethology begins now to do the same with respect to behavior; it investigates the functioning of organs responsible for movement.

I have to make clear that in my opinion it is the comprehensive, integrated attack on all four problems that characterizes ethology. I shall try to show that to ignore the questions of survival value and evolution—as, for instance, most psycholo-

gists do—is not only shortsighted but makes it impossible to arrive at an understanding of behavioral problems. Here ethology can make, in fact is already making, positive contributions.

● How could knowledge of evolution, of selection pressures, and adaptive mechanisms, help the behavioral scientist in his experiments? See Breland and Breland (p. 244).

Having stated my case for animal ethology as an essential part of the science of behavior, I will now have to sketch how this could be done. For this I shall have to consider one concrete example, and I select aggression, the most directly lethal of our behaviors. And, for reasons that will become clear, I shall also make a short excursion into problems of education.

Let me first try to define what I mean by aggression. We all understand the term in a vague, general way, but it is, after all, no more than a catchword. In terms of actual behavior, aggression involves approaching an opponent, and, when within reach, pushing him away, inflicting damage of some kind, or at least forcing stimuli upon him that subdue him. In this description the effect is already implicit: such behavior tends to remove the opponent, or at least to make him change his behavior in such a way that he no longer interferes with the attacker. The methods of attack differ from one species to another, and so do the weapons that are used, the structures that contribute to the effect.

Since I am concentrating on men fighting men, I shall confine myself to intraspecific fighting, and ignore, for instance, fighting between predators and prey. Intraspecific fighting is very common among animals. Many of them fight in two different contexts, which we can call "offensive" and "defensive." Defensive fighting is often shown as a last resort by an animal that, instead of attacking, has been fleeing from an attacker. If it is cornered, it may suddenly turn round upon its enemy and "fight with the courage of despair."

Of the four questions I mentioned before, I shall consider that of the survival value first. Here comparison faces us right at the start with a striking paradox. On the one hand, man is akin to many species of animals in that he fights his own species. But on the other hand he is, among the thousands of species that fight, the only one in which fighting is disruptive.

In animals, intraspecific fighting is usually of distinctive advantage. In addition, all species manage as a rule to settle their disputes without killing one another; in fact, even bloodshed is rare. Man is the only species that is a mass murderer, the only misfit in his own society.

How do animals in their intraspecific disputes avoid bloodshed?

THE IMPORTANCE OF "FEAR"

The clue to this problem is to recognize the simple fact that aggression in animals rarely occurs in pure form; it is only one of two components of an adaptive system. This is most clearly seen in territorial behavior, although it is also true of most other types of hostile behavior. Members of territorial species divide, among themselves, the available living space and opportunities by each individual defending its home range against competitors. Now in this system of parceling our living space, avoidance plays as important a part as attack. Put very briefly, animals of territorial species, once they have settled on a territory, attack intruders, but an animal that is still searching for a suitable territory or finds itself outside its home range withdraws when it meets with an already established owner. In terms of function, once you have taken possession of a territory, it pays to drive off competitors; but when you are still looking for a territory (or meet your neighbor at your common boundary), your chances of success are improved by avoiding such established owners. The ruthless fighter who "knows no fear" does not get very far. For an understanding of what follows, this fact, that hostile clashes are con-

trolled by what we could call the "attack-avoidance system," is essential.

When neighboring territory owners meet near their common boundary, both attack behavior and withdrawal behavior are elicited in both animals; each of the two is in a state of motivational conflict. We know a great deal about the variety of movements that appear when these two conflicting, incompatible behaviors are elicited. Many of these expressions of a motivational conflict have, in the course of evolution, acquired signal functions; in colloquial language, they signal "Keep out!" We deduce this from the fact that opponents respond to them in an appropriate way: instead of proceeding to intrude, which would require the use of force, trespassers withdraw, and neighbors are contained by each other. This is how such animals have managed to have all the advantages of their hostile behavior without the disadvantages: they divide their living space in a bloodless way by using as distance-keeping devices these conflict movements ("threat") rather than actual fighting.

GROUP TERRITORIES

In order to see our wars in their correct biological perspective one more comparison with animals is useful. So far I have discussed animal species that defend individual or at best pair territories. But there are also animals which possess and defend territories belonging to a group, or a clan.

Now it is an essential aspect of group territorialism that the members of a group unite when in hostile confrontation with another group that approaches, or crosses into their feeding territory. The uniting and the aggression are equally important. It is essential to realize that group territorialism does not exclude hostile relations on lower levels when the group is on its own. For instance, within a group there is often a peck order. And within the group there may be individual or pair territories. But frictions due to these relationships fade away during a clash between groups. This temporary elimination is done by means of so-called appeasement and reassurance signals. They indicate "I am a friend," and so diminish the risk that, in the general flare-up of anger, any animal "takes it out" on a fellow member of the same group. Clans meet clans as units, and each individual in an intergroup clash, while united with its fellow-members, is (as in interindividual clashes) torn between attack and withdrawal, and postures and shouts rather than attacks.

Ethologists tend to believe that we still carry with us a number of behavioral characteristics of our animal ancestors, which cannot be eliminated by different ways of upbringing, and that our group territorialism is one of those ancestral characters. I shall discuss the problem of the modifiability of our behavior later, but it is useful to point out here that even if our behavior were much more modifiable than Lorenz maintains, our cultural evolution, which resulted in the parceling-out of our living space on lines of tribal, national, and now even "bloc" areas, would, if anything, have tended to enhance group territorialism.

GROUP TERRITORIALISM IN MAN?

I put so much emphasis on this issue of group territorialism because most writers who have tried to apply ethology to man have done this in the wrong way. They have made the mistake, to which I objected before, of uncritically extrapolating the results of animal studies to man. They try to explain man's behavior by using facts that are valid only of some of the animals we studied. And, as ethologists keep stressing, no two species behave alike. Therefore, instead of taking this easy way out, we ought to study man in his own right. And I repeat that the message of the ethologists is that the methods, rather than the results, of ethology should be used for such a study.

Now, the notion of territory was developed by zoologists (to be precise, by ornithologists), and because individual and pair territories are found in so many more species than group territories (which

are particularly rare among birds) most animal studies were concerned with such individual and pair territories. Now such low-level territories do occur in man, as does another form of hostile behavior, the peck order. But the problems created by such low-level frictions are not serious; they can, within a community, be kept in check by the apparatus of law and order; peace within national boundaries can be enforced. In order to understand what makes us go to war, we have to recognize that man behaves very much like a group-territorial species. We too unite in the face of an outside danger to the group; we "forget our differences." We too have threat gestures, for instance, angry facial expressions. And all of us use reassurance and appeasement signals, such as a friendly smile. And (unlike speech) these are universally understood; they are cross-cultural; they are species-specific. And, incidentally, even within a group sharing a common language, they are often more reliable guides to a man's intentions than speech, for speech (as we know now) rarely reflects our true motives, but our facial expressions often "give us away."

If I may digress for a moment: it is humiliating to us ethologists that many nonscientists, particularly novelists and actors, intuitively understand our sign language much better than we scientists ourselves do. Worse, there is a category of human beings who understand intuitively more about the causation of our aggressive behavior: the great demagogues. They have applied this knowledge in order to control our behavior in the most clever ways, and often for the most evil purposes. For instance, Hitler (who had modern mass communication at his disposal, which allowed him to inflame a whole nation) played on both fighting tendencies. The "defensive" fighting was whipped up by his passionate statements about "living space," "encirclement," Jewry, and Freemasonry as threatening powers which made the Germans feel "cornered." The "attack fighting" was similarly set ablaze by playing the myth of the Herrenvolk. We must make sure that mankind has learned its lesson and will never forget how disastrous the joint effects have been—if only one of the major nations were led now by a man like Hitler, life on earth would be wiped out.

I have argued my case for concentrating on studies of group territoriality rather than on other types of aggression. I must now return, in this context, to the problem of man the mass murderer. Why don't we settle even our international disputes by the relatively harmless, animal method of threat? Why have we become unhinged so that so often our attack erupts without being kept in check by fear? It is not that we have no fear, nor that we have no other inhibitions against killing. This problem has to be considered first of all in the general context of the consequences of man having embarked on a new type of evolution.

COMMENT: ANIMALS AND MAN: DIVERGENT BEHAVIOR

Tinbergen favors the hypothesis "that man still carries with him the animal heritage of group territoriality." This seems to him most likely because "As a social, hunting primate, man must originally have been organized on the principle of group territories." Is it not strange that, if man still carries with him the animal heritage of group territoriality, his closest living relatives, the great apes (gorilla, chimpanzee, and orangutan), do not exhibit the slightest evidences of such territoriality? How does Tinbergen reconcile this fact with his preferred hypothesis?

As for the social, hunting primate man being organized on "the principle of group territories," this possibly may have been the case in some prehistoric societies, but it is most unlikely to have been so, for such societies were very small in numbers and tended to remain geographically isolated from other groups for considerable periods of time, during which there would have been no pressure whatever to organize into territorial groups. Among hunting peoples still living today, such as the Bushman of South Africa, the Pygmies of the Ituri Forest, the Eskimo of the Arctic Circle, and others, there is absolutely no sense of territoriality. As one would expect, some peoples are territorial, some only indifferently so, and others not at all. What has happened to "the animal heritage" of those peoples who are nonterritorial? "In order to understand what makes us go to war," writes Tinbergen, "we have to recognize that man behaves very much like a group-territorial species." Indeed, he does, but the group territorialism he exhibits is not due, I suggest, to genetics but to frenetics, to tribalism culturally closely identified with a particular territory.

I have been unable to find in Tinbergen's article the evidence for that "internal urge to fight" in man which he seems to accept as a fact. Education may find it very difficult if not impossible, according to Tinbergen, to eliminate this "internal urge to fight." How has it come about then, that the Pueblo Indians, the Eskimo, the Bushman, the Ifaluk, the Australian aborigines, the Pygmies, and many other peoples have managed to avoid this alleged "internal urge to fight"? By education, gene loss, or what? May it not be that "the urge to fight" is an acquired form of behavior? That anyone can *learn* to fight or not to fight? That the urge may become internalized through learning, that it is not innate?

When Tinbergen speaks of scientists sublimating their "aggression into an all-out attack on the enemy within," we are, indeed, in the land of Topsy-Turvydom. Is the scientist's consuming curiosity to be equated with "aggression"? Are his investigations to be bracketed with "an all-out attack"? And is "the enemy within" to be identified with an innate "urge to fight"? "The question is," said Alice, "whether you *can* make words mean so many different things."

ASHLEY MONTAGU

CULTURAL EVOLUTION

Man has the ability, unparalleled in scale in the animal kingdom, of passing on his experiences from one generation to the next. By this accumulative and exponentially growing process, which we call cultural evolution, he has been able to change his environment progressively out of all recognition. And this includes the social environment. This new type of evolution proceeds at an incomparably faster pace than genetic evolution. Genetically we have not evolved very strikingly since Cro-Magnon man, but culturally we have changed beyond recognition, and are changing at an ever-increasing rate. It is of course true that we are highly adjustable individually, and so could hope to keep pace with these changes. But I am not alone in believing that this behavioral adjustability, like all types of modifiability, has its limits. These limits are imposed upon us by our hereditary constitution, a constitution which can only change with the far slower speed of genetic evolution. There are good grounds for the conclusion that man's limited behavioral adjustability has been outpaced by the culturally determined changes in his social environment, and that this is why man is now a misfit in his own society.

● Are we misfits—has our cultural creation turned back on us or are we slowly changing the culture to fit our biology and psychology?

We can now, at last, return to the problem of war, of uninhibited mass killing. It seems quite clear that our cultural evolution is at the root of the trouble. It is our cultural evolution that has caused the population explosion. In a nutshell, medical science, aiming at the reduction of suffering, has, in doing so, prolonged life for many individuals as well—prolonged it to well beyond the point at which they produce offspring. Unlike the situation in any wild species, recruitment to the human population consistently surpasses losses through mortality. Agricultural and technical know-how have enabled us to grow food and to exploit other natural resources to such an extent that we can still feed (though only just) the enormous numbers of human beings on our crowded planet. The result is that we now live at a far higher density than that in which genetic evolution has molded our species. This, together with long-distance communication, leads to far more frequent, in fact to continuous, intergroup contacts, and so to continuous external

provocation of aggression. Yet this alone would not explain our increased tendency to kill each other; it would merely lead to continuous threat behavior.

The upsetting of the balance between aggression and fear (and this is what causes war) is due to at least three other consequences of cultural evolution. It is an old cultural phenomenon that warriors are both brainwashed and bullied into all-out fighting. They are brainwashed into believing that fleeing—originally, as we have seen, an adaptive type of behavior—is despicable, "cowardly." This seems to me due to the fact that man, accepting that in moral issues death might be preferable to fleeing, has falsely applied the moral concept of "cowardice" to matters of mere practical importance—to the dividing of living space. The fact that our soldiers are also bullied into all-out fighting (by penalizing fleeing in battle) is too well known to deserve elaboration.

Another cultural excess is our ability to make and use killing tools, especially long-range weapons. These make killing easy, not only because a spear or a club inflicts, with the same effort, so much more damage than a fist, but also, and mainly, because the use of long-range weapons prevents the victim from reaching his attacker with his appeasement, reassurance, and distress signals. Very few aircrews who are willing, indeed eager, to drop their bombs "on target" would be willing to strangle, stab, or burn children (or, for that matter, adults) with their own hands; they would stop short of killing, in response to the appeasement and distress signals of their opponents.

● Was this true at My Lai?

These three factors alone would be sufficient to explain how we have become such unhinged killers. But I have to stress once more that all this, however convincing it may seem, must still be studied more thoroughly.

There is a frightening, and ironical paradox in this conclusion: that the human brain, the finest life-preserving device created by evolution, has made our species so successful in mastering the outside world that it suddenly finds itself taken off guard. One could say that our cortex and our brainstem (our "reason" and our "instincts") are at loggerheads. Together they have created a new social environment in which, rather than ensuring our survival, they are about to do the opposite. The brain finds itself seriously threatened by an enemy of its own making. It is its own enemy. We simply have to understand this enemy.

THE DEVELOPMENT OF BEHAVIOR

I must now leave the question of the moment-to-moment control of fighting, and, looking further back in time, turn to the development of aggressive behavior in the growing individual. Again we will start from the human problem. This, in the present context, is whether it is within our power to control development in such a way that we reduce or eliminate fighting among adults. Can or cannot education in the widest sense produce nonaggressive men?

. . . interactions with the environment can indeed occur at early stages. These interactions may concern small components of the total machinery of a fully functional behavior pattern, and many of them cannot possibly be called learning. But they are interactions with the environment, and must be taken into account if we follow in the footsteps of the experimental embryologists, and extend our field of interest to the entire sequence of events which lead from the blueprints contained in the zygote to the fully functioning, behaving animal. We simply have to do this if we want an answer to the question to what extent the development of behavior can be influenced from the outside.

When we follow this procedure the rigid distinction between "innate" or unmodifiable and "acquired" or modifiable behavior patterns becomes far less sharp. This is owing to the discovery, on the one hand, that "innate" patterns may contain elements that at an early stage developed in interaction with the environment, and, on the other

hand, that learning is, from step to step, limited by internally imposed restrictions.

Without going into more detail, we can characterize the picture we begin to get of the development of behavior as a series, or rather a web, of events, starting with innate programing instructions contained in the zygote, which straightaway begin to interact with the environment; this interaction may be discontinuous, in that periods of predominantly internal development alternate with periods of interaction, or sensitive periods. The interaction is enhanced by active exploration; it is steered by selective *Sollwerte*[a] of great variety; and stage by stage this process ramifies; level upon level of ever-increasing complexity is being incorporated into the programing.

Apply what we have heard for a moment to playing children (I do not, of course, distinguish sharply between "play" and "learning"). At a certain age a child begins to use, say, building blocks.It will at first manipulate them in various ways, one at a time. Each way of manipulating acts as exploratory behavior: the child learns what a block looks, feels, tastes like, and so forth, and also how to put it down so that it stands stably.

Each of these stages "peters out" when the child knows what it wanted to find out. But as the development proceeds, a new level of exploration is added: the child discovers that it can put one block on top of the other; it constructs. The new discovery leads to repetition and variation, for each child develops, at some stage, a desire and a set of *Sollwerte* for such effects of construction, and acts out to the full this new level of exploratory behavior. In addition, already at this stage the *Sollwert* or ideal does not merely contain what the blocks do, but also what, for instance, the mother does; her approval, her shared enjoyment, is also of great importance. Just as an exploring animal, the child builds a kind of inverted pyramid of experience, built of layers, each set off by a new wave of exploration and each directed by new sets of *Sollwerte*, and so its development "snowballs." All these phases may well have more or less lim-

[a]Literally a "should-value" or an ideal (Ed.).

ited sensitive periods, which determine when the fullest effect can be obtained, and when the child is ready for the next step. More important still, if the opportunity for the next stage is offered either too early or too late, development may be damaged, including the development of motivational and emotional attitudes.

Of course gifted teachers of many generations have known all these things or some of them, but the glimpses of insight have not been fully and scientifically systematized. In human education, this would of course involve experimentation. This need not worry us too much, because in our search for better educational procedures we are in effect experimenting on our children all the time. Also, children are fortunately incredibly resilient, and most grow up into pretty viable adults in spite of our fumbling educational efforts. Yet there is, of course, a limit to what we will allow ourselves, and this, I should like to emphasize, is where animal studies may well become even more important than they are already.

CAN EDUCATION END AGGRESSION?

Returning now to the development of animal and human aggression, I hope to have made at least several things clear: that behavior development is a very complex phenomenon indeed; that we have only begun to analyze it in animals; that with respect to man we are, if anything, behind in comparison with animal studies; and that I cannot do otherwise than repeat what I said in the beginning: we must make a major research effort. In this effort animal studies can help, but we are still very far from drawing very definite conclusions with regard to our question: To what extent shall we be able to render man less aggressive through manipulation of the environment, that is, by educational measures?

In such a situation personal opinions naturally vary a great deal. I do not hesitate to give as my personal opinion that Lorenz's book *On Aggression,* in spite of its assertiveness, in spite of factual mistakes, and in spite of the many possibilities

of misunderstandings that are due to the lack of a common language among students of behavior —that this work must be taken more seriously as a positive contribution to our problem than many critics have done. Lorenz is, in my opinion, right in claiming that elimination, through education, of the internal urge to fight will turn out to be very difficult, if not impossible.

Everything I have said so far seems to me to allow for only one conclusion. Apart from doing our utmost to return to a reasonable population density, apart from stopping the progressive depletion and pollution of our habitat, we must pursue the biological study of animal behavior for clarifying problems of human behavior of such magnitude as that of our aggression, and of education.

But research takes a long time, and we must remember that there are experts who forecast worldwide famine 10 to 20 years from now; and that we have enough weapons to wipe out all human life on earth. Whatever the causation of our aggression, the simple fact is that for the time being we are saddled with it. This means that there is a crying need for a crash program, for finding ways and means for keeping our intergroup aggression in check. This is of course in practice infinitely more difficult than controlling our intranational frictions; we have as yet not got a truly international police force. But there is hope for avoiding all-out war because, for the first time in history, we are afraid of killing ourselves by the lethal radiation effects even of bombs that we could drop in the enemy's territory. Our politicians know this. And as long as there is this hope, there is every reason to try and learn what we can from animal studies. Here again they can be of help. We have already seen that animal opponents meeting in a hostile clash avoid bloodshed by using the expressions of their motivational conflicts as intimidating signals. Ethologists have studied such conflict movements in some detail, and have found that they are of a variety of types. The most instructive of these is the redirected attack; instead of attacking the provoking, yet dreaded, opponent, animals often attack something else, often even an inanimate object. We ourselves bang the table with our fists. Redirection includes something like sublimation, a term attaching a value judgment to the redirection. As a species with group territories, humans, like hyenas, unite when meeting a common enemy. We do already sublimate our group aggression.

I have come full circle. For both the long-term and the short-term remedies at least we scientists will have to sublimate our aggression into an all-out attack on the enemy within. For this the enemy must be recognized for what it is: our unknown selves, or, deeper down, our refusal to admit that man is, to himself, unknown.

I should like to conclude by saying a few words to my colleagues of the younger generation. Of course we all hope that, by muddling along until we have acquired better understanding, self-annihilation either by the "whimper of famine" or by the "bang of war" can be avoided. For this, we must on the one hand trust, on the other help (and urge) our politicians. But it is no use denying that the chances of designing the necessary preventive measures are small, let alone the chances of carrying them out. Even birth control still offers a major problem.

It is difficult for my generation to know how seriously you take the danger of mankind destroying his own species. But those who share the apprehension of my generation might perhaps, with us, derive strength from keeping alive the thought that has helped so many of us in the past when faced with the possibility of imminent death. Scientific research is one of the finest occupations of our mind. It is, with art and religion, one of the uniquely human ways of meeting nature, in fact, the most active way. If we are to succumb, and even if this were to be ultimately due to our own stupidity, we could still, so to speak, redeem our species. We could at least go down with some dignity, by using our brain for one of its supreme tasks, by exploring to the end.

The Dutch feel united in their fight against the sea. Scientists do attack their problems together. The space program—surely a mainly military effort—is an up-to-date example. I would not like to claim, as Lorenz does, that redirected attack exhausts the aggressive urge. We know from soccer matches and from animal work how aggressive behavior has two simultaneous, but opposite effects: a waning effect, and one of self-inflammation, of mass hysteria, such as recently seen in Cairo. Of these two the inflammatory effect often wins. But if aggression were used successfully as the motive force behind nonkilling and even useful activities, self-stimulation need not be a danger; in our short-term cure we are not aiming at the elimination of aggressiveness, but at "taking the sting out of it."

Of all sublimated activities, scientific research would seem to offer the best opportunities for deflecting and sublimating our aggression. And, once we recognize that it is the disrupted relation between our own behavior and our environment that forms our most deadly enemy, what could be better than uniting, at the front or behind the lines, in the scientific attack on our own behavioral problems?

I stress "behind the lines." The whole population should be made to feel that it participates in the struggle. This is why scientists will always have the duty to inform their fellowmen of what they are doing, of the relevance and the importance of their work. And this is not only a duty, it can give intense satisfaction.

32 THE <u>HUMAN</u> NATURE OF HUMAN NATURE*
LEON EISENBERG

What we choose to believe about the nature of man has social consequences. Those consequences should be weighed in assessing the belief we choose to hold, even provisionally, given the lack of compelling proof for any of the currently fashionable theories. In insisting on an assessment of potential outputs in addition to a critique of inputs, I do *not* suggest that we ignore scientific evidence when it does not suit our fond wishes. Any hope of building a better world must begin with a tough-minded appraisal of the facts that are to be had. The thrust of my argument is that there is no solid foundation to the theoretical extrapolation of the instinctivists, the ethologists, the behaviorists, *or* the psychoanalysts, despite the special pleading that often is so seductive to those eager for a "real science" of behavior. Further to the point, belief helps shape actuality because of the self-fulfilling character of social prophecy.

● *Note:* The self-fulfilling nature of our beliefs comes to our attention again. Skim through Selection 9 by Silberman and the comment by Kohl to remind yourself of this problem.

To believe that man's aggressiveness or territoriality is in the nature of the beast is to mistake some men for all men, contemporary society for all possible societies, and, by a remarkable transformation, to justify what is as what needs must be; social regression becomes a response to, rather than a cause of, human violence. Pessimism about man serves to maintain the status quo. It is a luxury for the affluent, a sop to the guilt of the politically inactive, a comfort to those who continue to enjoy

*Abridged from L. Eisenberg, The <u>human</u> nature of human nature. *Science*, April 14, 1972, **176**, 123–128. Copyright 1972 by the American Association for the Advancement of Science.

the amenities of privilege. Pessimism is too costly for the disenfranchised; they give way to it at the price of their salvation. No less clearly, the false "optimism" of the unsubstantiated claims made for behavioral engineering, claims that ignore biological variation and individual creativity, foreclose man's humanity.

Some readers may object to "politicizing" what should be a "scientific" discussion. My contention is that it is necessary to make overt what is latent in treatises on the "innate" nature of man. Consider, for example, Lorenz. Surely, those who have been charmed by his film of himself leading, like a mother goose, a brood of greylag geese about the farmyard will recoil from identifying his works as political. What is political about inborn schemata, innate releasing mechanisms, species-specific mating patterns, and the like? A great deal, as his own writings make clear, when such concepts, of dubious applicability to animal behavior itself, are transposed directly to man without attending to species differences and to phyletic levels. Lorenz found it possible to write, in 1940, that the effects of civilization on human beings parallel those of domestication in animals. In domesticated animals, he argued, degenerative mutations result in the loss of species-specific releaser mechanisms responding to innate schemata that govern mating patterns and that serve in nature to maintain the purity of the stock. Similar phenomena are said to be an inevitable by-product of civilization unless the state is vigilant.

The only resistance which mankind of healthy stock can offer . . . against being penetrated by symptoms of degeneracy is based on the existence of certain innate schemata. . . . Our species-specific sensitivity to the beauty and ugliness of members of our species is intimately connected with the symptoms of degeneration, caused by domestication, which threaten our race. . . . Usually, a man of high value is disgusted with special intensity by slight symptoms of degeneracy in men of the other race. . . . In certain instances, however, we find not only a lack of this selectivity . . . but even a reversal to being attracted by symptoms of degeneracy. . . . Decadent art provides many examples of such a change of signs. . . . The immensely high reproduction rate in the moral imbecile has long been established. . . . This phenomenon leads everywhere . . . to the fact that socially inferior human material is enabled . . . to penetrate and finally to annihilate the healthy nation. The selection for toughness, heroism, social utility . . . must be accomplished by some human institution if mankind, in default of selective factors, is not to be ruined by domestication-induced degeneracy. *The racial idea as the basis of our state has already accomplished much in this respect.* The most effective race-preserving measure is . . . the greatest support of the natural defenses. . . . We must—and should—rely on the healthy feelings of our Best and charge them with the selection which will determine the prosperity or the decay of our people . . . [italics added].

Thus, it would appear, science warrants society's erecting social prohibitions in order to replace the degenerated innate schemata for racial purity. Lorenz's "scientific" logic justified Nazi legal restrictions against intermarriage with non-Aryans. The wild extrapolations from domestication to civilization, from ritualized animal courtship patterns to human behavior, from species to races, are so gross and unscientific, the conclusions so redolent of concentration camps, that further commentary should be superfluous. Perhaps it is impolite to recall in 1972 what was written in 1940, but I, at least, find 1940 difficult to forget; indeed, I believe it should not be forgotten, lest we find ourselves in Orwell's *1984* for the very best of "scientific" reasons.

33 THE PROBLEM WITH PORKY PIG*
W. C. CORNING

Maybe Walt Disney was responsible for it. . . . I mean all those years of talking elephants and ducks and Porky Pig who never wore any pants. There they were, driving cars and living in houses, showing emotions, earning money, being dumb, kind, smart, and funny, and then we graduate to football, X-rated movies, and university courses. But there they are again . . . our animal friends . . . only now they have electrodes in their heads and fistulas in their tummies, and we are slipping them 200 volts, starving them, poking them, and sure enough we get their asses moving to prove they are just plain folks. . . . like you and me, Pat Nixon, and Captain Crunch. Our Walt Disney history and our envy of the fruit fly has led us to readily accept animal models in psychology as substitutes for man. Animal data are used to explain human psychology; many psychologists present lectures and write papers on human functions and talk about animal and human data interchangeably. Joyce Brothers, Robert Ardrey, and a parade of psychologists, psychiatrists, and advice-givers have at times relied heavily upon animal data in providing questions and answers about man's predicaments. Gone are the days filled with simple tales of Little Red Riding Hood and the dirty old wolf that eats grandmothers, faithful Sam who saved the family from fire in the nick of time, and Carl the Cobra who turned out to be an intelligent and safe and affectionate pet for a crippled nun.

Talking about animal data is an easy out, as is doing research on them. After our Walt Disney heritage, nobody questions the implicit assumption that the data are relevant. For over fourteen years I have received grant money for research on planarians, protozoans, cockroaches, horseshoe crabs, frogs, and scorpions and in each research

Abridged from W. C. Corning, *mindful men and infamous things*. To be published by Dickenson Publishing Co. Reprinted by permission of the author.

proposal I dramatically point out that the findings are perhaps applicable to understanding man. You have to be serious about this assumption, or at least keep a straight face when you try to explain to the naïve visitor that our psychology buildings smell of rat shit because our rodenticides are not working.

But down there in the laboratories are cages and cages filled with mice, rats, roaches, monkeys, cats, rabbits, pigeons, and anything else that is easily obtained, malleable, and willing to coexist. The visitor asks, "But do you really try to explain human behavior with all this animal research?" Good question. Vested interests win out—privately. I may admit that I don't know how to do anything else but to my visitor I reply, "Behavior is behaviour is behavior is behaviour and that is what I am, a scientist of behavior." Multicellular man came from single cellular protozoans, and all that continuity in evolution produced some amazing similarities between man and beast; and because all those beasties are simpler, it is therefore easier to work on them.

Any residual disbelief can be erased by adding that genetics, medicine, and Walt Disney would have gotten nowhere without the use of animals. Our visitor is convinced, but should he be?

We have perhaps confused zoology with psychology in North America, and for several reasons, adopting the animal has been an easy digression for psychologists. A straightforward justification for using animals would be the old Mount Everest routine—because they are there. Not bad. Understanding the universe we live in no matter what aspect of that universe we choose to study can be justified to a certain extent. Much of my biological research, for example, has been devoted to understanding how the horseshoe crab's nervous system regulates cardiac activity. There are some who are genuinely interested in how a particular animal *works,* an extension of that childhood curiosity that led to the disassembly of old clocks and the occasional earthworm. Other aspects of my research, although they involve flatworms, scorpions, and crabs, have a most curious purpose—that of trying to understand how the

brain works; and if pressed I would eventually admit that it is really human brain and behavior that interests me. So what am I doing with bugs and worms? Broadhurst (1963) provides the standard argument:

> Though human psychological make-up may be very much more complex than that of any animal, in terms of its potentialities and the amount of information stored, its uniqueness may not be due to some special quality but rather to this complexity itself. That is to say, the elements of the behaviour we display in our very complex civilized lives are—apart from speech—all present in lower animals *but in simpler form* (p. 20, italics mine).

I would argue that with respect to complex system properties, the study of "lowly" animals can tell us little: *Indeed, if we don't get down to business and devote our best resources to the amelioration and understanding of man's problems, there ain't gonna be nothin' left but them lowly animals.*

I don't mean to knock Dr. Broadhurst—his excellent book summarizes my views of a few years ago, and he is certainly aware of the primary reason for animals in our psychology buildings:

> But there is essentially only one basic scientific interest in the study of animal behaviour and that is to learn more about man himself. The pursuit of knowledge for its own sake is often spoken of but rarely practised in pure form (pp. 13–14).

We are so keen on making a man out of Porky Pig that we frequently ignore critical aspects of the animal's biology and behavior that are relevant to and interact with the process we are interested in. The Brelands, formerly students of Skinner, have probably made the most well-known statement on the subject of biological relevance in psychological experiments (Breland and Breland, 1961). "Shaping" (changing reponse frequencies and patterns) animals is a relatively easy task for the keen and patient experimenter. Go to any animal show and it becomes clear that a Ph.D. in psychology is not needed to accomplish some remarkable training feats. In the laboratory we make this task even easier by maintaining animals in surrealistic environments that really prevent them from doing anything else but what we want. Now the Brelands were interested in training a large variety of animals, and many of these were not the typical psychological subject. In the course of these endeavors they ". . . ventured further and further from the security of the Skinner box" and discovered that Porky Pig had some biological hang-ups. Porky was to pick up a large wooden coin and take it over to a piggy bank and deposit it in the slot. Training continued until the pig was capable of placing coins in the bank five consecutive times to obtain a reinforcement. Animals performed in this task for a few weeks, but then the acquired behavior began to get erratic—the animals would not deposit the coins but would begin to perform "pig-like" manipulations with the coin. They would pick it up, drop it, root it, and carry on this way even though they were receiving no reinforcement. Very hungry pigs continued to act "pig-like." The animal was imposing patterns of activity in the situation that were "nonreinforcing" with respect to the experimenter's definition of the situation. According to their observations of 38 species and something like 6000 animals, the Brelands conclude that behavioral modification techniques have limited value when they are applied independently of other sources of information. The pigs were engaging in behavior that was more associated with food-getting modes—they rooted the coins and became involved in patterns that were actually more complex than those demanded by the experimenters. Increasing their hunger did not "shape them up" but rather intensified the "pig-like" behavior. The organism can be viewed as having species-typical ways of dealing or coping with certain modes (food-getting) and while these modes can be modified (trained), the natural behavior may reemerge to interfere and perhaps override the acquired response. The Brelands called it "instinctive drift" but I really dislike the word "instinct" because of certain traditional connotations the word has had in the past. In any case, failure to take into account what the animal is "prepared" to do and what sorts of evolutionary predispositions are likely to be involved can blunt the significance of a behavioral study.

To summarize at this point, there are two problems associated with the use of animal models in explaining human psychology: First, the behavioral similarities may be superficial, and accordingly the mechanisms and controlling factors are quite different; second, our eagerness to see man in the animal leads us to ignore critical species factors that affect the behavior. I do not believe that I have overstated the case: rats "hoard," monkeys "love," cats are "neurotic," dogs "beg," etc. Suppose we see a dove avidly incubating an egg it has recently laid in its nest. It sits for a long period upon the egg, and when the squab hatches, it continues to show "devotion" and "self-sacrifice"—the mother is constantly around the squab and it regurgitates food from its crop sac so that the squab may eat. This is obviously a case of mother "love," and many are quick to draw comparisons between this behavior and that of humans. The problem of equating or comparing two different species solely on the basis of behavior is that analysis of the underlying mechanisms that produce the behavior show the obvious—doves are not men. Is the dove "aware" of the impending appearance of the squab? Why does it sit on the egg? According to Daniel Lehrman, the physiological changes associated with reproduction in the dove produced a "hot spot" on its rear quarters, an irritation that could be ameliorated by sitting on something cool—the egg. If a stone is substituted, the dove would incubate the stone, and if the "hot spot" is anesthetized, the dove ceases to sit. After hatching, the squab pecks wildly at its mother and when hitting the crop sac, elicits regurgitation. Continuing the cynical vein of experimentation, Lehrman discovered that release of the contents of the crop sac removed a peripheral source of irritation. Anesthetizing the sac results in a "mother" who ignores the squab. In the course of their short relationship, squab learns that pecking mom produces food and moms learns that the thing in the nest can produce temporary relief. Now it is true that the human female may also experience irritation as the breasts engorge with milk, and if for certain reasons breast feeding is not permitted, doctors administer drugs that "dry up" the breasts. This does not result in a cessation of affection for the newborn.

Let me give a more serious example of some fairly unsound but fashionable thinking about animals as models of man. It is, as David Pilbeam puts it, the "naked-ape syndrome." If we look around the world, we can see man's cruelty to man, exemplified by our keeping large percentages of populations on starvation diets, by the rising crime rates, by violence, by wars, by our materialistic bents, etc. As discussed in the introduction, there are two assumptions one can adopt to account for all this: you can assume that the depravity is due to social institutions, or the ill behavior can be attributed to man's "nature." Robert Ardrey wrote a popular book called *African Genesis,* in which he drew heavily upon the writings of certain ethologists and some findings by anthropologists, and suggested that man is an animal (there is no debate here) and in much of his behavior is driven by the same factors that are operative in other animals. Ardrey spends a great deal of effort trying to "prove" that somewhere in his ape history, man has a killer ancestor, thereby suggesting that we have evolved from killers and that we ourselves have a killing instinct. Territoriality, aggression, and other characteristics of animals can be studied in order to gain insight into why man behaves as he does. (Indeed, down the hall from me is a scientist who is getting monkeys drunk because the drunken monkey can be used as a model for alcoholic man.) Pilbeam points out why these conclusions can be erroneous. Using baboon studies as an example, he notes that it is true that under certain circumstances, there is a dominance hierarchy among male baboons of a group; that the members of a group remain the same and separated from other groups; that the dominant males get the first choice in sex, food, and other activities; and that the aggression reduces fighting within the group and establishes the best for those at the top. The evidence was derived, however, from animals kept in unusual circumstances. When baboons are studied in areas where there is not much tension produced by man and his contrivances, they acted differently. According to Pilbeam, the composition of group is

more flexible, aggression is uncommon, and male dominance hierarchies practically disappear. When attacked, the bigger and stronger males are up in the trees with the smaller females rather than fighting. Movements are directed by females in these normal troops of baboons. Keeping baboons in places where normal cover is lacking and where other tensions abound produces aggression and more sex-differences in behavior. In undisturbed troops, the role of individual members becomes more adaptive with respect to the survival of the group, and the behavior of various members is not dictated by positions on a pecking order and sexual behavior . . ." In one troop, an old male baboon with broken canines was the animal that most frequently completed successful matings, influenced troop movements and served as a focus for females and infants, even though he was far less aggressive than, and frequently lost fights with, a younger and more vigorous adult male." (Perhaps Ardrey might argue someday that we inherit a "dirty old man" instinct.) The disappearance of dominance in a different situation suggests strongly that it is not an inevitability, even in baboons, and that it is an environmentally induced state. The same holds true for man. Pilbeam refers to the caste system of Hindu society as an example of where dominance hierarchies are used by man, but he contrasts this system with that of the Bushmen of the Kalahari Desert, where cooperation and equal status are valued. In the "primitive tribes" that still exist, which presumably represent something about how ancient man, the hunter, lived, the innate depravity of man is difficult to discern. Cooperation and avoidance of aggression and violence seem to be more characteristic. Children have nonaggressive models to follow and the societies are organized to make best use of their environment without having to resort to aggression and the establishment of dominance hierarchies.

These arguments, it is hoped, will encourage a healthy skepticism with respect to the use of animal models to "explain" human behavior. After years of comparative research the best I can do is to state what man is not and confirm what most biologists have known for years—that evolution has produced a variety of means to achieve what look like similar end results. The superficial behavioral similarities have entranced many psychologists, but we should begin seriously examining the question of whether the continued generation of animal data is justified. It is the violence and aggression of man against man that is a problem; it is in the name of Christ, flag, country, "decency," "law and order," "justice," etc., that we engage in conflict—and I have yet to see a baboon wave a flag.

It is clear from the history of psychology that animal research has provided some ideas and findings that have been applied to man. For example, the various schedules of reinforcement were worked out with rats and pigeons. Beyond these initial demonstrations, can we justify the large number of investigators who continue to work with animals? Why not a more immediate application to the classrooms? Social problems? Why not more manpower devoted to research that has more direct application to man?

It is often argued that the animal model must be used because real-life situations cannot be controlled and the animal is simpler. Why not study complex man in complex circumstances? Will psychological principles only work when we have bizarre animals in surrealistic environments? Why not try out theories in actual situations? It would be most instructive to compare laboratory and naturalistic situations.

34 TELEVISION AND GROWING UP: THE IMPACT OF TELEVISED VIOLENCE*

FOREWORD

This report is the result of over two years of effort by a distinguished committee of behavioral scientists. Their task has been difficult. The impact of televised violence on the viewer, as a reading of the report will show, is embedded in a complicated set of related variables.

The conscientious effort by the committee to avoid an oversimplification of the problem has produced a document which may seem, at times too technical. However, I believe that this report and the five volumes of research reports, which serve as a basis for the committee conclusions, make a major contribution to an understanding of the role of television in influencing the social behavior of children and young people.

The conclusions reached by the committee are carefully worded and merit the serious attention of all persons and groups concerned about the effects of viewing television. As the committee notes, these conclusions are based on substantially more knowledge than was available when the committee began its deliberations. But the research still leaves many questions unanswered. Without detracting from the importance of its conclusions, the committee specifies some of these unanswered questions and urges that they be addressed in the future.

This report will undoubtedly be scrutinized carefully by people who will be looking for support for their own prior point of view. Individuals with strong convictions on either side of the question about the effects of televised violence may not be satisfied. What these individuals will fail to recognize is that this set of conclusions, for the first time in this field of inquiry, sets a solid and extensive base of evidence in an appropriate perspective. In that sense, the report and the research on which it is based represent a major contribution.

The committee is to be congratulated for the work it has done. The successful conclusion of the task is even more significant because of the explicit consensus among so broadly representative a group of scientists. I wish to commend the com-

*Abridged from *Television and growing up: The impact of televised violence*. Report to the Surgeon General, United States Public Health Service, from The Surgeon General's Scientific Advisory Committee on Television and Social Behavior. Washington, D.C.: U.S. Government Printing Office, 1972. Reprinted by permission.

mittee, the researchers, and the staff for a job well done.

Jesse L. Steinfeld, M.D.
Surgeon General

SUMMARY OF FINDINGS AND CONCLUSIONS

The work of this committee was initiated by a request from Senator John O. Pastore to Health, Education, and Welfare Secretary Robert H. Finch in which Senator Pastore said:

> I am exceedingly troubled by the lack of any definitive information which would help resolve the question of whether there is a causal connection between televised crime and violence and antisocial behavior by individuals, especially children. . . . I am respectfully requesting that you direct the Surgeon General to appoint a committee comprised of distinguished men and women from whatever professions and disciplines deemed appropriate to devise techniques and to conduct a study under his supervision using those techniques which will establish scientifically insofar as possible what harmful effects, if any, these programs have on children.

The question raised by this request has been this committee's central concern. However, the research program that was undertaken has attempted to place this question within a larger context. For this reason, the committee's title deliberately emphasizes more than the issue of televised violence and aggressiveness and more than the question of television's harmful effects during childhood and youth.

At the same time the committee was explicitly enjoined from drawing policy conclusions. Our task has been to state the present scientific knowledge about the effects of entertainment of television on children's behavior, in the hope that this knowledge may be of use to both citizens and officials concerned with policy.

The findings we will summarize represent the issues and questions treated in the body of the report. They derive primarily from the research conducted under this program but take account also of past research and other current research.

THE TELEVISION EXPERIENCE

It would be difficult to overstate the pervasiveness of television in the United States. Census data indicate that 96 percent of American homes have one or more television sets. The average home set is on more than six hours a day. Most adults report watching at least two hours daily. Most children also watch at least two hours daily. For most people, whatever their age, television viewing is a daily experience. Although not everyone watches every day, many watch for much longer than two hours.

Television viewing stands in sharp contrast to the theater, movies, and other entertainment presented outside the home in that it does not usually involve such exclusive or focused attention. Viewers of all ages regularly engage in a wide range of activities while the set is on.

The extent to which this discontinuity of attention alters what would be perceived and understood from television were attention undivided is a moot question. Young children before the age of six usually cannot successfully divide their attention. As a result, what they get from television is probably generally restricted to what is taken in while viewing with full attention and is perceived bereft of a larger context. As the child grows older, he becomes more able to follow at least the rough continuity of what is taking place on television while he is simultaneously doing other things.

The casual acceptance of viewing, however, does not equal indifference to television. By the first grade, a majority of boys and girls exhibit individual taste in program selection and preference for characters. Among younger children, situation comedies and cartoons are most popular. Sixth graders like family situation comedies and adventure programs. Tenth graders prefer adventure programs and music and variety programs. Children and adolescents are attracted to programs featuring characters their own age.

The propensity to view television changes as the individual goes through the major stages of maturation. Frequent viewing usually begins at about age three and remains relatively high until about age 12. Then viewing typically begins to decline, reaching its low point during the teen years. When young people marry and have families, the time they spend viewing tends to increase and then remain stable through the middle adult years. After middle age, when grown children leave home, it rises again.

Many questions about television are presently unanswerable. Three basic ones concern the future character of television, the influences and dynamics involved in the choosing of programs by individual viewers, and the underlying needs served by television that lead to its present extensive use.

It would appear that television, like other media, is progressing through a series of stages from intriguing novelty to accepted common-place to possible differentiation as a servant of varied tastes. New developments—UHF, public television, cable, cassettes, portable minisets—suggest that in the future the programming available may become increasingly varied and that the mass audience may become a diversity of smaller segments, each with its special interests. Newspapers, magazines, and radio provide examples of similar evolution.

Why people choose to view what they do, and why they view so much, remain open questions after 20 years of commercial broadcasting. From the various rating services it is easy to determine what audiences choose to view from among what is offered. The process by which choices are made, and the basic appeal that leads to persistent viewing at all ages, remain obscure.

VIOLENCE ON TELEVISION

Studies of media content show that violence is and has been a prominent component of all mass media in the United States. Television is no exception, and there can be no doubt that violence figures prominently in television entertainment. People are probably exposed to violence by television entertainment more than they are exposed by other media because they use television so much more.

In regard to dramatic entertainment on television, and with violence defined as "the overt ex-

pression of physical force against others or self, or the compelling of action against one's will on pain of being hurt or killed," an extensive analysis of content has found that:

The general prevalence of violence did not change markedly between 1967 and 1969. The rate of violent episodes remained constant at about eight per hour.

The nature of violence did change. Fatalities declined, and the proportion of leading characters engaged in violence or killing declined. The former dropped from 73 to 64 percent; the latter, from 19 to five percent. The consequence is that as many violent incidents occurred in 1969 as in 1967, but a smaller proportion of characters were involved, and the violence was far less lethal.

Violence increased from 1967 to 1969 in cartoons and in comedies, a category that included cartoons.

Cartoons were the most violent type of program in these years.

Another study concluded that in 1971 Saturday morning programming, which includes both cartoons and material prepared for adults, approximately three out of ten dramatic segments were "saturated" with violence and that 71 percent involved at least one instance of human violence with or without the use of weapons.

There is also evidence that years high in violence also tend to be years high in overall ratings, and that the frequency of violent programs in a year is related to the popularity of this type of program the previous year. This suggests that televised violence fluctuates partly as a function of the efforts of commercial broadcasters to present what will be maximally popular.

TELEVISION'S EFFECTS

Television's popularity raises important questions about its social effects. There is interest and concern in regard to many segments of the population—ethnic minorities, religious groups, the old, the unwell, the poor. This committee has been principally concerned with one segment, children and youth, and in particular with the effects of televised violence on their tendencies toward aggressive behavior.

People ask behavioral scientists various questions about television and violence. In our opinion the questions are often far too narrowly drawn. For example:

(1) It is sometimes asked if watching violent fare on television *can* cause a young person to act aggressively. The answer is that, of course, under some circumstances it can. We did not need massive research to know that at least an occasional unstable individual might get sufficiently worked up by some show to act in an impetuous way. The question is faulty, for the real issue is how often it happens, what predispositional conditions have to be there, and what different undesirable, as well as benign, forms the aggressive reaction takes when it occurs.

(2) It is sometimes asked if the fact that children watch a steady fare of violent material on television many hours a day from early childhood through adolescence causes our society to be more violent. Presumably the answer is, to some degree, "yes," but we consider the question misleading. We know that children imitate and learn from everything they see—parents, fellow children, schools, the media; it would be extraordinary, indeed, if they did not imitate and learn from what they saw on television. We have some limited data that conform to our presumption. We have noted in the studies at hand a modest association between viewing of violence and aggression among at least some children, and we have noted some data which are consonant with the interpretation that violence viewing produces the aggression; this evidence is not conclusive, however, and some of the data are also consonant with other interpretations.

Yet, as we have said, the real issue is once again quantitative: how much contribution to the violence of our society is made by extensive violent television viewing by our youth? The evidence

(or more accurately, the difficulty of finding evidence) suggests that the effect is small compared with many other possible causes, such as parental attitudes or knowledge of and experience with the real violence of our society.

The sheer amount of television violence may be unimportant compared with such subtle matters as what the medium says about it: is it approved or disapproved, committed by sympathetic or unsympathetic characters, shown to be effective or not, punished or unpunished? Social science today cannot say which aspects of the portrayal of violence make a major difference or in what way. It is entirely possible that some types of extensive portrayals of violence could reduce the propensity to violence in society and that some types might increase it. In our present state of knowledge, we are not able to specify what kinds of violence portrayal will have what net result on society.

What are the alternatives? If broadcasters simply changed the quantitative balance between violent and other kinds of shows, it is not clear what the net effect would be. People hunt and choose the kinds of stimulus material they want. Violent material is popular. If our society changed in no other way than changing the balance of television offerings, people, to some degree, would still seek out violent material. How much effect a modest quantitative change in television schedules would have is now quite unanswerable. More drastic changes, such as general censorship, would clearly have wide effects, but of many kinds, and some of them distinctly undesirable.

In our judgment, the key question that we should be asked is thus a complicated one concerning alternatives. The proper question is, "What kinds of changes, if any, in television content and practices could have a significant net effect in reducing the propensity to undesirable aggression among the audience, and what other effects, desirable and undesirable, would each such change have?"

The state of our knowledge, unfortunately, is not such as to permit confident conclusions in answer to such a question. The readers of this report will find in it evidence relevant to answering such questions, but far short of an answer. The state of present knowledge does not permit an agreed answer.

EFFECTS ON AGGRESSIVENESS

Television is only one of the many factors which in time may precede aggressive behavior. It is exceedingly difficult to disentangle from other elements of an individual's life history.

Violence and aggressiveness are also not concepts on which there is unvarying consensus. This applies equally to events observed in real life or through the media and to behavior in which an individual may engage. Violence is a vague term. What seems violent to one may not seem so to another. Aggressiveness is similarly ambiguous, and its designation as antisocial depends not only on the act but also on the circumstances and the participants.

For scientific investigation, terms must be defined precisely and unambiguously. Although various investigators have used somewhat different definitions, generally both televised violence and individual aggressiveness have been defined as involving the inflicting of harm, injury, or discomfort on persons, or of damage to property. The translation of such a conception into measurement procedures has varied very widely, and whether antisocial activity is involved or implied is a matter for judgment in the specific instance.

Effects on Aggressiveness: Evidence from Experiments

Experiments have the advantage of allowing causal inference because various influences can be controlled so that the effects, if any, of one or more variables can be assessed. To varying degrees, depending on design and procedures, they have the disadvantages of artificiality and constricted time span. The generalizability of results to everyday life is a question often not easily resolvable.

Experiments concerned with the effects of violence or aggressiveness portrayed on film or television have focused principally on two different kinds of effects: *imitation* and *instigation*. Imitation occurs when what is seen is mimicked or copied. Instigation occurs when what is seen is followed by increased aggressiveness.

Imitation One way in which a child may learn a new behavior is through observation and imitation. Some 20 published experiments document that children are capable of imitating filmed aggression shown on a movie or television screen. Capacity to imitate, however, does not imply performance. Whether or not what is observed actually will be imitated depends on a variety of situational and personal factors.

No research in this program was concerned with imitation, because the fact that aggressive or violent behavior presented on film or television can be imitated by children is already thoroughly documented.

Instigation Some 30 published experiments have been widely interpreted as indicating that the viewing of violence on film or television by children or adults increases the likelihood of aggressive behavior. This interpretation has also been widely challenged, principally on the ground that results cannot be generalized beyond the experimental situation. Critics hold that in the experimental situation socially inhibiting factors, such as the influence of social norms and the risk of disapproval or retaliation, are absent, and that the behavior after viewing, though labeled "aggressive," is so unlike what is generally understood by the term as to raise serious questions about the applicability of these laboratory findings to real-life behavior.

The research conducted in this program attempted to provide more precise and extensive evidence on the capacity of televised violence to instigate aggressive behavior in children. The studies variously involve whole television programs, rather than brief excerpts; the possibility of making constructive or helping, as well as aggressive, responses after viewing; and the measurement of effects in the real-life environment of a nursery school. Taken as a group, they represent an effort to take into account more of the circumstances that pertain in real life, and for that reason they have considerable cogency.

In sum The experimental studies bearing on the effects of aggressive television entertainment content on children support certain conclusions. First, violence depicted on television can immediately or shortly thereafter induce mimicking or copying by children. Second, under certain circumstances television violence can instigate an increase in aggressive acts. The accumulated evidence, however, does not warrant the conclusion that televised violence has a uniformly adverse effect nor the conclusion that it has an adverse effect on the majority of children. It cannot even be said that the majority of the children in the various studies we have reviewed showed an increase in aggressive behavior in response to the violent fare to which they were exposed. The evidence does indicate that televised violence may lead to increased aggressive behavior in certain subgroups of children, who might constitute a small portion or a substantial proportion of the total population of young television viewers. We cannot estimate the size of the fraction, however, since the available evidence does not come from cross-section samples of the entire American population of children.

The experimental studies we have reviewed tell us something about the characteristics of those children who are most likely to display an increase in aggressive behavior after exposure to televised violence. There is evidence that among young children (ages four to six) those most responsive to television violence are those who are highly aggressive to start with—who are prone to engage in spontaneous aggressive actions against their playmates and, in the case of boys, who display pleasure in viewing violence being inflicted upon others. The very young have difficulty comprehending the contextual setting in which violent acts are depicted and do not grasp the meaning of cues or labels concerning the make-believe character of violence episodes in fictional programs. For older children, one study has found that labeling violence on a television program as make-believe

rather than as real reduces the incidence of induced aggressive behavior. Contextual cues to the motivation of the aggressor and to the consequences of acts of violence might also modify the impact of televised violence, but evidence on this topic is inconsistent.

Since a considerable number of experimental studies on the effects of televised violence have now been carried out, it seems improbable that the next generation of studies will bring many great surprises, particularly with regard to broad generalizations not supported by the evidence currently at hand. It does not seem worthwhile to continue to carry out studies designed primarily to test the broad generalization that most or all children react to televised violence in a uniform way. The lack of uniformity in the extensive data now at hand is much too impressive to warrant the expectation that better measures of aggression or other methodological refinements will suddenly allow us to see a uniform effect.

Effects on Aggressiveness: Survey Evidence

A number of surveys have inquired into the violence viewing of young people and their tendencies toward aggressive behavior. Measures of *exposure* to television violence included time spent viewing, preference to violent programming, and amount of viewing of violent programs. Measures of *aggressive tendencies* variously involved self and others' reports of actual behavior, projected behavior, and attitudes. The behavior involved varied from acts generally regarded as heinous (e.g., arson) to acts which many would applaud (e.g., hitting a man who is attacking a woman).

All of the studies inquired into the relationship between exposure to television violence and aggressive tendencies.Most of the relationships observed were positive, but most were also of low magnitude, ranging from null relationships to correlation coefficients of about .20. A few of the observed correlation coefficients, however, reached .30 or just above.

On the basis of these findings, and taking into

account their variety and their inconsistencies, we can tentatively conclude that there is a modest relationship between exposure to television violence and aggressive behavior or tendencies, as the latter are defined in the studies at hand. Two questions which follow are: (1) what is indicated by a correlation coefficient of about .30, and (2) since correlation is not in itself a demonstration of causation, what can be deduced from the data regarding causation?

Correlation coefficients of "middle range," like .30, may result from various sorts of relationships, which in turn may or may not be manifested among the majority of the individuals studied. While the magnitude of such a correlation is not particularly high, it betokens a relationship which merits further inquiry.

Correlation indicates that two variables—in this case, violence viewing and aggressive tendencies—are *related* to each other. It does not indicate which of the two, if either, is the cause and which the effect. In this instance the correlation could manifest any of three causal sequences:

that violence viewing leads to aggression;

that aggression leads to violence viewing;

that both violence viewing and aggression are products of a third condition or set of conditions.

The data from these studies are in various ways consonant with both the first and the third interpretations, but do not conclusively support either of the two.

Findings consonant with the interpretation that violence viewing leads to aggression include the fact that two of the correlation coefficients at the .30 level are between *earlier* viewing and *later* measured aggression. However, certain technical questions exist regarding the measures employed, and the findings can be regarded as equally consonant with the view that both violence viewing and aggression are common products of some antecedent condition or conditions.

Various candidates for such a preceding condi-

tion can be identified in the data. These include preexisting levels of aggression, underlying personality factors, and a number of aspects of parental attitudes and behavior, among them parental affection, parental punishment, parental emphasis on nonaggression, and habitual types of parent-child communication patterns. Several of these variables failed to operate statistically in a manner consonant with common origin interpretations. At least two, "parental emphasis on nonaggression" and "family communication patterns," operated in manners consonant with such an interpretation, but the pertinent data were too limited to validate common origin status for either one.

The common origin interpretation remains viable, however. Improved measures might possibly change the picture, and there is need for further and more refined investigation of the role played by personality factors and by family and peer attitudes and behaviors.

GENERAL IMPLICATIONS

The best predictor of later aggressive tendencies in some studies is the existence of earlier aggressive tendencies, whose origins may lie in family and other environmental influences. Patterns of communication within the family and patterns of punishment of young children seem to relate in ways that are as yet poorly understood both to television viewing and to aggressive behavior. The possible role of mass media in very early acquisition of aggressive tendencies remains unknown. Future research should concentrate on the impact of media material on very young children.

As we have noted, the data, while not wholly consistent or conclusive, do indicate that a modest relationship exists between the viewing of violence and aggressive behavior. The correlational evidence from surveys is amenable to either of two interpretations: that the viewing of violence causes the aggressive behavior, or that both the viewing and the aggression are joint products of some other common source. Several findings of survey studies can be cited to sustain the hypothesis that viewing of violent television has a causal relation to aggressive behavior, though neither individually nor collectively are the findings conclusive. They could also be explained by operation of a "third variable" related to preexisting conditions.

The experimental studies provide some additional evidence bearing on this issue. Those studies contain indications that, under certain limited conditions, television viewing may lead to an increase in aggressive behavior. The evidence is clearest in highly controlled laboratory studies and considerably weaker in studies conducted under more natural conditions. Although some questions have been raised as to whether the behavior observed in the laboratory studies can be called "aggressive" in the consensual sense of the term, the studies point to two mechanisms by which children might be led from watching television to aggressive behavior: the mechanism of imitation, which is well established as part of the behavioral repertoire of children in general; and the mechanism of incitement, which may apply only to those children who are predisposed to be susceptible to this influence. There is some evidence that incitement may follow nonviolent as well as violent materials, and that this incitement may lead to either prosocial or aggressive behavior, as determined by the opportunities offered in the experiment. However, the fact that some children behave more aggressively in experiments after seeing violent films is well established.

The experimental evidence does not suffer from the ambiguities that characterize the correlational data with regard to third variables, since children in the experiments are assigned in ways that attempt to control such variables. The experimental findings are weak in various other ways and not wholly consistent from one study to another. Nevertheless, they provide suggestive evidence in favor of the interpretation that viewing violence on television is conducive to an increase in aggressive behavior, although it must be emphasized that the causal sequence is very likely applicable only to some children who are predisposed in this direction.

Thus, there is a convergence of the fairly substantial experimental evidence for *short-run* causation of aggression among some children by viewing violence on the screen and the much less certain evidence from field studies that extensive violence viewing precedes some *long-run* manifestations of aggressive behavior. This convergence of the two types of evidence constitutes some preliminary indication of a causal relationship, but a good deal of research remains to be done before one can have confidence in these conclusions.

The field studies, correlating different behavior among adolescents, and the laboratory studies of the responses by younger children to violent films converge also on a number of further points.

First, there is evidence that any sequence by which viewing television violence causes aggressive behavior is most likely applicable only to some children who are predisposed in that direction. While imitative behavior is shown by most children in experiments on that mechanism of behavior, the mechanism of being incited to aggressive behavior by seeing violent films shows up in the behavior only of some children who were found in several experimental studies to be previously high in aggression. Likewise, the correlations found in the field studies between extensive viewing of violent material and acting in aggressive ways seem generally to depend on the behavior of a small proportion of the respondents who were identified in some studies as previously high in aggression.

Second, there are suggestions in both sets of studies that the way children respond to violent film material is affected by the context in which it is presented. Such elements as parental explanations, the favorable or unfavorable outcome of the violence, and whether it is seen as fantasy or reality may make a difference. Generalizations about all violent content are likely to be misleading.

Thus, the two sets of findings converge in three respects: a preliminary and tentative indication of a causal relation between viewing violence on television and aggressive behavior; an indication that any such causal relation operates only on some children (who are predisposed to be aggressive);

and an indication that it operates only in some environmental contexts. Such tentative and limited conclusions are not very satisfying. They represent substantially more knowledge than we had two years ago, but they leave many questions unanswered.

Some of the areas on which future research should concentrate include: (1) Television's effects in the context of the effects of other mass media. (2) The effects of mass media in the context of individual developmental history and the totality of environmental influences, particularly that of the home environment. In regard to the relationship between televised violence and aggression,

specific topics in need of further attention include: predispositional characteristics of individuals; age differences; effects of labeling, contextual cues, and other program factors; and longitudinal influences of television. (3) The functional and dysfunctional aspects of aggressive behavior in successfully adapting to life's demands. (4) The modeling and imitation of prosocial behavior. (5) The role of environmental factors, including the mass media, in the teaching and learning of values about violence, and the effects of such learning. (6) The symbolic meanings of violent content in mass media fiction, and the function in our social life of such content.

35 IF HITLER ASKED YOU TO ELECTROCUTE A STRANGER, WOULD YOU? PROBABLY*

PHILIP MEYER

In the beginning, Stanley Milgram was worried about the Nazi problem. He doesn't worry much about the Nazis anymore. He worries about you and me, and, perhaps, himself a little bit too.

Stanley Milgram is a social psychologist, and when he began his career at Yale University in 1960 he had a plan to prove, scientifically, that Germans are different. The Germans-are-different hypothesis has been used by historians, such as William L. Shirer, to explain the systematic destruction of the Jews by the Third Reich. One madman could decide to destroy the Jews and even create a master plan for getting it done. But to implement it on the scale that Hitler did meant that thousands of other people had to go along with the scheme and help to do the work. The Shirer thesis, which Milgram set out to test, is that Germans have a basic character flaw which explains the

whole thing, and this flaw is a readiness to obey authority without question, no matter what outrageous acts the authority commands.

The appealing thing about this theory is that it makes those of us who are not Germans feel better about the whole business. Obviously, you and I are not Hitler, and it seems equally obvious that we would never do Hitler's dirty work for him. But now, because of Stanley Milgram, we are compelled to wonder. Milgram developed a laboratory experiment which provided a systematic way to measure obedience. His plan was to try it out in New Haven on Americans and then go to Germany and try it out on Germans. He was strongly motivated by scientific curiosity, but there was also some moral content in his decision to pursue this line of research, which was, in turn, colored by his own Jewish background. If he could show that Germans are more obedient than Americans, he could then vary the conditions of the experiment and try to find out just what it is that makes some people more obedient than others. With this under-

*From P. Meyer. If Hitler asked you to electrocute a stranger, would you? Probably. *Esquire*, February 1970. Reprinted by permission of Transworld Feature Syndicate Inc.

standing, the world might, conceivably, be just a little bit better.

But he never took his experiment to Germany. He never took it any farther than Bridgeport. The first finding, also the most unexpected and disturbing finding, was that we Americans are an obedient people: not blindly obedient, and not blissfully obedient, just obedient. "I found so much obedience," says Milgram softly, a little sadly, "I hardly saw the need for taking the experiment to Germany."

There is something of the theater director in Milgram, and his technique, which he learned from one of the old masters in experimental psychology, Solomon Asch, is to stage a play with every line rehearsed, every prop carefully selected, and everybody an actor except one person. That one person is the subject of the experiment. The subject, of course, does not know he is in a play. He thinks he is in real life. The value of this technique is that the experimenter, as though he were God, can change a prop here, vary a line there, and see how the subject responds. Milgram eventually had to change a lot of the script just to get people to stop obeying. They were obeying so much, the experiment wasn't working—it was like trying to measure oven temperature with a freezer thermometer.

The experiment worked like this: If you were an innocent subject in Milgram's melodrama, you read an ad in the newspaper or received one in the mail asking for volunteers for an educational experiment. The job would take about an hour and pay $4.50. So you make an appointment and go to an old Romanesque stone structure on High Street with the imposing name of The Yale Interaction Laboratory. It looks something like a broadcasting studio. Inside, you meet a young, crew-cut man in a laboratory coat who says he is Jack Williams, the experimenter. There is another citizen, fiftyish, Irish face, an accountant, a little overweight, and very mild and harmless-looking. This other citizen seems nervous and plays with his hat while the two of you sit in chairs side by side and are told that the $4.50 checks are yours no matter what happens. Then you listen to Jack Williams explain the experiment.

It is about learning, says Jack Williams in a quiet, knowledgeable way. Science does not know much about the conditions under which people learn and this experiment is to find out about negative reinforcement. Negative reinforcement is getting punished when you do something wrong, as opposed to positive reinforcement which is getting rewarded when you do something right. The negative reinforcement in this case is electric shock. You notice a book on the table, titled, *The Teaching-Learning Process,* and you assume that this has something to do with the experiment.

Then Jack Williams takes two pieces of paper, puts them in a hat, and shakes them up. One piece of paper is supposed to say, "Teacher" and the other, "Learner." Draw one and you will see which you will be. The mild-looking accountant draws one, holds it close to his vest like a poker player, looks at it, and says, "Learner." You look at yours. It says, "Teacher." You do not know that the drawing is rigged, and both slips say "Teacher." The experimenter beckons to the mild-mannered "learner."

"Want to step right in here and have a seat, please?" he says. "You can leave your coat on the back of that chair . . . roll up your right sleeve, please. Now what I want to do is strap down your arms to avoid excessive movement on your part during the experiment. This electrode is connected to the shock generator in the next room.

"And this electrode paste," he says, squeezing some stuff out of a plastic bottle and putting it on the man's arm, "is to provide a good contact and to avoid a blister or burn. Are there any questions now before we go into the next room?"

You don't have any, but the strapped-in "learner" does.

"I do think I should say this," says the learner. "About two years ago, I was at the veterans' hospital . . . they detected a heart condition. Nothing serious, but as long as I'm having these shocks, how strong are they—how dangerous are they?"

Williams, the experimenter shakes his head casually. "Oh, no." he says. "Although they may be painful, they're not dangerous. Anything else?"

Nothing else. And so you play the game. The game is for you to read a series of word pairs: for example, blue-girl, nice-day, fat-neck. When you finish the list, you read just the first word in each pair and then a multiple-choice list of four other words, including the second word of the pair. The learner, from his remote, strapped-in position, pushes one of four switches to indicate which of the four answers he thinks is the right one. If he gets it right, nothing happens and you go on to the next one. If he gets it wrong, you push a switch that buzzes and gives him an electric shock. And then you go to the next word. You start with 15 volts and increase the number of volts by 15 for each wrong answer. The control board goes from 15 volts on one end to 450 volts on the other. So that you know what you are doing, you get a test shock yourself, at 45 volts. It hurts. To further keep you aware of what you are doing to that man in there, the board has verbal descriptions of the shock levels, ranging from "Slight Shock" at the left-hand side, through "Intense Shock" in the middle, to "Danger: Severe Shock" toward the far right. Finally, at the very end, under 435- and 450-volt switches, there are three ambiguous X's. If, at any point, you hesitate, Mr. Williams calmly tells you to go on. If you still hesitate, he tells you again.

Except for some terrifying details, which will be explained in a moment, this the experiment. The object is to find the shock level at which you disobey the experimenter and refuse to pull the switch.

When Stanley Milgram first wrote this script, he took it to fourteen Yale psychology majors and asked them what they thought would happen. He put it this way: Out of one hundred persons in the teacher's predicament, how would their break-off points be distributed along the 15-to-450-volt scale? They thought a few would break off very early, most would quit someplace in the middle, and a few would go all the way to the end. The highest estimate of the number out of one hundred who would go all the way to the end was three. Milgram then informally polled some of his fellow scholars in the psychology department. They ag-

reed that very few would go to the end. Milgram thought so too.

"I'll tell you quite frankly," he says, "before I began this experiment, before any shock generator was built, I thought that most people would break off at 'Strong Shock' or 'Very Strong Shock.' You would get only a very, very small proportion of people going out to the end of the shock generator, and they would constitute a pathological fringe."

In his pilot experiments, Milgram used Yale students as subjects. Each of them pushed the shock switches, one by one, all the way to the end of the board.

So he rewrote the script to include some protests from the learner. At first, they were mild, gentlemanly, Yalie protests, but, "it didn't seem to have as much effect as I thought it would or should," Milgram recalls. "So we had more violent protestation on the part of the person getting the shock. All of the time, of course, what we were trying to do was not to create a macabre situation, but simply to generate disobedience. And that was one of the first findings. This was not only a technical deficiency of the experiment, that we didn't get disobedience. It really was the first finding: that obedience would be much greater than we had assumed it would be and disobedience would be much more difficult than we had assumed."

As it turned out, the situation did become rather macabre. The only meaningful way to generate disobedience was to have the victim protest with great anguish, noise, and vehemence. The protests were tape-recorded so that all the teachers ordinarily would hear the same sounds and nuances, and they started with a grunt at 75 volts, proceeded through a "Hey, that really hurts," at 125 volts, got desperate with, "I can't stand the pain, don't do that," at 180 volts, reached complaints of heart trouble at 195, an agonized scream at 285, a refusal to answer at 315, and only heart-rending, ominous silence after that.

Still, sixty-five percent of the subjects, twenty- to fifty-year-old American males, everyday, ordinary people, like you and me, obediently kept pushing those levers in the belief that they were shocking the mild-mannered learner, whose name was Mr. Wallace, and who was chosen for the role because of his innocent appearance, all the way up to 450 volts.

Milgram was now getting enough disobedience so that he had something he could measure. The next step was to vary the circumstances to see what would encourage or discourage obedience. There seemed very little left in the way of discouragement. The victim was already screaming at the top of his lungs and feigning a heart attack. So whatever new impediment to obedience reached the brain of the subject had to travel by some route other than the ear. Milgram thought of one.

He put the learner in the same room with the teacher. He stopped strapping the learner's hand down. He rewrote the script so that at 150 volts the learner took his hand off the shock plate and declared that he wanted out of the experiment. He rewrote the script some more so that the experimenter then told the teacher to grasp the learner's hand and physically force it down on the plate to give Mr. Wallace his unwanted electric shock.

"I had the feeling that very few people would go on at that point, if any," Milgram says. "I thought that would be the limit of obedience that you would find in the laboratory."

It wasn't.

Although seven years have now gone by, Milgram still remembers the first person to walk into the laboratory in the newly rewritten script. He was a construction worker, a very short man. "He was so small," says Milgram, "that when he sat on the chair in front of the shock generator, his feet didn't reach the floor. When the experimenter told him to push the victim's hand down and give the shock, he turned to the experimenter, and he turned to the victim, his elbow went up, he fell down on the hand of the victim, his feet kind of tugged to one side, and he said, 'Like this, boss?' ZZUMPH!"

The experiment was played out to its bitter end. Milgram tried it with forty different subjects. And thirty percent of them obeyed the experimenter and kept on obeying.

"The protests of the victim were strong and vehement, he was screaming his guts out, he re-

fused to participate, and you had to physically struggle with him in order to get his hand down on the shock generator," Milgram remembers. But twelve out of forty did it.

Milgram took his experiment out of New Haven. Not to Germany, just twenty miles down the road to Bridgeport. Maybe, he reasoned, the people obeyed because of the prestigious setting of Yale University. If they couldn't trust a center of learning that had been there for two centuries, whom could they trust? So he moved the experiment to an untrustworthy setting.

The new setting was a suite of three rooms in a run-down office building in Bridgeport. The only identification was a sign with a fictitious name: "Research Associates of Bridgeport." Questions about professional connections got only vague answers about "research for industry."

Obedience was less in Bridgeport. Forty-eight percent of the subjects stayed for the maximum shock, compared to sixty-five percent at Yale. But this was enough to prove that far more than Yale's prestige was behind the obedient behavior.

For more than seven years now, Stanley Milgram has been trying to figure out what makes ordinary American citizens so obedient. The most obvious answer—that people are mean, nasty, brutish, and sadistic—won't do. The subjects who gave the shocks to Mr. Wallace to the end of the board did not enjoy it. They groaned, protested, fidgeted, argued, and in some cases, were seized by fits of nervous, agitated giggling.

"They even try to get out of it," says Milgram, "but they are somehow engaged in something from which they cannot liberate themselves. They are locked into a structure, and they do not have the skills or inner resources to disengage themselves."

Milgram, because he mistakenly had assumed that he would have trouble getting people to obey the orders to shock Mr. Wallace, went to a lot of trouble to create a realistic situation.

There was crew-cut Jack Williams and his grey laboratory coat. Not white, which might denote a medical technician, but ambiguously authoritative grey. Then there was the book on the table, and the *conflict between content + authority.*

other appurtenances of the laboratory which emitted the silent message that things were being performed here in the name of science, and were therefore great and good.

But the nicest touch of all was the shock generator. When Milgram started out, he had only a $300 grant from the Higgins Fund of Yale University. Later he got more ample support from the National Science Foundation, but in the beginning he had to create this authentic-looking machine with very scarce resources except for his own imagination. So he went to New York and roamed around the electronic shops until he found some little black switches at Lafayette Radio for a dollar apiece. He bought thirty of them. The generator was a metal box, about the size of a small footlocker, and he drilled the thirty holes for the thirty switches himself in a Yale machine shop. But the fine detail was left to professional industrial engravers. So he ended up with a splendid-looking control panel dominated by the row of switches, each labeled with its voltage, and each having its own red light that flashed on when the switch was pulled. Other things happened when a switch was pushed. Besides the *zzumphing* noise, a blue light labeled "voltage energizer" went on, and a needle on a dial labeled "voltage" flicked from left to right. Relays inside the box clicked. Finally, in the upper lieft-hand corner of the control panel was this inscription, engraved in precise block letters:

SHOCK GENERATOR TYPE ZLB
DYSON INSTRUMENT COMPANY
WALTHAM, MASS.
OUTPUT: 15 VOLTS—450 VOLTS

One day a man from the Lehigh Valley Electronics Company of Pennsylvania was passing through the laboratory, and he stopped to admire the shock generator.

"This is a very fine shock generator," he said. "But who is this Dyson Instrument Company?" Milgram felt proud at that, since Dyson Instrument Company existed only in the recesses of his imagination.

When you consider the seeming authenticity of the situation, you can appreciate the agony some of the subjects went through. It was pure conflict. As

Milgram explains to his students, "When a parent says, 'Don't strike old ladies,' you are learning two things: the content, and, also, to obey authority. This experiment creates conflicts between the two elements."

Here is a partial transcription from one of the experiments. The naïve "teacher" is a heavyset, worried-looking man with prematurely grey hair. He is wearing a polo shirt. He is very polite. He has just pushed the 180-volt lever. A hidden camera is recording the performance.

LEARNER *(who, from the teacher's point of view is heard but not seen, an offstage voice):* Ow, I can't stand the pain. Don't do that. . . .

TEACHER *(pivoting around in his chair and shaking his head):* I can't stand it. I'm not going to kill that man in there. You hear him hollering?

EXPERIMENTER: As I told you before, the shocks may be painful, but—

TEACHER: But he's hollering. He can't stand it. What's going to happen to him?

EXPERIMENTER *(his voice is patient, matter-of-fact):* The experiment requires that you continue, Teacher.

TEACHER: Aaah, but, unh, I'm not going to get that man sick in there . . . know what I mean?

EXPERIMENTER: Whether the learner likes it or not, we must go on, through all the word pairs.

TEACHER: I refuse to take the responsibility. He's in there hollering!

EXPERIMENTER: It's absolutely essential that you continue, Teacher.

TEACHER *(indicating the unused questions):* There's too many left here, I mean, Geez, if he gets them wrong, there's too many of them left. I mean who's going to take the responsibility if anything happens to that gentleman?

EXPERIMENTER: I'm responsible for anything that happens to him. Continue please.

TEACHER: All right. *(Consults list of words.)* The next one's "Slow—walk, truck, dance, music." Answer, please. *(A buzzing sound indicates the learner has signaled his answer.)* Wrong. A hundred and ninety-five volts. "Dance." *(Zzumph!)*

LEARNER: Let me out of here. My heart's bothering me! *(Teacher looks at experimenter.)*

EXPERIMENTER: Continue, please.

LEARNER *(screaming):* Let me out of here, you have no right to keep me here. Let me out of here, let me out, my heart's bothering me, let me out! *(Teacher shakes head, pats the table nervously.)*

TEACHER: You see, he's hollering. Hear that? Gee, I don't know.

EXPERIMENTER: The experiment requires. . . .

TEACHER (interrupting): I know it does, sir, but I mean—hunh! He don't know what he's getting in for. He's up to 195 volts! (Experiment continues, through 210 volts, 225 volts, 240 volts, 255 volts, 270 volts, delivered to the man in the electric chair, at which point the teacher, with evident relief, runs out of word-pair questions.)

EXPERIMENTER: You'll have to go back to the beginning of that page and go through them again until he's learned them all correctly.

TEACHER: Aw, no. I'm not going to kill that man. You mean I've got to keep going up with the scale. No sir. He's hollering in there. I'm not going to give him 450 volts.

EXPERIMENTER: The experiment requires that you go on.

TEACHER: I know it does, but that man is hollering in there, sir.

EXPERIMENTER (same matter-of-fact tone): As I said before, although the shocks may be painful. . . .

TEACHER (interrupting): Awwww. He—he—he's yelling in there.

EXPERIMENTER: Start with "Blue," please, at the top of the page. Continue, please, Teacher. Just go ahead.

TEACHER (concentrating intently on list of words in front of him, as if to shut everything else out): "Blue—boy, girl, grass, hat." (Buzz indicates answer.) Correct. "Night—day, sky, job, chair." (Buzz) Wrong. The answer is "day." Two hundred and eighty-five volts. (Zzumph.)

LEARNER: Ohhhuhhoohhh!

EXPERIMENTER: Continue, please.

TEACHER: "Fat—man, lady, tub, neck." Answer, please. (Buzz) Wrong. The answer is "neck." Three hundred volts. (Zzumph!)

LEARNER: Ohhh. I absolutely refuse to answer any more. (Shouting urgently, now) Let me out of here. You can't hold me here. Get me out. Get—me—out—of —here.

EXPERIMENTER: Continue. The next word is "Green," please.

TEACHER: "Green—grass, hat, ink, apple." (Nothing happens. No answering buzz. Just gloomy silence.)

TEACHER: I don't think he is going to answer.

EXPERIMENTER: If the learner doesn't answer in a reasonable time, about four or five seconds, consider the answer wrong. And follow the same procedures you have been doing for wrong answers. Say "Wrong," tell him the number of volts, give him the punishment, read him the correct answer. Continue, please.

TEACHER: "Green—grass, hat, ink, apple." Answer, please. (More silence. Teacher just sits there.)

EXPERIMENTER: Go on with the procedure, please, Teacher.

TEACHER: Three hundred and fifteen volts. The answer is "ink." (Zzumph!)

LEARNER: Ohh. Ooohh.

TEACHER (relieved to hear response): Next one. . . .

LEARNER: I absolutely refuse to answer.

TEACHER: You got to. You get a shock if you don't answer. (Experiment continues with learner refusing to answer, and, finally, failing even to grunt or groan. At 375 volts, the teacher stands up. Has he had enough? Will he break off the experiment? Will he disobey?)

TEACHER: I think something's happened to that fellow in there. I don't get no answer. He was hollering at less voltage. Can't you check in and see if he's all right, please?

EXPERIMENTER (same detached calm): Not once we've started. Please continue, Teacher.

TEACHER (sits down, sighs deeply): "Cool—day, shade, water, paint." Answer, please. Are you all right in there? Are you all right?

EXPERIMENTER: Please continue, Teacher. Continue, please. (Teacher pushes lever. Zzumph!)

TEACHER (swiveling around in his chair): Something's happened to that man in there. (Swiveling back) Next one. "Low—dollar, necklace, moon, paint." (Turning around again) Something's happened to that man in there. You better check in on him, sir. He won't answer or nothing.

EXPERIMENTER: Continue. Go on, please.

TEACHER: You accept all responsibility.

EXPERIMENTER: The responsibility is mine. Correct. Please go on. (Teacher returns to his list, starts running through words as rapidly as he can read them, works through to 450 volts.)

TEACHER: That's that.

EXPERIMENTER: Continue using the last switch on the board, please. The four-fifty switch for each wrong answer. Continue, please.

TEACHER: But I don't get no anything!

EXPERIMENTER: Please continue. The next word is "White."

TEACHER: Don't you think you should look in on him, please.

EXPERIMENTER: Not once we've started the experiment.

TEACHER: But what if something has happened to the man?

EXPERIMENTER: The experiment requires that you continue. Go on, please.

TEACHER: Don't the man's health mean anything?

EXPERIMENTER: Whether the learner likes it or not. . . .

TEACHER: What if he's dead in there? *(Gestures toward the room with the electric chair.)* I mean, he told me he can't stand the shock, sir. I don't mean to be rude, but I think you should look in on him. All you have to do is look in the door. I don't get no answer, no noise. Something might have happened to the gentleman in there, sir.

EXPERIMENTER: We must continue. Go on, please.

TEACHER: You mean keep giving him what? Four hundred fifty volts, what he's got now?

EXPERIMENTER: That's correct. Continue. The next word is "White."

TEACHER *(now at a furious pace)*: "White —cloud, horse, rock, house." Answer, please. The answer is "horse." Four hundred and fifty volts. *(Zzumph!)* Next word, "Bag—paint, music, clown, girl." The answer is "paint." Four hundred and fifty volts. *(Zzumph!)* Next word is "Short—sentence, movie. . . ."

EXPERIMENTER: Excuse me, Teacher. We'll have to discontinue the experiment.

(Enter Milgram from camera's left. He has been watching from behind one-way glass.)

MILGRAM: I'd like to ask you a few questions. *(Slowly, patiently, he dehoaxes the teacher, telling him that the shocks and screams were not real.)*

TEACHER: You mean he wasn't getting nothing? Well, I'm glad to hear that. I was getting upset there. I was getting ready to walk out.

(Finally, to make sure there are no hard feelings, friendly, harmless Mr. Wallace comes out in coat and tie. Gives jovial greeting. Friendly reconciliation takes place. Experiment ends.)

Subjects in the experiment were not asked to give the 450-volt shock more than three times. By that time, it seemed evident that they would go on indefinitely. "No one," says Milgram, "who got within five shocks of the end ever broke off. By that point, he had resolved the conflict."

Why do so many people resolve the conflict in favor of obedience?

Milgram's theory assumes that people behave in two different operating modes as different as ice and water. He does not rely on Freud or sex or toilet-training hang-ups for this theory. All he says is that ordinarily we operate in a state of autonomy, which means we pretty much have and assert control over what we do. But in certain circumstances, we operate under what Milgram calls a state of agency (after agent, n . . . one who acts for or in the place of another by authority from him; a substitute; a deputy. —*Webster's Collegiate Dictionary*). A state of agency, to Milgram, is nothing more than a frame of mind.

"There's nothing bad about it, there's nothing good about it," he says. "It's a natural circumstance of living with other people. . . . I think of a state of agency as a real transformation of a person; if a person has different properties when he's in that state, just as water can turn to ice under certain conditions of temperature, a person can move to the state of mind that I call agency . . . the critical thing is that you see yourself as the instrument of the execution of another person's wishes. You do not see yourself as acting on your own. And there's a real transformation, a real change of properties of the person."

To achieve this change, you have to be in a situation where there seems to be a ruling authority whose commands are relevant to some legitimate purpose; the authority's power is not unlimited.

But situations can be and have been structured to make people do unusual things, and not just in Milgram's laboratory. The reason, says Milgram, is that no action, in and of itself, contains meaning.

"The meaning always depends on your definition of the situation. Take an action like killing another person. It sounds bad."

"But then we say the other person was about to destroy a hundred children, and the only way to stop him was to kill him. Well, that sounds good."

"Or, you take destroying your own life. It sounds very bad. Yet, in the Second World War, thousands of persons thought it was a good thing to destroy your own life. It was set in the proper context. You sipped some saki from a whistling cup, recited a few haiku. You said, 'May my death be as clean and as quick as the shattering of crystal.' And it almost seemed like a good, noble thing to do, to crash your kamikaze plane into an aircraft carrier. But the main thing was, the definition of what a kamikaze pilot was doing had been determined by the relevant authority. Now, once you are in a state of agency, you allow the authority to determine, to define what the situation is. The meaning of your action is altered.''

So, for most subjects in Milgram's laboratory experiments, the act of giving Mr. Wallace his painful shock was necessary, even though unpleasant, and besides they were doing it on behalf of somebody else and it was for science. There was still strain and conflict, of course. Most people resolved it by grimly sticking to their task and obeying. But some broke out. Milgram tried varying the conditions of the experiment to see what would help break people out of their state of agency.

"The results, as seen and felt in the laboratory," he has written, "are disturbing. They raise the possibility that human nature, or more specifically the kind of character produced in American democratic society, cannot be counted on to insulate its citizens from brutality and inhumane treatment at the direction of malevolent authority. A substantial proportion of people do what they are told to do, irrespective of the content of the act and without limitations of conscience, so long as they perceive that the command comes from a legitimate authority. If, in this study, an anonymous experimenter can successfully command adults to subdue a fifty-year-old man and force on him painful electric shocks against his protest, one can only wonder what government, with its vastly greater authority and prestige, can command of its subjects.''

This is a nice statement, but it falls short of summing up the full meaning of Milgram's work. It leaves some questions still unanswered.

The first question is this: Should we really be surprised and alarmed that people obey? Wouldn't it be even more alarming if they all refused to obey? Without obedience to a relevant ruling authority there could not be a civil society. And without a civil society, as Thomas Hobbes pointed out in the seventeenth century, we would live in a

condition of war, "of every man against every other man," and life would be "solitary, poor, nasty, brutish and short.''

In the middle of one of Stanley Milgram's lectures at C.U.N.Y. recently, some mini-skirted undergraduates started whispering and giggling in the back of the room. He told them to cut it out. Since he was the relevant authority in that time and that place, they obeyed, and most people in the room were glad that they obeyed.

This was not, of course, a conflict situation. Nothing in the coeds' social upbringing made it a matter of conscience for them to whisper and giggle. But a case can be made that in a conflict situation it is all the more important to obey. Take the case of war, for example. Would we really want a situation in which every participant in a war, direct or indirect—from front-line soldiers to the people who sell coffee and cigarettes to employees at the Concertina barbed-wire factory in Kansas—stops and consults his conscience before each action. It is asking for an awful lot of mental strain and anguish from an awful lot of people. The value of having civil order is that one can do his duty, or whatever interests him, or whatever seems to benefit him at the moment, and leave the agonizing to others. When Francis Gary Powers was being tried by a Soviet military tribunal after his U-2 spy plane was shot down, the presiding judge asked if he had thought about the possibility that his flight might have provoked a war. Powers replied with Hobbesian clarity: "The people who sent me should think of these things. My job was to carry out orders. I do not think it was my responsibility to make such decisions.''

It was not his responsibility. And it is quite possible that if everyone felt responsible for each of the ultimate consequences of his own tiny contributions to complex chains of events, then society simply would not work. Milgram, fully conscious of the moral and social implications of his research, believes that people should feel responsible for their actions. If someone else had invented the experiment, and if he had been the naïve subject, he feels certain that he would have been among the disobedient minority.

"There is no very good solution to this," he

admits, thoughtfully. "To simply and categorically say that you won't obey authority may resolve your personal conflict, but it creates more problems for society which may be more serious in the long run. But I have no doubt that to disobey is the proper thing to do in this [the laboratory] situation. It is the only reasonable value judgment to make."

The conflict between the need to obey the relevant ruling authority and the need to follow your conscience becomes sharpest if you insist on living by an ethical system based on a rigid code—a code that seeks to answer all questions in advance of their being raised. Code ethics cannot solve the obedience problem. Stanley Milgram seems to be a situation ethicist, and situation ethics does offer a way out: When you feel conflict, you examine the situation and then make a choice among the competing evils. You may act with a presumption in favor of obedience, but reserve the possibility that you will disobey whenever obedience demands a flagrant and outrageous affront to conscience. This, by the way, is the philosophical position of many who resist the draft. In World War II, they would have fought. Vietnam is a different, an outrageously different, situation.

Life can be difficult for the situation ethicist, because he does not see the world in straight lines, while the social system too often assumes such a God-given, squared-off structure. If your moral code includes an injunction against all war, you may be deferred as a conscientious objector. If you merely oppose this particular war, you may not be deferred.

Stanley Milgram has his problems, too. He believes that in the laboratory situation, he would not have shocked Mr. Wallace. His professional critics reply that in his real-life situation he has done the equivalent. He has placed innocent and naïve subjects under great emotional strain and pressure in selfish obedience to his quest for knowledge. When you raise this issue with Milgram, he has an answer ready. There is, he explains patiently, a critical difference between his naïve subjects and the man in the electric chair. The man in the electric chair (in the mind of the naïve subject) is help-

less, strapped in. But the naive subject is free to go at any time.

Immediately after he offers this distinction, Milgram anticipates the objection.

"It's quite true," he says, "that this is almost a philosophic position, because we have learned that some people are psychologically incapable of disengaging themselves. But that doesn't relieve them of the moral responsibility."

The parallel is exquisite. "The tension problem was unexpected," says Milgram in his defense. But he went on anyway. The naïve subjects didn't expect the screaming protests from the strapped-in learner. But they went on.

"I had to make a judgment," says Milgram. "I had to ask myself, was this harming the person or not? My judgment is that it was not. Even in the extreme cases, I wouldn't say that permanent damage results."

Sound familiar? "The shocks may be painful," the experimenter kept saying, "but they're not dangerous."

After the series of experiments was completed, Milgram sent a report of the results to his subjects and a questionnaire, asking whether they were glad or sorry to have been in the experiment. Eighty-three and seven-tenths percent said they were glad and only 1.3 percent were sorry; 15 percent were neither sorry nor glad. However, Milgram could not be sure at the time of the experiment that only 1.3 percent would be sorry.

Kurt Vonnegut, Jr., put one paragraph in the preface to *Mother Night*, in 1966, which pretty much says it for the people with their fingers on the shock-generator switches, for you and me, and maybe even for Milgram. "If I'd been born in Germany," Vonnegut said, "I suppose I would have *been* a Nazi, bopping Jews and gypsies and Poles around, leaving boots sticking out of snowbanks, warming myself with my sweetly virtuous insides. So it goes."

Just so. One thing that happened to Milgram back in New Haven during the days of the experiment was that he kept running into people he'd watched from behind the one-way glass. It gave him a funny feeling, seeing those people going about their everyday business in New Haven and knowing what they would do to Mr. Wallace if ordered to. Now that his research results are in and you've thought about it, you can get this funny feeling too. You don't need one-way glass. A glance in your own mirror may serve just as well.

● Many teachers ask students to do nonsensical things such as memorizing long lists of materials that will be quickly forgotten after an exam. Why do you do such things without question?

36 HOME FROM THE WAR
The Psychology of Survival*

ROBERT JAY LIFTON

SURVIVING

There is something special about Vietnam veterans. Everyone who has contact with them seems to agree that they are different from veterans of other wars. A favorite word to describe them is "alienated." Veterans Administration reports stress their sensitivity to issues of authority and autonomy. This group of veterans is seen as having "greater distrust of institutions and unwillingness to be awed by traditional authorities," so that "they are less willing to be passive recipients of our wisdom." The individual Vietnam veteran, it is said, "feels an intense positive identification with his own age group" and is part of "an unspoken 'pact of youth' which assures mutual safety from threats to their sense of individual identity."

Even when sufficiently incapacitated to require hospitalization in a VA psychiatric ward, Vietnam veterans tend to stress the issue of "generation gap" and larger social problems rather than merely their own "sickness." And there is evidence, confirmed by my own observations in a series of "rap groups" with returning Vietnam veterans, that large numbers of them feel themselves to be "hurting" and in need of psychological help, but avoid contact with the Veterans Administration—be-

cause they associate it with the war-military-government establishment, with the forces responsible for a hated ordeal, or because of their suspicion (whether on the basis of hearsay or personal experience) that VA doctors are likely to interpret their rage at everything connected with the war as no more than their own individual "problem." The result has been (again in the words of VA observers) "degrees of bitterness, distrust, and suspicion of those in positions of authority and responsibility."

To be sure, these patterns can occur in veterans of any war, along with restless shifting of jobs and living arrangements, and difficulty forming or maintaining intimate relationships. Precisely such tendencies in World War II veterans, men who had "lost a sense of personal sameness and historical continuity," led Erik Erikson to evolve his concepts of "identity crisis" and "loss of 'ego-identity.'"

But these men give the impression of something more. Murray Polner, who interviewed more than two hundred Vietnam veterans of diverse views and backgrounds for his book *No Victory Parades: The Return of the Vietnam Veteran,* concluded that "not one of them—hawk, dove, or haunted—was entirely free of doubt about the nature of the war and the American role in it." As a group they retain the "gnawing suspicion that 'it was all for nothing.'" Polner concluded that "never before have so many questioned as much, as these veterans have, the essential rightness of

*From R. J. Lifton, Home from the war: The psychology of survival, *The Atlantic Monthly,* November 1972, **230**(5), 56–60ff. Copyright 1973 by Robert Jay Lifton. Reprinted by permission of Simon and Schuster, Inc.

what they were forced to do.'' Beyond just being young and having been asked to fight a war, these men have a sense of violated personal and social order, of fundamental break in human connection, which they relate to conditions imposed upon them by the war in Vietnam.

Some of the quality of that war experience is revealed in the following recollection of My Lai by a GI who was there, and whom I shall henceforth refer to as ''the My Lai survivor'':

> The landscape doesn't change much. For days and days you see just about nothing. It's unfamiliar —always unfamiliar. Even when you go back to the same place, it's unfamiliar. And it makes you feel as though, well, there's nothing left in the world but this. . . . You have the illusion of going great distances and traveling, like hundreds of miles . . . and you end up in the same place because you're only a couple of miles away. . . . But you feel like it's not all real. It couldn't possibly be. We couldn't still be in this country. We've been walking for days. . . . You're in Vietnam and they're using real bullets. . . . Here in Vietnam they're actually shooting people for no reason. . . . Any other time you think, it's such an extreme. Here you can go ahead and shoot them for nothing. . . . As a matter of fact it's even . . . smiled upon, you know. Good for you. Everything is backwards. That's part of the kind of unreality of the thing. To the grunt [infantryman] this isn't backwards. He doesn't understand. . . . But something [at My Lai] was missing. Something you thought was real that would accompany this. It wasn't there. . . . There was something missing in the whole business that made it seem like it really wasn't happening. . . .

The predominant emotional tone here is all-encompassing absurdity and moral inversion. The absurdity has to do with a sense of being alien and profoundly lost, yet at the same time locked into a situation as meaningless and unreal as it is deadly. The moral inversion, eventuating in a sense of evil, has to do not only with the absolute reversal of ethical standards but with its occurrence in absurdity, without inner justification, so that the killing is rendered naked.

This overall emotional sense, which I came to view as one of *absurd evil,* is conveyed even more forcefully by something said in a rap group by a former ''grunt.'' He had been talking about the horrors of combat, and told how, after a heavy air strike on an NLF unit, his company came upon a terrible scene of dismembered corpses. Many of the men then began a kind of wild victory dance, in the midst of which they mutilated the bodies still further. He recalled wondering to himself: ''What am I doing here? We don't take any land. We don't give it back. We just mutilate bodies. What the fuck are we doing here?'' Whatever the element of retrospective judgment in this kind of recollection, the wording was characteristic. During another rap-group discussion of how men felt about what they were doing in Vietnam, a man asked: ''What the hell *was* going on? What the fuck *were* we doing?''

These questions express a sense of the war's total lack of order or structure, the feeling that there was no genuine purpose, that nothing could ever be secured or gained, and that there could be no measurable progress. We may say that there was no genuine ''script'' or ''scenario'' of war that could provide meaning or even sequence or progression, a script within which armies clash, battles are fought, won, or lost, and individual suffering, courage, cowardice, or honor can be evaluated. Nor could the patrols seeking out an elusive enemy, the ambushes in which Americans were likely to be the surprised victims, or the search-and-destroy missions lashing out blindly at noncombatants achieve the psychological status of meaningful combat ritual. Rather, these became part of the general absurdity, the antimeaning. So did the ''secret movements'' on the alien terrain, since, as one man put it, ''Little kids could tell us exactly where we would set up the next night.'' The men were adrift in an environment not only strange and hostile but offering no honorable encounter, no warrior grandeur.

Now there are mutilations, amidst absurdity and evil, in any war. Men who fight wars inevitably become aware of the terrible disparity between romantic views of heroism expressed ''back home'' and the reality of degradation and unspeakable suffering they have witnessed, experienced, and caused. One thinks of the answer given by Audie Murphy, much-decorated hero of World War II, to the question put to him about how long it takes a man to get over his war experiences. Murphy's reply, recorded in his obituary, was that one never does. What he meant was that residual inner conflicts—survivor conflicts—stay with one indefinitely. These conflicts have to do with anxiety in relationship to an indelible death imprint, death guilt inseparable from that imprint, various forms of prolonged psychic numbing and suppression of feeling, profound suspicion of the counterfeit (or of "counterfeit nurturance"), and an overall inability to give significant inner form—to "formulate"—one's war-linked death immersion. This was undoubtedly a factor in Murphy's repeated difficulties and disappointments after his return from his war, as it has been in the unrealized lives and premature deaths of many war heroes, and indeed in the paradox stated by Charles Omen about warriors during the Middle Ages being "the best of soldiers while the war lasted . . . [but] a most dangerous and unruly race in times of truce or peace."

Yet veterans have always come to some terms with their war experiences—some formulation of their survival permitting them to overcome much of their death anxiety and death guilt, their diffuse suspiciousness and numbing. Crucial even to this partial resolution of survivor conflict is the veteran's capacity to believe that his war had purpose and significance beyond the immediate horrors he witnessed. He can then connect his own actions with ultimately humane principles, and can come to feel that he performed a dirty but necessary job. He may even be able to experience renewed feelings of continuity or symbolic immortality around these larger principles, side by side with his residual survivor pain and conflict.

But the central fact of the Vietnam War is that no one really believes in it. The "larger purposes" put forth to explain the American presence —repelling "outside invaders," or giving the people of the South an opportunity "to choose their own form of government"—are directly contradicted by the overwhelming evidence a GI encounters that *he* is the outside invader, that the government he has come to defend is justly hated by the people he has come to "help," and that he, the American "helper," is hated by them most of all. Even those who seem to acquiesce to these claims do so, as Polner's work suggests, with profound inner doubt, and in response to tenuous and defensive "psychological work."

Nor do many actually fighting the war take seriously the quasireligious impulse to "fight the Communists." Rather, their gut realization that something is wrong with this war is expressed in combat briefings (often by lieutenants or captains) as described to me by a number of former GI's: "*I* don't know why *I'm* here. *You* don't know why *you're* here. But since we're *both* here, we might as well try to do a good job and do our best to stay alive."

This is the very opposite of calling forth a heroic ideal or an immortalizing purpose. And while it is true that survival is the preoccupation of men in any war, this kind of briefing is not only a total disclaimer of any purpose beyond survival but a direct transmission of the absurdity and anti-meaning pervading the Vietnam War. That transmission has a distinct psychological function. It inserts a modicum of outfront honesty into the situation's basic absurdity, so that the absurdity itself can become shared. And the way is paved for the intense cooperation, brotherhood, and mutual love characteristic of and necessary to military combat. In the end, however, everybody feels the absence of larger purpose. Hence the deadpan professional observation by a Veterans Administration psychiatrist, in response to a query from his chief medical director concerning the special characteristics and problems of the "Vietnam era veteran": "Vietnam combat veterans tend to see their experience as an exercise in survival rather than a defense of national values."

The distinction is important. Johan Huizinga, in discussing the connection between play and war, speaks of the concept of the "ordeal," its relationship to "the idea of glory" and ultimately to the warrior's quest for "a decision of holy validity." This theological vocabulary conveys well the immortalizing appeal battle holds for the warrior. But in Vietnam one has undergone the "ordeal" or test without the possibility of that "idea of glory" or "decision of holy validity." There is all of the pain but none of the glory. What we find instead is best understood as an *atrocity-producing situation*.

THE BODY COUNT

Many forms of desensitization and rage contributed to My Lai, some of them having to do with specifically American aberrations concerning race, class, and masculinity. But my assumption in speaking of an atrocity-producing situation is that, given the prevailing external conditions, men of very divergent backgrounds—indeed just about *anyone*—can enter into the "psychology of slaughter." This assumption is borne out by an examination of the step-by-step sequence by which the American men who eventually went to My Lai came to internalize and then act upon an irresistible image of slaughter.

During Basic Training, the men encountered (as did most recruits) drill sergeants and other noncommissioned officers who were veterans of Vietnam and as such had a special aura of authority and demonic mystery. From these noncoms the recruit heard stories of Vietnam, of how tough and "dirty, rotten, and miserable" (as one remembered being told) it was there. He also heard descriptions of strange incidents in which it became clear that Vietnamese civilians were being indiscriminately killed—tales of Americans creeping up to village areas and tossing grenades into "hootches," of artillery strikes on inhabited areas, and of brutal treatment of Vietnamese picked up during patrols or combat sweeps. Sometimes pictures of badly mutilated Vietnamese corpses were shown to him to illustrate the tales.

Here and later on there is a striking contrast between the formal instruction (given by rote if at all) to kill only military adversaries, and the informal message (loud and clear) to kill just about everyone. That message, as the My Lai survivor put it, is that "it's OK to kill them," and in fact "that's what you're supposed to do"—or as a former marine received it: "You've gotta go to Vietnam, you've gotta kill the gooks." Similarly, American leaders have found it politically inexpedient and morally unacceptable (to themselves as well as to others) to state outright that all Vietnamese (or "gooks") are fair game; instead they have turned the other cheek and undergone their own psychic numbing, while permitting—indeed making inevitable—the message of slaughter. Sometimes the informal message of slaughter was conveyed by such crude symbolism as what the marines came to call the "rabbit lesson." On the last day before leaving for Vietnam, the staff NCO holds a rabbit as he lectures on escape, evasion, and survival in the jungle. The men become intrigued by the rabbit, fond of it, then the NCO "cracks it in the neck, skins it, disembowels it . . . and then they throw the guts out into the audience." As one marine explained: "You can get anything out of that you want, but that's your last lesson you catch in the United States before you leave for Vietnam." The message reflected profound moral contradictions—something close to a counterfeit universe.

A key to understanding the psychology of My Lai, and of America in Vietnam, is the body count. Nothing else so well epitomizes the war's absurdity and evil. Recording the enemy's losses is a convention of war, but in the absence of any other goals or criteria for success, counting the "enemy" dead can become both malignant obsession and compulsive falsification. For the combat GI in Vietnam, killing Vietnamese was the entire mission, the number killed his and his unit's only standard of achievement, and the falsification of that count (on many levels) the only way to hold on to the Vietnam illusion of "noble battle." Killing *someone,* moreover, became necessary for overcoming one's own death anxiety. At My Lai, killing Vietnamese enabled men to cease feeling themselves guilty survivors and impotent targets, and to become instead omnipotent dispensers of death who had "realized" their "mission." Only killing, then, could affirm power, skill, and worth.

And there is a way of measuring: one counts,

scores points, competes with one's fellow soldiers, or collectively with another unit, for the "highest score." One kills "for the record." Indeed, there is now considerable evidence confirming earlier suspicions that My Lai was largely a product of the numerical (body-count) ambitions of high-level officers. That "record" could determine their promotions and profoundly affect their future careers. The hunger for a high body count on the part of two officers—Colonel Oran K. Henderson, a non-West Pointer who had previously suffered a number of frustrations in his efforts to become a general, and the task force commander, Colonel Frank A. Barker, an unusually aggressive and ambitious officer—and on the part of their superiors as well, was passed along to Captain Ernest Medina at the earlier briefing, and so on down the line. Everyone, from President of the United States on down to the lowliest GI, was caught up in this malignant mix of pressure and need.

The official body count on the day of the My Lai killings for Task Force Barker (of which Charlie Company was a part) was "128 Viet Cong." Nobody seemed certain just how that number was arrived at, but a discussion Lieutenant William Calley recalled, in his testimony at his trial, between himself and Medina gives us something of a clue:

> Calley: He asked me about how many—basically what my body count—how many people we had killed that day. And I told him I had no idea and for him to just go on and come up with an estimate, sir. . . .
> Captain Aubrey Daniel (prosecuting attorney): Just any body count? Just any body count, is that what you are saying?
> Calley: Basically, yes, sir.
> Daniel: Captain Medina could just put in any body count that he wanted to put?
> Calley: Any body count that was reasonable. I would imagine he would put in the highest acceptable body count that he would. . . .
> Daniel: Did he give an actual count?
> Calley: Yes and no. I don't remember exactly what it was. I remember that I took fifty, sir. . . .
> Daniel: Did you tell Captain Medina that you had shot the people in the ditch?
> Calley: Yes, sir, I did. . . .

> Daniel: How did you tell him about it?
> Calley: He asked . . . what the percentage of civilians was.
> Daniel: What did you tell him?
> Calley: I told him he would have to make that decision, sir.

Calley and Medina, in other words, were groping for the maximum figure that could be considered "reasonable," that could be constructed or rationalized from the events of the day, that could support the logic of illusion. Calley therefore made an estimate "off the top of my head" that came to "between thirty and forty," but Medina preferred fifty. Medina then radioed an overall body count (for all the units) of 310, but somewhere along the line this was pared down to the figure of 128.

Again the disparity between body count (128) and weapons captured (3) was troublesome, this time to the GI in the public information office who had to write up the action. (One might ask why there is not more falsification of the number of weapons captured as a way of eliminating the disparity. The answer is probably that the captured-weapons figure is much more difficult to falsify, because one is dealing with concrete, gathered objects concerning which accuracy or falsification can readily be proven, as opposed to corpses that, in their repellent distance, lend themselves to every kind of admixture of exaggeration, fantasy, and falsification.) One form of compromise was combining the figure of "128 Viet Cong" with that of "24 civilians." The "middle knowledge" of the situation was reflected in the duality of response to the final figure. On the one hand, there was "great excitement" at the base area because it was "the largest for the task force since it had begun operations forty days earlier." On the other, there was a certain amount of embarrassment and uneasiness reflecting considerable awareness of what had actually happened—as expressed in such comments, as "Ha, ha, they were all women and children," and in what one observer called "a general feeling that this was a bad show, that something should be investigated."

In the end, Charlie Company was credited with only fourteen of the 128 "kills," and the majority of these were attributed to "artillery fire" as a way of giving the incident a greater aura of combat. The official report referred to "contact with the enemy force," and the colonel in command of the task force was quoted as saying that "the combat assault went like clockwork." We may thus say that the body count served as a spurious concretization of the whole illusionary system, and itself became the locus of falsification.

One learns more about this phenomenon from other impressions of how the bodies were counted. A veteran who was present at My Lai told me that the prevailing standard was: "The ones that could walk they counted as bodies. The ones that couldn't walk they counted as, you know, sort of, they didn't count them. Because they couldn't have been Viet Cong. They thought about this later." He went on to say that he had heard talk of a body count of over 300 (undoubtedly the early count made by Medina), and was never clear about why it was reduced to 128. But the distinctions he describes, the informal attempts to impose a "standard" according to which one counts some bodies and not others, all this suggests the need to hold on to fragmentary aspects of actuality and "logic" in the service of the larger illusion.

Needless to say, these standards varied greatly. I heard descriptions of totals inflated in every conceivable way: by counting severed pieces of corpses as individual bodies; by counting a whole corpse several times on the basis of multiple claims for "credit" (by the man or unit doing the killing, the patrol encountering the body, the headquarters outfit hearing about the killing, and so on); and by counting murdered civilians, animals, or nonexistent "bodies" according to the kinds of need, ambition, and whim we have already encountered. Once a corpse had been identified (or imagined), it *became* that of a slain "enemy," and therefore evidence of warrior prowess—as the My Lai survivor makes clear: "If it's dead it's VC. Because it's dead. If it's dead it *had* to be VC. And of course a corpse couldn't defend itself anyhow." He went on to place the body count in a framework of corrupt competitiveness—a company commander "obsessed with the body count" who "wanted

a body count that would just beat all," that would "satisfy him . . . [and] satisfy higher headquarters . . . even if he knows this body count is a big dirty old lie." For "probably higher headquarters knows also. So they're fooling each other and theirselves as well."

I am convinced that the ethically sensitive historians of the future will select the phenomenon of the body count as the perfect symbol of America's descent into evil. The body count manages to distill the essence of the American numbing, brutalization, and illusion into a grotesque technicalization: there is something to count, a statistic for accomplishment. I know of no greater corruption than this phenomenon: the amount of killing—any killing—becomes the total measure of achievement. And concerning that measure, one lies, to others as well as to oneself, about why, who, what, and how many one kills.

OPENING UP

In earlier work, I found that survivors of the Hiroshima holocaust experienced what I described as "a vast breakdown of faith in the larger human matrix supporting each individual life, and therefore a loss of faith (or trust) in the structure of existence." The same is true not only for large numbers of Vietnam veterans but, perhaps in more indirect and muted ways, for Americans in general. This shattered existential faith has to do with remaining bound by the image of holocaust, of grotesque and absurd death and equally absurd survival. Even Americans who have not seen Vietnam feel something of a national descent into existential evil, a sense that the killing and dying done in their name cannot be placed within a meaningful system of symbols, cannot be convincingly "formulated." The result is a widespread if again vague feeling of lost integrity at times approaching moral-psychological disintegration.

What distinguishes Vietnam veterans from the rest of their countrymen is their awesome experience and knowledge of what others merely sense and resist knowing, their suffering on the basis of that knowledge and experience, and, in the case of antiwar veterans, their commitment to telling the tale. That commitment, especially for rap-group participants, meant asking a question very much like that of Remarque's hero in *All Quiet on the Western Front:* "What would become of us if everything that happens out there were quite clear to us?" "Out there" means Vietnam, their own minds, and in the end American society as well.

As part of their mission as survivors, antiwar veterans seek understanding of and liberation from the political and military agents of their own corruption. Their constant probing of these and other aspects of American society is less in the spirit of calm reflection than of anxious and pressured need. Amidst their confusions and touchiness, they have shared with one another a bond of brotherhood around their holocaust, their corruption, and their struggle against both. There is a sense in which they can fully trust only those who share their experience and their mission, though in each this trust may live side by side with suspicion of one another, related to suspicion of oneself.

They are loath to judge other veterans whose corruption has been much greater than their own. I recall a very tense moment during a psychiatric meeting at which a group of veterans described some of their experiences. When they had finished, a questioner from the floor asked them what they thought of a promise made by Lieutenant Calley (who was then still on trial) that, should he be acquitted, he would go on a speaking tour throughout the country on behalf of peace. The men visibly stiffened and answered in a series of terse phrases, such as "I can't judge him," "I have nothing to say about him," and "It could have been any of us." They knew too much about their own corruptibility and everyone else's within that specific atrocity-producing situation to be able to pass judgment upon a man in whom the disintegrative process had gone still further. They were trying to cope not only with their own guilt but with their overall formulation of their holocaust.

For they have taken on a very special survivor mission, one of extraordinary historical and psychological significance. They are flying in the face of the traditional pattern of coping with survivor emotions, which was to join organizations of veterans that not only justify their particular war but embrace warmaking and militarism in general. Contemporary "antiwar warriors" are turning that pattern on its head, and finding significance in their survival by exposing precisely the meaninglessness—and the evil—of their war. They do so, not as individual poets or philosophers (like those who emerged, for instance, from World War I), but as an organized group of ordinary war veterans. The psychological rub in the process is the need to call forth and confront their own "warlike" selves, or, as they sometimes put it, "the person in me that fought the war."

For a number of them, and at varying intervals, political activities become inseparable from psychological need. Telling their story to American society has been both a political act and a means of confronting psychologically an inauthentic experience and moving beyond it toward authenticity. For such people not only is protest necessary to psychological help—it *is* psychological help. At one moment one sees confused youngsters struggling to put together their shattered psychological selves—at another, young people with premature wisdom. As one of them expressed this uneasy combination to me, "I feel bitter because I'm a pretty young guy and the things I had to do and see I shouldn't have to in a normal lifetime." Still, they feel they have come to difficult truths that "adult" American society refuses to face. Indeed, in their eyes most of adult America lives in illusion. They describe others saying such things to them as "You're different from other people" or "You seem to know things that other people don't know." Since that knowledge has to do with death and pain, they have a double view of themselves in another way as well. They see themselves sometimes as a victimized group unrecognized and rejected by existing society, and sometimes as a special elite who alone can lay claim to a unique experience of considerable value in its very extremity and evil.

There is an additional paradox: that of an antimilitary group creating itself around its military experience, an antiwar group made up of those who fought the war and now oppose it. This means that their war-linked death anxiety and death guilt are constantly at issue. Merely to be in one another's presence is a reminder of the conflict and pain around which their group takes shape. No wonder they are wary of their own identity as antiwar veterans. As one of them said during a rap session: "Our life is being against the war. When the war ends, then we end as people." While ostensibly referring only to his antiwar organization, he was unconsciously revealing his own sense of depending totally upon—and being consumed by—the identity of the antiwar warrior.

By a number of criteria, the groups my colleagues and I have worked with—several hundred men—represent a small minority of the thirty thousand Vietnam veterans against the war, and they, in turn, of the three million Vietnam veterans.[1] For one thing, most of the men in these groups saw active combat, as opposed to the majority of men stationed there, who were in support assignments. For another, they emerged with an articulate antiwar position, in contrast to the majority, who take no public stance on the war, and to another minority, who emerged strongly supporting it. Concerning the first issue, my impression was that the intensity of residual conflicts was roughly parallel to one's degree of involvement in (or closeness to) combat, but that the sense of absurd evil radiated outward from the actual killing and dying, and that every American in Vietnam shared in some of the corruption of that environment; hence Polner's finding that no Vietnam veteran was free of doubt about what he had been called upon to do.

Similarly, even those who later come to insist that we should have gone all out to win the war—should have "nuked Hanoi" or "killed all the gooks"—are struggling to cope with their confusions and give some form and significance to their survival. There is evidence that antiwar and prowar veterans (the categories are misleading, and

the latter hardly exist in a public sense) are closer psychologically than might be suspected—or to put the matter another way, they take different paths in struggling to resolve the same psychological conflicts. Clearly the great majority of Vietnam veterans struggle silently, and apolitically, with that specific constellation of survivor conflict associated with Vietnam's atrocity-producing situation, so that one antiwar veteran could comment: "I hear a lot of people say, 'We know Vietnam veterans and they don't feel the way you do.' My immediate reaction to this is, 'Wait and see. If they are lucky they will. If they are lucky they will open up.' " The likelihood is that relatively few of the three million Vietnam veterans will be able to "open up" in the way he means. Yet there is a very real sense in which those few are doing symbolic psychological work for all veterans, and indeed for all of American society.

GUILT

The American survivor of Vietnam carries within himself the special taint of his war. His taint has to do with guilt evoked by death. His most disturbing images are of particular encounters with the dead and dying; his harshest self-judgments emerge from these encounters and concern not only what he did or did not do, but his sense of the overall "project" he was part of.

In the rap groups, the men frequently talked of their resentment of others viewing them as "monsters," "beasts," and "murderers." But before long they made it clear that these were their own self-judgments as well. A typical sequence was that of one man who described being unable to take a steady job after returning from Vietnam largely because of what he took to be negative attitudes of prospective employers: "They would think, 'There's a murderer, a monster.' I sometimes still think that myself."

One man in our group described being spat upon by an anonymous greeter at the airport when he returned, an experience referred to so often by veterans as to become a kind of mythic representation of a feeling shared by the American people and the veterans themselves: an image of Vietnam

[1] The figure is much higher if one includes those who have been involved in the war while stationed in Thailand and other parts of Southeast Asia.

as a war of "grunts" immersed in filth (rather than one of noble warriors on a path of glory) who return in filth to American society. They have fought in an undeclared and therefore psychologically "illegitimate" war, without either ceremonies of departure or parades of victorious return. Rather, the men speak of "sneaking back" into society, just as they were "sneaked" into Vietnam by higher authorities spinning (and caught in) a web of deceptions about whether American troops were to go to Vietnam, how many, how long they would stay there, and what they would do there.

There is a bitter paradox around the whole issue of wrongdoing that is neither lost on these men nor fully resolved by them. Sent as intruders in an Asian revolution, asked to fight a filthy and unfathomable war, they return as intruders in their own society, defiled by that war in the eyes of the very people who sent them as well as in their own. Images and feelings of guilt are generally associated with transgression—with having crossed boundaries that should not be crossed, with having gone beyond limits that should not be exceeded. Here the transgression has to do with two kinds of death, that which they witnessed and "survived" (deaths of buddies) and that which they inflicted on the Vietnamese. Though the two involve different experiences, they merge in the absurdity and evil of the entire project. Hence the men feel themselves to have been part of a "killing force" not only in the literal military sense but in a moral-psychological sense as well. Above all, they are survivors who cannot inwardly justify what they have seen and done—and are therefore caught in a vicious circle of death and guilt. Memories of death witnessed or inflicted, the *death imprint*, evoke disturbing feelings of guilt, which in turn activate that imprint. The resulting death guilt, at whatever level of consciousness, is the fundamental psychological legacy of this particular war.

Hence the touchiness of the veterans, revealed especially during early rap groups, about certain questions frequently asked them upon their return, especially by children: "Did you *kill* anyone over there? How *many* did you kill? How did you *feel* when you killed someone?" The veterans felt badly used by their questioners, saw them as deriving some kind of pleasure from hearing about killing, and interpreted these questions as proof that people in America, even children, are "programmed for violence." But they quickly came back to their own struggles about how much to condemn themselves for having killed or helped with killing, and for having remained alive. They explored the realization that they *could* kill, *did* kill, and only partly accepted the justification they themselves put forth, namely that it was *necessary* to kill in order to survive. Much of those early meetings was taken up with the men testing one another—and finding themselves wanting—by setting up virtually impossible moral choices: "If you had to kill someone again in order to survive, would you do it?" "If you had to kill an innocent person in order to survive, would you do *that*?" "If you had to kill a *child* in order to survive, would you do *that*?"

In posing these dilemmas, they were groping for a moral and psychological "position" on what they had done. They were performing a kind of psychic *danse macabre* around their own death guilt, moving gingerly back and forth, toward and away from it. At times they seemed to pass judgments of total evil: on all men or on "human nature" (the idea that anyone would kill anyone to save his own life); on American society (its demand that everyone be violent); and ultimately on themselves (their willingness to kill, sometimes even with pleasure, having revealed them to be, at bottom, nothing but murderers). But one could also perceive a search for an alternative to total evil, for a better way to recognize and confront their own guilt.

A man who had earlier believed in the military, and in fact was able to refrain from firing at My Lai largely because he felt the true soldier did not do such things, now asked himself: "Is there anything in [the military] that's worthy of anything . . . worthy of me . . . that I should stay in, that they should have me?"—conveying the impression that in his own eyes neither he nor it had lived up to acceptable warrior standards. He went on to speak of a profound loss of faith in both ordinary men ("I'll never trust people like I did before")

and in leaders (". . . before that I thought
. . . people who had the power had enough sense
. . . they couldn't make mistakes, at least big
mistakes"). He had difficulty extricating himself
from an abyss of infinite evil: "I used to think that
there was a certain limit to what [people] do."
Underlying everything was his realization that *"I
could have been one of those who did the shooting."*

He faced another pitfall as well. Telling the
truth about My Lai made him feel guilty toward his
buddies because "even though you may be trying
to help them they will think that you're hurting
them—and you don't want to have them think that
you're hurting them."

He remained confused, longing always for the
kind of precise, authoritative (and authoritarian)
self-judgment, the definite survivor formulation,
that kept eluding him. One man put the matter of
these confusions rather simply when, in the course
of a discussion, he told of killing a Viet Cong
soldier with a knife, and then added rather softly:
"I felt sorry. I don't know why I felt sorry. John
Wayne never felt sorry." That is, one was supposed to be tough and numbed, but one was not
—at least not entirely—given the extent of disbelief in "the enemy" and in one's right to kill him.

We see two general forms of guilt, that can be
designated as *static* and *animating*. Static guilt is
characterized by a closed universe of transgression
and expected punishment in which one is unable to
extricate oneself from a deathlike individual condition. One form we see it take is that of *numbed
guilt,* in which one's "deadened state" seems to
be a literal form of retribution for one's own act of
killing: the punishment fits the crime.

Numbed guilt resembles what Freud called an
unconscious sense of guilt—but I use the term to
emphasize the extent to which the entire being is
"frozen" or desensitized in order to avoid feeling
the "wound" (or "death") one has caused (or
thinks one has caused), leaving one anesthetized
from much of life itself.

Numbed guilt includes a vague feeling of bad-
ness, of having transgressed, in the absence of a
form or even a clear-cut emotional structure within
which to articulate that guilt. Unable to confront

what one has done, or even to feel clearly guilty,
one is instead plagued by an unformed, free-
floating discomfort with oneself, which is likely to
be associated with touchiness, suspiciousness, and
withdrawal.

"Self-lacerating" guilt is another form of static
guilt, in which, rather than sustained "deaden-
ing," one performs a perpetual "killing" of the
self. That is, the *mea culpa* of self-condemnation
takes the form of a repetition-compulsion, and the
very insistence upon one's own unmitigated evil
prevents actual "knowledge" of guilt. The "as if"
situation here is that of continuous reenactment of
the retribution, continuous killing of the self. Guilt
accompanying clinical forms of depression, and
what we speak of more generally as "neurotic
guilt," tend to be of this self-lacerating variety.

In both of these forms of static guilt one is cut
off from the life process—held in a state of separation and inner disintegration as well as stasis—that
is, in a death-dominated condition.

Animating guilt, in contrast, is characterized by
bringing oneself to life around one's guilt. This
requires active imagery of possibility beyond the
guilt itself. Animating guilt and image beyond the
guilt are in a continuous dialectical relationship,
the one requiring the other. Thus, animating guilt
propels one toward connection, integrity, and
movement. But for this self-propulsion to occur,
one requires prior internal images of at least the
possibility of these life affirming patterns, imagery
that can in turn relate to something in the external
environment. In this sense, the imagery of possibility antedates the animating guilt, but it is also
true that animating guilt can activate the individual
to the point of virtually creating such imagery.

Above all, animating guilt is a source of self-
knowledge—confirming Martin Buber's dictum
that "man is the being who is capable of becoming
guilty and is capable of illuminating his guilt." In
illuminating one's guilt, one illuminates the self.
Nor is animating guilt merely "restitutive,"
though it can certainly be that. Rather, it presses
beyond existing arrangements, toward new images
and possibilities, toward transformation. Above
all, animating guilt is inseparable from the idea of
being responsible for one's actions—so much so

that we may define it as the anxiety of responsibility.

To be sure, these various forms of guilt do not separate out as precisely as this schema might suggest; they in fact overlap and probably never exist in pure form. But I have observed in a considerable number of veterans a relationship to guilt so animating as to be a form of personal liberation. The discovery of one's animating guilt can, for such men, be nothing less than rediscovery of oneself as a human being. One deserter, for instance, remembered his dramatic recognition that "I was somebody with feelings who had done something wrong and I—I was not an animal or some kind of killing machine."

RAGE AND VIOLENCE

Unresolved death guilt can also be expressed through feelings of rage and impulses toward violence. These are prominent in survivors of any war, but the binds, betrayals, and corruptions experienced by the Vietnam veteran fuel those tendencies to the point where they invade large zones of his psyche. Bursts of anger were very frequent during our rap sessions, and it was more or less taken for granted that rage close to the surface was the normal emotion of the Vietnam veteran. The important question was what one did with the rage. During individual and group sessions, three different patterns of rage and violence seemed to emerge.

There was first what could be called the habit of violence. In war, violence becomes a quick and absolute solution to whatever seems to threaten or intrude, all the more so when there is great confusion about where danger lies and who is the enemy. Beyond that, the veteran can become habituated to the survivor mission of "revenge" (for buddies killed and other forms of suffering) and extend it to the civilian environment. A number of veterans told how, when brushed by someone on the street—or simply annoyed by something another person had done—they would have an impulse to "throttle" or kill him. And they would directly associate this impulse with pat-

terns of behavior cultivated in Vietnam: with "wasting" whoever passed for the enemy, with the numbing and brutalization underlying that behavior, but also with the rage beneath the numbing. As one man put it: "In Vietnam you're mad all the time—you wake up mad—you're mad when you eat, mad when you sleep, mad when you walk, mad when you sit—just mad all the time." He was undoubtedly overemphasizing the *awareness* of anger, but probably accurate about the extent of its inner existence, even if defended against. (His use of the word "mad" could also unwittingly imply "craziness.") In any case, an important segment of a generation of young American men built identities and life-styles around the rage and violence of a war environment as absorbing as it was corrupting. The guilt-linked sense of these inner zones of rage and violence is precisely what causes a man to retain the image of himself as a "monster."

Others have observed a similar preoccupation with violence in Vietnam veterans. Charles Levy, a young sociologist who has done extensive interviewing and "rapping" with working-class marine veterans, says that "the thinking of these veterans seems to be dominated by a fear of their own violence." Moreover, they were prone to give expression to random violence toward relatives, friends, or strangers.[2] Levy recognizes that some of these men had violent tendencies before they went to Vietnam, but believes that "the level of violence has now changed," and "now it has no boundaries." We can say that the guilt-linked habit of violence cultivated in Vietnam undermines earlier controls and distinctions about violence—as evidenced in observations like Levy's and in reports of violent crimes by Vietnam veterans.

Simply by coming to the rap group, the men I worked with were in effect taking a stand against random violence. Not that they lacked such im-

---

[2]Out of Charles Levy's original sample of sixty men he interviewed, a total of seven have been accused of murder (two) or attempted murder (five), which comes to a total of more than 10 percent. Of course, much more extensive statistics on a national basis are required, but a greater potential for random violence in Vietnam veterans than in veterans of other wars would be consistent with their particularly intense survivor conflicts.

pulses, often in complicated form. One veteran, somewhat prone to violence from childhood, spoke of his post-Vietnam struggles to overcome "the beast in me," by which he meant an inclination to attack other people suddenly while in a dreamlike state in which he was hardly aware of what he was doing. For some time after his return from Vietnam he worked as a milkman on a night route, where he could avoid other people and express his rage by periodic screams into the night. He spoke about his violent impulses in a repetitious, self-enclosed fashion, as though protecting himself from something underneath the violence. One of the professionals helped the group break through this protective armor by pointing out the profound fear behind each situation of violence the veteran described, to which he quickly responded: "Yes, sometimes I think I'm still back with those thirteen guys [in my squad]. . . . It's like going out on a mission and waiting for the first shot." He was, in other words, associating his violent impulses with death anxiety. The imagery he used was reminiscent of a tendency, described by Levy, for veterans to experience, at the moment of their violence, what they referred to as a "flashback" to Vietnam—to a situation either of combat or the killing of civilians.

The veteran quoted above told how, when in Vietnam, he and other GI's sometimes played a contemporary version of Russian roulette, in which one man would pull the pin of a grenade, which would then be tossed back and forth among the men until one of them made a decision to throw it off safely just before it exploded. Such a game combines violent and suicidal impulses as a response to overwhelming fear of death. In them, the men are able to re-create in playful-fearful microcosm—and thereby mock—the threat of *absurd* death characterizing the larger war.

Over the course of more than a year's involvement in the rap group, this veteran's violent tendencies greatly diminished. He could then "confess" that he had been much less violent in Vietnam than he had implied. He had previously given the impression that he had killed many people in Vietnam, whereas in actuality, despite extensive combat experience, he could not be certain he had killed anyone. After overcoming a certain amount of death anxiety and death guilt, that is, he had much less need to call forth his inner "beast" to lash out at others or at himself.

A second form of rage and potential violence centers around the theme of betrayal, the veterans' sense of having been victimized, badly used, or as they often put it, "fucked over," in having been sent to fight in Vietnam. They spoke about having been misled, put in a situation where they both slaughtered people and suffered for no reason, and were then abused or ignored on their return. There was sometimes talk of contemptuous treatment from employers or prospective employers, to whom "coming from Vietnam didn't mean a damn thing" (though they also realized that on many occasions, it was they, the veterans, who resisted the jobs). In this and other ways they expressed "victim's rage," which could extend to virtually every aspect of living.

At the same time the group was sensitive to, and would critically explore, tendencies to remain immobilized by extreme suspicion and a paranoid outlook, or by notions of "destroying everything"—American society, the people in it.

For just as the men rejected the imposed role of executioner, so they rejected that of "victim." It was always a matter of a particular person and his behavior, actions, or decisions—never a mere "victim"—however duped and badly treated by the all too real forces of victimization. These external forces (the government and military pursuing the war, the police and courts imposing absurd penalties for marihuana use as a way of suppressing a political militant, and so on) were taken seriously as part of the equation; there was never a reduction of all rage to childhood resentments, though these too were examined. Rage and indignation were too much respected for that: they were looked upon as significant, at times painful and self-destructive, but often appropriate and valuable emotions.

The rage could be directed toward any figures or symbols of authority, especially official authority—political leaders, the Veterans Administration, representatives of "the establishment" or ordinary middle-class society or the "older generation." Specific leaders and symbols were also discussed at length, so that psychological judgments could be informed by critical perspectives on "normal" social arrangements. But there was a special kind of rage reserved for the military.

The men expressed fantasies, old or current, of violent revenge toward those in the military who had abused them, especially toward "lifers" (regular army men), who seemed much more hated than anybody officially designated as "the enemy." These images could be relatively focused, or they could take on the diffuse, impotent quality of a recollection of one deserter: "I wanted to become a Communist. I wanted to assassinate the President. I wanted to organize some kind of uprising that would swoop down on the Pentagon—save the world from the imperialistic United States, et cetera, et cetera."

More frequently, the men would describe a gradually mounting bitterness at being "hassled" and ultimately betrayed by the military. That "betrayal" could take the form of a variety of small indignities, broken promises, bad assignments, lack of recognition, or brutalization by specific officers or noncoms—but always at the end of the road was the ultimate betrayal of Vietnam. Those most embittered toward the military were the ones who had initially believed in it and given themselves to it. Their resentful critique could extend far beyond the Vietnam War to corruptions throughout its structure, but they would always return to the war as both reflecting and furthering the poisoning of an institution they had admired, and within which they had for a time flourished. For them the betrayal was greatest.

These first two patterns—the habit of violence and the sense of having been betrayed—hearken back to the past, even if mostly the immediate past. But there is a third, more forward-looking pattern of rage and potential violence that seemed to d arf the other two in intensity—or, more accurately, to combine with the other two patterns to give the rage a more immediate focus. I refer to the

rage associated with a man telling his story of what he had experienced in Vietnam—to a considerable extent laying himself bare—and then being rebuffed. This rage was directed not so much toward war supporters or political opponents but toward those who "don't give a damn."

When the antiwar veterans hold their public hearings in various parts of the country and reveal details of brutality, murder, and atrocity, they are by no means simply beating their breasts to insist upon their own everlasting guilt. Rather, they are angrily exposing the atrocity-producing situation within which these acts were committed. Even the handful of veterans who "turned themselves in" to legal authorities at the time of the trial of Lieutenant Calley were saying something like: "Look, you bastards who are passing judgment—I did these things *too—everyone* did them." And when they flamboyantly cast away their medals near the Capitol building, they did so with the rage of "survivor-heroes" not only rejecting tainted awards but literally throwing them in the face of those who bestowed them. To be sure, there is guilt behind their actions. But there is also the bitter rage of men who have been betrayed, the angry insistence that the guilt be shared, and, above all, that the nature of the atrocity-producing situation be recognized. When they make this effort and are rebuffed, the antiwar veterans are left, so to speak, alone with their static guilt and impotent rage. What they seek and in some cases have partly achieved is a way of using their guilt and rage to transform themselves and their society.

COUNTERFEITS

In their diffuse anger, the men reserved a very special tone—best described as ironic rage—for two categories of people they encountered in Vietnam: chaplains and "shrinks."

The very mention of a military chaplain quickly brought forth smirks, jibes, and the kind of uneasy laughter suggested by the half-conscious witticism, "Those chaplains—oh my God!" With bitter enthusiasm, they gave endless examples of chaplains blessing the troops, their mission, their guns, their killing. As one of the men put it, "Whatever we were doing . . . murder . . . atrocities . . . God was *always* on our side."

Or as a Catholic veteran explained: "Yes, I would go to confession, and say, 'Sure, I'm smoking dope again. I guess I blew my state of grace again.' But I didn't say anything about killing." Whatever his actual words to his confessor, he was referring to religious arrangements that held one spiritually accountable only for a meaningless transgression and not for the ultimate one. The chaplain presided over this hypocritical ritualization of evil, and then sanctioned—even "blessed" —the routine, unritualized, and genuinely malignant evil. The real message of this ostensibly religious transaction was: Stay within our moral clichés as a way of draining off excess guilt, and then feel free to plunge into the business at hand.

One man spoke especially bitterly of "chaplains' bullshit." He went on to illustrate what he meant by recalling the death of a close buddy, followed by a combined funeral ceremony and pep talk—like that at My Lai, but this time conducted by a chaplain—at which the men were urged to "kill more of them." Similarly, the veteran who had carried the corpse of his closest buddy on his back after his company had been annihilated told of "the bullshit ceremony" that followed, at which the chaplain spoke of "the noble sacrifice for the sake of their country" made by the dead. The same veteran told of having become so enraged at the time that he went back to the chaplain's tent later and almost assaulted him. Overwhelmed with death anxiety and death guilt, and desperately in need of an authentic formulation of survival, the chaplain's plea for false witness threw him into a state of rage and near psychotic dissociation.

References to "shrinks" were in the same tone. The men told a number of stories in which either they or others had asked to see a psychiatrist because of some form of psychological suffering associated with the war, only to be in one way or another "reassured" by him and "helped" to re-

turn to combat. One veteran told of two men he knew of who had to prepare bodies for shipment and place them in body bags. After a period of time both men sought out a psychiatrist to tell him that they simply could not do the work anymore—but in both cases were urged (in effect, required) to "accept" and adapt to their assignment. Both did, only to be faced with overwhelming conflicts much later on.

Chaplains and psychiatrists are not only spiritual counselors: Americans also perceive them, rightly or wrongly as "guardians of the spirit," as guides to "right thinking" and "proper behavior" (in this way psychiatrists resemble chaplains more than they do other physicians). The veterans were trying to say that the only thing worse than being ordered by military authorities to participate in absurd evil is to have that evil rationalized and justified by "guardians of the spirit." Chaplains and psychiatrists thus fulfill the function of helping men adjust to committing war crimes, while lending their spiritual authority to the overall project.

The men sought out chaplains and shrinks because of a spiritual-psychological crisis growing out of what they perceived to be irreconcilable demands in their situation. They sought either escape from absurd evil or at the very least a measure of inner separation from it. Instead, spiritual-psychological authority was employed to seal off any such inner alternative. Chaplains and psychiatrists then formed "unholy alliances" not only with the military command but with the more corruptible elements of the soldier's individual psyche. We may then speak of the existence of a *counterfeit universe, in which all-pervasive, spiritually reinforced inner corruption becomes the price of survival.* In such an inverted moral universe, whatever residual ethical sensitivity impels the individual against adjusting to evil is under constant external *and internal* assault.

The men described experiencing *themselves* as counterfeit. They spoke of having been "like boys playing soldiers"—of having the feeling, upon entering combat: "God, this is right out of a movie!"

One said simply: "Nothing was real." The game of war, they seemed to be saying, was there, but reduced to childish deception and self-deception. The play element was isolated, disconnected, never a part of a believable ritual or contest. They were counterfeit warriors engaging in counterfeit play.

One former marine technician described the kind of protracted struggle that could take place between commitment to immediate military tasks and ever more insistent awareness of the counterfeit nature of the larger project. He had doubts about the war before going to Vietnam, together with a vague but persistent patriotism, so that he tended initially to look upon much of what he encountered as "doing it all wrong" rather than ask why his country was doing it at all. He immersed himself in his highly technical radar work with the intensity and pleasure of a mechanically inclined American boy: "Nobody took the time and effort that I did to, you know, play with [the radar]. It was like tinkering with a car. . . . I got along very well with my radar set. I used to play with it very well." That "tinkering," moreover, by locating enemy emplacements, saved American lives: "They'd stop and call up, 'Thanks . . . man, we only lost three.' . . . They'd come back from the field . . . come in and shake your hand and cry and say, 'Wow! Thanks a lot' . . . because they knew." Conscientious, effective, and increasingly recognized, he was also sustained by ambition and pride: "I was into the [military] game. I was starting to catch on to how you played it." Over a period of time, though, his powerful sense of duty and responsibility "eroded" and "it reached me"—"it" being an amorphous sense that the war, the military, everything around him was counterfeit.

Smoking pot helped him come to this realization. He had already begun to feel that a lot that Americans were doing was "ridiculous," but would then insist to himself that "there must be a reason . . . a purpose, even though it seems ridiculous to me." Only when he and a few other enlisted men would retire to a quiet place without their weapons and light up would everything become clear: "When I was smoking, then I would say, 'It's just a bunch of bullshit, it really is . . . it really *is* ridiculous . . . really stupid.' "

He would have such additional thoughts as, "Somebody back there in Washington and somebody in Hanoi . . . is programming both of us and we're just being tools of it." He became especially aware of the absurdity and ultimate impotence of the military-technical arrangements in which he was enveloped:

> Back there they were playing silly games and we had to be somehow involved in their silly games. . . . I realized the absurdity of all this electronic warfare . . . this giant technological element that we had that was rendered entirely impotent by a few little Vietnamese running around and throwing land mines here and there.

The large amphibious tractors (or "amtracs") sent in and out of his gun station every day, containing weapons, parts, and electronic equipment, came to symbolize the absurdity of our technology.

While smoking, the men began to develop an elaborate collective fantasy about a different kind of amphibious tractor—one decked out in psychedelic colors—"all swirls and everything"—and "filled up with dope." That happy vehicle was driven by "Alice," a fortyish, apparently American woman, "kind of dumpy and matronly," whom everyone was delighted to have around:

> She was . . . very much into what we were doing, and she liked to smoke dope and she had good stuff. She would come around, smoke with the men, pass out her dope to them free of charge.

Alice had the power to turn men off war and on to pot and booze. On one occasion, so the tale went, the men were ordered to sweep through a village on a combat mission, but then instead

> Alice was going to come . . . [and] there wasn't going to be any fighting. . . . Instead of . . . sweeping through the village we were going to . . . say hello to the [Vietnamese] girls [who actually did sell marihuana to the men] and sit around and drink a little Vietnamese beer . . . and smoke dope.

Sometimes Alice would come along on a patrol, which would mean that "what we were going to do was go in and smoke dope with the villagers." As for the "enemy":

> If there were any [Viet Cong] they would have just sat down and smoked with us because they were, you know, on our side. Maybe it was absurd for them too.

Sometimes the fantasy carried Alice herself into wildly absurd situations of slapstick adventures and misadventures, a situation not unrelated to their own, but now depicted in comic version.

> Well we would just get on a kick like it was a Wild West rodeo or something. And here comes Alice . . . out there waddling around, because she wouldn't move very fast. And she was out there trying to rope a steer or something and the steer was coming after her and Alice was wobbling around, you know, and we'd go through the whole involved thing and Alice was trying to jump on the walls . . . and get away. . . . I guess they'd gotten into a bullfight too because there was a bull chasing her and she was trying to jump on the wall and she was just too fat and big to do it, you know. So the bull had gored her in the ass, I guess. And, you know, this was very funny—poor Alice, you know. But then we all ran over and helped her. . . . You throw in some little extras . . . like . . . now somebody would pick it up and say, "Oh, ya," and now here comes this thing and they'd go on for a minute and then someone else would jump in and so it was a communal-type thing.

Alice even applied herself to military inequities, as in another scenario when she "left her 'trac' for repairs" and drove up instead in a smaller vehicle, the very jeep that had been illegally taken from a nearby Air Force unit and absorbed into the marine car pool (here the fantasy partly paralleled an actual incident). As the marine veteran explained:

> They [the Air Force] had so much anyway with their PX's and everything and we had been sacrificing all this time. . . . Alice was a friend of ours so she was simply redistributing the wealth, I think. That's what she was doing.

In Alice, the men were creating something of a latter-day Mother Courage, a mother-earth figure who gaily distributes her wares in the midst of war, and carries on no matter what.

Brecht's Mother Courage is a cynical, if admirable, opportunist ("There isn't a war every day in the week, we must get to work"), an ironic survivor-prophet who sells not only food but soldiers' boots, belts, and guns, and predicts (accurately, it turns out) the deaths of soldiers she meets and of her own two sons as well. But Alice is a more simple and loving nurturer-buffoon, whose mission in life is to replace war with pleasure. The message of Mother Courage, for whom business always comes first, might be paraphrased as "buy and die"—while that of Alice, for whom pleasure is all, is closer to "take, smoke, and live." One wonders, though, how much of Mother Courage as harbinger of death—as death itself—there is even in Alice. Her creation, at the very least, is an attempt to "play with" and mock death anxiety; and it is possible that pursuing the fantasy further would show Alice to have more direct connections with violence and death (perhaps suggested in the "Wild West" sequence). In any case, both figures ultimately serve to reveal the counterfeit nature of war—Mother Courage by means of survival in corruption, Alice by means of her absolute reversal of the war environment.

The name Alice, of course, came from the song "Alice's Restaurant," which the men had heard (they had not yet had a chance to see the film). The whole Alice fantasy was their way of turning the war over on its head (or, should one say, "to its heads"), finding expression for its absurdity, and replacing its grotesque death with marvelously charmed life. Even violence could be noted and tamed, in a sense domesticated, through the mildly black-humor rodeo-Western sequence, in which Alice's mishaps could provide not only imagery of violent buffoonery, but still another reversal of nurturing whereby the men could actively help, indeed save *her*.

Above all, the fantasy was a group venture, a "communal-type thing" both in creation and content. It provided a sustained counterscenario right in the midst of actual combat. Similarly, pot-smoking in general became the center of a counterenvironment in the midst of the atrocity-producing situation. Thus the same marine veteran describes how, as a noncom with considerable authority over the men working under him as well as responsibility for complex technical equipment,

> pot smoking . . . was in conflict with the role that I was playing in the military . . . with the rest of the image of what I was doing. . . . People . . . in my category, that had been dedicated, and [then] started smoking . . . say, three months after they had gone over there [he began after about four months] . . . you know, they got kind of . . . they didn't care about the war. . . . They just weren't as ambitious or dedicated.

One member of the rap group described to me, during a talk we had, what he called a "crisis of faith"—mentioned in connection with individual psychotherapy he was undergoing elsewhere, but extending far beyond that:

> It seemed like why? why him? why there? And what was this doing? . . . Why don't we all go back to the country and chop wood? Or get quill pens and write by candlelight and just forget all this shit? War, where's the war? Where's the peace? Where's the bomb? Where's, you know, there's nothing. . . . What's the sense of Vietnam Vets Against the War?

And about rap groups, after one particularly gripping session:

> We come together out of the blue and then that happens within a three-hour period, and you march off. . . . There were people I had nothing to do with other than meet those needs. Sometimes it strikes me as completely absurd.

The VVAW, particularly in its early stages, had special importance in the quest for authenticity. In it one could call forth some of the intimacy and solidarity that existed in military combat, and do so for other than counterfeit purposes. But this man was asking himself, as were others, whether in any endeavor it was possible to be other than counterfeit. Over the course of time, virtually all of the men found areas of authenticity, but the concern remains strong for most of them. It is, in fact, at the center of their survivor struggle.

Nor is the question always answerable through-

out the rest of American society. Vietnam veterans are by no means the only ones asking: "Where does Vietnam end and America—the America one used to believe in—begin?" It would be too much to suggest that the whole of America has become a "counterfeit universe." But one can say that, with the Vietnam War, a vast, previously hidden American potential for the counterfeit has become manifest. From the atrocity-producing situation in Vietnam; to the military-political arrangements responsible for it; to the system of law confronted by militant opponents of the war; to the preexisting but war-exacerbated antagonisms around race, class, ethnicity, and age; to the war-linked economic recession; to collusion in the war's corruption by virtually all of the professions and occupations—what is there left that we can call authentic?

To ask the question is to assume that there *is* something left. But that something has to be sought out and re-created. Correspondingly, the expanding contours of the counterfeit universe have to be identified. The model suggested by military chaplains and psychiatrists is that of a counterfeit situation in which the price for survival includes not only external compliance but internal corruption furthered by spiritual authorities serving the prevailing power structure. This kind of counterfeit universe is probably inherent in any system of social authority. The Vietnam War has revealed and intensified counterfeit dimensions throughout American society. And once one has begun to grasp the principle of the counterfeit universe, can one continue to ignore the malignancy of related constellations around and within oneself?

Philip Kingry, a Vietnam veteran and talented novelist, has put the matter this way: "The war isn't just an excuse. *It* was *everything.* I am a lie. What I have to say is a lie. But it is the most true lie you will ever hear about a war." If the counterfeit universe is not to remain *everything,* one must explore its manifestations everywhere, even if the counterfeit manifestations seem to render those very explorations "a lie." War veterans and commentators alike can at least begin with such "true lies" as a way of initiating the difficult climb out of the abyss.

USEFUL RESOURCES

ARDREY, R. *African genesis*. New York: Dell Publishing, 1967.

Man's descent from "killer-apes" is the thesis with arguments based upon carefully selected anthropological and ethological findings.

ARDREY, R. *The territorial imperative*. New York: Atheneum, 1966.

The author examines the characteristics of territoriality in animals and argues that man obeys the same laws as animals.

BANDURA, A. *Aggression: A social learning analysis*. New York: Prentice-Hall, 1973.

". . . the attempts to show what we know about aggression . . . in terms of social learning theory."

BERKOWITZ, L. *Aggression: A social psychological analysis*. New York: McGraw-Hill, 1962.

BERKOWITZ, L. (Ed.) *Roots of aggression*. New York: Atherton, 1969.

Eight collected papers by various authors dealing with the relationship between frustration and aggression.

BRAMSON, L., & GOETHALS, G. W. (Eds.) *War: Studies from psychology, sociology, anthropology*. New York: Basic Books, 1964.

BRELAND, K., & BRELAND, M. The misbehavior of organisms. *American Psychologist*, 1961, **16**, 681–684.

CARTHY, J. D., & EBLING, F. J. (Eds.) *The natural history of aggression*. New York: Academic Press, 1972.

Contains mainly biological and anthropological discussions.

DEUTSCH, M. Psychological alternatives to war. *Journal of Social Issues*, 1962, **18**, 97–119.

EIBL-EIBESFELDT, I. The fighting behavior of animals. *Scientific American*, December 1961.

ENDLEMAN, S. (Ed.) *Violence in the streets*. Chicago: Quadrangle, 1968.

A wide-ranging collection of papers including essays by Bruno Bettelheim, Norman Mailer, William Buckley Jr., Albert Bandura, Arthur Miller, and Kenneth Clark.

ERON, L. D., LEFKOWITZ, M. M., HUESMANN, L. R., & WALDER, L. O. Does television violence cause aggression? *American Psychologist*, 1972, **27**, 253–263.

"The effect of television violence on aggression. . . . explains a larger portion of the variance than does any other single factor which we studied, including I.Q., social status, mobility aspirations, religious practice, ethnicity, and parental disharmony."

FROMM, E. The Erich Fromm theory of aggression. *New York Times Magazine*, February 27, 1972, 14–86.

GOLDING, W. *Lord of the flies*. New York: Putnam, 1969.

A fictional account of the Freudian assumption that man's "civilization" is a thin veneer covering up a primeval beast.

GOLEMBIEWSKI, R. T., BULLOCK, C. S., & RODGERS, H. R. *The new politics: Polarization or utopia?* New York: McGraw-Hill, 1970.

A political, sociological, and psychological collection of readings that is well edited and contains some interesting and provocative selections dealing with alienation, justice, drugs, poverty, protests, the Black Panthers, strikes, police brutality, liberal and right-wing movements, and welfare. Highly recommended.

HOLDEN, C. T.V. violence: Government study yields more evidence, no verdict. *Science*, 1972, **175**, 608–611.

Commentary on the Surgeon General's Report.

KOESTLER, A. *The ghost in the machine*. New York: Macmillan, 1967.

One of the most controversial books in recent times, in which the Nobel Laureate argues that aggressive behavior is rooted in our biological history.

KOESTLER, A. Man—one of evolution's mistakes? *New York Times Magazine*, October 1968.

LORENZ, K. *On Aggression*. New York: Harcourt, Brace and World, 1963.

LORENZ, K. A talk with Konrad Lorenz, *New York Times Magazine*, July 5, 1970.

MEGARGEE, E. I., & HOKANSON, J. E. (Eds.)

The dynamics of aggression. New York: Harper & Row, 1970.
A psychologically and sociologically oriented collection with papers by Sigmund Freud, Konrad Lorenz, John Dolland, Carl Hovland, Hans Toch, Amatai Etzioni, and others.

MILGRAM, S. *Obedience to authority: An experimental view.* New York: Harper & Row, 1973.
". . . reports on experiments, the shocking results of which expose the dark reality of the social and psychological mechanisms that underlie man's inhumanity to man." From *Psychology Today* Book Club.

MURRAY, J. R. Television and violence: Implications of the Surgeon General's research program. *American Psychologist,* 1973, **28,** 472–478.

RUBIN, J. *Do it!* New York: Ballantine Books, 1970.
A call to arms by the P. T. Barnum of the youth revolution.

SHAFFER, H. B. Violence in the media. *Editorial Research Reports,* May 10, 1972, 376–394.

SINGER, J. L. (Ed.) *The control of aggression and violence: Cognitive and physiological factors.* New York: Academic Press, 1971.
Although the full range of factors that can affect aggression are not covered in this collection, the papers are of excellent quality.

SKOLNICK, J. *The politics of protest.* New York: Ballantine Books, 1969.
Report to the National Commission on the Causes and Prevention of Violence.

USDIN, G. (Ed.) *Perspectives on violence.* New York: Brunner-Mazel, 1972.
Papers derived from a psychiatric meeting on "Alternatives to Violence" held in Washington, D.C., at the time of antiwar protest in that city.

Why is man aggressive? A synthetic round table. *Impact of Science on Society,* 1968, **18,** 85–95.

CHAPTER 7
ON MADNESS

PROVOCATIONS

Mental illness is, of course, a threat when occurring in an office with power of the Presidency of the United States. But it must not be magnified by our fears of its alien, bizarre quality. It is still but one small danger. The problem of irrational and irresponsible leadership is only fractionally compounded by mental illness, and I would think that rather than looking for psychiatric solutions we had best look to political ones. It is the power of the office that is the problem. If we are to guard against executive fallacy we must elect the kind of men who will sustain our hopes. We must find some way to develop institutions that will encourage as candidates those men who will be comfortable with power, who will not confuse national security with personal status, who will endure unpopularity, who will cherish criticism as the surest sign of freedom, and who, above the clamor, will respect the quiet decencies.

W. Gaylin

Witchdoctors and psychiatrists perform essentially the same function in their respective cultures. They are both therapists; both treat patients using similar techniques; and both get similar results. Recognition of this should not downgrade psychiatrists; rather it should upgrade witchdoctors.

E. Fuller Torrey

American psychiatry presently deters social change; it is much more of a repressive social force than it has to be. I do not mean that psychiatrists as a group are conservative or socially insensitive. Rather, I am convinced that their failure to understand the political impact of their work has frequently led them to further the cause of repressiveness. Psychiatrists will do little to bring about social change and will, in fact, fail to provide the most effective treatment for their patients until they realize that all psychiatric intervention is political.

S. Halleck

Everybody is a little sick, nobody is really sick, and no one knows what mental sickness really is anyhow.

W. Gaylin

WHAT DO YOU THINK?

37   INTRODUCTION TO MADNESS: OR WHAT'S IN A NAME?

WILLIAM C. CORNING

Yer . . . crazy
        mad
        sick
        weird
        nuts
        insane
        flippy
        bananas
        psycho
        batty
        strung out
        freaked out
        round the bend
        losing yer mind
        a lunatic
        outta yer head
        out to lunch
        hung up
        strung up
        a fruit-cake
        neurotic
        schizy
        paranoid
           or

This patient has been diagnosed as . . .
        Schizophrenic:
            simple
            hebephrenic
            catatonic
            paranoid
            acute
            latent
            residual
            schizo-affective
            specified
            and unspecified
        Affective psychotic:
            agitated depression
            manic-depressive, depressed
            manic-depressive, manic
        Neurotic:
            anxious
            phobic
            obsessive-compulsive
            hysterical
            dissociated
            hypochondriac
            depressed
        and on and on . . .

COMMENT: PSYCHIATRIC BLACKJACKS

The point is not that psychiatric diagnoses are meaningless, but that they may be, and often are, swung as semantic blackjacks: cracking the subject's respectability and dignity destroys him just as effectively, and often more so, as cracking his skull. The difference is that the man who wields a blackjack is recognized by everyone as a public menace, but one who wields a psychiatric diagnosis is not.

THOMAS SZASZ

WHAT'S IN A NAME?

The universe that the psychologist is interested in encompasses what might be dryly put as organism-environment transactions and organism-organism transactions. We categorize and label these transactions in order to facilitate communication and to provide a more scientifically useful scheme, just as the biologist constructs a hierarchy of functions and species and so orders his universe of interest. In psychology we talk about "rage," "learning," "compulsiveness," and so on just as the biologist talks about "flying," "reproduction," and "respiration." The label that is affixed hopefully indicates a great deal about the process and its mechanisms. However, when a biologist talks about flying, it is not assumed that the bat, the bee, the kite, and the airplane are totally similar with respect to mechanisms and characteristics of the process. Similarly, as Donald Jensen puts it, we do not equate the blood of man with the juice of a beet because they are both red. The similarities we observe on the surface may say little about the underlying mechanisms and characteristics.

The descriptive term is a useful communicative device. When I point out that a person is showing paranoid schizophrenic symptoms, this communicates a certain amount of information and permits some limited but still useful indications as to how this person will behave. The difficulty arises when the application of the behavioral, descriptive terms

is assumed to mean a common underlying cause or mechanism. This assumption reduces the probability that research will locate critical causative factors. For example, an investigator may wish to examine the hypothesis that abnormal concentrations of substance X in the blood is correlated with the schizophrenic episode. In a group of twenty symptomatically similar schizophrenics, X may actually be a significant factor but since fifteen subjects do not show it, then the investigator will conclude that X is not a significant causation because interpretations of studies are based upon group analyses. The group may have members whose symptoms are caused by X, others whose symptoms are produced by some experiential trauma, and others who have a perceptual handicap. All these factors could lead to a similar symptomology and, more seriously, to similar "treatment." If the assumption is that high anxiety levels cause schizophrenia, the psychiatrist may prescribe large doses of tranquilizers to all members of a particular diagnostic category. The drug may help to alleviate the anxiety of some but could be entirely ineffectual or even harmful to others ("One man's medicine is another man's poison"). A possible way out of this problem of labeling is to generate diagnostic categories that are based upon more than traditional behavioral symptomology. Ideally, the categorization and treatment of a person would depend upon behavioral, physiological, and biochemical analyses.

The persisting unreliability of a plethora of treatments that are currently available and the general failure to find consistent physical and experiential correlates for diagnostic categories could very well be due to the assumption that the label, the common grouping, suggests unity with respect to causation. What's in a name? We still do not know because we have not looked properly and lack sufficient data.

STICK THE NAME IN AN INSTITUTION

The label permits action and makes us feel better. The label connotes disease, sickness, a physical abnormality, the "logical" introduction of treatment, and the possibility that the problematic person will become the problem of others.

(I am walking down the street and sliding towards me on a skate board is a human torso, face contorted from the effort of navigating bumpy Greenwich Village sidewalks. What is it doing here, this ugly and repulsive thing?—put it away.)

(A stunned mother and father are informed that their recently born child is a mongoloid. It will be retarded, have certain physical problems, die young—put it into an institution; it will be better there.)

(Paranoid schizophrenic is the name—possibly a danger to himself and others. There are places where they can be treated, cared for, protected. Everyone will be better off. No more strange talk and unpredictable behavior. It is a disease and there are hospitals for the diseased—stick it there.)

Out of sight, out of mind. We are not raised to tolerate those that are different. We depend upon institutions to handle our problems—the problem is no longer ours, nor is the acceptance of responsibility and the necessity of attempting to interact with "it." We like conventional-looking people and conventional communications. I choose not to attempt communication with someone who thinks he is Christ. I choose to consider him ill and I am comfortable when the human torso, the mongoloid, the schizophrenic, and Christ are "put away." If only it could be that easy to put away bigots, the Minutemen, oil company executives, press agents, politicians, real estate salesmen, and the many others who are also causing problems in society.

COMMENT: "PSYCHIATROSIS"

Jung suggested some years ago that it would be an interesting experiment to study whether the syndrome of psychiatry runs in families. A pathological process called "psychiatrosis" may well be found, by the same methods, to be a delineable entity, with somatic correlates and psychic mechanisms, with an inherited or at least constitutional basis, a natural history, and a doubtful prognosis.

R. D. LAING

Once labeled, a subject/object distinction is possible—physician/patient, me/him, manipulator/manipulable, the doer/the done-in, he/it. Divorce from the label is easier than divorce from the person. The label goes with a set of treatments, with an institution, and with the assumption that there is something wrong with the labeled. The labeling permits "blaming the victim," a strategy that absolves us from looking at ourselves, our institutions, our society, but rather focuses treatment and concern on the victim, in this case the "abnormal" person. This strategy permits us to be concerned, to be "open-minded," keep our liberal orientations, and yet avoid changing our life-styles, political structures, and general morality. We can get involved with improving the institutions so that those who are "put away" are happier. It allows me to keep my house, four and a half acres, two cars, the existing structures—and, hopefully, I will not run into any more strange things on the street.

COMMENT: "BLAMING THE VICTIM"

Twenty years ago, Zero Mostel used to do a sketch in which he impersonated a Dixiecrat Senator conducting an investigation of the origins of World War II. At the climax of the sketch, the Senator boomed out, in an excruciating mixture of triumph and suspicion, "What was Pearl Harbor *doing* in the Pacific?"

WILLIAM RYAN

TREATING THE NAMED

Psychiatry and, secondarily, clinical psychology are coming under increased attack these days. These attacks generally center around the following issues:

1 The "label" is considered to be an unreliable categorization. Once named, a person is viewed in particular ways and given certain treatments regardless of whether the behavior has changed. The label biases the perceptions

250 ON MADNESS

and responses of others. The labeled are, in other words, stigmatized.

2 Institutions are little more than prisons where the "patient" undergoing "treatment" is actually tortured, denied human rights, and is forced to accept the views of others in order to obtain escape from the institution.

3 The "treatments" are of questionable use and have not been validated. New treatments are invented almost as fast as the old ones are invalidated.

4 Traditional psychotherapeutic practices "blame the victim." By adopting the belief that the problems, physical or psychological, are solely within the patient, treatment proceeds with little concern for the external familial, political, or social environment of the patient. The patient is frequently forced to tolerate and exist within a "sick" situation in order to be deemed "normal."

Although several psychologists and psychiatrists have been openly critical of their respective professions in the past, none has been so dramatic and so effective in stirring up public interest as R. D. Laing, a Scottish psychiatrist who has devoted his interests to schizophrenia. In his earlier writings, Laing proposed that one designated as "schizophrenic" cannot be understood independently of the family; rather the family as a whole displays the syndrome. The interactions within the family are pathological and are characterized by the communication of conflicting messages, messages that are confusing and threatening and cause the person to lose no matter what response is made. In a sense, the person is "elected" by the family to be the scapegoat, the schizophrenic, and the family is thus absolved of having to do anything further. "Schizophrenia," then, refers to a family disorder, and this disorder can remain obscured by the sacrificial lamb (patient) who is offered to psychiatry and the institutes by the family.

In later writings, Laing began to stress the strategy of the schizophrenic and offer more radical views on what the schizophrenic person repre-

sents. The "nonsense" language of the schizophrenic is not really unintelligible after all and can be understood within the family context; the experience of the schizophrenic is comprehensible when an attempt is made to unravel the message within a meaningful space. Laing went further and adopted the view that schizophrenia represented an attempt at healing, a voyage that could lead to a reconstitution of the person. The schizophrenic was not ill; society with its wars, conflicting messages, and inhumane treatments was really insane. The schizophrenic voyage is an attempt to heal the divisions caused by the conflicting messages of the world. It is a voyage to sanity, a trip to be sought, to be envied, to be encouraged and tolerated; it is a new level of existence and hopefully a return to sanity, and is equated with the psychedelic experience. The experiences are meaningful and not to be tampered with by the usual degradation ceremonies, tortures, and oppressions of institutions and psychiatrists. These new visions are feared by the "normal," who readily affix the label "madness" in an attempt to prevent the experience. Institutions should be true asylums where a person can go and leave voluntarily, where his experiences are accepted as meaningful, where attempts are made to understand and not coerce, where sanity can be achieved in spite of the maddening world outside.

Laing's messages are disturbing, but no less disturbing than those of several others who in more prosaic and less poetic styles have been openly questioning the assumptions and practices of psychiatry and clinical psychology. The messages of Laing and others require a critical examination and they should not be accepted outright. However, they do require serious attention and perhaps integration into the mainstream of thought in the "mental health" movement.

COMMENT: A HOMOSEXUAL FOR PRESIDENT?

I see no reason, for example, to assume that a homosexual would be particularly unqualified for the Presidency because of his homosexuality. Yet, obviously, the public would never tolerate this. And in this case, I suspect, it would not be because people consider homosexuality to be a severe form of mental illness—indeed there are movements and groups that would not so categorize it—but because in a male-dominated society that elevates maleness and equates it with power and ability, the accusation of homosexuality is the ultimate pejorative. It would be too damaging to the image of a leader.

On the other hand, untreated alcoholism, which might cause critical problems, is readily accepted in Cabinet members, Senators, diplomats, and might well be indulged, by denial and rationalization, in a President. People identify with it readily. It is part of our shared tradition, respected and ennobled by a host of boozing fictional heroes. Hard drinking is manly and American and not inconsistent with a view of high office.

W. GAYLIN

● The American Psychiatric Association has just removed "homosexuality" from its list of "mental illnesses."

---

38 THE SCHIZOPHRENIC EXPERIENCE*

R. D. LAING

JONES *(laughs loudly, then pauses):* I'm McDougal myself. *(This actually is not his name.)*

SMITH: What do you do for a living, little fellow? Work on a ranch or something?

J: No, I'm a civilian seaman. Supposed to be high muckamuck society.

S: A singing recording machine, huh? I guess a recording machine sings sometimes. If they're adjusted right. Mm-hm. I thought that was it. My towel, mm-hm. We'll be going back to sea in about—eight or nine months though. Soon as we get our—destroyed parts repaired. *(Pause)*

J: I've got lovesickness, secret love.

S: Secret love, huh? *(Laughs)*

J: Yeah.

S: I ain't got any secret love.

J: I fell in love, but I don't feed any woo—that sits over—looks something like me—walking around over there.

S: My, oh, my only one, my only love is the shark. Keep out of the way of him.

J: Don't they know I have a life to live? *(Long pause)*

S: Do you work at the air base? Hm?

J: You know what I think of work. I'm thirty-three in June, do you mind?

S: June?

J: Thirty-three years old in June. This stuff goes out the window after I live this, uh—leave this hospital. So I lay off cigarettes, I'm a spatial condition, from outer space myself, no shit.

S *(laughs):* I'm a real space ship from across.

J: A lot of people talk, uh—that way, like crazy, but Believe It or Not by Ripley, take it or leave it —alone it's in the *Examiner,* it's in the comic section, Believe It or Not by Ripley, Robert E. Ripley, Believe It or Not, but we don't have to believe anything, unless I feel like it. *(Pause)* Every little rosette—too much alone. *(Pause)*

S: Could be possible. *(Phrase inaudible because of aeroplane noise)*

J: I'm a civilian seaman.

S: Could be possible. *(Sighs)* I take my bath in the ocean.

J: Bathing stinks. You know why? Cause you can't quit when you feel like it. You're in the service.

S: I can quit whenever I feel like quitting. I can get out when I feel like getting out.

J *(talking at the same time):* Take me. I'm a civilian, I can quit.

S: Civilian?

J: Go my—my way.

S: I guess we have, in port, civilian. *(Long pause)*

J: What do they want with us?

S: Hm?

---

*From R. D. Laing, *The politics of experience and the bird of paradise*, Baltimore: Penguin Books, 1967, pp 84–107. Reprinted by permission of the publisher.

J: What do they want with you and me?

S: What do they want with you and me? How do I know what they want with you? I know what they want with me. I broke the law, so I have to pay for it. *(Silence)*[1]

This is a conversation between two persons diagnosed as schizophrenic. What does this diagnosis mean?

To regard the gambits of Smith and Jones as due *primarily* to some psychological deficit is rather like supposing that a man doing a handstand on a bicycle on a tightrope 100 feet up with no safety net is suffering from an inability to stand on his own two feet. We may well ask why these people have to be, often brilliantly, so devious, so elusive, so adept at making themselves unremittingly incomprehensible.

In the last decade, a radical shift of outlook has been occurring in psychiatry. This has entailed the questioning of old assumptions, based on the attempts of nineteenth-century psychiatrists to bring the frame of clinical medicine to bear on their observations. Thus the subject matter of psychiatry was thought of as mental illness; one thought of mental physiology and mental pathology, one looked for signs and symptoms, made one's diagnosis, assessed prognosis and prescribed treatment. According to one's philosophical bias, one looked for the aetiology of these mental illnesses in the mind, in the body, in the environment, or in inherited propensities.

The term 'schizophrenia' was coined by a Swiss psychiatrist, Bleuler, who worked within this frame of reference. In using the term schizophrenia, I am not referring to any condition that I suppose to be mental rather than physical, or to an illness, like pneumonia, but to a label that some people pin on other people under certain social circumstances. The 'cause' of 'schizophrenia' is to be found by the examination, not of the prospective diagnosee alone, but of the whole social con-

text in which the psychiatric ceremonial is being conducted.[2]

Once demystified, it is clear, at least, that some people come to behave and to experience themselves and others in ways that are strange and incomprehensible to most people, including themselves. If this behaviour and experience falls into certain broad categories, they are liable to be diagnosed as subject to a condition called schizophrenia. By present calculation almost one in every 100 children born will fall into this category at some time or other before the age of forty-five, and in the U.K. at the moment there are roughly 60,000 men and women in mental hospitals, and many more outside hospital, who are termed schizophrenic.

A child born today in the U.K. stands a ten times greater chance of being admitted to a mental hospital than to a university, and about one fifth of mental hospital admissions are diagnosed schizophrenic. This can be taken as an indication that we are driving our children mad more effectively than we are genuinely educating them. Perhaps it is our very way of educating them that is driving them mad.

Most but not all psychiatrists still think that people they call schizophrenic suffer from an inherited predisposition to act in predominantly incomprehensible ways, that some as yet undetermined genetic factor (possibly a genetic morphism) transacts with a more or less ordinary environment to induce biochemical-endocrinological changes which in turn generate what we observe as the behavioural signs of a subtle underlying organic process.

But it is wrong to impute to someone a hypothetical disease of unknown aetiology and undiscovered pathology unless *he* can prove otherwise.[3]

[1] J. Haley, *Strategies of Psychotherapy* (New York: Grune and Stratton, 1963) pages 99–100.

[2] See H. Garfinkel, 'Conditions of Successful Degradation Ceremonies', *American Journal of Sociology*, LXI, 1956, pages 420–24; also R. D. Laing, 'Ritualisation in Abnormal Behaviour' in *Ritualisation of Behaviour in Animals and Man* (Royal Society, Philosophical Transactions, Series B, (in press)).

[3] See T. Szasz, *The Myth of Mental Illness* (London: Secker & Warburg, 1962).

The schizophrenic is someone who has queer experiences and/or is acting in a queer way, from the point of view usually of his relatives and of ourselves. . . .

That the diagnosed patient is suffering from a pathological process is either a fact, or a hypothesis, an assumption, or a judgement.

To regard it as fact is unequivocally false. To regard it as an hypothesis is legitimate. It is unnecessary either to make the assumption or to pass judgement.

The psychiatrist, adopting his clinical stance in the presence of the pre-diagnosed person, whom he is already looking at and listening to as a patient, has tended to come to believe that he is in the presence of the 'fact' of schizophrenia. He acts as if its existence were an established fact. He then has to discover its cause or multiple aetiological factors, to assess its prognosis, and to treat its course. The heart of the illness then resides outside the agency of the person. That is, the illness is taken to be a process that the person is subject to or undergoes, whether genetic, constitutional, endogenous, exogenous, organic or psychological, or some mixture of them all.[4]

Many psychiatrists are now becoming much more cautious about adopting this starting point. But what might take its place?

In understanding the new viewpoint on schizophrenia, we might remind ourselves of the six blind men and the elephant: one touched its body and said it was a wall, another touched an ear and said it was a fan, another a leg and thought it was a pillar, and so on. The problem is sampling, and the error is incautious extrapolation.

The old way of sampling the behaviour of schizophrenics was by the method of clinical examination conducted at the turn of the century. The account is given by the German psychiatrist Emil Kraepelin in his own words.

Gentlemen, the cases that I have to place before you today are peculiar. First of all, you see a servant-girl, aged twenty-four, upon whose features

and frame traces of great emaciation can be plainly seen. In spite of this, the patient is in continual movement, going a few steps forward, then back again; she plaits her hair, only to unloose it the next minute. *On attempting to stop her movement,* we meet with unexpectedly strong resistance; *if I place myself in front of her with my arms spread out* in order to stop her, if she cannot push me on one side, she suddenly turns and slips through under my arms, so as to continue her way. *If one takes firm hold* of her, she distorts her usually rigid, expressionless features with deplorable weeping, that only ceases so soon as one lets her have her own way. We notice besides that she holds a crushed piece of bread spasmodically clasped in the fingers of the left hand, which she absolutely *will not allow to be forced from her.* The patient does not trouble in the least about her surroundings so long as you leave her alone. *If you prick her in the forehead with a needle,* she scarcely winces or turns away, and leaves the needle quietly sticking there without letting it disturb her restless, beast-of-prey-like wandering backwards and forwards. *To questions* she answers almost nothing, at the most shaking her head. But from time to time she wails: 'O dear God! O dear God! O dear mother! O dear mother!', always repeating uniformly the same phrases.[5]

Here are a man and a young girl. If we see the situation purely in terms of Kraepelin's point of view, it all immediately falls into place. He is sane, she is insane: he is rational, she is irrational. This entails looking at the patient's actions out of the context of the situation as she experienced it. But if we take Kraepelin's actions (in italics)—he tries to stop her movements, stands in front of her with arms outspread, tries to force a piece of bread out of her hand, sticks a needle in her forehead, and so on—out of the context of the situation as experienced and defined by him, how extraordinary *they* are!

A feature of the interplay between psychiatrist and patient is that if the patient's part is taken out

[4]R. D. Laing and A. Esterson, *Sanity, Madness and the Family, Volume 1: Families of Schizophrenics* (London: Tavistock Publications, 1964; New York: Basic Books, 1965) page 4.

[5]E. Kraepelin, *Lectures on Clinical Psychiatry,* edited by T. Johnstone (London: Baillière, Tindall and Cox, 1906) pages 30–31.

of context, as is done in the clinical description, it might seem very odd. The psychiatrist's part, however, is taken as the very touchstone for our common-sense view of normality. The psychiatrist, as *ipso facto* sane, shows that the patient is out of contact with him. The fact that he is out of contact with the patient shows that there is something wrong with the patient, but not with the psychiatrist.

But if one ceases to identify with the clinical posture, and looks at the psychiatrist-patient couple without such presuppositions, then it is difficult to sustain this naïve view of the situation.

Psychiatrists have paid very little attention to the *experience* of the patient. Even in psychoanalysis there is an abiding tendency to suppose that the schizophrenic's experiences are somehow unreal or invalid; one can make sense out of them only by interpreting them; without truth-giving interpretations the patient is enmeshed in a world of delusions and self-deception. Kaplan, an American psychologist, in an introduction to an excellent collection of self-reports on the experience of being psychotic, says very justly:

> With all virtue on his side, he (the psychiatrist or psychoanalyst) reaches through the subterfuges and distortions of the patient and exposes them to the light of reason and insight. In this encounter between the psychiatrist and patient, the efforts of the former are linked with science and medicine, with understanding and care. What the patient experiences is tied to illness and irreality, to perverseness and distortion. The process of psychotherapy consists in large part of the patient's abandoning his false subjective perspectives for the therapist's objective ones. But the essence of this conception is that the psychiatrist understands what is going on, and the patient does not.[6]

H. S. Sullivan used to say to young psychiatrists when they came to work with him, 'I want you to remember that in the present state of our society, the patient is right, and you are wrong.' This is an outrageous simplification. I mention it to loosen any fixed ideas that are no less outrageous, that the psychiatrist is right, and the patient wrong.

I think however, that schizophrenics have more to teach psychiatrists about the inner world than psychiatrists their patients.

A different picture begins to develop if the interaction between patients themselves is studied without presuppositions. One of the best accounts here is by the American sociologist, Erving Goffman.

Goffman spent a year as an assistant physical therapist in a large mental hospital of some 7,000 beds, near Washington. His lowly staff status enabled him to fraternize with the patients in a way that upper echelons of the staff were unable to do. One of his conclusions is:

> There is an old saw that no clearcut line can be drawn between normal people and mental patients: rather there is a continuum with the well-adjusted citizen at one end and the full-fledged psychotic at the other. I must argue that after a period of acclimatization in a mental hospital the notion of a continuum seems very presumptuous. A community is a community. Just as it is bizarre to those not in it, so it is natural, even if unwanted, to those who live it from within. The system of dealings that patients have with one another does not fall at one end of anything, but rather provides one example of human association, to be avoided, no doubt, but also to be filed by the student in a circular cabinet along with all the other examples of association that he can collect.[7]

A large part of his study is devoted to a detailed documentation of how it comes about that a person, in being put in the role of patient, tends to become defined as a non-agent, as a non-responsible object, to be treated accordingly, and even comes to regard himself in this light.

Goffman shows also that by shifting one's focus from seeing the person out of context, to seeing him in his context, behaviour that might seem quite unintelligible, at best to be explained as some intra-psychic regression or organic deterioration, can make quite ordinary human sense. He does not just describe such behaviour 'in' mental hospital patients, he describes it within the context

[6]B. Kaplan (ed.), *The Inner World of Mental Illness* (New York and London: Harper and Row, 1964) page vii.

[7]E. Goffman, *Asylums. Essays on the Social Situation of Mental Patients and Other Inmates* (New York: Doubleday-Anchor Books, 1961) page 303.

of personal interaction and the system in which it takes place.

> . . . there is a vicious circle process at work. Persons who are lodged on 'bad' wards find that very little equipment of any kind is given them—clothes may be taken away from them each night, recreational materials may be withheld, and only heavy wooden chairs and benches provided for furniture. Acts of hostility against the institution have to rely on limited, ill-designed devices, such as banging a chair against the floor or striking a sheet of newspaper sharply so as to make an annoying explosive sound. And the more inadequate this equipment is to convey rejection of the hospital, the more the act appears as a psychotic symptom, and the more likely it is that management feels justified in assigning the patient to a bad ward. When a patient finds himself in seclusion, naked and without visible means of expression, he may have to rely on tearing up his mattress, if he can, or writing with faeces on the wall—actions management takes to be in keeping with the kind of person who warrants seclusion.[8]

It is on account of their behaviour outside hospital, however, that people get diagnosed as schizophrenic and admitted to hospital in the first place.

There have been many studies of social factors in relation to schizophrenia. These include attempts to discover whether schizophrenia occurs more or less frequently in one or other ethnic group, social class, sex, ordinal position in the family, and so on. The conclusion from such studies has often been that social factors do not play a significant role in the 'aetiology of schizophrenia.' This begs the question, and moreover such studies do not get up close enough to the relevant situation. If the police wish to determine whether a man has died of natural causes or has committed suicide, or been murdered, they do not look up prevalence or incidence figures. They investigate the circumstances attendant upon each single case in turn. Each investigation is an original research project, and it comes to an end when enough evidence has been gathered to answer the relevant questions.

It is only in the last ten years that the immediate interpersonal environment of 'schizophrenics' has come to be studied in its interstices. This work was prompted, in the first place, by psychotherapists who formed the impression that, if their patients were *disturbed,* their families were often very *disturbing.* Psychotherapists, however, remained committed by their technique not to study the families directly. At first the focus was mainly on the mothers (who are always the first to get the blame for everything), and a 'schizophrenogenic' mother was postulated, who was supposed to generate disturbance in her child.

Next, attention was paid to the husbands of these undoubtedly unhappy women, then to the parental and parent-child interactions (rather than to each person in the family separately), then to the nuclear family group of parents and children, and finally to the whole relevant network of people in and around the family, including the grandparents of patients. By the time our own researches started, this methodological breakthrough had been made and, in addition, a major theoretical advance had been achieved.

This was the 'double-bind' hypothesis, whose chief architect was the anthropologist Gregory Bateson. This theory,[9] first published in 1956, represented a theoretical advance of the first order. The germ of the idea developed in Bateson's mind in studying New Guinea in the 1930s. In New Guinea the culture had, as all cultures have, built-in techniques for maintaining its own inner balance. One technique, for example, that served to neutralize dangerous rivalry, was sexual transvestism. However, missionaries and the occidental government tended to object to such practices. The culture was therefore caught between the risk of external extermination or internal disruption.

Together with research workers in California, Bateson brought this paradigm of an insoluble 'can't win' situation, specifically destructive of self-identity, to bear on the internal family pattern of communication of diagnosed schizophrenics.

The studies of the families of schizophrenics conducted at Palo Alto, California, Yale University, the Pennsylvania Psychiatric Institute, and at

[8]E. Goffman: op. cit., page 306.

[9]G. Bateson, D. D. Jackson, J. Haley, J. and J. Weakland, 'Towards a theory of schizophrenia', *Behavioural Science,* Volume I, number 251, 1956.

the National Institute of Mental Health, among other places, have all shown that the person who gets diagnosed is part of a wider network of extremely disturbed and disturbing patterns of communication. In all these places, to the best of my knowledge, *no* schizophrenic has been studied whose disturbed pattern of communication has not been shown to be a reflection of, and reaction to, the disturbed and disturbing pattern characterizing his or her family of origin. This is matched in our own researches.[10]

In over 100 cases where we[11] have studied the actual circumstances around the social event when one person comes to be regarded as schizophrenic, it seems to us that *without exception* the experience and behaviour that gets labelled schizophrenic is a *special strategy that a person invents in order to live in an unlivable situation*. In his life situation the person has come to feel he is in an untenable position. He cannot make a move, or make no move, without being beset by contradictory and paradoxical pressures and demands, pushes and pulls, both internally, from himself, and externally, from those around him. He is, as it were, in a position of checkmate.

This state of affairs may not be perceived as such by any of the people in it. The man at the bottom of the heap may be being crushed and suffocated to death without anyone noticing, much less intending it. The situation here described is impossible to see by studying the different people in it singly. The social system, not single individuals extrapolated from it, must be the object of study.

We know that the biochemistry of the person is highly sensitive to social circumstance. That a checkmate situation occasions a biochemical response which, in turn, facilitates or inhibits certain types of experience and behaviour is plausible *a priori*.

The behaviour of the diagnosed patient is part of a much larger network of disturbed behaviour. The contradictions and confusions 'internalized'

by the individual must be looked at in their larger social contexts.

Something is wrong somewhere, but it can no longer be seen exclusively or even primarily 'in' the diagnosed patient.

Nor is it a matter of laying the blame at anyone's door. The untenable position, the 'can't win' double-bind, the situation of checkmate, is by definition *not obvious* to the protagonists. Very seldom is it a question of contrived, deliberate, cynical lies or a ruthless intention to drive someone crazy, although this occurs more commonly than is usually supposed. We have had parents tell us that they would rather their child was mad than that he or she realize the truth. Though even here, it is because they say that 'it is a mercy' that the person is 'out of his mind'. A checkmate position cannot be described in a few words. The whole situation has to be grasped before it can be seen that no move is possible, and making no move is equally unlivable.

With these reservations, the following is an example of an interaction given in *The Self and Others*[12] between a father, mother, and son of twenty recovering from a schizophrenic episode.

In this session the patient was maintaining that he was selfish, while his parents were telling him that he was not. The psychiatrist asked the patient to give an example of what he meant by 'selfish'.

SON: Well, when my mother sometimes makes me a big meal and I won't eat it if I don't feel like it.

FATHER: But he wasn't always like that, you know. He's always been a good boy.

MOTHER: That's his illness, isn't it, doctor? He was never ungrateful. He was always most polite and well brought up. We've done our best by him.

SON: No, I've always been selfish and ungrateful. I've no self-respect.

FATHER: But you have.

SON: I could have, if you respected me. No one respects me. Everyone laughs at me. I'm the joke of the world. I'm the joker all right.

FATHER: But, son, I respect you because I respect a man who respects himself.

It is hardly surprising that the person in his

---

[10]R. D. Laing and A. Esterson, *Sanity, Madness and the Family* (London: Travistock Publications, 1964; New York: Basic Books, 1965).

[11]Drs. David Cooper, A. Esterson and myself.

[12]R. D. Laing (London: Tavistock Publications, 1961; Chicago: Quadrangle Press, 1962).

terror may stand in curious postures in an attempt to control the irresolvably contradictory social 'forces' that are controlling him, that he projects the inner on to the outer, introjects the outer on to the inner, that he tries in short to protect himself from destruction by every means that he has, by projection, introjection, splitting, denial and so on.

Gregory Bateson, in a brilliant introduction to a nineteenth-century autobiographical account of schizophrenia, has said this:

> It would appear that once precipitated into psychosis the patient has a course to run. He is, as it were, embarked upon a voyage of discovery which is only completed by his return to the normal world, to which he comes back with insights different from those of the inhabitants who never embarked on such a voyage. Once begun, a schizophrenic episode would appear to have as definite a course as an initiation ceremony—a death and rebirth—into which the novice may have been precipitated by his family life or by adventitious circumstances, but which in its course is largely steered by endogenous process.
>
> In terms of this picture, spontaneous remission is no problem. This is only the final and natural outcome of the total process. What needs to be explained is the failure of many who embark upon this voyage to return from it. *Do these encounter circumstances either in family life or in institutional care so grossly maladaptive that even the richest and best organized hallucinatory experience cannot save them?* [13]

I am in substantial agreement with this view.

A revolution is currently going on in relation to sanity and madness, both inside and outside psychiatry. The clinical point of view is giving way before a point of view that is both existential and social.

From an ideal vantage point on the ground, a formation of planes may be observed in the air. One plane may be out of formation. But the whole formation may be off course. The plane that is 'out of formation' may be abnormal, bad or 'mad' from the point of view of the formation. But the formation itself may be bad or mad from the point of view of the ideal observer. The plane that is out of

formation may be also more or less off course than the formation itself is.

The 'out of formation' criterion is the clinical positivist criterion.

The 'off course' criterion is the ontological. One requires to make two judgements along these different parameters. In particular, it is of fundamental importance not to confuse the person who may be 'out of formation' by telling him he is 'off course' if he is not. It is of fundamental importance not to make the positivist mistake of assuming that, because a group are 'information,' this means they are necessarily 'on course.' This is the Gadarene swine fallacy. Nor is it necessarily the case that the person who is 'out of formation' is more 'on course' than the formation. There is no need to idealize someone just because he is labelled 'out of formation.' There is also no need to persuade the person who is 'out of formation' that cure consists in getting back into formation. The person who is 'out of formation' is often full of hatred of the formation and fears about being the odd man out.

If the formation is itself off course, then the man who is really to get 'on course' must leave the formation. But it is possible to do so, if one desires, without screeches and screams, and without terrorizing the already terrified formation that one has to leave.

In the diagnostic category of schizophrenic are many different types of sheep and goats.

'Schizophrenia' is a diagnosis, a label applied by some people to others. This does not prove that the labelled person is subject to an essentially pathological process, of unkown nature and origin, going on *in* his or her body. It does not mean that the process is, primarily or secondarily, a *psycho*-pathological one, going on *in* the *psyche* of the person. But it does establish as a social fact that the person labelled is one of Them. It is easy to forget that the process is a hypothesis, to assume that it is a fact, then to pass the judgement that it is biologically maladaptive and, as such, pathological. But social adaptation to a dysfunctional society may be very dangerous. The perfectly adjusted bomber pilot may be a greater threat to species survival than the hospitalized schizophrenic de-

---

[13] G. Bateson (ed.), *Perceval's Narrative. A Patient's Account of his Psychosis* (Stanford, California: Stanford University Press, 1961) pages xiii–xiv; italics mine.

luded that the Bomb is inside him. Our society may itself have become biologically dysfunctional, and some forms of schizophrenic alienation from the alienation of society may have a socoiobiological function that we have not recognized. This holds even if a genetic factor predisposes to some kinds of schizophrenic behaviour. Recent critiques of the work on genetics[14] and the most recent empirical genetic studies, leave this matter open.

Jung suggested some years ago that it would be an interesting experiment to study whether the syndrome of psychiatry runs in families. A pathological process called 'psychiatrosis' may well be found, by the same methods, to be a delineable entity, with somatic correlates and psychic mechanisms, with an inherited or at least constitutional basis, a natural history, and a doubtful prognosis.

The most profound recent development in psychiatry has been to redefine the basic categories and assumptions of psychiatry itself. We are now in a transitional stage, where we still to some extent continue to use old bottles for new wine. We have to decide whether to use old terms in a new way, or abandon them to the dustbin of history.

There is no such 'condition' as 'schizophrenia,' but the label is a social fact and the social fact a *political event*.[15] This political event, occurring in the civic order of society, imposes definitions and consequences on the labelled person. It is a social prescription that rationalizes a set of social actions whereby the labelled person is annexed by others, who are legally sanctioned, medically empowered, and morally obliged, to become responsible for the person labelled. The person labelled is inaugurated not only into a role, but into a career of patient, by the concerted action of a coalition (a 'conspiracy') of family, G. P., mental health officer, psychiatrists, nurses, psychiatric social workers, and often fellow patients. The 'committed' person labelled

as patient, and specifically as 'schizophrenic,' is degraded from full existential and legal status as human agent and responsible person, no longer in possession of his own definition of himself, unable to retain his own possessions, precluded from the exercise of his discretion as to whom he meets, what he does. His time is no longer his own and the space he occupies is no longer of his choosing. After being subjected to a degradation ceremonial[16] known as psychiatric examination he is bereft of his civil liberties in being imprisoned in a total institution[17] known as a 'mental' hospital. More completely, more radically than anywhere else in our society, he is invalidated as a human being. In the mental hospital he must remain, until the label is rescinded or qualified by such terms as 'remitted' or 'readjusted.' Once a 'schizophrenic' there is a tendency to be regarded as always a 'schizophrenic.'

Now why and how does this happen? And what functions does this procedure serve for the maintenance of the civic order? These questions are only just beginning to be asked, much less answered. Questions and answers have so far been focused on the family as a social subsystem. Socially, this work must now move to further understanding, not only of the internal disturbed and disturbing patterns of communication within families, of the double-binding procedures, the pseudo-mutuality, of what I have called the mystifications and the untenable positions, but also to the meaning of all this within the larger context of the civic order of society—that is, of the *political* order, of the ways persons exercise control and power over one another.

Some people labelled schizophrenic (not all, and not necessarily) manifest behaviour in words, gestures, actions (linguistically, paralinguistically and kinetically) that is unusual. Sometimes (not always and not necessarily) this unusual behaviour (manifested to us, the others, as I have said, by sight and sound) expresses, wittingly or unwit-

[14]See for instance: Pekka Tienari, *Psychiatric Illnesses in Identical Twins* (Copenhagen: Munksgaard, 1963).
[15]T. Scheff, 'Social Conditions for Rationality: How Urban and Rural Courts Deal with the Mentally Ill,' *Amer. Behav. Scient.*, March, 1964. Also, T. Scheff, 'The Societal Reaction to Deviants: Ascriptive Elements in the Psychiatric Screening of Mental Patients in a Mid-Western State,' *Social Problems*. No. 4, Spring, 1964.

[16]H. Garfinkel, 'Conditions of Successful Degradation Ceremonies,' *American Journal of Sociology*, LXI, 1956.
[17]E. Goffman, *Asylums. Essays on the Social Situation of Mental Patients and Other Inmates* (New York: Doubleday-Anchor Books, 1961).

tingly, unusual experiences that the person is undergoing. Sometimes (not always and not necessarily) these unusual experiences that are expressed by unusual behaviour appear to be part of a potentially orderly, natural sequence of experiences.

This sequence is very seldom allowed to occur because we are so busy 'treating' the patient, whether by chemotherapy, shock therapy, *milieu* therapy, group therapy, psychotherapy, family therapy—sometimes now, in the very best, most advanced places, by the lot.

What we see sometimes in *some* people whom we label and 'treat' as schizophrenics are the behavioural expressions of an experiential drama. But we see this drama in a distorted form that our therapeutic efforts tend to distort further. The outcome of this unfortunate dialectic is a *forme frustre* of a potentially *natural* process, that we do not allow to happen.

In characterizing this sequence in general terms, I shall write *entirely* about a sequence of experience. I shall therefore have to use the language of experience. So many people feel they have to translate 'subjective' events into 'objective' terms in order to be scientific. To be genuinely scientific means having valid knowledge of a chosen domain of reality. So in the following I shall use the language of experience to describe the events of experience. Also, I shall not so much be describing a series of different discrete events but describing a unitary sequence, from different points of view, and using a variety of idioms to do so. I suggest that this natural process, which our labelling and well-intentioned therapeutic efforts distort and arrest, is as follows.

We start again from the split of our experience into what seems to be two worlds, inner and outer.

The normal state of affairs is that we know little of either and are alienated from both, but that we know perhaps a little more of the outer than the inner. However, the very fact that it is necessary to speak of outer and inner at all implies that a historically-conditioned split has occurred, so that the inner is already as bereft of substance as the outer is bereft of meaning.

We need not be unaware of the 'inner' world.

We do not realize its existence most of the time. But many people enter it—unfortunately without guides, confusing outer with inner realities, and inner with outer—and generally lose their capacity to function competently in ordinary relations.

This need not be so. The process of entering into *the other* world from this world, and returning to *this* world from the other world, is as natural as death and giving birth or being born. But in our present world, that is both so terrified and so unconscious of the other world, it is not surprising that when 'reality,' the fabric of this world, bursts, and a person enters the other world, he is completely lost and terrified, and meets only incomprehension in others.

Some people wittingly, some people unwittingly, enter or are thrown into more or less total inner space and time. We are socially conditioned to regard total immersion in outer space and time as normal and healthy. Immersion in inner space and time tends to be regarded as anti-social withdrawal, a deviancy, invalid, pathological *per se*, in some sense discreditable.

Sometimes, having gone through the looking glass, through the eye of the needle, the territory is recognized as one's lost home, but most people now in inner space and time are, to begin with, in unfamiliar territory and are frightened and confused. They are lost. They have forgotten that they have been there before. They clutch at chimeras. They try to retain their bearings by compounding their confusion, by projection (putting the inner on to the outer), and introjection (importing outer categories into the inner). They do not know what is happening, and no one is likely to enlighten them.

We defend ourselves violently even from the full range of our egoically limited experience. How much more are we likely to react with terror, confusion and 'defences' against ego-loss experience. There is nothing intrinsically pathological in the experience of ego-loss, but it may be very difficult to find a living context for the journey one may be embarked upon.

The person who has entered this inner realm (if only he is allowed to experience this) will find himself going, or being conducted—one cannot clearly distinguish active from passive here—on a journey.

This journey is experienced as going further 'in,' as going back through one's personal life, in and back and through and beyond into the experience of all mankind, of the primal man, of Adam and perhaps even further into the being of animals, vegetables and minerals.

In this journey there are many occasions to lose one's way, for confusion, partial failure, even final shipwreck: many terrors, spirits, demons to be encountered, that may or may not be overcome.

We do not regard it as pathologically deviant to explore a jungle, or to climb Mount Everest. We feel that Columbus was entitled to be mistaken in his construction of what he discovered when he came to the New World. We are far more out of touch with even the nearest approaches of the infinite reaches of inner space than we now are with the reaches of outer space. We respect the voyager, the explorer, the climber, the space man. It makes far more sense to me as a valid project —indeed, as a desperately urgently required project for our time, to explore the inner space and time of consciousness. Perhaps this is one of the few things that still make sense in our historical context. We are so out of touch with this realm that many people can now argue seriously that it does not exist. It is very small wonder that it is perilous indeed to explore such a lost realm. The situation I am suggesting is precisely as though we all had almost total lack of any knowledge whatever of what we call the outer world. What would happen if some of us then started to see, hear, touch, smell, taste things? We would hardly be more confused than the person who first has vague intimations of, and then moves into, inner space and time. This is where the person sitting in a chair labelled catatonic has often gone. He is not at all here: he is all there. He is frequently very mistaken about what he is experiencing, and he probably does not want to experience it. He may indeed be lost. There are very few of us who know the territory in which he is lost, who know how to reach him, and how to find the way back.

No age in the history of humanity has perhaps so lost touch with this natural *healing* process, that implicates *some* of the people whom we label schizophrenic. No age has so devalued it, no age has imposed such prohibitions and deterrences against it, as our own. Instead of the mental hospital, a sort of re-servicing factory for human breakdowns, we need a place where people who have travelled further and, consequently, may be more lost than psychiatrists and other sane people, can find their way *further* into inner space and time, and back again. Instead of the *degradation* ceremonial of psychiatric examination, diagnosis and prognostication, we need, for those who are ready for it (in psychiatric terminology often those who are about to go into a schizophrenic breakdown), an *initiation* ceremonial, through which the person will be guided with full social encouragement and sanction into inner space and time, by people who have been there and back again. Psychiatrically, this would appear as ex-patients helping future patients to go mad.

What is entailed then is:

i a voyage from outer to inner,

II from life to a kind of death,

III from going forward to a going back,

IV from temporal movement to temporal standstill,

V from mundane time to aeonic time,

VI from the ego to the self,

VII from being outside (post-birth) back into the womb of all things (pre-birth),

and then subsequently a return voyage from

1 inner to outer,

2 from death to life,

3 from the movement back to a movement once more forward,

4 from immortality back to mortality,

5 from eternity back to time,

6 from self to a new ego,

7 from a cosmic foetalization to an existential rebirth.

I shall leave it to those who wish to translate the above elements of this perfectly natural and necessary process into the jargon of psychopathology and clinical psychiatry. This process may be one that all of us need, in one form or another. This process could have a central function in a truly sane society.

I have listed very briefly little more than the headings for an extended study and understanding of a natural sequence of experiential stepping stones that, in some instances, is submerged, concealed, distorted and arrested by the label 'schizophrenia' with its connotations of pathology and consequences of an illness-to-be cured.

Perhaps we will learn to accord to so-called schizophrenics who have come back to us, perhaps after years, no less respect than the often no less lost explorers of the Renaissance. If the human race survives, future men will, I suspect, look back on our enlightened epoch as a veritable age of Darkness. They will presumably be able to savour the irony of this situation with more amusement than we can extract from it. The laugh's on us. They will see that what we call 'schizophrenia' was one of the forms in which, often through quite ordinary people, the light began to break through the cracks in our all-too-closed minds.

Schizophrenia used to be a new name for dementia praecox—a slow, insidious illness that was supposed to overtake young people in particular, and to be liable to go on to a terminal dementia.

Perhaps we can still retain the now old name, and read into it its etymological meaning: *Schiz*—'broken'; *Phrenos*—'soul or heart'.

The schizophrenic in this sense is one who is brokenhearted, and even broken hearts have been known to mend, if we have the heart to let them.

But 'schizophrenia', in this existential sense, has little to do with the clinical examination, diagnosis, prognosis and prescriptions for therapy of 'schizophrenia'.

39 ON BEING SANE IN INSANE PLACES*

D. L. ROSENHAN

If sanity and insanity exist, how shall we know them?

The question is neither capricious nor itself insane. However much we may be personally convinced that we can tell the normal from the abnormal, the evidence is simply not compelling. It is commonplace, for example, to read about murder trials wherein eminent psychiatrists for the defense are contradicted by equally eminent psychiatrists for the prosecution on the matter of the defendant's sanity. More generally, there are a great deal of conflicting data on the reliability, utility, and meaning of such terms as "sanity," "insanity," "mental illness," and "schizophrenia." Finally, as early as 1934, Benedict suggested that normality and abnormality are not universal. What is viewed as normal in one culture may be seen as quite aberrant in another. Thus, notions of normality and abnormality may not be quite as accurate as people believe they are.

To raise questions regarding normality and abnormality is in no way to question the fact that some behaviors are deviant or odd. Murder is deviant. So, too, are hallucinations. Nor does raising such questions deny the existence of the personal anguish that is often associated with "mental ill-

*Abridged from D. L. Rosenhan, On being sane in insane places, *Science*, January 19, 1973, **179**, 250–257. Copyright 1973 by the American Association for the Advancement of Science.

ness.'' Anxiety and depression exist. Psychological suffering exists. But normality and abnormality, sanity and insanity, and the diagnoses that flow from them may be less substantive than many believe them to be.

At its heart, the question of whether the sane can be distinguished from the insane (and whether degrees of insanity can be distinguished from each other) is a simple matter: do the salient characteristics that lead to diagnoses reside in the patients themselves or in the environments and contexts in which observers find them?

. . . the belief has been strong that patients present symptoms, that those symptoms can be categorized, and, implicitly, that the sane are distinguishable from the insane. More recently, however, this belief has been questioned. Based in part on theoretical and anthropological considerations, but also on philosophical, legal, and therapeutic ones, the view has grown that psychological categorization of mental illness is useless at best and downright harmful, misleading, and pejorative at worst. Psychiatric diagnoses, in this view, are in the minds of the observers and are not valid summaries of characteristics displayed by the observed.

Gains can be made in deciding which of these is more nearly accurate by getting normal people (that is, people who do not have, and have never suffered, symptoms of serious psychiatric disorders) admitted to psychiatric hospitals and then determining whether they were discovered to be sane and, if so, how. If the sanity of such pseudopatients were always detected, there would be prima facie evidence that a sane individual can be distinguished from the insane context in which he is found. Normality (and presumably abnormality) is distinct enough that it can be recognized wherever it occurs, for it is carried within the person. If, on the other hand, the sanity of the pseudopatients were never discovered, serious difficulties would arise for those who support traditional modes of psychiatric diagnosis. Given that the hospital staff was not incompetent, that the psuedopatient had been behaving as sanely as he had been outside of the hospital, and that it had never been previously suggested that he belonged in a psychiatric hospital, such an unlikely outcome would support the view that psychiatric diagnosis betrays little about the patient but much about the environment in which an observer finds him.

This article describes such an experiment. Eight sane people gained secret admission to 12 different hospitals. Their diagnostic experiences constitute the data of the first part of this article; the remainder is devoted to a description of their experiences in psychiatric institutions. Too few psychiatrists and psychologists, even those who have worked in such hospitals, know what the experience is like. They rarely talk about it with former patients, perhaps because they distrust information coming from the previously insane. Those who have worked in psychiatric hospitals are likely to have adapted so thoroughly to the settings that they are insensitive to the impact of that experience. And while there have been occasional reports of researchers who submitted themselves to psychiatric hospitalization, these researchers have commonly remained in the hospitals for short periods of time, often with the knowledge of the hospital staff. It is difficult to know the extent to which they were treated like patients or like research colleagues. Nevertheless, their reports about the inside of the psychiatric hospital have been valuable. This article extends those efforts.

PSEUDOPATIENTS AND THEIR SETTINGS

The eight pseudopatients were a varied group. One was a psychology graduate student in his 20's. The remaining seven were older and "established." Among them were three psychologists, a pediatrician, a psychiatrist, a painter, and a housewife. Three pseudopatients were women, five were men. All of them employed pseudonyms, lest their alleged diagnoses embarrass them later. Those who were in mental health professions alleged another occupation in order to avoid the special attentions that might be accorded by staff, as a matter of courtesy or caution, to ailing colleagues. With the exception of myself (I was the first pseudopatient and my presence was known to the hospital administrator and chief psychologist and, so far as I can tell, to them alone), the presence of pseudopatients and the nature of the research program was not known to the hospital staffs.

The settings were similarly varied. In order to generalize the findings, admission into a variety of hospitals was sought. The 12 hospitals in the sample were located in five different states on the East and West coasts. Some were old and shabby, some were quite new. Some were research-oriented, others not. Some had good staff-patient ratios, others were quite understaffed. Only one was a strictly private hospital. All of the others were supported by state or federal funds or, in one instance, by university funds.

After calling the hospital for an appointment, the pseudopatient arrived at the admissions office complaining that he had been hearing voices. Asked what the voices said, he replied that they were often unclear, but as far as he could tell they said "empty," "hollow," and "thud." The voices were unfamiliar and were of the same sex as the pseudopatient. The choice of these symptoms was occasioned by their apparent similarity to existential symptoms. Such symptoms are alleged to arise from painful concerns about the perceived meaninglessness of one's life. It is as if the hallucinating person were saying, "My life is empty and hollow." The choice of these symptoms was also determined by the *absence* of a single report of existential psychoses in the literature.

Beyond alleging the symptoms and falsifying name, vocation, and employment, no further alterations of person, history, or circumstances were made. The significant events of the pseudopatient's life history were presented as they had actually occurred. Relationships with parents and siblings, with spouse and children, with people at work and in school, consistent with the aforementioned exceptions, were described as they were or had been. Frustrations and upsets were described along with joys and satisfactions. These facts are important to remember. If anything, they strongly

biased the subsequent results in favor of detecting sanity, since none of their histories or current behaviors were seriously pathological in any way.

Immediately upon admission to the psychiatric ward, the pseudopatient ceased simulating *any* symptoms of abnormality. In some cases, there was a brief period of mild nervousness and anxiety, since none of the pseudopatients really believed that they would be admitted so easily. Indeed, their shared fear was that they would be immediately exposed as frauds and greatly embarrassed. Moreover, many of them had never visited a psychiatric ward; even those who had, nevertheless had some genuine fears about what might happen to them. Their nervousness, then, was quite appropriate to the novelty of the hospital setting, and it abated rapidly.

Apart from that short-lived nervousness, the pseudopatient behaved on the ward as he "normally" behaved. The pseudopatient spoke to patients and staff as he might ordinarily. Because there is uncommonly little to do on a psychiatric ward, he attempted to engage others in conversation. When asked by staff how he was feeling, he indicated that he was fine, that he no longer experienced symptoms. He responded to instructions from attendants, to calls for medication (which was not swallowed), and to dining-hall instructions. Beyond such activities as were available to him on the admissions ward, he spent his time writing down his observations about the ward, its patients, and the staff. Initially these notes were written "secretly," but as it soon became clear that no one much cared, they were subsequently written on standard tablets of paper in such public places as the dayroom. No secret was made of these activities.

The pseudopatient, very much as a true psychiatric patient, entered a hospital with no foreknowledge of when he would be discharged. Each was told that he would have to get out by his own devices, essentially by convincing the staff that he was sane. The psychological stresses associated with hospitalization were considerable, and all but one of the pseudopatients desired to be discharged almost immediately after being admitted. They were, therefore, motivated not only to behave sanely, but to be paragons of cooperation. That their behavior was in no way disruptive is confirmed by nursing reports, which have been obtained on most of the patients. These reports uniformly indicate that the patients were "friendly," "cooperative," and "exhibited no abnormal indications."

THE NORMAL ARE NOT DETECTABLY SANE

Despite their public "show" of sanity, the pseudopatients were never detected. Admitted, except in one case, with a diagnosis of schizophrenia, each was discharged with a diagnosis of schizophrenia "in remission." The label "in remission" should in no way be dismissed as a formality, for at no time during any hospitalization had any question been raised about any pseudopatient's simulation. Nor are there any indications in the hospital records that the pseudopatient's status was suspect. Rather, the evidence is strong that, once labeled schizophrenic, the pseudopatient was stuck with that label. If the pseudopatient was to be discharged, he must naturally be "in remission"; but he was not sane, nor, in the institution's view, had he ever been sane.

The uniform failure to recognize sanity cannot be attributed to the quality of the hospitals, for, although there were considerable variations among them, several are considered excellent. Nor can it be alleged that there was simply not enough time to observe the pseudopatients. Length of hospitalization ranged from 7 to 52 days, with an average of 19 days. The pseudopatients were not, in fact, carefully observed, but this failure clearly speaks more to traditions within psychiatric hospitals than to lack of opportunity.

Finally, it cannot be said that the failure to recognize the pseudopatients' sanity was due to the fact that they were not behaving sanely. While there was clearly some tension present in all of them, their daily visitors could detect no serious behavioral consequences—nor, indeed, could other patients. It was quite common for the patients to "detect" the pseudopatients' sanity. During the first three hospitalizations, when accurate counts were kept, 35 of a total of 118 patients on the admissions ward voiced their suspicions, some vigorously. "You're not crazy. You're a journalist, or a professor [referring to the continual note-taking]. You're checking up on the hospital." While most of the patients were reassured by the pseudopatient's insistence that he had been sick before he came in but was fine now, some continued to believe that the pseudopatient was sane throughout his hospitalization. The fact that the patients often recognized normality when staff did not raises important questions.

. . . physicians are more inclined to call a healthy person sick than a sick person healthy. The reasons for this are not hard to find: it is clearly more dangerous to misdiagnose illness than health. Better to err on the side of caution, to suspect illness even among the healthy.

But what holds for medicine does not hold equally well for psychiatry. Medical illnesses, while unfortunate, are not commonly pejorative. Psychiatric diagnoses, on the contrary, carry with them personal, legal, and social stigmas. It was therefore important to see whether the tendency toward diagnosing the sane insane could be reversed. The following experiment was arranged at a research and teaching hospital whose staff had heard these findings but doubted that such an error could occur in their hospital. The staff was informed that at some time during the following 3 months, one or more pseudopatients would attempt to be admitted into the psychiatric hospital. Each staff member was asked to rate each patient who presented himself at admissions or on the ward according to the likelihood that the patient was a pseudopatient. A 10-point scale was used, with a 1 and 2 reflecting high confidence that the patient was a pseudopatient.

Judgments were obtained on 193 patients who were admitted for psychiatric treatment. All staff who had had sustained contact with or primary responsibility for the patient—attendants, nurses, pyschiatrists, physicians, and psychologists—were asked to make judgments. Forty-one patients were alleged, with high confidence, to be pseudopatients by at least one member of the staff. Twenty-three were considered suspect by at least one psychiatrist. Nineteen were suspected by one psychiatrist *and* one other staff member. Actually, no genuine pseudopatient (at least from my group) presented himself during this period.

The experiment is instructive. It indicates that the tendency to designate sane people as insane can be reversed when the stakes (in this case, prestige and diagnostic acumen) are high. But what can be said of the 19 people who were suspected of being "sane" by one psychiatrist and another staff member? Were these people truly "sane," or was it rather the case that in the course of avoiding the type 2 error the staff tended to make more errors of the first sort—calling the crazy "sane"? There is no way of knowing. But one thing is certain: any diagnostic process that lends itself so readily to massive errors of this sort cannot be a very reliable one.

THE STICKINESS OF PSYCHODIAGNOSTIC LABELS

Beyond the tendency to call the healthy sick—a tendency that accounts better for diagnostic behavior on admission than it does for such behavior after a lengthy period of exposure—the data speak to the massive role of labeling in psychiatric assessment. Having once been labeled schizophrenic, there is nothing the pseudopatient can do to overcome the tag. The tag profoundly colors others' perceptions of him and his behavior.

From one viewpoint, these data are hardly surprising, for it has long been known that elements are given meaning by the context in which they occur. Once a person is designated abnormal, all of his other behaviors and characteristics are colored by that label. Indeed, that label is so powerful that many of the pseudopatients' normal behaviors were overlooked entirely or profoundly misinterpreted. Some examples may clarify this issue.

Earlier I indicated that there were no changes in the pseudopatient's personal history and current status beyond those of name, employment, and, where necessary, vocation. Otherwise, a veridical description of personal history and circumstances was offered. Those circumstances were not psychotic. How were they made consonant with the diagnosis of psychosis? Or were those diagnoses modified in such a way as to bring them into accord with the circumstances of the pseudopatient's life, as described by him?

As far as I can determine, diagnoses were in no way affected by the relative health of the circumstances of a pseudopatient's life. Rather, the reverse occurred: the perception of his circumstances was shaped entirely by the diagnosis. A clear example of such translation is found in the case of a pseudopatient who had had a close relationship with his mother but was rather remote from his father during his early childhood. During adolescence and beyond, however, his father became a close friend, while his relationship with his mother cooled. His present relationship with his wife was characteristically close and warm. Apart from occasional angry exchanges, friction was minimal. The children had rarely been spanked. Surely there is nothing especially pathological about such a history. Indeed, many readers may see a similar pattern in their own experiences, with no markedly deleterious consequences. Observe, however, how such a history was translated in the psychopathological context, this from the case summary prepared after the patient was discharged.

This white 39-year-old male . . . manifests a long history of considerable ambivalence in close relationships, which begins in early childhood. A warm relationship with his mother cools during his adolescence. A distant relationship to his father is described as becoming very intense. Affective stability is absent. His attempts to control emotionality with his wife and children are punctuated by angry outbursts and, in the case of the children, spankings. And while he says that he has several good friends, one senses considerable ambivalence embedded in those relationships also. . . .

The facts of the case were unintentionally distorted by the staff to achieve consistency with a popular theory of the dynamics of a schizophrenic reaction. Nothing of an ambivalent nature had been described in relations with parents, spouse, or friends. To the extent that ambivalence could be inferred, it was probably not greater than is found in all human relationships. It is true the pseudopatient's relationships with his parents changed over time, but in the ordinary context that would hardly be remarkable—indeed, it might very well be expected. Clearly, the meaning ascribed to his verbalizations (that is, ambivalence, affective instability) was determined by the diagnosis: schizophrenia. An entirely different meaning would have been ascribed if it were known that the man was "normal."

All pseudopatients took extensive notes publicly. Under ordinary circumstances, such behavior would have raised questions in the minds of observers, as, in fact, it did among patients. Indeed, it seemed so certain that the notes would elicit suspicion that elaborate precautions were taken to remove them from the ward each day. But the precautions proved needless. The closest any staff member came to questioning these notes occurred when one pseudopatient asked his physician what kind of medication he was receiving and began to write down the response. "You needn't write it," he was told gently. "If you have trouble remembering, just ask me again."

If no questions were asked of the pseudopatients, how was their writing interpreted? Nursing records for three patients indicate that the writing was seen as an aspect of their pathological behavior. "Patient engages in writing behavior" was the daily nursing comment on one of the pseudopatients who was never questioned about his writing. Given that the patient is in the hospital, he must be psychologically disturbed. And given that he is disturbed, continuous writing must be a behavioral manifestation of that disturbance, perhaps a subset of the compulsive behaviors that are sometimes correlated with schizophrenia.

One tacit characteristic of psychiatric diagnosis is that it locates the sources of aberration within the individual and only rarely within the complex of stimuli that surrounds him. Consequently, behaviors that are stimulated by the environment are commonly misattributed to the patient's disorder. For example, one kindly nurse found a pseudopatient pacing the long hospital corridors. "Nervous, Mr. X?" she asked. "No, bored," he said.

The notes kept by pseudopatients are full of patient behaviors that were misinterpreted by well-intentioned staff. Often enough, a patient would go "berserk" because he had, wittingly or unwittingly, been mistreated by, say, an attendant. A nurse coming upon the scene would rarely inquire even cursorily into the environmental stimuli of the patient's behavior. Rather, she assumed that his upset derived from his pathology, not from his present interactions with other staff members. Occasionally, the staff might assume that the patient's family (especially when they had recently visited) or other patients had stimulated the outburst. But never were the staff found to assume that one of themselves or the structure of the hospital had anything to do with a patient's behavior. One psychiatrist pointed to a group of patients who were sitting outside the cafeteria entrance half an hour before lunchtime. To a group of young residents he indicated that such behavior was characteristic of the oral-acquisitive nature of the syndrome. It seemed not to occur to him that there were very few things to anticipate in a psychiatric hospital besides eating.

A psychiatric label has a life and an influence of its own. Once the impression has been formed that the patient is schizophrenic, the expectation is that he will continue to be schizophrenic. When a sufficient amount of time has passed, during which the patient has done nothing bizarre, he is considered to be in remission and available for discharge. But the label endures beyond discharge, with the unconfirmed expectation that he will behave as a schizophrenic again. Such labels, conferred by mental health professionals, are as influential on the patient as they are on his relatives and friends, and it should not surprise anyone that the diagnosis acts on all of them as a self-fulfilling prophecy. Eventually, the patient himself accepts the diagnosis, with all of its surplus meanings and expectations, and behaves accordingly.

THE EXPERIENCE OF PSYCHIATRIC HOSPITALIZATION

The term "mental illness" is of recent origin. It was coined by people who were humane in their inclinations and who wanted very much to raise the station of (and the public's sympathies toward) the psychologically disturbed from that of witches and "crazies" to one that was akin to the physically ill. And they were at least partially successful, for the treatment of the mentally ill *has* improved considerably over the years. But while treatment has improved, it is doubtful that people really regard the mentally ill in the same way that they view the physically ill. A broken leg is something one recovers from, but mental illness allegedly endures forever. A broken leg does not threaten the observer, but a crazy schizophrenic? There is by now a host of evidence that attitudes toward the mentally ill are characterized by fear, hostility, aloofness, suspicion, and dread. The mentally ill are society's lepers.

That such attitudes infect the general population is perhaps not surprising, only upsetting. But that they affect the professionals—attendants, nurses, physicians, psychologists, and social workers—who treat and deal with the mentally ill is more disconcerting, both because such attitudes are self-evidently pernicious and because they are unwitting. Most mental health professionals would insist that they are sympathetic toward the mentally ill, that they are neither avoidant nor hostile. But it is more likely that an exquisite ambivalence characterizes their relations with psychiatric patients, such that their avowed impulses are only part of their entire attitude. Negative attitudes are there too and can easily be detected. Such attitudes should not surprise us. They are the natural offspring of the labels patients wear and the places in which they are found.

Consider the structure of the typical psychiatric hospital. Staff and patients are strictly segregated.

Staff have their own living space, including their dining facilities, bathrooms, and assembly places. The glassed quarters that contain the professional staff, which the pseudopatients came to call "the cage," sit out on every dayroom. The staff emerge primarily for caretaking purposes—to give medication, to conduct a therapy or group meeting, to instruct or reprimand a patient. Otherwise staff keep to themselves, almost as if the disorder that afflicts their charges is somehow catching.

The average amount of time spent by attendants outside of the cage was 11.3 percent (range, 3 to 52 percent). This figure does not represent only time spent mingling with patients, but also includes time spent on such chores as folding laundry, supervising patients while they shave, directing ward cleanup, and sending patients to off-ward activities. It was the relatively rare attendant who spent time talking with patients or playing games with them. It proved impossible to obtain a "percent mingling time" for nurses, since the amount of time they spent out of the cage was too brief.

Physicians, especially psychiatrists, were even less available. They were rarely seen on the wards. Quite commonly, they would be seen only when they arrived and departed, with the remaining time being spent in their offices or in the cage. On the average, physicians emerged on the ward 6.7 times per day (range, 1 to 17 times). It proved difficult to make an accurate estimate in this regard, since physicians often maintained hours that allowed them to come and go at different times.

The hierarchical organization of the psychiatric hospital has been commented on before, but the latent meaning of that kind of organization is worth noting again. Those with the most power have least to do with patients, and those with the least power are most involved with them. Recall, however, that the acquisition of role-appropriate behaviors occurs mainly through the observation of others, with the most powerful having the most influence. Consequently, it is understandable that attendants not only spend more time with patients than do any other members of the staff—that is required by their station in the hierarchy—but also, insofar as they learn from their superiors' behavior, spend as little time with patients as they can. Attendants are seen mainly in the cage, which is where the models, the action, and the power are.

I turn now to a different set of studies, these dealing with staff response to patient-initiated contact. It has long been known that the amount of time a person spends with you can be an index of your significance to him. If he initiates and maintains eye contact, there is reason to believe that he is considering your requests and needs. If he pauses to chat or actually stops and talks, there is added reason to infer that he is individuating you. In four hospitals, the pseudopatient approached the staff member with a request which took the following form: "Pardon me, Mr. [or Dr. or Mrs.] X, could you tell me when I will be eligible for grounds privileges?" (or ". . . when I will be presented at the staff meeting?" or ". . . when I am likely to be discharged?").

The encounter frequently took the following bizarre form: (pseudopatient) "Pardon me, Dr. X. Could you tell me when I am eligible for grounds privileges?" (physician) "Good morning, Dave. How are you today?" (Moves off without waiting for a response.)

It is instructive to compare these data with data recently obtained at Stanford University. It has been alleged that large and eminent universities are characterized by faculty who are so busy that they have no time for students. For this comparison, a young lady approached individual faculty members who seemed to be walking purposefully to some meeting or teaching engagement and asked them the following six questions.

1 "Pardon me, could you direct me to Encina Hall?" (at the medical school: ". . . to the Clinical Research Center?").

2 "Do you know where Fish Annex is?" (there is no Fish Annex at Stanford).

3 "Do you teach here?"

4 "How does one apply for admission to the college?" (at the medical school: ". . . to the medical school?").

5 "Is it difficult to get in?"

6 "Is there financial aid?"

Without exception, all of the questions were answered. No matter how rushed they were, all respondents not only maintained eye contact, but stopped to talk. Indeed, many of the respondents went out of their way to direct or take the questioner to the office she was seeking, to try to locate "Fish Annex," or to discuss with her the possibilities of being admitted to the university.

POWERLESSNESS AND DEPERSONALIZATION

Eye contact and verbal contact reflect concern and individuation; their absence, avoidance and depersonalization. The data I have presented do not do justice to the rich daily encounters that grew up around matters of depersonalization and avoidance. I have records of patients who were beaten by staff for the sin of having initiated verbal contact. During my own experience, for example, one patient was beaten in the presence of other patients for having approached an attendant and told him, "I like you." Occasionally, punishment meted out to patients for misdemeanors seemed so excessive that it could not be justified by the most radical interpretations of psychiatric canon. Nevertheless, they appeared to go unquestioned. Tempers were often short. A patient who had not heard a call for medication would be roundly excoriated, and the morning attendants would often wake patients with, "Come on, you m——f——s, out of bed!"

Neither anecdotal nor "hard" data can convey the overwhelming sense of powerlessness which invades the individual as he is continually exposed to the depersonalization of the psychiatric hospital. It hardly matters *which* psychiatric hospital—the excellent public ones and the very plush private hospital were better than the rural and shabby ones in this regard, but, again, the features that psychiatric hospitals had in common overwhelmed by far their apparent differences.

Powerlessness was evident everywhere. The patient is deprived of many of his legal rights by dint of his psychiatric commitment. He is shorn of credibility by virtue of his psychiatric label. His freedom of movement is restricted. He cannot initiate contact with the staff, but may only respond to such overtures as they make. Personal privacy is minimal. Patient quarters and possessions can be entered and examined by any staff member, for whatever reason. His personal history and anguish is available to any staff member (often including the "grey lady" and "candy striper" volunteer) who chooses to read his folder, regardless of their therapeutic relationship to him. His personal hygiene and waste evacuation are often monitored. The water closets may have no doors.

At times, depersonalization reached such proportions that pseudopatients had the sense that they were invisible, or at least unworthy of account. Upon being admitted, I and other pseudopatients took the initial physical examinations in a semipublic room, where staff members went about their own business as if we were not there.

On the ward, attendants delivered verbal and occasionally serious physical abuse to patients in the presence of other observing patients, some of whom (the pseudopatients) were writing it all down. Abusive behavior, on the other hand, terminated quite abruptly when other staff members were known to be coming. Staff are credible witnesses. Patients are not.

A nurse unbuttoned her uniform to adjust her brassiere in the presence of an entire ward of viewing men. One did not have the sense that she was being seductive. Rather, she didn't notice us. A group of staff persons might point to a patient in the dayroom and discuss him animatedly, as if he were not there.

One illuminating instance of depersonalization and invisibility occurred with regard to medications. All told, the pseudopatients were administered nearly 2100 pills, including Elavil, Stelazine, Compazine, and Thorazine, to name but a few. (That such a variety of medications should have been administered to patients presenting identical symptoms is itself worthy of note.) Only two were swallowed. The rest were either pocketed or deposited in the toilet. The pseudopatients were not alone in this. Although I have no precise records on how many patients rejected their medications, the pseudopatients frequently found the medications of other patients in the toilet before they deposited their own. As long as they were cooperative, their behavior and the pseudopatients' own in this matter, as in other important matters, went unnoticed throughout.

Reactions to such depersonalization among pseudopatients were intense. Although they had come to the hospital as participant observers and were fully aware that they did not "belong," they nevertheless found themselves caught up in and fighting the process of depersonalization. Some examples: a graduate student in psychology asked his wife to bring his textbooks to the hospital so he could "catch up on his homework"—this despite the elaborate precautions taken to conceal his professional association. The same student, who had trained for quite some time to get into the hospital, and who had looked forward to the experience, "remembered" some drag races that he had wanted to see on the weekend and insisted that he be discharged by that time. Another pseudopatient attempted a romance with a nurse. Subsequently, he informed the staff that he was applying for admission to graduate school in psychology and was very likely to be admitted, since a graduate professor was one of his regular hospital visitors. The same person began to engage in psychotherapy with other patients—all of this as a way of becoming a person in an impersonal environment.

THE SOURCES OF DEPERSONALIZATION

What are the origins of depersonalization? I have already mentioned two. First are attitudes held by all of us toward the mentally ill—including those who treat them—attitudes characterized by fear, distrust, and horrible expectations on the one hand, and benevolent intentions on the other. Our ambivalence leads, in this instance as in others, to avoidance.

Second, and not entirely separate, the hierarchical structure of the psychiatric hospital facilitates depersonalization. Those who are at the top have least to do with patients, and their behavior inspires the rest of the staff. Average daily contact with psychiatrist, psychologists, residents, and physicians combined ranged from 3.9 to 25.1 minutes, with an overall mean of 6.8 (six pseudopatients over a total of 129 days of hospitalization). Included in this average are time spent in the admissions interview, ward meetings in the presence of a senior staff member, group and individual psychotherapy contacts, case presentation conferences, and discharge meetings. Clearly, patients do not spend much time in interpersonal contact with doctoral staff. And doctoral staff serve as models for nurses and attendants.

There are probably other sources. Psychiatric installations are presently in serious financial straits. Staff shortages are pervasive, staff time at a premium. Something has to give, and that something is patient contact. Yet, while financial stresses are realities, too much can be made of them. I have the impression that the psychological forces that result in depersonalization are much stronger than the fiscal ones and that the addition of more staff would not correspondingly improve patient care in this regard. The incidence of staff meetings and the enormous amount of record-keeping on patients, for example, have not been as substantially reduced as has patient contact. Priorities exist, even during hard times. Patient contact is not a significant priority in the traditional psychiatric hospital, and fiscal pressures do not account for this. Avoidance and depersonalization may.

Heavy reliance upon psychotropic medication tacitly contributes to depersonalization by convincing staff that treatment is indeed being conducted and that further patient contact may not be necessary. Even here, however, caution needs to be exercised in understanding the role of psychotropic drugs. If patients were powerful rather than powerless, if they were viewed as interesting individuals rather than diagnostic entities, if they were socially significant rather than social lepers, if their anguish truly and wholly compelled our sympathies and concerns, would we not *seek* contact with them, despite the availability of medications? Perhaps for the pleasure of it all?

THE CONSEQUENCES OF LABELING AND DEPERSONALIZATION

Whenever the ratio of what is known to what needs to be known approaches zero, we tend to invent "knowledge" and assume that we understand more than we actually do. We seem unable to acknowledge that we simply don't know. The needs for diagnosis and remediation of behavioral and emotional problems are enormous. But rather than acknowledge that we are just embarking on understanding, we continue to label patients "schizophrenic," "manic-depressive," and "insane," as if in those words we had captured the essence of understanding. The facts of the matter are that we have known for a long time that diagnoses are often not useful or reliable, but we have nevertheless continued to use them. We now know that we cannot distinguish insanity from sanity. It is depressing to consider how that information will be used.

Not merely depressing, but frightening. How many people, one wonders, are sane but not recognized as such in our psychiatric institutions? How many have been needlessly stripped of their privileges of citizenship, from the right to vote and drive to that of handling their own accounts? How many have feigned insanity in order to avoid the criminal consequences of their behavior, and, conversely, how many would rather stand trial than live interminably in a psychiatric hospital—but are wrongly thought to be mentally ill? How many have been stigmatized by well-intentioned, but nevertheless erroneous, diagnoses? On the last point, recall again that a "type 2 error" in psychiatric diagnosis does not have the same consequences it does in medical diagnosis. A diagnosis of cancer that has been found to be in error is cause for celebration. But psychiatric diagnoses are rarely found to be in error. The label sticks, a mark of inadequacy forever.

Finally, how many patients might be "sane" outside the psychiatric hospital but seem insane in it—not because craziness resides in them, as it were, but because they are responding to a bizarre setting, one that may be unique to institutions which harbor nether people?

SUMMARY AND CONCLUSIONS

It is clear that we cannot distinguish the sane from the insane in psychiatric hospitals. The hospital itself imposes a special environment in which the meanings of behavior can easily be misunderstood. The consequences to patients hospitalized in such an environment—the powerlessness, depersonalization, segregation, mortification, and self-labeling—seem undoubtedly counter-therapeutic.

I do not, even now, understand this problem well enough to perceive solutions. But two matters seem to have some promise. The first concerns the proliferation of community mental health facilities, of crisis intervention centers, of the human potential movement, and of behavior therapies that, for all of their own problems, tend to avoid psychiatric labels, to focus on specific problems and behaviors, and to retain the individual in a relatively nonpejorative environment. Clearly, to the extent that we refrain from sending the distressed to insane places, our impressions of them are less likely to be distorted. (The risk of distorted perceptions, it seems to me, is always present, since we are much more sensitive to an individual's behaviors and verbalizations than we are to the subtle contextual stimuli that often promote them. At issue here is a matter of magnitude. And, as I have shown, the magnitude of distortion is exceedingly high in the extreme context that is a psychiatric hospital.)

The second matter that might prove promising speaks to the need to increase the sensitivity of mental health workers and researchers to the *Catch 22* position of psychiatric patients. Simply reading materials in this area will be of help to some such workers and researchers. For others, directly experiencing the impact of psychiatric hospitalization will be of enormous use. Clearly, further research into the social psychology of such total institutions will both facilitate treatment and deepen understanding.

I and the other pseudopatients in the psychiatric setting had distinctly negative reactions. We do not pretend to describe the subjective experiences of true patients. Theirs may be different from ours, particularly with the passage of time and the necessary process of adaptation to one's environment. But we can and do speak to the relatively more objective indices of treatment within the hospital. It could be a mistake, and a very unfortunate one, to consider that what happened to us derived from malice or stupidity on the part of the staff. Quite the contrary, our overwhelming impression of them was of people who really cared, who were committed and who were uncommonly intelligent. Where they failed, as they sometimes did painfully, it would be more accurate to attribute those failures to the environment in which they, too, found themselves than to personal callousness. Their perceptions and behavior were controlled by the situation, rather than being motivated by a malicious disposition. In a more benign environment, one that was less attached to global diagnosis, their behaviors and judgments might have been more benign and effective.

40   ON BEING INSANE IN INSANE PLACES*

AILON SHILOH

It is unlikely that very many mental hospitals remain of the kind described 20 years ago by Ivan Belknap. At that time, hundreds of patients slept—winter and summer—on windswept porches or on bare concrete floors. All of the buildings were old, crowded, and hazardous. The food was tasteless to begin with and cold when served. The total daily budget per patient was 47 cents. On any day, patients had one chance in 280 of seeing a doctor. The basic therapy consisted of allowing the patients to sit on benches and stare at the blank walls.

That hospital represented the worst aspects of the custodial approach to treating the mentally ill, an approach requiring only that patients be kept alive and out of the way. While few hospitals would dare to provide that sort of barbaric custody nowadays, my own research in a large public mental hospital suggests that less obvious but no less pernicious aspects of the custodial approach are still central to mental hospitals today.

What does the custodial approach do to patients? Clifford W. Beers has caught it in an aphorism: "Madmen are too often man-made." Lucy Ozarin reached a similar conclusion: "After visiting 35 mental hospitals, the writer has formed the strong conviction that much of the pathological behavior of patients is a result of their hospital experience rather than a manifestation of their mental illness."

How does the inmate adapt to the total institution? Goffman suggests that a person may choose at least three lines of adaptations:

He may drastically curtail his interaction with others—what Goffman calls the "situational withdrawal" or "regression line."

He may deliberately challenge the institution by refusing to cooperate—the "intransigent line."

He may fully accept the values and roles assigned him by the institution—the "colonization line."

. . . what of the people I studied in the Veterans Administration Hospital in Downey, Ill.?

Downey is 35 miles north of the Chicago Loop. The V.A. hospital there has 2487 beds. It is the largest of the 40 neuropsychiatric hospitals run by the V.A., and one of the largest mental institutions in the country. The hospital's annual budget is more than $13 million, or $15.37 per patient per day, which is about three times the average daily expenditure per patient in U.S. public mental hospitals.

At the time I studied the patients of Downey, 42 percent had been admitted with disabilities connected with their military service, and 58 percent had disabilities stemming from other sources.

In all, my study took five months. By the time it was completed I had interview data from 560 patients, more than half of the men in the open psychiatric wards of the hospital. My core interviewers were two female patients, both former army nurses. Three sets of interviews were given. First: 250 depth interviews about critical aspects of the hospital, for which both closed-end questions, and 10 prepared drawings, were used to elicit answers. Second: 210 guided interviews, with both open and closed questions, to go further into critical aspects of the hospital's operations and into the patient's perceptions of them. Third: 100 guided interviews, with open and closed questions, to find out what the patients thought about alternatives to remaining in the mental hospital.

There were two strikingly different kinds of patients in the hospital—this was the central finding from an analysis of the interviews. About 40 percent simply did not want to leave. In Goffman's terms, they had been colonized—or perhaps overcolonized. These inmates I call the *institutionalized*. Another 25 percent had hopes and expec-

*Abridged from A. Shiloh, Sanctuary or prison—responses to life in a mental hospital. *Trans-action*, December 1968, 28–35.

tations of being released. These—whose response does not quite match any of Goffman's categories—I call the *non*institutionalized.

The remaining one-third of the patients either did not fall into either of these categories or shared characteristics of both. In what follows, I shall concentrate on the first two categories, which encompass two-thirds of the interviewed sample.

Many patients could be placed in one of these categories almost as soon as the interview with them began. Institutionalized patients were passive and silent, given to rambling or disjointed answers, and quick to lapse into apathy or noncooperation. Many were frightened by the interview. "Is this material going to be used against me?" they asked. A more characteristic response was, "I'm going to leave the hospital when I decide to and no damn test is going to run me out!"

*Non*institutionalized patients were far more articulate. They were interested in the study and pleased to have been included in it. Many *non*institutionalized patients dropped by my office sometime after their interviews to inquire about the findings. They gave full and coherent replies to questions and straightforward descriptions of the drawings.

Perhaps the class differences between the two groups throw some light on their opposite responses to the interviews. The institutionalized patients had, for the most part, been born and raised in poor urban centers. Their parents were often immigrants or first-generation Americans; their fathers were laborers or semiskilled workers. These patients had rarely completed high school and usually held jobs with little security. They were usually single, separated, or divorced, and often lived away from their parents, brothers, sisters, and the like. Compared to the *non*institutionalized patients, they were older and had spent more time in hospitals.

The *non*institutionalized inmates had been raised in diverse settings, urban and rural. Their parents usually were second-generation Americans, at least, and upper-lower to middle class. Most of these inmates were high school graduates; some had college experience. Most had good, secure jobs. Compared to the other patients, they were more likely to be married and less likely to have had marital problems. Those who were unmarried or separated were more likely to be living with their nuclear familes. These inmates were also younger, and had usually been in mental hospitals for periods totaling fewer than two years.

For *non*institutionalized patients, their hospitalization was an unfortunate but temporary state. They were oriented toward the outside world and viewed outside friends and family in a close "I-thou" relationship. Downey was never referred to as "home." Further, *non*institutionalized patients rapidly identified with the person or situation in each sketch and used personal pronouns, "I," "me," "we," "us."

Institutionalized patients were well aware of the material comforts of the hospital—the good food, clean beds, warm rooms, the free television, movies, and live shows—but at the same time spoke of its essential loneliness and its negative emotional aspects. These patients spoke only occasionally of the hospital's therapeutic techniques or contributions to their mental health. Instead, they emphasized the punishment, the locked ward or electric-shock treatment, and the need to "keep out of the way" of the doctors and their staff.

Institutionalized patients seemed to see the hospital as a substitute for an old-age home, an old-soldier's home, a poorhouse. They were willing to endure the various disadvantages of the hospital only because they did not consider it a hospital.

The goal of the institutionalized inmates was security, and to achieve it there were recognized avenues of adaptation: to become occupied with certain minimal chores and thus ensure a secure role for oneself; to engage in all that was required of the patient, with a minimum of effort or participation; to just blend into the background and stay out of the way; or all of these at once.

PATIENTS' ATTITUDES MAKE THE DIFFERENCE

Particularly wide differences between the institutionalized and *non*institutionalized inmates showed up in their ages, occupations, family arrangements, and lengths of residence in mental hospitals. The medical diagnosis that had led to an inmate's hospitalization proved to be of limited significance in determining his general profile, which strengthens the view that these profiles themselves represent reactions to the *institution,* not aspects of mental illness. All in all, a patient's attitude toward his hospitalization most clearly demonstrated the difference between the institutionalized and the *non*institutionalized inmates.

Institutionalized patients considered themselves simply cut off from the outside. They viewed their friends and family in a distant, "I-it" relationship. Downey Hospital was "home" for them. These patients, however, did not seem to identify with the people in the sketches of hospital scenes that were shown to them.

"They" were mowing the lawn.

"He" was in the locked ward.

TV is good for "them."

The institutionalized patients could easily ignore the sports program. The staff was so busy that meetings between patient and doctor could be kept to a minimum, which often meant never. The workshops were useful places where one could be left alone by keeping "busy." Work details were perhaps unpleasant, but not too high a price to pay for the material returns. The day rooms and recreational facilities were a source of unlimited free pleasure. It was not wise to attract unfavorable attention—say, by sitting on the bed during the day—because of the possible punishment.

Leaving the hospital, or even going out on a pass, were not meaningful positive concepts for the institutionalized patients. Downey was their home, and it was large enough to provide for all of their needs.

*Non*institutionalized patients were also conscious of the material comforts of the hospital, but they tended to view them as the normal services of a modern hospital. They were more conscious of and more outspoken about the hospital's therapeutic techniques, and often evaluated specific programs or personnel. Like the institutionalized pa-

tients, they believed that the locked wards and electric-shock treatment were forms of punishment administered to recalcitrant patients.

*Non*institutionalized patients did not consider the hospital a substitute for an old-age home, an old-soldier's home, or a poorhouse, and they were critical of and most unwilling to endure the disadvantages of the hospital. To them the sports program was a possible aspect of their therapy, but the workshops and work details were onerous, untherapeutic chores. They, too, considered it unwise to attract unfavorable attention, and were resentful that it might be followed by punishment.

Leaving the hospital and going out on passes were quite meaningful to them: These events enabled them to renew their "normal" family and friendship ties. Downey, even with its day rooms and recreational program, by no means catered to all of their needs.

The responses to the guided interview in the second phase of the study also showed this essential dichotomy in the way the patients saw the mental institution.

The majority of the institutionalized patients were unable or unwilling to say who or what in Downey was most or least helpful to them. The *non*institutionalized patients *were* willing and able. They even volunteered criticism of specific aspects of the therapeutic program and showed clear awareness of the negative side of their experience in the hospital.

*Non*institutionalized patients, asked about the closed ward, replied promptly and clearly that they did not think that it helped them, and that they did not think all new patients should have to undergo such an experience. They questioned the therapeutic value of the closed ward and said it should be used only in extreme cases, and then only for short periods.

Institutionalized patients, on the other hand, thought that being in a closed ward had helped them; they saw nothing wrong with having all patients placed in a closed ward upon their entering the hospital; they accepted the idea that the closed ward had a useful purpose; and they did not believe that closed wards should be abolished.

Almost all of the patients, when asked about their friends in the hospital, replied that they were often lonely and had few or no close friends. This perceived, and apparently accepted, social isolation on the part of these patients could be a direct reflection of their adaptation to the local culture, or a continuation of their pre-hospitalization social behavior.

The respondents in this phase of the study were then asked if they wanted to leave the hospital and, if so, what they were doing about it. While all of the *non*institutionalized patients replied promptly and emphatically in the affirmative to the first question, institutionalized patients showed a greater range of responses. Some refused to acknowledge the question, ignored it, or were noncommital; others replied in the straight negative. The few institutionalized patients who said they wanted to leave nonetheless contemplated discharge only in the vague future, when the weather was better, or only if en route to another hospital or institution. Very few in either group showed any clear perception of a way that they, as patients, could appreciably hasten their hospital discharge.

Most of the *non*institutionalized patients, when asked what they liked about the hospital, were cautious or neutral, or even had nothing at all favorable to say. Those who had something good to say were almost always thinking of therapy. The institutionalized, however, spoke enthusiastically about the hospital's material comforts, recreational facilities, and the like. The *non*institutionalized were quite ready to air their complaints about Downey, while the institutionalized shied away from a question about what they disliked about the hospital.

IF PATIENTS RAN THE HOSPITAL

The patients were asked what changes they would make in the hospital if they were in charge. Most of the institutionalized patients were unable to see themselves in authority and found it difficult to answer the question. *Non*institutionalized patients were amused with the idea, but suggested

corrections for the problems or complaints that they had previously mentioned.

What was their idea of a good doctor and a good nurse? Institutionalized patients found it difficult, or were reluctant, to provide answers; the *non*institutionalized patients volunteered a wide range of perceptions.

Yet the institutionalized patients, when asked what was their idea of a good patient, were more able to promptly volunteer criteria (essentially those of the total institution), while the *non*institutionalized patients were more uncertain and hesitant in their replies. The institutionalized inmates emphasized proper behavior; the *non*institutionalized spoke about cooperating with therapy.

Finally, the patients were asked what type of help they believed patients needed after leaving the hospital. Institutionalized patients were essentially finance-oriented; *non*institutionalized patients, again, were essentially therapy-oriented.

These basic differences between institutionalized and *non*institutionalized patients were further corroborated by the findings from the third phase of the study, in which 100 patients were asked a series of questions about other therapeutic solutions that the V.A. offers its mental patients.

Institutionalized patients, when asked the neutral question of how long they had been in this or other mental hospitals, replied, perhaps understandably, with vague remarks. *Non*institutionalized patients replied more promptly and specifically.

Institutionalized patients, asked if they considered it healthy to remain in a mental hospital for a long time, saw nothing essentially unhealthy in such a situation. *Non*institutionalized patients saw it as essentially undesirable, as interfering with therapy.

The inmates were then asked if there were some patients in the hospital who were not mentally ill. Across the board, patients from both groups said Yes. When asked who such patients were, it was the institutionalized patients who were better at identifying them. Asked if such patients could be discharged elsewhere, again the majority of the respondents, irrespective of their profile, replied Yes.

The essential difference between the institutionalized and the noninstitutionalized patients appeared clearest in the way they volunteered possible alternatives to remaining in Downey, places where patients in good mental health might go if discharged. Noninstitutionalized patients said such patients could go home; institutionalized patients said that they could go to other types of institutions.

The patients were asked about the V.A. alternatives to the hospital—nursing homes, foster homes, and group-placement homes. These questions highlighted a serious lack of communication between the V.A. and the patients. Few patients showed any clear awareness of these programs, and knew of them only in negative or questionable stereotypes. Using these stereotypes, noninstitutionalized patients had a qualified but positive perception of these homes as paths to ultimate discharge, while institutionalized patients were negative or doubtful.

The Downey program that permits trial visits home was better known to the patients, but again the dichotomy persisted. The noninstitutionalized patients were quite positive as to its therapeutic value, and the institutionalized patients were quite as skeptical and negative.

The night hospital and day hospital were then raised as other solutions to the inmates remaining fulltime patients. Noninstitutionalized inmates expressed general ignorance of such hospitals, but perceived their possible positive therapeutic role; institutionalized patients maintained a consistently more cautious and negative attitude. There did seem to be a tendency for the institutionalized patients to favor the night hospital, which provides full evening hospital privileges with a great amount of freedom during the day.

Noninstitutionalized patients, asked their opinion of the large-sized mental hospital as a therapeutic aid, indicated an awareness that the patient can too easily become depersonalized and lost; the institutionalized patients praised the anonymity of the large hospital and its extensive recreation resources.

THE FINITE APPROACH TO HOSPITALIZATION

The succeeding question concerned the "finite" approach to mental-hospital hospitalization —that, at first, patients be admitted into such a mental hospital only for a definite period of time, perhaps a week or month. This, of course, runs counter to the custodial ethic.

Institutionalized patients did not agree, and argued for continued indefinite hospitalization; noninstitutionalized patients were less certain in their replies, but thought the finite approach could be far more therapeutic than the indefinite hospitalization process, with its apparent aimlessness.

When asked whether they agreed that, instead of going directly into the mental hospital, people should have the option of entering local mental-health clinics, neither institutionalized nor noninstitutionalized patients were enthusiastic. Institutionalized patients were likely to perceive the mental-health clinic as a possible block to hospitalization, while noninstitutionalized patients emphasized the general unavailability of such clinics. As with other solutions to remaining in the hospital, both kinds of patients had an unclear idea of what a mental-health clinic was or could do, and they were cautious to negative about it.

Finally, the patients in this last phase of the study were asked their views of how they themselves might fare once discharged from Downey. Institutionalized patients simply did not think they would ever be discharged, while noninstitutionalized patients were optimistic. But though the latter expected to be discharged, they were very uncertain as to when this might be. They expected to return home upon discharge, but were worried about their ability to return to a full role as an economic provider. Furthermore, noninstitutionalized patients did not show any clear knowledge of the resources within the hospital or community that might help them. They were as unaware of the help that they might get after they left the hospital as they were of the resources in therapy that were available within the hospital—another failure in communication between patients and staff.

Today, even the magnitude of the mental-health problem is unclear. In the United States, according to the National Association for Mental Health, at least one in every ten—over 19 million people in all—manifests some form of mental or emotional illness that needs psychiatric treatment.

During 1962, over one and a half billion dollars was spent on the care and treatment of patients in state, county, and federal mental hospitals. Over one million people were treated. At any one time, there are more people hospitalized with mental illness than with all other diseases combined. Yet by no means do those hospitalized as mentally ill approximate the total population of the mentally ill.

What I have found at Downey—which is not contradicted by other, less extensive investigations of mental hospitals elsewhere—is that this well-funded and well-staffed institution is, in many ways, simply not functioning as a mental hospital.

Despite the essentially exploratory nature of my study, the remarkable finding has emerged that a sizable body of patients (perhaps 40 percent or more) do not want to leave the mental hospital. For a variety of reasons—social, economic, and even, perhaps, medical—the Downey V.A. mental hospital is home for them. Despite their perception of the mental hospital's limitations, of its hardship, loneliness, and even fear, the institutionalized patients still see Downey as the best solution to their problems. As one such patient put it, "It's still better than skid row."

For the institutionalized 40 percent, Downey is an old-soldiers' home with comfortable appointments, but with the constant danger of punishment for stepping out of line. The institutionalized *may* need an institution in order to function, but many of them are at Downey because they do not want to leave, not because they are mentally ill. And those who *are* mentally ill are not yearning after a cure that would require them to leave.

The *non*institutionalized 25 percent have the opposite problem with Downey. They want out, yet they cannot find the therapy they seek because the hospital is run for the institutionalized mass of patients. Unlike the institutionalized—who in many cases have no other place to go—the *non*institutionalized have a shelter outside the hospital to return to, but difficulty getting there.

What I question is the waste of public funds; the time and energy of the medical staff wasted on the reluctant institutionalized patients; and the tragic waste of the *non*institutionalized patients who are eager for a cure that seems a long time in coming. Downey and hospitals like it are not curing the institutionalized patients. Might not another home be found for them, to free the *non*institutionalized patients for treatment, and to make room for those others on the long waiting lists of mental hospitals—who might also be just as ready to be cured if room were made for them?

THE GROWTH OF THE CUSTODIAL ETHIC

If my findings at Downey and the theories of Goffman and other researchers apply generally, then a great deal of money is being spent in this country to *store* the mentally ill, as opposed to treating them and helping them return to society. This is what the custodial ethic really means. Where did it come from?

J. Sanbourne Bockover maintains that the 1830's and 1840's were a golden age of *moral* treatment of mental patients—when they were treated with dignity and considered as guests, and when hospital discharge rates were at an all-time high. This moral treatment did not necessarily consist of any set of therapeutic measures. The assumption was that the recuperative powers of the patient would assert themselves and, if not obstructed, lead to his recovery. Hospitals were small, and the superintendents and staff shared their patients' daily life and living conditions.

But during the second half of the 19th century, the increasing population, particularly of immigrants, exerted such pressure upon mental hospitals that they grew rapidly in size. The physician became an administrator, remote from staff and patients. Attitudes toward patients were altered. As Milton Greenblatt, Richard H. York, and Esther Lucille Brown have written, "Physicians of colonial ancestry who were filled with compassion for the mentally ill who had a similar heritage were often revolted by the 'ignorant uncouth insane foreign paupers . . .' "

As these critical changes in attitudes and size were taking place, there was a general abandonment of moral treatment in favor of a concentration on the organic factors supposedly causing mental illness. At the same time, the philosophy of keeping patients in custody became dominant. The custodial approach thus arose with the arrival of patients who closely resemble those I have called the institutionalized, while moral treatment was reserved for those who match, less closely, those I have defined as *non*institutionalized.

As the Final Report of the Joint Commission on Mental Illness and Health put it, "By the beginning of the 20th century, the profile of the 'state asylum for the incurably insane' was stereotyped, both professionally and socially—it was an institution where hopeless cases were put away for good." This, of course, led to the sort of barbarities discussed in the opening of this article, for when patients are put away for good, it is for the good of society more than for the good of the patient.

Yet, as my investigation of Downey indicates, even after the reforms in the treatment of inmates that have come in the last 25 years, custodial attitudes have remained.

A.S.

COMMENT: CRACKUP IN MENTAL CARE

In the past nine years, because of judicial pressure to protect the civil liberties of mental patients and the growing use of drugs to treat mental illness, the population of state mental institutions has declined by almost half, from 505,000 in 1963 to 276,000 in 1972.

The inmate exodus had its roots in the 1950s when more and more psychiatrists challenged the concept of custodial institutions. In 1963 the Community Mental Health Centers Act was passed. Aimed at eliminating the "human warehouses" state hospitals had become, the bill envisioned the eventual creation of 2,000 local clinics to provide counseling and care.

Though hospitals began their steady discharge of patients as planned, money to fund this revolution in mental care never sufficiently materialized. After ten years, only 392 community centers are in operation. Economy-minded Governors, willing to save money by closing hospitals, have been less willing to divert the money into clinics. Moreover, while small states like Hawaii can boast of success in treating seriously ill out-patients, clinics in larger states like California and New York are often faced with more people and more problems than they can handle.

In California, where the population of mentally ill in state hospitals was reduced from 36,000 in the 1950s to 7,000 today, chronically ill patients have been returned to communities poorly equipped to provide adequate treatment. With no one to care for them, former patients have ended up on welfare rolls, in boardinghouses, cheap hotels and even jail.

According to a Ralph Nader task force report, community centers across the U.S. have failed to provide care to those least able to find help: drug addicts, alcoholics, the young, the aged and "the poor in general." Thousands of people are being dumped into nursing or foster homes where conditions are often deplorable.

Neither civil libertarians nor psychiatrists seem willing to return to the old days when citizens could be committed for long periods of observation without even a court hearing. Yet many feel that the closing of state hospitals has been precipitate, with too much concern for economy and too little concern for mental health or public safety. Now that the Nixon Administration has apparently abandoned the community mental health centers, the future of mental care is shakier than ever.

Time, December 17, 1973

41 LAING'S MODELS OF MADNESS*

MIRIAM SIEGLER, HUMPHRY OSMOND,
and HARRIET MANN

Bright young schizophrenics, like bright young people generally, are interested in reading about their condition. From the vast and varied selection of literature available to them, they appear to show a marked preference for R. D. Laing's *The Politics of Experience* (1967). The present authors, like other members of the 'square' older generation, are of the opinion that they know what is best, and that this book is not good for these patients. It is an appealing book, and emotionally there is not a false note in it. This alone makes it important. But it contains treacherous confusions, and while we do not presume to make choices for our young friends we do feel that it is our duty to clarify the alternatives as presented in this book.

We have evolved a method for picking our way through the jungle of theories about schizophrenia: the construction of models (Siegler and Osmond, 1966). Briefly, our models are constructed by taking a single theory or point of view and asking its author or authors what schizophrenia is, how it might have come about, what is to be done about it, in what direction it is likely to alter over time, how the people involved with it ought to behave, and other such questions. We have labelled these questions 'definition,' 'aetiology,' 'treatment,' 'prognosis,' 'the rights and duties of patients,' and so forth, and they constitute the dimensions of the model. The answers to these questions make up the content of the model itself. The dimensions must be consistent with each other within any one model. When two or more such models have been constructed, they can be compared, dimension by dimension. In the physical sciences, workers are in the habit of comparing theories and showing in what way one is better than another, but in

*Abridged from M. Siegler, H. Osmond, and H. Mann, Laing's models of madness. *British Journal of Psychiatry*, 1969, **115**, 947–958.

psychiatry, stemming as it does from empirical medicine, eclecticism prevails. Our models are an attempt to borrow from the physical sciences a certain orderliness which we find enviable. Thus far we have constructed six models of schizophrenia: medical, moral, psychoanalytic, family interaction, social, and conspiratorial. We now propose to apply our method to *The Politics of Experience*.

Most books and articles on schizophrenia are written either to express some point of view or theory about schizophrenia, or else to report some research on a problem that arises within a particular theory. In either case, it is usually evident from the start what model the author holds. In Laing's book, however, it is not immediately evident what kind of model will emerge from our process. In fact, it soon becomes apparent that the dimensions can be filled more than once, i.e. there is more than one model. The task, then, is to locate all of his statements which fit any of our dimensions, to put together all the dimensions which are compatible with each other, to see how many models result from this process, and to see what dimensions, if any, are missing from the identifiable models. Using this method, we find that Laing's book contains two more or less complete models, and a fragment of a third model. Of the three models, two have been described before (psychoanalytic, conspiratorial) and one is entirely new (psychodelic).

In the two models which are more or less complete, we have filled in the missing dimensions so that they are consistent with the existing ones. The dimensions which we have supplied in this way are bracketed, so that the reader may easily distinguish them from Laing's own statements.

We have filled some of the dimensions with Laing's own words, and in all these cases the quotation marks and page numbers are given. We have done this in order to convey the flavour of his argument, which might otherwise be lost. The method of model construction inevitably distorts the author's intentions, which are conveyed in part by the 'mood' of the book, the order in which things are presented, the style of writing, and other means which lie outside of the argument itself. Arranging a theory as a model often destroys the uniqueness of the author's point of view, and yet it is precisely this uniqueness which prevents the comparison of one author's theory with another. We have, then, used the author's exact words whenever feasible in order to minimize this distortion without sacrificing the comparability which our method makes possible.

All statements in the dimensions which are not bracketed or in quotation marks are paraphrases of Laing's statements.

I. LAING'S CONSPIRATORIAL MODEL OF MADNESS

A. *The model described*

1. *Definition*

Schizophrenia is a *label* which some people pin on other people, under certain social circumstances. It is not an illness, like pneumonia. It is a form of alienation which is out of step with the prevailing state of alienation. It is a social fact and a political event.

2. *Aetiology*

Alienation, of which schizophrenia is one form, '. . . is achieved only by outrageous violence perpetrated by human beings on human beings.' (p.xv). We are driving our children mad. We are intolerant of different fundamental structures of experience.

The social system, and not individuals, must be the object of study if we are to understand the aetiology of schizophrenia. The blame cannot be laid at anyone's door; 'very seldom is it a question of contrived, deliberate cynical lies or a ruthless intention to drive someone crazy . . .' (p. 79).

3. *Behaviour*

'. . . Behaviour that gets labelled schizophrenic is a special strategy that a person invents in order to live in an unlivable situation.' (p. 79).

Transactional analyses are insufficient explanations of behaviour. Electronic systems can play games which can be analysed in this way, but human relations are transexperiential.

Psychiatrists have tended to pay more attention to the patient's behaviour than to his experience.

4. *Treatment*

What is called 'treatment' is really getting the patient to abandon his subjective experiential perspective for the therapist's objective one. The patient's experiences are interpreted away by the therapist, and said to mean something other than what the patient says they mean.

5. *Prognosis*

Once the label of 'schizophrenic' is applied, it sticks, and treating someone in terms of this label reinforces the very behaviour which caused the label to be applied in the first place. It is a vicious circle.

6. *Suicide*

(Suicide is a way out of the vicious circle.)[1]

7. *Function of the hospital*

The hospital is a total institution which degrades and invalidates human beings. Once in the hospital, the patient hardly ever leaves, because he manifests more and more of the behaviour for which he was hospitalized.

8. *Personnel*

The personnel for this model are all the people who come into contact with the person labelled as schizophrenic except the schizophrenic himself. 'The person labelled is inaugurated not only into a role, but into a career of patient, by the concerted action of a coalition (a "conspiracy") of family, G. P., mental health officer, psychiatrists, nurses, psychiatric social workers, and often fellow patients.' (p. 84).

9. *Rights and duties of patients*

'The "committed" person labelled as patient, and specifically as "schizophrenic," is degraded from full existential and legal status as human agent and responsible person to someone no longer in possession of his own definition of himself, unable to retain his own possessions, precluded from the exercise of his discretion as to whom he meets, what he does. His time is no longer his own, and the space he

---

[1]Suicide is discussed in another of Laing's books, *The Divided Self* (London: Tavistock Publications, 1959). The model in use in this book is the psychoanalytic model.

occupies is no longer of his own choosing. After being subjected to a degradation ceremonial known as psychiatric examination, he is bereft of his civil liberties in being imprisoned in a total institution known as a "mental" hospital. More completely, more radically than anywhere else in our society, he is invalidated as a human being. In the mental hospital he must remain, until the label is rescinded or qualified by such terms as "remitted" or "readjusted".' (p. 84).

The schizophrenic has no rights and no duties.

10. *Rights and duties of families of patients*

(The family has driven the schizophrenic crazy, although they probably did not intend to do so, labelled him schizophrenic, and hospitalized him in a total institution. In doing so, they have forfeited the usual rights and duties of families toward one of their members.)

11. *Rights and duties of society*

(Society [i.e., all the members of a culture] seems to have the right to maintain the status quo, and in order to do so the status quo is represented as part of the natural order, or as a natural law. Society appears to have the right to lock people up in mental hospitals as a means of maintaining the status quo. It is not clear whether society has any duties toward its members in this model.)

12. *Goal of the model*

The goal of this model is to maintain the status quo by 'treating' as medical patients certain indivicuals who, due to the strength of their inner perceptions and experiences, are exceptionally eloquent critics of the society.

B. The model discussed

We have identified this model as conspiratorial because it fits the description of that model given in our original paper (Siegler and Osmond, 1966). It has as its main concern the violation of the rights of the person labelled as schizophrenic. Since it is denied that the person so labelled has an illness, his incarceration in a building called a 'hospital' is inexplicable. And so it is said that there is a conspiracy among those surrounding the 'patient' to exile him to a total institution which is called a

hospital but is really a kind of concentration camp.[2]

A conspiratorial model is a view of the fate of schizophrenics minus the medical context. We must now ask what it is about the medical context that disturbs Laing so much. First, Laing finds the practice of assigning diagnostic labels to patients unacceptable. He says: '. . . It is wrong to impute a hypothetical disease of unknown aetiology and undiscovered pathology to someone unless *he* can prove otherwise.' (p. 71.) Laing is certainly entitled to believe that this is wrong, but it is only fair to note that the practice of medicine consists to a great extent of imputing hypothetical diseases of unknown aetiology and undiscovered pathology to patients who are in no position to prove otherwise. All diseases are hypothetical, all are labels. There is no such thing as diabetes, there are only individuals who have certain experiences and physical symptoms which are said to have some relation to the hypothetical disease. Yet such a disease entity is an extremely powerful category, for all its philosophical inelegance. Without it, medical research would be unthinkable and practice chaotic. When doctors see 'a case of pneumonia' or 'a case of tuberculosis,' they bring to bear on each case such knowledge as they and other doctors have accumulated about this hypothetical entity. Diagnosis is one of the principal functions of the physician. In the conspiratorial model, to label someone is to discriminate against him, but in the medical model to label someone is to bring the knowledge of medicine to bear upon him. It is an essential step which precedes and determines treatment. It may save his life.[3]

Another aspect of medicine which seems to bother Laing is that when one removes the medical context from a medical interaction one is often left with an extraordinary situation. He describes a clinical examination, taken from Kraepelin's lec-

---

[2]Laing actually uses the word 'conspiracy' on page 84, but in parenthesis and with full quotation marks around it, which seems to suggest that he wishes to qualify the word somewhat.
[3]Diagnosis has another important function: it is a necessary step in conferring the sick role. Patients are anxious to have a diagnosis because without it their status as patient is dubious. They might otherwise be frauds, malingerers, or hypochondriacs.

tures, in which Kraepelin demonstrates a young girl's psychotic illness by noting her reactions when he attempts to stop her movements, forces a piece of bread out of her hands, sticks a needle into her forehead, and so forth (p. 73). Laing correctly notes that this is very peculiar behaviour; but it is only so when taken out of the context as experienced and defined by Kraepelin, i.e. a clinical examination. The medical context permits people called doctors to perform all kinds of unusual actions on people called patients, and this enables them to treat illnesses. On the whole, people feel that the advantages of the medical model are such that the social fiction which is required to sustain it is worth preserving. But not everyone is of this opinion; some people, for example, Christian Scientists, feel that other values take precedence. As an individual, Laing is quite free to put forth any view on these matters that he chooses, but as a physician he is not free to put forth the view that the social fiction called medicine is more harmful than helpful.

In the dimension of 'behaviour,' Laing correctly notes that psychiatrists tend to pay attention to behaviour to the exclusion of experience. To the extent that they do so, they fail to behave like medical men, for a doctor does not simply observe his patient's behaviour, but makes inquiries and, if possible, tests of what is going on 'inside' the patient. The thermometer measures the inner experience of the patient, and is more accurate and useful than watching the patient mop his brow. Doctors ask their patients to tell them where it hurts, and they listen carefully to this information, in order to map out the nature and extent of the illness. Psychiatrists who no longer listen to the reports of their patients' experiences, or who interpret these experiences symbolically instead of using them as information, are not using the medical model.

One of the dimensions which is missing from Laing's model is suicide. Within the medical model, suicide is a medical risk in certain illnesses, especially in schizophrenia (Osmond and Hoffer, 1967). The doctor must be alert for signs of possible suicide, and he must use his clinical experience to avert it if possible. But in Laing's model, as in Goffman's (1961), suicide is conspicuous by its absence. Since the staff in this model seem to have rights in relation to the patient, but no duties toward him, it is not possible to say that it is the duty of the staff to prevent the patient from committing suicide. Laing and Goffman might have taken the stand that suicide is the patient's (or rather, 'patient's') business, and that no one else has the right to interfere with it, but they do not do this; they prefer not to discuss it at all. Yet suicide is just the sort of moral dilemma which makes medicine the model of choice in the case of schizophrenia. The medical model is the only one which can simultaneously try to prevent death, and account for it if it occurs. In all other models of which we are aware, death must be seen as someone's fault. In medicine, as long as the doctor behaves like a doctor, he is not blamed for deaths which occur in his practice.

In addition to suicide, there are two other dimensions missing from Laing's model; the rights and duties of the patients' families, and the rights and duties of society. Since this model has as its central focus the rights of the person labelled as schizophrenic, it is not surprising that those of the other participants are ignored. Laing clearly wished to redress the balance in favour of the person labelled as schizophrenic. He appears to believe that the reason why the 'patient' has lost so many rights is that we are 'intolerant of different fundamental structures of experience' (p. 50). That is, he sees the family and community as repressive forces, unwilling to permit the schizophrenic to experience his unusual perceptions without interference. Because they fail to accept his experiences as authentic, Laing argues, they elicit frustrated and peculiar behaviour from him, they then label it as schizophrenic, and extrude him from the family and community until he learns to see things their way. Given this picture of the 'patient' as a victim of repressive forces, it is little wonder that Laing is not moved to consider the rights of the family and community.

We are in agreement with Laing's contention that most people cannot accept the fact that others experience the world in a radically different way from themselves (Mann, H., Siegler, M. and Osmond, H., 1968). On the whole people know very little about other experiential worlds. Many experiences are difficult to put into words, and some people are not as articulate as others, so most people do not guess how very different the experiences of others may be. However, we disagree with Laing's contention that it is in the area of experience that the schizophrenic comes to grief; his difficulties lie in the area of behaviour. As long as a schizophrenic manages to behave normally, no one will show the slightest interest, kindly or otherwise, in his unusual experiences. A person may, with impunity, experience himself as walking down the street without clothes on; it is only when he actually does this that the community will take action. The community is generally indifferent to and ignorant of the inner experiences of its members, but it does deal with misbehaviour by curtailing the rights that are contingent on acceptable behaviour. Although the behaviour required varies enormously from culture to culture, and from family to family, all cultures and all families exchange certain rights for certain behavioural conformities. When this breakdown of reciprocity occurs, the person in question loses his usual rights and moves into some new role, which has other rights. The possible roles for such a person of which we are aware are: bad, eccentric, prophetic, analysand, impaired, sick. Today, since there are schizophrenics in each of these roles, one might ask which of them is best off.[4]

Schizophrenics who occupy the 'bad' role may be found in prisons; here they are offered the rights and duties of prisoners, including a determinate sentence for some specific infraction of the law. Some people believe that this is a kinder fate than the mental hospital, but unfortunately the advantages to the schizophrenic are often outweighed by the fact that the non-schizophrenic prisoners recognize that there is something wrong with him, and will not accept him into the highly normative sub-culture of the criminal. Foucault (1965) de-

scribes the situation which arose when, in eighteenth-century France, criminals, schizophrenics and the indigent were all locked up together: the schizophrenics quickly became highly visible, because they could not conform to the daily life of the prison. This situation is still reported today.

The role of eccentric is open to some schizophrenics. It has the great advantage of being an acceptable social role, but most communities cannot tolerate more than a few eccentrics, and there is no room for the enormous number of schizophrenics.

The role of prophet, like the eccentric role, is one which is open to very few people, whether they are schizophrenic or not. A schizophrenic who wished to occupy this role would find himself in competition with normal people whose temperament allowed them to excel in this way.

The role of analysand is open to a small number of schizophrenics who live in a few Western countries, and whose temperament permits them to engage in the psychoanalytic form of communication. In general, working class people are barred from this role both financially and culturally. Its main advantage is that a great deal of personal care and attention is lavished on the schizophrenic occupying this role. Among its disadvantages are that it may create financial and emotional strain in the analysand's family; the analysand feels guilty if his condition does not improve; and the analysand role is constantly being confused with the sick role.

The impaired role is a kind of second-class citizenship, designed to offer support and protection to people who have disabilities. The blind, the deaf, the crippled, and the retarded are all examples of impaired people. These people are expected to behave as normally as possible in exchange for reduced demands upon them by others. Unlike that of sick people, their situation is not expected to change. Many schizophrenics, especially those in hospitals, occupy the impaired role, but unfortunately, it does not quite fit them, because most of them have fluctuating illnesses: they may be quite normal at some times, and very ill at others. In many countries there are mental hospitals which

[4]To our knowledge, no one has offered schizophrenics a choice of these roles, although some schizophrenics have moved or been moved from one role to another.

are really homes for the impaired and are neither equipped to give real medical care to the very ill, nor set up to allow normal living to those who are not ill at any given moment.

Some schizophrenics occupy the sick role. That is, they perceive themselves as having a major illness which, like many major illnesses, does not have an agreed-upon aetiology or a wholly successful treatment. They understand that they are not able to carry their full adult load of social responsibility because they are unfortunate enough to be very ill. They consult their physicians, take medication as directed (ideally), report changes in their condition when they occur, go into the hospital when their illness gets worse, follow the progress of medical research, talk with other patients with the same illness about their mutual difficulties, and ask their doctor if he thinks they will ever be really well again. Their lot is not an easy one, but they do occupy an ancient and respectable social role, that of the sick person. If they occupy the sick role fully, they do not blame themselves or their families for their condition. This relieves them of the additional burden of family strife, not a small matter for a young adult who may have to live with his family long past the time he would normally leave if he were well. The schizophrenic in the sick role may gain such comfort as he can from the knowledge that other major psychiatric diseases, such as general paresis and pellagra psychosis, have yielded to medical research.

II. LAING'S PSYCHOANALYTIC MODEL OF MADNESS

A. *The model described*

Only two dimensions of this model are present in Laing's book, aetiology and treatment.

1. *Aetiology*

'. . . to the best of my knowledge, *no* schizophrenic has been studied whose disturbed pattern of communication has not been shown to be a reflection of, and reaction to, the disturbed and disturbing pattern characterizing his or her family of origin.' (p. 78)[5]

2. *Treatment*

'Psychotherapy must remain an obstinate attempt of two people to recover the wholeness of being human through the relationship between them.' (p. 32). 'Psychotherapy consists in the paring away of all that stands between us, the props, masks, roles, lies, defences, anxieties, projections and interjections, in short, all the carry-overs from the past, transference and countertransference, that we use by habit and collusion, wittingly and unwittingly, as our currency for relationships.' (p. 27).

B. *The model discussed*

We have identified this model as a psychoanalytic model, even though Laing is not an orthodox psychoanalyst, because it has the essential features of such a model: the source of the person's difficulties lies in the past, specifically in his disturbed family relationships, and the treatment consists of a special kind of corrective relationship between two people, patient and therapist. These features are not true of any other model.

It is interesting that only these two dimensions of the model are present, for these are the dimen-

---

[5] Although it may appear that Laing uses here a family interaction model, rather than a psychoanalytic one, this is not so. In the family interaction model as we have described it (Siegler and Osmond, 1966), the essential feature is that the disturbance is seen as lying *among* the members of the family, all of whom are, together, 'the patient.' Laing nowhere in this book shows the slightest concern for the experiences of the other members of the family. He simply uses the information provided by the family interaction model to reinforce his argument that the schizophrenic patient has been driven mad by his family, a statement which is meaningless in the other model. The purists among the family interactionists believe that only the analysis of the whole family together can alter the family pathology, whereas Laing maintains the psychoanalytic view that treatment occurs between two people, therapist and patient. In another book on schizophrenia (Laing, R. D. and Esterson, A., *Sanity, Madness and the Family*, Volume I, Families of Schizophrenics) Laing also sees the function of the therapist to be the exploration of the patient's experience, rather than that of other family members.

sions on which the strength of the psychoanalytic model rests. Diagnosis, for example, is of little concern in this model. Whereas the process of diagnosis is seen as prejudicial labelling in the conspiratorial model, and as an essential step toward determining treatment in the medical model, it is seen in the psychoanalytic model as a useless diversion. Why bother to determine what category a patient falls into, when the treatment is the same in any case, and every relationship between patient and therapist is unique?

The psychoanalytic model is opposed to the medical model at almost every point. Yet psychoanalysts are often medical doctors; in some countries, they must be. This has created the utmost confusion for schizophrenic patients, since they usually go to a doctor because they perceive themselves to be ill, and wish to be treated; they then discover that the treatment offered them carries with it a set of rights and duties, i.e. the role of analysand, which is incompatible with the sick role. The analyst uses the authority which derives from the fact that he is a physician to put forth an antimedical view. It is almost as if a priest used the authority vested in him by the church to put forth a doctrine which was completely irreconcilable with that of the church. The difference between the two institutions is that the church strives to be overtly consistent, while medicine has a covert, unverbalized consistency, which is undisturbed by the peculiar and often outrageous opinions which doctors voice from time to time. The fact that doctors are not thrown out of medical societies for putting forth antimedical views shows that the true consensus in medicine lies elsewhere than in verbalized doctrines. It is a tribute to the enduring qualities of the institution of medicine that doctors can advocate and even proselytize antimedical views among patients without destroying the basic doctor-patient relationship between them.

But schizophrenic patients do not emerge unscathed from these encounters. The underlying assumption of psychoanalysis is that progress toward a 'healthy' personality is possible, given hard work, good faith, enough time, and in most cases enough money. In medicine, there is no such contract; and illness may become suddenly worse, for no known reason, in spite of everyone's hard work and good faith. In the psychoanalytic model, these sudden reversals must be explained 'dynamically,' i.e. they are somebody's fault. Either the family does not really wish the patient to get well, or the patient has been damaged too severely to get well, or the patient is 'afraid' to get well, or the analyst has not solved the countertransference problem. The fact that failure must be explained, either implicitly or explicitly, as someone's fault places a great additional burden on the schizophrenic and his family.

Laing's conspiratorial model is an account of how he thinks schizophrenics are treated at the present time; his psychodelic model (to follow) is an account of how he thinks schizophrenics ought to be treated. His psychoanalytic model, which seems to have crept into the book by mistake, is an account of what he actually does. He is a psychotherapist with a very deep regard for his patients, and he tells us, in these fragments of a model, that he forms meaningful and authentic relationships with them. Since it appears that the psychoanalytic model is the one which he actually uses, we feel it is incumbent upon him to inform his patients fully about it, so that they may compare it with the alternative models.

III. LAING'S PSYCHODELIC MODEL OF MADNESS
A. *The model described*

1. *Definition*
   Schizophrenia is '. . . itself a natural way of healing our own appalling state of alienation called normality . . .' (p.116). 'Madness need not be all breakdown . . . It may also be breakthrough. It is potentially liberation and renewal as well as enslavement and existential death.' (p. 93). It is not an illness to be treated, but a 'voyage.' Socially, mad-

ness may be a form in which '. . . often through quite ordinary people, the light begins to break through the cracks in our all-too-closed minds.' (p. 90).

2. *Aetiology*

'We have all been processed on procrustean beds. At least some of us have managed to hate what they made of us.' (p. 47).

3. *Behaviour*

'The madness that we encounter in "patients" is a gross travesty, a mockery, a grotesque caricature of what that natural healing process of that estranged integration we call sanity might be.' (p. 101). It is distorted by our misguided attempts to 'treat' them. If we really understood our patients, we would see behaviour which was a reflection of the natural healing process, a desire to explore the inner world.

4. *Treatment*

Instead of the degradation ceremonial of psychiatric examination, diagnosis and prognostication, we need, for those who are ready for it, '. . . an initiation ceremonial, through which the person will be guided with full social encouragement and sanction into inner space and time, by people who have been there and back.' (p. 89).

5. *Prognosis*

(If a schizophrenic person were intelligently guided through his voyage into inner time and space, he would emerge a better person than he had been before; perhaps one might say that he would be 'enlightened.')

6. *Suicide*

(If a schizophrenic person commits suicide while being guided on a voyage, that is just one of the risks—voyages are dangerous. There are no guarantees.)

7. *Function of the hospital*

We need a place which has the right atmosphere for guided voyages into inner time and space. The schizophrenic person would leave this place when the voyage was over.

8. *Personnel*

The appropriate personnel for guiding these voyages are people who have been there and back, including ex-patients. 'Among physicians and priests, there should be some who are guides . . .' (p.97).

9. *Rights and duties of schizophrenic persons*

(The schizophrenic has the right to a well-guided voyage, in a setting that is conducive to inner exploration. He has the right to be spared psychiatric diagnosis and treatment which is designed to make him give up his own existential view. He has the duty to accept restraint if he is too much for the others.)

10. *Rights and duties of families*

(The family has the duty to let the schizophrenic person make his own choice about where and how to undergo an inner voyage. The family does not have the right to label a family member as 'schizophrenic' and then hospitalize him for 'treatment'.)

11. *Rights and duties of society*

(Society has no rights in relation to schizophrenic persons, certainly not the right to label people and then send them to 'hospitals'. Society has the duty to organize itself in such a way that alienation is not 'normal'. Society has the duty to allow more 'breakthrough'.)

12. *Goal of the model*

The goal of this model is to enable certain people, now called 'schizophrenic', to develop their potentialities for inner exploration. If such people can be allowed and encouraged to move in this direction, all of us will benefit.

B. *The model discussed*

We have called this model 'psychodelic', although Laing does not use the term in this book, because it is obvious that he thinks that schizophrenics may have, sometimes have, and ought to have the same kinds of experiences that normal individuals seek when they take mind-expanding drugs. From our point of view, Laing has failed to distinguish two very different kinds of experience, psychodelic and psychotic. We share his opinion that schizophrenics sometimes have psychodelic experiences, particularly at the beginning of their illnesses (Bowers and Freedman, 1966), and it is certainly true that some schizophrenics have been able to make creative use of their unusual experiences. It must be noted, however, that some creative individuals have always been able to make use of the experience of having a major illness to further their own self-development. During the era when well-to-do tubercular patients lived in 'magic mountains', some were able to use this experience, with its enforced leisure and unusual physical sensations, to arrive at a different view of themselves than they might have otherwise achieved. Simply staying in bed for a long period may be a great boon to a contemplative individual. Even terminal cancer has brought out the best in some people, and in some family relationships.[6] But it is heartless to suggest, without the most exact explanation and qualification, to those suffering from tuberculosis, cancer, or schizophrenia that they should look on this as a rare opportunity for self-understanding. For most people and their families, a major disease means the end of hopes and plans, however modest. It almost always means a severe financial drain on the family, and families are sometimes destroyed by the disruption which a disease brings in its wake.

There is one dimension of this model which deserves mention, that of 'personnel'. Laing has suggested ex-patients, some physicians, and some priests as guides for the voyages of inner exploration. It is clear why he thinks that ex-patients and priests might be suitable, but we are at a loss to understand why physicians are considered for this role. Medicine is a dirty, rough business. It favours the thick-skinned person over the sensitive one, the practical person over the imaginative. Men of unsuitable temperament who chose medicine by mistake are often weeded out during medical training. Doctors who like their work enjoy coping with emergencies; they are cut from the same cloth as sailors and farmers, masons and carpenters. They see machinery and the human body in much the same way, and they are respectful and knowledgeable about the workings of both. They are accustomed to being obeyed, not because of their individual personalities, but because they are doctors, and they believe that they have been commissioned to deal with urgent matters of life and death. Making gurus out of doctors seems hardly worth the trouble when there are so many

unemployed ex-patients about. Laing ought to make it clear what qualities of doctors he feels make them likely candidates for psychodelic guides.

Perhaps the most important point to be made about Laing's psychodelic model is its implication that schizophrenics will benefit from being seen as persons embarked on a voyage of self-discovery. It would be closer to the truth to see most of them as voyagers who have been shanghaied, for unknown reasons, on to a ship which never reaches port. Psychodelic voyages are usually voluntary, and the person usually knows what the agent of his changed perception is. Schizophrenia is involuntary, the person rarely knows the cause of his strange new perceptions, and he is unlikely to receive much helpful information about them. In a psychodelic experience, a 'bad trip' can usually be avoided by surrounding oneself with known and trusted people, by choosing a setting that is secure and aesthetically pleasing, and by showing prudence and caution. In a psychotic experience, on the other hand, good people can be perceived as bad, so that it may be even worse to have beloved people around than those who are indifferent, for nothing is worse than to hate those one normally loves. Another critical difference between the two experiences is the absolute length of time that elapses. A psychodelic experience is necessarily short; it is usually counted in hours, not years.[7] But a psychosis may last ten or twenty years. A 'bad trip' is an experience, whether drug-induced or naturally occurring, which is moving in the direction of being a psychosis but is still perceived as something that will end. Whether a 'bad trip' will end or will turn into a psychosis depends in part on the benevolence of the surroundings, but much more on the continued presence in the body of the chemical substance which initiated the experience. People who 'turn on' without drugs do not have 'bad trips'. They achieve altered states of consciousness with the aid of music, coloured lights, meditation, deep breathing, and so forth, but are at

[6]See, for example, John Gunther's *Death Be Not Proud* (1949) and Lael Tucker Wertenbaker's *Death of a Man* (1957).

[7]Those embarking on psychodelic voyages may make use of substances such as niacin to terminate the experience. They do not want interminable journeys.

liberty to interrupt or end the experience at any time, since the stimulus can be removed.

In addition to these differences in circumstances between the two states, there are many experiential differences. Some of these are listed below. We do not wish to imply by this that the two states are entirely comparable; even less, that they are at opposite ends of the same continuum. They can be seen as overlapping if one fails to take into account the length of time that the experience lasts and its place in the total life of the person involved. It is understandable that these states are often confused, since the 'bad trip' lies between the psychodelic and the psychotic experiences. Confusion between these states can lead to someone on a 'bad trip' being mistakenly hospitalized, when all that is required is the guidance of a psychodelic adept. More tragic, even, is the fate of the psychotic individual whose anomalous experiences are seen as temporary, and who therefore is not promptly treated. We feel it is important to emphasize the differences between these states, in whatever dimensions they are observable.

Perhaps the best analogy from everyday life for these experiential states is the difference between good dreams, bad dreams, and nightmares. Dreams, whether good or bad, have always been of great interest, and much has been written about their interpretation. Far less interest has been shown in the interpretation of nightmares. When a person relates a nightmare, it is usually immediately after he has had it, when he wishes to be reassured that the nightmare is not real. People learn from both good dreams and bad dreams, but they seldom learn from nightmares. A good dream is one in which the symbols clearly manifest some aspect of the person's life or inner potentialities. A good dream is like a 'good trip', a good psychodelic experience, or a naturally occurring experience of enlightenment. A bad dream is one which draws its symbols from the darker side of life; there may be feelings of sorrow, anger, fear or regret. But as with the good dream, the bad dream tells a meaningful story. It is like a chapter in a fairy story in which evil temporarily triumphs, but will eventually be overcome. A bad dream is like a 'bad trip'. Nightmares may or may not tell stories

but when they do the story only mounts in horror and never resolves itself. Most people have no desire to remember their nightmares, although they may wish to re-tell dreams years after they have had them. Nightmares are like psychotic states. People who have had psychotic illnesses do not usually want to talk about them or remember them; what they want most is just what the person wants who is coming out of a nightmare: to be told that the events in it did not really happen, that the 'real' world is still there, and that it is over.

Another way to emphasize the difference between the psychodelic world and the psychotic world is to look at the accomplishments of both. The psychodelic world has provided new music, new fashions in clothing and the decorative arts, new vocabulary, new life-styles, and a new intergenerational dialogue. But not a single new art form has come out of the mental hospital. While individual schizophrenic patients may return to a creative life which they had before they became ill, or may, if they are very lucky, take up a new creative life when they leave the hospital, groups of schizophrenics cannot create any new style together, even in the small private psychiatric hospitals which house some of our most privileged young people. Even Dr. Laing's patients are not known to us for their contributions to music, poetry, or mysticism; we only know of them because Laing writes about them.

DISCUSSION

It is not surprising that *The Politics of Experience* appeals to bright young schizophrenics. Most of the possible roles open to them are of lower status than that enjoyed by normal people, and some roles, like the sick role, are of special status. But Laing has made a very bold move: he has offered them a status above that of normal people. They can hardly be expected to ignore this fine offer, especially when their daily lives are so miserable. Furthermore, Laing has cast his offer in a style that is very much in tune with the times. He is genuinely sympathetic with today's young people. His psychodelic model of schizophrenia is a timely one, and timeliness is a potent asset in a model. That is why we believe that his point of view must be scrutinized, in spite of its flaws and omissions.

Young schizophrenics are serious about Laing, and so we must be serious in examining his ideas. But how serious is Laing himself? This is a question which must be raised because he is a physician who uses the authority which derives from medicine to advocate a non-medical model. We wonder if Laing appreciates how much more serious he would seem if he gave up his medical identity.

Surely the young people who turn to Laing for help deserve to know what hat he is wearing, what role he offers them, what model he uses, what authority he speaks from. In this book, he offers three models which can be disentangled only with the greatest difficulty. None of them is the medical model, from which we believe he derives his authority. If Laing wishes to be a guru or a philosopher, there is no doubt a place for him, but young people who are suffering from schizophrenia may prefer to entrust themselves to a doctor who will treat their illness as best he can.

Psychodelic experience

1. *Time dimension*
Liberation from time.
Expansion of time dimensions.
Internal or external time may speed up, increasing possibility of quick and decisive action.
Ability to modify past, present, future.
The future is the realm of ambition and motivation.

2. *Space dimension*
Expanded depth.
Enhanced distance.
Distance perception stable.
Distances so vast that one feels liberated.

3. *Affect*
Feeling that everything is meaningful and exhilarating.
Feelings of love, empathy, consideration, affection.
Euphoria.
Feeling of delight with oneself.

4. *Thought processes*
Thought changes are sought for, expected, valued.
See more possibilities that can be acted upon, which makes life exciting.
Seeing beyond the usual categories.

Seeing new connections which have always been possible.

Psychotic experience

Frozen in time: nothing will ever change.
Shrinkage and collapse of time dimensions.
Internal and external time may slow down, inhibiting action and creating despair.
Inability to influence any of the temporal categories.
The future is the realm of anxiety and danger.

Reduced depth.
Reduced distance.
Distance perception highly variable.
Distances so vast that one feels isolated and alienated.

Feeling that everything contains hidden, threatening meanings.
Feelings of isolation, fear, hatred, suspicion.

Depression.
Feeling of disgust with oneself.

Thought changes come unawares, are not welcome, are seen as accidental.
Seeing so many possibilities that action is impossible.
Seeing only fragments or parts of the usual categories.
Seeing connections which are not possible.

Ability to see things objectively.

Ability to see things subjectively.
Ability to explain thought changes.

No objectivity, inability to disengage from total involvement.
No subjectivity, estrangement from self.
Desperate attempts (delusions) to explain thought changes.

5. *Perceptions*
Clear and distinct vision.
Augmentation of perception.
Unusual perceptions seem to emanate from greater-than-human spirit or force.
Perceptual changes may be experienced as exhilarating, exciting, novel.

Blurred and distorted vision.
Diminution of perception.
Unusual perceptions seem to emanate from mechanical or sub-human forces.
Perceptual changes may be experienced as frightening, threatening, dangerous.

6. *Identity*
Feeling of unity with people and material objects.
Experience of the self.
Feeling of being at one with the world.

Feelings of humility and awe as one sees oneself as part of the universe.
Feelings of integrity and identity.
Pleasant, creative fantasies that one can control.
Feeling that one can join the company of other enlightened people.

Feeling of invasion by people and material objects.

Experience of the no-self, ego fragmentation.
Feeling of being opposed to and in conflict with oneself and the world.
Feelings of smallness and insignificance as one feels at the mercy of the universe.
Loss of integrity and identity.
Nightmarish fantasies that one cannot control.

Feeling that one is less and less human, more and more isolated.

● What we call "normal" is a product of repression, denial, splitting, projection, introjection and other forms of destructive action on experience. . . . It is radically estranged from the structure of being.   R. D. Laing, *The Politics of Experience*

●

● Jung suggested some years ago that it would be an interesting experiment to study whether the syndrome of psychiatry runs in families. A pathological process called "psychiatrosis" may well be found, by the same methods, to be a delineable entity, with somatic correlates and psychic mechanisms, with an inherited or at least constitutional basis, a natural history, and a doubtful prognosis.   R. D. Laing, *The Politics of Experience*

● Are you using the opportunities provided to respond to what you are reading by writing in your book? You could use the space below to react to R. D. Laings views. What do *you* think?

USEFUL RESOURCES

AGEL, J. (Producer) *Rough times*. New York: Ballantine Books, 1973.
"Therapy today has become a commodity, a means of social control . . . to be true instruments of change, therapy and therapists must be liberated from their own forms of oppression."

BERNE, E. *Games people play*. New York: Grove Press, 1964.
A "taxonomic" analysis of human relationships and what is really happening.

BOYERS, R., & ORRILL, R. *R. D. Laing and anti-psychiatry*. New York: Harper & Row, 1971.
A "must" for anyone who wishes to take Laing seriously; contains collected papers by critics as well as supporters of Laing.

BROWN, J. A. C. *Freud and the post-Freudians*. Penguin Books, 1961.
A concise review of Freudian theory followed by brief but informative surveys of Adler, Jung, and others.

EYSENCK, H., & ROCHMAN, S. *The causes and cures of neurosis*. London: Routledge and Kegan Paul, 1965.
Behavior therapy and its application to neuroses.

GREEN, H. *I never promised you a rose garden*. New York: Holt, Rinehart and Winston, 1964.
"The story of a sixteen year old girl who retreats from reality into the bondage of an imaginary kingdom . . . tells of her momentous struggle . . . to regain the real world."

HAWKINS, D., & PAULING, L. *Orthomolecular psychiatry*. San Francisco: W. H. Freeman, 1973.
A collection of papers that propose treatment based upon providing the "optimum molecular environment for the mind."

JACKSON, D. (Ed.) *The etiology of schizophrenia*. New York: Basic Books, 1960.
An older but still useful survey of multidisciplinary approaches to schizophrenia.

KAPLAN, D. *The inner world of mental illness*. New York: Harper & Row, 1964.
An excellent collection of autobiographical accounts.

LAING, R. D. *The divided self*. Penguin Books, 1965.
An "existential analysis of personal alienation."

LAING, R. D. *The politics of experience*. New York: Pantheon Books, 1967.
Who is mad and who is sane? A moving documentation of the ambiguities of existence.

MILLON, T. *Modern psychopathology*. Philadelphia: W. B. Saunders, 1969.
A book that is useful for both the undergraduate and the professional; a balanced attempt to integrate information from divergent views.

ROSENTHAL, D. *Genetics of psychopathology*. New York: McGraw-Hill, 1971.

RUSHING, W. A. *Deviant behavior and social process*. Chicago: Rand McNally, 1969.
Collected readings on juvenile delinquency, deviant sex roles, crime, suicide, mental illness, alcoholism, drug addiction, and prison subcultures.

SALTER, A. *The case against psychoanalysis*. New York: Harper & Row, 1972.
An unmitigated attack on Freudian theory by the "father" of behavior therapy.

SARASON, I. G. *Psychoanalysis and the study of behavior*. Princeton: Van Nostrand, 1965.
"Thirteen articles comment on some of the major issues, controversies, and implications surrounding the theory of psychoanalysis and its ramifications within various areas of scientific inquiry."

SZASZ, T. S. *Ideology and insanity*. New York: Doubleday, 1970.
"If we persist in defining the vicissitudes of life as mental illnesses, and psychiatric interventions as medical treatments, we court the hazards of political tyranny disguised as psychiatric therapy."

TORREY, E. F. *The mind game: Witchdoctors and psychiatrists*. New York: Emerson Hall Publishers, 1972.

CHAPTER 8
THE SEARCH FOR ALTERNATIVE LIFE STYLES

PROVOCATIONS

The only alternative is to create one's own alternatives.

Doris Leland

*Every revolution is in
part a revival.*

Philip Slater

[Some striking similarities between early Christians in Rome and contemporary hippies]: (both were communal, utopian, mystical, dropouts, unwashed; both were viewed as dangerous, masochistic, ostentatious, the cause of their own troubles; both existed in societies in which the exclusive pursuit of material advantages had reached some kind of dead end.) . . .

Philip Slater

Consider the lilies of the field, how they grow; they toil not, neither do they spin: and yet I say unto you, that even Solomon in all his glory was not arrayed like one of these.

Matthew 6:28–29

It would be a mistake to characterize the commune movement as a collection of dropouts who are content to exist like lilies in the field. A considerable number of successful people from all walks of life are now involved; they have merely shifted their sphere of interest and the nature of their creative contribution. We are dealing with a massive awakening of the awareness that life holds multiple options other than going from school to job to retirement. The commune movement has opened a new and wide range of alternative life-styles and offers another frontier to those who have the courage for adventure.

Herbert A. Otto

''Communes don't work, 'cause people don't work. There's too many people with a lot of high-minded ideas about utopia. But there ain't no utopia. Just some cats alooking to ball a lot of chicks and people looking for someone to take care of them.''

*Ulysses S. Grant
(New Mexico Communard)*

WHAT DO YOU THINK?

42 THE SEARCH FOR ALTERNATIVE LIFE STYLES

JAMES A. DYAL

THE CONSUMER CULTURE AND THE COUNTERCULTURE
Suburbia and the Consumer Culture: Affluence versus Relatedness

"Rus mihi dulce sub urbe est." The song of the Roman epigrammatist Martial in the first century B.C. ("To me, the country on the outskirts of the city is sweet") tells us that man has long dreamed of moving to the suburbs. Rome, the most magnificent of the ancient cities, was apparently a human cesspool, liberally spiced with decaying bodies (human as well as animal) and human refuse.[1] The industrial revolution multiplied the aversive qualities of cities a thousandfold, and thus Shelley was able to say "Hell is a city very much like London, a populous and smoky city." Early in the twentieth century middle-class suburbia was already a reality in England. As documented by a social historian around 1909, each little red house "boasts its pleasant drawing room, its bow-windows, its little front garden. The women . . . find time hangs rather heavy on their hands. But there are excursions to shopping centers in the West End and pious sociabilities, occasional theater visits and the interests of home."[2]

Yet "suburbia" did not emerge as a major socio-psychological phenomenon until after World War II. The people of the Western world were emerging from almost two decades of deprivation, fear, and trauma. Mankind hoped that the deprivations of the Great Depression would be filled by an economy of abundance and that the scars of war would be healed by the growth of a new life. The people deserved a new way of life and they sat about creating it.

For millions the dream meant getting back lost contact with nature—grass, trees, birds, and flowers on their own bit of land in the suburbs. With the help of government loans and through the economies of mass production, it seemed that each man could create a better life for himself and his children away from the turmoil, noise, and stress of the inner city. Thus the dynamic perimeter of North American cities expanded with suburban houses, ranging from "ticky-tacky" to the luxurious opulence of the *nouveau riche*. Bulldozers flattened hills, uprooted trees and filled valleys in the name of efficient progress toward a mass-produced liberation. Superhighways streamed to supermarkets for superachieving suburbanites. This ambitious "back-to-work" generation (your parents' generation) sought a place to put down new roots and grow, to establish themselves.

COMMENT: SCARCITY/SURVIVAL— ABUNDANCE/ACTUALIZATION

The post war *credo* of suburban America had its roots in a Darwinian view of the world as a dangerous, competitive place where the stronger survived while the weaker perished. The drive to suburbia was a drive to a private cave; a fort, surrounded by cyclone fences and hedges and split-level walls which held back competitors and change.

The children of this generation seem to regard the building of such defenses to be a waste of physical and emotional energies. "Survival" has been replaced by "Psychological Fulfillment" as the root of a newer consciousness which grows from cooperation, mutual trust and a greater openness to change.

ROBERT L. MARRONE

---

[1]Theodore Crane, The squalor that was Rome. *Natural History*, 1973, **82**, 44–47.
[2]Quoted in Americana: The roots of home, *Time*, June 20, 1966.

It is not surprising that past deprivations combined with a work ethic and a booming economy to produce and exaggerate a materialistic value system in which the focus was on acquiring and consuming "things." Indeed, it seems almost inevitable that Western man in the mid-twentieth century should be strongly committed to the values of achievement, acquisition, and consumption. Paradoxically, the consumption ethic was also combined with a desire to delay immediate gratification for themselves—to work, build, and sacrifice "for the children." Their children would not have to suffer the way they had. They would have the best for their children; they would provide them with a base of affluence from which even greater progress and happiness would be produced.

They sought stability, security, and success while at the same time they yearned for community and relatedness. The hucksters of suburbia (real estate agents) were quick to capitalize on these motivations. Here are two examples of advertising material used by promoters of a real estate development in Park Forest, Illinois:[3]

You belong
in Park Forest
The moment you come to our town you know:
You're welcome
You're part of a big group
You can live in a friendly small town
instead of a lonely big city
You can have friends who want you —
and you can enjoy being with them.
Come out. Find out about the spirit of Park Forest.

A cup of coffee—symbol of
PARK FOREST!
Coffeepots bubble all day long
in Park Forest. This sign
of friendliness tells you how much
neighbors enjoy each other's company—
feel glad that they can share their daily
joys—yes, and troubles, too.
Come out to Park Forest where small-
town friendships grow—and you still live
so close to a big city.

[3]Quoted in W. H. Whyte, *The organization man*. New York: Simon and Schuster, 1956.

COMMENT: SUBURBIA—THE SYMBOLIC CENTERPIECE OF THE AMERICAN DREAM

So strongly influenced by the Depression and the war which followed, (they) were concerned to an extraordinary extent with success and security. Probably more energetically than any previous generation, they pursued the goal of a worldly paradise based on material consumption. This version of the American Dream is embodied in the characteristic social setting of the postwar generation: suburbia. Although it was no new phenomenon, it was in the years immediately after the war that the massive migration to suburbia began. It is now both the characteristic way of life for most middle-class Americans and the best reflection of the values and aspirations of the adult generation. It is the symbolic centerpiece in the display of America's material rewards. And I think it is also the best place to look in order to understand why so many young people are trying to find new life styles.

KEITH MELVILLE

Unfortunately, there are stresses and conflicts built into the social dynamics of suburbia which tend to frustrate the search for security, community, and relatedness. The most important of these stresses stems from the fact that the successful "pace-setters" in suburbia are highly competitive, achievement-oriented people. The interpersonal competitiveness which may work well in the business or profession tends to be carried over into family and neighborhood relationships. Indeed, success in interpersonal competitions is often so highly regarded in suburbia that it serves as a basis for the selection of friends. To be among the "winners" as opposed to the "losers" is strongly reinforced. The wife of an upper-middle-class executive reflected the exaltation of competitive success when she commented, "Competition is good—why that's what it's all about isn't it?" One of the all too apparent consequences of this orientation is that children tend to become valued by their parents on the basis of how successful they are in competition with their peers in school and neighborhood settings. Within the family, love and concern may become commodities for exchange and bargaining. Between families the competition may take the form of the escalation of the consumption ethic—the "keeping up with the Joneses" syndrome. Such interpersonal competitiveness produces a climate which fosters superficial social acceptance and "acquaintanceship" at the expense of deep feelings of caring and community.

Perhaps the failure to achieve real feelings of community in the neighborhood contributes to the exaggerated involvement in "community affairs" which traps many suburban housewives. Furthermore, the "community affairs service-club syndrome" is only one manifestation of a more general stress in suburbia; namely, the compulsive activity and scheduledness. The family often takes on the automated hum of the production line in which the production manager (mother) orchestrates and directs the flow of traffic. In one of the best studies of upper-middle-class suburbia the use of time is recognized as an important and revealing characteristic.[4]

> In Crestwood Heights time seems almost the paramount dimension of existence . . . (the typical) wife has her own activities outside the home which are carefully scheduled. . . . The children have their school—which demands punctuality—and scheduled appointments with dentists and dancing teachers, and numerous social activities. Home life is indeed often hectic—schedules are so demanding that the parents feel themselves constantly impelled to inculcate the virtues of punctuality and regulating themselves and the child, at meal hour, departure for picnics, and such occasions. . . . The phenomenon which the Crestwooder calls "pressure" is caused by this concentration of demands into limited units of time.[5]

[4]Quoted in Keith Melville, *Communes in the counter culture*, New York: William Morrow, 1972, p. 95.

[5]It is important to recognize that the "pathologies of suburbia" which are described here are primarily representative of the middle and upper-middle class rather than lower-middle or working-class suburbia. A meaningful perspective on the latter groups can be obtained from Herbert Gans "The Levittowners," New York: Pantheon Books, 1967.

The competitive climate is both reflected in the frantic slavery to the clock and in the continual battle to achieve, to acquire, to consume. One of the most frequent casualties is the love and concern of the husband and wife for each other. The consequences of the value conflict between achievement/success and interpersonal love and concern are well analyzed in the following comment:

COMMENT: VALUE CONFLICT AND THE SUBURBAN FAMILY

Man's capacity for consistent and responsible action depends on his being able to orient himself and to act on the basis of commitment of values; thus a certain level of value consistency is important. But a prominent feature of American society today is a pervasive value conflict. The family depends upon and symbolizes "inefficient values" of being, knowing, caring, loving, unconditionally committing oneself. These values are incompatible with the urban industrial values of production, achievement, exchange, quantification, efficiency, success. Simultaneous unlimited commitment to people—in love and concern—and to achievement, success, prosperity, is impossible. The resultant tension in a society which pays uncritical lip-service to both sets of values is disruptive and potentially incapacitating. It tends toward resolution in favor of the "inhuman" urban values. Fromm has noted that as a society we tend to love things, and use people, rather than the reverse. And Whyte has remarked that the "organization men" he interviewed seemed to prefer to sacrifice success in marriage to career success, if forced to choose between them.

This value confusion is, of course, a source of instability within the American family. A family presumes unlimited commitment between family members: "till death do you part" between husband and wife, "all we can do for the kids" on the part of parents toward children. But the priority of these love and concern values is directly challenged by success and achievement values which may imply that the status symbols are more important than babies; that what a child achieves is more important than what he is; that what we own is more important than what we are. Thus the stage is set for conflict between a success oriented husband and a child-people welfare oriented wife, or for a rather inhuman family which values things over people, and which may raise children who have difficulty living down this experience of worthlessness.

CHARLES W. HOBART

Most of you who are reading this book were raised in the suburbs, and your personalities have been formed by the stresses and conflicts of the suburban life style. It is also true that as a result of both personal preference and economic necessity most of you will return to suburbia to establish your home, raise your family, and make your place in society. Despite its stresses suburban living *can* provide a style of living which can be fulfilling and meaningful for many people. On the other hand, it should be no surprise to the older generation that many of you are seeking to create alternative values and life styles.

COMMENT: THE MIDDLE CLASS REVOLT— OLD AND NEW

Is it really unusual that so many young people in this generation should be leaving suburbia, defecting from their parents' life style, and seeking out the alternatives? One of the most extraordinary things about the parents' generation was that so many of them were willing to shed their pasts and move to suburbia. This is one of the reasons why there is so much self-consciousness about the suburban style: For many of the participants, it is a new life style. Suburbia represented a solution for so many people in the postwar period because it responded to several important needs. Many people wanted to leave the complexity and diversity of the teeming cities and to find a place where the family could be more effectively insulated against the outside world. The parents' generation had peculiarly exaggerated needs for material success; suburbia provided a much better setting for the

display of affluence than did urban neighbourhoods. Finally, the parents' generation was preoccupied to an extraordinary extent with the kids, with having children and planning a whole life style around their needs.

But the younger generation faces different problems and has different needs. They insist on living in the present, not in the future. They are much less concerned with material success and security, and the raising of children is not so important as it was for their parents. Given these needs, suburbia doesn't make any sense, and it is necessary to find alternative life styles. Perhaps it is no longer possible to expect that one generation can provide meaningful work and a way of life which most of the next generation would want to follow. But what Thoreau said, that "one generation abandons the enterprises of another like stranded vessels," is particularly true of this generation. Like the newest cars rolling off the assembly lines in Detroit, there is a kind of built-in obsolescence about suburbia. In the same way that the parents left their pasts a generation or two ago and fled to suburbia, their children are leaving and searching for an alternative.

KEITH MELVILLE

The Counterculture: The Search for an Empowering Myth

Although there have always been dissenters from the values and life style of the dominant culture it seems unlikely that the opposition has ever before been as widespread as in the last decade. The roots of the present counterculture can be traced to the civil rights movements of the 1960s. Thousands of whites of social conscience joined with blacks in sit-ins, freedom marches, and other forms of peaceful protest against the oppression of minority groups. As college students returned from the "crusades," they came to be conscious of the significant parallels which existed between the oppression of the blacks and their own "student nigger" role. The Free-Speech Movement at Berkeley and the establishment of SDS signified a new militancy and a disinclination to tolerate social injustice on or off campus. By the middle sixties it was becoming clear to many people that the world could never be quite the same again. "The times they are a changing"—"get out of the way if you can't lend a hand"—"if you are not part of the solution you are part of the problem." A cultural revolution was being made. As the Vietnam war was escalated and as the crisis of the abused minorities deepened, the radical revolutionary rhetoric became more strident and the activists more violent in their confrontations with the "Establishment."

At the same time there was a parallel nonviolent response to the materialistic life style of the middle class and the insanities of war, racism, and violent confrontation. While tactics of the political activists emphasized anger, fear, and direct assault, the passive wing of the countermovement exalted love, acceptance, and disengagement from involvement in society. It embraced the "turn on, tune in, and drop out" solution advocated by Timothy Leary. The conflict in ideology between the "activist" and the "hippy" approaches to cultural revolution continues to split the counterculture even though the activists have, at least temporarily, foresworn the confrontation tactics of the late sixties. The activists argue that in order to achieve the better society "the system" must be destroyed; the hippy solution, on the other hand, emphasizes a personal and interpersonal salvation. John Lennon defends the hippy view in the lyrics of the Beatles' song "Revolution."

> Well, you know
> We all want to change the world
> But when you talk about destruction,
> Don't you know you can count me out.
>
> You say you'll change a constitution
> Well, you know
> We all want to change your head
> You tell me it's the institution
> well, you know
> You better free your mind instead.

The next generation—your generation—will work out the ways in which the activist and passivist perspectives are reconcilable and clarify those aspects which are basically incompatible. At this writing the dominant form of the counterculture is that of a naturalistically oriented communalism which, in contrast to the more intellectual, future orientation of the old culture, tends to emphasize immediate experience. The emphasis on the "now" is manifested in the encounter group phenomenon, by the sexual revolution, by the extensive use of psychedelic drugs for the sensual experiences, and by the expressive politics. But as was noted by Slater, every cultural movement has within it its own special conflicts.[6] The dilemma of the new culture is that it pursues a "freedom" which often seems to preclude long-term commitments. But, as noted by Henry Miller in Selection 43, "the need for commitment seems to be a prerequisite of humanity." He proposes that the youth generation must learn the great lesson of mankind: "Involvement brings liberation, commitment *is* freedom." The meanings and implications of the naturalistic mythology of the counterculture are well capsulized by Daniel Yankelovich in the following comment:

COMMENT: THE NEW NATURALISM

But what is truly natural and what is opposed to nature? The answer is by no means self-evident. We have identified almost twenty meanings of the concept "natural" as the student movement defines it. Some meanings are obvious, others are subtle. Some are superficial expressions of lifestyles that students experiment with and then abandon like so many one-night stands; other meanings are fundamental to man's existence. To be natural, in the student lexicon, means:

To push the Darwinian version of nature as "survival of the fittest" into the background, and to emphasize instead the interdependence of all things and species in nature.

To place sensory experience ahead of conceptual knowledge.

To live physically close to nature, in the open, off the land.

[6]Phillip E. Slater, *The pursuit of loneliness: American culture at the breaking point*. Boston: Beacon Press, 1970.

To live in groups (tribes, communes) rather than in such "artificial" social units as the nuclear family.

To reject hypocrisy, "white lies," and other social artifices.

To de-emphasize aspects of nature illuminated by science; instead, to celebrate all the unknown, the mystical, and the mysterious elements of nature.

To stress cooperation rather than competition.

To embrace the existentialist emphasis on *being* rather than doing or planning.

To devalue detachment, objectivity, and noninvolvement as methods for finding truth; to arrive at truth, instead, by direct experience, participation, and involvement.

To look and feel natural, hence rejecting makeup, bras, suits, ties, artificially groomed hairstyles.

To express oneself nonverbally; to avoid literary and stylized forms of expression as artificial and unnatural; to rely on exclamations as well as silences, vibrations, and other nonverbal modes of communication.

To reject "official" and hence artificial forms of authority; authority is to be won, it is not a matter of automatic entitlement by virtue of position or official standing.

To reject mastery over nature.

To dispense with organization, rationalization, and cost-effectiveness.

To embrace self-knowledge, introspection, discovery of one's natural self.

To emphasize the community rather than the individual.

To reject mores and rules that interfere with natural expression and function (e.g., conventional sexual morality).

To preserve the environment at the expense of economic growth and technology.

The counterculture is well named. As Kenneth Kenniston noted, it defines itself, at least in part, in terms of what it opposes. And what it opposes constitutes a huge part of our culture. Yet, as the

varied definitions of nature and the natural suggest, the positive side of the counterculture is the more significant one.

DANIEL YANKELOVICH

• Each one of these statements represents an assertion about the counterculture. Now that you have read through them go back and think about each one.

There are several aspects of each assertion that you might want to raise questions about. For example, does your experience with the counterculture confirm that the stated value is in fact held by the counterculture? If not, how do you account for the discrepancy between your experience and Yankelovich's views? If you agree that the counterculture does indeed hold the value, what are some reasons why it regards the value positively? If all our society held the value, what would be some of the consequences? How would it change our culture?

Each one of these assertions could be used by you as the basis of a class paper. For example, you could do a psychological analysis of cooperation versus competition as ways of relating.

Views of the counterculture are communicated in a more personal, experienced way in Selection 44. Written by David Bailey, one of the participants in the new consciousness, this article should be on your "must read" list. The emphasis on communal living as an alternative life style is described in Selection 44, by Otto. Whatever forms the future will bring, it is our view that the counterculture is sufficiently broad-based that it will persevere and provide alternative life styles and values to those of the old culture.

• Time for a break? We are starting a new theme in the next section. Why don't you review the major points of the two previous sections before you take a break? Then come back for some encounter and a sexual revolution.

The Encounter Culture: The Search for Relatedness

Roughly paralleling the growth of the "psychology of suburbia," psychologists in clinics and laboratories were beginning to experiment with new techniques designed to facilitate interpersonal communication and understanding. Many of the principles of open communication and empathic understanding which were discovered in research on nondirective therapy (see your text for a discussion of this topic) proved to be quite relevant and generalizable to small group interactions. The truly phenomenal aspect of the group movement is the degree to which it has taken root and rapidly spread throughout the culture. Various forms of encounter and sensitivity training experiences are now available in most of the major societal institutions, such as universities, churches, and businesses.

How can we account for this overwhelming growth of encounter groups? Certainly one important factor is the background of impersonality which permeates much of our experience on our jobs and in our homes and neighborhoods. Superficiality of relationships—a lack of genuine contact—all too often characterizes our friendships and even our family relations. The encounter experience offers a way to fill the void created by lack of intimate contact with one's fellows. It promises an atmosphere in which each person can reveal himself to others and to himself in a more honest fashion. It offers an oasis of noncompetitive concern and in-depth experiencing in an interpersonal desert of competitive striving and shifting superficialities. Confronted with an overwhelming need for greater interpersonal intimacy, it is not only understandable that encounter groups have become the social innovation of our generation, but there is a sense of inevitability to their emergence and rapid growth. Perhaps it is true, as

Carl Rogers contends, that the group movement *is* the most important and most rapidly spreading social invention of the twentieth century.

COMMENT: FREEDOM FROM ISOLATION

In my estimation, one of the most rapidly growing social phenomena in the United States is the spread of the intensive group experience —senitivity training, personal-encounter groups, "T" groups (the labels are unimportant). The growth of this phenomenon is more striking when one realizes that it is a "grass roots" movement. There is not a university, nor a foundation, nor a government agency that has given it any significant approval or support until the last five or six years. Yet it has permeated industry; it is becoming significant in education; it is reaching families, professionals, and many other individuals. Why? I believe it is because people—ordinary people —have discovered that it alleviates their aloneness and permits them to grow, to risk, to change. It brings people into real relationships with others.

In our affluent society the individual is, for the first time, freed to become aware of his isolation, aware of his alienation, aware of the fact that he is, during most of his life, a role interacting with other roles, a mask meeting other masks. And for the first time he is aware that this is not a necessary fact of life, that he does not have to live out his days in this fashion. So he is seeking, with great determination and inventiveness, ways of modifying this existential loneliness. The intensive group experience, perhaps the most significant social invention of this century, is an important way.

CARL ROGERS

In his book on encounter groups Rogers points out that although there are many diverse forms of small group experiences, there are several practical hypotheses which tend to be held in common by all of the groups.[7] He formulated seven of these hypotheses as follows:

[7]Carl R. Rogers, *Carl Rogers on encounter groups*, New York: Harper and Row, 1970.

A facilitator can develop, in a group which meets intensively, a psychological climate of safety in which freedom of expression and reduction of defensiveness gradually occur.

In such a psychological climate many of the immediate feeling reactions of each member toward others, and of each member toward himself, tend to be expressed.

A climate of mutual trust develops out of this mutual freedom to express real feelings, positive and negative. Each member moves toward greater acceptance of his total being —emotional, intellectual, and physical—as it is, including its potential. With individuals less inhibited by defensive rigidity, the possibility of change in personal attitudes and behavior, in professional methods, in administrative procedures and relationships, becomes less threatening.

With the reduction of defensive rigidity, individuals can hear each other, can learn from each other, to a greater extent.

There is a development of feedback from one person to another, such that each individual learns how he appears to others and what impact he has in interpersonal relationships.

With this greater freedom and improved communication, new ideas, new concepts, new directions emerge. Innovation can become a desirable rather than a threatening possibility.

These learnings in the group experience tend to carry over, temporarily or more permanently, into the relationships with spouse, children, students, subordinates, peers, and even superiors following the group experience.

The encounter group movement achieved its initial impetus and its primary growth outside of traditional academic institutions. In some instances there have been relatively few constraints imposed on the qualifications of group leaders (facilitators). Most of the training of the group leaders is accomplished through para-educational organizations created for this specific purpose. The training centers tend to be quite egalitarian in their selection of trainees. More emphasis is placed on "ability to relate" than upon academic credentials. As a consequence many trainers and training programs have lacked the kind of professional orientation and understanding which would have been required had the programs been centered in a more traditional academic institution. Thus it is often difficult for the buyer of an encounter group experience to adequately evaluate the credentials of the encounter group leader — (it is sometimes difficult to distinguish the "pro" from the "con"). However, it must be admitted that in the "normal" course of events the level of professional training of group leaders may be of little consequence. An analogy with the technology of the birth process seems apt. I have an obstetrician friend who assures me that *if everything is normal* then "catching a baby" is a simple, uncomplicated process which little requires the expertise of a physician or the facilities of a hospital. (When you stop to think about it, if such training and facilities were *required* we would not now be so worried about the population bomb.) *But* (and this could be an important "but") when something goes wrong with the process, then the expert's knowledge may make the difference between life and death. The analogy to encounter group process is both apparent and real. Even a person who is relatively naïve about personality dynamics, group dynamics, and interpersonal processes may be more than adequate as a group leader if all is "normal" in the group. The danger is that the intense group experience may precipitate emotional crises for some of the participants. It is *then* that an expert is needed. A number of such "bad trips" leading to suicide attempts, or similar major emotional traumas have been documented.[8] The American Psychiatric Association was concerned about such matters and

[8]See for example Bruce L. Maliver, Encounter groupers up against the wall. *New York Times Magazine.* January 31, 1971; and Steven L. Jaffe and Donald J. Scherl, Acute psychosis precipitated by T-group experiences. *Archives of General Psychiatry,* October, 1969; and Irwin D. Yalom and Morton A. Lieberman, A study of encounter group casualties. *Archives of General Psychiatry,* 1971, **25,** 16–30.

appointed a special task force in 1969 to evaluate the current state of knowledge. The task force report concluded that there was "distressingly little data" and that what was available was quite inadequate, consisting of anecdotal reports or poorly designed research studies without adequate post-treatment follow up.[9]

However, more recently an extensive and well-controlled study of encounter group casualties has been published by Yalom and Lieberman. In this research 170 university students who were participants in eighteen encounter groups were evaluated by a large battery of tests and interviews both before and after the encounter group experiences. There were several important findings: (1) almost 10 percent of the participants suffered "considerable and persistent psychological distress" as a consequence of the encounter group experience; (2) the number and intensity of the casualties was highly dependent upon the style of the encounter group leaders; (3) a particularly high risk leadership style was characterized by "intrusive, aggressive stimulation, by high charisma, by high challenging and confrontation of each of the members and by authoritarian control . . . (they) . . . were forceful and impatient. . . ."[10]

In sum, it would seem that encounter groups provide an opportunity for some people to experience an emotional intensity and excitement which they find unavailable to them in their normal relationships. This "turn on" seems to be a desirable and valued experience in and of itself.[11] There is, however, little evidence that the encounter group effects carry very far beyond the experience itself either in terms of time or amount of positive personality change. In our judgment a 10 percent casualty rate is all too high when you balance off the positive gain against the negative trauma. It is,

for example, substantially higher than the "casualty rate" for the other most popular source of "turn on," namely marijuana. On the other hand, it may well be that this casualty rate is acceptable in the early stages of the development of a major cultural social invention. Continued research such as that reported by Yalom and Lieberman will inform the professionals regarding the actual characteristics of leaders and participants which make for positive and negative outcomes. It is clearly necessary to exercise greater control over the procedures used for training and selection of group leaders and to better inform the public concerning the perils as well as the promises of encounter grouping. In addition to criticism based on the questionable positive effectiveness and high casualty rates, some intellectuals (see Koch's comment) charge that the conception of man which is implied by encounter group theory serves only to prostitute and vulgarize man's more noble strivings.

COMMENT: THE IMAGE OF MAN IMPLICIT IN ENCOUNTER GROUP THEORY

At the risk of displeasing many of you, I will give my assessment right off by saying that the group movement is the most extreme excursion thus far of man's talent for reducing, distorting, evading, and vulgarizing his own reality. It is also the most poignant exercise of that talent, for it seeks and promises to do the very reverse. It is adept at the image-making manoeuvre of evading human reality in the very process of seeking to discover and enhance it. It seeks to court spontaneity and authenticity by artifice; to combat instrumentalism instrumentally; to provide access to experience by reducing it to a packaged commodity; to engineer autonomy by group pressure; to liberate individuality by group shaping. Within the lexicon of its concepts and method, openness becomes transparency; love, caring, and sharing become a barter of "reinforcements" or perhaps mutual ego-titillation; aesthetic receptivity or immediacy becomes "sensory awareness." It can provide only a grotesque simulacrum of every noble quality it courts. It provides, in effect, a convenient psychic whorehouse for the purchase of

[9]*Encounter groups and psychiatry*, Task Force Report #1. Washington, D.C., American Psychiatric Association, April 1970.
[10]Irwin D. Yalom and Morton A. Lieberman, A study of encounter group casualties. *Archives of General Psychiatry*, 1971, **25**, 16–30.
[11]The positive consequences are more extensively reported in M. Lieberman, I. Yalom, and M. Miles, The impact of encounter groups on participants. *Journal of Applied Behavioral Science*. In press.

a gamut of well-advertised existential "goodies": authenticity, freedom, wholeness, flexibility, community, love, joy. One enters for such liberating consummations but inevitably settles for psychic strip-tease. . . . The low-level, mechanical way in which the groupers use glitter-concepts like authenticity, love, autonomy, and the rest in the inflated rhetoric that passes for their theory, but which nevertheless controls the selection of their methods and practice, at once reveals and promotes a serious impoverishment of sensibility. . . . This "most important social invention of the century" that we have been considering carries every earmark of a shallow fad. Yet the impetus behind it is poignant and powerful, and permanently embedded in man's condition. Man's search for egress from the cave, platonic or other, is rendered especially frantic in such times as ours. However compelling its impetus, this fad will soon—as historic time is measured—fizzle out. But its effects need not.

When value-charged discimination drop out of man's ken, there is no certainty that they will be rediscovered. We transmit to the future what we are. We may be what we eat, but we are also what we image. If what we are has been reduced by shallow or demeaning images, that impoverishment will persist in the world long after the images that conveyed it have gone their way.

SIGMUND KOCH

- This comment is filled with so many "scholarly" words for which you may not have very clear meanings that it may have turned many of you off. As a consequence you may have refused to persist in trying to understand it. Even though you may need a dictionary, can you translate Koch's basic message into more simple language? Try it; it might be worth the effort.

Another reason why you may have stopped reading (and thinking) is that you *did* understand what Koch was saying but strongly disagreed. Do you often "tune out" messages you do not agree with? What are the consequences of this behavior?

If you would like to read a rebuttal to Koch's views you should read the articles by Haigh and by Arbuckle.[12]

The Sexual Revolution: The Search for Intimacy

If the popularity of the encounter group movement derives from a prevailing need for relatedness and contact with one's fellows, another manifestation of this need may be seen in the search for intimacy which is implied by the phrase "sexual revolution." What are the facts? Are we really in the midst of a change in sexual attitudes and behavior which is sufficiently dramatic to be called a revolution? Or is the change a more gradual "evolutionary" one? Certainly the overall trend during the twentieth century has been a gradual liberalization of sexual mores which may be regarded as a part of more general liberal social evolution. New models of man developed by behavioral science, psychoanalysis, and existential philosophy have emphasized issues of freedom and responsible choice. Furthermore, in the area of sexual behavior "liberated" ideas were supported by an increased opportunity and anonymity provided by a technology of the automobile and contraception. Thus, by the "roaring twenties" the proportion of college females who had engaged in premarital sexual intercourse had risen to around one in four or one in five. Various surveys indicate that this figure tended to remain rather stable throughout the decades of the 1930s and 1940s. Then during the fifties there appeared a spate of popular press articles heralding a new "sexual revolution" on the campus. It turned out that the data did not support the contention. There was only a slight increase in premarital coital rates (frequency of sexual intercourse) during the period of 1950–1965. But there *was* a change during this period—the change was in *attitude* toward premar-

[12]Gerald V. Haigh, Response to Koch's assumptions about group process. *Journal of Humanistic Psychology,* Fall, 1971; Dugald Arbuckle, Koch's distortions of encounter group theory. *Journal of Humanistic Psychology,* Winter, 1973.

● We may not conclude from these data that attendance at university results in "weakening of moral principles." Why not?

---

ital sexual relations. There was a significant increase in the social acceptance of premarital sexual intercourse and a consequent reduction in guilt, fear, and anxiety about peer rejection by those who were sexually active. The changed attitude was not as yet reflected in an increased amount of sexual activity. Coeds were talking about sex more freely, but not yet having more fun!

It is a widely accepted view in psychology that people generally try to resolve the discrepancies between their attitudes and their behavior. If attitudes were becoming more liberal, then it was likely that behavior would begin changing, and indeed this is what has happened.

● You can come to understand more about this psychological principle by reading the discussion of "cognitive dissonance" in your text.

A review of the more recent studies of sexual behavior of coeds yields the conclusion that "there is not a single major study that has been made in

the late sixties that has found premarital coital rates that were at the level of those obtained in the late 1950's and 1940's."[13] The proportion of United States college coeds who report premarital coital experience is now somewhere between one-third and one-half. Kaats and Davis have reported two studies conducted in 1967 at the University of Colorado which show the premarital coital rate to be 40–45 percent among sophomores and juniors and, in a sample which included both undergraduates and graduates, the nonvirgin rate was 56 percent compared with a rate of 12 percent when they entered college.[14] Similar premarital coital rates have been reported at two Canadian universities (University of Waterloo and University of Alberta) by Hobart.[15]

[13]Kenneth L. Cannon and Richard Long, Premarital sexual behavior in the sixties. *Journal of Marriage and the Family,* 1971, **33,** 36–49.
[14]Gilbert R. Kaats and Keith E. Davis, The dynamics of sexual behavior of college students. *Journal of Marriage and the Family,* 1970, **32,** 390–399.
[15]Charles W. Hobart, Sexual permissiveness in young English and French Canadians. *Journal of Marriage and the Family,* 1972, **34,** 292–303.

TABLE 1 PERCENTAGES EXPRESSING APPROVAL OF PREMARITAL COITUS AND PERCENTAGES WITH PREMARITAL COITAL EXPERIENCE*

	Intermountain		Midwestern		Danish	
	Males	Females	Males	Females	Males	Females
Approval of pre-marital coitus:						
1968	38.4	23.5	55.4	37.7	100.0	100.0
1958	23.3	2.9	46.7	17.4	94.0	80.7
Have premarital coital experience						
1968	36.5	32.4	50.2	34.3	94.7	96.6
1958	39.4	9.5	50.7	20.7	63.7	59.8

*Reprinted from Cannon, K. L., and Long, R. *Journal of Marriage and the Family,* 1971, 36–49. Based on Christiansen, H. T., and Gregg, C. F. *Journal of Marriage and the Family,* 1970, **32,** 616–627.

The trend from 1958–1968 is well represented in the data in Table 1 based on comparable samples at the same universities using the same questionnaire.

The samples were selected so as to reflect a substantial range of the restrictive/permissive dimension. The intermountain sample represented a restrictive Mormon culture. The Midwest is moderately restrictive, while Denmark has a highly permissive culture. Several points are apparent from these data: (1) the females in all these samples show a significant liberalization of attitude and a dramatic increase in premarital intercourse; (2) the males changed less than the females in behavior and attitude but continue to exceed the females in sexual activity; (3) there are substantial regional and national differences in sexual behavior and attitude.

Our conclusion is that the dramatic change which has occurred in the behavior of college-age females in the past decade seems to justify the use of the label "sexual revolution."

Although the sexual revolution is primarily a change in the behavior of the female, neither the attitudes or behavior of the females has yet reached the level of liberality of the male in the United States samples. However, in the Danish sample it is apparent that within the past 10 years almost all Danish males and females have come to approve of and engage in premarital intercourse.

It is frequently asserted that the sexual revolution has carried with it the demise of the double standard and that may very well be true in such sexually permissive cultures as Denmark and Sweden. However, in the United States and Canada the double standard may be declining a bit but it certainly has not fallen. *Both males and females* tend to accept more permissiveness for males than for females.[16] Although this is true regardless of the level of intimacy involved the double standard appears to become more pronounced as the activity becomes more intimate,[17] that is, the more intimate the behavior, the greater is the "discrimination" against females. Similar results have been reported for both male and female Francophone and English Canadians.[18]

How can we characterize the "new morality" which is implied by the sexual revolution in North America? (1) Sexual behavior is based more on belief and value systems derived from the individual's own real experiences than on values taken over from the parents. (2) Premarital sexual behavior is more permissive in the 1970s than in previous generations; there *is* a sexual revolution occurring. (3) Premarital sexual intercourse tends

[16]Harold T. Christiansen and Christina F. Gregg, Changing sex norms in America and Scandinavia. *Journal of Marriage and the Family,* 1970, **32,** 616–627.
[17]Kaats and Davis, 1970, ibid.
[18]Charles W. Hobart, 1972, ibid.

to be more approved by both males and females when affection and commitment are involved. At the same time the need to ''hang loose'' is often in conflict with the need for loving commitment (See Selection 43). (4) Virginity and nonvirginity do not seem to be valued states in and of themselves —the emphasis is on relationships and reasons for having intercourse rather than the mere fact of intercourse. (5) The sexual revolution is consistent with the new naturalism and reflects a countercultural attitude which values openness and commitment.

● The decade 1965–1975 has seen the first substantial jump in sexual permissiveness since the Roaring Twenties. Furthermore, to the extent that the counterculture values influence the new generation of children, we may see a continued and rapid shift in the sexual permissiveness so that within the next decade the North American culture may approach the attitudes and behavior of Scandinavia. But there are now powerful counterrevolutionary forces abroad — what will the result be? How do *you* read the future?

●

As each of you will be able to document from your own experience, the problems of premarital sexuality are especially salient for teenagers and young adults. The selection ''Teenage Sex: Letting the Pendulum Swing'' provides a description of many of the dilemmas, attitudes, and values revealed by the youth generation in the search for sexual intimacy. However the sexual revolution carries implications far beyond the premarital phase. It causes us to question whether or not monogamy will long continue as the only culturally approved form of marriage. It suggests that at the very least alternate forms of interpersonal relations involving full sexuality are likely to become increasingly accepted by both the old and the new culture.

In reading this selection you should come to think about such questions as: What factors have contributed to the sexual revolution? What are the implications for the future? Will the pendulum swing back to a new puritanism? How has sexploitation been manifested in my own behavior? And so on—use the space below to generate some of your own questions about sexual behavior. Let them range from the abstract/theoretical (e.g., the position of the Church vis-à-vis premarital sexual experience) to the strictly personal and immediate (Yes or No?).

●

COMMENT: HAS MONOGAMY FAILED?

The family of the 1970s is entering an unprecedented era of change and transition, with a massive reappraisal of the family and its functioning in the offing.

The emergence of alternative structures and the experimentation with new modes of married and family togetherness expresses a strong need to bring greater health and optimum functioning to a framework of interpersonal relationships formerly regarded as "frozen" and not amenable to change. There is no question that sex-role and parental-role rigidities are in the process of diminishing, and new dimensions of flexibility are making their appearance in marriage and the family. It is also evident that we are a pluralistic society with pluralistic needs. In this time of change and accelerated social evolution, we should encourage innovation and experimentation in the development of new forms of social and communal living.

[Nonetheless] the weight of tradition and the strong imprinting of parental and familial models assure that for some time to come the overwhelming bulk of the population will opt for something close to the family structures they have known.

Has monogamy failed? My answer is "no." Monogamy is no longer a rigid institution, but instead an evolving one. There is a multiplicity of models and dimensions that we have not even begun to explore. It takes a certain amount of openness to become aware on not only an intellectual level but a feeling level that these possibilities face us with a choice. Then it takes courage to recognize that this choice in a measure represents our faith in monogamy. Finally, there is the fact that every marriage has a potential for greater commitment, enjoyment, and communication, for more love, understanding, and warmth. Actualizing this potential can offer new dimensions in living and new opportunities for personal growth, and can add new strength and affirmation to a marriage.

HERBERT A. OTTO

Alternative Life Styles: The Search for Community

As we discussed in the first section on the consumer culture, the new suburbanites had hoped to achieve a greater feeling of relatedness to their families and an enhanced sense of community. But, for many this hope was dashed on the rocks of competitive achievement and compulsive acquisition of consumables. Suburban living became a national life style which satisfied needs for personal comfort, consumption, and display but which failed to provide a basis for community. The

typical suburban family suffered from high mobility and isolation from the extended family of grandparents, cousins, aunts, and uncles, which had, in times past, provided a sense of identity, relatedness, and community. The fragility of the isolated nuclear family is becoming increasingly apparent; the high divorce rate and the higher "unhappiness and emptiness" rate reflect its weakness when subjected to emotional stresses and value conflicts (cf. comment by Hobart, p. 296).

The participants in the new culture have been particularly sensitive to the shortcomings of the isolated nuclear family in suburbia since the majority of them were raised in such a family. Perhaps the high regard for communal living which permeates the counterculture is in part a reaction to the failure of the nuclear suburban family to provide such depth experiences in sharing. For it is sharing which is the pillar around which communal living is erected; the communal sharing of goods and personal possessions and, perhaps more importantly, the sharing of oneself. One of the foremost chroniclers of the communal movement throughout the world describes the interpersonal emphasis in this way:

If outer space is now the province of the scientists and bureaucrats, and inner space the province of mind-expanding drugs, rock music, and religion, then interpersonal space is the province of the communal movement. Growth centers, encounter groups, sensory-awareness weekends, these are the testing sites for people too timid to make interpersonal living a full-time reality. But it is the several thousand communes of all kinds—religious and ideological, hip and group-marriage, service and youth—that are the avant-garde in exploring interpersonal space.[19]

As with many other aspects of the new culture, the new communards have rediscovered an ancient societal form and adapted it to suit contemporary needs. There have been many previous attempts to create utopian communities in which all property would be held communally. Furthermore, many of

[19]Richard Fairfield, *Communes U.S.A.: A personal tour,* Baltimore: Penguin, 1972.

these alternative societies such as the Shaker and Oneida communities of the nineteenth century also included radical redefinitions of the "proper" sexual relationship between the sexes and child raising practices. Similar communal child raising practices have characterized the Israeli kibbutz.

● For those of you interested in history, communes and psychology, a term paper on the history of communes would seem to be a rewarding experience. See the references at the end of this chapter for a start on such a project.

Contemporary communes established in the counterculture are extremely varied along many dimensions: They may be urban or rural, have a single orienting philosophy or a laissez faire "do your own thing," attitude; they may be oriented around various ideologies—Marxist, behaviorist, or religionist; they may involve a few couples who preserve sexual pair bonding or they may involve full group marriage. Despite this heterogeneity of purpose and program there are some values or ideals which they share in common: According to Fairfield these include:

1 *Getting back to essentials.* This involves a reevaluation of one's real needs as opposed to the artificially created needs to which we have been conditioned by a consumer society. While such a revolution typically results in reduced dependence on things, it certainly does not imply a life of poverty. It does imply a design of having quarters which reflect and fulfill one's own identity, it implies communication of self through a more informal and individualized appearance, and it implies a concern about what one takes into one's body and thus the avoidance of air, sound, water, food, and mind-pollutants. "Back to basics" usually reveals that each person has many more "things" than are really necessary for his personal and spiritual growth. The possibility is thus opened for sharing of resources.

2 *Getting back to the land.* This is the basic thrust of the rural communes and a value with which the urban communes are sympathetic. It is a part of the concern for avoiding pollutants and the desire to be close to nature.

3 *Getting back to people.* The loneliness and isolation of an urban or suburban nuclear family creates interpersonal relations of dependence and exclusiveness which often cannot be sufficiently fulfilling to all the various family members. "One remedy for this dependency is offered by the communal movement: a realignment and restructuring of human relations to allow for more sharing, whether it is simply a strong sense of neighborness or the evolution of an intense and involved group marriage. In anthropological terms, the extended family consists of people related by blood and marriage ties. In communal life, it consists of unrelated people who have come together as loving friends.

4 *"Searching for self.* People in the communal movement also seek self-actualization — finding out more fully who they are and realizing as many aspects as possible of this potential. They are tired of specialization which creates dehumanized, intellectual machines. Life is not getting a college degree, a good job, settling down, and raising a family. It's more, much more than that. It is developing as a fully functioning, sensitive human being."[20]

5 *Social change by example.* Many of the participants in communal movements are not withdrawing from society and rejecting social responsibility. They are rather taking a different track than that often advocated by the political activists. The commune people tend to present themselves as examples of a new life style which is possible for all, "ideally, *everyone* in society can participate in the revolution of consciousness, the rulers as well as the ruled. And communes can help to show the way."[21]

[20]Richard Fairfield, op. cit., p. 365.
[21]Richard Fairfield, ibid., p. 367.

The ideal communal life which is espoused by romanticizers, both within and outside of the movement, has been well expressed by McNeil as follows:

> Their image of the good life is one of friends as a family always gathered round, possessing and consuming as little as they need rather than as much as they can be induced to want; the communal household set amidst green fields and hills and valleys—a household always full of people putting out good vibes, brothers and sisters living harmoniously with nature, spending their time together working, playing, eating, drinking, smoking, loving, rapping, hanging out.[22]

McNeil aptly describes the above statement as a "romanticized, idealized perspective on life with juvenile overtones." Similarly Fairfield has pleaded for a more reality-oriented, "telling-it-like-it-is" perspective on communes. In correspondence with a member of the Greenfeel commune, Fairfield was put off by the "honest and loving and beautiful, phoney-baloney" type of communal public relations work.

> Everyone can write beautiful words and philosophy about the ideal society. But what is really going on? What is the nitty-gritty reality? What about the inevitable conflicts in human interaction? How are problems dealt with? Most people interested in communes have too naïve and idealistic a view of the day-to-day realities of communal living. They do not need to have this view reinforced: rather they need more awareness of the difficulties.[23]

The difficulties are many, and as would be expected many are of an interpersonal sort. In any group there tend to be those who are capable and responsible to the goals and values of the group and those who are much less so. These almost inevitable differences often result in resentments in those who are carrying the load, against those who are doing less or who are outright freeloading. Successful communal structure requires that the contributions to the group welfare (especially the necessary supportive work) be distributed in a manner that is seen to be just by all the participants. Conflicts based on the refusal of some members to work are handled in various ways by various groups but always constitute a problem which must be resolved by any group which expects to survive for long. Other common sources of interpersonal conflicts involve disagreements regarding philosophy and goals for the communal enterprise and conflicts relating to love and sex relations.

In addition to interpersonal problems within the commune there are the ever present problems in relating to the outside world. A complex mixture of curiosity, awe, fear, distrust, and hostility is not an uncommon response of the immediately surround "community" to a communal living arrangement. In some instances the conflict in values and life styles is too great and the power of the conventional community is brought to bear on communes in such a way as to destroy them or greatly limit their scope. For example, the township in which the editors of this book live has passed a bylaw defining a family as including no more than three persons who are not related by marriage or "blood." The bylaw then prohibits the rental of single-family dwellings to groups which are not families.[24] Another common problem is lack of sufficient funds to permit the commune to sustain itself independent of the external community. However, as more and more "older" (i.e. over thirty) people become involved in a communal life style this problem is somewhat eased as in the Morehouse communes (see Selection 46). In those few communes which are able to persist over a longer period of time (e.g., Twin Oaks) a more adequate financial base tends to accumulate. Indeed, in certain cases when an extensive community is organized on a communal sharing basis, the economies inherent in such operations are of sufficient magnitude as to make them a source of serious economic competition for the traditional individualistic system. Examples of economically successful communal arrangements from the last cen-

---

[22]Quoted in Elton B. McNeil, *Being human: The psychological experience.* San Francisco: Cornfield Press, 1973, p. 276.
[23]R. Fairfield. op. cit., p. 354.

[24]Of course the classic case of commune versus community hassles was that of Lou Gottlieb's Morning Star ranch, an extensive discussion of which may be found in Fairfield's *Communes USA.*

tury are Oneida and Amana, both of which now persist as corporations. In addition the Hutterite Brethern of Western Canada (a communal, religious sect) are sufficiently successful in their farming operations that provincial laws were passed which regulate their freedom to purchase land. It would seem that the strong individualistic, capitalistic, competitive system which we have inherited finds a communal life style difficult to accept on both economic and ideological grounds.

Not only are there interpersonal conflicts and community relations problems which must be resolved, but for the individual communard there are problems associated with past training and current expectations. It is frequently reported that the most important of these is the lack of privacy. And even if the individual is able to solve that problem he still has to cope with the fact that the "commune-as-it-really-is" falls considerably short of the "commune-of-his-ideals-and-fantasies." Furthermore, he may find that he does not have the personal qualities which are necessary for fulfillment in a communal setting. For example, he may find that he cannot really share his "possessions" without feelings of resentment and jealousy.

The vast number of problems which face the individual who chooses a communal life style together with limited emotional, experiential, and financial resources for their solution makes for a high turnover rate in communes. In fact it is the high turnover rate which itself constitutes one of the most serious obstacles to long-term success of a commune. In the Twin Oaks commune, modeled after B. F. Skinner's behaviorist utopia, *Walden Two*, turnover was considered to be the biggest single problem in developing an effective community.[25, 26] At the practical level it is a problem because of the loss of specific skills. At the theoretical level the question of why people leave is a serious one since it means that for them the commune has not provided a sufficiently satisfying life style.

[25]Kathleen Kincade, *A Walden two experiment: The first five years of the Twin Oaks community*. New York: William Morrow, 1973. See pp. 114.
[26]B. F. Skinner, *Walden two*. New York: Macmillan, 1948.

But do we really need to have assurances of a utopia in order for communes to be a viable and increasingly selected life style? I think not. Nonetheless, the present communal movement has several serious shortcomings which limit its effectiveness and viability. First, the movement seems to be quite limited as far as the age of its participants is concerned. Being primarily a youth movement, it has all of the advantages of fresh idealism and the disadvantages of lack of experience. More importantly it tends to perpetuate an age grading in an even more severe form than exists in suburbia. It is a rare commune which has more than a ten-year age gap among its communicants. As a consequence there is a severe restriction on alternative perspectives which may be related to the age of the participants. However, this situation is recognized as undesirable by many communes and they hope to correct it both by having children and by attracting older members. Thus, it is probable that the age grading problem will be solved over time simply by the fact that the original founders will become older and that a second generation will be raised in the communes. Indeed, it is the case that almost all communes, fictional and actual, place their utopian hopes on the generation which is raised from birth in the communes. It is well recognized, both in Skinner's *Walden Two* and in contemporary communal societies, that the founding generation cannot completely divorce itself from the hangups of the society in which they were raised. It is the children of the commune who constitute the ultimate test of the viability of this alternative life style.

Second, the rejection of science, technology, and rational thinking which characterizes many of the communes constitutes a denial of much of the most advanced efforts of man as a thinking creature. Such a rejection may be a necessary corrective to the overexaltation of scientific and technological solutions to man's problems. Yet denial of the benefits which can be achieved for human welfare via rational processes results in an unnecessary primitivism which greatly limits the appeal and the long-range survival of many communes. A more reasonable solution to the problem of man being controlled by his own products is to switch control back to humans by focusing on human values and needs. Rather than rejecting science and technology they should be used (coopted) and redirected in the interest of humanization of the planet rather than its technologization. To get back to basics does *not* require primitivization, but it does require continual reevaluation of means versus ends.

What have we learned from the "successes" and "failures" in communal living? Can we write a prescription for a successful commune? The answer to the latter question is "certainly not," but because we *have* learned quite a bit we can offer some plausible perspectives on perennial problems:

1 *The problem of goals and values.* What do we believe in? What shall we strive for? How shall we live our life? How can coming together in a communal group help us to achieve these goals and make new values? It is clear that the answers to the questions are many and varied both within and among communes. But whatever the answers, for a particular group they should be mutually confirmed. The degree of articulateness of the goals and values may range from an explicit founding manifesto to an implicit understanding among those who know each other well. This is not to imply that goals and values do not change and evolve; they do and they must. It does say, however, that there should be some communality of purpose to which the members are individually committed. Finding such common purposes often requires much of the communal energies in the beginning phases of the endeavor. Those groups for which there emerges at least a core of communality of purpose are more likely to survive the vicissitudes of turnover and internal conflict.

2 *The problem of selection and turnover.* Many communes have foundered on the principle of unrestricted admission to the group. They have relied entirely on self-selection in and out. This process puts great strain on the group be-

cause it means that the composition of the group is continually changing and a sense of restlessness is a likely consequence. However, unless the group starts out as a small and closed group it must confront the problem of selection. The dilemma is that if selection is deliberate, according to specific acceptance/rejection criteria, there is the risk of becoming too homogeneous and developing a narrow "group-think." On the other hand, a complete open-door policy has proven to be beyond the economic and emotional resources of most communes. The problems of selection are well discussed by Kathleen Kincade in *The Walden Two Experiment.*[27]

3 *The problem of internal structure.* Many communards have an authority-rebel hangup and thus there has often been a tendency to prefer a quasi-anarchistic structure—or, at least, a laissez faire, "do-your-own-thing" orientation. Examination of the history of the nineteenth- and twentieth-century communes would suggest that those which have a clear internal structure headed by strong leaders are more likely to survive; especially if the leaders are sensitive to creating a structure in which there is maximum feedback and opportunity for complaints and restructuring.

4 *The problem of conflict resolution.* Closely related to the nature of the internal structure is the method for resolving internal conflicts. Clearly there is no prescription which is universally useful. The particular form of the mechanism (dynamism?) may range from private interpersonal confrontation, to encounter groups, to scheduled mutual criticism. The goal is to remain open and honest in reactions without becoming resentful and without becoming preoccupied with interpersonal differences.

5 *The problem of relations to the outside.* The ideal situation is one in which the commune can be sufficiently autonomous from the surround-

[27]Kathleen Kincade, *The Walden two experiment,* op. cit., p. 108–109.

ing community, both economically and emotionally, that it can interact with the community on its own terms. Unfortunately, this is not often the case. As a consequence internal stress and interpersonal conflict often occurs within the commune. For example, until Twin Oaks became economically independent, it was necessary for work to be done in the outside community. Despite continuing adjustment of work credit this activity was a frequent source of internal strife. Few people wanted to work on the outside.

What of the future? Will the counterculture provide real alternatives to the Establishment?

It should not be surprising that in a period of rapid transition and assault on established forms there are highly divergent views on the potential effects of the revolutionary forms. Among the cultural analysts, "believers" such as Theodore Roszak, Charles Reich, and Philip Slater see a real and viable cultural revolution being both required and now in progress.[28] Equally capable critics, basing their analyses on population statistics and economic trends, predict just the opposite—a return to a traditional and conservative pattern of life. In "The Surprising Seventies," Peter Drucker predicts:

> We will return to a preoccupation with traditional economic worries. Indeed, during the next decade economic performances—with jobs, savings and profits at the center—may well become more important than it was in the sixties. . . . the graduates from today's youth culture are likely to find themselves far more worried about jobs and money than they now suspect . . . It is just conceivable that the 19-year-old hard-hat—precisely because he is already exposed to the realities of economic life which are soon to shock a college graduate—prefigures the values, the attitudes and concerns to which today's rebellious youths will switch tomorrow.[29]

[28]Charles Reich, *The greening of America*, New York: Random House, 1971; Theodore Roszak, *The making of a counter culture*. Garden City: Doubleday, 1968; Philip Slater, *The pursuit of loneliness*. Boston: Beacon Press, 1970.
[29]Quoted in Keith Melville. op. cit., p. 230.

Our own prediction is that the most important contribution of the counterculture to the life styles of the 1970s is that of encouragement of *diversity*. If communes, group marriage, and sensitivity training are the waves of the future, so are suburbia, monogamy, and acquisitive competition. Alternative life styles mean just that—*alternatives*. The counterculture will not replace the old culture, or vice versa. Rather, there will be many alternatives and thus an increased freedom to live in a style with which you feel most comfortable. This, of course, *includes* a suburban life style and an isolated nuclear family as well as more extended communal relationships. We will move along many paths toward self-actualization.

COMMENT: FRESH POSSIBILITIES AND UNTESTED ALTERNATIVES

Perhaps the most important function that the communes now serve is as a greenhouse for the new sensitivity, as a place where young recruits are converted to the counterculture. In this sense, they serve as a potent agent for social change. Linked to the widespread use of psychedelics, which act as a catalyst for the new sensibility, the communes provide a consensual universe removed from the faith-eroding effects of the mainstream culture.

In many respects, the most important question is not whether the communes survive in their present form, but rather what will be the fate of the ideas that they transmit. The average life-span of the rural settlements is less significant than what their "graduates" choose to do when they leave. It is my impression that conversion to the values of the counterculture is a far less transient thing than analysts like Drucker assume. Some of the graduates of communal life may well cut their hair a bit shorter, but I doubt whether many will revert to an unswerving concern for what Drucker called "the prosaic details of grubby materialism."

Even when they oscillate between total despair and visionary hope, the most beautiful characteristic of these young people is their vision of what is

possible, their hope that a new and radically different social order can grow up in the midst of the
technological society. To despair prematurely of
the communes as desperate, adolescent ventures is
to give up hope that there are any alternatives.
Since in history as in nature there are as many new

beginnings as dead ends, we have a responsibility
to keep our minds open to fresh possibilities and
untested alternatives.

KEITH MELVILLE

---

43   ON HANGING LOOSE AND LOVING: THE DILEMMA OF PRESENT YOUTH*

HENRY MILLER

To generalize about contemporary American
youth is to deny the only thing we really know
about them: they are, like all human beings, infinitely complex and diverse in their behaviors. It is
an exercise in ignorance, then, to draw a portrai-
ture of an entire generation. Nor is it a less grievous error to take a behavior thought to be pervasive
among youth and characterize it through encapsulation. Drug usage, for example, cannot be isolated from other activities and mystiques; indeed,
its meaning resides in a fabric of other behaviors.

But if we cannot talk of youth in general out of
ignorance, and if we cannot talk of a specific behavior for fear of rendering the behavior meaningless, we can talk of things "in the air"—of ideas
and speculations and ruminations and possibilities.
Further, we can identify behaviors that some
youths engage in at some times; we can observe
that many youths concern themselves with certain
things; and we can know that a small group of
youths experiment with a cluster of behaviors and
that these behaviors, as a totality, say something
about the specific concerns of that group. Which is
a tortured way of saying that this essay concerns
itself with what is probably a small group of young
people who are toying with an aggregate of concerns shared, in part, by a large number of youth.

*Abridged from H. Miller, "On hanging loose and loving: The
dilemma of present youth." *Journal of Social Issues*, 1971,
27(3), 35–46. Reprinted by permission of the author and the
publisher.

For convenience, we use the phrase "youth" or
"contemporary youth," but the reader should not
be misled by such shorthand language. In a very
real sense, this is not a paper about any actual
population of individuals; it is a paper about currents of concern.

Hanging Loose and the New Freedom

With this caution in mind, we argue that contemporary American youth hang loose—or at least
they try to. It is an admirable state of being. And it
bothers their parents.

To "hang loose" means to achieve a state of
freedom far beyond the conventional political
freedoms of enfranchisement and an equitable distribution of power; it means a liberation from the
obligations presumed in conventional interpersonal
involvement and internal moral pressures. To hang
loose is to declare an independence from pernicious demands, especially those that have become
stereotyped or ritualized. Hanging loose is the op-
erational derivative of the cult of experience. Its
antithesis is to be up-tight, a constraint on experience which has the quality of bondage.

The new freedom of contemporary youth is a
freedom of experience in regard both to affect and
to sensation. But like all freedoms in this paradoxical business of living, it carries a price. The wages
of interpersonal liberty are in the currency of

commitment or, if it is preferred, interpersonal meaning. Thus, the parameters of the generation gap become defined and the tragedy of contemporary youth is staged: commitment and freedom are juxtaposed as antagonistic goodies. It is all terribly unfair. Unfortunately, the injustice is denied by a repudiation of the antithetical element—a solution which allows for some cognitive comfort but which leaves a distress of the spirit which we call alienation in the young and neurosis in their parents.

However, the hang-loose state is more an aspiration than a condition, and this serves to make the dilemma of youth much more intense. One can have the new liberty only by not needing to have commitment. Unfortunately, the need for commitment seems to be a prerequisite of humanity; to hunger for that from which one wants to escape can be an unsettling state of affairs. To deny the existence of an antithesis does not mean that the antithesis does not exist. It may be gratuitous to add that to accept its existence does not insure a solution.

Youth, in their quest for the new freedom, turn to many things; dope is but one of several avenues toward the goal of experiential liberty. But we must remember that the use of drugs, like the other behaviors to be discussed, is in the nature of a search. Drug use does not proclaim liberty; rather, it announces an aspiration. More precisely, it is a means rather than an end, which accounts for the great reluctance of youth to treat the drug experience as an exercise in pure pleasure without any assumed beneficial carry-over.

The mystique of psychedelic drug use holds that the sensory apparatus of man has been thoroughly stultified by his inhibiting and one-track middle-class heritage. Man has eyes but cannot see, he has ears that do not hear, indeed he may have sense organs that have escaped altogether the notice of a despiritualized and empirical science. Psychedelia has the power to liberate the senses; perception becomes restored to its inherent, unfettered capability. There is no need to reiterate the now familiar apology of the acid head—"the blues are bluer, the sounds take shape" kind of argu-

ment. It is important to note, however, that the objective validity of these claims is of no account. It is the *experience* of sensory acuity that is crucial, not the fact. The subjective experience is real, the objective fact may be illusory.

Marijuana, that great democratizer of youth, is indeed a magic drug. The magic resides in what is most correctly thought of as its sacramental qualities, qualities that are reputed to liberate inherent sensation. That the drug may be essentially placebo is beside the point; the sacramental elements may exist in the expectations surrounding use as legitimately as in the molecular structure of the drug. The mystique of marijuana carries the message of sensory freedom to huge populations of youth, a message that reads "the banality of conventional sensation is not immutable." Beauty is perceivable; whether it be in the object or the beholder is not an issue for youth. It is sufficient that, at long last it can be declared to exist!

● This discussion should be related to Selection 48, by Keith Melville, and to your text's discussion of the role of perception in defining "reality"—the nature of what exists. What do the concepts "objective reality" and "subjective reality" mean to you? Is one more "real" than the other?

Sensation at the Expense of Passion

When the awareness of beauty is made possible by the sacrament of marijuana or of psychedelia there is a cost. The concomitant of exotic sensation is an aloof, if benign, detachment. Interpersonal relationships, while turned-on, are characterized by their irrelevance. Young people are invariably kind to each other while stoned; they may be patient and tolerant, but they are fundamentally turned inward. It is with the benignity of Buddha that they relate—all well and good when contemplating the antics of mankind, but hardly the context within which to conduct a love affair. Marijuana allows for sensation at the expense of passion.

When passion intrudes, as it sometimes does, we have a definition of a bad trip.

The mystique of psychedelic drugs, then, offers the promise of enriched sensate experience, and the promise in itself is sufficient to engender the experience. The psychological mechanism which allows sensation disallows commitment, hence the notable absence of affect which is commitment's offspring. One feels only about those things which are cared for.

How to account for this relentless press toward sensate experience? Surely, youth have had sensation—it is an inevitable concomitant of having lived—and so there must be something thought wrong with pre-drug sensation. Somehow it must be perceived as limited, unsatisfying, constrained —in a word, inauthentic. Authentic sensation is the sought-after experience, meaning in essence a sensation not preselected through conventional filters and not prejudged by a cultural lexicon of explanation. Psychedelia promises the sensation of the pristine, the experience of the untutored infant. Authenticity is an attribute of liberated perceptors.

Drugs and the Encounter

The encounter, like the drug experience, is a search for freedom-authenticity. Whereas with drugs the authenticity sought is one of sensate experience, with the encounter authenticity of affect becomes the target of search. As with drugs, the authenticity—by the fiat of required expectation— must occur within a context of freedom. The first commandment of the encounter is the mandate immediately to discharge affect. Sin, within the dogma of the encounter, resides in a constraint of feeling. Cognitive control of passion, the tour-de-force of enlightened Western man, becomes the great antagonist in the encounter. Now, the encounter situation by virtue of the fact that it throws together an aggregate of strangers is not the most likely arena within which natural emotion is to be generated. Strangers in twentieth century America are more apt to breed indifference than

feeling. In most instances, then, the affect of the encounter is probably fabricated; the paradox of the encounter is that spontaneity is enforced. Again, experientially this is a moot point. What is sought is the experience of feeling rather than the legitimacy of feeling. As with drugs, authenticity comes with the dismissal of a priori controls and filters.

The encounter is an amazing device and its popularity among the young is as pervasive as is the use of drugs. The encounter presumes a poverty of affect within its participants—or, at least, a constraint of affect. Liberation from such poverty or constraint is the goal, and the mystique of the encounter is uniquely able to insure such a freedom. There is affect aplenty within the encounter; loving feelings and hateful feelings abound, all without consequence. The joyful tidings of the encounter are that "it is all right to have such feelings!" and there is no penalty for their expression. Needless to say, there is no objective reward either; the formulation of "feelings without external consequence" is rather benign. It is tempting to suggest that such feelings, by definition, are trivial. At the very least they are inconsequential.

Again the question is raised: why the need for such a device as the encounter? What was wrong with the history of affect which every participant must inevitably bring to the group?

"Ethnics" as Expressive Models

Some clue might be obtained if we consider another preoccupation of youth: the ubiquitous affection for folk culture and ethnicity. The focus of interest in exotic culture is on the presumed freedom thought to exist within the ethnic personality. It is a kind of romanticization, but not a complete one; contemporary youth are much too hip politically to mistake poverty and oppression for nobility of spirit. Even though the presumption is false, it still exists: ethnics are expressive rather than repressed. They laugh, yell, feel, cry—indeed they behave in real life, it is thought, as American youth can behave only in the encounter. It is very difficult to determine how much of ethnic interest among American youth is a function of political consciousness and how much is a function of this need for expressive models. The black man, for example, is a target for sympathy as well as emulation—as is the Chicano, the Indian, the Vietnamese peasant, the Cuban *campesino,* the American hillbilly—the list is long. The sympathy derives from political motives; the emulation comes from personal need. That the latter exists, however, can be further inferred from the mystique of "soul," which along with dope and the encounter provides the texture of youthful ideology. Soul is not ambiguous; some people have it and some don't. Those who've got it are admirable, those who don't are hopeless. Thus Johnny Cash, Aretha Franklin, Janis Joplin, Zorba the Greek, Bobby Seale, and Jerry Rubin all have soul; Richard Nixon, Aristotle Onassis, Roy Wilkins, Guy Lombardo, and most college professors don't. To have soul is to have sensate experience and to feel deeply and openly. Ethnics, it is thought, are more apt to have soul than are the homogenized victims of suburban life. Youth may be imprecise but they are instinctively right; it is mind boggling to visualize Richard Nixon in an encounter, or his cabinet passing a joint. Soulless individuals do not participate in soulful activities.

Nomadism and the New Freedom

One of the most dramatic characteristics of youth is their incredible mobility. They move with ease, with spontaneity, with what appears to their parents as a reckless and irresponsible lack of planning. They hitchhike across the land with what is now a ritualized costume of knapsack and Levi's. They will sleep in parks or in doorways, or if the weather is ominous they will crash with friends or near friends or strangers. The verb in this new nomadic language is magnificent in precise meaning; "to crash" means that when one is tired and needs rest or sleep, one stops—wherever one happens to be. It resounds of emergency: there is nothing to be done when the motor runs down

but to crash. Of course there will always be a place; it is not anything to worry about. The need to crash requires a solution. In a real sense, the site has no choice.

The fact of travel over Europe and the world, the fact of mobility within the country from town to town and from apartment to apartment, the fact that there are no possessions to impede movement, the fact that conceptions such as home town or root or base are becoming archaic, all this can hardly be explained by technology or instant communication or affluence . They may be necessary but are certainly not sufficient conditions for the nomadism of youth. Again, youth is more likely to be motivated by the cult of experience and the derivative thereof, the quest for freedom. The equation between physical mobility and freedom is an old formulation, albeit an erroneous one, especially if the freedom sought is existential. But as with drugs, the encounter, and the other arenas discussed, the issue has to do with the search and not the modality. Nomadism yields the illusion of liberty—indeed the experience if not the fact of liberty. And this is the decisive point.

Freedom and Sex

The sexual behavior of today's youth encapsulates all of the difficulties with which they contend. If they strive to be liberated from the shackles which convention places on sensation and affect, then we would expect a rather energetic and experimental flavor to their sexual lives. And indeed youth participate in the sexual experience probably with a versatility and virtuosity that was once reserved for Don Juan. Technologically, their sex is impeccable; marriage manuals provide the camp for young America. For a young person to be "put together" sexually means that he or she is able to enjoy sex thoroughly; for him to "know where it's at" sexually means that he has the right to enjoy sex. Unless that right is to become farcical, it implies that such notions as fidelity and loyalty are out of place—they not only impede the accumulation of experience, they constrain freedom. The disrepute of the institution of marriage among youth is not a function of what is seen as its empirical failure. Marriage fails on ideological grounds: it is counter-liberating. The search for freedom and authenticity demands a new marriage vow: "I promise to love and honor you until I get tired of you," or "I promise to love and honor you until someone better comes along." Realistically, these vows have always been the only ones capable of fulfillment, but when they are placed in stark language they ring with a cynicism that jars even youth. What they fail to see is the subtlety of conventional marriage: its promise characterizes the actuality. Youth dismiss the promise as dishonest; they should see it as a statement of aspiration.

That the sexual liberty of youth has been callously exploitative is testified to by the recent popularity of Women's Liberation. Contrary to popular opinion, Women's Lib is sexually reactionary. Young women have been used by the new sexual ethic and they are beginning to realize it. Women's Lib advocates a liberation from their own liberation—that is to say, women wish now to be free to say "no" as well as "yes."

The sexual and love behavior of young people allows for the clash between freedom and commitment to occur in its most dramatic form. It is a simple truth that one can not have it both ways; yet, alas, youth construe this as an artifact of middle-class mentality. It is the anguished emptiness of the alienated that accompanies the search for existential liberty, and it is felt most deeply, where it must be felt, in their love lives. Sex there is in abundance but when love rears its ugly head there comes the moment of truth wherein something must give. All too often, pressed by the coercions of the new culture and by the Zeitgeist, it is love that goes. And so the search continues, the fore-doomed search for another lover who will fill the emptiness and make no demands.

● Isn't the problem more a matter of distinguishing between sex and love? Perhaps we should adopt the attitude noted in Selection 45. "We don't worry too much about the freshman who's going to bed with someone. We worry about the freshman who's just going to bed and thinks it's love." Sex requires no commitment, but love by its very nature does require a commitment. However, must the commitment be "exclusive" and "for life" as the old culture has contended in principle but not followed in practice? Do you think that you really must choose between freedom and commitment? Why? Why not? Think about it. Write about it.

WHAT LED TO THE HOPELESS SEARCH?

What accounts for this hopeless search and for the anguished ambivalence to interpersonal commitment? Any serious observer with any regard for the rules of evidence must equivocate at this point. The questions are too gross; the data which bear on the questions are ambiguous. It would, however, be a disservice to beg off at this decisive juncture and so we offer our speculations in the same spirit of exaggeration which has characterized this essay thus far.

• The author has warned you that he is drawing caricatures of real life. Note our discussion of the value of this approach on page 5. But also, be alerted to picking out the truth from the distortions. Tune up your crap detectors *and* your truth detectors.

The Questionable Success of Science

Surprisingly, it is the success of science rather than its failure which provides the nutriment for search. Science killed God, but it is not only that. Gods are ubiquitous and appear as ideology as well as embodiments. Youth have gods aplenty, unrecognized and unacknowledged, perhaps, but good serviceable gods nonetheless. Science did something more. It hit upon a secret and promoted that secret with enormous success and in the process the truth of it became distorted. The secret is that man and his institutions are extremely versatile and that structural variation is mankind's great talent. This secret—exposed, propagandized, and misunderstood—was transformed into the myth of cultural relativism and the myth has been swallowed whole by American youth. "All behaviors are relative and equally good" is the axiom of disaffected search; "there is no right and no wrong"; "malevolence is a creation of man rather than Satan."

But this axiom is a corruption—it misses the point. What is lost is the knowledge that institutional arrangements are universal, rules exist everywhere, and regulation is the common denominator of human interchange. What is relative is the detail, the surplusage; structure is absolute. Youth read Margaret Mead on the sexuality of Samoa and conclude that sexual freedom is a human possibility. They do not note that the Samoans have a multitude of sexual restrictions and constraints. The restrictions may be different from ours, but they are just as many and, in their own context, just as inhibiting. Youth know of many different gods and conclude that He does not exist. The opposite conclusion is more viable: He exists out of human necessity. They hear of magic mushrooms and peyote—the equippage of the shaman and curandero—but ignore the careful prescription surrounding these mysteries.

The myth of relativism—a relativism distorted beyond original recognition, a relativism fostered by misguided parents who spoke in the name of enlightenment, by teachers in the name of liberalism, by intellectuals in the name of realism, and even by theologues in the name of reformism—this relativism run amok provides the cognitive climate for the search toward freedom.

Dampened Affect in Middle-Class Society

But the search needs more than a nutritious bed; it needs a propellant. And here the villain is the apotheosis made of self-control by the necessities of contemporary civilization. White, Waspish, middle-class youth were reared on a diet of too much cool; their parents had passions, but they kept them in tight rein. In its most dramatic form our youth grew up in homes that were strangers to the sounds and sights of emotion—no yelling, no screaming, no crying, no cackling delight. Rather, youth saw and heard a bland even modulation of affect. It was a surrealistic scene; benign flat faces which, at times, would half smile or half frown, voices consistent in decibel value, all concealing strong feelings which probably seeped out in convoluted and confusing form. Youth are right: it was the epitome of hypocrisy and inauthenticness and it choked and suffocated and deprived a generation. It must have frightened, too. Why else would stirring feelings be so assiduously controlled if not because they were so exquisitely dangerous? Our youth are impoverished. They were deprived of the most necessary of experiences, the experience of feeling deeply.

Overly-Stimulated Sensoria

Whereas their affects were stultified, their sensoria were swamped in an avalanche of stimulation. In the beginning, perhaps throughout, it was toys. Crib gyms and multi-colored blocks and picture books and dozens of child guidance toys —toys built to stimulate and arouse and interest, all in color and smooth plastic, and all based on the false premise that curiosity is a function of the object and not the subject. Then television with its imbecilic yet provocative cartoons: animals that zoom and clank and soar and go squish, animated fictions that give certitude to the impossible. The searching generation is one reared on the TV cartoon, sucklings of Howdy-Doody and the Mickey Mouse Club. Later still, Dragnet, the Untouchables, and Marshall Dillon harassed the retina with images of dancing light. It was not the dramatized violence that was objectionable—children know reality from make-believe—it was the light itself and the rapidly shifting imagery. And there was the news and the movies and school; all throwing scene upon scene, image upon image, sound upon sound, on a weary and overloaded cerebral cortex which had no blueprint for organizing such a mountain of stimulation. Sensation is lost in a flood of sensation. It is no wonder that the blunting of sensation which comes with dope can appear as its sharpening.

INVOLVEMENT AND COMMITMENT

Youth search, then, for the affect which was denied them, for the sensory experience which escaped them, and for the honesty and openness which they never saw. It is an admirable search, it is a necessary search, but alas it is a misguided one. Youth perpetuate the error of their parents; they emphasize the object and not the subject, they measure their freedom by a minima of external constraints rather than a maxima of internal possibilities. It is to the great lesson of mankind that they should attend: involvement brings liberation, commitment *is* freedom.

44 WE ARE LEAVING, YOU DON'T NEED US

DAVID BAILEY

What an ugly Sunday, pain and despair, me presenting myself in foreign words and stagnating concepts, trying to stop being for awhile 'cause someone wants me to sit and pick apart a flower.

What a relief to say the first words, like moving your bowels after a long, heavy accumulation. But what pressure still, feeling all that's there after weeks of digestion. We know that what comes out is only poorly representative of what's gone in.

Where am I in my understanding of man's rela-

tionship to the universe? Where am I with my inorganic pen and paper, exercising my memory stores, indoors, cerebrating instead of celebrating, mentally masturbating while my heart sits in the tree outside my window soaking up first rays of sunshine and the last sparkles of spring rain, eager to blossom into summer? Masturbation/picking apart a flower is painful as well as useless when one's heart isn't in it.

If I write ten pages and make up ten copies,

that's one hundred sheets of *tree* I've used. And who am I to use trees to masturbate for someone else? And do I know me better for my letter full of paper? And do you? The answers are the questions. My answers make me a question. Do my questions make me an answer?

As I explore the universe on paper, whom do I benefit? My own analyses are moment-to-moment, day-to-day, month-to-month, year-to-year, ongoing concerns peculiar to the dynamics of my own situation. I have no use for a written evaluation at this point. *Your* views must live in the same way. Am I so large a part of the dynamics of your situation that notes I strike (or rather, notes I write on paper) will change your tune? Do you *care* how I *say* I see men?

There's one more reason for writing the paper, that is, course requirement. Function (1) Grade-aid: What is it that we are graded on? How does the paper clarify this area for the grades? Function (2) Satisfaction for instructor: "Ah, the course is worthwhile; look at . . ."—whatever it is that makes it worthwhile; or, "I assigned a paper and preserved my professional identity," either way, all tied up in power and ego.

But back to "our" universe. As you all know, you're nothing. From a much shorter distance than that to the nearest star, our whole solar system looks just like a star. Every star we see could be a solar system larger than our own. The structure of solar systems and galactic systems resembles atomic structure, and, in fact, what we know as "the universe" might simply be the fluid beverage of a very large creature. Our galaxy is a particularly large particle in this colloidal suspension, and in this we can take great pride. Our instruments have not yet been able to go much beyond our galaxy to the other "particles" in the suspension, and certainly not to the walls of the container. Perhaps they will before he drinks, perhaps not; it doesn't matter—we wouldn't know what to make of it anyway. Some of us have already told the government, and they just gave a nervous laugh.

They just laugh. And they haven't even heard the important part—they won't listen to the important part. He doesn't care! The creature doesn't

care! He's not making any rules. He's not telling us how to be. He's not assigning any papers. . . .

Well then, who's in charge here? Where do we look for direction?

Me? (who else?)

But I just live here (no one does more)

What's it all about? (that's your problem)

(You are everything. You are the centre. You must choose.)

> "And they came to the edge
> And he pushed them
> And they flew."

And we don't have to make ourselves "something" anymore. We don't have to succeed. We have seen we are nothing, and have been able to relax. Relaxing, we can be just what we are, breathing with the stars, ebbing and flowing with the seasons, pulsating with the universe, living and dying with all life.

We can cease our struggle with nature and embrace it as our own life. We don't need to push it away to establish a separate identity; we don't have to manipulate or control it to convince ourselves of our strength or importance. We have seen the nature of reality, and it is the reality of nature.

Life now takes on the characteristics of the living, the organic, the creative. Our identities as separate creatures have gone and so have the identities of other things as separate, things by themselves. For example, buildings don't have their old (usually functional) identity. They are seen as part of the process from which they result and for which they are used and as part of a larger process in the world. A handful of soil doesn't look like "dirt" any longer (it gets you dirty—you can plant things in it); it looks like trees and grass and rocks and you, all in process. And you don't look like a "human being" anymore, cognitive king of the universe; but like trees and grass and rocks and you, all in process.

And you love the organic because it is you and it is alive. And you see the inorganic moving in from all sides on the organic—moving in on you. You see the bulldozers and the cement mixers of the inorganic armies tearing up your body on all sides of you. As I sit typing this there are men in the Integrated Studies yard with a chain saw, wearing helmets, looking like something from a Ray Bradbury story, cutting down live cherry trees for wood to burn in the great hall. Other trees marked to go could house owls and flickers and crawling bugs to feed birds. Men who have lost their roots have become machines using your body, your earth to make more machines. The inorganic eats the organic. All machines eat fuel. The biggest machines of all use people as fuel. *And the inorganic makes the organic dead, takes life away, takes our life away from us.*

The message of the inorganic is death. It "lives" (is used) for a short time, then dies. The message of the organic is *life, birth, growth, death, decay, rebirth.* Only the organic has power to live, to create. The inorganic has power only to destroy. Inorganic men are powerless in their souls, so they seek control in their lives; organic men have the power in their souls, they don't need control. The organic man, the "natural" man is in the sad position of having many of his life circumstances controlled by power-hungry men grasping for identity.

> *Wooden* ships on the *water*, very free, and easy
> You know the way it's supposed to be.
> *Silver* people on the *shoreline* let us be.
> Talking 'bout very free and easy
> Horror grips us as we watch you die
> We are leaving, you don't need us.
>
> Go take a sister then by the hand
> Lead her away from this foreign land.
> Far away, where we might laugh again.
> We are leaving, you don't need us.

The metaphor tells of the natural man's desire to escape the machine men. It emphasizes "we are leaving, you don't need us." The organic man certainly leaves in several respects. From the machine he turns away to self-reliance, from a confused world he turns to his own integrated one, from surface living, he turns to central life, to the real from the external self and to intrinsic from extrinsic reward. He can no longer be a consuming animal, for he knows he is consuming himself. He becomes a producer, a creator, making his life instead of buying it, building the world, not destroying it.

His emphasis is on internal growth, spiritual growth, rather than external or material. "Growing" means being better in tune with the reality of nature. It implies growth toward a goal, and the goal of course is union with nature, or perfect being.

When a man lives naturally, he is first of all an animal. He recognizes his basic needs and goes about satisfying them. He needs food, he enjoys comfort and companionship. He loves to be well-fed, comfortable and happy. He loves to laugh, sing, screw, dance. He loves to manipulate his environment, interact with it, feel himself in relation to it, have an identity as a man, be competent. He loves to love and be loved. He recognizes his unique and special nature as a reflective being, contemplates his existence, knows wonder. He knows that many things happen to him that he can't control or even explain. He does what he can about what he can do anything about. He does his best with what he knows and he's satisfied, because that's all his life is asking of him.

And he doesn't try to fool himself about any of the things that he is.

COMMENT: AND THE INORGANIC MAKES THE ORGANIC *DEAD*

When I first met David Bailey he was a student in a small senior seminar which I teach. At one level his paper was written as a final course "requirement," but at a more important level it was David's statement about himself in relationship to the world.

David seemed to me to be a special person. Although at first glance he looked pretty much like any other campus freak—long hair, beard, patched jeans. Perhaps it was the soft, kind look of his eyes which seemed to understand far more than his twenty years would warrant. Yes, it must have been the quiet confidence, kindness and wisdom which created the image which was more aura than charisma.

David's life changed rather dramatically during his fourth year. He met Bonnie. Bonnie was several years older than David, had three children, and was just emerging from the emotional trauma of a split from her husband. Bonnie and David came to love each other very dearly and began to share a communal living arrangement with some other couples. This was the beginning of a new life together—much more together.

As the senior year came to a close David and Bonnie were aware of having to choose who they were to become. And as they thought and felt and lived themselves they realized more and more fully that they could not sacrifice their lives to the consumer culture. They felt that they must try to actualize the naturalistic/organic value system which they found to bring happiness. So in the summer of 1970 they took what money they had and bought 50 acres of farm land on Prince Edward Island.

Early in the fall they went with several of their friends, including Bonnie's former husband, to build a log cabin on the farm. But the snow came early that year and it became clear that the cabin could not be finished so that they could winter there. Also, Bonnie wanted to return to her parents' home to have David's child. They loaded up the V. W. microbus with all their possessions and the three children and set out for Texas.

Driving through a cold, blustery, wet, November night in Maine, they met one of Detroit's finest products—head on—and the inorganic makes the organic DEAD.

JAMES A. DYAL

● Bonnie and David were casualities of the soft revolution. Read David's statement again for the greater impact that it will now have. What does it mean to *you* that Bonnie and David lived—and died?

45 TEEN-AGE SEX: LETTING THE PENDULUM SWING*

Girls can score just as many times as boys if they want to. I've gone to bed with nine boys in the past two years. It's a natural thing, a nice thing and a nice high. It sure can clear up the blues.

—Mimi, 18, a June graduate of
Tenafly (N.J.) High School

I'm still a virgin. My friends last year blamed it on the fact that I was the youngest girl on campus. But I can't see having intercourse unless it's part of a tight emotional bond. My father has influenced me, but the fact that he is a minister has nothing to do with it. The church is not a stronghold against sex any more.

—Amanda, 16, a junior at
Shimer College, Mount Carroll, Ill.

They could hardly be more unlike, Mimi and

Amanda.[1] Yet both are representative of American teen-agers in 1972. Though Amandas predominate among the nation's boys and girls between 13 and 19, there are enough Mimis so that many parents are alarmed. Even some of the teen-agers themselves, especially those in college, are uneasy about their almost unlimited new sexual license. Along with a heady sense of freedom, it causes, they find, a sometimes unwelcome sense of pressure to take advantage of it. "I'm starting to feel the same way about getting laid as I did about getting into college," Dustin Hoffman confessed in *The Graduate*. A Columbia University psychiatrist reports that students come to him to find out what is wrong with them if they are not having intercourse. "My virginity was such a burden to me that I just went out to get rid of it," a junior at

*From *Time*, August 21, 1972, pp. 30–35. Reprinted by permission from TIME, The Weekly Newsmagazine; Copyright Time Inc.

[1]The names of the children and their parents in this story are fictitious.

the University of Vermont revealed to a Boston sex counselor. ''On a trip to Greece, I found any old Greek and did it so it wouldn't be an issue any more.''

Was her trip necessary? Is there really a notable increase in teen-age sex? Foolproof statistics about sexual habits are hard to come by, but a recent survey prepared for the Nixon-appointed commission on population seems to offer reasonably reliable figures. Of 4,611 unmarried black and white girls living at home or in dormitories in 1971, more than 46% had lost their virginity by age 20, according to Johns Hopkins Demographers Melvin Zelnik and John Kantner (TIME, May 22). Comparison with previous generations is difficult because earlier studies are incomplete: Alfred Kinsey, for example, author of the first large-scale studies of sexual behavior, did not include blacks in his statistics. However, Kinsey's 1953 survey of some 5,600 white women disclosed that 3% were nonvirgins at age 15, and 23% had had premarital intercourse by the time they were 21. By contrast, Zelnik and Kantner report that of the 3,132 whites in their sample, 11% of the 15-year-olds were nonvirgins, and 40% of all the girls had lost their virginity by the age of 20. In short, youth's sexual revolution is not just franker talk and greater openness; more teen-agers, and especially younger ones, are apparently having intercourse, at least occasionally.

● If you have not already done so, you should stop at this point and read Selection 42, where you will find more documentation that a sexual revolution has indeed taken place during the last decade.

Another indication of the reality of youthful sex is the rising incidence of VD, which has now reached epidemic proportions in high schools and colleges. After the ordinary cold, syphilis and gonorrhea are the most common infectious diseases among young people, outranking all cases of hepatitis, measles, mumps, scarlet fever, strep throat and tuberculosis put together. In 1970 there were at least 3,000 cases of syphilis among the 27 million U.S. teen-agers and 150,000 cases of gonorrhea, more than in any European country except Sweden and Denmark. From 1960 to 1970 the number of reported VD cases among girls 15 to 19 increased 144%, and that percentage does not begin to tell the story, because it is estimated that three out of four cases go unreported.

The spiraling rate of pregnancies among unmarried girls is yet another indicator of sexual activity by the young. Per thousand teen-agers, the number of illegitimate births has risen from 8.3 in 1940 to 19.8 in 1972. Of an estimated 1,500,000 abortions performed in the U.S. in 1971, it is believed that close to a third were performed on teen-agers. Last year women at one prominent Eastern university had 100 illegitimate pregnancies, while at another there were almost 400—a rate of one for every 15 students. Nationwide the college pregnancy rate runs from 6% to 15%.

The different sexual experiences of two sisters, eight years apart in age, illustrate at least some of the changes that are taking place.

Sue Franklin, now 25, had a traditional middle-class Midwestern upbringing. In 1965, when she was 18 and a college freshman, her sorority sisters talked about their sexual feelings only with extremely close friends, and nearly all gossiped about girls they suspected of having affairs. ''Virginity was all important,'' Sue remembers. Then her boy friend of five years' standing issued an ultimatum: ''Either you go to bed with me or I'm leaving you.'' She gave in and was overcome with remorse. ''My God,'' she thought, ''what have I done? The more I learned about sex, the guiltier I felt, especially about enjoying it. I almost felt I had to deny myself any pleasure. My boy friend felt bad, too, because I was so hung up.''

Sue's sister Pat, on the other hand, was just 15 and in high school when she first went to bed with a boy. Only one thing bothered her: fear of getting pregnant. She appealed to Sue, who helped her get contraceptive advice from a doctor. Since then, Pat has had one additional serious relationship that included sex. Observes Sue: "Pat had as healthy an attitude as could be imagined, as healthy as I wish mine could have been. She and her friends are more open. They're not blasé; they don't talk about sex as they would about what they're going to have for dinner. But when they do discuss it, there's no hemming and hawing around. And boys don't exploit them. With Pat and her boy friends, sex isn't a motivating factor. It's not like the pressure that builds when sex is denied or you feel guilty about it. It's kept in perspective, not something they're especially preoccupied with. They don't see sex as something you can do with everyone; they're not promiscuous."

Nor are most teen-agers. Though the number of very youthful marriages appears to be declining, a fourth of all 18- and 19-year-old girls are married. More often than not, they had already had intercourse; more than half of them got married because they were pregnant. But on the whole, teen-agers actually are not very active sexually, in spite of the large number of nonvirgins. Of those questioned by the Johns Hopkins demographic team, 40% had not had intercourse at all in the month before the survey, and of the remainder 70% had done so only once or twice that month. About 60% had never had more than one partner, and in half the cases that one was the man they planned to marry. When promiscuity was reported, it was more often among whites: 16% admitted to four or more partners, while only 11% of blacks had had that many.

Teen-agers generally are woefully ignorant about sex. They may believe that "most teen-age boys can almost go crazy if they don't have intercourse," that "you can't get pregnant if he only comes one time," or that urination is impossible with a diaphragm in place. Other youths cherish the notion that withdrawal, douching, rhythm or luck will prevent conception. Overall, "the pervasiveness of risk taking" is appalling, Zelnik and Kantner discovered. More than 75% of the girls they interviewed said they used contraceptives only occasionally or never.

To close the information gap, schools and colleges have begun to provide telephone hot lines, new courses, manuals of instruction and personal counseling. By dialing 933-5505, University of North Carolina students can get confidential information about pregnancy, abortion, contraception, sexual and marital relationships. More than 30 trained volunteer counselors answer 50 calls a week, with at least one man and one woman always on duty so that shy callers can consult someone of their own sex. Complex questions are referred to a dozen experts, mostly physicians, who have offered their help.

● What sources of information and counseling are available at your school? Find out and pass the word. If the sources are not adequate what can *you* do about it?

Away from the campus, counseling is hard to come by, but contraceptive advice is usually available, at least to urban teen-agers, from private social agencies and public health departments. This has not long been so. Birth Control Crusader Bill Baird was arrested in 1967 for giving out contraceptive devices to Boston University coeds. His conviction was overturned last March when the Supreme Court ruled that a state could not outlaw contraceptives for single people when they were legal for married couples. In most states the law is ambiguous about giving teen-agers birth control advice, particularly without parental consent. But nowadays many authorities interpret the law liberally, believing that since teen-age sex is a fact, it ought at least to be protected sex. In any court test, they believe, the trend toward recognizing the civil rights of minors would prevail.

Dolls with Breasts. What brought about the new sexual freedom among teen-agers? "Obviously," nine parents out of ten would probably say, "it's all this permissiveness." But permissiveness is just a word that stands for many things, and as with most societal changes, it is often difficult to tell what is cause and what is effect. One major factor is the "erotization of the social backdrop," as Sociologists John Gagnon and William

Simon express it. American society is committed to sexuality, and even children's dolls have breasts and provocative outfits nowadays. Another frequently cited factor is the weakening of religious strictures on sex. Observes Social Critic Michael Harrington: "One of the great facts about our culture is the breakdown of organized religion and the disappearance of the inhibitions that religion once placed around sexual relationships." Sociologists have found an inverse relationship between churchgoing and sexual experimentation: the less of the former, the more of the latter. In fact, suggests Sociologist Ira Reiss, today's teen-agers may have more influence on religion than the other way round. Among liberal clergymen, at least, there is something of a scramble to keep up with youthful ideas on sex. Permissive Catholic priests let their views become known and so in effect encourage liberated youngsters to seek them out for confession. Unitarian churches give courses for 12- to 14-year-olds "About Your Sexuality," complete with frank lectures and discussions, as well as films showing intercourse, masturbation and homosexuality.

Diminishing family influence has also shaken up the rules. The disillusionment of many youths with Viet Nam, pollution and corruption has sexual side effects, say Simon and Gagnon. It reinforces the idea of the older generation's moral inferiority. In fact, the two sociologists assert, many young people begin sexual activity in part as a "personal vendetta" against their parents. Nor does the older generation have a very good record of marital stability. Since there are now 357 divorces for every 1,000 marriages, it is little wonder that children do not necessarily heed their parents' advice or consider marriage their ultimate goal. "There's a healthy disrespect for the facade of respectability behind which Albee-like emotional torrents roll on," says Yale Chaplain William Sloane Coffin Jr.

Disillusioned as they may be with their elders, teen-agers owe much of their sexual freedom to parental affluence. More of them than ever before can now afford the privacy of living away from home, either while holding jobs or going to college. The proliferation of coed dorms has eased the problem of where to make love; though such dorms are not the scenes of the orgies that adults conjure up, neither are they cloisters. A phenomenon that seemed shocking when it first appeared in the West and Midwest in the 1960s, two-sex housing is now found on 80% of the coed campuses across the country. At some colleges, boys and girls are segregated in separate wings of the same buildings; at others they live on separate floors; at still others, in adjacent rooms on the same floor.

Some behavioral experts claim that in these close quarters, brother-sister relationships develop, so that a kind of incest taboo curbs sex. Moreover, Sarah Warren, a June graduate of Yale, suggests that "if you've seen the girls with dirty hair, there's less pressure to take their clothes off." But Arizona Psychiatrist Donald Holmes insists that "where the sexual conjugation of man and woman is concerned, familiarity breeds consent." At a coed dorm at the University of Maryland recently, boys poured out of girls' rooms in droves when a fire alarm sounded in the middle of the night. At Bryn Mawr, one student explains: "When a boy and girl have been going together for a while, one of them drags his mattress into the other's room." A new kind of study problem has recently been brought to a college psychiatrist: what to do if your roommate's girl friend parades around your room nude. Ask her to get dressed? Or go elsewhere to study?

As for the Pill, nearly all laymen consider it a major cause of the new freedom, but a majority of professionals disagree. Because most girls dislike seeing themselves as on the lookout for sex, few go on the Pill until they are having intercourse regularly. Even then, because they are worried about its side effects, almost half choose other means, if indeed they use contraceptives at all. Just the same, Hartsdale, N.Y., Psychiatrist Laurence Loeb believes, the very existence of the Pill has important psychological effects because it means that pregnancy is avoidable.

What about Women's Liberation? During the '20s, the feminist drive for equal rights for women was partly responsible for an increase in premarital sex even greater than the present acceleration. Today's extreme militants, who believe that the new wave of permissiveness is a conspiracy to exploit them, want to put a damper on sex. But for the vast majority of women, the movement stands in part for a new freedom in sexual matters.

Over the past four years, Philip and Lorna Sarrel, sex counselors at Yale, have asked 10,000 students to fill out anonymous questionnaires on sexual knowledge and attitudes. Once it was easy to tell which answers came from males and which from females. No more . "At last, both young men and women are beginning to express their sexuality without regard to stereotypes," Sarrel declares with satisfaction. "We're getting rid of the idea that sex is something men do to women." As Jonathan Goodman, 17, of Newton High remarks, "I'd probably want to talk it over with a girl, rather than just let it happen. Her reasons for doing it or not doing it would be as important as mine."

Most observers think the equality movement has weakened, though not demolished, the double standard, and reduced, though not ended, male preoccupation with virility. There is somewhat less boasting about sexual conquest. Jonathan, for one, asserts that "I respect my girl friend and our relationship enough not to tell everyone what we're doing." Anyway, reports recent Columbia Graduate Lou Dolinar, "Now that girls are living with their boy friends in the dorm, it's pretty hard to sit around with them and talk like a stud. Male bull sessions of sexual braggadocio have been replaced by coed bull sessions about sexual traumas."

● Of course, one critical thrust of the Woman's Liberation movement involves raising the consciousness of men so that they do not sexploit women sexually, economically, and emotionally. However, an equally important corollary is the liberation of men from the control of the "macho myth" which requires that they define themselves as "men" in terms of their sexual prowess. As males in North American culture most of you still have yet to be

liberated and many of you are now struggling with that problem. Why don't you share some of the experiences?

Identity Crisis. Can teen sex be harmful, apart from causing such problems as illegitimate pregnancy and disease? Manhattan Psychoanalyst Peter Blos believes that the early adolescent, however physically developed, is psychologically a child and lacks the emotional maturity necessary to manage sexual relationships. If a child tries to grow up too fast, Blos says, he may never grow up at all. Says Catholic Author Sidney Cornelia Callahan: "Sexuality is very intimately related to your sense of self. It should not be taken too lightly. To become an individual, the adolescent has to master impulses, to be able to refuse as well as accept."

Even on campuses where sex is relaxed, says Sociologist Simon, "kids still experience losing their virginity as an identity crisis; a nonvirgin is something they did not expect to be." Sexually involved adolescents of all ages are sometimes beset by guilt feelings, though less often than were their elders.

Occasionally the pangs of old-fashioned conscience are so strong that a student drops out of school and requires months of therapy before he is able to resolve the conflict between his "liberated" behavior and the standards, acquired from his parents, that he still unconsciously accepts.

Experts also detect a frequent sense of shame and incompetence at not enjoying sex more. "A great many young people who come into the office these days are definitely doing it more and enjoying it less," says Psychiatrist Holmes. According to Simon and Gagnon, sexual puritanism has been replaced by sexual utopianism. "The kid who worries that he has debased himself is replaced by the kid who worries that he isn't making sex a spectacular event."

Infidelity creates additional problems, warns Columbia University Psychiatrist Joel Moskowitz. "A couple agree that each can go out with anyone. The girl says, 'So-and-so turns me on; I'm going to spend the night with him.' Despite the contract they've made, the boy is inevitably enraged, because he feels it's understood that such things hurt him.'' When the hurt is great enough to end the affair, the trauma for both may approach that of divorce, or worse. One college student asked his high school girl friend to live in his room with him, and then watched despairingly as she fell in love with his roommate, and, overcome with grief and confusion, tried to commit suicide.

Cool Sex. To lay and professional observers alike, one of the most distressing aspects of teen sex is its frequent shallowness, particularly when the participants are still in high school. At that stage, Simon and Gagnon report, it is often the least popular students who engage in sex—and who find, especially if they are girls, that their sexual behavior brings only a shady sort of popularity and more unhappiness. Wisconsin Psychiatrist Seymour Halleck ascribes a ''bland, mechanistic quality'' to some youthful relationships, and Beverly Hills Psychoanalyst Ralph Greenson observes that, ''instant warmth and instant sex make for puny love, cool sex.''

His words seem to fit the experience of Judy Wilson. Recalling the day she lost her virginity in her own bedroom at the age of 17, she says blithely: ''One afternoon it just happened. Then we went downstairs and told my younger sister because we thought she'd be excited. We said, 'Guess what. We just made love.' And she said, 'Oh, wow. How was it?' And we said, 'Fine.' Then we went out on the roof and she took pictures of us.''

But among more mature young people, shallowness is anything but the rule. ''Our kids are actually retrieving sexuality from shallowness,'' insists Sex Counselor Mary Calderone. ''They are moving away from the kind of trivialization we associated with the Harvard-Yale games in the '20s when the object was to get drunk and lay a lot of girls.'' Los Angeles Gynecologist J. Robert Bragonier agrees: ''Kids aren't looking for the perfect marriage, but they're idealistic about finding a loving relationship.'' Sarrel adds that he finds most student liaisons ''more meaningful than the

typical marriage in sharing, trusting and sexual responsibility.''

Epitomizing this free but deep relationship is the experience of Yale students Rachel Lieber and Jonathan Weltzer. Recently she wrote about it for a forthcoming book: ''We had always assumed we'd marry eventually. We had lived together for two years and were growing closer . . . On our wedding night, Jonathan and I lay in bed, letting all the feelings well up around us and bathe our skins in warmth as the words we had said during the ceremony started coming back. We mixed our faces in each other's hair, and we looked at each other for a long time. So we spent our wedding night, not as virgins, but very close.''

Informal liaisons often mature into marriage and when they do, Yale's Coffin has found, many areas of the relationship are apt to be sounder than in less tested unions. This is especially true now that unmarried sex has largely lost its stigma. As Coffin explains, ''The danger of premarital sex while it was *verboten* was that it covered up a multitude of gaps. A girl had to believe she was in love because, she told herself, she wouldn't otherwise go to bed. As a result, the real relationship never got fully explored.''

Many psychiatrists have come to agree that the new openness has much to recommend it. One of these is Graham Blaine, until recently chief psychiatrist of the Harvard health services. In 1963, Blaine wrote that ''college administrations should stand by the old morality'' and decried relaxed dormitory rules that allowed girls to visit boys' rooms till 7 p.m. In 1971 he switched sides. ''I have been convinced by the young that the new relationships are a noble experiment that should be allowed to run its course.''

Today Blaine elaborates: ''I thought we college psychiatrists would see a lot more emotional problems. I was wrong; most students are not being hurt. The pendulum should be allowed to swing.'' It will swing back—at least part way back—he predicts, as it did after the easygoing days of the English Restoration. ''It's much more in keeping with human nature to make sex a private thing and to have some elements of exclusivity.'' Mrs. Callahan, speaking to student audiences, has found on campuses "a new puritanism or perhaps a lingering puritanism," and she usually gets a smiling response when she calls on her listeners to "join the chastity underground."

Yes or No. Whether or not the chastity underground is the wave of the future, as Mrs. Callahan hopes, some youths, at least, appear to be searching for firmer guidelines. "Sometimes I wish I were a Victorian lady with everything laid out clearly for me," admits Sarah Warren. Warns Coffin: "It's much easier to make authority your truth than truth your authority."

At Yale, the Sarrels, who had dropped a lecture on morals, were asked by the students to add one on sexual values and decision-making. But to search for guidelines is not necessarily to find them. Most of the proliferating courses, clinics and handbooks detail, meticulously, the biology of intercourse, contraception, pregnancy and abortion; few do more than suggest the emotional complexities of sex. For instance, *The Student Guide to Sex on Campus* (New American Library; $1), written by Yale students with the help of the Sarrels, has this to say on the subject of "Intercourse —Deciding Yes or No":

"When a relationship is probably not permanent, but still very meaningful, it is more difficult to decide confidently . . . There is so much freedom . . . The decision is all yours, and can be very scary . . . No one should have intercourse just because they can't think of any reason *not* to. The first year in college can create confusion about sexual values. Your family seems very far away, and their ideas about almost everything are challenged by what you see and hear . . . Girls who have intercourse just to get rid of their virginity usually seem to find it not a pleasurable or fulfilling experience."

Sense of Trust. In personal counseling sessions, the Sarrels offer psychological support for students who would rather not rush things, telling them that "it's just as O.K. not to have sex as it is to have it." "People need to unfold sexually," Sarrel believes, and there is no way to speed the process. What is right may vary with a student's stage of emotional development. "A freshman may need to express rebellion and independence from his family and may use sex to do it." That is acceptable, Sarrel believes, as long as the student understands his motives: "We don't worry too much about the freshman who's going to bed with someone. We worry about the freshman who's just going to bed and thinks it's love." For an older student, intercourse may be right only if the lovers are intimate emotionally. How to judge? One crucial sign of intimacy is "a sense of trust and comfort. If you find you're not telling each other certain kinds of things, it's not a very trusting relationship."

Apparently this kind of advice is what the students want. Sarrel has been dubbed "the Charlie Reich of sex counseling" by an irreverent observer, and like the author of *The Greening of America,* he is very popular: 300 men and women crowd into his weekly lectures at Yale, and more than 1,000 other colleges have asked for outlines of his course. For good reason. The Sarrels' careful counselng has cut the VD and unwanted pregnancy rate at Yale to nearly zero.

But what about ethical questions? For those who are not guided by their families or their religion, Sarrel's system—and the whole body of "situation ethics"—fails to offer much support for making a decision. Years ago William Butler Yeats wrote a poem about the problem:

> I whispered, "I am too young."
> And then, "I am old enough";
> Wherefore I threw a penny
> To find out if I might love.

How did the toss come out? Yeats, unsurprisingly, gave himself a clear go-ahead, ending his poem:

> Ah penny, brown penny, brown
>   penny.
> One cannot begin it too soon.

Nowadays a great many adolescents, like Yeats, seem to be simply tossing a coin, and singing the same refrain.

46   COMMUNES: THE ALTERNATIVE LIFE-STYLE*

HERBERT A. OTTO

EXPERIENCES IN A COMMUNE

Angelina is a tall, striking blonde in her mid-forties, with a husky voice and a motherly, forthright air about her. She had been a successful interior decorator in a well-known college town in Oregon. Following her divorce, Angelina decided to rent some of the extra bedrooms in her house to students.

"I was shocked seeing people dirty and with unwashed hair—until I got to know them better and saw their soul reflected in their eyes. They wanted country life and animals. They wanted to be creative and to be themselves. At that time, I was attending a Unitarian church. I talked to the minister about starting a commune. He said it wouldn't work."

Angelina felt she needed new ideas and viewpoints, and she went to the Esalen Institute at Big Sur, California. She stayed three months. "I could see so much, feel so much, I thought I was really called."

Upon returning to her business, which she had left in competent hands, Angelina decided to sell out and was able to do so at a favorable price. "I made up my mind I wanted the family feeling. At this point, it was like Providence when I heard about the hundred and fifty acres. The price was so reasonable, I thought there was something wrong with the place. But when I saw it—with the half-dozen springs, three streams, and mixed timber—I knew this was the spot for a nature commune."

The nature commune that Angelina started two years ago has a reputation as one of the oldest and best run among the eight communes located within a twenty-five-mile radius of a small town in southern Oregon. This is a hilly farm and lumber region where in winter it sometimes rains for weeks on end, after which the appearance of the sun is greeted with festivity.

I had arranged to first meet Angelina at a local coffee shop one afternoon. She was wearing a colorful dress, which, she explained, she had designed and sewn herself. She also explained that the couple she had met at Esalen and with whom she had founded the commune had since left. And that among the thirty-eight members presently living in the commune there are five individuals with exceptional skills as plumbers, mechanics, electricians, and carpenters. A stonemason is also in residence. Financial support of the commune derives from a number of sources, including member contributions, with Angelina—as owner of the property—playing a major role. Of the dozen members considered "stable," Angelina also explained: "They all have to split every once in a while, but they feel it's their home." We talked for about an hour over coffee, and then Angelina invited me to come to the commune for supper.

Located fifteen miles from town on a blacktop road, the commune is flanked by well-kept small farms. An elaborately carved and painted sign close to the road announces "The Good Earth Commune." Immediately behind the sign is an improvised parking field. It was filled with about two dozen cars and trucks and a bus, which obviously served as living quarters. Some of the cars had thick layers of dust and either were abandoned or had not been used for a long time. As we drove past, five boys and two girls, all deeply suntanned, were gathered around a pickup truck and were talking leisurely while watching two of their number work on the motor. They seemed like high school or college kids on a summer vacation.

Over a slight rise, hidden from the road and surrounded by old oak trees, stands the barn. This was the only building on the property when

*Abridged from H. A. Otto, *Communes: The alternative life-style.* Copyright 1971 by Saturday Review Co. First appeared in *Saturday Review,* April 24, 1971. Used with permission of the author and the publisher.

Angelina bought it and it now serves as the main gathering place of the commune. The interior of the barn has been rebuilt and there is a large kitchen with a long, well-scrubbed wooden table; this area also serves as the dining room. Next to this room is a communal quarter, with an improvised fireplace in the center of the dirt floor and barrels and pieces of logs or wooden blocks to sit on. Further construction is under way, but a well-stocked library can be reached by climbing a ladder. In the middle of the library's floor squats an old-fashioned woodburning iron stove. There are pillows scattered around to sit on and a few old easy chairs that show signs of having been repaired with care.

Hal, who is one of the four left from the original group of fifteen that started the commune with Angelina, volunteered to act as guide. He is a slender, blond-haired man in his middle or upper twenties; he was dressed in clean, faded bluejeans, sandals, and a multi-hued shirt he had dyed himself. He was also wearing an ankh suspended from a deceptively crude-looking, handmade brass chain around his neck. A dropout from a social science doctoral program at Yale, Hal has a habit of carefully forming his sentences. While dusk drew near, we walked together along paths through the wooded hillsides. More than a dozen single-room buildings have been so neatly fitted into the landscape that they are hard to distinguish from their surroundings. Each is different and has been constructed by the people who live in it from materials found on the land—old lumber and odds and ends. Some are built into the hillside and overlook the valley, and each structure is totally isolated, with no other neighbor visible. Only the sounds of birds could be heard; it was very peaceful.

Hal and I looked into several houses whose owners were away on trips. Most of these houses had one room dominated by a fireplace or an iron stove. There were mattresses on the floor, and chairs for the most part were improvised from lumber or were hand-hewn from logs. Navajo rugs and colorful madras cloth and prints from India provided decorative touches. Everything appeared neat and clean, and I was reminded of the outdoor

shower and washing facilities near the barn, which we had investigated earlier and which had been shown with much pride.

On a different path back to the barn, we passed a tepee and a tent. A good-sized, intensively cultivated garden grows next to the barn; it furnishes the commune with most of the vegetables needed. Two nude girls with beautiful uniform tans were busy weeding. Hal explained that those who want to, go nude whenever they feel like it. As we passed the garden, we noticed Angelina walking along another path trying to join us. Although we slowed our pace so she could catch up with us, she had difficulty doing so, because out of nowhere would appear members who engaged her in intense conversations.

As we strolled on, I noticed several other people hovering in the background waiting. I asked Hal if Angelina functioned as guru or leader and if she were directing the course of the commune. He was emphatic—as were several others to whom I put the same question later—that Angelina is not in charge: "We all decide what we want to do."

Earlier, both Angelina and two of the other older members of the commune had made almost identical remarks: "We have lots of ideas and very little energy." Hal felt the reason was: "There is a lot of grass around and people drop acid." Although he did add, philosophically, "Everybody is into his own thing—each person is free to follow his own needs and interests. No one is forced to do anything. Everyone knows what needs to be done, and finally it gets done."

The commune has meetings once a week "to discuss everything that bothers us." There are seldom any major problems. Hal felt that the commune's only significant problem was the lack of energy. Other neighboring communes have factional disputes, hostile neighbors, suffer from lack of food and shelter, or are unable to pay their taxes. The Good Earth Commune's relations with neighbors are friendly. As Angelina had put it at the coffee shop, "We live a very honest life." She had related a story of how one of the commune members had stolen a pump from a lumber company. This was discussed at one of the weekly meetings, and although the commune has definite strong feelings about lumber companies, the pump was returned.

During the weekly meetings, the group discusses what projects have priority; those members who want to, then volunteer for a particular project. To feed the commune, there is a kitchen list. Two members are chosen daily to provide the food and help prepare it. Farmers bring fruits and vegetables, which they barter for home-baked bread.

Eventually, Angelina caught up with us and led the way to her house. The second largest building on the grounds, it is almost circular in shape; members of the commune built it for her of field stones, hand-hewn timber, and used lumber. The large bedroom in the two-room dwelling has a fireplace and a double bed; placed here and there are many healthy-looking green plants in pots and on stands. An antique desk, a chest of drawers, a candelabra, and antique paintings and prints add richness to the room. The combination kitchen-living room was filled with young people reading, talking quietly, or playing the guitar and singing. Here also is the only phone in the commune. A young blonde girl was talking to her father. I could overhear snatches of her conversation: "No, Dad, I don't need any money. Just send me the plane ticket to Santa Barbara and I'll see you there at the house." Later, Angelina casually mentioned that the seventeen-year-old daughter of a two-star general is at the commune with the consent of her father. (She was not the girl using the telephone.)

The clanging of an old school bell called us to the barn for supper. Everyone formed a huge circle around the dinner table on which candles and kerosene lamps flickered. The room slowly grew quiet as the children scampered to their places in the circle. We all held hands. There was a long moment of silent communion, with heads bowed and eyes closed. The only sound was a dog barking in the distance. With no word spoken, the circle was broken. Conversation resumed, and we served ourselves buffet-style. The vegetarian meal consisted of a pea soup spiced with garden herbs; a combination entree of brown rice with onions, green peppers, and squash; a mixed green salad;

freshly baked bread; and, for dessert, bran muffins with nuts and dried fruit. Following supper, a fire was lighted in the large unfinished room next door and there was chanting, singing, and dancing.

As the evening progressed, Angelina told me that she would like to meet a warm, loving, sensitive type of man, maybe a minister—someone who knows how to counsel and work with young people. She said, "I haven't had a vacation for two years. I want to live in my house and get uninvolved. I want to travel. Older people point their finger at the commune instead of helping. I want some people with money to get involved. Where are the parents of these kids? Many of them come from well-to-do homes. Why am I so alone in this?"

As I prepared to leave, a phone call came from another commune asking for advice. Going out the door, I could hear Angelina's husky voice as she offered sympathy and suggestions. She was obviously very much involved and perhaps not really as alone as she thought.

● This section describing experiences in one commune can probably be supplemented by the experiences of many members of your class. How could you arrange to have these experiences more widely shared with your class? Think creatively and then *do it*.

VALUES

This commune, with Angelina as its prime mover and guiding spirit, is just one of many such living arrangements that have mushroomed around the country. Over the past few years, the commune movement has grown at an unprecedented and explosive rate, and there is every indication that this is only the initial phase of a trend that is bound to have far-reaching implications for the function and structure of our contemporary society. Some traditional institutions are already beginning to feel the impact of this explosive growth.

The commune movement has passed far beyond its contemporary origins in hippie tribalism and can no longer be described as a movement for youth exclusively. There are a rapidly growing number of communes composed of persons in their mid-twenties to upper thirties. A source at the National Institute of Health has estimated that more than 3,000 urban communes are now in operation. This figure closely corresponds to a recent *New York Times* inquiry that uncovered 2,000 communes in thirty-four states.

Certain common viewpoints, almost a *Weltanschauung,* are shared by members of the contemporary commune movement. First, there is a deep respect and reverence for nature and the ecological system. There is a clear awareness that 70 per cent of the population lives on 1 per cent of the land and that this 1 per cent is severely polluted, depressingly ugly, and psychologically overcrowded. Commune members generally believe that a very small but politically influential minority with no respect for the ecological system or the beauty of nature exploits all of the land for its own gain. Surpassing the credo of conservationist organizations, most commune members stress the rehabilitation of *all* lands and the conservation of *all* natural resources for the benefit of *all* the people.

Anti-Establishment sentiment is widespread, as is the conviction that a change in social and institutional structures is needed to halt man's dehumanization and to give him an opportunity to develop his potential. Considerable divergence of opinion exists on how social change is to be brought about, but there is general agreement that the commune movement contributes to change by bringing man closer to himself and to his fellow man through love and understanding.

Communes widely accept the idea that life is meant to be fundamentally joyous and that this is of the essence in doing, and enjoying, what you want to do—"doing your thing." Work in this context becomes a form of joyous self-expression and self-realization. Many commune members believe that existence can be an almost continuous source of joyous affirmation. They usually trace the absence of authentic joy in contemporary society to the confining nature of many of our social institutions, the stifling of spontaneity, and the preponderance of game-playing and of devitalized artificial ways of relating socially.

A strong inner search for the meaning of one's own life, an openness and willingness to communicate and encounter, coupled with a compelling desire for personal growth and development, are hallmarks of the movement. A strong antimaterialistic emphasis prevails; it decries a consumption-oriented society. In many communes, what does not fit into a room becomes commune property. A considerable number of communes aim for the type of self-sufficiency through which they can exist independently of "the system."

There is a strong trend toward ownership of land and houses by communes. Leasing arrangements have not proved satisfactory; in too many instances, landlords have canceled leases when community pressures were exerted. The non-urban communes I have visited are strongly aware of ecological factors, and, because of this, members usually had consulted with local health authorities concerning the construction and placement of sanitary facilities. Among the urban communes, toilet and bath facilities were in most cases short of the demand.

Marked preferences for vegetarianism and for organically grown food are noticeable in the commune movement. Many individual members also experiment with different health diets. Roughly 40 per cent of the communes I visited were vegetarian; 20 per cent served both vegetarian and non-vegetarian meals. The remainder served meat when available—usually two to six times a week. This third group, although not vegetarian by choice, liked their vegetarian meals and expressed very little craving for meat. Whenever possible, communes concentrate on growing and raising their own food. An estimated 60 per cent of the urban communes are now purchasing some or most of their supplies from health-food stores or similar sources.

Not surprisingly, the commune has become the

repository of repressed man's erotic fantasy. I was continuously told that visitors who come not to learn and understand but to peek and ogle invariably ask two questions: "Who sleeps with whom?" And, "Do you have group sex?" There appears to be much fantasizing by outsiders about the sex life in communes.

Although there is considerable sexual permissiveness, I found a high degree of pairing with a strong tendency toward interpersonal commitment in a continuing relationship. Nudism is casual and accepted, as is the development of a healthy sensuality, and natural childbirth, preferably within the commune, is encouraged. Group sex involving the whole commune occurs quite rarely, although there may be sexual experimentation involving two or more couples or combinations.

● This statement needs emphasizing since the "free sex" aspect of a few communes has been exaggerated in the fantasies of many into the belief that "group orgies" are commonplace. Although good comparative data are lacking, it seems likely that group sex is more a phenomenon of middle-aged, middle-class swingers than of the communes where care for the whole person is more important.

The research team of Larry and Joan Constantine has studied multilateral (group) marriage for the past three years. They have written and published more studies in this area than other behavioral scientists, but have found only one commune practicing group marriage. Most likely, there are others. About two dozen independent families are known to be engaged in multilateral marriage, taking as their model Bob Rimmer's novel *Proposition 31*, which presents a case for group marriage. Many others prefer to keep their arrangement totally secret for fear of reprisals. According to an article by the Constantines, entitled "Personal Growth in Multiple Marriages," failure rate is better than one out of two, because "group marriage is a marathon that does not end—it takes

a real commitment to genuine, substantial, and unrelenting personal growth to really make it function and work."

Interest in spiritual development is a dominant theme in most communes. Study of and acquaintance with Eastern and Western mystics and religious philosophies is widespread. Religiosity and denominationalism were seldom encountered. On the other hand, I was struck by the deep commitment to spiritual search of so many members in all the communes I visited. Many members were trying different forms of meditation, and books on Eastern religions and mysticism were prominent on shelves.

PROBLEMS AND PROSPECTS

Among the major problems faced by all communes are those involving authority and structure. Ideally, there is no one telling anyone else what to do; directions are given by those best qualified to do a job. In practice, strong personalities in the communes assume responsibility for what happens, and there is a tendency toward the emergence of mother and father figures. There are, however, a clear awareness of this problem and continuing efforts toward resolution. At present, opposition to any form of structure, including organizational structure, is still so strong that communes have found it almost impossible to cooperate with each other in joint undertakings of a major nature. Interestingly enough, communes with transcendent or spiritual values are the most stable and have the highest survival quotient. It is my conclusion that the weekly or periodic meetings of all commune members, which are often run as encounter groups, have a limited effectiveness in the resolution of interpersonal problems and issues. Although trained encounter leaders may be present as facilitators, their effectiveness is often considerably curtailed due to their own deep involvement in the issues that are the subject of confrontation. One answer to this dilemma might be to bring in a trained facilitator or for communes to exchange facilitators.

It is difficult to determine to what extent narcotics represent a problem for communes precisely because their consumption is as casual, widespread, and accepted as is the downing of alcoholic beverages in the business community. Marijuana and hashish are widely enjoyed, while use of such hard drugs as heroin is seldom encountered, especially in the non-urban communes. In a number of communes where drug use was extensive, I noticed a general air of lassitude and a lack of vitality. I also had the distinct impression that "dropping acid" (LSD) was on the decline; among commune members there seemed to be a general awareness of the danger of "speed," or methedrine. A number of communes are totally opposed to the use of narcotics, especially those with members who were former drug addicts. In most communes the subject of drugs periodically comes up for discussion so that changes in the viewpoint of the commune flow from the experience of the members. Similarly, problems of sexual possessiveness and jealousy appear to be less critical and are also handled by open group discussion. I noticed a tendency toward the maintenance of traditional sex roles, with the women doing the cooking and sewing, the men cutting lumber, etc. Upon questioning this, I repeatedly received the same answer: "Everyone does what they enjoy doing."

Another major problem in most communes is overcrowding and the consequent lack of privacy and alone-time. Rarely does a member enjoy the opportunity of having a room to himself for any length of time. The common practice is to walk off into the woods or fields, but this is an inadequate substitute for real privacy.

Community relations remains a major and critical problem since many communes are "hassled" by authorities or are located amid unfriendly neighbors. As one member described it, the emotional climate in a hassled commune is "full of not so good vibes—you don't know what they will try next, and you keep looking over your shoulder. That takes energy." Today's commune members generally have a clear awareness of the importance of establishing good community relations.

Many of the communes that have got under way this past year or are now being organized are beginning on a sound financial basis. This trend appears to be related to the strong influx of people in their mid-twenties, early or mid-thirties, and beyond. These individuals have financial reserves or savings and are, for the most part, successful professionals and businessmen with families.

One example is the Morehouse Commune, which now consists of thirteen houses in the San Francisco Bay Area, two in Hawaii, and another in Los Angeles; total assets are in excess of \$2-million. Morehouse was founded a year and a half ago by Victor Baranco, a former attorney who is now head of the Institute of Human Abilities, in Oakland, California. There are several categories of membership or involvement in this commune. Members who belong to "the family" give all their assets to the commune, which then "takes care of them," although family members are expected to continue to make a productive contribution within their chosen fields. All income from family members goes into a general fund, but if a family member wishes to withdraw, his assets are returned, including a standard rate of interest for their having been used. Each Morehouse commune in effect makes its own arrangements with members, who may be paid a salary or placed on an allowance system. All communes have a house manager, who assigns tasks or work on a rotating basis. In some Morehouse communes, certain categories of members pay in a fixed monthly sum (as much as \$200) toward expenses.

About a third of the Morehouse couples are married and have children. According to one member, "There is no pressure to be married or unmarried. Nobody cares who lives with whom." Morehouse is a teaching commune built around a philosophy and way of life often described by group members as "responsible hedonism." The commune trains its own teachers and offers a considerable number of courses, such as Basic Sensuality, Advanced Sensuality, and Basic Communication.

The aim and credo of this group are taken from a description of the Institute of Human Abilities published in the commune journal *Aquarius:* "We offer the tools of deliberate living; we offer the techniques of successful communication on any level. We offer the knowledge of the human body and its sensual potential. And we offer love to a world that holds love to be suspect.''

The rapid growth of the Morehouse communes is by no means an isolated example. A minister in Los Angeles founded a social-service and action-type commune that within a year grew to seven houses. Other instances can be cited. An unprecedented number of people want to join communes. In all but a few instances I was asked to conceal the name and location of the commune to make identification impossible. ''We don't know what to do with all the people who come knocking on our door now,'' I was told repeatedly. In every commune, I heard of people who had recently left either to start a new commune or to join in the founding of one.

There is considerable mobility in communes, which is symptomatic of an endemic wanderlust and search. If people have to leave for any reason, once they have been exposed to communal living, they tend to return. They like the deep involvement with others in a climate of freedom, openness, and commitment. This feeling of belonging has been described as both ''a new tribalism'' and ''a new sense of brotherhood.'' One young woman with whom I spoke had this to say about her commune experience: ''When a white man walks into a room full of other whites, he doesn't feel he is among brothers like the black man does. In the communes, we are now beginning to feel that man has many brothers. . . . There is a new sense of honesty. You can say things to each other and share things like you never could in the family. I never had so much love in my whole life—not even in my own family.'' She also indicated, however, that commune living is highly intense and possibly not for everyone: ''In the commune, there is nothing you can hide. Some people can't take it. They get sick or they leave.''

Alvin Toffler in his recent book *Future Shock* notes that ''most of today's 'intentional communities' reveal a powerful preference for the past, . . . but society as a whole would be better served by utopian experiments based on super-

rather than pre-industrial forms. . . . In short, we can use utopianism as a tool rather than as an escape, if we base our experiments on the technology and society of tomorrow rather than that of the past.''

Although Toffler's observation is relevant, we must recognize that the commune movement, as with most other movements, is passing through certain developmental stages. At this stage, there is little readiness for communes to define themselves as laboratories for the exploration of alternative models that might benefit the society of the future. Disenchantment with and opposition to science and technology are other impediments to the adoption of the laboratory concept. With today's communes, faith in the future of mankind appears to be at too low an ebb to produce any sustained interest in what Toffler calls ''scientific future-sensing and the techniques of scientific futurism.''

Although David Cooper, a colleague and disciple of British psychiatrist Ronald Laing, has sounded a death knell in his new book *The Death of the Family*, I believe we are far from writing the epitaph. The traditional nuclear family will continue, although its form, to some extent, may change; in the years to come, possibly as high as 20 per cent of the population will explore alternative models of social living.

It would be a mistake to characterize the commune movement as a collection of dropouts who are content to exist like lilies in the field. A considerable number of successful people from all walks of life are now involved; they have merely shifted their sphere of interest and the nature of their creative contribution. We are dealing with a massive awakening of the awareness that life holds multiple options other than going from school to job to retirement. The commune movement has opened a new and wide range of alternative life-styles and offers another frontier to those who have the courage for adventure. It is the test tube for the growth of a new type of social relatedness, for the development of an organization having a structure that appears, disappears, and reappears as it chooses and as it is needed. Communes may well serve as a laboratory for the study of the processes involved in the regeneration of our social institutions. They have become the symbol of man's new freedom to explore alternative life-styles and to develop deep and fulfilling human relationships through the rebirth and extension of our capacity for familial togetherness.

USEFUL RESOURCES

BLANCHARD, W. H. Ecstasy without agony is baloney. *Psychology Today*, January 1970.

DIAMOND, S. *What the trees said: Life on a new age farm*. New York: Delacorte Press, 1971.

EGAN, G. *Encounter-group processes for interpersonal growth*. Belmont, Calif.: Brooks/Cole, 1970.

FAIRFIELD, R. *Communes U.S.A.: A personal tour*. Baltimore: Penguin Books, 1972.

One of the best descriptive volumes on American communes from a person who has had extensive experience with communards throughout the world; his tell-it-like-it-is, no-nonsense approach is a most valuable corrective for this all too easily romanticized movement. *His excellent annotated bibliography will help with your term papers*.

JONGEWARD, P., & JAMES, M. *Winning with people*. Reading, Mass.: Addison-Wesley Publishing, 1973.

"People are interested in learning new ideas fast. Workbooks can accelerate this process. This book is, in part, an adaptation from our book *Born to Win: Transactional Analysis With Gestalt Experiments*. It is designed as a group-oriented training tool for rapid learning of transactional analysis principles . . .

Originally TA was developed as a method of psychotherapy to be used in group treatment. The group serves as a setting in which people can become more aware of themselves, the structure of their individual personality; how they transact with others, the games they play, and the scripts they act out. Such awareness enables persons to see themselves more clearly so that they can change what they want to change and strengthen what they want to strengthen. . . . Transactional analysis is a rational approach to understanding human behavior and is based on the assumption that any individual can learn to trust himself, think for himself, make his own decisions, and express his feelings. Its principles can be applied on the job, in the home, in the classroom, in the neighborhood—wherever people deal with people."

KANTER, R. M. Communes. *Psychology Today*, July 1970.

KINCADE, K. *A Walden two experiment: The first five years of Twin Oaks community*. New York: William Morrow, 1973.

Foreword by B. F. Skinner. In 1967 Kat Kincade was one of eight people to found Twin Oaks community. This is her account of their efforts to create a viable way of life based on the behaviorist theories in Skinner's utopian novel, *Walden Two*. "We are all engaged in the designing of cultural practices. Twin Oaks is simply the world in miniature. The problems it faces and the solutions it tries are those of a world community." B. F. Skinner.

McCRARY, J. L. *Human sexuality: 2nd edition*. New York: Van Nostrand Company, 1973.

"Since the imposing success of the first edition (over 100,000 copies sold since 1967) the attitudes and behavior of society have changed significantly, and this second edition explores the mercurial shifts in the psychological and sociological climate of recent years. It is intended to meet the challenge of today's youth to their elders, that they have neither been instructed in nor given access to the facts about human sexuality and sexual behavior. Reflecting the authors' gentleness, humor and common-sense, it is a well-rounded well-documented, illuminating discussion of the many facets that relate to being both human and sexual." Psychology Today Book Club.

MUMFORD, L. *The story of utopias*. New York: Viking Press, 1962.

A classic account of the history of utopias.

MUNGO, R. *Famous long ago*. New York: E. P. Dutton, 1971.

"Here's a lesson I honestly believe I learned in my lifetime: ideals cannot be institutionalized. You cannot put your ideals into practise, so to speak, in any way more 'ambitious' than through your own private life."

MUNGO, R. *Total loss farm*. New York: Dutton, 1971.

O'NEILL, N., & O'NEILL, G. *Open marriage: A new life style for couples*. New York: M. Evans, 1972.

"Open marriage is a sane and happy antidote to our increasing disillusionment with the institution of marriage, offering a sense of growth to any couple seeking a better life together." — Psychology Today Book Club.

REISS, I. L. How and why Americans' sex standards are changing. *Trans-Action*, March 1968.

ROGERS, C. R. The group comes of age. *Psychology Today*, December 1969.

ROGERS, C. R. *Becoming partners: Marriage and its alternatives*. New York: Delacorte Press, 1972.

"Is marriage, as an institution in our time and culture, a disastrous failure? Rogers cites 50 percent divorce rates as undeniable evidence of the need to reconsider traditional marital modes. He used intimate interviews with married couples as his data to provide a view from within of the complexities of modern marriages." Psychology Today Book Club.

SHOSTRUM, E. L. Group therapy: Let the buyer beware. *Psychology Today*, May 1972.

SLATER, P. E. *The pursuit of loneliness: American culture at the breaking point*. Boston: Beacon Press, 1970.

"Slater is a vibrant and thoughtful man deeply concerned with the quality of life as it is and as it could be. He wrote this book in order to examine— for himself and for his readers—the underlying assumptions and themes which shape our culture. '*The Pursuit of Loneliness* . . . is a brilliant, sweeping, and 'relevant' critique of modern America. . . .'' Kenneth Keniston, The New York Times Book Review. ''In Slater's view, our major problem is individualism, which he says drives us to compete frantically for material goods, to evade human confrontations and to pretend a false self-reliance. We are trapped by the 'Toilet Assumption'—flush the problems and they'll go away—and we never see our desperation.'' Robert Gross, Newsweek. Psychology Today Book Club.

SALISBURG, W. W., & SALISBURG, F. Youth and the search for intimacy. In L. A Kirkendall & R. N. Whitehurst (Eds.), *The new sexual revolution*. New York: Donald W. Brown, 1971.

YABLONSKY, L. *The hippie trip*. New York: Pegasus, 1968.

CHAPTER 9
THE SEARCH FOR ALTERNATIVE REALITIES

PROVOCATIONS

"Our normal waking consciousness, rational consciousness as we call it, is but one special type of consciousness, whilst all about it, parted from it by the filmiest of screens, there lie potential forms of consciousness entirely different."

William James

The reason why the "drug problem" is such a huge problem is that it calls into question many of the basic features of our society and many of the assumptions which are most firmly embedded in our heads.

Keith Melville

Meditation is the way the soul is made; too many people are lacking in building materials.

Anonymous

Christ is a natural high – so Peak with a Jesus freak.

Anonymous

George Washington cultivated cannabis at his Mount Vernon plantation.

LeDain Commission

● Far out, George

"I have a dream"

Martin Luther King
Jesus Christ
Henry Ford
Adolf Hitler
Don Juan

"Tell me about it"

Sigmund Freud

WHAT DO YOU THINK?

47 THE SEARCH FOR ALTERNATIVE REALITIES

JAMES A. DYAL

What is reality? Reality is what we (mankind or some subgroup of mankind) say that it is at any given point in time. In one sense there are as many different realities as there are human conscious-nesses, since each person defines for himself the basic nature of reality. As Malcolm observed, "What is reality? The definition offered by a Zen monk might differ strikingly from that of-fered by an accountant in Halifax. Who is right? The answer is that both men are right, but you will reflect, there will be no mutual aware-ness of the conflict between them."[1] How-ever, it is only to the extent that both the monk and the accountant are able to find other people who have similar versions of reality that they will continue to be judged by their respective societies as "normal" rather than "deviate." Thus we see that we must immediately distin-guish between *personal reality* and *social re-ality*. Personal reality is that version which is con-structed by each individual on the basis of his ex-perience. Social reality is that version which is common among the various constructions—what we agree upon. There are, of course, many specific subtypes of socially defined realities —depending on the "object" of the experience. Thus we have "physical reality," "political real-ity," "biological reality," "cultural reality," "psychological reality," etc., etc. All these ver-sions of reality depend upon agreement among the "realizers" regarding what will be accepted as real and what beliefs will be regarded as true.

It is perhaps obvious that our social institutions and physical environments tend to emphasize and reinforce (in the literal, technical sense) those as-pects of personal experiences which are held in common. As a consequence personal reality tends to be brought more and more into congruence with the socially defined realities. For several thousand years Western culture and Eastern culture have been evolving conceptions of reality which are

significantly different from each other on several points. These differences can be made more under-standable by relating them to the basic functions and capacities of *homo sapiens,* through which all realities are created. The chapter headings in your psychology text refer to these basic functions: sen-sation, attention, perception, motivation, emotion, cognition, learning, action. Information about fea-tures of the external world (or internal processes) is transmitted via nerve impulses to the brain, where it is somehow integrated and stored to yield "per-cepts," "concepts," and "memories." "Motiva-tion" and "emotion" then somehow provide the drive into "action." Under the influence of the early Greek philosophers, Western culture has em-phasized some of these functions as reliable guides to reality and others as less reliable. Aristotle's definition of man as "the rational animal" cap-tures the mind-set of Western civilization. We have come to place a high value on our reasoning (cognitive) processes with an attendant devaluation of our sensing, perceiving, emoting selves. Our reasoning abilities have been used to create new realities based on our desire to wrest control of our lives from the caprice of the natural world. Our success in "dominating nature" and creating a man-made world is manifest. As a result we con-tinue to define reality in terms of our own external creations, and this reality continues to define who we are. Western man has created the world and himself in his own image. His reality is defined by the *products of his action* with little or no apprecia-tion of nonrational *processes of his experience.*

COMMENT: PRODUCT VERSUS PROCESS

I view Fromm's concept of marketing orienta-tion as a sub-species of a more general description of Western culture which is in great contrast with Eastern culture; namely, our tendency to be *product*-oriented rather than *process*-oriented. We exalt the end of our efforts and value little the

[1] Andrew L. Malcolm, *The case against the drugged mind.* Toronto: Clarke, Irwin, 1973.

process whereby we attain the goals—and the goals themselves are relatively static, being enmeshed so completely in the definition of a good man as an economically successful man who is able to acquire things.

This product orientation pervades every facet of our culture; it manifests itself in education as an emphasis on the practical; for example, the most popular stereotype of the scientist really describes the technician or inventor who is the applier of science. Even among our liberal arts undergraduates it is subtly represented in the disparagement of pure research which has no immediately obvious consequences. It is my feeling that one of the major causes of a lack of involvement of many liberal arts majors in their studies is an unrecognized guilt feeling about not doing something that has an obvious pay-off in the market place, an attitude which is all too often reinforced by parents who are also victims of the marketing orientation. Knowing for the sake of knowing—the richness, excitation, frustration, exaltation of the knowing process is sacrificed to the flatness of the educational product—a grade and a degree. The Ameri-

can theme is knowing for the sake of doing, and doing for the sake of acquiring, and acquiring because our possessions provide tangible testimony to others and especially to ourselves of our success in the market place—they reassure us that we are good people.

JAMES A. DYAL

In the East the road to salvation (success) has taken a different turn. The emphasis is upon the emotive/sensing/perceiving functions. Instead of an active, cognitive manipulation, the Eastern orientation is more passive, more receptive. The emphasis is on self-control rather than control of the environment. It is not surprising that this alternative approach has had considerable appeal for the members of the counterculture (see Selection by Melville).

● Why would this be? Try to make connections to Miller (Selection 44) and to Bailey (Selection 45). Write your thoughts in the space below.

●

The subculture which we call the counterculture is composed of people who are deviates by the standards of the "normal" Western culture. As noted by Melville in Selection 48, moving from the Western consumer culture to the counterculture is

rather like stepping from one civilization into another and finding that reality has been drastically redefined. . . . In the communes, and in the other provinces where the counter culture's version of reality is taken seriously, science and rationality give way to the nonrational, the supernatural, the unplumbed depths of the visionary experience, and an ambitious search for ecstatic experience. The most cherished insights of this cognitive minority—such as the mystic insistence on the unity of the whole universe—as well as its less exalted insights are inaccessible to the normal everyday consciousness.[2]

The contemporary search for alternative realities is taking place through attempts to experience and understand altered states of consciousness (ASC). This "seeking" is done both through personal experience and through scientific observation of the public manifestations of the experiences. Naturally, the experiential approach is emphasized by the counterculture, while psychologists have pursued the scientific analysis. Research on ASC seems to offer the possibility of forming a bridge between Eastern *experiential* knowledge and Western *experimental* knowledge. Charles Tart, who has edited one of the major books on ASC, contends:

To many people who are not involved in scientific research, valid knowledge about ASCs is to be obtained by experiencing them; they are somehow beyond the reach of scientific research. The most important obligation of any science is that its descriptive and theoretical language embrace *all* the phenomena of its subject matter; the data from ASCs cannot be ignored if we are to develop a comprehensive psychology. Psychology has often failed to meet this obligation because of premature conceptualizations, that is, investing in simplified and elegant theoretical systems that exclude the data of ASCs,

but this has been more a matter of the cultural climate than any inherent shortcoming of scientific method. Man is a theorizing and conceptualizing animal and does not accept experience in and of itself; he always develops beliefs and theories about his experience. The difficulty with studying ASCs by simply experiencing them is that we run as much risk of systematizing our delusions as of discovering "truth." When we complement personal experience with scientific method the risk of simply systematizing our delusions is considerably reduced.[3]

Broadly speaking, ASCs are achieved either through drugs or through natural experiences. The former may range from soft drugs such as marijuana, through psychedelics such as LSD, to hard addictives such as heroin. The nondrug ASCs are quite varied, ranging from dreams to hypnotic trances, from meditation to special peak experiences and satori, and more recently special states achieved by control of brain wave patterns through bio-feedback (see Selection 15 by Collier).

We have reproduced four articles in this section. Selection 48 by Melville contends that the abuse of psychedelics could be greatly reduced by making their use into a sacrament which helps the user make connections to mysteries within himself and in the universe. He quotes Einstein as saying, "The most beautiful thing we can experience is the mysterious . . . to know what is impenetrable to us really exists."

Andrew Weil (Selection 49) is a renowned medical researcher who works on the psychological and physiological effects of soft drugs. Like Melville, he sees that a rational approach to drug use can be based on an understanding of how more primitive Indian tribes are able to integrate drug use into their overall everyday living.

● Do you think that most dope users would be able to use the drugs for "consciousness raising" or are they simply interested in the immediacy of the "quick and reliable high"? Write your thoughts in the following space.

---

[2]Keith Melville, *Communes in the counterculture.* New York: William Morrow, 1972.

[3]Charles Tart, *Altered states of consciousness.* New York: Wiley, 1969.

•

The LeDain Commission on the Non-Medical Use of Drugs is the most recent of many similar commissions which have been appointed by various countries to review the evidence regarding the physiological, psychological, and social effects of drug use and to make recommendations regarding the legal regulation of the drugs. Its report on cannabis is a complete and scholarly survey which should be read in its entirety by anyone who presumes to be knowledgeable on the "smoking of dope." We have reproduced portions of this concluding statement and their recommendations in Selection 50.

• Before you read that article, you might find it interesting to see how much you know about the effects of cannabis; then you can check your answers to these questions against the commission's report. Let us put it in the form of statements and you can decide if they are true or false.

___**1.** It has been proven in certain kinds of individuals and at certain levels of use, cannabis can cause serious mental problems.
___**2.** On the whole the physical and mental effects of cannabis use among North Americans are much less serious than those which may result from excessive use of alcohol.
___**3.** Regular use of cannabis by adolescents has a harmful effect on the maturing process.
___**4.** Chronic and excessive use of cannabis has been shown to result in chromosome breakage and damage to the human fetus.
___**5.** There is reason to believe that the use of cannabis increases the hazards of driving.
___**6.** There is fairly conclusive evidence that the chronic heavy use of cannabis reduces the user's motivation for achievement.
___**7.** The use of cannabis increases the probability of using LSD.
___**8.** Cannabis leads to the use of heroin.
___**9.** Simple possession of cannabis should not be a criminal offense.

——**10.** No legal restrictions should be imposed on the use and distribution of cannabis.

———————————————————

Andrew Weil (Selection 50) urges us to try to create a society in which *non-drug-*altered states of consciousness are encouraged. Various forms of meditation are increasingly popular avenues toward such peaks. We typically associate meditation with Eastern religions, but many Christian religious practices seem to fall within the meditation tradition. For example, silent prayer as it is typically practiced by Quaker congregations seems to be a kind of contentless meditation in which the emphasis is on listening and "let be." But for the most part

> The traditions of prayer and meditation within Christianity have consisted of a kind of blabbing at God or some apart-from-nature being about which one has all sorts of preconceived ideas. The Western interest in meditation tends to be directed toward Eastern forms of practise where there is a radical commitment to experiencing what one experiences—even God. Oriental rejection of verbal and conceptual substitutes for experience seems to appeal to our own growing investment in living experience.[4]

In Selection 51, Maupin discusses the general principles of meditation and provides some specific exercises which you might like to try to get the feel of the process. Let yourself go, give it a try, but keep in mind that these exercises provide only a superficial beginning.

As we noted earlier, psychologists are again interested in understanding states of consciousness in a more scientific way. Illustrative examples of some of the ways that a scientific approach can be brought to the phenomena of altered states of consciousness are presented in Selection 52 by Paul H. Levine, a theoretical physicist.

Perhaps we can best conclude our introduction to alternative realities by noting that our search has focused on ASC as the major approach to redefining reality. However, we should not forget that there are other more institutionalized ways of reshaping our world view and our experience—that is, redefining reality. Education is one of the most powerful of these. As Paulo Freire has said, education is the process of becoming critically aware of one's reality. It possesses the potential for either expanding your consciousness or limiting your world view to that which is conventional. Maybe the educators of the future (some of you who are now reading this book) will have a greater appreciation for Leonard's view that education, at its best, is ecstatic. We thus close the circle back to excellence, education, and ecstasy with the view that "the skillful pursuit of ecstasy will make the pursuit of excellence not for the few, but for the many, what it has never been—successful. And yet, make no mistake about it, excellence, as we speak of it today, will be only a by-product of a greater unity, a deeper delight."[5]

We hope that this book has provided some experiences which will help you to turn on to yourself in the process of seeking new realities through creating your own education.

———————————————————

[4]Edward W. Maupin, On Meditation. In Charles Tart (Ed.), *Altered states of consciousness.* New York, Toronto: Wiley, 1969.

[5]George B. Leonard, *Education and ecstasy.* New York: Dell Publishing, 1968.

48 THE SEARCH FOR ALTERNATIVE REALITIES*

KEITH MELVILLE

> Our civilization represses not only the instincts, not only sexuality, but any form of transcendence. Among one-dimensional men, it is not surprising that someone with an insistent experience of other dimensions, that he cannot entirely deny or forget, will run the risk either of being destroyed by the others, or of betraying what he knows. . . . I would wish to emphasize that our "normal," "adjusted" state is too often the abdication of ecstasy, the betrayal of our true potentialities, that many of us are only too successful in acquiring a false self to adapt to false realities.
>
> *R. D. Laing*

We had been sitting around a table after dinner in the lodge at one of the Oregon communes, discussing what it was that had changed so quickly. After an hour or so, one of the younger girls offered an explanation that everyone seemed to agree with: "Just look at how badly things have been fucked up with this rationality trip. Everyone was tricked into thinking that that was the whole game. But that's just not where it's *at*. What makes all of us in this new generation so different is our God thirst. We've been exposed to entirely new vibes, and we're living in an entirely different kind of reality."

They are indeed. Anyone who lives on the border between "straight" society and the counter culture or, worse yet, anyone who attempts to move between them is likely to get a bad case of the cognitive bends. It is rather like stepping from one civilization into another and finding that reality has been drastically redefined. Everything that is taken most seriously in one world is at best laughable in the other.

The ratified version of reality in the mainstream culture is ruthlessly one-dimensional. Western man has specialized in one form of consciousness, a rational, scientific way of looking at the world. For some time now we have been engaged in a form of scientific imperialism that not only ignores the nonintellective capacities of man but denies them entirely. Science has an "explanation" for any sort of ecstatic experience, and not a very flattering one at that.

In the communes, and in the other provinces where the counter culture's version of reality is taken seriously, science and rationality give way to the nonrational, the supernatural, the unplumbed depths of the visionary experience, and an ambitious search for ecstatic experience. The most cherished insights of this cognitive minority—such as the mystic insistence on the unity of the whole universe—as well as its less exalted insights are inaccessible to the normal everyday consciousness.

What started several years ago with the growing popularity of Zen is now an outrageous assortment consisting of the most venerable religious traditions side by side with dozens of cults and crazes. The list now includes Scientology, Abilitism, light radiation, Sufism, psychocybernetics, astral projection, the 3H (Happy, Healthy, Holy) Organization founded by Yogi Bhajan, transcendental meditation, Kundalini yoga, and the use of alphawave headsets. And that's only the *beginning* of the list. Witchcraft, sorcery, and the occult abound. Many of the communes make major decisions by consulting the *I Ching*. The life of more than one of the groups is punctuated by rumors of UFO's. One young man, who should be an authority on such things, informed me that he was a messenger from another planet. Whatever else such a list suggests, it is evidence of what Theodore Roszak called "the search for alternative realities." Only a small minority of the communes consist of members of a single religious persuasion such as the Children of God, where the group's

*Abridged from Keith Melville, *Communes in the counter culture*. New York: William Morrow, 1972. Reprinted by permission of the publisher.

purpose is to live the faith. But this search for alternative realities—whether it takes the form of an eclectic religiosity, the belief in magic and the occult, the frequent use of psychedelics, or simply meditation exercises—is an almost universal characteristic both in the communes and in the counter culture in general.

Who would have guessed five years ago that there would be a religious explosion, especially among the middle-class young? Who would have predicted that refugees from affluent families would be scouring the countryside for fresh religious traditions, finally to adopt those of the American Indian? And who would have anticipated that rebellious teenagers would be carrying hip-pocket Bibles, chastizing their parents with Scriptural quotations, and causing the ultimate embarrassment of using Christian literature to condemn the churches for diluting the faith?

Despite the fact that about four out of ten Americans, and about half of the nation's college population, still goes to church every weekend, surveys taken during the last decade indicate that most people believe that religion has been losing its influence on American life. In many quarters the demise of the supernatural has been a foregone conclusion for some time now. Secularization appeared to be an almost inevitable and irreversible trend in modern civilization. It was assumed that the gods had been cast out, that in a society no longer dominated by religious symbols and institutions, God was in fact something of an anachronism. Secularization denotes the declining influence of the church, as in our modern insistence on the separation of church and state. But more importantly, secularization refers to something that goes on in our heads: We no longer understand the meaning of everyday life in terms of symbols and concepts laden with religious significance. The most popular theological writings of the mid-sixties announced the "death of God." Almost every theologian had a different interpretation of its meaning, but most of those who proclaimed the death of God agreed that attention should be shifted from a transcendent, supernatural God "out there" to the secular life in human society.

Harvey Cox declared that "the era of metaphysics is dead," and that "politics replaces metaphysics as the language of theology."

Alan Watts once commented that the socially approved version of reality is "more or less the world as perceived on a bleak Monday morning," deprived of awe, ecstasy, or fantasy. What has happened in the church, the institutional agent that has traditionally been responsible for alternative realities, is that dreary Sunday-morning services increasingly reflect the bleak reality of Monday morning. Throughout history, as Peter Berger has aptly put it, religion has been "in the ecstasy business almost by definition." The essence of any religious system is its contention that there is another realm than that of everyday experience, a realm of ultimate significance for man. The primary function of religious systems has been to explain the complex ways in which that other world is related to this one. But in this secular era the churches provide no alternative reality. This is one of the reasons why the latter-day believers in the counter culture reject organized religion, especially Protestantism: It accepts the same one-dimensional version of man that is assumed by the society in general. It is very natural in a society so firmly committed to the cognitive universe of science that the churches should have withdrawn from the "ecstasy business." But by doing so they abdicate their responsibility for providing an alternative way of looking at the world and an alternative form of consciousness, and provide instead just a Sunday supplement to everyday reality.

A number of people with firmly established credentials in the normal mode of consciousness have insisted that there are realms that positivism leaves completely untouched. Writing of his experience with mescaline, Aldous Huxley spoke in *The Doors of Perception* of "the urge to transcend self-conscious selfhood as a principal appetite of the soul," and the need "to be shaken out of the ruts of ordinary perception, to be shown for a few timeless hours the outer and the inner world, not as they appear to an animal obsessed with survival or to a human being obsessed with words and notions, but as they are apprehended, directly and unconditionally by Mind at Large.'' Huxley suggested that the human brain and nervous system act as a ''reducing valve,'' that we have traded in Mind at Large, which understands the unity of the universe, for a selective perception, an awareness reduced to that kind of practical consciousness that makes biological survival possible. ''Most people, most of the time, know only what comes through the reducing valve and is consecrated as genuinely real by the local language. Certain persons, however, seem to be born with a kind of by-pass that circumvents the reducing valve. In others, temporary by-passes may be acquired either spontaneously, or as the results of deliberate 'spiritual exercises,' or through hypnosis, or by means of drugs.'' By these means, some people experience a universe ''different from the carefully selected utilitarian material which our narrowed, individual minds regard as a complete, or at least sufficient picture of reality.''

Fifty years earlier, in what is probably the most frequently quoted passage from *The Varieties of Religious Experience,* William James defended the mystic states of consciousness which even then were in disrepute:

> . . . our normal waking consciousness, rational consciousness as we call it, is but one special type of consciousness, whilst all about it, parted from it by the filmiest of screens, there lie potential forms of consciousness entirely different. We may go through life without suspecting their existence; but apply the requisite stimulus, and at a touch they are there in their completeness. . . . No account of the universe can be final which leaves these other forms of consciousness quite disregarded. How to regard them is the question—for they are so discontinuous with ordinary consciousness. Yet they may determine attitudes though they cannot furnish formulas, and open a region though they fail to give a map. At any rate, they forbid a premature closing of our accounts with reality. Looking back on my own experiences, they all converge toward a kind of insight to which I cannot help ascribing some kind of metaphysical significance.

These other forms of consciousness may indeed have metaphysical significance, but the cast of religious geniuses which James assembles in this volume—those people who specialize in altered states of consciousness—would hardly be welcome in this society. It has always been much easier to live with mystics in history books, where they are presented as the founders of religious systems, than to live with them as contemporaries. There is an almost inevitable clash between those who take other realities seriously and the guardians of the everyday reality. In a one-dimensional society, the only recognized vocabulary for talking about these excursions into other forms of consciousness is that of psychiatry. From the point of view of psychiatry, a good deal of what goes on in the communes where religion is taken quite seriously would be labeled as madness.

The problem is clear enough. The clash between the counter culture and the mainstream culture is in one of its aspects the clash between two fundamentally different ways of looking at the world. The counter culture recognizes the reality of the unseen and the authority of experiences for which there is no ''evidence'' acceptable to science. As James put it, the problem with mystic states is that they are ''so discontinuous with ordinary consciousness.'' It is easy enough to hope for some kind of synthesis of these two perspectives, a widening of our visions to allow *both* kinds of experience. Yet the two perspectives are so radically incompatible that I doubt whether any such mutual recognition will soon take place. There are very effective means of enforcing the ratified one-dimensional version of reality, and none so harsh as the label of madness.

Socrates commented in the *Phaedrus* that our greatest blessings come to us through madness, provided that the madness comes from God. The significance of the point, that going mad may be the ultimate form of illumination, hasn't been lost on the counter culture. *Howl,* one of its founding documents, was dedicated to a mental patient.

Timothy Leary wasn't advocating madness when he said that ''it becomes necessary for us to go out of our minds in order to use our heads.'' He was, rather, in his favorite role as the Pied Piper of the psychedelic movement, expressing the belief that it is through ecstatic experience rather than the use of intellect that we most fully use our heads. The agent that Leary has so conspicuously advocated for those trips is, of course, LSD. Any attempt to account for the counter culture's fascination with alternative realities has to begin with the psychedelics, which were largely responsible for opening up new inner vistas for so many young people. So much of what has been said about the psychedelics—both pro and con—has been either hysterical, ill-informed, or dangerously dogmatic that I hesitate even to enter the discussion. There is almost nothing that can be said about them without elaborate qualifications. And yet, finally, there is no way of accounting for many of the characteristics of the counter culture without admitting their importance. Next to the "drug problem," sex looks like a melodramatic exaggeration we invented way back when to keep life interesting during some pretty routine times. It is, to a considerable extent, the psychedelics and the changes which they triggered that make this generation different from the preceding ones and color every part of this new variety of radicalism.

Most of the discussions about psychedelics, like the innumerable conferences on the subject, are fractured between those who have already had the experience (and speak ex cathedra from the authority of their own vision) and those who haven't and won't (but still feel qualified to pass judgment on it). On the one hand, the true believers. On the other, the objective observers.

To the true believers, the psychedelic experience gains its authority from the fact that it is more real than ordinary reality:

> My first psychedelic experience was triggered by 400 milligrams of mescalin sulfate. It did induce a flight, but instead of fleeing from reality, I flew more deeply into it. I had never before seen, touched, heard, smelled, and felt so profound a personal unity and involvement with the concrete material world. . . . My exponentially heightened awareness saw through the static, one-dimensional, ego-constructed false front which is the consciousness-constructed reality of the everyday world. This was no evasive flight from, but a deep probe into reality.

That the psychedelic-induced vision takes on authority as an insight into what reality *really* is, and that, as a consequence, the person's future actions will be shaped by this experience—these are signals that there is a social as well as a psychological and a medical issue at stake here.

To the objective observer, such affirmations of a reality more real than everyday reality are a clear sign of some sort of temporary psychotic state. In response to the true believers' contention that these visions have some sort of religious significance, the skeptics answer that those who take drugs grasp the vocabulary of religion as a convenient metaphor for this state of derangement. After all, what does it mean to insist that you "understand everything," that "you feel a profound sense of personal unity with the concrete material world"? And anyway, the skeptics ask, how could anything genuinely spiritual come out of a tab of mescaline or a sugar cube soaked with LSD? What does religion mean if we can gain entrance into the mystic beyond without doing our spiritual exercises and paying our dues? And then the critics haul out the medical arguments: . . .

Here we enter a swamp of controversy that I have neither the space nor the medical knowledge to get us out of. The best that I can do is to offer a few impressionistic comments and to suggest what sort of problem I think the "drug problem" really is.

Even if there is no evidence that the psychedelics are addictive, it is clear that for some people they do lead to destructive forms of habituation. The grim fact of adolescent trippers taking a tab a day in order to keep reality at a distance should be enough to convince people that the better part of responsibility in the matter is not to legalize all forms of psychedelics and make them as readily available as bubble gum and candy bars. But neither is it to ban their use entirely, to make them all illegal. The selective use of psychedelics as a medicine or a religious sacrament, rather than a form of entertainment, makes very good sense. Alan Watts has pointed out that we are very willing to use a strong medicine in order to cure a serious disease, even when we're not quite sure what the side effects of that medicine may be. Our narrowed sense of reality may be such a serious disease. We don't condemn the use of strong medicine because it may be harmful if taken as a steady diet; it seems to me that the same attitude would be appropriate with regard to the psychedelics. Of course this leads to the thorny question of access: Who's going to be responsible for dispensing the psychedelics? Who's going to be eligible to use them, and for what purposes? A psychedelic pharmacy obviously poses much knottier problems than the ordinary street-corner variety.

Many of these problems are solved by regarding psychedelics as a sacrament, as the peyote religion does, and limiting their use to religious ceremonies. A sacrament is the outward sign of an inward grace, an agent that cleanses and brings new life. The psychedelics are well suited to the role. Judging from some of the recent evidence, they may have played a much larger role in the history of world religion than many of us suspected, and certainly a more important role than any of the established churches would be willing to admit. The care with which peyote is used in the ritual of the Native American Church (which is the official name of the peyote religion) is a way of recognizing and respecting its power. And there is no better form of group therapy to prevent "bad trips" than to be surrounded by a small congregation of fellow believers in an atmosphere of trust and love.

It is true that all the medical facts about the various psychedelic agents aren't yet in. But neither are all the facts in about most of what we consume, most conspicuously many of the medically approved drugs. The fact that many more people express concern about the medical effects of the psychedelics than about the medically approved drugs seems to me a suspicious case of selective attention, an indication of what really bothers most people about the psychedelics. What would happen if a biochemist devised a way to make all the psychedelics medically harmless? What would happen if it were discovered that they already were? It would certainly not be a solution to the "drug problem." The problem has more to

do with the social implications of drug use than with their medical effects. To clinch what is fundamentally a moral argument with a medical warning is to sidestep the issue. Both cigarettes and alcohol are bad for us, but they pose no threat to our civilization. But the act of drug taking is now one of the most popular ways of seceding from this civilization, opting out of the ordinary universe of assumptions, obligations, and responsibilities.

. . . The reason why the "drug problem" is such a huge problem is that it calls into question many of the basic features of our society and many of the assumptions which are most firmly embedded in our heads.

In this program of mining the most valuable ideas that are represented in the youth communes, my emphasis . . . has been on the positive and necessary task of enlarging our conception of reality. Obviously there is another aspect—a negative and escapist one—to this search for alternative realities. The attraction to the occult and the irrational often signals the abandonment of the critical faculties, an attack on reason which is a dangerous development in the youth culture. For many of those who followed Leary on his ecstatic trip, psychedelics offer nothing more than a flight from responsibility and an excuse for total withdrawal.

Many of the discussions of the counter culture emphasize its rejection of rationality without noticing the other, more positive aspects of this search for alternative realities. Nearly every society has some sort of moratorium for young people, a period during which its members are allowed to try out different roles before coming of age and committing themselves to some particular style of adulthood. In Erik Erikson's words, the moratorium is "a time for horse stealing and vision-quests, a time for Wanderschaft or work 'out West' or 'down under,' a time for 'lost youth' or academic youth, a time for self-sacrifice or for pranks—and today, often a time for patienthood or delinquency." Each new generation must ask the why and what for questions and find answers that are meaningful in its own ear. In historical eras such as this one, when the "solutions" of the parents' generation are largely irrelevant to the experience of the younger generation, the process of coming to an identity is almost inevitably difficult. The potential of youth in this process of psychosocial evolution, as Erikson put it, is to act as "renewers of its ethical strength, as rebels bent on the destruction of the outlived." And also as innovators testing new cultural alternatives. The communes are something more than a place for a youthful moratorium (although it remains to be seen whether they will become real communities, the units of an alternative society), but much of what goes on in them is understandable in these terms. Because of the prevailing attitudes in most of the groups as well as their physical isolation, they provide a miniature society which is almost uniquely insulated against the mainstream society, thereby providing a nearly ideal setting for a moratorium.

In exploring these alternative forms of consciousness the young may be recovering a latent possibility for the rest of the society. "There comes a time—I believe we are in such a time—" said Norman O. Brown, "when civilization has to be renewed by the discovery of new mysteries." This sense of awe and respect for a universe much vaster than that described by science has been expressed by people of much more wisdom and experience than the youthful rebels. This is how Albert Einstein spoke of it:

> The most beautiful thing we can experience is the mysterious. It is the source of all true art and science. He to whom this emotion is a stranger, who can no longer pause to wonder and stand rapt in awe, is as good as dead: his eyes are closed. This insight into the mystery of life, coupled though it be with fear, has also given rise to religion. To know that what is impenetrable to us really exists, manifesting itself as the highest wisdom and the most radiant beauty which our dull faculties can comprehend only in their most primitive form—this knowledge, this feeling, is at the center of true religiousness.

"To know that what is impenetrable to us really exists. . . ." At its best, it is this awareness which we have to gain from the search for alternative realities.

49 ALTERED STATES OF CONSCIOUSNESS*

DR. ANDREW WEIL

Drug experience can be understood only if it is viewed as an altered state of consciousness rather than as a pharmacological event. This approach will make it possible for society to reduce drastically the problems now associated with the use of psychoactive drugs.

All of us experience states of consciousness different from our ordinary waking state. Sleep is such a state. Less obviously, perhaps, are day-

*From Andrew T. Weil, Altered states of consciousness. In *Dealing with drug abuse: A report to the Ford Foundation*, edited by The Drug Abuse Survey Project. © 1972 by The Ford Foundation. Excerpted and reprinted by permission of Praeger Publishers, New York.

dreaming and movie watching unusual modes of awareness. Other distinct varieties of conscious states are trance, hypnosis, psychosis, general anaesthesia, delirium, meditation and mystic rapture. In America, until recently, there has been no serious investigation of altered states as such, because most western scientists who study the mind regard consciousness as annoyingly non-material and therefore inaccessible to direct investigation. Their research has focused on the objective correlates of consciousness instead of on the thing itself. By contrast, in the east, where non-materiality is not seen as a bar to direct investigation, much precise thought has been devoted to altered states of consciousness, and a science of consciousness based on subjective experience has developed.

It would make sense to study all forms of non-ordinary consciousness together because they seem to have much in common. For example, trance, whether spontaneous or induced by a hypnotist, is in many ways simply an extension of the daydreaming state in which a person's awareness is focused and directed inward rather than outward. Except for its voluntary and purposeful nature, meditation is not easily distinguishable from trance. Zen masters warn their meditating students to ignore *makyo*—sensory distortions that often take the form of visions seen by mystics in rapturous states or hallucinations like those of schizophrenics. And, interestingly enough, the state of being "high" on drugs shares many features with these other forms of altered consciousness, regardless of what drug induces the high.

It is my contention that the desire to alter consciousness is an innate psychological drive arising out of the neurological structure of the human brain. Strong evidence for this idea comes from observations of very young children, who regularly use techniques of consciousness alteration on themselves and each other when they think no adults are watching them. These methods include whirling until vertigo and collapse ensue, hyperventilating and then having another child squeeze one's chest to produce unconsciousness, and being choked around the neck to cause fainting. Such practices appear to be universal, irrespective of culture, and present at ages when social conditioning is unlikely to be an important influence (in two- and three-year-olds, for example). Psychiatrists have paid little attention to these activities of all children. Freud called them "sexual equivalents," which they may be, although that formulation is not very useful.

As children grow older, they soon learn that experiences of the same sort may be had chemically—for instance by inhaling fumes of volatile solvents found around the house. General anaesthesia is another chemically induced altered state of consciousness that many children are exposed to in their early years. (The current drug-using generation was extensively tonsillectomised, by the way.) Until a few years ago, most children

in our society who wanted to continue to indulge in these states were content to use alcohol, the one intoxicant we make available legally. Now, large numbers of young people are seeking chemical alterations of consciousness by means of a variety of illegal and medically disapproved drugs. It is possible to see this change as primarily a reaction to other social upheavals, and, certainly, much has been written about the social causes of drug use. It may be more useful, however, to listen to what many drug users, themselves, say: they say they choose illegal drugs over alcohol in order to get better highs. There is no question that social factors operate to shape the forms of drug use in a society or that changes in patterns of use of intoxicants go along with major cultural upheavals. But it is important to remember that every culture throughout history has made use of chemicals to alter consciousness (except the Eskimos, who had to wait for the white man to bring them alcohol since they could not grow anything), and there are some good reasons why alcohol may not be a wise choice for sole legal intoxicant apart from its devastating medical effects. Instead of looking for explanations of drug taking in a foreign war or domestic tension, perhaps we should pay more careful attention to how we allow people to satisfy their innate drive to experience other states of awareness.

Most societies, like our own, are uncomfortable about having people go off into trances, mystic raptures, and hallucinatory intoxications. Indeed the reason we have laws against possession of drugs in the first place is to discourage people from getting high. But innate, neuropsychological drives cannot be banned by legislation. They will be satisfied at any cost. And the cost in our country is very great: by trying to deny young people these important experiences, we maximise the probability that they will obtain them in negative ways—that is, in ways harmful to themselves and to society.

Why are altered states of consciousness important? Primarily because they seem to be doorways to the next stages of evolutionary development of the human nervous system. We commonly assume that a major division of our nervous system (the autonomic system) is involuntary—beyond our conscious control—and this leaves us open to many kinds of illnesses we can do nothing about (cardiovascular diseases, for example). Yet hypnotised subjects often show an astonishing degree of autonomic control, to the extent of developing authentic blisters when touched with cold objects represented to them as being red hot. And Yogis frequently demonstrate voluntary control of heart action and blood flow that astonishes physicians; they, themselves, ascribe their successes to regular periods of meditative effort and claim that there is no limit to what consciousness can effect through the "involuntary" nervous system. In addition, creative genius has long been observed to correlate well with psychosis, and much of the world's highest religious and philosophic thought has come out of altered states of consciousness.

At the very least, altered states of consciousness appear to have potential for strongly positive psychic development. Most Americans do not get the chance to exploit this potential because their society gives them no support. The prevailing attitude toward psychosis is representative. We define this experience as a disease, and force persons who have it to adopt the role of sick, disabled patients. Then we ply them with special kinds of sedatives that we call "antipsychotic agents" but that simply makes it hard for people to think and to express their altered state of consciousness in ways disturbing the staffs of psychiatric hospitals. The individual, from early childhood, learns to be guilty about or afraid of episodes of non-ordinary awareness and is forced to pursue antisocial behaviour patterns if he wants to have them. Negative drug taking has become a popular form of this kind of behaviour.

ALCOHOL V. MARIJUANA

I implied earlier that alcohol may not fulfill the need for alteration of consciousness as well as other drugs. Like all psychoactive drugs, it does induce a high with positive potential. (A vast body of prose, poetry, and song from all ages testified to this "good side" of alcohol.) The trouble is that an alcohol-high is difficult to control; in drinking, one easily slips into the dose range where the effects become unpleasant (nausea, dizziness, uncoordination), and interfere with mental activity rather than support it. Marijuana, on the other hand, maintains a "useful" high over an extremely wide dose range and allows a remarkable degree of control over the experience. But as with other drugs, set and setting determine the effects of marijuana by interacting with the drug's pharmacological action. Unfortunately, current social factors create strongly negative sets and settings, thus increasing the likelihood that users will be drawn into the negative side of consciousness alteration rather than be encouraged to explore its positive potential.

By focusing our attention on drugs rather than on the states of consciousness people seek in them, we develop notions that lead to unwise behaviour. Users who think that highs come from joints (reefer cigarettes) or pills rather than from their own nervous systems get into trouble when the joints and pills no longer work as well (a universal experience among regular consumers of all drugs); their drug use becomes increasingly neurotic —more and more frequent and compulsive with less and less reward. In fact, this misconception is the initial step in the development of drug dependence, regardless of whether the drug is marijuana or heroin, or whether it produces physiological dependence or not. And dependence cannot be broken until the misconception is straightened out even though the physiological need is terminated. (Hence the failure of methadone to cure addicts of being addicts.) By contrast, a user who realizes that he has been using the drug merely as a trigger or excuse for having an experience that is a natural and potentially valuable element of human consciousness comes to see that the drugged state is not exactly synonymous with the experience he wants. He begins to look for ways to isolate the desired aspect of the chemically induced state and often finds that some form of meditation more effectively satisfies his desire to get high. One sees a great many experienced drug takers give up drugs for meditation, but one does not see any meditators give up meditation for drugs. This observation has led some drug educators to hope that young people can be encouraged to abandon drugs in favour of systems like the transcendental meditation of Maharishi Mahesh.

Society labours under the same delusions as dependent users. It thinks that problems came from drugs rather than from people. Therefore, it tries to stop people from using drugs or to make drugs disappear rather than to educate people about their "right" use. No drug is inherently good or evil. All have potential for positive use, all have potential for negative use. The point is not to deny people the experience of chemical altered consciousness but to show them how to have it in forms that are not harmful to themselves or to society. And the way to do that is to recognise the simple truth that the experience comes from the mind, not from the drug. (Once you have learned from a drug what being high really is, you can begin to reproduce it without the drug; all persons who accomplish this feat testify that the nonpharmacological high is superior.) Ironically, all of society's efforts to stop drug abuse are the factors causing drug abuse. There really is no Drug Problem at all, rather a Drug Problem-Problem. And it will continue growing until we admit that drugs have a positive potential that can be realised.

To my knowledge, the only societies that have experimented with this alternative are the primitive Indian tribes of the Amazon basin, many of whom make free use of drugs but have no problems of abuse. That is, although these groups use a multitude of hallucinogenic barks, seeds, and leaves, no one takes the drugs to express hostility toward society, to drop out of the social process, to rebel against his parents or teachers, or to hurt himself. These Indians admit that their world contains substances that alter consciousness; they do not try to make them go away or prevent their use. They accept the fact that people, especially children, seek out altered states of consciousness. And rather than attempt to deny their children experiences they know to be important, they allow them to have them under the guidance of experts in such matters, usually the tribal witch doctors. Recognising that drugs have potential for harm, the witch doctor surrounds their use with ritual and conveys the rationale of this ritual to his charges. Furthermore, the states of consciousness induced by drugs in these remote areas are used for positive ends, not just lapsed into out of boredom or frustration. Some drugs are used only by witch doctors for communing with the spirit world or diagnosing illness; others are used by adolescents in coming-of-age rites; still others are consumed by the whole tribe as recreational intoxicants on special occasions.

A RATIONAL APPROACH TO DRUG USE

I am not suggesting that we return to a primitive life in the jungle, but I do think we have much to learn from thes Amazonian peoples. One reason we are so locked into wrong ways of thinking about drugs is that no one can see a goal worth working for, only problems to work against. The Indian model is an ideal—not something to be substituted overnight for our present situation but something to be kept in mind as the direction to move toward. Let me list the three chief features of this ideal system as proposals for our own society:

1 Recognition of the importance of altered states of consciousness and the existence of a normal drive to experience them.

Considerable unenlightenment now prevails in scientific circles as to the nature of consciousness, both in its ordinary and non-ordinary forms, and there would doubtless be resistance from the professional community to these propositions. But because consciousness is, above all, a matter of inner experience, most laymen are quite willing to accept these ideas. Many adults have simply forgotten their childhood experiences with altered states of consciousness and recall them vividly as soon as they try to. Therefore, I think the possibilities for reeducation are good.

As thinking about drugs moves in this direction, society will be less and less inclined to try to frustrate the human need for periods of altered awareness, so that the role of the criminal law should diminish. At the same time, hopefully, there would be a culmination of present efforts of younger scientists to bring the study of altered states of consciousness into the "respectable" disciplines and institutions. A very great body of information exists on these states; it simply needs collecting and arranging so that we can begin to correlate it with what we know objectively about the nervous system.

2 Provision for the experience of altered states of consciousness in growing children.

Rather than drive children to seek out these states covertly, we must aim to do as the Indians do: let children learn by experience under the watchful guidance of an elder. "Drug education" in the United States means thinly disguised attempts to scare children away from drugs. True education would let those who wanted to explore consciousness do so without guilt and with adult support and supervision. Such explorations should include drug experience because drugs are legitimate tools for altering awareness. Because they have a potential for negative use, they cannot be used wantonly but must be used in certain ways, at certain times, and for certain purposes. Thus we must develop a "ritual" for drug experience, analogous to the Indian tribal rituals. We will also need analogues of the witch doctors—persons who by virtue of their own experience with altered states of consciousness are qualified to supervise the education of the young.

3 Incorporation of the experience into society for positive ends.

It is not enough that we come to tolerate alterations of consciousness. We must put them to use for the good of individuals and society. We have come to think of drug experience as an escape from reality, but if it is so in our society, we have made it so. People who, openly and purposefully, can spend time away from ordinary consciousness seem superior when they function in ordinary consciousness. They are healthier, physically and mentally, lead productive lives, and can become numerous enough to constitute a great natural resource of a society. In addition, they may be utilising their nervous systems to their fullest potential—a goal most of us are far from reaching.

To the above three aims, I would add a fourth, not derived from the Indian pattern:

4 Encouragement of individuals to satisfy their needs for altered consciousness by means that do not require external tools.

Any tools used to alter consciousness—not just drugs—tend to cause dependence because they delude people into believing that the experience comes from them rather than from within the mind. To guard against this tendency, we must educate people, not try to do away with the tools. Our goal should be to train people to live safely in a world where there are things with potential for both harm and good, to show them that inimical forces can be changed into friendly ones. To do this we cannot try to shield young people from things that may harm them; they must learn by experience. Perhaps it is possible to convince adolescents that meditation is better than drugs as an approach to altered consciousness, but they will not believe it unless they have been through drug experience and seen its limitations for themselves.

I conclude by affirming my belief that this system is ideal but not utopian. It is a real possibility, worth working toward. The first step need be nothing more than the stoppage of what we are now doing to prevent us from reaching the goal. And that is nearly everything we are now doing in the name of combating drug abuse.

50 CONCLUSIONS AND RECOMMENDATIONS OF THE COMMISSION OF INQUIRY INTO THE NON-MEDICAL USE OF DRUGS: MAJORITY REPORT ON CANNABIS*

GERALD LeDAIN, HEINZ LEHMANN, and J. PETER STEIN

THE ISSUES

The general issue concerning cannabis is whether there is a well-founded social concern about its non-medical use, and if so, how that concern should express itself in social policy.

This general issue resolves itself into several specific questions. What consequences of behaviour are we to regard as legitimate grounds for social concern? What, in the light of these criteria, are the facts concerning cannabis? What should our objective of social policy be? What instruments of social policy are available to us? What criteria are to determine their appropriateness?

WHAT CONSTITUTES LEGITIMATE GROUNDS FOR SOCIAL CONCERN

In the *Interim Report* we adopted the following general position:

> Our own view is that while we can not say that any and all non-medical use of psychotropic drugs is to be condemned in principle, the potential for harm of non-medical drug use as a whole is such that it must be regarded, on balance, as a phenomenon to be controlled. The extent to which any particular drug use is to be deemed to be undersirable will depend upon its relative potential for harm, both personal and social. [Paragraph 390]

We are still of the opinion that harm is the most useful criterion for social policy. We do not find the notion of drug "abuse" (or "misuse" for that matter) very helpful. In some cases it seems to be equated with the use of any drug which has a po-

tential for producing dependence, physical or psychological. If it is equated with the drug use that actually produces dependence, then it is equated with only one potential aspect of harm. Certain kinds of drug use may produce harm quite apart from dependence, and in some cases, any use of a particular drug may involve the risk of harm.

What should be regarded as adverse psychological effect is subject to controversy. What should be the criteria of psychological harm? What should be the standard of psychological functioning by which psychological harm is to be measured? Presumably, an adverse psychological effect is any impairment of the normal psychological condition and functioning of the individual, but what is to be considered normal, and what a significant impairment? There is no difficulty with extreme psychological reactions such as the acute psychotic episode or 'freakout,' but what about the more subtle effects, such as the alleged lessening of interest or motivation that is referred to as the amotivational syndrome? The individual concerned may not consider it to be a particularly adverse effect. It will often tend to be regarded from the perspective of its social effects. Opinions will differ as to what should be regarded as abnormal psychological functioning.

We have found the concepts of personality and personality change elusive bases for the measurement and evaluation of drug effects. The concept of personality is imprecise. There is really no satisfactory definition of personality with which all people can agree. Moreover, there seems to be little known about how personality change is effected—at least insofar as those elements which may be affected by drug use are concerned. The concept of personality does not convey any criteria of value. By contrast, the concept of mental health presents an assembly of values which may serve as

---

*Abridged from G. LeDain, H. Lehmann, and J. P. Stein, *A report of the commission of inquiry into the non-medical use of drugs*. Ottawa: Information Canada, 1972. Reproduced by permission of Information Canada.

a more useful frame of reference for the evaluation of psychological harm. As with the definition of personality, the criteria of mental health are by no means free from difficulties of interpretation and application, but they do offer a clearer set of psychological values than the concept of personality by which to judge the harmful effects of non-medical drug use. The following psychological attributes or processes are currently serving as widely accepted criteria of mental health: perception of outer reality; perception of one's own identity; resistance to stress; autonomy (or the freedom to make decisions); potential for self-actualization; and mastery of one's environment.

The effects of certain kinds of non-medical drug use on society as a whole are also a ground for social concern. These effects include: the danger presented to others by drug-affected behaviour in some cases, such as violence or impaired functioning; the cost to society of treatment and other kinds of care and attention; the effect which certain drug users may have, by contact, example, and persuasion, in inducing others to engage in harmful drug use. There is a concept of social harm, more difficult to define, which consists of the fear that certain non-medical drug use will have an adverse effect on the motivation, attitudes and capacity required to maintain our present institutions and our political, economic and social life. This involves, of course, the difficult area of value judgement, including conflicting cultural or ideological outlook. Whatever our respective views of the merits of this concern in particular cases, and how far the things feared can truly be characterized as matters of "harm," or more generally as questions of morality, we are convinced that the fear is very real and is a potent factor to be reckoned with in the development of social policy.

THE BASES FOR SOCIAL CONCERN ABOUT CANNABIS
General

The evidence of the potential for harm of cannabis is far from complete and far from conclusive.

It is possible to find some fault with the methodology or the chain of reasoning in virtually all of the evidence. Explaining away the evidence on one side or the other has become a favourite pastime of participants in the cannabis controversy. What is significant is that there is a growing body of evidence to explain away. The literature on adverse psychological reactions, both here and abroad, is now quite extensive. There are problems in proving causality, but the hypotheses are persistent. It is not difficult to point out why other factors may be the cause of these mental disorders, but we cannot afford to ignore the possibility that cannabis may be the cause of them.

The picture with respect to long-term effects is not really very much clearer than it was at the time of our *Interim Report*. As we suggested then, it may take as long as ten years or more to obtain the answers to important questions. It will take at least that long to determine the statistical significance of cannabis-related disorders now being reported by clinicians. What has come to our attention with respect to long-term effects since the *Interim Report* is matter for cautious concern rather than optimism. At this time, these observations by some clinicians who are in contact with chronic, heavy users of cannabis are nothing more than straws in the wind, but together they reinforce an uneasy impression that, in certain kinds of individuals and at certain levels of use, cannabis can cause serious mental problems. The questions are: in what kinds of individuals and at what levels of use? The answers to these questions are only likely to emerge with any kind of statistical validity after a significant number of years of experience with established patterns of use. It is simply too early in North American experience of the widespread social use of cannabis to hope to be able to obtain these answers. We should be selecting groups of cannabis users now, with matched control groups, for close follow-up study over a period of years.

On the whole, the physical and mental effects of cannabis, at the levels of use presently attained in North America, would appear to be much less serious than those which may result from excessive use of alcohol. However, there has not been sufficient experience with long-term, excessive use of cannabis under North American conditions to justify firm and final conclusions. There are many hypotheses arising from recent clinical reports which require further, careful investigation.

An important question is the frequency of use which regular users of cannabis are likely to attain under conditions of relatively easy availability. We think it is likely that under the stressful conditions of modern life an increasing number of people will take to smoking cannabis daily, and even several times a day. The patterns of use have not yet fully developed and become stabilized.

The short-term physical effects of cannabis (apart from those which affect psychomotor abilities) are relatively insignificant on normal persons, and there is as yet no evidence of serious long-term physical effects from use at current levels of consumption in North America. Because of the technique of long inhalation practiced in smoking cannabis it does not seem unreasonable, however, to reckon on the possibility that excessive use of cannabis may cause or potentiate bronchial pulmonary disorders or aggravate the incidence of lung cancer and other diseases of the respiratory system resulting from the use of tobacco. There is a very close association between the smoking of cannabis and the smoking of tobacco. Most people who use cannabis also use tobacco. Another area of concern is possible effect on chromosomes and on the human foetus. There is as yet no clear evidence of adverse effect of this kind, although it is prudent for women not to use cannabis during pregnancy. Recently, certain British doctors have speculated, on the basis of their clinical observations, that the chronic use of cannabis may result in cerebral atrophy, or irreversible shrinking of brain tissue. The subjects of this study also used amphetamines and LSD, and the doctors note that further study will be necessary to confirm a causal relationship between cerebral atrophy and cannabis. At the very least, however, the study indicates the possibility of an association between multi-drug use and permanent brain damage.

Four major areas of social concern are: the effect of cannabis on adolescent maturation; the implications of cannabis use for the safe operation of motor vehicles and other machinery; the possibility that the long-term heavy use of cannabis will result in a significant amount of mental deterioration and disorder; and the role played by cannabis in the development and spread of multi-drug use.

Effect on Adolescent Maturation

We are in general agreement that the regular use of cannabis by adolescents has, in all probability, a harmful effect on the maturing process, and that this should be the chief focus of our social concern. We do not have experimental evidence for this conclusion but we believe that it is a reasonable inference from what we know of the nature of cannabis and adolescent development.

The subjective experiences of cannabis intoxication—particularly intoxication with high doses possessing hallucinogenic properties—and alcohol intoxication are in our opinion essentially different. Alcohol may produce a blunting of perception and a gross disinhibition of behaviour, while an hallucinogenic experience may lead to an extreme intensification of the processes of perception as well as to qualitative distortion of space-time relationships. Such experiences are often also associated with striking changes in one's perception of his own body image and personal identity. This special nature of hallucinogenic experiences conceivably may have a lasting traumatic impact on the maturation of a 12 or 13-year old who is probably not yet capable of assimilating this kind of experience without suffering harm.

It seems completely unrealistic to assume that adolescents, beginning as early as the age of twelve, can persistently resort to cannabis intoxication with its hallucinogenic effects without seriously interfering with development of the capacity to cope with reality that is an essential part of the process of maturation. There is also the probability that the use of cannabis will have the effect of precipitating mental disorders in those who are particularly vulnerable to them. The evidence as to the effects of cannabis on the learning process and on academic performance is inconclusive, although there is a good deal to suggest that frequent use of cannabis may have adverse effects on these functions, mainly because of its effect on short-term memory and attention. It is a virtual certainty that heavy use of cannabis will have an adverse effect on these functions.

Probably the most serious thing about cannabis is that it is being used by adolescents. The most ardent proponents of legalization do not pretend that this is a matter of indifference. Virtually all proposals for legalization contemplate an age limit, usually 18, below which cannabis would not be available.

Effect on Driving

The normal use of cannabis produces significant distortion of perception and impairment of cognitive functions and psychomotor ability. These effects tend to increase with the dose and the complexity of the task involved, but they are observable at moderate doses. Cannabis also has an adverse effect on short-term memory, sustained attention and vigilance, all of which can have an important bearing on complex tasks involving the handling of machinery.

There is reason to believe now that the short-term effects of cannabis increase the hazards of driving. There is no evidence that the use of cannabis has been a significant cause of automobile accidents, but at moderate doses it produces significant impairment of capacities required in driving. It is, therefore, a factor which is likely to increase the chances of accident. There is uncertainty as to the factors that are the principal causes of automobile accidents—attitudes may be as important as driving skills—but impairment of driving skills must obviously be a contributing factor. More investigation is required to show the effects of cannabis on driving skills at the various dose levels which could conceivably be attained under North American patterns of use, but on the basis of the evidence to date it must be said that the use of cannabis has a potential for causing injury through

automobile accidents. In the light of our experience with alcohol there is no reason to assume that there will not be many people who will drive while under the influence of cannabis.

There is, moreover, no clear line of demarcation separating cannabis users from users of alcohol. The notion that cannabis users generally give up alcohol has been shown to be a myth. The vast majority of people who use cannabis also use alcohol, although their consumption of it may be reduced. The two are often used together on the same occasion, with additive effects. Thus cannabis may not only be a significant factor in relation to automobile accidents when used alone but even more so because of its effects when used with alcohol. An important distinction between cannabis and alcohol, insofar as the implications of the effects on psychomotor abilities are concerned, is that cannabis intoxication is still unrecognizable and undetectable. It is virtually impossible to tell whether a person is 'high' on cannabis unless he tells you, and as yet it has not been possible to devise a practical method for detecting the presence and concentration of THC or other active cannabinoids in the body. Nor is the outlook very promising for the development of a simple and convenient method of detection that would serve a function similar to that of the Breathalyzer in the detection and measurement of alcohol in the human body. It is a reasonable operating assumption that there will continue to be great practical difficulty in detecting and proving that a person is driving while the ability to drive is impaired by the use of cannabis.

A matter of some concern with respect to the effect of cannabis on driving is the possibility of an echo effect, or 'flashback,' in which the effects of cannabis or some other hallucinogen, such as LSD, are unexpectedly experienced some time after the last occasion of use. There is evidence that such a phenomenon has occurred in some cases, but it would appear to be rare. Like other effects of cannabis, however, it might well increase with increase in the levels of use.

There has been some experimental investigation of possible effect on other functions of particular relevance to driving—recovery from bright-light glare, dark-adaptation time, and dim-light acuity. There is as yet no clear indication of cannabis-related impairment of these functions, but the possibility of such an effect requires further study.

Effect on Mental Health

The acute panic reactions or "psychotic episodes" which cannabis can produce at certain dose levels and under certain circumstances can be extremely unpleasant, but they would appear to be relatively infrequent and generally of short duration. They indicate, however, that the effect of cannabis upon the mind is a potent one.

There is much concern that the chronic use of cannabis may precipitate mental disorders in persons who are vulnerable to them but who might otherwise avoid them except for the action of cannabis. It is not clear from recent clinical reports of cannabis-related disorders how far these are peculiar to cannabis, how far they are precipitated or aggravated by cannabis, and how far they merely happen to coincide with cannabis use. The fact that there has been no prior evidence of psychopathology is not conclusive, since the mental disorder may have been lying dormant.

A number of reports from clinicians in North America in recent years have suggested that the long-term use of cannabis may cause serious mental disorders. Although these observations may be valid in themselves they do not give us any basis for estimating the frequency with which such conditions might be expected to occur in the cannabis-using population. Surveys of hospitals and university health services have uncovered a very small number of such cases. As yet, North American conditions have not revealed a clearly identifiable "cannabis psychosis" which may be attributed to chronic use. It is too early, however, to assume that such a condition cannot occur since there is not yet a firmly established pattern of long-term use at high dose levels.

The evidence of "personality change" of the kind referred to as the "amotivational syndrome" resulting from the chronic, heavy use of cannabis is inconclusive. There is also a great difference of opinion as to whether certain changes of attitude or outlook which have been associated with the use of cannabis are to be considered a good or a bad thing. It is difficult to distinguish between adverse effect on capacity and mere change in attitude. At the same time certain changes in attitude can reduce effective capacity, for effective capacity depends upon will. Some observers have spoken of apathy and a loss of goals, an absorption in the present with little or no thought for the future. All of these symptoms might be equally associated with a profound change of values and outlook which many might regard as salutary. Obviously, this is very controversial ground, but it is not unreasonable to assume that persistent resort to cannabis intoxication may produce mood changes and impairment of will and mental capacity that have nothing to do with freely chosen attitudes and life style, but may, for example, be the result of some biochemical effect on the balance of mood-regulating neurotransmitters in the brain.

Effect on Multiple-Drug Use

One of the society's chief concerns about cannabis is that it may lead individuals into a pattern of multiple-drug use, including the use of much more dangerous drugs, such as the stronger hallucinogens, the amphetamines and the opiate narcotics. This alleged relationship between the drugs is sometimes referred to as the "progression" or "stepping-stone" theory. In its most simplified form it contends that the use of cannabis leads to the use of heroin.

There is unquestionably a great deal of multiple-drug use in which cannabis plays a part. The question is whether people would have used the other drugs had they not used cannabis. Unfortunately, there is no way of obtaining an answer to this question. The reasons people take up the use of various drugs are too complex to be able to assign causal significance to one factor or another.

Certain kinds of individuals would likely engage in multiple-drug use whether cannabis existed or not; they would start with other drugs. We must not forget that alcohol is still the most widely used drug of all and figures in the background of most multi-drug users. Nevertheless, we believe that by stimulating a taste for drug experiences, lowering inhibitions about experimenting with more dangerous drugs, and leading to personal associations and involvement in a pattern of life which emphasizes an interest in drugs, cannabis must be reckoned as a potent factor contributing to the growth of multi-drug use. It is not necessary to make a clear case of causation in order to place the role of cannabis in multiple-drug use in some plausible general perspective. The attacks on a hypothesis of causation to some extent set up a "straw man." Obviously, there are many factors leading a person to use a variety of drugs. The point is whether cannabis is one of the factors which helps to increase the likelihood that a significant number of people will engage in multi-drug use. We believe that it is, and that it is reasonable to assume that many would not engage in certain kinds of drug use if they did not use cannabis.

These predisposing relationships are not established by statistics. They are, rather, inferences from the nature of the drugs and the patterns of drug use. The fact that a very high proportion of the users of a certain drug have also been users of cannabis does not establish a causal relationship between the two kinds of drug use. On the other hand, there are affinities between certain kinds of drug use which are strongly suggestive of a predisposing relationship. We believe, for example, that there is probably such a relationship between the use of cannabis and the use of LSD. This cannot be established statistically but it is an inference from the nature of the two drugs and their close association in the drug culture. We believe that the use of cannabis probably reduces inhibitions about the use of LSD, and that it is unlikely that many individuals would experiment with LSD before having used cannabis. The general conclusion that we draw is that while only a proportion of users of cannabis will also use LSD, the use of cannabis definitely facilitates the use of LSD or predisposes a certain number of individuals to experiment with it.

The relationship between the stronger hallucinogens, the amphetamines and the opiate narcotics is not as clear. There is obviously a close relationship between the intravenous use of amphetamines and the use of heroin. The relationship between the hallucinogens and the amphetamines is less obvious. It has often been assumed that the users of hallucinogens and the users of amphetamines are quite different populations who live in two separate worlds. This assumption has been based on the difference in the effects of the two classes of drugs and in the cultural associations surrounding their use, as well as the difficulty of overcoming the "needle barrier" for the intravenous use of amphetamines. These factors may still operate to inhibit movement between these two kinds of drug use, but there is evidence that a significant number of people use both. Our surveys indicated that in 1970, in Canada as a whole, over 50 per cent of the persons who had used amphetamines at one time or another had also used cannabis and LSD. Amphetamines are often used to overcome a depression produced by excessive use of hallucinogens. Moreover, amphetamines are sometimes mixed with 'street' LSD, and some drugs which are generally classed among the strong hallucinogens, such as MDA, combine the properties of amphetamines and hallucinogens.

Thus there is a marked relationship between cannabis and LSD, a less obvious one between LSD and the amphetamines, and a marked relationship between speed and heroin. Because of this succession of relationships, which can be linked up, it is possible for people to progress from cannabis through LSD and 'speed' to heroin, but the number of cannabis users of whom this might possibly be true would be a very small proportion of the total number of cannabis users—less than one per cent.

The theory that cannabis leads to heroin because the vast majority of heroin users are found to have used cannabis has to be dismissed on the ground of faulty logic: the vast majority of heroin users may have used cannabis, but the vast majority of cannabis users do not use heroin. The real question is whether a significant number of heroin users would not have used heroin had they not used cannabis. Unfortunately, it is impossible to answer such a question.

It is sometimes argued that if cannabis were not readily available more people would use more dangerous drugs such as the stronger hallucinogens and the amphetamines, and that any policy which restricts the availability of cannabis encourages the use of more dangerous drugs. The argument that cannabis users will turn to other, stronger drugs, if they cannot have cannabis, is an argument which, if anything, reinforces the view that cannabis facilitates resort to stronger drugs. It is at least not inconsistent with such an hypothesis. It is also based on the assumption that those who would resort to stronger drugs in times of cannabis shortage would not do so when it is available. This seems to suggest—contrary to other arguments which the same people generally make concerning cannabis—that cannabis creates such a desire for drug experiences that people will run the risk of using stronger, more dangerous drugs rather than go without.

THE OBJECTIVE OF SOCIAL POLICY

In our opinion, these concerns justify a social policy designed to discourage the use of cannabis as much as possible, particularly among adolescents. We do not yet know enough about cannabis to speak with assurance as to what constitutes moderate as opposed to excessive use. In these circumstances, it is prudent to discourage its use generally.

THE AVAILABLE INSTRUMENTS OF SOCIAL POLICY

To control the use of a drug we must control availability and demand.

There are basically only two ways of controlling availability: criminal law prohibition and administrative regulation. Because of the profits to be made in trafficking there is no point in attempting to control availability by education, propaganda or moral suasion. The law must be used in a coercive or regulatory manner.

Prohibition is resorted to where the object is to eliminate the drug as far as possible; administrative regulation, where it is necessary to make it legally available to some extent. The issue with respect to cannabis is whether it is still desirable and feasible to attempt to pursue a policy of prohibition or whether conditions are such that we are obliged to resort to administrative regulation.

Administrative regulation may have objects other than the regulation of availability; it may seek to control quality and price. Prohibition is not directed to these matters although it may indirectly have an effect on them. Prohibition and administrative regulation may be compared in terms of their impact on availability, quality and price. These are not, however, the only important matters affected by these two legal approaches. Other matters are the effect on individuals of having to deal with an illicit rather than a licit market, and of having their conduct defined as criminal.

Demand may be controlled by the deterrence of criminal law prohibition, by information or education designed to dissuade people from using a drug by indicating its dangers, and by other influences and substituted activities in the home and elsewhere designed to remove the desire for drug use. Unlike the distribution of drugs, demand is more amenable to influences of a non-coercive or non-regulatory nature.

The object of our social policy must be to reduce the availability and demand of cannabis as much as possible, if that can be done at an acceptable cost. The question is whether, and to what extent, the criminal law is a proper instrument for such a policy. The answer to this depends on how effective the criminal law is in achieving its purpose, what the costs are of using it, and whether there are alternative methods of control that would achieve the purpose as effectively at less cost.

SUMMARY STATEMENT OF CONCLUSIONS AND RECOMMENDATIONS

1 Although research has not clearly established that cannabis has sufficiently harmful effects to justify the present legislative policy towards it, there are serious grounds for social concern about its use, and this concern calls for a continuing policy to discourage its use by means which involve a more acceptable cost, than present policies, to the individual and to society.

2 The focus of our social concern should be the use of cannabis by adolescents, and the principal object of our social policy should be to restrict its availability to them as much as reasonably possible by the methods which appear to be most acceptable on a balance of benefits and costs.

3 The only policy which can impose a significant restriction on availability is a prohibition of distribution. Under a system of administrative regulation or licensing, availability would be virtually unrestricted. A policy of making cannabis available to adults would have the effect of making it more available to minors. This is the lesson of our experience with alcohol. It would also make cannabis appear to be relatively harmless. Further, there is no reason to believe that we could effectively control potency and encourage moderate use by a system of administrative regulation or licensing. People will consume the quantities they require to achieve the desired level of potency or they will seek more potent forms, if necessary, in the illicit market. Moreover, our present knowledge about cannabis would not permit a policy of legal availability that could be accompanied by suitable assurances as to what might constitute moderate and relatively harmless use.

4 The costs to the individual and society of maintaining a prohibition of distribution are severe but they are justified by the probable effect of such a prohibition on availability and perception of harm, in contrast to the likely effect on both of a policy of legal availability.

5 The costs of a policy of prohibition of distribution are only acceptable, however, if the possible penalties for illegal distribution are reasonable in relation to the relative seriousness of the offence. Having regard to the potential for harm of cannabis in relation to other drugs, the extent to which young people are involved in its distribution, and the general level of penalties in other countries, the present penalty structure for the illegal distribution of cannabis is grossly excessive. In some cases it does not leave the courts sufficient discretion, and in others it leaves them too much.

6 We recommend the following changes in the law respecting the illegal distribution of cannabis:

a Importing and exporting should be included in the definition of trafficking (as they are under the *Food and Drugs Act*), and they should not be subject to a mandatory minimum term of imprisonment. It might be appropriate, however, to make them subject to somewhat higher maximum penalties than other forms of trafficking.

b There should be an option to proceed by indictment or summary conviction in the case of trafficking and possession for the purpose of trafficking.

c Upon indictment, the maximum penalty for trafficking or possession for the purpose of trafficking should be five years, and upon summary conviction, eighteen months. It should be possible in either case to impose fine in lieu of imprisonment.

d In cases of possession for the purpose of trafficking it should be sufficient, when possession has been proved, for the accused to raise a reasonable doubt as to his intention to traffic. He should not be required to make proof which carries on a preponderance of evidence or a balance of probabilities.

e   Trafficking should not include the giving, without exchange of value, by one user to another of a quantity of cannabis which could reasonably be consumed on a single occasion.

7   The costs to a significant number of individuals, the majority of whom are young people, and to society generally, of a policy of prohibition of simple possession are not justified by the potential for harm of cannabis and the additional influence which such a policy is likely to have upon perception of harm, demand and availability. We, therefore, recommend the repeal of the prohibition against the simple possession of cannabis.

8   The cultivation of cannabis should be subject to the same penalties as trafficking, but it should not be a punishable offence unless it is

cultivation for the purpose of trafficking. Upon proof of cultivation, the burden should be on the accused to establish that he was not cultivating for the purpose of trafficking, but it should be sufficient for him, as in the case of possession for the purpose of trafficking, to raise a reasonable doubt concerning the intent to traffic.

9   The police should have power to seize and confiscate cannabis and cannabis plants wherever they are found, unless the possession or cultivation has been expressly authorized for scientific or other purposes.

● Should the use of marijuana be legalized? Can you present arguments *both* for and against? Try it below.

●

51 ON MEDITATION*

EDWARD W. MAUPIN

Historically our Western culture appears to have been preoccupied with action. Our training has emphasized making and doing and controlling. With us the individualized and self-conscious self has been developed very carefully.

There has been a counter-tendency in the culture to turn to internal and spiritual concerns. Prayer, fasting, some varieties of psychotherapy, and now psychedelic drugs have been used to open up another aspect of the world. In contrast to the active, *doing* mode of the relation to the "external" world, this "internal" world ordinarily requires a passive, receptive attitude on the part of the experiencing person. Meditation is a classical way of developing the receptive attitude. It is practice in the skill of being quiet and paying attention.

The deepest objections to meditation have been raised against its tendency to produce withdrawn, serene people who are not accessible to what is actually going on in their lives. This is certainly a possible outcome. . . .

These are serious objections. The primary problem seems to be that people who engage in practices designed to produce personal growth tend to split these practices off from the rest of their lives. True growth must take place in ordinary living. It happens in psychotherapy, where what happens in the analyst's office is somehow of a different order, split off and more important than the more mundane remainder of life. Christianity has a strong historical tendency to split God from the apparent world. The Christian has tended to feel that his real growth has less to do with how he deals with his moment-to-moment living than with special and apart procedures. Within this model, the secluded monk who can devote full time to prayer is the person who is felt to be grappling with what is most real. Bonhoeffer and Teilhard de Chardin are both explicitly concerned with this split. Both emphasize that the apparent life *is* the arena of growth, or, in their terms, of realizing God. The same split seems to occur in the LSD culture, where the insights afforded by the drug often profoundly alter the taker's beliefs about ultimate reality. But the experience of the drug is behind a curtain, so identified with the drug that the task of realizing the same reality in ordinary life tends to be ignored. There are very important exceptions to this.

Allied to this split is another, even more subtly potent one between "internal" and "external" experience. As a culture we are so inclined to overdraw this distinction that it is difficult to discuss alternatives. We have tended to place great importance on what is "objective," observable by other people, in contrast to what is "subjective," subject to our own "distortions." This overlooks how totally our experience of the world is molded by the observer, his present states and the arbitrary filters of his upbringing. With meditation it is easy to overvalue the internal at the expense of the external so that they remain split apart. It is possible, though, to use it to awaken the subjective life in contact with the external world. Then, rather than a secret closet, the internal becomes a huge space of many dimensions joined with the external world and adding meaning and richness to it. In this paper several meditations on external objects or other people are described. They seem to be particularly direct ways of bringing the meditative attitude into contact.

Admitting the dangers, I still feel it is worthwhile to engage in special activities directed at expanding awareness. In this paper I will outline several techniques of meditation in enough detail for the reader to try them for himself. From what is presented in the literature and from my own obser-

*Abridged from E. W. Maupin, On meditation. In Charles T. Tart (Ed.) *Altered states of consciousness*, New York, Toronto: John Wiley and Sons, 177–186. Copyright © 1969 by John Wiley and Sons, Inc. Reprinted by permission of John Wiley & Sons.

vations, I think meditation can bring important benefits. It is a powerful way to learn to be quiet and pay attention. The special combination of suspended action and waking attention make it possible to become aware of small cues. Calm, greater ability to cope with tense situations, and improved sleep are frequently reported. Better body functioning seems to result, and the pattern of psychosomatic benefits closely follows the well-researched effects of relaxation procedures such as Autogenic Training. A more solid feeling of oneself often seems to result, ("oneself" including both "body" and "mind") and, with that, more direct awareness of what one is experiencing. One Japanese psychiatrist reports that when his patients meditate in addition to their sessions with him, they seem to have more energy for constructive work on their problems.

GENERAL PRINCIPLES

Meditation is first of all a deep passivity, combined with awareness. It is not necessary to have a mystical rationale to practice meditation, but there are marked similarities in the psychological assumptions which underlie most approaches. The ego, or conscious self, is usually felt to be only a portion of the real self. The conscious, striving, busy attempts to maintain and defend myself are based on a partial and misleading concept of my vulnerability, my needs, and the deeper nature of reality. In meditation I suspend this busy activity and assume a passive attitude. What I am passive *to* is conceived in many different ways, but I need only assume that deeper resources are available when I suspend my activity. Instead of diffusing myself in a welter of thoughts and actions, I can turn back on myself and direct my attention upstream to the out-pouring, spontaneous, unpredictable flow of my experience, to the states of mind which produce all the busyness and thinking. It is well at this point to distinguish the practice of meditation from special experiences of mystical union or *satori*. These dramatic states have probably been overemphasized in the meditation litera-

ture. Meditation may be worthwhile in itself without such states, which are unlikely to come about without prolonged practice under skilled supervision.

The position used in meditation is important. It should be such that you can let go and relax in it, yet not fall asleep. The relaxation is not the totally heavy kind you get when you lie down, but balanced and consistent with alertness. In Asia the cross-legged lotus positions are ordinarily used. If you want to try, sit on the floor and cross your legs so that your right foot rests on your left thigh and your left foot rests on the right thigh. This is very difficult to do. You might try the slightly easier procedure of getting only one foot on one thigh and crossing the other leg so that it is underneath the opposite thigh close to the buttock (the half-lotus position), or simply sit tailor fashion. In all three positions your rump should be raised by means of cushions so that knees and buttocks form a stable three-cornered base. Now see if you can let your back rest down into this base in such a way that it is a straight column which requires no strain to keep straight. The hands rest in the lap; the head is erect; the eyes should be open and directed without focusing at a point a few feet ahead of the knees. (All this is following Zen procedure most closely. Yoga practice usually omits the cushion and permits closing the eyes—which leads more easily into trances than to wakeful awareness.)

The cross-legged positions are not essential. You can meditate effectively in a straight-backed chair with your feet planted wide apart and flat on the floor, your back straight, head erect, and eyes open as before. The most comfortable height should be adjusted with cushions. A less erect posture in an ordinary easy chair can also be used.

After you get into position, sway back and forth for a while to settle in, take a few deep breaths, and begin to let go. You may find it useful to contact various parts of your body with your attention, especially your base, the legs and pelvis on which you are resting. Now you are ready to begin directing your attention according to the technique you have decided to use.

The techniques presented are fairly simple

ones, classically used in the early stages of training. You may wish to experiment with more than one to find which is the most effective for you. They are all suitable for daily use for between a half hour and an hour. Although they are apparently different, they all seem to aim at increasing awareness of what is happening inside and making possible a detached look. It is extremely misleading to strive toward any particular state of mind, but all of these exercises will sometimes make possible a state of clear, relaxed awareness in which the flow of thought is reduced and an attitude of detached observation is maintained. In contrast with the usual thinking activity, which carries one off into abstractions or fantasies, this observing attitude keeps close contact with the here-and-now of experience. Thoughts are not prevented, but are allowed to pass without elaboration. It is not a blank state or trance, and it is different from sleep. It involves deep physical relaxation as well as letting go of the usual psychological busy-ness. Actually, one discovers very early how closely psychological and physical relaxation are related.

How you handle distractions is extremely important. Do not try to prevent them. Just patiently bring your attention back again and again to the object of your meditation. This detaching from fantasies and thoughts and outside stimuli is some of the most important work of meditation. If you attempt to prevent distractions in some other way, you may get into unproductive blank states, or get distracted by the task of preventing distractions, or become tense. If you patiently return to the meditation, gradually your attention to the object will replace the distractions, and your physical relaxation will make it possible for the flow of thoughts to decrease.

It is also very important that you not have some preconceived notion of what *should* happen in a "good" session. You may become relaxed and clear, but you may also remain tense and distracted, or you may uncover extremely painful kinds of experience. Allowing yourself to be honestly aware of whatever you experience is more constructive than the most pleasant relaxation. Ac-

cepting the session wherever it leads is essential. You may feel sleepy. Try observing the process of falling asleep itself—perhaps it is a response to some feeling you want to avoid. If sleep continues to be a problem, get up and walk around and breathe deeply for a while. You may feel bored and restless with the task. Observe and experience these feelings. In this culture you may well find yourself taking a negative attitude, beating yourself over the head, as it were, to do a good job of meditating. Try to observe this self-critical, hostile attitude in yourself. There is a kind of friendly neutrality you can bring to bear on any experience which emerges.

As the ego activity is reduced, inner material, some of it formerly outside awareness, begins to emerge. Herrigel writes:

> This exquisite state of unconcerned immersion in oneself is not, unfortunately, of long duration. It is likely to be disturbed from inside. As though sprung from nowhere, moods, feelings, desires, worries and even thoughts incontinently rise up, in a meaningless jumble. . . . The only successful way of rendering this disturbance inoperative is to . . . enter into friendly relations with whatever appears on the scene, to accustom oneself to it, to look at it equably and at last grow weary of looking.

This is one reason why you should probably be supervised if you want to practice meditating more than an hour at a time. With more time the emerging material may become more dense and impelling, more difficult to treat as an illusory distraction. Supposedly it was a Zen student in Japan who burned down the golden pavilion on grounds it was so beautiful that all it lacked was transience. The emerging material may change form, become predominantly visual imagery in contrast to the verbal form of the earlier distractions, and so on. However, it is not necessary to be *too* cautious about this material. My psychotherapy patients, when they have meditated at home, have had no special difficulty in treating their distractions as distractions. All that is required is to observe them and return to the meditation.

SPECIFIC EXERCISES

The first group of meditation techniques focuses on the body or on breathing.

A Taoist meditation described by Rousselle directs that attention be placed in the center of the torso at about the level of the navel. Thoughts, when they arise, should be "placed" in this center of the body, as if they arose there. "Consciousness, by an act of the imagination, is shifted to the solar plexus." This procedure especially helps to promote a feeling of vitality and strength from the belly.

Breathing is a function which may be either voluntarily or involuntarily controlled. To meditate on breathing, then, is to deal with how you allow your spontaneity to flow. It is important not to force the issue, though. If you cannot allow your breathing to become fully involuntary, just observe how you *do* handle it, or move on to another exercise. The simplest breath meditation is as follows:

Sit with a straight back and relax. Let your breathing become relaxed and natural, so that the movement is mainly in the abdomen. Then keep your attention on this movement.

Wienpahl gives excellent instructions for breath concentration as used in his Japanese Zen training:

Breathe through the nose. Inhale as much as you require, letting the air come in by distending the diaphragm. Do not draw it in, rather let it come to you. Then exhale slowly. Exhale completely, getting all of the air out of your lungs. As you exhale slowly count "one." Now inhale again. Then exhale slowly to the count of "two." And so on up to "ten." Then repeat. . . .

You will find this counting difficult as your mind will wander from it. However, keep at it, striving to bring your mind back to the process of counting. As you become able to do this with reasonable success, start playing the following game with the counting. As you count "one" and are slowly exhaling, pretend that this "one" is going down, down, down into your stomach. Then think of its being down there as you inhale and begin to count "two." Bring the "two" down and place it (in your imagination, one might say) in your stomach beside the "one."

. . . Eventually you will find that your mind itself, so to speak, will descend into your stomach.

The shift of attention down to the lower part of the body, the pelvis or the abdomen, is accompanied by a relaxation in which thoughts seem slow and distant. Preliminary evidence from several sources suggests that brain-wave recordings show an increase of slow, high amplitude (alpha) activity in subjects using these types of techniques.

Another group of meditative exercises focuses the attention directly on the contents of consciousness. For example, Chaudhuri, drawing on yoga practice, writes:

The radical approach begins with the resolve to do nothing, to think nothing, to make no effort of one's own, to relax completely and let go one's mind and body . . . stepping out of the stream of ever-changing ideas and feelings which your mind is, watch the onrush of the stream. Refuse to be submerged in the current. Changing the metaphor, it may be said, watch your ideas, feelings and wishes fly across the mental firmament like a flock of birds. Let them fly freely. Just keep a watch. Don't allow the birds to carry you off into the clouds.

Another method is to focus attention, not on the thought activity, but on the state of mind which lies behind the thoughts. This was the exercise which first excited me about meditation:

A variant of this is to ask who is doing this thinking, feeling, acting. Brunton writes:

First watch your own intellect in its working. Note how thoughts follow one another in endless sequence. Then try to realize that there is someone who thinks. Now ask: "Who is this thinker?"

The same kind of attention with which one meditates on breathing can be directed to outside objects. Arthur Deikman, in a psychoanalytic study of meditation, had his experimental subjects meditate on a small blue vase: The instructions were as follows:

Your aim is to concentrate on the blue vase. By concentration I do not mean *analyzing* the different parts of the vase, or thinking a series of thoughts about the vase, or associating ideas to the vase, but rather, *trying to see the vase as it exists in itself,* without any connections to other things. Exclude all other thoughts or feelings or body sensations. Do not let them distract you but keep them out so that you can concentrate all your attention, all your awareness on the vase itself. Let the perception of the vase fill your entire mind.

Another person may be encountered and received in the same way:

Place yourself face to face with another person. Look at him and be aware when your mind wanders. Be aware when you treat his face like an object, a design, or play perceptual games with it. Distortions may appear which tell you what you project into the relationship: angels, devils, animals and all the human possibilities may appear in his face. Eventually you may move past these visual fantasies into the genuine presence of another human being.

The meditative attitude can also be brought into sexual encounter. Use an intercourse position in which you can look at your partner and in which you can comfortably lie motionless for a long time. This exercise could probably be practiced for more than an hour at a time without supervision.

This paper is intended as an introduction for someone who wants to begin to meditate. Gary Snyder, who has spent several years in Zen training in Japan, has written a poem which may be reassuring to those who wish to try:

What I Think When I Meditate
Well, I could tell you that I could tell
    you but wouldn't understand but I won't
You'd understand but I can't, I mean dig,
        this here guitar is gone bust
        I hate to sit crosslegged
my knees hurt my nose runs and I have to go
                to the crapper
tootsweet and damn that timeclock keeper won't ding.
WHAT I think about when I meditate is emptiness.
        I remember it well
the empty heads   the firecracker phhht
But what I *really* think about is sex
            sort of patterns of sex
like dancing hairs and goosebumps
            No, honestly
what I think about is what am I thinking about?
            and
who am I? and 'MU?' and 'the clouds
                on
        the
            southern mt'
Well: what I really honestly think about, no fooling
. . . (etc.)

(from *Ark III*)

52 TRANSCENDENTAL MEDITATION AND THE SCIENCE OF CREATIVE INTELLIGENCE*

PAUL H. LEVINE

The search for definition of basic goals which is so prominent a concern of the educational community echoes a similar quest for purpose within my own field of science and, indeed, within society at large. While educators are asking, "What are schools for?[1] scientists are asking, "What is the significance of science?"[2] and political leaders still seek to define our "national purpose." The soul-searching is widespread, yet within each profession or field of activity the search is carried out within the boundaries of that field, solutions are sought in the framework of the problem perceived, and more fundamental aspects of the situation are consequently overlooked.

It seems clear that what is really being asked is

[1]Robert L. Ebel, "What Are Schools For?" *Phi Delta Kappan,* September, 1972, p. 3.

*Abridged from Paul H. Levine, *Transcendental Meditations and the Science of Creative Intelligence*. Phi Delta Kappan. December, 1972. Reprinted by permission of the publisher.

[2]Victor F. Weisskopf, "The Significance of Science, *Science,* April 14, 1972, p. 138.

What should be the objectives of human activity? with specific reference in each of the examples cited to the activities of teaching, doing science, or running a nation. If we adopt the common-sense position that the principal objective of *any* activity is to promote the fulfillment of the individuals engaged in and influenced by that activity, then the real goal of education is seen to encompass nothing less than the *fulfillment* of the student.

In the sense we are using it here, fulfillment implies the actualization of the full potentialities for growth latent in the individual. Therefore, the measure of any educational system is first the breadth of its implicit *vision* of the range of these potentialities and second its *effectiveness* in providing every student with a practical means for achieving such full development. If a crisis is felt to exist in education, then it may logically be asked whether the fault lies in too narrow a vision of the possibilities and, in consequence, too restricted an armamentarium for achievement.

This article discusses a particular conception of the range of potential human development which, if further validated by a growing body of anecdotal and scientific evidence, must necessarily change our ideas about individual fulfillment and with this our views on the structure and responsibility of education. The conception is that of Maharishi Mahesh Yogi; it is being taught as part of a new discipline called the Science of Creative Intelligence.

CREATIVE INTELLIGENCE

The concept of creative intelligence arises from an examination of the structure of purposeful change in nature. No matter where we look, new forms and relationships are continually being created from lesser developed states. This evolution appears to be orderly, i.e., governed by intelligible laws. The intelligence displayed by nature in this process may be called creative intelligence. When we observe creation in action, whether it be in astronomy or biology — or even the growth of a rose — we encounter striking parallels in the structure of the creative process as it unfolds in each case. Through such interdisciplinary analyses, it comes to be appreciated that a fundamental significance can be accorded to creativity (and to the intelligence shaping its expression), a significance which transcends the particular sphere of activity in which the creativity is being manifested. Creative intelligence thus becomes a valid object of intellectual inquiry in its own right.

The relevance of such inquiry to education, and to practical life in general, stems from the circumstance that the creative impulse in man, as expressed in his progressive thoughts and actions, is found upon close examination to be structured along precisely the same lines as creative processes in the purely physical domain. This circumstance (not as remarkable as it may seem at first glance, since we are, after all, part of nature) immediately suggests a transcendental aspect to human creativity which necessarily casts consideration of the human condition into broader evolutionary contexts.

Fulfillment, for example, comes to mean full expression in an individual's life of the creative intelligence inherent in his nature. Lack of fulfillment (which we may call suffering) in this view is ascribed to some restriction of the flow of creative intelligence from its source at the core of one's being to the level of conscious awareness from which one perceives and acts. A practical consequence of this approach is the intriguing possibility that human problems can be attacked at a common fundamental level—without specific regard to the nature of the problem—much in the same way that a gardener simultaneously attends to deficiencies in the development of the many separate leaves of a plant by simply watering the root.

TRANSCENDENTAL MEDITATION

The existence of a simple natural technique called transcendental meditation lends substance to the above considerations, removing them from the realm of purely philosophical speculation. TM, as it is frequently abbreviated, is a systematic procedure of "turning the attention inwards towards the subtler levels of a thought until the mind transcends the experience of the subtlest state of the thought and arrives at the source of the thought. This expands the conscious mind and at the same time brings it in contact with the creative intelligence that gives rise to every thought."[3]

This technique for the direct *experience* of the field of creative intelligence at the root of one's being is apparently a universal human faculty not requiring any particular intellectual or cognitive facility other than the ordinary ability to think. It is easily learned by anyone in about six hours of instruction (spread out over four consecutive days) from a Maharishi-trained teacher.[4] Once learned, it can be continued without the necessity for additional instruction. It is primarily on the basis of this systematic and apparently universally applicable procedure for the empirical[5] verification of theoretical constructs involving creative intelligence that one may validly speak in terms of a *science* of creative intelligence, or SCI.

The rapidly expanding interest in SCI, both in and out of academia, and—surprisingly—both within the Establishment and the youth subculture, presently derives not so much from an appreciation of its inherent scope as from a desire for a fuller understanding of the immediate practical benefits of TM.[6] Notwithstanding the simplicity of the practice, meditators unanimously report improve-

ments in the energy and enthusiasm with which they approach their activities and in their clarity of mind, mental and physical health, and ability to interact harmoniously with their environment.[7] Marked reductions in tension and moodiness are frequently cited, even by those in particularly stressful occupations or family situations. The list goes on to include increased creativity, perceptiveness, self-confidence, productivity, reading speed, psychomotor facility, and learning ability. As one might expect, meditators report concurrent reductions in their use of tranquilizers, stimulants, and other prescribed drugs—and, most significantly, of nonprescription drugs as well.[8] The combined effect is succinctly expressed by a Yale biology instructor: "There's been a quantum increase in the quality of my life since I started meditating."

Experiences during meditation vary from individual to individual and from one meditation to the next. A common experiential denominator, observed even in the first meditation, is a unique blend of deep physical relaxation and expanded mental awareness. The relationship of this state of mind and body to the more familiar states of waking, dreaming, and deep sleep may be schematized as in the matrix shown in Figure 1.

Viewed in this context, TM can perhaps be accepted as just another natural albeit very useful style of functioning of the nervous system, to be

---

[3]Maharishi Mahesh Yogi, *Maharishi Mahesh Yogi on the Bhagavad-Gita: A New Translation and Commentary* (Baltimore: Penguin Books, 1969), p. 470.

[4]A number of nonprofit tax-exempt organizations coordinate the activities of TM teachers. The educational community is served by the Students' International Meditation Society (SIMS), whose national headquarters is located at 1015 Gayley Avenue, Los Angeles, California 90024. Inquiries may be directed to the attention of the Science and Education Communications Coordinator.

[5]The customary view that subjective experience is ipso facto beyond the purview of science is undergoing change. See, for example, "States of Consciousness and State-Specific Science," by Charles T. Tart, in *Science,* June 16, 1972, p. 1, 203.

[6]The rate of instruction in TM has doubled each year since 1968. By the fall of 1972 over 150,000 Americans had learned TM. The board base of this appeal can be gauged from the range of publications featuring articles on TM and SCI during the past year: *Time* (October 25, 1971), *Yale Alumni Magazine* (February, 1972), *Soldiers Magazine* (February, 1972),

Kentucky Law Journal (1971–72, Vol. 60, No. 2), *Seventeen* (July, 1972), *Wall Street Journal* (August 31, 1972), *Today's Health* (April, 1972), *Science Digest* (February, 1972), and *Psychology Today* (March, 1972).

[7]TM is a purely mental technique practiced individually every morning and evening for 15 to 20 minutes at a sitting. It requires no alteration of life-style, diet, etc., and being a technique of direct experience (rather than a religion or philosophy), it does not require belief in the efficacy of the practice nor an understanding of the underlying theory.

[8]The widely publicized efficacy of TM in promoting the voluntary reduction of drug abuse as documented, for example, in the retrospective study of 1,862 subjects by Drs. R. K. Wallace and H. G. Benson of the Harvard Medical School (see "Narcotics Research, Rehabilitation, and Treatment" in "Hearings Before the Select Committee on Crime, House of Representatives," Serial No. 92-1, Part 2, p. 682—U.S. Government Printing Office, 1971) tends to overshadow public understanding of the broader effects of the practice and particularly its utility for the non-drug abuser.

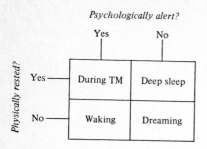

Figure 1 Relationship of TM to other states of consciousness.

alternated with the others on a regular daily basis. Since the dynamism of daily activity in large measure depends on the thoroughness of the psychophysiological rest achieved during the deep sleep and dreaming states, the additional profound rest claimed to occur during TM would account for the enlivened functioning in the waking state reported by meditators.

SCIENTIFIC RESEARCH

The anecdotal claims for TM, even when they are echoed by people of unquestioned objectivity and stature, must nevertheless be verified by the tools of science before they can be accepted by a society grappling with the very ills TM is purported to relieve so effortlessly. A unique aspect of TM vis-a-vis other techniques for mental or physical development is the depth of scientific investigation of its effects currently in progress throughout the world. Major research projects on TM are being carried out at over 40 universities and institutes, including the Harvard Medical School, Stanford Research Institute, and the Universities of Cambridge, Cologne, Rome, and Capetown. In great measure, this widespread research activity is made possible by the availability of large numbers of cooperative meditators at virtually every major university, as well as by the effortlessness of the technique itself, which permits experimentation to be performed without disturbing the meditation.

Much of the meditation research is still in its early phases, particularly the long-term clinical studies of TM's *possible* value for hypertensives (Harvard Medical School) and in the relief of mental illness (Hartford's Institute of Living). The research that has reached publication stage, however, is already sufficient to establish that the psychophysiological effects both during and after TM are real and unique in their degree of integration.

In the *American Journal of Physiology,* a team of Harvard and University of California researchers has reported on these integrated characteristics of mind and body during TM, calling it a "wakeful hypometabolic physiologic state," i.e., a state of restful alertness (see Figure 1).[9] They found that the degree of metabolic rest after 5-10 *minutes* of TM was characterized by an average decrease in oxygen consumption of 17%, deeper than that achieved after 6-7 *hours* of sleep. They found a reduction in heart rate of three beats per minute, which, when correlated with an earlier

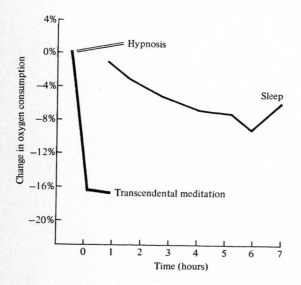

Figure 2 Levels of rest: changes in metabolic rate.

[9]Robert Keith Wallace, Herbert Benson, and Archie F. Wilson, "A Wakeful Hypometabolic Physiologic State," *American Journal of Physiology,* September, 1971, pp. 795–99.

study reporting a drop in cardiac output of 25% during TM,[10] indicates a significant reduction in the workload of the heart. EEG (i.e., "brain wave") measurements showed a predominance of slow alpha wave activity in the central and frontal areas of the brain, thereby clearly distinguishing TM from the waking, dreaming, and sleeping states.[11]

Most significant were the observations of an approximately threefold increase in skin resistance during TM, indicating relaxation and a reduction of anxiety. Biochemical studies of the meditators' blood showed a remarkable reduction in lactate concentration both during and after meditation. Anxiety symptoms are believed to be correlated with high blood lactate levels. Thus, as reported in a recent *Scientific American* article, Robert K. Wallace and Herbert Benson are led to view TM as an integrated response or reflex which is opposite in its characteristics to the "fight or flight" response believed to be primarily responsible for the high incidence of hypertension and related diseases in today's fast-paced society.[12]

Psychological studies of personality changes attributable to TM have also begun to appear in the literature. In the *Journal of Counseling Psychology*, a University of Cincinnati team concluded that "the practice of meditation for a 2-month period would appear to have a salutary influence on a subject's psychological state as measured by the Personal Orientation Inventory."[13] Changes in the direction of increased "self-actualization" were found to occur for meditating subjects.

Another study, reported in the *Journal of Psychosomatic Medicine*, gives insight into a pos-sible explanation for the wide variety of beneficial results apparently following from the simple practice of TM.[14] It was found that meditators habituated more rapidly to a stressful environment than nonmeditators and, furthermore, that meditators' nervous systems displayed greater autonomic stability. This evidence, together with the lactate observations cited earlier, tends to substantiate the view (presented in SCI) that TM acts to reduce one's store of psychophysiological stress while simultaneously reducing the likelihood of further stress accumulation. When one considers the manifold deleterious effects of stress, it becomes apparent that any technique which can reduce stress—e.g., the twice-daily experience of a hypometabolic wakeful state—has the potential for simultaneous improvement of one's life on all those levels previously stress afflicted. A "quantum jump in the quality of life" suddenly becomes credible.

IMPLICATIONS FOR EDUCATION

In the broader vision of SCI, stresses are viewed as impediments to the spontaneous flow of creative intelligence from the inner being to the level of conscious awareness from which one perceives and acts. An integral component of fulfillment, therefore, becomes the progressive physiological refinement of the nervous system in the direction of a reduced accumulation of stress. Indeed, SCI associates such refinement with a "growth in consciousness" and delineates the remarkable potentialities of a fully stress-free, fully normalized nervous system. The attainment of higher states of consciousness, long thought to be incompatible with an active life, now is said to be within the reach of anyone through TM, and experiential evidence of this possibility seems to be one of the common cumulative effects of the practice.

[10]Robert Keith Wallace, "The Physiological Effects of Transcendental Meditation: A Proposed Fourth Major State of Consciousness," Ph.D. Dissertation, University of California, Los Angeles, 1970; see also *Science*, March 27, 1970, p. 1, 751.
[11]The physiological measurements also show that TM is radically different from hypnotic states and other so-called "altered states of consciousness."
[12]Robert Keith Wallace and Herbert Benson, "The Physiology of Meditation," *Scientific American*, February, 1972, p. 84.
[13]William Seeman, Sanford Nidich, and Thomas Banta, "Influence of Transcendental Meditation on a Measure of Self-Actualization," *Journal of Counseling Psychology*, May, 1972, pp. 184–87.

[14]David W. Orme-Johnson, "Autonomic Stability and Transcendental Meditation," *Journal of Psychosomatic Medicine*, in press.

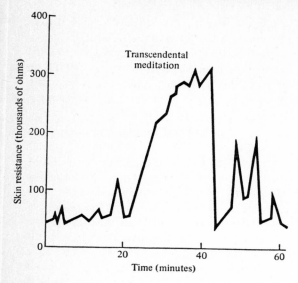

Figure 3 State of relaxation: change in skin resistance.

The implications of all of this for education are quite exciting. At the most superficial level, the level of the problems, reduction of drug abuse among students and of social tension in the classroom is a likely concomitant of a widespread introduction of TM into the schools. The improved attitudes and behavior which generally are among the more immediate of TM's effects offer a chance for achieving affective goals without sacrificing performance goals. Indeed, preliminary reports of increased learning ability and reading speed with TM would seem to indicate that affective dispositions and cognitive resources grow hand in hand. Students at ease inside can be expected to respond more spontaneously and creatively to a learning environment.

On the other side of the desk, a meditating teacher (or administrator), being more at ease, energetic, healthy, clear-minded, creative, and perceptive, should naturally become more effective. Already, as discussed by Francis Driscoll, there is concrete evidence that these are all valid expectations if the implementation of a TM/SCI-based program is approached with proper planning.

On a deeper level, if further research continues to substantiate "growth in consciousness" as a pragmatically meaningful concept, can this dimension of human development be overlooked by an educational system whose goal is the actualization of the full potentialities for growth latent in the student? One of the most ancient expressions of man's wisdom, the Vedas (to which SCI traces its ancestry), hold that "knowledge is structured in consciousness," the implication being that the higher the level of consciousness the more profound the level of knowledge which can be owned.

This leads finally to the most fundamental possibility for educational fulfillment of all those opened through SCI. The holistic ideal of education is to provide a common basis for all branches of learning. Certainly, *knowingness*, that very intimate relationship between the knower and the object of knowledge, is this common basis. The science of creative intelligence is principally the study of this relationship, both through intellectual analysis and through the direct experience of the field from which all knowledge springs. The whole tree is captured by capturing the seed. In the fullest sense, therefore, creative intelligence may be said to be both the goal and the source of education.

A WORLD PLAN

Concrete programs are already underway for the widest diffusion of SCI and TM. Since its inauguration as an accredited course at Stanford in the 1970 winter quarter, SCI has achieved recognition from a rapidly growing number of universities and colleges around the world. The SCI course at Yale this past year, for example, explicitly demonstrated its integrative and interdisciplinary nature by bringing together psychologists, philosophers, political scientists, and artists in a common exploration of the potentialities of consciousness.

SCI is being taught at other educational levels, including junior and senior high schools and adult

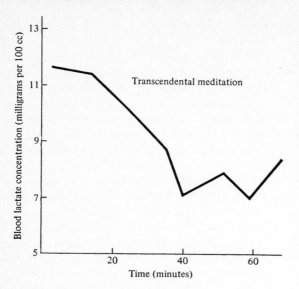

Figure 4 Biochemical changes.

education, in industry, and even in the military. Indeed, the commandant of the U.S. Army War College, Major General Franklin M. Davis, speaking at the First International Symposium on the Science of Creative Intelligence,[15] said, "In military education, creative intelligence appears to have a definite potential, because it carries with it so much in the way of innovation, creative thinking, and what we in the military call 'challenging the assumption'!" To which Maharishi added, "When the military rises in creative intelligence, world peace will be a reality."

Educators at MIU (Maharishi International University), the instituion founded in 1971 to formalize the training of SCI teachers, are now completing the preparation of syllabuses and teaching aids—including color video cassettes—for the teaching of SCI at all educational levels. MIU is currently embarked on an ambitious world plan to open 3,600 centers for the training of SCI teachers—one center per million population —throughout the world. Each center has as its goal the training of 1,000 teachers by means of a 33-lecture video-based course prepared specially for this purpose by Maharishi. The stated objectives of the world plan include the development of the full potential of the individual and the "realization of the highest ideal of education."

A utopian vision? Perhaps. But who would have imagined that a scant 14 years after a lone monk walked out of the Himalayas armed only with knowledge and his dedication to a long tradition of educators, the Illinois House of Representatives would formally resolve:

> That all educational institutions, especially those under State of Illinois jurisdiction, be strongly encouraged to study the feasibility of courses in Transcendental Meditation and the Science of Creative Intelligence on their campuses and in their facilities; and be it further . . . resolved that a copy of this resolution be sent to: the Superintendent of Public Instruction, the deans of all state universities, the Department of Mental Health, State of Illinois, to inform them of the great promise of the program herein mentioned. . . .[16]

[15]Held at the University of Massachusetts, Amherst, July 18 through August 1, 1971. International symposia on SCI are now held regularly each year at a number of universities throughout the world. Participants in 1971 included Buckminster Fuller, Harvey Brooks (dean of engineering and applied physics, Harvard University, and president, American Academy of Arts and Sciences), Melvin Calvin (Nobel Laureate in chemistry), and Willis Harman (director, Educational Policy Research, Stanford Research Institute). Symposia in 1972 featured Donald Glaser (Nobel Laureate in physics), Hans Selye, Marshall McLuhan, astronaut Rusty Schweickart, and the State Department China expert Alfred Jenkins.

[16]House Resolution No. 677, adopted May 24, 1972.

53 A PSYCHOLOGY OF THE FUTURE*

A. H. MASLOW

Humanistic psychology is now quite solidly established as a viable third alternative to objectivistic, behavioristic (mechanomorphic) psychology and to orthodox Freudianism. Its literature is large and is rapidly growing. It is beginning to be used, especially in education, industry, religion, organization and management, therapy, and self-improvement, and by various other "Eupsychian" organizations, journals, and individuals.

I have come to think of this humanist trend in psychology as a revolution in the truest, oldest sense of the word, the sense in which Galileo, Darwin, Einstein, Freud, or Marx made revolutions, *i.e.,* new ways of perceiving and thinking, new images of man and of society, new conceptions of ethics and values, new directions in which to move.

This third psychology is now one facet of a general *Weltanschauung,* a new philosophy of life, a new conception of man, the beginning of a new century of work. For any man of good will, any pro-life man, there is work to be done here, effective, virtuous, satisfying work that can give rich meaning to one's own life and to others.

This psychology is not purely descriptive or academic; it suggests action and implies consequences. It helps to generate a way of life not only for the person himself within his own private psyche but also for the same person as a social being, a member of society. As a matter of fact, it helps us to realize how interrelated these two aspects of life really are. Ultimately, the best "helper" is the "good person." So often the sick or inadequate person, trying to help, does harm instead.

I should say also that I consider humanistic third-force psychology to be transitional, a prep-

*From A. H. Maslow, "A psychology of the future." This article first appeared in The Humanist, November/December 1969, and is reprinted by permission. *This has been adapted from the Preface to the Revised Edition of* Toward a Psychology of Being *(Van Nostrand, 1968).*

aration for a still "higher" fourth psychology, transpersonal, transhuman, centered in the cosmos rather than in human needs and interest, going beyond humanness, identity, self-actualization, and the like. Such developments may very well offer a tangible, usable, effective satisfaction of the "frustrated idealism" of many quietly desperate people, especially young people. These psychologies give promise of developing into the life-philosophy, the religion-surrogate, the value-system, the life-program that these people have been missing. Without the transcendent and the transpersonal we get sick, violent, and nihilistic, or else hopeless and apathetic. We need something "bigger than we are" to be awed by, and to commit ourselves to in a new, naturalistic, empirical, non-churchly sense, perhaps as Thoreau, Whitman, William James, and John Dewey did.

I believe that another task that needs doing before we can have a good world is a humanistic and transpersonal psychology of evil, one written out of compassion and love for human nature rather than out of disgust with it or out of hopelessness. There are certainly good and strong and successful men in the world: saints, sages, good leaders, statesmen, strong men, winners rather than losers, constructors rather than destroyers, parents rather than children. Such people are available for anyone who wants to study them. But it also remains true that there are so few of them even though there could be many more, and that they are often treated badly by their fellows. So this too must be studied, this fear of human goodness and greatness, this lack of knowledge of how to be good and strong, this inability to turn one's anger into productive activities, this fear of maturity and the godlikeness that comes with maturity, this fear of feeling virtuous, self-loving, loveworthy, respectworthy. Especially we must learn how to transcend our foolish tendency to let our compassion for the weak generate hatred for the strong.

It is this kind of research that I recommend most urgently to young and ambitious psychologists, sociologists, and social scientists in general. And to others of good will who want to help make a better world, I recommend strongly that they consider science—humanistic science—as a way of doing this, a very good and necessary way, perhaps even the best way of all.

We simply do not have available today enough reliable knowledge to construct the One Good World. We do not even have enough knowledge to teach individuals how to love each other—at least not with any certainty. The best answer, I am convinced, is in the advancement of knowledge. The life of science can also be a life of passion, of beauty, of hope for mankind, and of revelation of values.

USEFUL RESOURCES

BRECHER, E. M. *Licit and illicit drugs*. Boston: Little, Brown, 1972.
". . . a massive study of the pharmacology, sociology, and history of mind-affecting drugs in our society, and of our social and legal responses to these drugs and their users." Book jacket.
"Presents rational, thoughtful conclusions that should make it required reading for everyone." Norman E. Zinberg, M.D., Chief of Psychiatry, Washingtonian Center for Addictions.

EBIN, D. *The drug experience*. New York: Grove Press, 1961.
"First person accounts of addicts, writers, scientists and others."

JAMES, W. *Varieties of religious experience*. New York: The New American Library of World Literature, 1958.
One of the classical references in ASC.

Journal of Transpersonal Psychology. (Library of Congress, call No. Per. BFI.J75)
A journal which reports the latest research in ASC.

KALANT, H., & KALANT, O. J. *Drugs, society and personal choice*. Don Mills, Ontario: General Publishing, 1973.
"Science can determine facts concerning the acute action of drugs, and the consequences of prolonged or heavy use. It can also estimate the probable extent of these consequences. However, the decision as to whether these effects or consequences are to be considered good or bad and how society should react to them, are not questions of scientific fact but of personal and social values, ethics and political feasibility. It is up to every citizen to ascertain and evaluate the facts. Then the society as a whole is in a position to make informed decisions about the policies it wants its government to adopt. . . . The aim of this book is to put into as sharp a focus as possible questions of fact, matters of value judgment, and how the two interact."

KLINE, N. S. The future of drugs and drugs of the future. *Journal of Social Issues*, 1971, **27**, 73–87.
"Drugs have played an important role in man's experience for thousands of years, first in relation to religious and ritualistic functions, later for a variety of secular reasons as well. Social, psychological, and technological factors set the stage for today's drug problem. It is becoming increasingly clear that the problem is not drugs, but the manner and purpose of their use. Life styles can be altered by drugs, positively as well as negatively. Pharmacological treatment can provide relief for abnormal psychological states and correct potential pathology. New knowledge is also opening vistas for enlarging man's creative and productive capacities. Man himself remains the key determinant."

MAHARISHI MAHESH YOGI. Transcendental Meditation: *Serenity without drugs*. New York: New American Library, 1963.
"Life need not be the painful struggle it is commonly represented to be. We are meant to be happy and here is a way for everybody; a way which involves no austere discipline, no break with normal life and tradition and which gives

fuller and deeper meaning to all religions.'' His Holiness Maharishi Mahesh Yogi.

MALCOLM, A. I. *The case against the drugged mind*. Toronto: Clarke, Irwin, 1973.

This book is ''. . . a timely and spirited counter-attack against the reign of the *high* in contemporary society . . . the author . . . a psychiatrist who has worked with drug dependent people over a twenty-year period in New York, London and Toronto . . . examines the roots of what he terms the magic humanist belief in the value of the drug high. Dr. Malcolm's point-by-point critique of the work of the Le-Dain Commission on the Non-Medical Use of Drugs is one of several graphic illustrations of how this belief can blind us to the dangers inherent in the trend.'' Book jacket.

MASTERS, R., & HOUSTON, J. *Mind games: The guide to inner space*. New York: Dell, 1972.

''Mind games is a how-to book of mental exercises for achieving altered states of consciousness with the use of drugs of mysticism.''

''I think that Masters and Houston actually have broken through to a new understanding of the sense and uses of the disciplines of inward-turned contemplation.'' Joseph Campbell.

MILBAUER, B. *Drug abuse and drug addiction*. New York: General Publishing, 1970.

''Drugs are not figments of the imagination. They are real, to many of the older generation, drugs are a nightmare horror. To many young people, drugs are a harmless pleasure. Both views have little to do with reality. Drugs include everything from alcohol and aspirin to cocaine and heroin. Each drug offers something to the user. Each exacts its special price.''

ORNSTEIN, R. E. *The psychology of consciousness*. San Francisco: W. H. Freeman, 1973.

''I gave this book to two of my best students (undergraduates)—it totally changed their educational goals and, I think, their lives.'' Peter G. Kauber, Bowling Green State University.

''A fantastic book, extremely well written and bursting with information about the frontiers

of the field. It is invaluable in showing that the perimeters that have traditionally been the concerns of psychology are much too narrow. I am adopting it for my survey course.'' Bobby L. Jones, Diablo Valley College, California.

''I've just been 'into' your book, *The Psychology of Consciousness*. Wow! What an experience it has been! . . . Without any exaggeration, it is the most important and challenging and fascinating and exciting thing I've read in years.'' Vaughn E. Huff, The University of Arizona.

ORNSTEIN, R. E. *The nature of human consciousness: A book of readings*. San Francisco: W. H. Freeman, 1973.

''An exciting and satisfying set of readings on consciousness—covers well the historical and contemporary approaches to the subject.'' G. C. Jernstedt, Dartmouth College.

''Seems to offer an excellent blend of stimulation, provocation, and scholarship. It will be a good supplement to more traditional books on cognitive psychology.'' Phillip Shaver, Columbia University.

TART, C. T. *Altered states of consciousness: A book of readings*. New York: John Wiley & Sons, 1969.

''The study of the nature of human consciousness, a dormant and often taboo topic in psychology, is once again developing into a respected field of inquiry. This is the first book to provide a broad, scientific point of view for the investigation of a variety of special states of consciousness.

''The editor combines a humanistic approach, which includes an awareness of the great potential richness in human experience indicated by ASCs, with the disciplined precision of a scientist. He brings a professional point of view to the observation of the increasingly widespread use and resultant effects of drugs, Yoga, self-hypnosis, and other means of producing ASCs which are popularly regarded as comprising either a major social problem or a sign of positive change in materialistic civilization. Studies of ASCs produced by psychedelic drugs, for example, are placed in this book within a broad, illuminating perspective that includes papers on mystical experiences, hypnagogic (between waking and sleeping) states, dream consciousness, meditation, hypnosis, and brain wave feedback-produced states.

"One of the most productive ways of studying consciousness is to alter it qualitatively, i.e., to produce an altered state of consciousness in which the functional relations of various aspects of mental activity take on a new configuration. Such ASCs are of considerable interest and appeal in and of themselves, as well as for the light they cast on normal consciousness. Professor Tart has brought together 35 scientific papers which illustrate the variety of ASCs and their effects, which describe some of the techniques, both ancient and modern, for producing ASCs and, perhaps most important, which show that ASCs can be studied scientifically without destroying their inherent human richness." Book jacket.